R E A D I N G S

CANADIAN
HISTORY
PRE-CONFEDERATION

READINGS IN CANADIAN HISTORY

PRE~CONFEDERATION

R. DOUGLAS FRANCIS/DONALD B. SMITH

THIRD EDITION

Holt, Rinehart and Winston of Canada, Limited
Toronto

Canadian Cataloguing in Publication Data

Main entry under title:
Readings in Canadian history,
3rd ed.
Includes bibliographical references.

Contents: [v. 1.] Pre-Confederation — [v. 2.]
Post-Confederation.
ISBN 0-03-922691-3 (v. 1) ISBN 0-03-922692-1 (v. 2)

1. Canada - History. I. Francis, R. D. (R. Douglas),
1944- . II. Smith, Donald B., 1946-

FC164.R43 1990   971   C89-094789-9
F1026.R43 1990

Publisher: David Dimmell
Developmental Editor: Iris Coupe
Publishing Services Manager: Karen Eakin
Editorial Co-ordinator: Marcel Chiera
Copy Editor: Darlene Zeleney
Cover and Interior Design: John Zehethofer
Typesetting and Assembly: True to Type Inc.
Printing and Binding: Metrolitho Inc.

Cover: *Canoes in a Fog, Lake Superior, 1869*, by Frances Ann Hopkins. 55.8.1,
NA-1081-3, in the collection of the Glenbow Museum, Calgary, Alberta. Reproduced by permission.

Printed in Canada

1 2 3 4   93 92 91 90

Preface

In this third edition of our two-volume *Readings in Canadian History*, as in the previous two editions, our concern is to provide a collection of articles suitable for introductory Canadian history tutorials. This has meant selecting topics related to the major issues dealt with in such history courses, and providing useful readings of a general nature. We have once again included material that deals with the various regions of the country, and selected, whenever possible, readings that reflect new research interests among Canadian historians. Consequently, we have changed some of the topics, and many of the readings. Unfortunately, these new additions have necessitated the elimination of worthwhile readings in the second edition due to a limitation of space. Still, we hope that this edition will continue to meet the needs of introductory students in Canadian history.

This volume includes two or three selections on each of fifteen topics, thus providing instructors flexibility in choosing readings. Short introductions to each topic set the readings in an historical context and offer suggestions for further readings. It is our hope that this reader will contribute to increased discussion in tutorials, as well as complement course lectures and, where applicable, textbooks.

In this edition we have included several popular historical articles from *Horizon Canada* and the National Museum of Civilization's Visual History Series. Although these essays appear in an undocumented form, we have added them because they provide good summaries of the respective topics and are written by experts in the field.

In preparing the reader, we and the publisher have both sought advice from a number of Canadian historians. Their comments have been generously given and have greatly improved the original outline. We would like in particular to thank Douglas Baldwin of Acadia University, Olive Dickason of the University of Alberta, Carol Wilton-Siegel of York University, John Eagle of the University of Alberta, and Hugh Johnston of Simon Fraser University for their detailed comments on our draft for the third edition. Many other individuals made valuable suggestions, and we are indebted to John Belshaw of Cariboo College, Margaret Conrad of Acadia University, Beatrice Craig of the University of Ottawa,

Chad Gaffield of the University of Ottawa, Marcel Martel of Glendon College, York University, Thomas Socknat of the University of Toronto, Robert Sweeny of Memorial University, Duncan McDowell of Carleton University, and Peter Ward of the University of British Columbia. Heartfelt thanks also go to Dave Dimmell, Steve Payne, Iris Coupe, John Caldarone, and Marcel Chiera of Holt, Rinehart and Winston for their help and constant encouragement towards the completion of this third edition and to Darlene Zeleney who edited the book. Finally, we wish to thank those Canadian historians who consented to let their writings be included in this reader. Their ideas and viewpoints will greatly enrich the study and appreciation of Canadian history among first- and second-year university students.

Douglas Francis
Donald Smith
Department of History
University of Calgary

Publisher's Note to Instructors and Students

This textbook is a key component of your course. If you are the instructor of this course, you undoubtedly considered a number of texts carefully before choosing this as the one that will work best for your students and you. The authors and publishers of this book spent considerable time and money to ensure its high quality, and we appreciate your recognition of this effort and accomplishment. Please note the copyright statement.

If you are a student, we are confident that this text will help you to meet the objectives of your course. You will also find it helpful after the course is finished, as a valuable addition to your personal library. So hold on to it.

And since we want to hear what you think about this book, please be sure to send us the stamped reply card at the end of the text. This will help us to continue publishing high-quality books for your courses.

Contents

List of Maps

Topic One

The Native Peoples and Early European Contact

The Europeans who came to North America looked upon it as an empty continent, completely open for settlement. In reality Indian tribal groups claimed and inhabited almost every part of the "New World," from the Gulf of Mexico to the Arctic coast, from the Atlantic to the Pacific. There were over fifty such groups in Canada alone.

In the pre-European period there existed no common designation for the whole country, nor even a single name for the native inhabitants. The "Indians" of Canada owed their allegiance to their family, their band, their village, their tribe, and — in the case of several tribes — to their confederacy. But they had no concept of a pan-Indian identity. Each tribe spoke its own language and regarded its own members as "the people." This lack of a perceived common identity contributed to their failure to resist the Europeans. But certainly other factors contributed as well: the reliance of some native groups on European manufactured trade goods, fur-trade rivalries, colonial wars, and the catastrophic drop in population due to exposure to European diseases.

In their article, "The Indians of Northeastern North America," Jacques Rousseau and George W. Brown present a sketch of the native groups of eastern Canada at the time of white contact, showing how the Europeans' arrival both improved, and at the same time fatally weakened, the native societies. Anthropologist Bruce Trigger, in "The French Presence in Huronia: The Structure of Franco-Huron Relations in the First Half of the Seventeenth Century," follows the fortunes of the Hurons, one of the native groups that came into the closest contact with French fur traders in the seventeenth century.

Diamond Jenness' dated *Indians of Canada* (Ottawa: King's Printer, 1932; numerous editions since) should be supplemented by the useful survey by Alan D. McMillan entitled *Native Peoples and Cultures of Canada: An Anthropological Overview* (Vancouver: Douglas and McIntyre, 1988). A good collection of articles on Canada's native peoples, edited by R. Bruce Morrison and C. Roderick Wilson, is *Native Peoples: The Canadian Experience* (Toronto: McClelland and Stewart, 1986). Anthropologist Alice B. Kehoe provides an overview in her *North American Indians: A Comprehensive Account* (Englewood Cliffs, N.J.: Prentice-

Hall, 1981). Thomas Y. Canby's "The Search for the First Americans," *National Geographic* 156, 3 (September 1979): 330–63, is an interesting account of recent archaeological work in the Americas. J.V. Wright's *Six Chapters of Canada's Prehistory* (Ottawa: National Museums of Canada, 1976), reviews what is currently known of the Canadian Indian before the arrival of the European.

A very good introduction to the subject of early French–Indian relations in the Americas is Olive Patricia Dickason's *The Myth of the Savage and the Beginnings of French Colonialism in the Americas* (Edmonton: University of Alberta Press, 1984). Other introductory texts are Alfred G. Bailey's *The Conflict of European and Eastern Algonkian Cultures, 1504–1700* (1937; second edition published by the University of Toronto Press, 1969); the short booklet by Bruce Trigger, *The Indians and the Heroic Age of New France*, Canadian Historical Association, Historical Booklet no. 30 (Ottawa: CHA, 1977) and his *Natives and Newcomers: Canada's 'Heroic Age' Reconsidered* (Kingston and Montreal: McGill-Queen's University Press, 1985); and the first chapter, entitled "Native Peoples and the Beginnings of New France to 1650," in Brian Young and John A. Dickinson's *A Short History of Quebec: A Socio-Economic Perspective* (Toronto: Copp Clark, 1988), 11–34. Extremely useful maps appear in R. Cole Harris, ed., *Historical Atlas of Canada*, vol. 1, *From the Beginning to 1800* (Toronto: University of Toronto Press, 1987).

Students interested in pursuing the subject further should consult James Axtell, ed., *The Indian Peoples of Eastern America: A Documentary History of the Sexes* (New York: Oxford, 1981) and his *The Invasion Within: The Contest of Cultures in Colonial North America* (New York: Oxford University Press, 1985); Cornelius Jaenen, *Friend and Foe: Aspects of French–Amerindian Cultural Contact in the Sixteenth and Seventeenth Centuries* (Toronto: McClelland and Stewart, 1976); Bruce Trigger, *The Children of Aataentsic: A History of the Huron People to 1660*, 2 vols. (Montreal: McGill-Queen's, 1976); and Basil Johnston, *Ojibway Heritage* (Toronto: McClelland and Stewart, 1976).

Two interesting books on the early fur trade have recently appeared. Calvin Martin's *Keepers of the Game: Indian–Animal Relationships and the Fur Trade* (Berkeley, California: University of California Press, 1978), should be supplemented by Shepard Krech's edited work, *Indians, Animals and the Fur Trade: A Critique of Keepers of the Game* (Athens, Georgia: University of Georgia Press, 1981).

The Europeans' early attitudes toward Indian sovereignty are reviewed in Brian Slattery's "French Claims in North America, 1500–59," *Canadian Historical Review*, 59 (1978): 139–69; Olive Patricia Dickason's "Renaissance Europe's View of Amerindian Sovereignty and Territoriality," *Plural Societies* 8, 3–4 (1977): 97–107; and W.J. Eccles' "Sovereignty-Association, 1500–1783," *Canadian Historical Review* 65 (1984): 475–510. Leslie C. Green and Olive Dickason review the ideology of the European occupation of the Americas in *The Law of Nations and the New World* (Edmonton: University of Alberta Press, 1989).

How did the Europeans' view of land and nature differ from that of the Indians? In what ways would their attitudes lead to misunderstandings with the Indians? The questions of Indian sovereignty and the right to self-determination are important issues today.

The Indians of Northeastern North America*

JACQUES ROUSSEAU and GEORGE W. BROWN

This volume of the Dictionary contains the biographies of 65 Indians. In many ways they are a group apart. For almost all of them the information is fragmentary. Like fireflies they glimmer for a moment before disappearing again into the dark forest of unrecorded history. More important, their stories must be extracted almost entirely from records which are not their own. The history of the Americas as we know it is the white man's history, written of necessity from his own records; The Indians' oral tradition has added a little, but not a great deal; archaeology in recent years has added much, but most significantly on the pre-white period. We can now begin, however, to understand more fully the tremendous drama of interracial and intercultural conflict, with all its tragic consequences, which followed the white man's "discovery" of the Americas. Here biography can help us, since the stories of individual Indians often give us clearer glimpses of these conflicts and tensions than we might otherwise have, for they are revealed to us in human terms and not as impersonal forces. For this reason the number of Indians included in this volume has on the whole leaned to the generous side.

Of the first natives met by Europeans in what is now Canada we have no individual records, though there are numerous references to such meetings in explorers' accounts. Amongst the Amerinds the Eskimos belong to a distinct linguistic and cultural family and were mainly encountered in the explorations of Hudson Bay, though they are mentioned also in the Norse sagas. Contacts with them were, however, brief and sporadic.

At the beginning of the historical period the Eskimos had penetrated as far south as Havre-Saint-Pierre (formerly Pointe-aux-Esquimaux), on the north shore of the St. Lawrence. The first Indians of the Gulf region

3

*From *Dictionary of Canadian Biography*, vol. 1, *1000–1700*. Copyright 1966 by University of Toronto Press. Reprinted by permission of University of Toronto Press.

encountered by the early explorers were the Beothuks. Probably belonging to a distinct linguistic family, with a population of about 500 persons at the time of their discovery, they were entirely confined to Newfoundland. Their treatment by the whites in the early period was deplorable, members of the tribe being regarded as little better than animals by the Newfoundland fishermen who hunted them down. No missionaries

4

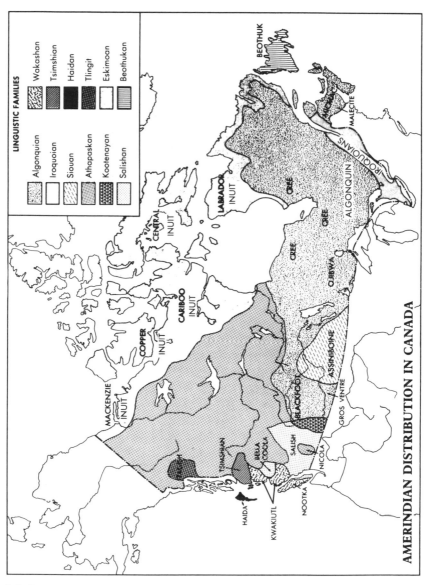

P.G. Cornell, J. Hamelin, F. Ouellet, and M. Trudel, *Canada: Unity in Diversity* (Toronto, 1967), 14.

were ever sent to the Beothuks and no colonist of the island ever learned their language. The tribe finally disappeared about the middle of the 19th century (*see* J.P. Howley, *The Beothuks or Red Indians, the aboriginal inhabitants of Newfoundland* (Cambridge, 1915); Jacques Rousseau, "Le dernier des Peaux-rouges," *Cahiers des Dix*, 27 (1962): 47-76).

It is when we come to the Amerinds of the mainland that we find records of large numbers of identifiable persons from whom a representative selection for a volume such as this can be made. Northeastern North America was, however, a very large area stretching from Acadia westward through the entire region of the St. Lawrence and Great Lakes; and it is essential, as a background for the Indian biographies, that we recall that in the 17th century the Indians of this region present an often confusing mosaic of shifting tribes and bands at various levels of culture and with great differences in their ways of life. Beyond this also, if we are to have any true appreciation of the tension and tragedy in which both the Indian and the white man became involved, we must have some understanding of the basic rhythms and patterns of life which affected Indian thought and action.

5

In the northeastern region there were, broadly speaking, two linguistic groupings of Indian tribes: the Algonkian, migratory and primarily dependent on hunting and fishing; and the Iroquoian, semi-sedentary and semi-agricultural. Occupying the northern, and by far the larger, part of the region, were the many tribes of the Algonkian family. Farthest to the east were the Micmacs and the Malecites, inhabiting at the time of their discovery what is now the province of Nova Scotia, including Cape Breton Island, northern New Brunswick, and Prince Edward Island. The boundary between them was the height of land separating the waters that flow into the Saint John River from those that enter the Gulf of St. Lawrence; the Malecite territory extended to the shore of the St. Lawrence opposite present-day Tadoussac, and included also part of the state of Maine. The Malecites and several Algonkian tribes to the southward formed the Abenaki Confederacy (including, among others, the Passamaquoddy, Penobscot, and possibly the Sokoki Indians), which allied itself in the 17th century with the French against the Iroquois Confederacy and the English colonists of the Atlantic seaboard.

North of the St. Lawrence and east of the St. Maurice were the Montagnais; while further east along the north shore of the Gulf and stretching north into Labrador over a very great area were the roving bands of the closely related, and at times almost indistinguishable, Naskapis. West of the St. Maurice and occupying the Ottawa River basin were the Algonkians. Still further west were the Ottawas, on the route toward Georgian Bay; the Nipissings in the vicinity of Lake Nipissing; and the Chippewas or Ojibwas to the north around Lake Superior. North also of the Algonkians and Ojibwas, occupying the watershed of James Bay and stretching westward into present-day Saskatchewan, were the many roving bands of Crees.

The Algonkian peoples are usually described as migratory because so many individual tribes ranged more or less continually over wide expanses in search of game — moose, deer, caribou, smaller animals which were trapped — and fish. They also used wild plants to augment their diet and in certain places they gathered wild rice and made maple syrup in season. A few tribes also practised horticulture on a small scale, planting maize, beans, and squash. Food was generally plentiful during the summer months but many of the tribes experienced severe food shortages in the winter.

Because the Algonkians were migratory, their material possessions were, of necessity, portable. Baskets and other containers were woven or made out of bark or wood. The single-family peaked or dome-shaped lodge or wigwam, as it is called, was the basic form of shelter used throughout the area. With its covering of birch-bark rolls, woven rush mats, or skins, this type of house was easy to assemble and dismantle. For winter travel, the Algonkians used the toboggan and snow-shoes and for summer expeditions, the graceful birch-bark canoe, one of the great Indian contributions to water transportation in North America.

The important socio-economic unit was the band, although there were tribal divisions which were known and recognized. Bands varied in size from a few families to several hundred individuals. In many ways, the Algonkian peoples inclined to individualism — so much so that they have been described by many authorities as "atomistic." The recognized leader of the band was usually an experienced hunter, noted for his astuteness and good judgement. In some instances, these positions were hereditary in a powerful family (descent among these people was through the male line). A particularly gifted man might become chief of the tribe when a number of bands joined in the conduct of war, in negotiations with other tribes, or with the white men's governments. At the local level, however, it was more often the shaman who exerted the greatest influence.

With the rise of the fur trade, the Algonkians found their knowledge of the forest and the habits of the fur-bearing animals most valuable, as trapping became their major occupation. It was the European traders who introduced them to iron tools, guns, kettles, brandy, and other facets of white culture. In exchange, the traders received the pelts of lynx, otter, marten, fox, and, most important of all, beaver. In becoming trappers, the Algonkians had to relinquish much of their traditional woodland economy as they settled around the trading-posts. Thus they became dependent on the fur market, with all its vicissitudes, and were exposed to many evil aspects of European civilization, alcoholism in particular. Their participation in the fur trade as allies of the French involved them in conflicts with the Iroquois and, ultimately, dragged them into the struggle between England and France for North America itself.

In considerable contrast to the life of the Algonkians was that of the Iroquoian tribes, most prominent among whom in the early 17th century were the Hurons located south of Georgian Bay, and the Iroquois of the Five Nations Confederacy occupying the territory south of the St. Lawrence and Lake Ontario from the Richelieu River almost to Lake Erie. Situated in these well-watered and fertile regions of present-day southern Ontario and western New York, they had an hospitable environment for an extensive agricultural economy. Here they were able to grow maize, their principal crop, as well as beans, squash, pumpkins, tobacco, and other vegetable products, some in considerable quantity. The surrounding woodlands furnished them with a number of wild plants, game animals (deer in particular), and fish.

A rich, well-documented ethnohistorical literature describes the role of these peoples in the 17th century but their history before contact with the white man evokes considerable debate among archaeologists. It is now believed that the Hurons and the Iroquois shared a common origin in the south, having pushed into the region of the Great Lakes from the southwest, following the line of the Ohio and splitting on lakes Erie and Ontario, some going to the north side of these lakes, some to the south. In 1534 Cartier found Iroquois on the lower St. Lawrence; but, in the interval between then and the coming of Champlain in 1608, they went back to the position south of the river which in the 17th century became a "buffer zone" between New France and the English colonies on the Atlantic seaboard.

7

Leagued in the Huron or Wyandot Confederacy were four tribes: Attignaouantan (Bear), Attingneenougnahak (Cord), Ahrendarrhonon (Rock), and Tahontaenrat (Deer). Adjoining the Hurons were other Iroquoian tribes: the Tobacco Nation or Petuns to the west, and the Neutrals to the south along the north shore of Lake Erie. The famous Iroquois Confederacy consisted in the 17th century of five tribes: the Mohawks farthest east toward the Richelieu River, and westward from them the Oneidas, Onondagas, Cayugas, and Senecas. South and west of the Senecas were the Eries, another Iroquoian tribe.

All these Iroquoian peoples lived in rather permanent villages which were abandoned after an occupancy of 10 to 15 years. These villages were usually situated on high ground near some source of water and were fairly large, attaining populations of several hundreds or more. Most were protected by a log palisade. The houses were multiple-family units, appropriately called "long-houses" because of their rectangular shape, and usually accommodated eight to ten families each, although some have been reported to house from 20 to 30 families.

The household was the basic unit of Iroquoian social organization, which may be described technically as a maternal lineage, with descent reckoned through the female line. The core of any household consisted of a number of females descended from a common ancestress. When a man married, he occupied his wife's house. Authority in these households was vested in an old woman. While not constituting a true mat-riarchate, these older women did exert a great deal of influence, par-ticularly in the political sphere.

The clan, a larger kin group, consisted of a number of households and resembled somewhat a great family. Clansmen considered themselves siblings, intermarriage between them was prohibited, custom dictated that they aid one another in time of need, they held property as a cor-porate group, they redressed injuries to one another and avenged deaths. Most of the clans bore animal names, Bear, Wolf, and Turtle being almost universal.

The significant political unit was the tribe. It had a name, occupied a defined territory, and possessed a council of chiefs or sachems. Lin-guistic affinity and a common way of life did not, however, necessarily imply friendly intercourse. The Hurons, who became the irreconcilable enemies of the Iroquois, their linguistic and cultural kin, were on much better terms with the Algonkians, originally migratory hunters, speaking an alien dialect. Thus it was that by the time the white man arrived confederacies had been founded, the purpose of which was to maintain peace among the member tribes. The Five Nations referred to their con-federacy as the "League of the Iroquois" or "the great peace." Its foun-ders were the half-legendary Dekanahwideh and Hiawatha. In this system those tribes which were not members of the League were theoretically considered at war with it.

The institutional structure of the League of the Iroquois was described in symbolic terms derived from the long-house, certain tribes being "keepers of the door," etc. The kinship bonds of the maternal line, rep-resenting the household, were extended across the member tribes, which were themselves divided into clans. Since certain clans extended across various tribes, it then followed that quarrelling between clan "brothers" would theoretically be unthinkable.

The decisions of the league were made by a federal council composed of 50 sachems, whose positions were hereditary in the female line. It was the old women who decided which eligible male relative would ac-tually inherit. Indeed the older women, the heads of the households, made most of the decisions, while the men holding the titles of authority carried them out. The five tribes comprising the league did not, it might be noted, enjoy equal representation. The Senecas, for example, were represented by 8 sachems and the Onondagas by 14, with the three re-maining tribes ranging in between. The requirement that decisions be unanimous offset this unequal representation, however. Sachems enjoyed high repute. Indeed, aside from warfare, the office of sachem was the only means whereby a man might gain prestige.

Eloquence was one of the prime qualifications for a great sachem. Ora-tory and the recitation from memory of the great legends surrounding the founding of the league were outstanding attractions at the annual meeting of the Federal Council held at Onondaga, New York. As an aid to memory, wampum belts were used, combinations of black and white beads (made from clam and other shells), signifying important ideas and events. At times wampum was also used as a form of currency.

Although members of the league did, on occasion, join one another to wage concerted war (the destruction of the Hurons is a case in point), the greater part of their military activities smacked of the vendetta. A few warriors would combine to conduct a raid, making the most of sur-prise attack. Scalps were taken and prisoners brought back to the village, where they were either killed or adopted. Each household which had lost a member had the right to select a captive to fill the vacancy. Death by torture was the fate of the remainder. To die without showing the slightest indication of pain was considered ideal behaviour and victims were supposed to exhibit contempt for their captors by presuming to enjoy the tortures they received. Whatever their warfare, small- or large-scale, during the historic period, the Iroquois suffered great losses, wit-ness a passage in the Jesuit *Relations* to the effect that Huron and Al-gonkian captives made up two-thirds of the Oneida tribe in 1668 (R. G. Thwaites, ed., *The Jesuit Relations and Allied Documents* (73 vols.; Cleveland 1896–1901), 51:123).

Such in sketchiest outline are a few suggestions about the nature of Indian society at the time of the white man's arrival, but even these will help us to understand why the impact of the 17th-century European culture on that of the Indian profoundly altered every aspect of Indian life and thought. That any remnants of Indian culture survived is a trib-ute to its strength and to the loyalty of the Indians to their traditions. The nature and devastating effects of this clash of cultures can be un-derstood better now than by any observer at the time, though there are many penetrating recorded observations by both Indians and whites, es-pecially by persons like Marie de l'Incarnation and some of the Jesuits, for example, in their letters, relations, and journals.

For the Indians of northeastern North America there were three vital areas where they suffered the full impact of the culture clash: first, the ideological, in which their religious beliefs and tribal organization were shaken to their very roots and the authority and influence of chiefs and medicine-men were gravely weakened; second, the economic, in which the fur trade caused a revolution affecting every aspect of daily life, sowing discord among the tribes, and finally erupting into the fur-trade wars; and third, political, where the imperial rivalries of French and English relentlessly dragged the Indians into the white men's struggles for military supremacy. In each of these areas the results were inevitably far more profound and tragic for the Indians than for the whites. From the first limited contacts with the early explorers, subsequently multiplied a thousand-fold across the whole continent, the Indians found their an-cient ways completely disrupted, and social and moral disintegration,

9

aggravated by brandy and disease, began to haunt them. M. André Vachon in his "L'eau-de-vie dans la société indienne," Canadian Historical Association, *Report* (1960–61), 26–27, has vividly described this revolution:

"Indian society, which was extremely primitive, was in no way prepared for contact with Europeans. The Indian's first meeting with the white man was a brutal shock for him. Suddenly he discovered a world, the dimensions of which bore no relation to his own: the iron blades of the white men had more cutting power than the Indian's flint knives; their canoes were immense; their fire-arms killed from a distance with a noise like thunder. Surely the spirits on the side of the white men were infinitely more powerful than any others the Indian had ever encountered. Accustomed as he was to explaining natural phenomena in supernatural terms, the Indian recoiled from this first clash with western and Christian civilization, profoundly shaken in the very core of his existence — his religion.

10

"As these contacts with the white man became more frequent and prolonged, the Indian soul suffered a corresponding attrition. At first the French gave knives, axes, and kettles to the Indians in order to win their friendship. But this contact with European goods completely upset the Indian way of life. They could not resist the metal tools, so superior to their own in utility and convenience, which were, in their minds, imbued with power and strength, and they adopted them immediately. In consequence, they forsook their traditional crafts, they ceased to make their own weapons and utensils, they modified their methods of hunting to suit the new weapons. The French traded clothing, as well, in return for furs, also food and brandy. Each time the Indians accepted a European product, they abandoned a portion of their own culture. Little time elapsed before they became the slaves of the fur traders, for they were forced to bring more and more furs to the company stores in order to get all the new goods they needed. The Indian who, hitherto, had hunted only to satisfy his own limited needs, faced the brutal fact that he now lived in a competitive society which already had completely altered his life pattern . . . little by little, certain fundamental traditions were forgotten; and the demoralized Indian, conscious of his decline, gradually lost the will to live.

"Brandy, without question, played its part in this disintegration of the Indian culture. But we must guard against the temptation to isolate this element and to exaggerate its importance. Brandy was only one of the many factors which combined to bring about the physical and spiritual deterioration of the Indian."

The predominant influence in the ideological sphere was the impact made by the missions, initiated by the Recollets and later taken over by the Jesuits. The primitive Indians found it well-nigh impossible to reconcile the two dominant motives for the white man's penetration of their continent: the search for material wealth and the conversion of pagan souls. Neither motive seemed reasonable to men who provided merely for the material needs of the moment and who possessed an integrated system of belief peculiarly adapted to the natural environment in which it had evolved. Moreover, the Indians were further confused by a secular authority which revealed its will to them, sometimes through the black-robes, sometimes through Onontio (the governor), and sometimes through the traders. This multiple standard in the ideologies and behaviour of the white men was to make an indelible impression on the Indian. The ensuing clash of interests and cultural values was to beget a fatal violence at the very foot of the altar and does much to explain the obstacles encountered by both the missionaries and those whom they sincerely wished to aid in bridging the gulf separating the palaeolithic from the modern age. Many persons, both Indians and whites, whose lives are described in this volume found themselves struggling, often helplessly, with complex and almost insoluble problems created by this pioneer phase of Canadian history.

11

The Hurons and their fate, as allies of the French, provide perhaps the best and most tragic example of the results which followed the deep penetration of a primitive, indigenous culture by a European one, so far removed from it by centuries of civilization. Coming in a spirit of the utmost devotion and willing to suffer every hardship, even torture and death, the missionaries found themselves facing the baffling problem of bringing new concepts, religious and secular, to a people whose ways and language, in the beginning at least, they did not understand. And, an added difficulty, they soon found themselves, as important representatives of the small, educated minority in the colony, inextricably and often unwillingly involved in civil and commercial policy; in the disputes over the fur trade and the sale of brandy; and in the bitter Indian military conflicts which destroyed the Huron country and, for a time, threatened even the existence of New France itself.

Despite a high mortality rate, the native population had maintained its equilibrium before the arrival of the white men. Infectious diseases, hitherto unknown, were introduced by the Europeans, causing a catastrophic drop in population.

A too hasty judgement might attribute to warfare the numerical decline of the Indians. The majority succumbed first of all to these new diseases carried by the whites. When the Huron nation first allied itself with the French, its population numbered 30 000 in contrast with the Iroquois total of 15 000. Measles raged among the Hurons in 1634, which was soon followed by smallpox and some other unnamed epidemic. In 1640 the Hurons numbered no more than 12 000, while the Iroquois population remained substantially the same. This epidemiological disparity has its own explanation. The Huron and Algonkian allies, with their families, paid regular visits to the trading-posts of New France, camping there for weeks at a time, in contact with the colonists and thus exposed to fresh contagion. The French missionaries and traders, on their part, freely frequented the Indian villages, whereas the Dutch and English more rarely penetrated to the Iroquois country. The Mohawks lived in the forest heart and many a long portage was necessary before their emissaries arrived to complete their brief transactions at Fort Orange (Albany, N.Y.). Solitary and on foot, in a hurry to return home, they were better able to avoid contagion than were entire households, travelling in canoes and prepared to stay for an extended period. The Iroquois family was not welcome at Fort Orange, a fact which saved it. The Dutch supplied fire-arms to the Iroquois after 1643 but the French, fearing revolt, refused to arm their non-Christian Indian allies. In 1649, when the Five Nations gave the final blow to the Hurons, disease had already conquered them. History often overwhelms its victims. The Hurons and the Iroquois had been equal, both belonging to the same race, speaking the same language, with the same characteristics and social structure (*see* Jacques Rousseau, "Les premiers Canadiens," *Cahiers des Dix* 25 (1960): 9–64).

12

The geographical location of the Iroquois in the western part of what is now the state of New York gave them an important military advantage, enabling them to attack from the south, with relative impunity, the routes along the St. Lawrence and Lake Ontario, both vital links in the French communications with the *pays d'en haut* (the up-country), their major fur supply, to which the Iroquois also sought access. Thus the Iroquois had a motive for aggression and the base from which to launch it, whereas the Hurons had no interest in attacking their neighbours to the south.

Unlike the Hurons, the Iroquois were in a strategic position for diplomatic bargaining with more than one European government. Although the Iroquois were caught, against their will, in the conflicts and rivalries between the French on the St. Lawrence and the Dutch (after 1664 the English) of the Hudson River valley and New York, their strong military position (though it proved vulnerable in the long run) allowed them through most of the 17th century to play off the Dutch or the English against the French and thus to gamble for high stakes in the fur trade, with all the diplomatic and oratorical arts in which their leaders excelled.

"Are there practical persons who believe that Champlain would have done better to form an alliance with the Iroquois? Others maintain that his idealism led him to take the side of the Hurons and Algonkins, exposed as they were to the foul deeds of the cruel Iroquois. Neither of these views is well founded. Champlain wanted to explore west from New France, to discover the route to China, and to create an agriculturally self-sufficient colony; but in the beginning he favoured the fur trade, the economic base for the young nation and the justification for the existence of the Compagnie des Cent-Associés, at that time masters of Canada. The north country harboured the finest furs — and the water routes leading into it were controlled by the Algonkins and the Hurons.

The latter were, therefore, much more useful to the colony than were the Iroquois. The Hurons, moreover, profited from the same social structure as the Iroquois and they exceeded them by 10 000 to 15 000 men. The facts of the situation dictated Champlain's choice. But these tribes also had their problems. To participate in the fur trade they needed military aid against the Iroquois, with whom they had been at war for a half-century. Their enemies wanted to force them to join the Confederacy of the Five Nations. Independence is a prize for which a high price must be paid" (Rousseau, "Les premiers Canadiens," 50).

For the fur trade the geographical location of the Iroquois during the 17th century was less favourable than that of the Hurons. They could not fall back on the rich resources to the west when their own fur supply became exhausted, and occupying the coveted Indian position of middleman between the hunting tribes or bands and the European purchasers, French, Dutch, or English, was thus beyond their reach. From the 1620's on, the European demand for furs was insatiable and the Hurons controlled access to the northern and western fur supply. They carefully prevented even the French from contacts at first hand with the Tobacco and Neutral nations which were their trading partners and with the Nipissings to the north who provided them with furs. For a brief period, the Allumette Island tribe (Algonkian), which inhabited an island in the Ottawa River, athwart the Huron–French trade route, cherished commercial ambitions, in spite of its numerical inferiority, but it was never successful in supplanting the Hurons, although its members were sufficiently powerful to exact tribute from the river traffic. Indian manoeuvres to control the fur trade are well illustrated by the career of the infamous Oumasasikweie.

13

In the 1630's and 1640's, however, it was the Hurons who demonstrated, collectively and most strikingly, the powerful position of the middleman. Located just south of the Precambrian Shield they were able to build up a trading empire among the Algonkian tribes stretching from the Great Lakes to the St. Maurice River, and even beyond it to the Saguenay, and northward to Hudson Bay. Their trading canoes loaded with their own and European goods, they threaded their way through the lakes and rivers of this great area, bartering for furs which would then be carried down to Montreal and Quebec, the Ottawa being the principal convoy route. From their neighbours, the Neutral and Tobacco nations, who were jealously guarded against contact with the French, the Hurons obtained native products such as corn and tobacco to supplement their own articles of barter with the Algonkian tribes.

It was this Huron trading empire, already weakened by disease, which, along with the Jesuit missions, the Iroquois destroyed in 1649-50, so completely indeed that the Hurons ceased to exist as a people, their remnants being dispersed among the tribes north and west with some seeking refuge on the île d'Orléans, later moving into Quebec itself and then, after ten years, to Notre-Dame-de-Foy, three or four miles west of Quebec.

"Of the 50 000 Hurons, Neutrals, and Eries who were in existence at the time the colony was founded, there remained only a remnant; in Oklahoma the Wyandots, their descendants, numbered scarcely 378 in 1905 and at Lorette, in the neighbourhood of Quebec, there were 835 Hurons in 1953. The majority of the fugitives merged with the Iroquois; Father Le Moyne encountered 1000 among the Onondagas in 1653. Three years later, the Iroquois presented an ultimatum to the vanquished in the vicinity of Quebec: assimilation or war to the death? The majority of Hurons bowed before this threat" (Rousseau, "Les premiers Canadiens," 51). So completely did they lose their identity that the Iroquois fighting against Dollard at the Long Sault in 1660 could include adopted Hurons in their ranks. The dialogue between Dollard's Hurons and those of the enemy, as reported by Louis Taondechoren, an Indian who escaped from the massacre, would tend to confirm this.

After 1650 the Iroquois never fully reaped the reward of replacing the Hurons in the fur trade, for the Ottawas fell heir to much of the Huron trade. The fierce forays of the Iroquois continued, however, far to the north and east, with ambuscades which at times closed the Ottawa to the fur convoys and with attacks on the settlements along the St. Lawrence which threatened the very existence of New France. Not until the arrival and campaign (1665–66) of the Carignan-Salières regiment under the Marquis de Tracy did the colony gain even a partial security in the military sense. Even then the long record of negotiations, treaty-making, and alternate intervals of war and peace did not end. It spanned, in fact, the entire 17th century, and spilled over into the 18th, for the Iroquois were then no less deeply involved in the Anglo-French wars and in the campaigns of the American Revolution. Thus the Iroquois provide the most striking example of the impact made on the Indians of northeastern North America by the white man's imperial rivalries, which dominated the new continent as well as the old.

What part geographical location and the fur trade played in the 17th century Iroquois history is impossible to determine exactly. That both had a very great influence there is no question, even if one cannot accept the too rigidly deterministic explanation put forward, for example, by George T. Hunt in *The Wars of the Iroquois* (Madison, 1940). Between Hurons and Iroquois, even though they were linguistically and culturally closely related, there were important contrasts in ideologies and institutions. The Iroquois, for example, never responded as deeply to Christianity as did the Hurons. Missionary projects were not attempted by the Dutch and English, while French efforts, religious as well as secular, were centred north of the St. Lawrence and from this base expanded into the Mississippi regions. The devoted but tragic and unsuccessful attempt of Father Jogues to found a mission in the Mohawk country

14

was too slight and temporary an episode to affect the course of Iroquois cultural development. Whatever the explanation, the Iroquois were successful in defending themselves to some extent against catastrophic cultural changes, so that even today their descendants form a distinct cultural entity. Doubtless geographical location, leadership, the internal strength of Iroquois tradition and institutions, and other less tangible factors all played a part in their survival as a people. Of particular institutional significance was the famous Confederacy of the Five Nations. Although it was a voluntary association and its members acted with great freedom both in war and in peace, it undoubtedly had a cohesive influence, especially, it would appear, after 1660.

The clash of cultures, while affecting the Indian more drastically, also had its impact on the European, a stranger at first in the unfamiliar environment of the New World. Indeed, he owed to the Indian his own survival in these harsh surroundings. Cartier's description of his voyage of 1534 is our first authentic account of Indian-European contacts in northeastern North America. In it he described the Iroquoians whom he met in Gaspé Bay, explained their customs, and mentioned maize, a plant under cultivation there. The two young Indians, Domagaya and Taignoagny, taken to France with the reluctant permission of their father, Donnacona, became in the next year the first Canadian interpreters at Stadacona. Through their good offices Cartier was able to learn something of the Great River of Canada, notably that it was *not* a strait leading into the Sea of Cathay. The cartographers of the Old World, drawing the first maps of Canada, were greatly indebted to the invaluable information collected from the Indians. From the Indians also, Cartier learned the spectacular cure for scurvy which beset his men in the winter of 1535–36 (Jacques Rousseau, "L'annedda et l'arbre de vie," *Revue d'histoire de l'Amérique française* 8 (1954): 171–212).

The first and probably the most important contribution of the Indian to the white man was in exploration. It was the Indian, his canoe, his snow-shoes, and his interpreters (many of them children of the first unions between the French and Indian women) that enabled Champlain, Jolliet, La Vérendrye, and many others to thread their way towards *les pays d'en haut*, sometimes by streams which were little more than a trickle, and thus to discover a continent. It was also through the lore of the Indian and his knowledge of the fur-bearing animals that the *coureurs-de-bois* were able to make themselves at home in the forest and ultimately to build a commercial venture of world-wide importance, the development of which forms a dominant theme in early Canadian history.

The Indians' knowledge of native plants became of great importance to the European. Tobacco, maize, all types of squash or pumpkin, and beans, were unknown in Europe before Columbus. The Hurons made oil from the sunflower which they used to grease their hair. Champlain discovered the Jerusalem artichoke in eastern Canada but it was the his-

15

torian, Marc Lescarbot, who introduced it into Europe. The Canadian Indians were familiar with maple syrup though maple sugar, the *sucre du pays* was unknown to them. Some Indian foods have been incorporated into the European-American cuisine, such as corn cooked on the cob and in other ways, for example, as succotash (a mixture of Indian corn and boiled beans, a favourite dish in New England); game cooked with wild rice; and, finally, certain methods of making bread stuffs which had been perfected in the northern forests, much to the benefit of the modern explorers. The native peoples of Central and South America alone have given more than 100 plants to world agriculture and thus transformed the commerce and cuisine of the Old World. The potato, called *patate* in French-Canada and in several provinces of France, comes from Peru. Carib Indians contributed the manioc and the sweet potato. The pimento provided the principal condiment in Mexico and was highly esteemed there as a vegetable. Some species of cotton were cultivated in New Mexico. And among other species which came from the recently discovered continent were the tomato, cocoa, peanuts, the pineapple, the avocado, and arrow root.

The French and English languages have also borrowed from the Indian dialects; in English, for example, *pow-wow, canoe, tepee, chipmunk, moose, hominy, squash, tamarack,* etc. In French no less than 100 words have been adopted, among them *canot, tobagane, wigwam,* and more than 25 names of plants and animals in the province of Quebec alone.

Thus the 65 Indian biographies in this volume are only a slight reminder of the part played by the Indians in Canada's early development, a token tribute to a host of other unnamed Indians. Unknown contributors to today's culture, obscure heroes who fell in many battles, interpreters and canoe-men, they helped literally to haul half a continent into the modern age. It is to this anonymous multitude that Canadian history owes some of its most striking pages.

The French Presence in Huronia: The Structure of Franco-Huron Relations in the First Half of the Seventeenth Century*

BRUCE G. TRIGGER

Few studies of Canadian history in the first half of the seventeenth century credit sufficiently the decisive role played at that time by the coun-

*From the *Canadian Historical Review* 49 (1968): 107–141. Reprinted by permission of the University of Toronto Press.

try's native peoples. The success of European colonizers, traders, and missionaries depended to a greater degree than most of them cared to admit on their ability to understand and accommodate themselves not only to native customs but also to a network of political and economic relationships that was not of their own making. Traders and missionaries often were forced to treat Algonkians and Iroquoians as their equals and sometimes they had to acknowledge that the Indians had the upper hand. If the Europeans were astonished and revolted by many of the customs of these Indians (often, however, no more barbarous than their own), they also admired their political and economic sagacity.[1] Indeed, one Jesuit was of the opinion that the Huron were more intelligent than the rural inhabitants of his own country.[2] If the missionary or fur trader felt compelled to understand the customs of the Indians, the modern historian should feel no less obliged to do so.

In order to appreciate the role that the Indians played in the history of Canada in the first half of the seventeenth century, it is necessary to study their customs and behaviour and the things they valued. Because their way of life differed from that of the Europeans, the fur traders and missionaries who interacted with them frequently became amateur anthropologists, and some of them became very good ones. For some tribes the documentation amassed by these early contacts is extensive and of high quality. For no tribe is this truer than for the Huron.[3] From the detailed picture of Huronia that emerges from these studies, it is possible to ascertain the motives that prompted the behaviour of particular Indians, or groups of Indians, in a manner no less detailed than our explanations of those which governed the behaviour of their European contemporaries. I might add, parenthetically, that historians are not alone to blame for the failure to utilize anthropological insights in the study of early Canadian history. Iroquoian ethnologists and archaeologists have tended to avoid historical or historiographic problems. Only a few individuals, such as George T. Hunt, have attempted to work in the no man's land between history and anthropology.

Two explanations have been used by anthropologists and historians to justify the existing cleavage between their respective studies. One of these maintains that when the Europeans arrived in eastern North America, the native tribes were engaged in a struggle, the origins and significance of which are lost in the mists of time and therefore wholly the concern of ethnohistorians. Because of this, there is no reason for the historian to try to work out in detail the causes of the conflicts and alliances that existed at that time.[4] Very often, however, the struggle between different groups is painted in crude, almost racist, terms (and in complete contradiction to the facts) as one between Algonkian- and Iroquoian-speaking peoples, the former being an indigenous population, mainly hunters, the latter a series of invading tribes growing corn and living in large villages. It should be noted that such a simplistic ex-

17

planation of European history, even for the earliest periods, would now be laughed out of court by any competent historian. The alternative hypothesis suggests that European contact altered the life of the Indian, and above all the relationships among the different tribes, so quickly and completely that a knowledge of aboriginal conditions is not necessary to understand events after 1600.[5] From an *a priori* point of view, this theory seems most unlikely. Old relationships have a habit of influencing events, even when economic and political conditions are being rapidly altered. Future studies must describe in detail how aboriginal cultures were disrupted or altered by their contact with the Europeans, rather than assume that interaction between Indians and Europeans can be explained as a set of relationships that has little or no reference to the native culture.

We will begin by considering developments in Huronia prior to the start of the fur trade.

The Huron

When the Huron tribes were described for the first time in 1615,[6] they were living in the Penetanguishene Peninsula and the part of Simcoe County that runs along Matchedash Bay between Wasaga Beach and Lake Simcoe. The Huron probably numbered twenty to thirty thousand, and, according to the most reliable of the descriptions from the Jesuit missionaries,[7] they were divided into four tribes that formed a confederacy similar in its structure to the league of the Iroquois.[8] The Attignaouantan or Bear tribe, which included about half of the people in the confederacy, lived on the western extremity of Huronia. Next to them lived the Attingueenougnahak, or Cord tribe, and the Tahontaenrat or Deer tribe. Farthest east, near Lake Simcoe, were the Ahrendarrhonon or Rock nation. The Tionnontate, or Petun, who spoke the same language as the Huron and were very similar to them, inhabited the country west of Huronia near the Blue Mountain. The Petun, however, were not members of the Huron confederacy and prior to the arrival of the French, they and the Huron had been at war. Another Iroquoian confederacy, the Neutral, lived farther south between the Grand River and the Niagara frontier. Except for a few Algonkian bands that lived west of the Petun, there do not appear to have been any other Indians living in southern Ontario, except in the Ottawa Valley. The uninhabited portions of the province were the hunting territories of the Huron, Neutral, and Petun and also served as a buffer zone between these tribes and the Iroquois who lived south of Lake Ontario.

The Huron, like other Iroquoian tribes, grew corn, beans, and squash. These crops were planted and looked after by the women, who also gathered the firewood used for cooking and heating the houses. Contrary to popular notions the men also made an important contribution to the tribal economy, inasmuch as it was they who cleared the fields for planting (no small task when only stone axes were available) and who caught the fish which were an important source of nutrition. Because of the high population density, the areas close to Huronia appear to have been depleted of game, and expeditions in search of deer had to travel far to the south and east.[9] In general, hunting appears to have been of little economic importance among the Huron.

Huron villages had up to several thousand inhabitants and the main ones were protected by palisades made of posts woven together with smaller branches. Inside large villages there were fifty or more longhouses, often 100 feet or more in length, made of bark attached to a light wooden frame. These houses were inhabited by eight to ten very closely related families. Families that traced themselves back to a common female ancestor formed a clan which was a political unit having its own civil chief and war leader. Each tribe in turn was made up of a number of such clans and the clan leaders served on the tribal and confederal councils.[10]

19

The events that led to the formation of the Huron confederacy are not well understood. The Huron themselves said that it began around AD 1400 with the union of the Bear and Cord tribes and grew thereafter through the addition of further lineages and tribes. Archaeologically it appears that, although one or more of the Huron tribes was indigenous to Simcoe County, other groups moved into historic Huronia from as far away as the Trent Valley, the Toronto region, and Huron and Grey counties to the west.[11] Two tribes, the Rock and the Deer, had been admitted to the confederacy not long before the arrival of the French.

Historians frequently have asserted that it was fear of the Iroquois that prompted the Huron to seek refuge in this remote and sheltered portion of Ontario.[12] While this may be why some groups moved into Huronia, it is clear that in prehistoric times the Huron outnumbered the Iroquois and probably were not at any military disadvantage. For this reason ethnologists have begun to seek other explanations to account for the heavy concentration of population in Huronia in historic times. An abundance of light, easily workable soil may be part of the answer. Since the Huron lacked the tools to work heavier soils, this advantage may have outweighed the tendency towards drought and the absence of certain trace minerals in the soil which now trouble farmers in that area.[13] Huronia also lay at the south end of the main canoe route that ran along the shores of Georgian Bay. North of there the soil was poor and the growing season short, so that none of the tribes depended on agriculture. They engaged mainly in hunting and fishing, and tribes from at least as far away as Lake Nipissing traded surplus skins, dried fish, and meat with the Huron in return for corn, which they ate in the winter when other food was scarce.[14]

As early as 1615 the French noted that Huronia was the centre of a well-developed system of trade. Hunt, however, seems to have seriously overestimated both the extent of this network and the degree to which the Huron were dependent on it.[15] The main trade appears to have been with the hunting peoples to the north who happened to be Algonkian-speaking. The other Iroquoian tribes had economies similar to that of the Huron, so that with the exception of a few items, such as black squirrel skins, which came from the Neutral country, and tobacco from the Petun, trade with the other Iroquoian tribes was of little importance. Trade with the north, however, brought in supplies of dried meat, fish, skins, clothing, native copper, and "luxury items" such as charms, which were obtained in exchange for corn, tobacco, fishing nets, Indian hemp, wampum, and squirrel skins.[16] Although manufactured goods, as well as natural products, flowed in both directions, the most important item the Huron had for export undoubtedly was corn. In 1635 Father Le Jeune described Huronia as the "granary of most of the Algonkians."[17]

Whole bands of northerners spent the winters living outside Huron villages, trading furs and dried meat with their hosts in return for corn. The Huron assumed a dominant position in these trading relationships and the Jesuits record that when the Algonkians had dealings with them, they did so in the Huron language since the latter did not bother to learn Algonkian.[18] The social implications of such linguistic behaviour cannot be lost on anyone living in present-day Quebec. In the French accounts the Algonkians appear to have been better friends of the Rock tribe than they were of the Bear.[19]

Considerable quantities of European trade goods that are believed to date between 1550 and 1575 have been found in Seneca sites in New York State.[20] Since both archaeological and historical evidence suggests that there was contact between the Huron and the tribes that lived along the St. Lawrence River in the sixteenth century,[21] it is possible that trade goods were arriving in Huronia in limited quantities at this time as well. In any such trade the Algonkin tribes along the Ottawa River would almost certainly have been intermediaries. It is thus necessary to consider the possibility that trade between the Huron and the northern Algonkians originally developed as a result of the Huron desire to obtain European trade goods.

There are a number of reasons for doubting that trade with the northern tribes had a recent origin. For one thing, the rules governing trade were exceedingly elaborate. A particular trade route was recognized as the property of the Huron tribe or family that had pioneered it, and other people were authorized to trade along this route only if they had obtained permission from the group to which it belonged.[22] Thus, since the Rock were the first Huron tribe to establish relations with the French on the St. Lawrence, they alone were entitled by Huron law to trade with them.[23] Because of the importance of this trade, however, the Rock soon "shared" it with the more numerous and influential Bear, and with the other tribes of Huronia.[24] The control of trade was vested in a small number of chiefs, and other men had to have their permission before they were allowed to engage in it.[25] An even more important indication of the antiquity of Huron contact with the north is the archaeological evidence of the Huron influence on the native cultures of that region, which can be dated as early as AD 900 and is especially evident in pottery styles.[26] Taken together, these two lines of evidence provide considerable support for the hypothesis of an early trade.

In the historic period the Huron men left their villages to visit other tribes in the summers, while their women were working in the fields. Profit was not the only reason for undertaking long voyages. The Jesuits report that many travelled into distant regions to gamble or to see new sights — in short for adventure. Trading expeditions, like war, were a challenge for young men.[27] Trading between different tribes was not always a safe and uncomplicated business and, for all they had to gain from trade during the historic period, the Huron frequently were hesitant to initiate trade with tribes of whom they had only slight acquaintance.

The dangers that beset intertribal contacts were largely products of another institution, as old, if not older than trade — the blood feud. If a man was slain by someone who was not his kinsman, his family, clan, or tribe (depending on how far removed the murderer was) felt obliged to avenge his death by slaying the killer or one of the killer's relatives. Such action could be averted only by reparations in the form of gifts paid by the group to which the murderer belonged to that of the murdered man. When an act of blood revenge actually was carried out, the injured group usually regarded it as a fresh injury; thus any killing, even an accidental one, might generate feuds that would go on for generations. This was especially true of intertribal feuds.[28]

The Huron and Five Nations had both suppressed blood feuds within their respective confederacies, but only with great difficulty. When quarrels arose between individuals from tribes not so united, they frequently gave rise to bloodshed and war. The chances of war were also increased because skill in raiding was a source of prestige for young men who therefore desired to pursue this activity.[29] If it were possible, prisoners captured in war were taken back to their captors' villages to be tortured to death, partly as an act of revenge, but also as a sacrifice to the sun or "god of war."[30] These three motives — revenge, individual prestige, and sacrifice — were common to all the Iroquoian-speaking peoples of the northeast and to many of their neighbours, and generated and sustained intertribal wars over long periods of time. Indeed, where no close political ties existed, such as those within the Huron confederacy, and where there were no mutually profitable trading relationships, war between tribes appears to have been the rule. The Huron were almost invariably at war with one or more of the Five Nations, and prior to the

21

development of the fur trade (when they started to carry French goods to the south and west) they appear to have been at war with the Neutral and Petun as well.[31]

On the other hand, when a trading relationship developed between the Huron and some neighbouring tribe, every effort was made to control feuds that might lead to war between them. The payment that was made to settle a blood feud with the Algonkians was greater than that made to settle a feud inside the confederacy,[32] and the dearest payment on record was made to the French in 1648 to compensate them for a Jesuit *donné* murdered by some Huron chiefs.[33]

A second method of promoting stable relations between tribes that wished to be trading partners appears to have been the exchange of a few people both as a token of friendship and to assure each group that the other intended to behave properly. Very often, these hostages appear to have been children. Although this custom is never explicitly described by the early French writers, the evidence for its existence is clear-cut. A Huron, whose sons or nephews (sister's sons and therefore close relatives) were sent to the Jesuit seminary in Quebec, boasted that they were relatives of the French and for this reason hoped for preferential treatment when they went to trade on the St. Lawrence.[34] Others said they had "relatives" among the Neutral and Petun and one man is reported as leaving his daughter with these relatives.[35] The priests and lay visitors who came to Huronia in early times were treated as kinsmen by the Huron, and families and individuals were anxious to have them live with them,[36] no doubt because the Huron regarded these visitors as pledges of good faith whose association with a particular family would establish good relations between that family and the French officials and traders downriver. The presentation of young children to Jacques Cartier at a number of villages along the St. Lawrence suggests, moreover, that this custom may have been an old one.[37]

The Huron thus not only traded with other tribes prior to the start of the fur trade, but also, in common with other tribes in the northeast, had developed a code or set of conventions that governed the manner in which this trade was conducted. Being a product of Indian culture, this code was designed to deal with specifically Indian problems. We will now turn to the French attempts to adapt themselves to the native trading patterns after Champlain's first encounter with the Indians in 1608.

Early Franco-Huron Relations

In 1608, the year Champlain established a trading post at Quebec, he was visited by the representatives of some Algonkin tribes from the Ottawa Valley and, in order to win their respect for him as a warrior and to secure their goodwill, he agreed to accompany them the following year on a raid against their chief enemy, the Iroquois.[38] The regions to the north gave promise of more pelts and ones of better quality than did the Iroquois country to the south and fighting with a tribe alongside its enemies was an effective way of confirming an alliance.[39] Thus Champlain's actions seem to have been almost inevitable. At the same time he probably also hoped to drive Iroquois raiders from the St. Lawrence Valley and to open the river as a valuable trade artery.[40]

When the Ottawa River Algonkin returned the next year, they were accompanied by a party of Huron warriors from the Rock tribe. In later times the Huron informed the Jesuits that they had first heard of the French from the Algonkians early in the seventeenth century, and as a result of this had decided to go downriver to meet these newcomers for themselves.[41] Very likely Champlain's account and the Huron one refer to the same event. Some of the Ottawa River Algonkin, who were already probably in the habit of wintering in Huronia, may have tried to recruit Huron warriors for their forthcoming expedition against the Iroquois, and the Huron, prompted by curiosity and a desire for adventure, may have agreed to accompany them to Quebec.

23

Champlain was keenly interested at this time both in exploring the interior and in making contacts with the people who lived there. Learning the size of the Huron confederacy and their good relations with the hunting (and potentially trapping) peoples to the north, Champlain realized their importance for the development of the fur trade and set out to win their friendship. The Huron, on the contrary, were at first extremely hesitant in their dealings with the French,[42] in part because they had no treaty with them and also because they regarded the French as allies of the Algonkin, who might become hostile if they saw the Hurons trying to establish an independent relationship with them.

The ambiguity of the Huron position can be seen in the exchange of children that was arranged in 1610. At that time the Huron gave Champlain custody of a boy, who was to go to France with him, and in exchange they received a young Frenchman. When the Huron departed, however, the French boy (probably Etienne Brûlé) did not leave with them, but stayed with Iroquet, an Algonkin chief from the lower Ottawa.[43] Iroquet, however, seems to have been one of the Algonkin who was in the habit of wintering in Huronia. Thus a three-sided exchange seems to have been arranged in which the Huron laid the basis for a friendly relationship with the French, but one that was subordinate to, and dependent upon, their relationship with the Algonkin.

As trade with the French increased, the Huron began to appreciate French goods and to want more of them. Metal awls and needles were superior to native bone ones, and iron arrowheads could penetrate the traditional shields and body armour of their enemies. Metal kettles were easier to cook in than clay pots and metal knives were much more efficient than stone ones. Clearing fields and cutting wood was easier when stone axes were replaced by iron hatchets. Luxury items, such as cloth and European beads, were soon sought after as well.[44]

The growing demand for these products in a population that numbered between twenty and thirty thousand no doubt made the Huron anxious to establish closer relations with the French, without, if possible, having to recognize the Ottawa River Algonkin as middlemen or to pay them tolls to pass through their lands.[45] Since the principal item that the French wanted was beaver pelts,[46] the Huron probably also began to expand their trade with the north at this time in order to secure these furs in larger quantities. In return for these furs, they carried not only corn and tobacco but also French trade goods to their northern trading partners. The tribes north of Lake Huron seem to have continued to trade exclusively with the Huron rather than seeking to obtain goods from the French. No doubt this was in part because Huronia was nearby and reaching it did not require a long and hazardous journey down the Ottawa River. Such a journey would have been time-consuming, if not impossible, for a small tribe. More importantly, however, they wanted corn for winter consumption which the Huron, but not the French, were able to provide. Although there is no documentary evidence to support this suggestion, it seems likely that increasing supplies of corn permitted these hunters to devote more time to trapping and relieved them of some of their day-today worries about survival.[47] Thus the growth of the fur trade may have led the northern groups to concentrate on trapping and the Huron to devote more of their energy to producing agricultural surpluses to trade with the north.[48] On at least one occasion, the Huron were providing even the French at Quebec with needed supplies of food.[49] In the 1640s their close friends and trading partners, the Nipissing, were travelling as far north as James Bay each year in order to collect the furs which they passed on to the Huron.[50]

In spite of the Huron desire for French goods and their ability to gather furs from the interior, the development of direct trade between Huronia and the St. Lawrence required the formation of a partnership that was expressed in terms the Indian could understand. Without continual assurances of goodwill passing between Huron and French leaders and without the exchange of gifts and people, no Huron would have travelled to Quebec without fear and trepidation. Even after many years of trade, Hurons going to Quebec felt safer if they were travelling with a Frenchman whom they knew and who could be trusted to protect their interests while they were trading.[51] Champlain understood clearly that treaties of friendship were necessary for successful trading partnerships with the Indians. For this reason he had been willing to support the Algonkin and Montagnais in their wars with the Mohawk and, since it was impossible to be friendly with both sides, had maintained his alliance with these northern tribes in spite of Iroquois overtures for peace.[52] The cementing of a treaty with the various Huron tribes was clearly the main reason he visited Huronia in 1615, a visit made in the face of considerable opposition from the Ottawa River Algonkin.[53]

Quite properly in Huron eyes, Champlain spent most of his time in Huronia with the Rock tribe. This had been the first of the Huron tribes to contact him on the St. Lawrence and therefore had a special relationship with the French according to Huron law. When he accompanied a Huron war party on a traditional, and what appeared to him as an ill-fated raid against the central Iroquois, Champlain was resorting to a now-familiar technique for winning the friendship of particular tribes.[54] What Champlain apparently still did not realize was that the aim of these expeditions was adventure and taking prisoners, rather than the destruction of enemy villages.[55] The Huron were undoubtedly far more pleased with the results of the expedition than Champlain was.

From 1615 on, a number of Frenchmen were living in Huronia; their main purpose in being there was to encourage the Huron to trade.[56] Many of these young men, like the coureurs de bois of later times, enjoyed their life among the Indians and, to the horror of the Catholic clergy, made love to Huron women and probably married them according to local custom. The rough and tumble ways of individuals like Etienne Brûlé endeared them to their Huron hosts and this, in turn, allowed them to inspire confidence in the Indians who came to trade. It has been suggested that the main reason these men remained in Huronia was to persuade the Huron to trade in New France rather than to take their furs south to the Dutch who had begun to trade in the Hudson Valley after 1609.[57] This explanation seems unlikely, however. Until 1629 most of the Dutch trade appears to have been confined to the Mahican.[58] Although the Dutch were apparently anxious to trade with the "French Indians" as early as 1633, the Mohawk were not willing to allow them to do so unless they were in some way able to profit from the trade themselves.[59] This the Huron, who had a long-standing feud with the Iroquois, were unwilling to let them do.

The main job of the early coureurs de bois appears to have been to live in Huronia as visible evidence of French goodwill and as exchanges for the Huron youths who were sent to live with the French.[60] In this capacity they were able to encourage the Indians to engage in trade. Each year some of them travelled downriver with the Huron to see that the Algonkin did not prevent the passage of their canoes or scare the Huron off with stories of disasters or plots against them in Quebec.[61] They also acted as interpreters for the Huron and aided them in their dealings with the traders.[62] Except for the years when the Mohawk blockaded the Ottawa River, the Huron sent an annual "fleet" or series of fleets to Quebec bearing the furs they had collected.[63] It is unfortunate that the records do not supply more information on these fleets, particularly about who organized them and what was their tribal composition. The fleets left Huronia in the spring and returned several months later. When the St. Lawrence was blocked by the Iroquois, the Hurons made their way to Quebec over the smaller waterways that led through the Laurentians.[64]

The Recollet and Jesuit missionaries who worked in Huronia between 1615 and 1629 were accepted by the Huron as part of the Franco-Huron trading alliance and as individuals whose goodwill was potentially advantageous in dealing with the traders and authorities in Quebec. That they lacked interest except as shamans is evident from Gabriel Sagard's statement that it was hard to work among any tribe that was not engaged in trade (i.e., bound by the Franco-Huron alliance).[65] The priests appear to have restricted their missionary activities to caring for the needs of the French traders in Huronia and trying to make some converts among the Indians. Their preaching, as far as it was understood, did not appear to present a challenge or affront to the Huron way of life, although the customs of the priests were strange to the Indians, who found these men austere and far less appealing than the easy-going coureurs de bois.[66] For obvious reasons, relations between the priests and local traders were not good and Sagard claims that among other things the latter often refused to help the missionaries learn native languages.[67] The most serious charge that the priests levelled at these traders was that their behaviour sowed confusion and doubt among the Huron and impeded the spread of the Christian faith among them.[68] These early experiences convinced the Jesuits that to run a mission in Huronia properly the priests must control those Europeans who were allowed to enter the country.

In the early part of the seventeenth century the colony of New France was nothing more than a trading post and its day-to-day existence depended upon securing an annual supply of furs.[69] Not understanding the long-standing hostility between the Huron and the Iroquois, the French were apprehensive of any move that seemed likely to divert furs from the St. Lawrence to the Hudson Valley. The French made peace with the Mohawk in 1624 and French traders did business with them, an arrangement that no doubt pleased the Mohawk as it made them for a time less dependent on the Dutch and therefore gave them more bargaining power in their dealings with Albany.[70] Nevertheless, the French became extremely alarmed about a peace treaty that the Huron negotiated with the Seneca in 1623. This appears to have been one of the periodic treaties that the Huron and Iroquois negotiated in order to get back members of their respective tribes who had been taken prisoner, but not yet killed, by the enemy.[71] As such, it was probably perfectly harmless to French interest. Nevertheless the situation was judged sufficiently serious for a delegation of eleven Frenchmen, including three clerics, to be sent to the Huron country.[72] Various writers have followed Jean Charlevoix in saying that this delegation was instructed to disrupt the new treaty. Charlevoix, however, wrote long after the event took

26

place and is not an unbiased witness.[73] It seems more likely that the
expedition had as its main purpose simply the reaffirming of the alliances
made between Champlain and the various Huron chiefs in 1615. In actual
fact the Huron probably had no thought of trading with the Iroquois
at this time. To the chagrin of the Dutch, the Mohawk were firm in
their refusal to allow the northern tribes to pass through their country
to trade on the Hudson. The Huron undoubtedly felt that direct trade
with the French, even if they were farther from Huronia than the Dutch,[74]
was preferable to trade via the Mohawk with the Europeans in New
York State.

The very great importance that the Huron attached to their trade with
the French even at this time is shown by their efforts to prevent potential
rivals, such as the Petun or Neutral, from concluding any sort of formal
alliance with the French. Neither group seems to have constituted much
of a threat, since the Petun had to pass through Huron territory in order
to paddle north along the shore of Georgian Bay[75] and the Neutral, who
do not seem to have had adequate boats, would have had to travel down
the St. Lawrence River to Quebec — en route the Mohawk would have
either stolen their furs or forced them to divert most of the trade to
the south.[76] The Huron do not seem to have minded well-known coureurs
de bois occasionally visiting the Neutral or other tribes with whom they
traded, but when, on his visit to the Neutral in 1626, Father de La
Roche Daillon proposed an alliance between them and the French, the
Huron spread rumours about the French that brought an end to the
proposed treaty.[77] The ease with which the Huron did this, and repeated
the manoeuvre in 1640–41,[78] is an indication both of the insecurity that
tribes felt in the absence of a proper treaty with foreigners and of the
importance that the Huron placed on their privileged relationship with
the French. These observations reinforce our conclusion that coureurs
de bois did not live in Huronia simply to dissuade the Huron from going
to trade with either the Mohawk or the Dutch, but instead were a vital
link in the Franco-Huron alliance and necessary intermediaries between
the Huron and the French fur traders in Quebec. Such were the services
for which Brûlé received a hundred pistoles each year from his
employers.[79]

Franco-Huron trade increased in the years prior to 1629. Undoubtedly
the Huron were growing increasing reliant on European goods, but it
is unlikely that they were ever completely dependent on trade during
this period. There is no evidence that the British occupation of Quebec
led them to trade with New Holland or with the Iroquois. Several renegade Frenchmen, including Brûlé, remained in Huronia and probably
encouraged the Huron to trade with the British.[80] It was during this
period that Brûlé was murdered by the Huron living in Toanché. Since
he was given a proper burial it is unlikely that he was tortured to death
and eaten as Sagard reports.[81] More likely, he was killed in a brawl with

the Huron among whom he lived. That he was killed during the British occupation of New France does not, however, seem to be without significance. Until the French withdrawal he had been protected not only by his popularity but more importantly by the Franco-Huron alliance. Once the French had departed, he was on his own.

The Jesuits Take Control

The Compagnie des Cent-Associés, which took effective control of the affairs of New France after the colony was retroceded to France in 1632, was different from earlier trading companies in that its members were more interested in missionary work than their predecessors had been. At this time the Society of Jesus also managed to obtain the *de facto* monopoly over missionary activities in New France that it was to hold for many years.[82] The Jesuits brought about a number of changes in policy with regard to Huronia. In particular, they were much more anxious to evangelize the Huron *as a people* than the Recollets had been.[83] As their prime goal they sought to lead the entire confederacy toward the Christian religion, rather than to convert individuals. Moreover, as a result of the strong influence they wielded at the French court, they were in a better position to command the support of officials and fur traders.[84] For the first while after they returned to the Huron country, the Jesuits continued many of the mission practices that had been current prior to 1629, such as sending Indian children to their seminary at Quebec.[85] As their knowledge of the Huron language and of the country improved (in both cases as a result of systematic study) they gradually began to modify their work along lines that were more in keeping with their general policy.[86]

A major *bête noire* of the missionaries prior to 1629 was the French traders who lived in Huronia and set a bad example for the natives. In order to assure unity of purpose for their work, the duties that formerly had been carried out by these coureurs de bois were taken over by lay brothers, workmen, and *donnés* directly subject to Jesuit supervision.[87] Later accusations that the Jesuits were engaged in the fur trade seem to have sprung largely from this action. The oft-repeated claim that priests were vital to the fur trade in Huronia is obviously without foundation. The coureurs de bois, who had lived in Huronia for many years, not only had functioned effectively during this period without missionary support but also appear to have been substantially more popular and more effective in their dealings with the Huron than the priests had been. The Jesuits wished to be rid of this group principally to assure that the French living in Huronia would not be working at cross-purposes. The trading companies apparently were willing to allow the Jesuits to have their own way in this matter, but in return it was necessary that the laymen attached to the Jesuit mission discharge at least the most vital functions of organizing the annual trade which the coureurs de bois had done heretofore.[88] The reasons that the Jesuits had for wanting to be rid of the coureurs de bois were clearly religious, not economic.

The Jesuits' connections with the fur trade did not arise, however, simply from their desire to be rid of the coureurs de bois; they also depended on it not only to get into Huronia but also for their personal safety so long as they remained there. The Huron were obviously not at all interested in what the Jesuits had to teach, and on several occasions after 1634 they made it clear that they preferred the former coureurs de bois to the Jesuits and their assistants.[89] In 1633, and again in 1634, they offered a whole series of excuses, including the hostility of the Algonkin from Allumette Island, as reasons for not taking the Jesuits home with them.[90] Moreover, fearing revenge for the death of Brûlé, they were unwilling to allow their children to remain as seminarians at Quebec.[91] In 1634 Champlain made the official French position clear when he informed the Huron that he regarded the Jesuits' presence in their country as a vital part of a renewed Franco-Huron alliance, at the same time expressing the hope that they would someday agree to become Christians.[92] Since the Huron wanted to renew their former trading relationship with the French, they agreed to accept the priests as a token of this alliance. Henceforth they were bound by treaty to allow the Jesuits to live among them and to protect the priests from harm. The thought of having these individuals who were so respected by the French in Huronia and under their control must also have given the Huron confidence in their dealings with the French who remained in Quebec.

Although the Jesuits travelled to Huronia in 1635 in canoes that belonged to members of the Cord and Rock tribes, they were put ashore rather unceremoniously in the territory of the Bear tribe, where Brébeuf had worked previously and where Brûlé had been murdered.[93] It is not clear whether the Jesuits had wanted to go to this region or were left there by their Rock and Cord hosts who did not want to take them to their own villages. It is possible that the Bear, who were the most powerful of the Huron tribes, exerted their influence to have the Jesuits left among them. In this regard it is perhaps not without meaning that the Jesuits previously had discussed with the Indians the possibility of their settling in Ossossané, the chief town of the Bear nation.[94] Brébeuf was welcomed by the villagers of Ihonitiria, among whom he had lived before, and the Jesuits decided to settle in that village both because it was close to the canoe route to New France and also in order to persuade the villagers that they bore them no ill will for having murdered Brûlé. The latter, the Jesuits said, was regarded by the French as a traitor and debauched renegade.[95] Nevertheless, his murder haunted the Huron, and even some neighbouring tribes,[96] who feared that it might lead to war with the French. Such fears may have been responsible for the dispute that the Jesuits observed between certain villages of the Bear tribe shortly after their arrival in Huronia.[97]

It would appear that according to native custom the Jesuits coming to Huronia had a right to expect they would receive free food and lodgings. This would have been in return for similar care given by the French to the young seminarists in Quebec.[98] In Huron eyes the latter had been exchanged as tokens of good faith in return for the Jesuits and their assistants.[99] In fact, the Huron provided food and shelter for the Jesuits only rarely. The missionaries had to purchase or provide these things for themselves and found the Huron demanding payment of some sort for most of their services.[100]

For a time after their return to Huronia the Jesuits were the objects of friendly public interest and their presence and goodwill were sought after, in part because individual Hurons sought to obtain favours in Quebec through their commendation, in part because the services people performed for the Jesuits, and even attendance at religious instruction, were rewarded with presents of trade goods and tobacco. The latter, although a native product, was scarce in Huronia at the time.[101] Since all of the priests (except perhaps Brébeuf) were struggling to learn the Huron language, most of the missionary activities during the first few years were confined to the Bear country. Only a few trips were made into more distant areas of Huronia.[102]

The Epidemics of 1635 to 1640

The first serious trial for the Jesuits, and for the Franco-Huron alliance, occurred between the years 1635 and 1640. An unspecified disease, either measles or smallpox, was present in Quebec the year the Jesuits returned to Huronia and it followed the Huron fleet upriver. This was the beginning of a series of epidemics which swept away more than half the Huron population in the next six years.[103] These new maladies were especially fatal to children and old people. Because they were fatal to the latter group, many of the most skilful Huron leaders and craftsmen, as well as the people most familiar with native religious lore, perished.[104] The loss of children may well have meant that the proportion of men of fighting age in the Huron population was below normal by the end of the next decade.

The Jesuits, who wished to save the souls of dying children, frequently baptized them, both with and without their parents' permission. The Huron, being unclear about the Jesuits' intention in doing this, observed that children tended to die soon after baptism and came to suspect that the Jesuits were practising a deadly form of witchcraft.[105] The rumour revived that the Jesuits had been sent to Huronia to seek revenge for Brûlé's murder,[106] a rumour which gained credence from pictures of the torments of hell that the Jesuits displayed in their chapel and from the ritual of the mass (which the Huron understood had something to do with eating a corpse).[107] According to Huron law, sorcerers could be killed without a trial, and in times of crisis extensive pogroms appear to have been unleashed against persons suspected of this crime.[108] Nevertheless, while individuals threatened to murder the Jesuits and on one occasion a council of the confederacy met to try the Jesuits on a charge of witch-craft,[109] none of the Frenchmen in Huronia was killed.

Although the majority of the people were frightened of the Jesuits and believed that they were working to destroy the country, their leaders repeatedly stressed that they could not afford to rupture the Franco-Huron alliance by killing the French priests.[110] One well-placed chief said that if the Huron did not go downriver to trade with the French for even two years, they would be lucky if they found themselves as well off as the [despised] Algonkians.[111] While this statement was a bit of rhetoric, it stresses the importance of the fur trade to the Huron at this time and their growing reliance on French trade goods. During the entire course of the epidemics only one village, apparently a small one, was willing to give up the use of trade goods, and hence presumably to sever relations with the French.[112] Instead, the Huron resorted to in-direct means to persuade the Jesuits to leave Huronia *voluntarily*. Chil-dren were encouraged to annoy them, their religious objects were be-fouled, and occasionally they were personally threatened or mistreated.[113] The Jesuits noted, rather significantly, that these persecutions diminished before the annual trip downriver or after the return of a successful fleet.[114] The French officials in Quebec were aware of the dangerous situation in which the Jesuits found themselves, but as long as feelings ran high in Huronia, these authorities could do no more than to try to spare them from the worst excesses of Huron anger. They did this by threatening to cut off trade if the Jesuits were killed.

By 1640 the serious epidemics in Huronia were over. That summer, the new governor of Canada, Charles Huault de Montmagny, took action to "punish" the Huron who came to Quebec for their bad treatment of the Jesuits.[115] It is not clear what form this punishment took, but it appears that in the course of his dealings with them he made it clear that he considered their bad treatment of the Jesuits had terminated the existing alliance. At the same time he offered to renew the alliance, but only on the clear understanding that the Jesuits would continue to live in Huronia and work there unmolested. This is the first time, to our knowledge, that French officials had injected a positive element of threat into their dealings with the Huron. Presumably, the great losses in manpower and skills that the Huron had suffered and their consequent increasing dependence on trade and French support made such action possible. The Huron were in good health and expecting an abundant harvest; hence, many of the anxieties that had plagued them in recent years were dispelled. Because of this they were once more in a good mood and, hence, under the protection of a renewed Franco-Huron alliance the Jesuits found themselves free not only to continue the mission work among them but also to intensify their efforts.[116]

Already during the final crisis of 1639, the Jesuits had decided to establish a permanent centre for their missionary work in the Huron area. This centre was foreseen as serving various functions. Not only would it provide a refuge in time of danger (such as they lacked in 1639), but it also would allow them to put up buildings of European design. It had not been economical to construct these in the Huron villages which shifted their location about once every decade. The Jesuits' centre was thus designed to be a further example of European culture in the heart of Huronia, a focus from which new ideas could diffuse to the local population. Gradually, pigs, fowl, and young cattle were brought upriver from Quebec and European crops were grown in the fields nearby.[117] The residence of Ste Marie acquired a hospital and a burial ground and became a place where Christian Indians could come for spiritual retreats and assembly on feast days.[118] Being located apart from any one village, and near the geographical centre of the confederacy, it was better able, both from a political and a geographical point of view, to serve as a mission centre for all Huronia. (During the worst years of the epidemics the Jesuits had remained for the most part in the northwest corner of Huronia.) In 1639 the Jesuits also made a survey and census of the country prior to setting up a system of missions that would carry the Christian message to all of the Huron tribes and, as far as possible, to other tribes as well.[119]

The Jesuits had thus weathered a difficult period. It is clear that they had been allowed to enter Huronia and to continue there only because of the Franco-Huron alliance. That they were not killed or expelled from Huronia at the height of the epidemics is an indication of how dependent the Hurons were becoming on the fur trade and how much the alliance with the French meant to them. It also indicates that the Huron leaders were able to restrain their unruly followers in order to preserve good relations with New France.[120] Evidence of lingering malice towards the priests can be seen in the events that came to light on the visit of Fathers Brébeuf and Chaumonot to the Neutral country in the winter of 1640–41. There the priests learned that the Huron had offered the Neutral rich presents, if they would kill the missionaries.[121] In this way the Huron hoped to destroy two of the "sorcerers" who had been tormenting their nation without endangering the French alliance. They also had other motives, however. The proposed murder, so long as it was not traced back to the Huron, would put the Neutral in a bad light and would prevent Brébeuf from pursuing any dealings with the Seneca. Although there is no evidence that Brébeuf planned to visit the Seneca, a rumour had spread that having failed to kill the Huron with witchcraft he now was seeking to turn their enemies loose upon them.[122]

A Crisis in Huron–Iroquois Relations

If the year 1640 marked the end of the persecution of the Jesuits in Huronia, unknown to them and to their Huron hosts, it also marked the beginning of a crisis that was to destroy Huronia. Beaver had become rare in the Huron country and most of the skins they traded with the French came from neighbouring tribes to the north.[123] A similar decline in the beaver population of New York State seems to have reached a point of crisis by 1640. That year the number of pelts traded at Fort Orange is reported to have dropped sharply.[124] While it is possible that at least part of the decline was the result of clandestine traders cutting into official trade, most commentators agree that it was basically related to the exhaustion of the supply of beaver in the Iroquois' home territory.[125]

33

While this hypothesis is not well enough documented that it can be regarded as certain, it seems a useful one for explaining Iroquois behaviour during the next few years. There is little doubt that after 1640 the Iroquois were preoccupied with securing new sources of pelts. The main controversy concerning their relations with their neighbours during this period centres on whether they were seeking to obtain furs by forcing the Huron to share their trade with them[126] or were attacking their neighbours in order to secure new hunting territories. Although Trelease[127] supports the latter theory, the data he uses apply for the most part to a later period and come mainly from sources in New York State and New England. Contemporary Canadian evidence definitely seems to rule out his claims; indeed if his hypothesis were true, the events leading to the destruction of Huronia would make little sense at all.

Trelease's theory finds its main support in claims made by the Iroquois in the early part of the eighteenth century that they had conquered Ontario and adjacent regions as beaver hunting grounds. In the treaty of 1701, in which the Iroquois placed their "Beaver ground" under the protection of the King of England, the Iroquois said explicitly that they had driven the indigenous tribes from this area in order to hunt there.[128] Trelease errs, however, in assuming that the reasons the Iroquois gave for conquering this territory in 1701 were the same as those they actually had for doing so half a century earlier. There is no doubt that in 1701 the Iroquois (mainly the Seneca) were hunting beaver in Ontario, but since the Huron country was reported in the 1630s to be as hunted out as their own it is illogical to assume that they attacked this region in 1649 in order to secure more hunting territory. The Huron beaver supplies they sought to capture were those coming by trade from the north. Only after their attacks failed to capture the western fur trade and after Ontario was deserted for a time allowing the restoration of the local beaver population did the Iroquois begin to hunt there. Since they lacked historical records, it is not surprising that by 1701 the Iroquois believed

34

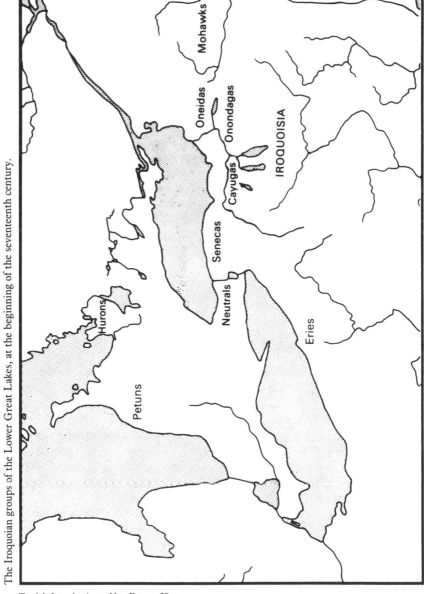

The Iroquoian groups of the Lower Great Lakes, at the beginning of the seventeenth century.

Trudel, *Introduction to New France*, 28.

the use that they were making of Ontario at the present time was the same reason they had for attacking the tribes there long before. The attacks the Iroquois launched against the Petun and Neutral, following their attack on the Huron, offer no opposition to this theory. Although these groups had not participated in the fur trade prior to 1649, there was considerable danger that with the Huron gone they would attempt to do so. Hence, their dispersal was also necessary.

Trelease's theory thus fails to provide an acceptable explanation of events in Canada in the middle of the seventeenth century. It seems much more likely that the Iroquois, and mainly the Mohawk, began by trying to force the Huron to trade with them and that only latterly, when their efforts in this direction were unsuccessful, did they decide to destroy the Huron (and their neighbours) as an intermediary group.

The Mohawk began to intimidate the Huron by harassing those travelling along the Ottawa River — a tactic that had the additional advantage of providing a supply of captured furs. In 1642 Iroquois raiders spread fear and terror throughout all of the Huron villages,[129] and in 1644 they succeeded in preventing contact between Quebec and Huronia.[130] The increasing number of guns that the Iroquois were acquiring from the Dutch, English, and Swedish colonies along the Atlantic seaboard gradually gave them military superiority over the Huron, among whom the French had limited and controlled the sale of guns.[131] In 1644 the French despatched more than twenty soldiers to Huronia to protect the Huron over the winter and assure the arrival of their furs in Quebec the next spring.[132] The Mohawk were also harassing the French in the St. Lawrence Valley who were moved the next spring to discuss peace, both to assure their own safety and to re-open the river to trade. Although the subsequent treaty of 1645 was with the French, the Mohawk seem to have interpreted it as involving a commitment that in the future the Huron would trade with them as well as with the French.[133] The Huron, however, had no intention of doing this, and the French, who may not have perceived clearly what the Mohawk wanted, did not want to encourage them to divert trade. The main French reason for the treaty with the Mohawk was the short-term one of opening the river. The French had little to offer the Iroquois in return and refused to sell them guns, the one item they wanted.[134] When it became clear to the Mohawk that the Huron did not intend to trade with them, they renewed their attack on Huronia and on the Huron fleet.

The Development of a Christian Faction

While this dangerous crisis in intertribal relations was boiling up, a situation was developing in Huronia that put a new strain on the Franco-Huron alliance.

35

Prior to 1640, most Christian converts were Hurons on the point of death, many of whom knew nothing about Christian theology but who hoped that baptism would save their lives.[135] At one point during the epidemics a Huron version of the rite of baptism became part of a native healing cult that was said to be inspired by a native deity who had revealed himself as the real Jesus.[136] In these rites the sick were sprinkled with water as part of an orgiastic ceremony typical of traditional Huron healing rituals. After 1640, however, the Jesuits began to convert increasing numbers of people who were in good health. Many were men of importance, whose conversions made that of their families, friends, and tribesmen easier.[137] In order to prevent backsliding, the Jesuits at first made it a policy to baptise (except in cases of extreme ill health) only adults who had provided substantial proof of their devotion to Christianity and whose family life seemed to be stable.[138]

Many factors seem to have induced people to convert: some admired the bravery of the Jesuits, others wished to be able to follow a Christian friend to heaven, still others noted in their names a theological term that the Jesuits were using.[139]

Although economic motives were not the only ones involved in conversion, it is noteworthy that at least a few Huron became Christians to avoid participation in pagan feasts, which required them to give away considerable amounts of property in the form of presents and entertainment.[140] A far larger number of people hoped through conversion to receive preferential treatment in their dealings with traders and officials in New France.[141] In 1648, when only 15 per cent of the Huron were Christian, half of the men in the Huron fleet were either converts or were preparing for baptism.[142] Those who traded with the French in Quebec not only were more exposed to French culture and to Christianity than were those who remained at home but also had more to gain from good relations with the French. Commercial considerations may also explain why the Jesuits generally found it easier to convert men than women.

While stressing the practical economic motives that certainly motivated many conversions, personal and cultural factors should not be ignored. The Huron were increasingly dependent on French culture and in the eyes of many, but (as we shall see) certainly not all, of the Huron the priest was coming to replace the native sorcerer as an object of awe and respect. This did not, however, lead the Huron to lose faith in themselves or in their culture, as it did in many other tribes.[143] Supported by the respect shown by the Jesuits for the Huron people and for much of their culture, many Huron converts appear to have been imbued with a sincere zeal to change and reform their own culture. No doubt the size of the Huron confederacy and its isolation from unsupervised contact with the Europeans did much to prevent the deterioration in self-confidence that is obvious among many weaker tribes. Had other circumstances not been adverse, I think it would have been possible for the Jesuits to have transformed Huronia successfully into a nation that was both Christian and Indian.

For a time the growing number of Huron converts posed no serious problems for the rest of society, although individual converts were frequently taunted and sometimes expelled from their longhouses with much resulting personal hardship.[144] (A woman who had been a member of a pagan healing society was threatened with death when after conversion she refused to perform in the society.[145]) Threats and assassination no doubt were the fate of other converts. The Jesuits and their assistants, however, were no longer attacked or molested in any way.[146] It appears that at least some headmen surrendered their political office on becoming Christians, since they felt that the obligation to participate in Huron festivals which these offices entailed was contrary to their new faith.[147] In this and in other ways the nascent Christian community avoided for a time the possibility of an open clash with the large pagan majority.

Gradually, however, a rift began. Some Christians refused, for example, to be buried in their tribal ossuaries, which in effect was to deny membership in their village or tribe.[148] They also refused to fight alongside pagans in the war parties but instead formed their own detachments, no doubt because of the religious implications of traditional Iroquoian warfare.[149] As the number of converts grew, men retained their political offices after conversion, but appointed deputies to handle the religious functions traditionally associated with them.[150] As the number of Christians who held these important offices continued to grow, the split between pagans and Christians became increasingly a political issue.

The Jesuits, for their part, now set as their immediate goal the Christianizing of an entire village.[151] Significantly the most promising town was Ossossané where the Jesuits had been working for a long time. This town, belonging to the Bear tribe, was also the political centre of the Huron confederacy.[152] In 1648 they achieved their objective. By then the majority of people in Ossossané were converts. And that winter the chiefs of the village refused to allow the people who remained pagan to celebrate the traditional festivals, and they appointed a Jesuit as the chief headman of the village, with the right to act as a censor of public morals.[153]

The Pagan Reaction and the Destruction of Huronia

Although in 1645 such social revolutions were still several years in the future, many of the pagans had already begun to fear for the survival of their traditional customs and beliefs.[154] Undoubtedly a large number of these people were genuinely attached to the old ways and for this reason alone resented the growth of Christianity. It is also possible that many chiefs who wished to remain pagan began to fear a decline in their own influence as Christians began to play a stronger role in the life of the country. They probably resented the closer contacts that Christian chiefs had with the French and feared that these contacts would be used as a source of power. As a result of these fears and rivalries, pagan and Christian factions began to develop within the various tribes and villages throughout Huronia.[155]

Although the documentation in the Jesuit Relations is scanty, there appears to have been a considerable variation in attitude towards the Jesuits and Christianity among the different Huron tribes. The Bear, among whom the Jesuits had lived for the longest time and whose main town, Ossossané, had a large and rapidly growing Christian community, seem to have been the most pro-Christian and pro-French.[156] The Cord probably had much the same sort of attitude.[157] The Rock and Deer tribes, however, seem to have been considerably less friendly. The Jesuits report that the former tribe, being the easternmost, had suffered most from the attacks of the Iroquois and was therefore the most inclined to seek peace with their traditional enemies. The Rock were also described, however, as a tribe with a strong aversion to the faith who never had been converted.[158] The Deer had a reputation among the Jesuits for being sorcerers,[159] and one assumes from this that they gave the missionaries a bad time. Both of these tribes joined the Iroquois of their own free will after the break-up of Huronia in 1649.[160] Despite this variation, however, there were people in all the Huron tribes who were starting to have misgivings about the future of Huronia and who resented the changes that the French alliance was bringing about.

After 1645 these sentiments seem to have led to the formation of a sizable anti-French party, which apparently found a certain amount of support everywhere in Huronia, except perhaps in Ossossané. This marked a new development in French–Huron relations, all previous opposition having been to the priests resident in Huronia rather than to the French in general. Supporters of this party seem to have reasoned that Christianity was a threat to Huronia, that Christianity flourished because the Jesuits were able to work there under the terms of the Franco-Huron alliance, and that the best way to save the country (and enhance the power of the pagan chiefs at the expense of their Christian rivals) was therefore to expel the Jesuits, break off the alliance, and begin trading with the Iroquois. In this way, not only would the traditional culture of Huronia be saved, but the attacks of the Iroquois, which had been growing in intensity,[161] could be brought to an end. Thus for the first time a respectable body of opinion in Huronia came to believe that an alliance with enemies who shared similar beliefs and culture was preferable to one with strangers seeking to change the Huron way of life. The threat that was facing the traditionalists made the thought of trading with their old enemies and rivals seem much less unpleasant than it had been a few years previously.

The first plan for a rapprochement with the Iroquois was well conceived and sought to exploit internal differences within the Iroquois confederacy for the Hurons' own advantage. Since the treaty of 1645 had
failed to obtain the furs they wanted, the Mohawk were likely to be
suspicious of, if not hostile to, further Huron blandishments. The Seneca
likewise were unfriendly because of recent Huron attacks on them.[162]
The Onondaga, however, had long enjoyed the position of being the
chief tribe in the confederacy and were increasingly jealous of the Mohawk, who were exploiting their close contacts with the Dutch and the
English in an effort to dominate the league.[163] It is therefore no surprise
that it was through the Onondaga that the Huron attempted to make
peace with the Iroquois.

The Jesuits did not record, and may not have known, the exact nature
of the treaty that the Huron were trying to negotiate. The presence of
a clause promising that the Huron would trade furs with the Iroquois
is suggested by a remark, attributed to the Andaste or Susquehannock
(who were allies of the Huron and sent ambassadors to the Onondaga
to argue on their behalf), that such a treaty would promote the trade
of all these tribes with one another.[164] It is also significant that among
the Huron the Bear tribe was the one most opposed to this treaty.[165]
The Jesuits said this was because the Bear had suffered less from Iroquois
raids than had the other Huron tribes, but a second reason could be
that the Christians who were more numerous in this tribe than in the
others, saw in these negotiations a clear threat to the Franco-Huron alliance and to their own power and well-being. Negotiations continued
for some time, but were terminated in January 1648, when a party of
Mohawk warriors slew a Huron embassy on its way to the chief Onondaga
town to arrange the final terms of the treaty.[166] A distinguished Onondaga
chief, who had remained in Huronia as a hostage, committed suicide
when he learned what the Mohawk had done.[167]

There seems little reason to doubt the honesty of the Onondaga in
these negotiations. The Mohawk probably attacked the Huron embassy
because they were angry that negotiations were being conducted with
the Onondaga rather than with them. The Mohawk may also have believed that the Huron were trying to deceive the Onondaga and that
the only way of dealing with the Huron confederacy was to destroy it.
In any case, the Mohawk managed to bring the first major political offensive of the anti-French faction in Huronia to an ignominious
conclusion.

Even though this first effort had failed, at least some Huron apparently
believed that a rapprochement with the Iroquois still was possible. Indeed, either because they were totally convinced of the necessity of ap-
peasing the Iroquois or because of their extreme hatred of the Christians,
a minority seems to have become convinced that a break with the French
was a precondition for further negotiation. The group responsible for
the next move was led by six, apparently distinguished, chiefs from three

39

villages.[168] Unfortunately, these village are unnamed. The chiefs decided to make a public issue of the question of a continued Franco-Huron alliance through the simple expedient of killing a Frenchman. They do not appear to have designated any particular victim and their henchmen slew Jacques Douart, a *donné* whom they encountered not far from Ste Marie. Once Douart was slain, the conspirators issued a proclamation calling for the banishment from Huronia of the French and all of the Huron who insisted on remaining Christian.[169] An emergency council was convened (apparently from all over the country) and for several days these proposals were debated. On the one side were the Christians and those pagans who felt that the Franco-Huron alliance should continue; on the other the traditionalists who had stirred up the trouble and no doubt some other Hurons who hated neither Christianity nor the French, but who felt that a peace treaty with the Iroquois was important enough to be worth the termination of the French alliance. Among the latter must have been many refugees from the Rock tribe which had been forced to abandon its villages as a result of Iroquois attacks only a short time before.[170] The pro-French party finally won the debate and the Jesuits in turn agreed to accept the traditional Huron compensation for a murder, in this case one hundred beaver skins.[171] The ritual presentation of this settlement made clear that it was designed to reaffirm and protect the Franco-Huron alliance which the unprecedented actions of these chiefs had endangered. Thus ended what appears to have been the last attempt to rupture the Franco-Huron alliance.

During the summer of 1648 the Seneca attacked and destroyed the large town of St. Joseph. As the situation grew more serious the Huron turned increasingly to the French for help and the number of conversions increased sharply.[172] As in 1644, a few French soldiers were sent to winter in Huronia. These soldiers, so long as they remained in Huronia, were believed sufficient to hold off the Iroquois, but they had been instructed to return to Quebec with the Huron fleet in the spring.[173] As the military situation in Huronia grew more desperate, the French in Quebec became increasingly anxious to profit as much as possible while they still could. In the summer of 1649, a party of over thirty coureurs de bois made a flying trip to Huronia and returned to Quebec bringing with them 5000 pounds of beaver.[174]

In the spring of 1649 the Iroquois unleashed the attack that resulted in the death of Fathers Lalemant and Brébeuf and brought about the dispersal of the Huron confederacy. Many factors contributed to the Iroquois victory, but their superior number of guns was undoubtedly the most important.[175] Hunt has suggested that the Huron were so given over to trading by 1649 that virtually all of their food was imported from the Neutral and Petun tribes and that the main factor in their defeat was therefore the cutting of their supply routes.[176] This suggestion is entirely without foundation. Agriculture was a woman's occupation and little affected by increasing trade. While men may have spent more time trading, the importation of iron axes made it easier to cut trees and hence there was no problem clearing the forests for agriculture. There are frequent references to the Huron as engaged in agricultural activities in the years prior to 1649 and one of the reasons the Iroquois returned to Huronia in the spring of 1650 was to prevent the planting of crops.[177] Driven from their homes and deprived of food, the Hurons scattered and their trading monopoly came to an end. It is interesting that large numbers of Huron, particularly from the Rock and Deer tribes, migrated to the Iroquois country and settled there. The latter tribe settled *en masse* among the Seneca, where they lived in their own village and retained their separate customs for a long time.[178] Their tribal affiliations suggest that these refugees were for the most part traditionalists and probably among them were many of the people who had been the most hostile to the French during the last years of the Jesuit mission. This hostility explains how these groups were so easily adopted by the people who had destroyed their homeland.

41

For the Jesuits the destruction of Huronia was the end of their first dream of leading a nation to Christianity in the heart of the Canadian forest. At least once in the Relations they mentioned the work their colleagues were accomplishing in Paraguay and compared this work with their own.[179] The chance had been lost of converting a people to Christianity while allowing them to retain their language and those institutions and customs that were not incompatible with their new faith. Because they were writing for a patriotic French audience, the Jesuits have little to say about the constitutional status of the Huronia they wished to create. Nevertheless, it seems clear that what they aimed at was not so much a French colony as an Indian state, which under Jesuit leadership could blend the good things of Europe with those already in the native culture. A Catholic Huronia would of necessity have been allied with France, the only Catholic power in eastern North America. Years later Louis de Buade de Frontenac probably came closer to a basic truth than he realized when he accused the Jesuits at Quebec of disloyalty because they kept the Indians apart from the French and taught them in their own language.[180]

The fur trade was the one means by which the Jesuits could gain admittance to Huronia and the only protection they had while working there. Ties with fur traders and government officials in Quebec were thus vital for the success of the Huron mission, but these ties do not seem to have prevented the Jesuits from seeking to serve the best interests of their Huron converts and Huronia at large — as they perceived these interests. To reverse the equation and say that the Jesuits were in Huronia mainly *for the purpose* of serving either the fur trade or the French government does not accord with anything we know about their activities.

In the short run the destruction of Huronia was a serious setback for New France. For a time the fur trade, on which the well-being of the colony depended, was cut to practically nothing. The Iroquois, on the other hand, seem to have achieved less than they hoped for from the destruction of Huronia. The western tribes soon became involved in a protracted war with the Erie[181] and tribal jealousies rent the confederacy. As a result of these jealousies the four western tribes began to trade with the French to avoid travelling through Mohawk towns to reach the Dutch.[182] By 1654 the French were starting to put together the rudiments of a new trading network north of the Great Lakes.[183] The remnants of the Huron and Petun who had remained in this area, and more importantly the Ottawa, an Algonkian tribe, played a major role in pushing this trading network to the west in the years that followed.[184] As the population of New France increased, the young men of the colony, with or without official permission, joined in this trade. Thus the destruction of Huronia was neither a total nor a permanent disaster for New France and certainly it did not help to save North America for Protestantism and the Anglo-Saxons, as at least one eminent historian has suggested.[185]

A more serious question is what would have happened had the anti-French party in Huronia been successful. Had they been able to organize an effective resistance to the Huron Christians and conclude a treaty with the Iroquois, the trade from the north might have been diverted permanently from the St. Lawrence into the Hudson Valley. Had that happened (and as Sagard and Le Clercq indicate the people in Quebec knew it well[186]) the chances of the infant French colony surviving even for a short time would have been slim. Instead of the destruction of Huronia tipping the balance of power in favour of the English, its survival might well have led to a Huron–Iroquois alliance that would have resulted in the destruction of New France and the end of the French presence in North America.

42

NOTES

This paper is based in part on research carried out with the assistance of Miss A. Elaine Clark during the academic year 1965–66. Miss Clark's assistance was made possible through a research grant provided by the French Canada Studies Programme of McGill University.

[1] See, e.g., Samuel de Champlain's comment on the sagacity of the Indians in trade (H.P. Biggar, ed., *The Works of Samuel de Champlain* (6 vols.; Toronto, 1922–36), 2: 171), and Jean de Brébeuf, Gabriel Lalemant, and Francesco Bressani on the efficacy of Huron law (R.G. Thwaites, ed., *The Jesuit Relations and Allied Documents* (73 vols.; Cleveland, 1896–1901), 10: 215; 28: 49–51; 38: 277).

[2] Thwaites, ed., *Relations* 18: 21. A similar statement is made by Paul Ragueneau (29: 281).

[3] Invariably, however, these early witnesses of Indian culture were interested in rather limited aspects of Indian life and tended to interpret Indian culture in terms of their own. Because of this, a valid assessment of these early records requires a comparative knowledge of Indian culture in later times. The groundwork for our understanding of seventeenth-century Huron culture is thus the work of several generations of ethnologists and ethnohistorians in Canada and the United States. The best résumé of Huron culture is Elisabeth Tooker, *An Ethnography of the Huron Indians, 1615–1649* (Washington, 1964). For a shorter and less complete synopsis see W.V. Kinietz, *The Indians of the Western Great Lakes, 1615–1760* (Ann Arbor, 1940).

[4] F. Parkman, *The Jesuits in North America in the Seventeenth Century* (Centenary Edition, Boston, 1927), 3, 4, 435, 436; G.E. Ellis, "Indians of North America," in J. Winsor, ed., *Narrative and Critical History of America* (8 vols.; Boston and New York, 1884–89), 1: 283.

[5] G.T. Hunt, *The Wars of the Iroquois: A Study in Intertribal Relations* (Madison, 1940), 4, 19.

[6] Biggar, ed., *Works of Champlain* 3: 49–51; 4: 238–44.

[7] Thwaites, ed., *Relations* 16: 227.

[8] L.H. Morgan, *League of the Ho-de-no-sau-nee, or Iroquois* (Rochester, 1851; reprinted New Haven, 1954). For a briefer description, see Morgan's *Houses and House-life of the Indian Aborigines* (Washington, 1881; reprinted with original pagination Chicago, 1965), 23–41.

[9] Meat remained largely a festive dish, commonest in winter and spring (G.M. Wrong, ed., *Sagard's Long Journey to the Country of the Hurons* (Toronto, 1939), 82; Thwaites, ed., *Relations* 17: 141–43).

[10] Thwaites, ed., *Relations* 16: 227–29. See also Elisabeth Toker, "The Iroquois Defeat of the Huron: A Review of Causes," *Pennsylvania Archaeologist* 33 (1963): 115–23, especially 119, 120.

[11] J.V. Wright, *The Ontario Iroquois Tradition* (Ottawa, 1966), 68–83. For information concerning the movements from the west I am indebted to a personal communication from Dr. Wright.

[12] See, for example, D. Jenness, *The Indians of Canada* (5th ed.; Ottawa, 1960), 280.

[13] B.G. Trigger, "The Historic Location of the Hurons," *Ontario History* 54 (1962): 137–48. For physiographic conditions, see L.J. Chapman and D.F. Putnam, *The Physiography of Southern Ontario* (2nd ed.; Toronto, 1966), 299–312.

[14] Biggar, ed., *Works of Champlain* 3: 52, 53. On the importance of corn meal among the northern hunters see Wrong, ed., *Sagard's Long Journey*, 268.

[15] Hunt, *Wars of the Iroquois*, 53–65.

[16] For the reference to squirrel skins see Thwaites, ed., *Relations* 7: 13; to nets, 6: 309.

[17] Thwaites, ed., *Relations* 8: 15.

[18] Wrong, ed., *Sagard's Long Journey*, 86.

[19] For a hostile statement about the Bear by the Algonkins, see Thwaites, ed., *Relations* 10: 145.

[20] C.F. Wray and H.L. Schoff, "A Preliminary Report on the Seneca Sequence in Western New York State, 1550-1687," *Pennsylvania Archaeologist* 23 (1953): 53–63.

[21] Colonel James F. Pendergast (personal communication) reports finding considerable evidence of Huron influence in late Iroquoian sites along the St. Lawrence River. These probably date from the sixteenth century or only a little earlier. For the historical evidence of contacts between the St. Lawrence Iroquoians and the interior of Ontario, see H.P. Biggar, ed., *The Voyages of Jacques Cartier* (Ottawa, 1924), 170–71, 200–202.

[22] Thwaites, ed., *Relations* 10: 225.

[23] Thwaites, ed., *Relations* 20: 19.

[24] Thwaites, ed., *Relations* 20: 19. In 1640 Lalemant reported that the Rock still considered themselves the special allies of the French and were inclined to protect them. This attitude changed after the Jesuits became more active in the interior of Huronia.

[25] Wrong, ed., *Sagard's Long Journey*, 99. Sagard says that a special council decided each year the number of men who could go out from each village. For more on the control of trade by old and influential men, see Thwaites, ed., *Relations* 14: 39.

[26] J.V. Wright, "A Regional Examination of Ojibwa Culture History," *Anthropologica* N.S. 7 (1965): 189–227.

[27] Thwaites, ed., *Relations* 5: 241.

[28] The Huron claimed that their feud with the Iroquois had been going on fifty years prior to 1615 (Biggar, ed., *Works of Champlain* 5: 78).

[29] Thwaites, ed., *Relations* 23: 91.

[30] Wrong, ed., *Sagard's Long Journey*, 159–61. For comparative discussions of Iroquoian warfare see Nathaniel Knowles, "The Torture of Captives by the Indians of Eastern North America," *Proceedings of the American Philosophical Society* 82 (1940): 151–225; R.L. Rands and C.L. Riley, "Diffusion and Discontinuous Distribution," *American Anthropologist* 58 (1958): 274–97.

[31] For the wars with the Petun, see Thwaites, ed., *Relations* 20: 43. Even at the time of Sagard's visit, there was a threat of war with the Neutral (Wrong, ed., *Sagard's Long Journey*, 151, 156, 157).

[32] Thwaites, ed., *Relations* 33: 243.

[33] Thwaites, ed., *Relations* 33: 239–49.

[34] Thwaites, ed., *Relations* 13: 125. The Bear Tribe wanted the French to participate in their Feast of the Dead so that they could thereby claim them as relatives (10: 311).

[35] Thwaites, ed., *Relations* 27: 25; 20: 59.

[36] Chretien Le Clercq, *First Establishment of the Faith in New France*, trans. J.G. Shea, 2 vols. (New York, 1881), 1: 97; Wrong, ed., *Sagard's Long Journey*, 71.

[37] Biggar, ed., *Voyages of Cartier*, 132-3, 143. The custom of giving children to Cartier may have arisen, on the other hand, as a result of the Indians observing Cartier's predilection for kidnapping Indians. In 1534 he had seized the two sons of Donnaconna, the chief of Stadacona.

[38] The fact that the Huron and Algonkians both were at war with the Five Nations naturally pitted the French against these latter tribes. Presumably Champlain's decision to side with the Huron and Algonkians was based on his conviction that it was impossible to maintain satisfactory relations with both sides, as well as on the economic factors mentioned in the text. For a discussion of the

43

origins of the hostility between the Algonkians and Five Nations, see B.G. Trigger, "Trade and Tribal Warfare on the St. Lawrence in the Sixteenth Century," *Ethnohistory* 9 (1962): 240-56.

[39] For Champlain's own comment on Indian expectations in this regard, see Biggar, ed., *Works of Champlain* 2: 70, 71, 110.

[40] H.A. Innis, *The Fur Trade in Canada* (2nd ed.; Toronto, 1956), 23-26.

[41] Thwaites, ed., *Relations* 15: 229. The first Huron chief to have dealings with the French was Atironta of the Rock tribe.

[42] Biggar, ed., *Works of Champlain* 2: 188, 189, 193. For a more general reference see 2: 254.

[43] Biggar, ed., *Works of Champlain* 2: 141; 4: 118, 119. This interpretation is reinforced by Champlain's statement that the boy was brought back by 200 Huron on June 13, 1611 (2: 186; 4: 136).

[44] For comments on the Indians' desire for European manufactured goods, see Innis, *Fur Trade*, 16-19; Hunt, *Wars of the Iroquois*, 4, 5.

[45] For examples of Algonkin harassment of Huron trade along the Ottawa River and various Algonkin attempts to imperil French-Huron relations (particularly by the Algonkin from Allumette Island) see Biggar, ed., *Works of Champlain* 5: 102; Wrong, ed., *Sagard's Long Journey*, 262; Thwaites, ed., *Relations* 5: 239; 7: 213; 8: 83, 99; 9: 271; 10: 77; 14: 53. The Montagnais also tried to intimidate the Huron, mainly to get free corn (Wrong, ed., *Sagard's Long Journey*, 265-68).

[46] Innis, *Fur Trade*, 3-6, 11-15.

[47] This is essentially the kind of relationship that existed between trading companies and Indian trappers in the north in more recent times.

[48] Champlain reports that the Huron produced large food surpluses which he says were meant to carry them over years of poor crops (Biggar, ed., *Works of Champlain* 3: 155-56). At least a part of these surpluses was used for trade.

44

[49] Le Clercq, *Establishment* 1: 298.

[50] Thwaites, ed., *Relations* 35: 201. There is good evidence, however, that the Nipissing were travelling north even earlier (Biggar, ed., *Works of Champlain* 2: 80).

[51] Le Clercq, *Establishment* 1: 211; Wrong, ed., *Sagard's Long Journey*, 244.

[52] Biggar, ed., *Works of Champlain* 5: 73-80; Hunt, *Wars of the Iroquois*, 69.

[53] The Huron had invited Champlain to visit their country as early as 1609 (Biggar, ed., *Works of Champlain* 2: 105). His attempt to travel up the Ottawa River in 1613 was brought to an end by the opposition of the Algonkin, among other things. Marcel Trudel (*Histoire de la Nouvelle-France*, vol. 2, *Le Comptoir, 1604-1627* (Montreal, 1966), 198-201) may be correct when he suggests that the Algonkin stirred up trouble between Champlain and Vignau in order to protect their trading interests in the interior.

[54] Although Champlain visited all the major Huron villages, he returned repeatedly to Cahiague, a Rock village. He also spent more time there than anywhere else. Lalemant reports that in 1640 his reputation was still very much alive among the Rock (Thwaites, ed., *Relations* 20: 19).

[55] Biggar, ed., *Works of Champlain* 3: 66, 69,73; 4: 254-66; also Hunt, *Wars of the Iroquois*, 20.

[56] Since most of the available data about this period was recorded by priests, we have little information about these men, and practically none from a friendly source. For what there is see, Biggar, ed., *Works of Champlain* 5: 101, 108, 129, 131, 132, 207; Le Clercq, *Establishment* 1: 205; Wrong, ed., *Sagard's Long Journey*, 194-95; Thwaites, ed., *Relations* 5: 133; 6: 83; 14: 17, 19; 18: 45; 20: 19; 25: 85.

[57] A.W. Trelease, *Indian Affairs in Colonial New York: The Seventeenth Century* (Ithaca, 1960), 30.

[58] Trelease, *Indian Affairs*, 46. Intermittent hostilities between the Mahican and Mohawk kept the latter from Fort Orange prior to the stunning defeat of the Mahican in 1628 or 1629 (48).

[59] Trelease, *Indian Affairs*, 52-54; Thwaites, ed., *Relations* 8: 59-61; Hunt, *Wars of the Iroquois*, 34. In 1638 the Huron told the Jesuits that "Englishmen" had come as far as Montreal telling the Indians that the Jesuits were the cause of sickness in Huronia (and no doubt attempting to trade with them or divert trade to the south) (Thwaites, ed., *Relations* 15: 31.)

[60] See, e.g., Biggar, ed., *Works of Champlain* 5: 101, 207.

[61] Biggar, ed., *Works of Champlain* 5: 108. On the usefulness of having Frenchmen accompany the fleet see Wrong, ed., *Sagard's Long Journey*, 262. Sagard reports that in the 1620s the Iroquois refrained from attacking Huron flotillas when they knew Frenchmen were travelling with the Indians (261).

[62] These were at least the functions that the Huron expected Frenchmen who had lived in Huronia would perform. The *coureurs de bois* are frequently referred to as interpreters (Biggar, ed., *Works of Champlain* 3: 168-72).

[63] Wrong, ed., *Sagard's Long Journey*, 249-56.

[64] This route apparently had been used in prehistoric times as well (Biggar, ed., *Voyages of Cartier*, 200-201, as interpreted by Innis, *Fur Trade*, 22).

[65] Edwin Tross, ed., *Histoire du Canada et voyages que les Frères mineurs Recollets y ont faicts pour la conversion des infidèles depuis l'an 1615 . . .*, by G. Sagard (4 vols.; Paris, 1866), 1: 42. This statement refers to the visit Le Caron made with Champlain. On the Huron desire to have the priests act as go-betweens in their trade with the French see Wrong, ed., *Sagard's Long Journey*, 244; Le Clercq, *Establishment* 1: 211.

[66] The Indians often were reluctant to take missionaries back to Huronia with them (Thwaites, ed., *Relations* 4: 221). Some priests, however, became personally popular with the Huron. The popularity of Father Brébeuf during his initial stay in Huronia is evident from the welcome he received when he returned in 1634.

[67] This claim appears in the *Dictionary of Canadian Biography*, vol. 1, *1000 to 1700* (Toronto, 1966), 133. It appears to be based on Sagard's comments on the behaviour of an interpreter named Nicolas Marsolet. Although Marsolet refused to teach the Montagnais language to the Recollets, he later agreed to instruct the Jesuits (Tross, ed., Histoire du Canada 2: 333).

[68] It is perhaps significant that the main complaint was about the sexual behaviour of these men rather than the sale of alcohol to the Indians (cf. André Vachon, "L'Eau-de-vie dans la société indienne," Canadian Historical Association, *Report*, 1960, 22–32). Alcohol does not appear to have been a serious problem in Huronia, no doubt because the Huron did not at this time feel their culture threatened by European contacts. The Jesuits' distaste for these men is reiterated in the Jesuit Relations, particularly when they are compared with the *donnés* and other men who served in Huronia under Jesuit supervision after 1634. See Thwaites, ed., *Relations* 6: 83; 14: 19; 15: 85; 17: 45.

[69] Trudel, *Histoire de la Nouvelle-France* 2: 405–434.

[70] Trelease, *Indian Affairs*, 52; Hunt, *Wars of the Iroquois*, 69–70.

[71] Thwaites, ed., *Relations* 33: 121.

[72] Le Clercq, *Establishment* 1: 204; Tross, ed., *Histoire du Canada*.

[73] There is nothing in Sagard or Le Clercq that implies that the priests were instructed to disrupt this treaty, as Hunt implies. Trudel (*Histoire de la Nouvelle-France* 2: 370) says that it was necessary to send Father Le Caron and the other Frenchmen to Huronia to prevent a commercial treaty between the Huron and the Iroquois. It is my opinion that the prospect of this treaty was a figment of the imagination of the French in Quebec and never a real possibility (see text below).

[74] On the Mohawk refusal to let the French Indians pass through their country to trade with the Dutch see Trelease, *Indian Affairs*, 52–53; Hunt, *Wars of the Iroquois*, 34. Trudel's (*Histoire de la Nouvelle-France* 2: 364–66) suggestion that the Huron were about to trade with the Dutch and that the French who stayed in Huronia did so to prevent this seems unlikely in view of the traditional enmity between the Huron and the Iroquois. To reach Albany the latter would have had to travel through the tribal territory of the three eastern Iroquois tribes. Mohawk opposition to this seems to have effectively discouraged the Huron from attempting such trade.

[75] Sagard says that the Huron did not permit other tribes to pass through their territory without special permission (Wrong, ed., *Sagard's Long Journey*, 99). The Jesuits say categorically that the Huron did not permit the Petun to trade with the French (Thwaites, ed., *Relations* 21: 177).

[76] For a reference about canoes see Hunt, *Wars of the Iroquois*, 51.

[77] Le Clercq, *Establishment* 1: 267. The Huron spread evil rumours about the Jesuits among the Petun when the Jesuits tried to do mission work there in 1640 (Thwaites, ed., *Relations* 20: 47–51).

[78] Thwaites, ed., *Relations* 21: 207–15. At first the priests pretended to be traders. This pretence, however, failed.

[79] Biggar, ed., *Works of Champlain* 5: 131.

[80] The French later describe him as a traitor (Thwaites, ed., *Relations* 5: 241).

[81] Tross, ed., *Histoire du Canada* 2: 431. For a description of his proposed reburial see Thwaites, ed., *Relations* 10: 307–309.

[82] G. Lanctot, *A History of Canada*, vol. 1 (Toronto, 1963), 148–9.

[83] It appears that one reason the Recollets received little support from the trading companies was that their policy of settling migratory Indians and of wanting Huron converts to settle in Quebec conflicted with the traders' own interests (Le Clercq, *Establishment* 1: 111).

[84] The support of Governor Montmagny appears to have been particularly effective (Thwaites, ed., *Relations* 21: 143; 22: 309, 311).

[85] Thwaites, ed., *Relations* 10: 33; 11: 97, 109, 111, 113; 13: 9; 14: 125 161, 231, 235, 255. On the discontinuation of the seminary, see 24: 103. During the first two years the Jesuits were back in Huronia they were struggling to orient themselves and to understand the nature of Huron society better. At first they tended to be rather patronizing. They gave advice on military matters (10: 53) and, failing to understand the nature of Huron politics, felt that their intervention was needed to mediate disputes among the different tribes (9: 273; 14: 17, 21). Later, when they realized how the Huron did things and that intervention was unnecessary, these efforts ceased.

[86] One example is the decision to seek to baptize older men — and especially influential ones (Thwaites, ed., *Relations* 15: 109).

[87] For Jesuit policy regarding lay assistants in Huronia, see Thwaites, ed., *Relations* 21: 293–303. See also 6: 81, 83; 15: 157; 17: 45; 20: 99; 25: 85; 27: 91.

[88] Parkman, *Jesuits in North America*, 465–67. Concerning early charges of Jesuit participation in the fur trade and a declaration by the directors of the Company of New France concerning their innocence, see Thwaites, ed., *Relations* 25: 75.

[89] Thwaites, ed., *Relations* 14: 17–19. For a clear statement that the Jesuits were aware that their presence in Huronia depended on the traders' ability to coerce the Huron to let them stay, see 34: 205. Soon after the Jesuits returned to Huronia, Brébeuf wrote that they won the esteem of the Indians by giving them arrowheads and helping them to defend their forts (34: 53). He hoped that the confidence won by these actions would permit the Jesuits eventually to "advance the glory of God."

45

[90] The main reason seems to have been that the French had detained a Huron who was implicated in killing a Frenchman in Huronia (Thwaites, ed., *Relations* 6: 19). It is interesting to note that the Huron also made it clear they wanted Frenchmen with guns instead of, or at least alongside, the priests (7: 217).

[91] Thwaites, ed., *Relations* 9: 287.

[92] Thwaites, ed., *Relations* 7: 47. The officials in Quebec continued to exhort the Huron to become Christians (17: 171).

[93] Thwaites, ed., *Relations* 8: 71, 91, 99.

[94] That was in July 1633 (Thwaites, ed., *Relations* 5: 259). The people of Ossossané continued to press the Jesuits to move there.

[95] Thwaites, ed., *Relations* 8: 99, 103–105. They also stayed at Ihonitiria because they felt it better to start work in a small village rather than a large and important one (8: 103). Ossossané was also unsatisfactory as its inhabitants were planning to relocate the village the next spring (8: 101).

[96] Thwaites, ed., *Relations* 5: 239; 8: 99; 10: 309; 14: 99–103.

[97] For an account of this dispute and the Jesuits' attempts to resolve it, see Thwaites, ed., *Relations* 10: 279–81, 307; 14: 21. No mention is made of the dispute after 1637, so presumably it was patched up. Brébeuf mentions elsewhere that, as a result of Brûlé's murder, other Huron were threatening the people of Toanché (the village where he was killed) with death (8: 99). The bad relations between Ossossané and the village of Ihonitiria (which was inhabited by Toanchéans) were exacerbated in 1633 when the latter became angry at the efforts of the chiefs of Ossossané to persuade all the Jesuits to settle in their village (5: 263).

46

[98] Presents were also given to the Huron both as tokens of goodwill and to ensure the good treatment of the Jesuits.

[99] For a discussion of the financial help the Jesuits expected to receive from the trading company see Thwaites, ed., *Relations* 6: 81–83. The financial support of the mission is discussed in Parkman, *Jesuits in North America*, 465–67.

[100] Thwaites, ed., *Relations* 10: 249; 13: 141; 17: 95; 18: 19, 97.

[101] Thwaites, ed., *Relations* 10: 301.

[102] One of these trips was to visit the father of a young convert named Amantacha who lived at St. Joseph (Thwaites, ed., *Relations* 8: 139). A careful tabulation by Miss Clark of the places the Jesuits mention visiting each year and the amount of attention given to each village in Huronia shows clearly that prior to 1640 their activities were confined to the Bear nation and particularly to the Penetang Peninsula. After that time their mission work spread into all parts of Huronia.

[103] To less than twelve thousand.

[104] Thwaites, ed., *Relations* 19: 123, 127; 8: 145–47. The high mortality rate among children is an over-all impression gained from reading the relations of the years 1636–40. It also corresponds with what is known about similar epidemics among other Indian groups.

[105] Thwaites, ed., *Relations* 19: 223.

[106] Thwaites, ed., *Relations* 14: 17, 53, 99–103.

[107] Thwaites, ed., *Relations* 39: 129.

[108] Thwaites, ed., *Relations* 19: 179.

[109] Thwaites, ed., *Relations* 15: 59–67.

[110] At all times the Huron leaders appear to have been convinced that killing a priest or one of their assistants would terminate the Franco-Huron alliance.

[111] Thwaites, ed., *Relations* 13: 215, 217. For a French statement emphasizing the Huron dependence on trade goods see 32: 179 (1647–48).

[112] Thwaites, ed., *Relations* 15: 21.

[113] Thwaites, ed., *Relations* 15: 51.

[114] Thwaites, ed., *Relations* 15: 55; 17: 115.

[115] Thwaites, ed., *Relations* 21: 143; 22: 310.

[116] Thwaites, ed., *Relations* 21: 131.

[117] One heifer and a small cannon arrived in 1648 (Thwaites, ed., *Relations* 32: 99).

[118] Thwaites, ed., *Relations* 26: 201.

[119] Concerning the establishment of Ste Marie and the mission system see Thwaites, ed., *Relations* 19: 123–65.

[120] There is a considerable amount of other evidence concerning the coercive power of Huron chiefs. See B.G. Trigger, "Order and Freedom in Huron Society," *Anthropologica* N.S. 5 (1963): 151–69.

[121] Thwaites, ed., *Relations* 21: 213. About the same time the Huron were spreading bad reports concerning the Jesuits among the Petun (20: 54) with whom they had recently made a new treaty of friendship (20: 43). These rumours were spread by Huron traders.

[122] Thwaites, ed., *Relations* 30: 75–77. So bitter was the Huron opposition to Brébeuf after he returned to Huronia that the Huron mission was compelled to send him down to Quebec until the situation quieted down (23: 35).

[123] The Jesuit Relation of 1635 records that the beaver was already totally extinct in the Huron country and that all the skins they traded with the French were obtained elsewhere (Thwaites, ed., *Relations* 8: 57).

[124] Trelease, *Indian Affairs*, 118–20; Hunt, *Wars of the Iroquois*, 32–34. For a later source see Jean Talon cited in Hunt, *Wars of the Iroquois*, 137.

[125] Hunt, *Wars of the Iroquois*, 32–34; Trelease, *Indian Affairs*, 118.

[126] This theory was first advanced by C.H. McIlwain in 1915. It was taken up in Innis, *Fur Trade*, 34–36 and Hunt, *Wars of the Iroquois*, 32–37, 74.

[127] Trelease, *Indian Affairs*, 120.

[128] E.B. O'Callaghan, ed., *Documents Relative to the Colonial History of the State of New York* . . . (15 vols.; Albany, 1853–87), 4: 908.

[129] Thwaites, ed., *Relations* 23: 105.

[130] Hunt, *Wars of the Iroquois*, 76.

[131] Tooker, "Defeat of the Huron," 117–18.

[132] Thwaites, ed., *Relations* 26: 71; 27: 89, 277. Brébeuf returned to Huronia at this time.

[133] Hunt, *Wars of the Iroquois*, 77–78.

[134] For the Iroquois desire to obtain French guns, see the evidence presented in Hunt, *Wars of the Iroquois*, 74.

[135] Thwaites, ed., *Relations* 10: 13; 13: 171.

[136] Thwaites, ed., *Relations* 20: 27–31.

[137] Thwaites, ed., *Relations* 20: 225; 26: 275.

[138] Thwaites, ed., *Relations* 15: 109. For the later relaxation of these requirements see 33: 145–47.

[139] Thwaites, ed., *Relations* 19: 191.

[140] Thwaites, ed., *Relations* 17: 111; 23: 129.

[141] Concerning this preferential treatment see Thwaites, ed., *Relations* 20: 225, 227.

[142] Thwaites, ed., *Relations* 32: 179.

[143] Vachon, "L'Eau-de-vie."

[144] Thwaites, ed., *Relations* 23: 67, 127; 26: 229. Pagan women also attempted to seduce Christian men to persuade them to give up their faith (30: 33). The Relation of 1643 mentions that some converts lived for six months at Quebec to avoid facing temptation in their homeland (24: 121).

[145] Thwaites, ed., *Relations* 30: 23.

[146] Thwaites, ed., *Relations* 21: 131.

[147] Thwaites, ed., *Relations* 23: 185.

[148] Thwaites, ed., *Relations* 23: 31.

[149] For another reference to the Huron–pagan rift see Thwaites, ed., *Relations* 23: 267.

[150] Thwaites, ed., *Relations* 28: 89. For other acts of Christian assertiveness around this time see 29: 263–69; 30: 63.

[151] Thwaites, ed., *Relations* 25: 85.

[152] Tross, ed., *Histoire du Canada* 1: 200; Thwaites, ed., *Relations* 5: 259.

[153] Thwaites, ed., *Relations* 34: 105, 217.

[154] For one incident see Thwaites, ed., *Relations* 30: 61–63. Various cults also arose that appear to have been aimed at organizing ideological resistance to Christianity. One was the cult of a forest monster (30: 27); the second was more explicitly anti-Christian (30: 29–31).

[155] As one Huron put it, "I am more attached to the church than to my country or relatives" (Thwaites, ed., *Relations* 23: 137). The Jesuits also observed that it was hard to be a good Christian and a good Huron (28: 53).

[156] Thwaites, ed., *Relations* 26: 217. The Jesuits had noted the special inclination of the Bear tribe to receive Christianity as early as 1636 (10: 31).

[157] After the destruction of Huronia the Cord were very loyal to the French. They were the only Huron tribe that refused to leave Quebec to go and live with the Iroquois (Thwaites, ed., *Relations* 43: 191). Prior to 1640, the Cord were not at all friendly with the Jesuits (17: 59); their change in attitude seems to have come about soon after (21: 285; 23: 151; 26: 265).

[158] Thwaites, ed., *Relations* 42: 73. Concerning their early desire for peace with the Iroquois see 33: 119-121.

[159] Thwaites, ed., *Relations* 17: 89.

[160] Thwaites, ed., *Relations* 36: 179. The Deer lived among the Seneca in their own village and on good terms with their hosts (44: 21). Many Rock people including the Indians of Contarea, lived among the Onondaga (42: 73).

[161] For evidence of incipient deterioration in morale and the beginning of the abandonment of Huronia in the face of Iroquois attack, see Thwaites, ed., *Relations* 30: 87; 33: 83–89.

[162] Thwaites, ed., *Relations* 33: 125. Hunt (*Wars of the Iroquois*, 72) notes that in 1637 the Huron had broken a peace treaty with the Seneca.

[163.] Thwaites, ed., *Relations* 33: 71, 123.

[164] Thwaites, ed., *Relations* 33: 131.

[165] Thwaites, ed., *Relations* 33: 119–21.

[166] Thwaites, ed., *Relations* 33: 125.

[167] Thwaites, ed., *Relations* 33: 125-27. He probably did this through anger at his allies and to show the innocence of the Onondaga. He might also have committed suicide to avoid Huron vengeance directed against his person, but this would have been construed as an act of cowardice. It is unlikely that the Onondaga would have exposed an important chief to almost certain death had they not been negotiating in good faith.

[168] Thwaites, ed., *Relations* 33: 229.

[169] Thwaites, ed., *Relations* 33: 231.

[170] Thwaites, ed., *Relations* 33: 81.

[171] Thwaites, ed., *Relations* 33: 233–49.

[172] Thwaites, ed., *Relations* 34: 227.

[173] Thwaites, ed., *Relations* 34: 83.

[174] Lanctot, *History of Canada* 1: 194, based on Thwaites, ed., *Relations* 34: 59–61.

[175] Tooker, "Defeat of the Hurons," 117–18; Innis, *Fur Trade*, 35–36. For the effective use of firearms by the Iroquois see Thwaites, ed., *Relations* 22: 307. The Jesuits saw the danger of growing Iroquois firepower as early as 1642 (22: 307) but the French officials in Quebec never developed a policy to counteract it. The restiveness of the Huron pagans may be one reason why the French did not want too many guns in Huron hands, even if they were being sold only to Christians.

[176] Hunt, *Wars of the Iroquois*, 59.

[177] Thwaites, ed., *Relations* 35: 191.

[178] Thwaites, ed., *Relations* 36: 179; 44: 21; 45: 243. Many of the Rock nation, particularly from Contarea, were later found living with the Onondaga (42: 73).

[179] Thwaites, ed., *Relations* 12: 221. The work in Paraguay is also mentioned in 15: 127.

[180] G. Lanctot, *A History of Canada* 2 (Toronto, 1964), 63.

[181] Hunt, *Wars of the Iroquois*, 100–102.

[182] Thwaites, ed., *Relations* 41: 201–203, and 44: 151; Hunt, *Wars of the Iroquois*, 99, 100.

[183] Thwaites, ed., *Relations* 40: 215; Lanctot, *History of Canada* 1: 212–13. On the lack of furs in Montreal in 1652–53 see Thwaites, ed., *Relations* 40: 211.

[184] Hunt, *Wars of the Iroquois*, 102–103.

[185] Parkman, *Jesuits in North America*, 550–53.

[186] Tross, ed., *Histoire du Canada* 3: 811; Le Clercq, *Establishment* 1: 204.

Topic Two

The Impact of the Fur Trade

French fur traders preceded the English within the boundaries of present-day Canada by nearly a century. Then in 1670 Charles II granted a royal charter to the "Company of Adventurers of England trading into Hudson Bay." The Hudson's Bay Company, as it became known, gained an exclusive monopoly (among English subjects) over the fur trade in "Rupertsland" — all the territory whose rivers drained into Hudson Bay. Rupertsland, named after Prince Rupert, the Hudson's Bay Company's first governor, comprised almost half of present-day Canada.

Until the conquest in 1760 French traders operating out of Montreal opposed the Hudson's Bay Company's monopoly. Thereafter a new challenge arose when British traders working out of Montreal allied with the French to form the North West Company. Only after the forced union of the two companies in 1821 did the Hudson's Bay Company have a practical monopoly of the northern fur trade, and then it truly enjoyed the rights and privileges granted to it in 1670.

The Woodland Indians welcomed the French and English traders with their iron manufactured goods — axes, knives, spears, and kettles. These durable items made hunting, cooking, and warfare much easier and more efficient than with their former implements of stone, wood, and bone. As a result of the trade, however, the Cree Indians living near the Hudson's Bay Company's posts on Hudson and James Bay came to rely on the white newcomers. Did the European fur traders, and in particular the Hudson's Bay Company, exploit the native peoples? Arthur Ray examines the Indians' role in the exchange in his essay "Fur Trade History as an Aspect of Native History."

An important consequence of the fur traders' arrival was the rise of a mixed-blood, or Métis, population, the result of the white fur traders' intermarriage with Indian women. Until recently, historians of the fur trade ignored the role of these Indian wives. Sylvia Van Kirk analyses their contribution in "'Women in Between': Indian Women in Fur Trade Society in Western Canada."

The fur trade also quickly developed on the Pacific Coast, reached by Europeans in the 1770s. It remained a maritime operation (until the early nineteenth century) and one in which the Pacific Coast Indians had the upper hand, as Robin Fisher describes in "Indian Control of the Maritime Fur Trade and the Northwest Coast."

E.E. Rich has written the standard account of the Hudson's Bay Company and its rivals in *The Fur Trade and the Northwest to 1857* (Toronto: McClelland and Stewart, 1967). Also of interest is W.J. Eccles' "The Fur Trade and Eighteenth-Century Imperialism," *William and Mary Quarterly*, 3rd series, 40 (1983): 341-62. The first notable study of the fur trade is H.A. Innis, *The Fur Trade in Canada* (1930; reprint edition, New Haven: Yale University Press, 1962). A.J. Ray provides a more recent study in his *Indians in the Fur Trade* (Toronto: University of Toronto Press, 1974). Dan Francis has written a very readable account of the personalities of the fur trade in Western Canada, *Battle for the West: Fur Traders and the Birth of Western Canada* (Edmonton: Hurtig, 1982). Three scholarly analyses that focus on the fur trade in a specific region are Dan Francis and Toby Morantz' *Partners in Furs: A History of the Fur Trade in Eastern James Bay, 1600-1870* (Kingston: McGill-Queen's University Press, 1983); Paul C. Thistle's *Indian-European Trade Relations in the Lower Saskatchewan River Region to 1840* (Winnipeg: University of Manitoba Press, 1986); and J.C. Yerbury's *The Subarctic Indians and the Fur Trade, 1680-1860* (Vancouver: University of British Columbia Press, 1986). A survey of recent literature dealing with the Indians' involvement in the fur trade will be found in "The Indian and the Fur Trade: A Review of Recent Literature," by Jacqueline Peterson with John Afinson, *Manitoba History* 10 (1985): 10-18. An excellent popular summary of the fur trade is the beautifully illustrated *Where Two Worlds Meet: The Great Lakes Fur Trade* (St. Paul: Minnesota Historical Society, 1982), by Carolyn Gilman. For a good short overview consult the chapters entitled "The First Businessmen: Indians and the Fur Trade" and " 'A Mere Business of Fur Trading,' 1670-1821" in Michael Bliss, *Northern Enterprise: Five Centuries of Canadian Business* (Toronto: McClelland and Stewart, 1987), 33-54, 79-108.

Sylvia Van Kirk, in *"Many Tender Ties": Women in Fur-Trade Society, 1670-1870* (Winnipeg: Watson and Dwyer, 1980), and Jennifer S.H. Brown, in *Strangers in Blood: The Fur Trade Company Families in Indian Country* (Vancouver: University of British Columbia Press, 1980), have written two excellent accounts of women in the fur trade. Olive Patricia Dickason has taken a pan-Canadian view of the rise of a mixed-blood population in her "From 'One Nation' in the Northwest to 'New Nation' in the Northwest: A Look at the Emergence of the Metis," *American Indian Culture and Research Journal*, 6,2 (1982):1-21. For a survey of the history of the Métis, see D. Bruce Sealey and Antoine S. Lussier, *The Métis: Canada's Forgotten People* (Winnipeg: Manitoba Métis Federation Press, 1975).

The history of the Indians' involvement in the fur trade on the Pacific Coast is covered in Wilson Duff's *The Indian History of British Columbia* (Victoria: Provincial Museum of British Columbia, 1964). More recent studies include Robin Fisher's *Contact and Conflict: Indian-European Re-*

lations in British Columbia, 1774–1890 (Vancouver: University of British Columbia Press, 1977) and Theodore J. Karamanski's *Fur Trade and Exploration: Opening the Far Northwest, 1821–1852* (Vancouver: University of British Columbia Press, 1983).

Fur Trade History as an Aspect of Native History*

ARTHUR J. RAY

Howard Adams, among others, has made the point that the dominant white Euro-Canadian culture has projected racist images of the Indians that, "are so distorted that they portray natives as little more than savages without intelligence or beauty."[1] He argued further that the Indians "must endure a history that shames them, destroys their confidence, and causes them to reject their heritage.[2] There is a great deal of truth in Adams's statements, and clearly a considerable amount of historical research needs to be done to correct these distorted images. One important aspect of any new meaningful Indian history necessarily will be concerned with the involvement of the Indian peoples in the fur trade and with the impact of that participation upon their traditional cultures as well as those of the European intruders. Work in this area will be important not only because it holds a potential for giving us new insights into Indian history, but also because it should serve to help establish Indian history in its rightful place in the mainstream of Canadian historiography. As some of Canada's most prominent historians have emphasized, the fur trade was a molding force in the economic, political, and social development of Canada,[3] and the Indian peoples played a central role in this enterprise. For these reasons Indian history should not simply be devoted to recounting the manner in which the aboriginal peoples of Canada were subjugated and exploited, but it must also consider the positive contribution that the Indian peoples made to the fur trade and, hence, to the development of Canada. If this positive contribution is recognized, it should help destroy some of the distorted images that many Canadians have of Indians and their history.

Given that fur trade history and Indian history are inextricably bound together, several questions immediately arise. How much attention have historians devoted to the roles that the Indians played in the fur trade in the considerable body of fur trade literature that already exists? What images of the Indian peoples emerge from this literature? What aspects of Indian involvement have yet to be explored fully?

51

*An article from *One Century Later: Western Canadian Reserve Indians since Treaty 7*, edited by Ian A.L. Getty and Donald B. Smith. Copyright 1978 by University of British Columbia. Reprinted by permission.

Until relatively recently the Indian peoples have not figured prominently in works dealing with the fur trade.[4] Rather, they generally appear only as shadowy figures who are always present, but never central characters, in the unfolding events.[5] In part, this neglect appears related to the fact that historians have been primarily concerned with studying the fur trade as an aspect of European imperial history or of Canadian business and economic history.[6] And, reflecting these basic interests, the considerable biographical literature that fur trade research has generated deals almost exclusively with Euro-Canadian personalities.[7] Relatively few Indian leaders have been studied to date.[8]

Although the tendency to consider the fur trade primarily as an aspect of Euro-Canadian history has been partly responsible for the failure of scholars to focus on the Indians' role in the enterprise, other factors have been influential as well. One of the basic problems with most studies of Indian–white relations has been that ethno-historians and historians have taken a retrospective view. They see the subjugation of the Indian peoples and the destruction of their lifestyles as inevitable consequences of the technological gap that existed between European and Indian cultures at the time of contact.[9] From this technological-determinist perspective, the Indian has been rendered as an essentially powerless figure who was swept along by the tide of European expansion without any real hope of channeling its direction or of influencing the character of the contact situation. The dominance of this outlook has meant that in most fur trade studies the Indian has been cast in a reflexive role. Reflecting this perspective, until recently most ethno-historical research has been approached from an acculturation-assimilation point of view. The questions asked are generally concerned with determining how Indian groups incorporated European technology as well as social, political, economic, and religious customs into their traditional cultures.

While also interested in these issues, historians have devoted a considerable amount of attention toward outlining the manner and extent to which Euro-Canadian groups, particularly missionaries and government officials, helped the Indians to adjust to the new socio-economic conditions that resulted from the expansion of Western cultures into the new world.[10] Often historical research has taken a certain moralistic tone, assuming that members of the dominant white society had an obligation to help the Indians adopt agriculture and European socio-economic practices and moral codes, so that the Indian peoples could fit into the newly emerging social order.[11] Thus, historians who undertake these types of studies are frequently seeking to determine whether or not the traders, missionaries, and government officials had fulfilled their obligations to help "civilize" the Indian.

Granting that much good work has been done in the above areas, it is my opinion that many new insights into Indian history can be obtained if we abandon the retrospective, technological-determinist outlook and devote more attention to an examination of Indian involvement in the fur trade in the context of contemporary conditions. Such an approach would necessarily recognize that the nature of the trading partnerships that existed between Indian groups and various European interests changed substantially over time and place, making it difficult, frequently misleading, and certainly premature, given the amount of research that still needs to be done, to make any sweeping statements at this time about the nature of Indian–white relations in the context of the Canadian fur trade.

In order to pursue this work effectively, two courses of action need to be followed — one is not currently popular, and the other is extremely tedious. First, students of Indian history need to abandon the assumption that the Indians were ruthlessly exploited and cheated in all areas and periods by white traders. At present this is a very popular theme for both Indian and liberal white historians. All of us have heard the story many times of how the Indians sold Manhattan Island for a few pounds of beads, and we have been informed of the many instances when Indians parted with valuable furs for trinkets and a drink. But, why are we never informed of what the Indians' perceptions of trade were? It may well be that they too thought they were taking advantage of the Europeans. For example, in 1634, when commenting on Montagnais beaver trapping in eastern Canada, Father Le Jeune wrote:

> The Castor or Beaver is taken in several ways. The Savages say it is the animal well-beloved by the French, English and Basques, — in a word, by the Europeans. I heard my [Indian] host say one day, jokingly, *Missi picoutau amiscou*, "The Beaver does everything perfectly well, it makes kettles, hatchets, swords, knives, bread; and in short, it makes everything." He was making sport of us Europeans, who have such a fondness for the skin of this animal and who fight to see who will get it; they carry this to such an extent that my host said to me one day, showing me a beautiful knife, "The English have no sense; they give us twenty knives like this for one Beaver skin."[12]

While there is no denying that European abuses of Indians were all too common, there are several things wrong with continually stressing this aspect of the fur trade and Indian history. As the previous quote suggests, it gives us only half the story. Of greater importance, by continually focusing only on this dimension of the trade, we run the serious risk of simply perpetuating one of the images in Indian historiography that Adams, among others, most strongly objects to, namely, the view that the Indians were little more than "savages without intelligence." It also glosses over a fundamental point that must be recognized if the Indian is to be cast in an active and creative role. We must not forget that the Indians became involved in the fur trade by their own choice. Bearing that in mind, an objective and thorough examination of the archival records of the leading trading companies, admittedly a wearisome task, gives considerable evidence that the Indians were sophisticated traders, who had their own clearly defined sets of objectives and conventions for carrying on exchange with the Europeans.

This can be demonstrated by following several lines of inquiry. One of these involves attempting to determine the kind of consumers the Indians were at the time of initial contact and how their buying habits changed over time. Probably one of the most striking pictures that emerges from an examination of the early correspondence books of the Hudson's Bay Company is that, contrary to the popular image, the Indians had a sharp eye for quality merchandise and a well-defined shopping list. In short, they were astute consumers and not people who were easily hoodwinked.

If this is doubted, the early letters that the traders on Hudson Bay sent to the governor and committee of the Hudson's Bay Company in London should be read carefully. A substantial portion of almost every letter deals with the subject of the quality of the company's trade goods and with the Indians' reactions to it. Not only do these letters reveal that the Indians could readily recognize superior merchandise, but they also indicate that the Indians knew how to take advantage of the prevailing economic situation to improve the quality of the goods being offered to them. The following quote, typical of those that were written in the period before 1763, demonstrates the point and at the same time indicates one of the problems that is associated with carrying on research of this type. On 8 August 1728, Thomas McCliesh sent a letter from York Factory to the governor and committee in London informing them:

> I have sent home two bath rings as samples, for of late most of the rings [which] are sent are too small, having now upon remains 216 that none of the Indians will Trade. I have likewise sent home 59 ivory combs that will not be traded, they having no great teeth, and 3900 large musket flints and small pistol flints, likewise one hatchet, finding at least 150 such in three casks that we opened this summer which causes great grumbling amongst the natives. We have likewise Sent home 18 barrels of powder that came over in 1727, for badness I never saw the like, for it will not kill fowl nor beast at thirty yards distance: and as for kettles in general they are not fit to put into a Indian's hand being all of them thin, and eared with tender old brass that will not bear their weight when full of liquid, and soldered in several places. Never was any man so upbraided with our powder, kettles and hatchets, than we have been this summer by all the natives, especially by those that borders near the French. Our cloth likewise is so stretched with the tenter-hooks, so as the selvedge is almost tore from one end of the pieces to the other. I hope that such care will be taken so as will prevent the

like for the future, for the natives are grown so politic in their way
of trade, so as they are not to be dealt by as formerly . . . and I
affirm that man is not fit to be entrusted with the Company's interest
here or in any of their factories that does not make more profit
to the Company in dealing in a good commodity than in a bad.
For now is the time to oblidge [*sic*] the natives before the French
draws them to their settlement.[13]

From McCliesh's letter one gets the impression that few of the goods
on hand were satisfactory as far as the Indians were concerned. Taken
out of context, comments of this type, which are common in the correspondence from the posts, could be construed to indicate that the governor and committee of the Hudson's Bay Company hoped to enhance
their profits by dealing in cheap, poor quality merchandise whenever
possible. However, such a conclusion would distort the reality of the
situation and overlook important developments that were underway in
the eighteenth century. If one examines the letters that the governor
and committee sent to the Bay during the same period, as well as the
minutes of their meetings in London and correspondence with British
manufacturers and purchasing agents, other important facts emerge.

55

These other documents reveal that from the outset the governor and
committee were concerned with having an array of the types and quality
of goods that would appeal to the Indians. From the minute books of
the company we learn that in the earliest years of operations the London
directors relied heavily upon the experience and judgement of Pierre-
Esprit Radisson to provide them with guidance in developing an inventory of merchandise that would be suitable for their posts in Canada.
Radisson helped choose the patterns for knives, hatchets, guns, and so
forth that manufacturers were to use, and he was expected to evaluate
the quality of items that were produced for the company.[14] The governor
and committee also sought the expertise of others in their efforts to maintain some quality control. For instance, in 1674 they attempted to enlist
the services of the gunsmith who inspected and approved the trade guns
of the East India Company.[15] They wanted him to evaluate the firearms
that the Hudson's Bay Company was purchasing.

In their annual letters to the posts on the Bay, the governor and committee generally asked the traders to comment on the goods that they
received and to indicate which, if any, manufacturer's merchandise was
substandard. When new items were introduced, the directors wanted to
know what the Indians' reactions to them were.

The question that no doubt arises is, if the governor and committee
were as concerned with the quality of the products they sold, as suggested
above, then why was there a steady stream of complaints back to London
about their goods? Before a completely satisfactory answer to this question can be given, a great deal more research needs to be done in these
records. However, several working hypotheses may be put forth at this

time for the sake of discussion and research orientation. In developing its inventory of trade goods, the Hudson's Bay Company, as well as other European groups, had to deal with several problems. One of these was environmental in character. Goods that may have been satisfactory for trade in Europe, Africa, or Asia, often proved to be unsuitable in the harsh, subarctic environment. This was especially true of any items that were manufactured of iron. For example, one of the problems with the early flintlocks was that the locks froze in the winter.[16]

The extremely cold temperatures of the winter also meant that metal became brittle. Hence, if there were any flaws or cracks in the metal used to make mainsprings for guns, gun barrels, knives, hatchets, or kettles, these goods would break during the winter. In this way the severe environment of the subarctic necessitated very rigid standards of quality if the goods that were offered to the Indians were going to be satisfactory. These standards surely tested the skills of the company's suppliers and forced the company to monitor closely how the various manufacturers' goods held up under use.

Besides having to respond to environmental conditions, the traders also had to contend with a group of consumers who were becoming increasingly sophisticated and demanding. As the Indians substituted more and more European manufactures for traditional items, their livelihood and well-being became more dependent upon the quality of the articles that they were acquiring at the trading posts. This growing reliance meant that the Indians could no longer afford to accept goods that experience taught them would fail under the stress of hard usage and the environment, since such failures could threaten their survival. It was partly for these reasons that the Indians developed a critical eye for quality and could readily perceive the most minute defects in trade merchandise.

Indian groups were also quick to take advantage of competitive conditions. They became good comparison shoppers and until 1821 used European trading rivalries to force the improvement of quality and range of goods that were made available to them. For example, during the first century of trade on Hudson Bay, the Indians frequently brought to Hudson's Bay Company posts French goods that they judged to be superior to those of English manufacture. The Indians then demanded that the Hudson's Bay Company traders match or exceed the quality of these items or risk the loss of their trade to the French. Similar tactics were used by the Indians in later years whenever competition was strong between Euro-Canadian groups. Clearly such actions were not those of "dumb savages," but rather were those of astute traders and consumers, who knew how to respond to changing economic conditions to further their own best interests. The impact that these actions had on the overall profitability of the trade for Euro-Canadian traders has yet to be determined.

The issue of profits raises another whole area of concern that is poorly understood and should be studied in depth. To date we know little about

AT THE PORTAGE.
Hudson's Bay Company's Employés on their annual Expedition.

National Archives of Canada / C3610.

Hudson's Bay Company's employees with their stock and canoes, from *Picturesque Canada* (1882).

how the economic motivations of the Europeans and the Indians influenced the rates of exchange that were used at the posts. In fact, there is still a great deal of confusion about the complicated system of pricing goods and furs that was used in Canada. We know that the Hudson's Bay Company traders used two sets of standards. There was an official rate of exchange that was set by the governor and committee in London which differed from the actual rate that was used at the posts. Of importance, the traders advanced the prices of their merchandise above the stated tariff by resorting to the use of short measures. Contemporary critics of the Hudson's Bay Company and modern native historians have attacked the company for using such business practices, charging that the Indians were thereby being systematically cheated, or to use the modern expression, "ripped off."[17] But was this the case? Could the company traders have duped the Indians over long periods of time without the latter having caught on? Again, common sense and the record suggests that this was not the case.

58

The traders have left accounts of what they claimed were typical speeches of Indian trading leaders. One central element of all of these addresses was the request by these leaders that the traders give the Indians "full measure and a little over."[18] Also, the Indians usually asked to see the old measures or standards. Significantly, the Indians do not appear to have ever challenged the official standards, while at the same time they knew that they never received "full measure." What can we conclude from these facts?

In reality, the official standards of trade of the Hudson's Bay Company, and perhaps those of other companies as well, served only as a language of trade, or point of reference, that enabled the Indians and the traders to come to terms relatively quickly. The traders would not sell goods at prices below those set in the official standard. The Indian goal, on the other hand, was to try to obtain terms that approximated the official rate of exchange. An analysis of the Hudson's Bay Company post account books for the period before 1770 reveals that the company traders always managed to advance prices above the standard, but the margin of the advance diminished as the intensity of French opposition increased.[19] And even under monopoly conditions such as existed in Western Canada before the 1730's, the Hudson's Bay Company traders were not able to achieve an across-the-board increase that exceeded 50 per cent for any length of time.[20] This suggests strongly that the Indians successfully used competitive situations to improve the terms of trade and that they had their limits. If prices were advanced beyond a certain level, the Indians must have perceived that their economic reward was no longer worth the effort expended, and they broke off trade even if there was no alternative European group to turn to.

These remarks about the *overplus* system apply to the period before 1770. What we need to know is the extent to which the Indians were able to influence the rates of exchange during the time of bitter Hudson's Bay Company and North West Company rivalry. A preliminary sample of data from that period suggests their impact was much greater and that range of price variation was much more extreme than in the earlier years. Similarly, it would be helpful to have some idea what effect the re-establishment of the Hudson's Bay Company's monopoly after 1821 had on trade good prices and fur values in Western Canada. Being able to monitor prices under these contrasting conditions would enable us to obtain some idea of how the Indians were coping with the changing economic situation and how their responses influenced the material well-being of the different tribal groups.

Although this sample of the early accounting records shows that the Indians were economic men in the sense that they sought to maximize the return they obtained for their efforts, the same documents also indicate that, unlike their European counterparts, the Indians did not trade to accumulate wealth for status purposes. Rather, the Indians seem to have engaged in trade primarily to satisfy their own immediate requirement for goods. On a short-term basis their consumer demand was inelastic. In the early years this type of response was important in two respects. It was disconcerting to the European traders in that when they were offered better prices for their furs, the Indians typically responded by offering fewer pelts on a per capita basis. This type of a supply response was reinforced by gift-giving practices. Following the Indian custom, prior to trade tribal groups and the Europeans exchanged gifts. As rivalries for the allegiance of the Indians intensified, the lavishness of the gifts that the traders offered increased.

59

The ramifications that Indian supply responses to rising fur prices and to European gift-giving practices had for the overall conduct of the fur trade have yet to be fully explored. Clearly the costs that the Europeans would have had to absorb would have risen substantially during the periods when competition was strong, but to date no one has attempted to obtain even a rough idea of the magnitude by which these costs rose during the time of English–French or Hudson's Bay Company–North West Company rivalry. Nor has serious consideration been given to the manner in which such economic pressures may have favoured the use and abuse of certain trade articles such as alcohol and tobacco.

Concerning the use of alcohol, the excessive consumption of this drug was an inevitable consequence of the manner in which the economies of the Indian and European were linked together in the fur trade and of the contrasting economic motives of the two groups. As rivalries intensified, the European traders sought some means of retaining their contacts with the Indians, while at the same time keeping the per capita supply of furs that were obtained at as high a level as was possible. However, in attempting to accomplish the latter objective, the Europeans faced a number of problems. The mobile life of the Indians meant that their ability to accumulate material wealth was limited, especially in the early years when the trading posts were distant from the Indians' homelands. And, there were social sanctions against the accumulation of wealth by individual Indians.[21] To combat these problems, the traders needed to find commodities that could be transported easily or, even better, consumed at the trading post.

Unfortunately, alcohol was ideal when viewed from this coldly economic perspective. It offered one of the best means of absorbing the excess purchasing power of the Indians during periods of intensive competition. Furthermore, alcohol could be obtained relatively cheaply and diluted with water prior to trade.[22] Hence, it was a high profit trade item, an article that helped the traders hold down their gift-giving expenses, and it could be consumed at the forts. Given these characteristics, the only way that the abusive use of alcohol in trade could have been prevented in the absence of a strong European or native system of government was through monopoly control.

The traditional Indian consumer habits and responses to rising fur prices were important in another way. They were basically conservationist in nature although not intentionally so. By trapping only enough furs to buy the goods they needed in the early years, the pressures that the Indians exerted on the environment by their trapping activities were far less than they would have been had the objective been one of accumulating wealth for status purposes. If the latter had been the primary goal, then the Indians would have been tempted to increase their per capita supply of peltry as fur prices rose, since their purchasing power was greater.

In light of the above, the period between 1763 and 1821 is particularly interesting and warrants close study. During that period Euro-Canadian trading rivalries reached a peak, and one of the consequences of the cut-throat competition that characterized the time was that large territories were over-hunted and trapped by the Indians to the point that the economies of the latter were threatened.[23] The question is, had the basic economic behaviour of the Indians changed to such an extent that it facilitated their over-killing fur and game animals? Or, was the heavy use of addictive consumables such as alcohol and tobacco a major factor in the destruction of the environment?

Yet another aspect of the fur trade that has received too little attention is the connection that existed between the European and eastern North American markets and the Western Canadian operations of the trading companies. It needs to be determined how prices for trade goods and furs in these markets, as well as transportation costs, influenced rates of exchange at the posts. For instance, it has become popular to cite cases where European traders advanced the prices of certain articles by as much as 1000 per cent over what it cost the companies to buy them in Europe. Similarly, accounts of occasions when the Indians received a mere pittance for valuable furs[24] are common. But, it is rarely reported, and indeed it is generally not known, what percentage of the total gross revenues of a company were made by buying and selling such items. Nor is it known if losses were sustained on the sales of other commodities. Equally important, there is not even a rough idea of what the total overhead costs of the companies were at various times. Hence, their net profit margins remain a mystery, and what was considered to be a reasonable profit margin by European standards in the seventeenth, eighteenth, and early nineteenth centuries is not known. Answers to all of these questions must be found before any conclusions can be reached about whether or not the Indian or the European trader was being "ripped off."

And indeed, the Indian side must be considered when dealing with this question and when attempting to understand how the trading system responded to changing economic conditions. Even though Harold Innis pointed out that Indian trading specialists played a crucial role in the development and expansion of the fur trade, a common view of the Indians in the enterprise is still one that portrays them basically as simple trappers who hunted their own furs and accepted whatever prices for these commodities that the traders were willing to give them. The fact of the matter is that the records show that in the period before 1770, probably 80 per cent of all of the furs the Europeans received in central Canada came from Indian middlemen who acquired their peltry through their own trading networks.

Furthermore, these middlemen charged the Europeans substantially more for these furs than they had paid to obtain them from the trapping bands with whom they dealt. In turn, the middlemen advanced the prices for their trade goods well above the levels they had been charged by the Europeans, sometimes by margins of almost 1000 per cent.

These practices of the Indian middlemen raise a difficult question. If the Indians were not engaged in the trade to accumulate wealth, as suggested earlier, then why did the middlemen advance their prices to the extent that they did? Did their price levels simply enable them to maintain a material standard that they had become accustomed to? Before this question can be answered, a great deal more needs to be known about the problems that the Indian middlemen had to cope with in their efforts to acquire and transport goods and furs. A clearer understanding of their motives for engaging in the trade is also required. For example, why did some Indian groups quickly assume the middleman role while others were apparently content to continue as trappers? How did middlemen groups fare, economically, in comparison with trapping groups?

The Indians played a variety of other roles in the fur trade. They served as provision suppliers, canoe builders, canoe and boat men, and farm labourers around the posts, to name only a few. The Indians quickly assumed these roles as economic conditions changed, rendering old positions obsolete and opening up new opportunities.

This brings to mind another broad research area that should be explored more fully than it has been to date. It deals with determining how the various Indian groups perceived and responded to changing economic situations. Work in this area would serve to destroy another distorted image that many Euro-Canadians have of Indian societies, namely, the view that these societies are rigid and incapable of responding to change. Historically there is little evidence to support such a notion for the period before 1870. While the fur trade was a going concern and the Indians were not tied to the reserves and shackled with bureaucratic red tape, they made many successful adaptations to new circumstances. More needs to be written about this aspect of Indian history. If this work is done, perhaps a picture will emerge that shows the Indians to be innovative, dynamic, and responsive people, whose creativity and initiative have been thwarted in the post-treaty period.

62

In conclusion, this paper has focused upon the early phases of the Western Canadian fur trade, and the discussion has been restricted primarily to the economic dimension of trade. However, this restriction is justified because many of the problems of Indian–white relations are rooted in the past. Also, many of the distorted images that Euro-Canadians currently hold regarding Indians, thereby causing problems in the relationships between the two groups, have been generated and perpetuated by the manner in which the fur trade history has been written. Correcting these images requires starting at the beginning, and it is not simply a matter of rewriting what has already been done. New research has to be conducted in the various archival collections across the country and records that have received little attention to date, such as accounting records, need to be exhaustively explored. In conducting this research and presenting our results, the urge to overcompensate for past wrongs and inaccuracies by placing the Indian on a pedestal must be resisted. If the latter course of action is taken, a new mythology that will not stand the test of time will be created. Even more serious, it would probably serve only to perpetuate the warped images that such research set out to destroy, because it would fail to treat the Indians as equals with their own cultures and sets of values. Finally, if one of the objectives of studying the fur trade is to attempt to obtain a better understanding of Indian–white relations, it must be based on solid objective historical research.

NOTES

I would like to thank Charles A. Bishop, SUNY-Oswego, James R. Gibson and Conrad Heidenrich, York University, and Carol Judd, Ottawa, for commenting on earlier drafts of this paper. The author, of course, is responsible for this paper.

[1] Howard Adams, *Prison of Grass* (Toronto: New Press, 1975), 41.
[2] Adams, *Prison of Grass*, 43.

3 The most notable example was probably Harold Innis. See H.A. Innis, *The Fur Trade in Canada* (1930; reprint ed., New Haven: Yale University Press, 1962), 386–92.

4 See, for example, Innis, *The Fur Trade*; A.S. Morton, *The History of the Canadian West to 1870–71*, 2nd ed. (Toronto: University of Toronto Press, 1973); and E.E. Rich, *The Fur Trade and the Northwest to 1857* (Toronto: McClelland and Stewart, 1967).

5 C. Jaenen, *Friend and Foe* (Toronto: McClelland and Stewart, 1976), 1–11.

6 Innis and Rich deal extensively with the fur trade as an aspect of imperial history. See Innis, *The Fur Trade*, 383; and Rich, *Fur Trade and Northwest*, xi and 296. Several corporate histories have been written. See as examples, L.R. Masson, *Les Bourgeois de la Compagnie du Nord-Ouest*, 2 vols. (1889–90; reprint ed., New York: Antiquarian Press, 1960); E.E. Rich, *The History of Hudson's Bay Company, 1670–1870*, 2 vols. (London: Hudson's Bay Record Society, 1958–59); and W.S. Wallace, *Documents Relating to the North West Company* (Toronto: Champlain Society, 1934).

7 One of the problems, of course, is that biographical details regarding Indian personalities are few. The historical record often does not provide information regarding births, deaths, and family relationships of Indian leaders.

8 There are some notable exceptions such as Dempsey's study of Crowfoot and Sluman's of Poundmaker. See H. Dempsey, *Crowfoot: Chief of the Blackfoot* (Edmonton: Hurtig, 1972); and N. Sluman, *Poundmaker* (Toronto: McGraw-Hill Ryerson, 1967).

9 This point of view was perhaps most strongly expressed by Diamond Jenness. See Diamond Jenness, "The Indian Background of Canadian History," Canada, Department of Mines and Resources, National Museum of Canada Bulletin No. 86 (Ottawa, 1937), 1–2; and Diamond Jenness, *Indians of Canada*, 6th ed. (Ottawa: National Museum of Canada, 1963), 249. See also George F. Stanley, "The Indian Background of Canadian History," Canadian Historical Association, *Papers* (1952), 14.

10 A notable example of this interest as it pertains to Western Canada is the early work of Frits Pannekoek. See Frits Pannekoek, "Protestant Agricultural Missions in the Canadian West in 1870" (M.A. thesis, University of Alberta, 1970). More recently, Pannekoek has begun to consider the divisive role these groups played in terms of race relations in Western Canada. See Frits Pannekoek, "The Rev. Griffiths Owen Corbett and the Red River Civil War of 1869–70," *Canadian Historical Review* 57 (1976): 133–49.

11 A notable exception to this viewpoint is that expressed by Stanley in 1952. He pointed out that programmes oriented towards assimilating the Indians into the dominant white society lead to cultural extinction of the former group. This is offensive to any people having a strong sense of identity. See Stanley, 21.

12 R.G. Thwaites, ed., *The Jesuit Relations and Allied Documents*, vol. 6 (New York: Pagent Book Company, 1959), 297–99.

13 K.G. Davies, ed., *Letters from Hudson Bay*, 1703–40 (London: Hudson's Bay Record Society, 1965), 136.

14 E.E. Rich, ed., *Minutes of the Hudson's Bay Company*, 1671–74 (Toronto: Champlain Society, 1942), 26–27, 58–59.

15 Rich, *Minutes*, 91.

16 A.J. Ray, *Indians in the Fur Trade* (Toronto: University of Toronto Press, 1974), 75.

17 For example, in the eighteenth century Arthur Dobbs charged that the company advanced the prices of its goods above the Standards of Trade to such an extent that it discouraged the Indians from trading. Arthur Dobbs, *An Account of the Countries Adjoining to Hudson's Bay in the Northwest Part of America* (London, 1744), 43. More recently the company has been attacked for its pricing policy by Adams, *Prison of Grass*, 24.

18 C.E. Heidenreich and A.J. Ray, *The Early Fur Trades: A Study in Cultural Interaction* (Toronto: McClelland and Stewart, 1976), 82–83.

19 A.J. Ray, "The Hudson's Bay Company Account Books as Sources for Comparative Economic Analyses of the Fur Trade: An Examination of Exchange Rate Data," *Western Canadian Journal of Anthropology* 6, 1 (1976): 44–50.

20 The principal exception was at Eastmain where the prevailing rates exceeded the 50 per cent markup level from the late 1690's until about 1720. However, it should be pointed out that French opposition was relatively weak in this area. See Ray, "Hudson's Bay Company Account Books," 45–50.

21 For example, one of the virtues of Indian leaders was generosity. And, generalized reciprocity or sharing was practised amongst band members. These values and practices served to discourage any individual, regardless of his position, from accumulating wealth in excess of that of his kinsmen.

22 Generally, alcohol was diluted with water by a ratio of one-quarter to one-third at the Hudson's Bay Company posts in the eighteenth century. See Davies, *Letters from Hudson Bay*, 268.

23 Ray, *Indians in the Fur Trade*, 117–24.

24 Adams, *Prison of Grass*, 51; and Susan Hurlich, "Up Against the Bay: Resource Imperialism and Native Resistance," *This Magazine* 9, 4 (1975): 4.

"Women in Between": Indian Women in Fur Trade Society in Western Canada*

SYLVIA VAN KIRK

In attempting to analyse the life of the Indian woman in fur trade society in Western Canada, especially from her own point of view, one is immediately confronted by a challenging historiographical problem. Can the Indian woman's perspective be constructed from historical sources that were almost exclusively written by European men? Coming from a non-literate society, no Indian women have left us, for example, their views on the fur trade or their reasons for becoming traders' wives.[1] Yet if one amasses the sources available for fur trade social history, such as contemporary narratives, journals, correspondence, and wills, a surprisingly rich store of information on Indian women emerges. One must, of course, be wary of the traders' cultural and sexual bias, but then even modern anthropologists have difficulty maintaining complete objectivity. Furthermore, the fur traders had the advantage of knowing Indian women intimately — these women became their wives, the mothers of their children. Narratives such as that of Andrew Graham in the late eighteenth century and David Thompson in the nineteenth, both of whom had native wives, comment perceptively on the implications of Indian–white social contact.[2] The key to constructing the Indian woman's perspective must lie in the kinds of questions applied to data;[3] regrettably the picture will not be complete, but it is hoped that a careful reading of the traders' observations can result in a useful and illuminating account of the Indian women's life in fur trade society.

The fur trade was based on the complex interaction between two different racial groups. On the one hand are the various Indian tribes, most importantly the Ojibway, the Cree, and the Chipewyan. These Indians may be designated the "host" group in that they remain within their traditional environment. On the other hand are the European traders, the "visiting" group, who enter the Northwest by both the Hudson's Bay and St. Lawrence-Great Lakes routes. They are significantly different from the Indians in that they constitute only a small, all-male fragment of their own society. For a variety of factors to be discussed, this created a unique situation for the Indian women. They became the "women in between" two groups of males. Because of their sex, Indian women were able to become an integral part of fur trade society in a

*From the Canadian Historical Association, *Historical Papers* 1977, 30–47. Copyright by the Canadian Historical Association. Reprinted by permission.

sense that Indian men never could. As country wives[4] of the traders, Indian women lived substantially different lives when they moved within the forts. Even within the tribes, women who acted as allies of the whites can also be observed; certain circumstances permitted individual women to gain positions of influence and act as "social brokers" between the two groups.

It is a major contention of this study that Indian women themselves were active agents in the development of Indian–white relations.[5] A major concern then must be to determine what motivated their actions. Some themes to be discussed are the extent to which the Indian woman was able to utilize her position as "woman in between" to increase her influence and status, and the extent to which the Indian woman valued the economic advantage brought by the traders. It must be emphasized, however, that Indian–white relations were by no means static during the fur trade period.[6] After assessing the positive and negative aspects of the Indian woman's life in fur trade society, the paper will conclude by discussing the reasons for the demise of her position.

65

I

Miscegenation was the basic social fact of the western Canadian fur trade. That this was so indicates active cooperation on both sides. From the male perspective, both white and Indian, the formation of marital alliances between Indian women and the traders had its advantages. The European traders had both social and economic reasons for taking Indian mates. Not only did they fill the sexual void created by the absence of white women,[7] but they performed such valuable economic tasks as making moccasins and netting snowshoes that they became an integral if unofficial part of the fur trade work force.[8] The traders also realized that these alliances were useful in cementing trade ties; officers in both the Hudson's Bay and North West companies often married daughters of trading captains or chiefs.[9] From the Indian point of view, the marital alliance created a reciprocal social bond which served to consolidate his economic relationship with the trader. The exchange of women was common in Indian society where it was viewed as "a reciprocal alliance and series of good offices . . . between the friends of both parties; each is ready to assist and protect the other."[10] It was not loose morality or even hospitality which prompted the Indians to be so generous with their offers of women. This was their way of drawing the traders into their kinship circle, and in return for giving the traders sexual and domestic rights to their women, the Indians expected equitable privileges such as free access to the posts and provisions.[11] It is evident that the traders often did not understand the Indian concept of these alliances and a flagrant violation of Indian sensibilities could lead to retaliation such as the Henley House massacre in 1755.[12]

But what of the women themselves? Were they just pawns in this exchange, passive, exploited victims? Fur trade sources do not support this view; there are numerous examples of Indian women actively seeking to become connected with the traders. According to an early Nor'Wester, Cree women considered it an honour to be selected as wives by the voyageurs, and any husband who refused to lend his wife would be subject to the general condemnation of the women.[13] Alexander Ross observed that Chinook women on the Pacific coast showed a preference for living with a white man. If deserted by one husband, they would return to their tribe in a state of widowhood to await the opportunity of marrying another fur trader.[14] Nor'Wester Daniel Harmon voiced the widely held opinion that most of the Indian women were "better pleased to remain with the White People than with their own Relations," while his contemporary George Nelson affirmed "some too would even desert to live with the white."[15] Although Alexander Henry the Younger may have exaggerated his difficulties in fending off young Indian women, his personal experiences underline the fact that the women often took the initiative. On one occasion when travelling with his brigade in the summer of 1800, Henry was confronted in his tent by a handsome woman, dressed in her best finery, who told him boldly that she had come to live with him as she did not care for her husband or any other Indian. But Henry, anxious to avoid this entanglement partly because it was not sanctioned by the husband whom he knew to be insatiably jealous, forced the woman to return to her Indian partner.[16] A year or so later in the lower Red River district, the daughter of an Ojibway chief had more luck. Henry returned from New Year's festivities to find that "Liard's daughter" had taken possession of his room and the devil could not have got her out."[17] This time, having become more acculturated to fur trade life, Henry acquiesced and "Liard's daughter" became his country wife. The trader, however, resisted his father-in-law's argument that he should also take his second daughter because all great men should have a plurality of wives.[18]

The fur traders also comment extensively on the assistance and loyalty of Indian women who remained within the tribes. An outstanding example is the young Chipewyan Thanadelthur, known to the traders as the "Slave Woman."[19] In the early eighteenth century, after being captured by the Cree, Thanadelthur managed to escape to York Factory. Her knowledge of Chipewyan made her valuable to the traders, and in 1715-16, she led an H.B.C. [Hudson's Bay Company] expedition to establish peace between the Cree and the Chipewyan, a necessary prelude to the founding of Fort Churchill. Governor James Knight's journals give us a vivid picture of this woman, of whom he declared: "She was one of a Very high Spirit and of the Firmest Resolution that ever I see any Body in my Days."[20]

Post journals contain numerous references to Indian women warning the traders of impending treachery. In 1797, Charles Chaboillez, having been warned by an old woman that the Indians intended to pillage his post, was able to nip this intrigue in the bud.[21] George Nelson and one of his men only escaped an attack by some Indians in 1805 by being "clandestinely assisted by the women."[22] It appears that women were particularly instrumental in saving the lives of the whites among the turbulent tribes of the Lower Columbia.[23] One of the traders' most notable allies was the well-connected Chinook princess known as Lady Calpo, the wife of a Clatsop chief. In 1814, she helped restore peaceful relations after the Nor'Westers had suffered a raid on their canoes by giving them important information about Indian custom in settling disputes. Handsome rewards cemented her attachment to the traders with the result that Lady Calpo reputedly saved Fort George from several attacks by warning of the hostile plans of the Indians.[24]

The reasons for the Indian women's actions are hinted at in the traders' observations. It was the generally held opinion of the traders that the status of women in Indian society was deplorably low. As Nor'Wester Gabriel Franchère summed it up:

> Some Indian tribes think that women have no souls, but die altogether like the brutes; others assign them a different paradise from that of men, which indeed they might have reason to prefer . . . unless their relative condition were to be ameliorated in the next world.[25]

Whether as "social brokers" or as wives, Indian women attempted to manipulate their position as "women in between" to increase their influence and status. Certainly women such as Thanadelthur and Lady Calpo were able to work themselves into positions of real power. It is rather paradoxical that in Thanadelthur's case it was her escape from captivity that brought her into contact with the traders in the first place; if she had not been a woman, she would never have been carried off by the Cree as a prize of war. Once inside the H.B.C. fort, she was able to use her position as the only Chipewyan to advantage by acting as guide and consultant to the Governor. The protection and regard she was given by the whites enabled Thanadelthur to dictate to Indian men, both Cree and Chipewyan, in a manner they would not previously have tolerated. Anxious to promote the traders' interests, she assaulted an old Chipewyan on one occasion when he attempted to trade less than prime furs; she "ketcht him by the nose Push'd him backwards & call'd him fool and told him if they brought any but Such as they ware directed they would not be traded."[26] Thanadelthur did take a Chipewyan husband but was quite prepared to leave him if he would not accompany her on the arduous second journey she was planning to undertake for the Governor.[27] It is possible that the role played by Thanadelthur and subsequent "slave women" in establishing trade relations with the whites may have enhanced the status of Chipewyan women. Nearly a century later, Alexander Mackenzie noted that, in spite of their burdensome existence, Chipewyan women possessed "a very considerable influence in the traffic with Europeans."[28]

Lady Calpo retained a position of influence for a long time. When Governor Simpson visited Fort George in 1824, he found she had to be treated with respect because she was "the best News Monger in the Parish"; from her he learned "More of the Scandal, Secrets and politics both of the out & inside of the Fort than from Any other source."[29] Significantly, Lady Calpo endeavoured to further improve her rank by arranging a marriage alliance between the Governor and her carefully raised daughter. Although Simpson declared he wished "to keep clear of the Daughter," he succumbed in order "to continue on good terms with the Mother."[30] Many years later, a friend visiting the Columbia wrote to Simpson that Lady Calpo, that " 'fast friend' of the Whites" was still thriving.[31]

As wives of the traders, Indian women could also manoeuver themselves into positions of influence. In fact, a somewhat perturbed discussion emerges in fur trade literature over the excessive influence some Indian women exerted over their fur trader husbands. The young N.W.C. [North West Company] clerk George Nelson appears to have spent long hours contemplating the insolvable perplexities of womankind. Nelson claimed that initially Cree women when married to whites were incredibly attentive and submissive, but this did not last long. Once they had gained a little footing, they knew well "how to take advantage & what use they ought to make of it."[32] On one of his first trips into the interior, Nelson was considerably annoyed by the shenanigans of the Indian wife of Brunet, one of his voyageurs. A jealous, headstrong woman, she completely dominated her husband by a mixture of "caresses, promises & menaces." Not only did this woman render her husband a most unreliable servant, but Nelson also caught her helping herself to the Company's rum. Brunet's wife, Nelson fumed, was as great "a vixen & hussy" as the tinsmith's wife at the market place in Montreal: "I now began to think that women were women not only in civilized countries but elsewhere also."[33]

Another fur trader observed a paradoxical situation among the Chipewyan women. In their own society, they seemed condemned to a most servile existence, but upon becoming wives of the French-Canadian voyageurs, they assumed "an importance to themselves and instead of serving as formerly they exact submission from the descendants of the Gauls."[34] One of the most remarkable examples of a Chipewyan wife rising to prominence was the case of Madam Lamallice, the wife of the brigade guide at the H.B.C. post on Lake Athabasca. During the difficult winter of 1821–22, Madam Lamallice was accorded a favoured position because she was the post's only interpreter and possessed considerable influence with the Indians.[35] George Simpson, then experiencing his first winter in the Indian Country, felt obliged to give in to her demands for extra rations and preferred treatment in order to prevent her defection. He had observed that the Nor'Westers' strong position was partly due to the fact that " . . . their Women are faithful to their cause and good Interpreters whereas we have but one in the Fort that can talk Chipewyan."[36] Madam Lamallice exploited her position to such an extent that she even defied fort regulations by carrying on a private trade in provisions.[37] A few years later on a trip to the Columbia, Governor Simpson was annoyed to discover that Chinook women when married to the whites often gained such an ascendancy "that they give law to their Lords."[38] In fact, he expressed general concern about the influence of these "petticoat politicians" whose demands were "more injurious to the Companys interests than I am well able to describe."[39] The Governor deplored Chief Factor James Bird's management of Red River in the early 1820s because of his habit of discussing every matter "however trifling or important" with "his Copper Cold Mate," who then spread the news freely around the colony.[40] Too many of his officers, Simpson declared, tended to sacrifice business for private interests. Particular expense and delay were occasioned in providing transport for families. Simpson never forgave Chief Factor John Clarke for abandoning some of the goods destined for Athabasca in 1820 to make a light canoe for his native wife and her servant.[41]

It is likely that Simpson's single-minded concern for business efficiency caused him to exaggerate the extent of the Indian women's influence. Nevertheless, they do seem to have attempted to take advantage of their unique position as women "in between" two groups of men. This fact is supported by the traders' observation that the choice of a husband, Indian or white, gave the Indian woman leverage to improve her lot. Now she could threaten to desert to the whites or vice versa if she felt she were not being well-treated:

> She has always enough of policy to insinuate how well off she was while living with the white people and in like manner when with the latter she drops some hints to the same purpose.[42]

Although Chipewyan women who had lived with the voyageurs had to resume their former domestic tasks when they returned to their own people, they reputedly evinced a greater spirit of independence.[43] Considerable prestige accrued to Chinook women who had lived with the traders; upon rejoining the tribes, they remained "very friendly" to the whites and "never fail to influence their connections to the same effect."[44]

From the Indian woman's point of view, material advantage was closely tied to the question of improved influence or status. The women within

69

the tribes had a vested interest in promoting cordial relations with the whites. While George Nelson mused that it was a universal maternal instinct which prompted the women to try to prevent clashes between Indian and white,[45] they were more likely motivated by practical, economic considerations. If the traders were driven from the country, the Indian woman would lose the source of European goods, which had revolutionized her life just as much if not more than that of the Indian man. It was much easier to boil water in a metal kettle than to have to laboriously heat it by means of dropping hot stones into a bark container. Cotton and woolen goods saved long hours of tanning hides. "Show them an awl or a strong needle," declared David Thompson, "and they will gladly give the finest Beaver or Wolf skin they have to purchase it."[46]

Furthermore, it can be argued that the tendency of the Indians to regard the fur trade post as a kind of welfare centre was of more relevance to the women than to the men. In times of scarcity, which were not infrequent in Indian society, the women were usually the first to suffer.[47] Whereas before they would often have perished, many now sought relief at the companies' posts. To cite but one of many examples: at Albany during the winter of 1706, Governor Beale gave shelter to three starving Cree women whose husband had sent them away as he could only provide for his two children.[48] The post was also a source of medical aid and succour. The story is told of a young Carrier woman in New Caledonia, who having been severely beaten by her husband managed to struggle to the nearest N.W.C. post. Being nearly starved, she was slowly nursed back to health and allowed to remain at the post when it became apparent that her relatives had abandoned her.[49] The desire for European goods, coupled with the assistance to be found at the fur trade posts, helps to explain why Indian women often became devoted allies of the traders.

In becoming the actual wife of a fur trader, the Indian woman was offered even greater relief from the burdens of her traditional existence. In fact, marriage to a trader offered an alternative lifestyle. The fur traders themselves had no doubt that an Indian woman was much better off with a white man. The literature presents a dreary recital of their abhorrence of the degraded, slave-like position of the Indian women. The life of a Cree woman, declared Alexander Mackenzie, was "an uninterrupted success of toil and pain."[50] Nor'Wester Duncan McGillivray decided that the rather singular lack of affection evinced by Plains Indian women for their mates arose from the barbarous treatment the women received.[51] Although David Thompson found the Chipewyan a good people in many ways, he considered their attitudes toward women a disgrace; he had known Chipewyan women to kill female infants as "an act of kindness" to spare them the hardships they would have to face.[52]

The extent to which the fur traders' observations represent an accurate reflection of the actual status of Indian women in their own societies presents a complex dilemma which requires deeper investigation. The cultural and class biases of the traders are obvious. Their horror at the toilsome burdens imposed upon Indian women stems from their narrow, chivalrous view of women as the "frail, weaker sex." This is scarcely an appropriate description of Indian women, particularly the Chipewyan who were acknowledged to be twice as strong as their male counterparts.[53] Furthermore, while the sharp sexual division of labour inflicted a burdensome role upon the women, their duties were essential and the women possessed considerable autonomy within their own sphere.[54] Some traders did think it curious that the women seemed to possess a degree of influence in spite of their degraded situation; indeed, some of the bolder ones occasionally succeeded in making themselves quite independent and "wore the breeches".[55]

A possible way of explaining the discrepancy between the women's perceived and actual status is suggested in a recent anthropological study of the Mundurucú of Amazonian Brazil. In this society, the authors discovered that while the official (male) ideology relegates women to an inferior, subservient position, in the reality of daily life, the women are able to assume considerable autonomy and influence.[56] Most significantly, however, Mundurucú women, in order to alleviate their onerous domestic duties, have actively championed the erosion of traditional village life and the concomitant blurring of economic sex roles which have come with the introduction of the rubber trade. According to the authors, the Mundurucú woman "has seen another way of life, and she has opted for it."[57]

This statement could well be applied to the Indian woman who was attracted to the easier life of the fur trade post. In the first place, she now became involved in a much more sedentary routine. With a stationary home, the Indian woman was no longer required to act as a beast of burden, hauling or carrying the accoutrements of camp from place to place. The traders often expressed astonishment and pity at the heavy loads which Indian women were obliged to transport.[58] In fur trade society, the unenviable role of carrier was assumed by the voyageur. The male servants at the fort were now responsible for providing firewood and water, although the women might help. In contrast to Indian practice, the women of the fort were not sent to fetch home the produce of the hunt.[59] The wife of an officer, benefiting from her husband's rank, enjoyed a privileged status. She herself was carried in and out of the canoe[60] and could expect to have all her baggage portaged by a voyageur. At Fond du Lac in 1804 when the wife of N.W.C. *bourgeois* John Sayer decided to go on a sugar-making expedition, four men went with her to carry her baggage and provisions and later returned to fetch home her things.[61]

While the Indian woman performed a variety of valuable economic tasks around the post, her domestic duties were relatively lighter than they had traditionally been. Now her energies were concentrated on making moccasins and snowshoes. As one Nor'Wester declared, with the whites, Indian women could lead "a comparatively easy and free life" in contrast to the "servile slavish mode" of their own.[62] The prospect of superior comforts reputedly motivated some Spokan women to marry voyageurs.[63] The ready supply of both finery and trinkets which *bourgeois* and voyageurs were seen to lavish on their women may also have had an appeal.[64] Rival traders noted that luxury items such as lace, ribbons, rings and vermilion, which "greatly gain the Love of the Women," were important in attracting the Indians to trade.[65] The private orders placed by H.B.C. officers and servants in the 1790s and later include a wide range of cloth goods, shawls, gartering, earrings and brooches for the women.[66] When taken by a trader, *à la façon du pays*, it became common for an Indian woman to go through a ritual performed by the other women of the fort; she was scoured of grease and paint and exchanged her native garments for those of a more civilized fashion. At the N.W.C. posts, wives were clothed in "Canadian fashion," which consisted of a shirt, short gown, petticoat and leggings.[67]

The traders further thought that Indian women benefited by being freed from certain taboos and customs which they had to bear in Indian society. Among the Ojibway and other tribes, for example, the choicest part of an animal was always reserved for the men; death, it was believed, would come to any woman who dared to eat such sacred portions. The Nor'Westers paid little heed to such observances. As Duncan Cameron sarcastically wrote: "I have often seen several women living with the white men eat of those forbidden morsels without the least inconvenience."[68] The traders were also convinced that Indian women welcomed a monogamous as opposed to a polygamous state. Polygamy, several H.B.C. officers observed, often gave rise to jealous and sometimes murderous quarrels.[69] It is possible, however, that the traders' own cultural abhorrence of polygamy[70] made them exaggerate the women's antipathy toward it. As a practical scheme for the sharing of heavy domestic tasks, polygamy may in fact have been welcomed by the women.

II

Thus far the advantages which the fur trade brought to Indian women have been emphasized in order to help explain Indian women's reactions to it. It would be erroneous, however, to paint the life of an Indian wife as idyllic. In spite of the traders' belief in the superior benefits they offered, there is evidence that fur trade life had an adverse effect on Indian women. Certainly, a deterioration in her position over time can be detected.

First there is the paradox that the supposedly superior material culture of the fur trade had a deleterious effect on Indian women. It was as if, mused Reverend John West, the first Anglican missionary, "the habits

72

of civilized life" exerted an injurious influence over their general con-
stitutions.[71] Apart from being more exposed to European diseases, the
Indian wives of traders suffered more in childbirth than they had in
the primitive state.[72] Dr. John Richardson, who accompanied the Franklin Expedition of the 1820s, noted that not only did Indian women now
have children more frequently and for longer periods, but that they were
more susceptible to the disorders and diseases connected with pregnancy
and childbirth.[73] It was not uncommon for fur traders' wives to give
birth to from eight to twelve children, whereas four children were the
average in Cree society.[74]

The reasons for this dramatic rise in the birth rate deserve further
investigation, but several reasons can be advanced. As recent medical
research had suggested, the less fatiguing lifestyle and more regular diet
offered the Indian wife could have resulted in great fecundity.[75] The
daily ration for the women of the forts was four pounds of meat or fish
(one half that for the men);[76] when Governor Simpson jokingly remarked
that the whitefish diet at Fort Chipewyan seemed conducive to procreation he may have hit upon a medical truth.[77] Furthermore, sexual activity
in Indian society was circumscribed by a variety of taboos, and evidence
suggests that Indian men regarded their European counterparts as very
licentious.[78] Not only did Indian women now have sex more often, but
the attitudes of European husbands also may have interfered with traditional modes of restricting family size. The practice of infanticide was,
of course, condemned by the whites, but the Europeans may also have
discouraged the traditional long nursing periods of from two to four years
for each child.[79] In their view this custom resulted in the premature
aging of the mothers,[80] but the fact that Indian children were born at
intervals of approximately three years tends to support the recent theory
that lactation depresses fertility.[81]

The cultural conflict resulting over the upbringing of the children must
have caused the Indian women considerable anguish. An extreme example of the tragedy which could result related to the Chinook practice
of head-flattening. In Chinook society, a flat forehead, achieved by strap-
ping a board against the baby's head when in its cradle, was a mark
of class; only slaves were not so distinguished. Thus it was only natural
that a Chinook woman, though married to a fur trader, would desire
to bind her baby's head, but white fathers found this custom abhorrent.
The insistence of some fathers that their infants' heads not be flattened
resulted in the mothers murdering their babies rather than have them
suffer the ignominy of looking like slaves. Gradually European preference
prevailed. When Governor Simpson visited the Columbia in the early
1820s, he reported that Chinook wives were abiding by their husbands'
wishes and no cases of infanticide had been reported for some years.[82]

In Indian society, children were the virtual "property" of the women
who were responsible for their upbringing;[83] in fur trade society, Indian
women could find themselves divested of these rights. While the traders

73

acknowledged that Indian women were devoted and affectionate mothers, this did not prevent them from exercising patriarchal authority, particularly in sending young children to Britain or Canada so that they might receive a "civilized" education.[84] It must have been nearly impossible to explain the rationale for such a decision to the Indian mothers; their grief at being separated from their children was compounded by the fact that the children, who were especially vulnerable to respiratory diseases, often died.[85]

It is difficult to know if the general treatment accorded Indian women by European traders met with the women's acceptance. How much significance should be attached to the views of outside observers in the early 1800s who did not think the Indian woman's status had been much improved? Some of the officers of the Franklin Expedition felt the fur traders had been corrupted by Indian attitudes toward women; Indian wives were not treated with "the tenderness and attention due to every female" because the Indians would despise the traders for such unmanly action.[86] The first missionaries were even stronger in denouncing fur trade marital relations. John West considered the traders' treatment of their women disgraceful: "They do not admit them as their companions, nor do they allow them to eat at their tables, but degrade them *merely* as slaves to their arbitrary inclinations."[87] Such statements invite skepticism because of the writers' limited contact with fur trade society, and in the case of the missionaries because of their avowedly hostile view of fur trade customs. Furthermore, the above statements project a European ideal about the way women should be treated, which apart from being widely violated in their own society, would have had little relevance for Indian women. It is doubtful, for example, that the Indian women themselves would have viewed the fact that they did not come to table, a custom partly dictated by the quasi-military organization of the posts, as proof of their debased position.[88] The segregation of the sexes at meals was common in Indian society, but now, at least, the women did not have to suffice with the leftovers of the men.[89]

Nevertheless, there is evidence to suggest that Indian women were misused by the traders. In Indian society, women were accustomed to greater freedom of action with regard to marital relationships than the traders were prepared to accord them. It was quite within a woman's rights, for example, to institute a divorce if her marriage proved unsatisfactory.[90] In fur trade society, Indian women were more subject to arbitrary arrangements devised by the men. Upon retiring from the Indian Country, it became customary for a trader to place his country wife and family with another, a practice known as "turning off." Although there was often little they could do about it, a few cases were cited of women who tried to resist. At a post in the Peace River district in 1798, the Indian wife of an *engagé*, who was growing tired of wintering *en derouine*, absolutely rejected her husband's attempt to pass her to the man who agreed to take his place.[91] At Fort Chipewyan in 1800, the estranged wife of the voyageur Morin foiled the attempt of his *bourgeois* to find her a temporary "protector"; she stoutly refused three different prospects.[92] Indian women also did not take kindly to the long separations which fur trade life imposed on them and their European mates. Although the Indian wife of Chief Factor Joseph Colen was to receive every attention during his absence in England in the late 1790s, Colen's successor could not dissuade her from taking an Indian lover and leaving York Factory.[93]

Indian wives seem to have been particularly victimized during the violent days of the trade war when rivals went so far as to debauch and intimidate each other's women. In 1819 at Pelican Lake, for example, H.B.C. servant Deshau took furs from a N.W.C. servant and raped his wife in retaliation for having had his own wife debauched by a Nor'Wester earlier in the season.[94] A notorious instance involved the Indian wife of H.B.C. servant Andrew Kirkness at Isle à la Crosse in 1810–11. In the late summer, this woman in a fit of pique had deserted her husband and sought refuge at the Nor'Westers' post. She soon regretted her action, however, for she was kept a virtual prisoner by the Canadians, and all efforts of the H.B.C. men to get her back failed. The upshot was that Kirkness himself deserted to the rival post, leaving the English in dire straits since he was their only fisherman. Kirkness was intimidated into remaining with the Nor'Westers until the spring with the threat that, should he try to leave, "every Canadian in the House would ravish his woman before his eyes." Eventually Kirkness was released, but only after his wife had been coerced into saying that she did not want to accompany him. As the H.B.C. party were evacuating their post, the woman tried to escape but was forcibly dragged back by the Nor'Westers and ultimately became the "property" of an *engagé*.[95]

Such abusive tactics were also applied to the Indians. By the turn of the century, relations between the Indians and the Nor'Westers in particular showed a marked deterioration. In what seems to have been a classic case of "familiarity breeding contempt," the Nor'Westers now retained their mastery through coercion and brute force and frequently transgressed the bounds of Indian morality. An especially flagrant case was the Nor'Westers' exploitation of Chipewyan women at its posts in the Athabasca district. By the end of the eighteenth century, they had apparently built up a nefarious traffic in these women; the *bourgeois* did not scruple at seizing Chipewyan women by force, ostensibly in lieu of trade debts, and then selling them to the men for large sums.[96] The situation became so bad that the Chipewyan began leaving their women behind when they came to trade, and when Hudson's Bay traders appeared on Lake Athabasca in 1792, the Indians hoped to secure their support and drive out their rivals. The English, however, were too weak to offer any effective check to the Nor'Westers who continued to assault

75

both fathers and husbands if they tried to resist the seizure of their women. Since they were not powerful enough to mount an attack, the Chipewyan connived at the escape of their women during the summer months when most of the traders were away. Resentful of their treatment, many of the women welcomed the chance to slip back to their own people so that the summer master at Fort Chipewyan was almost solely pre-occupied with keeping watch over the *engagés* women.[97] By 1800 at least one voyageur had been killed by irate Chipewyan, and the *bourgeois* con-templated offering a reward for the hunting down of "any d—nd rascal" who caused a Frenchman's woman to desert.[98]

The Indians appear to have become openly contemptuous of the white man and his so-called morality. A northern tribe called the Beaver In-dians took a particularly strong stand. At first they had welcomed the Canadians but, having rapidly lost respect for them, now forbade any intercourse between their women and the traders.[99] Elsewhere individual hunters boycotted the traders owing to the maltreatment of their women.[100] Sporadic reprisals became more frequent. Whereas Indian women had previously played a positive role as a liaison between Indian and white, they were now becoming an increasing source of friction be-tween the two groups. Governor Simpson summed up the deteriorating situation:

> It is a lamentable fact that almost every difficulty we have had with Indians throughout the country may be traced to our interference with the Women of the Forts in short 9 murders out of 10 Committed on Whites by Indians have arisen through Women.[101]

Although there is little direct evidence available, it is possible that the Indian women themselves were becoming increasingly dissatisfied with their treatment from the whites. In spite of the initiative which the women have been seen to exercise in forming and terminating re-lationships with the traders, there were undoubtedly times when they were the unwilling objects of a transaction between Indians and white men. Certainly not all Indian women looked upon the whites as desirable husbands, a view that was probably reinforced with experience. George Nelson did observe in 1811 that there were some Indian women who showed "an extraordinary predilection" for their own people and could not be prevailed upon to live with the traders.[102]

The increasing hostility of the Indians, coupled with the fact that in well-established areas marriage alliances were no longer a significant factor in trade relations, led to a decline in the practice of taking an Indian wife. In fact in 1806, the North West Company passed a ruling prohibiting any of its employees from taking a country wife from among the tribes.[103] One of the significant factors which changed the traders' attitudes toward Indian women, however, was that they were now no longer "women in between." By the turn of the century a sizeable group

76

of mixed-blood women had emerged and for social and economic reasons, fur traders preferred mixed-blood women as wives. In this way the Indian women lost their important place in fur trade society.

The introduction of the Indian woman's perspective on Indian-white relations serves to underscore the tremendous complexity of inter-cultural contact. It is argued that Indian women saw definite advantages to be gained from the fur trade, and in their unique position as "women in between," they endeavoured to manipulate the situation to improve their existence. That the limits of their influence were certainly circumscribed, and that the ultimate benefits brought by the traders were questionable does not negate the fact that the Indian women played a much more active and important role in the fur trade than has previously been acknowledged.

NOTES

[1] The lack of written Indian history is, of course, a general problem for the ethnohistorian. Indeed, all social scientists must rely heavily on the historical observations of the agents of white contact such as fur traders, explorers, and missionaries. Little seems to have been done to determine if the oral tradition of the Indians is a viable source of information on Indian-white relations in the fur trade period.

[2] Glyndwr Williams, ed., *Andrew Graham's Observations on Hudson's Bay, 1769-91* (London: Hudson's Bay Record Society, vol. 27, 1969); Richard Glover, ed., *David Thompson's Narrative, 1784-1812* (Toronto: Champlain Society, vol. 40, 1962).

[3] A fascinating study which indicates how the application of a different perspective to the same data can produce new insights is *Women of the Forest* by Yolanda and Robert Murphy (New York, 1974). Based on field work conducted twenty years earlier in Amazonian Brazil, the authors found that by looking at the life of the Mundurucú tribe from the woman's point of view, their understanding of the actual as opposed to the official functioning of that society was much enlarged.

[4] Marriages between European traders and Indian women were contracted according to indigenous rites derived from the Indian custom. For a detailed explanation, see Sylvia Van Kirk, " 'The Custom of the Country': An Examination of Fur Trade Marriage Practices," in L.H. Thomas, ed., *Essays in Western History* (Edmonton, 1976), 49-70.

[5] See Murphy, *Women of the Forest*, Ch. 6, for a useful comparison. Mundurucù women actively welcomed the social change brought about by the introduction of the rubber trade into their traditional economy.

[6] An instructive study of the Indians' economic role in the fur trade is provided by Arthur Ray in *Indians in the Fur Trade* (Toronto, 1974). He shows that the Indian played a much more active, although changing role in the dynamics of the fur trade than had previously been acknowledged.

[7] H.B.C. men were prohibited from bringing women to Hudson Bay. It was not until the early nineteenth century that the first white women came to the Northwest.

[8] In 1802 H.B.C. men defended their practice of keeping Indian women in the posts by informing the London Committee that they were "Virtually your Honors Servants," H.B.C. Arch., B.239/b/79, fos. 40d-41. For a discussion of the important economic role played by native women in the fur trade, see Sylvia Van Kirk, "The Role of Women in the Fur Trade Society of the Canadian West, 1700-1850," unpublished Ph.D. thesis, University of London, 1975.

[9] H.B.C. Arch., Albany Journal, 24 Jan. 1771, B.3/a/63, f. 18d; "Connolly vs. Woolrich, Superior Court, 9 July 1867, *Lower Canada Jurist* 11: 234.

[10] Charles Bishop, "The Henley House Massacres," *The Beaver* (Autumn 1976): 40.

[11] Bishop, "The Henley House Massacres," 39. For a more technical look at the socio-economic relationship between the Indians and the traders, see the discussion of "balanced reciprocity" in Marshall Sahlins, *Stone Age Economics* (Chicago, 1972), Ch. 5.

[12] In this instance the Indian captain Woudby attacked Henley House because the master was keeping two of his female relatives but denying him access to the post and its provisions.

[13] Alexander Henry, *Travels and Adventures in Canada and the Indian Territories, 1760-1776*, ed. Jas. Bain. (Boston, 1901), 248.

[14] Alexander Ross, *The Fur Hunters of the Far West*, vol. 1 (London, 1855), 296-97.

[15] W. Kaye Lamb, ed., *Sixteen Years in the Indian Country: The Journal of Daniel Williams Harmon, 1800-1816* (Toronto, 1957), 29; Toronto Public Library, George Nelson Papers, Journal 1810-11, 24 April 1811, 42.

16 Elliot Coues, ed., *New Light on the Early History of the Greater North West: The Manuscript Journals of Alexander Henry and David Thompson, 1799–1814*, (Minneapolis, 1965), 71–73.

17 Coues, *New Light*, 163.

18 Coues, *New Light*, 211.

19 For a detailed account of the story of this woman, see Sylvia Van Kirk, "Thanadelthur," *The Beaver* (Spring 1974): 40–45.

20 Van Kirk, "Thanadelthur," 45.

21 Public Archives of Canada (P.A.C.), Masson Collection, Journal of Charles Chaboillez, 13 Dec. 1797, 24.

22 Nelson Papers, Journal and Reminiscences 1825–26, 66.

23 Ross, *Fur Hunters* 1: 296.

24 Coues, *New Light*, 793; Frederick Merk, ed., *Fur Trade and Empire: George Simpson's Journal, 1824–25* (Cambridge, Mass., 1931), 104.

25 Gabriel Franchère, *Narrative of a Voyage to the Northwest Coast of America, 1811–14*, ed. R.G. Thwaites (Cleveland, Ohio, 1904), 327.

26 Van Kirk, "Thanadelthur," 44.

27 Van Kirk, "Thanadelthur," 45.

28 W. Kaye Lamb, ed., *The Journals and Letters of Sir Alexander Mackenzie* (Cambridge, Eng., 1970) 152.

29 Merk, *Fur Trade and Empire*, 104.

30 Merk, *Fur Trade and Empire*, 104–105.

31 H.B.C. Arch., R. Crooks to G. Simpson, 15 March 1843, D. 5/8, f. 147.

32 Nelson Papers, Journal 1810–11, pp. 41–42.

33 Nelson Papers, Journal 1803–04, 10–28 *passim*.

34 Masson Collection, "An Account of the Chipwean Indians," 23.

35 E.E. Rich, ed., *Simpson's Athabasca Journal and Report, 1820–21* (London, H.B.R.S., vol. 1, 1938), 74.

36 Rich, *Athabasca Journal*, 231.

37 H.B.C. Arch., For Chipewyan Journal 1820–21, B.39/a/16, fos. 6–21d. *passim*.

38 Merk, *Fur Trade and Empire*, 99.

39 Merk, *Fur Trade and Empire*, 11–12, 58.

40 H.B.C. Arch., George Simpson's Journal, 1821–22. D.3/3, f.52.

41 Rich, *Athabasca Journal*, 23–24; see also Merk, *Fur Trade and Empire*, 131.

42 "Account of Chipwean Indians," 23–24.

43 "Account of Chipwean Indians," 23.

44 Ross, *Fur Hunters* 1: 297.

45 Nelson Papers, Journal and Reminiscences 1825–26, 66. Nelson claimed that around 1780 some Indian women had warned the Canadian pedlars of impending attack because in their "tender & affectionate breast (for women are lovely all the world over) still lurked compassion for the mothers of those destined to be sacrificed."

46 Glover, *Thompson's Narrative*, 45. Cf. with the Mundurucú women's desire for European goods, Murphy, *Women of the Forest*, 182.

47 Samuel Hearne, *A Journey to the Northern Ocean*, ed. Richard Glover (Toronto, 1958), 190.

48 H.B.C. Arch., Albany Journal, 23 Feb. 1706, B.3/a/1, f. 28.

49 Ross Cox, *The Columbia River*, ed. Jane and Edgar Stewart (Norman, Okla., 1957), 377.

50 Lamb, *Journals of Mackenzie*, 135.

51 A. S. Morton, *The Journal of Duncan McGillivray . . . at Fort George on the Saskatchewan, 1794–95* (Toronto, 1929), 60.

52 Glover, *Thompson's Narrative*, 106.

53 Hearne, *Journey to Northern Ocean*, 35: "Women," declared the Chipewyan chief Matonabee, "were made for labour; one of them can carry, or haul, as much as two men can do."

54 There has been a trend in recent literature to exalt the Indian woman's status by pointing out that in spite of her labour she had more independence that the pioneer farm wife. See Nancy O. Lurie, "Indian Women: A Legacy of Freedom," *The American Way* 5 (April 1972): 28–35.

55 Morton, *McGillivray's Journal*, 34; L.R.F. Masson, *Les Bourgeois de la Compagnie du Nord-Ouest* 1: 256.

56 Murphy, *Women of the Forest*, 87, 112.

57 Murphy, *Women of the Forest*, 202.

58 Lamb, *Journals of Mackenzie*, 254; Glover, *Thompson's Narrative*, 125.

59 Masson Collection, Journal of John Thomson, 15 Oct. 1798, p. 10.

60 J.B. Tyrrell, *Journals of Samuel Hearne and Philip Turnor, 1774–92* (Toronto, Champlain Society, vol. 21, 1934), 252.

61 Michel Curot, "A Wisconsin Fur Trader's Journal, 1803–04," *Wisconsin Historical Collections* 20: 449, 453.

62 Nelson Papers, Journal 1810–11, 41: Reminiscences, Part 5, 225.

63 Cox, *Columbia River*, 148.

64 Coues, *New Light*, 914; Ross, *Fur Hunters* 2: 236.

65 Tyrrell, *Journals of Hearne and Turnor*, 273.

66 H.B.C. Arch. Book of Servants Commissions, A.16/111 and 112 *passim*.

[67] Lamb, *Sixteen Years*, 28–29.

[68] Masson, *Les Bourgeois* 2: 263.

[69] Hearne, *Journey to Northern Ocean*, 80; Williams, *Graham's Observations*, 158.

[70] Alexander Ross, *Adventures of the First Settlers on the Oregon or Columbia River* (London, 1849) 280–81: Glover, *Thompson's Narrative*, 251.

[71] John West, *The Substance of a Journal during a residence at the Red River Colony, 1820–23* (London, 1827), 54.

[72] The traders were astonished at the little concern shown for pregnancy and childbirth in Indian society, see for example Lamb, *Journals of Mackenzie*, 250, and Williams, *Graham's Observations*, 177.

[73] John Franklin, *Narrative of a Journey to the Shores of the Polar Sea, 1819–22* (London, 1824), 86.

[74] Franklin, *Narrative of a Journey*, 60. The Indian wives of Alexander Ross and Peter Filder, for example, had thirteen and fourteen children respectively.

[75] Jennifer Brown, "A Demographic Transition in the Fur Trade Country," *Western Canadian Journal of Anthropology* 6, 1: 68.

[76] Cox, *Columbia River*, 354.

[77] J.S. Galbraith, *The Little Emperor* (Toronto, 1976), 68.

[78] Nelson Papers, Reminiscences, Part 5, p. 155.

[79] Brown, "A Demographic Transition," 67.

[80] Margaret MacLeod, ed. *The Letters of Letitia Hargrave* (Toronto, Champlain Society, vol. 28, 1947), 94–95; Alexander Ross, *The Red River Settlement* (Minneapolis, 1957), 95, 192.

[81] Brown, "A Demographic Transition," 65.

[82] Merk, *Fur Trade and Empire*, 101.

[83] Williams, *Graham's Observations*, 176, 178.

[84] Ross, *Adventures on the Columbia*, 280; W.J. Healy, *Women of Red River* (Winnipeg, 1923), 163–66.

[85] Lamb, *Sixteen Years*, 138, 186.

[86] Franklin, *Narrative of a Journey*, 101, 106.

[87] West, *Red River Journal*, 16.

[88] Cox, *Columbia River*, 360.

[89] Hearne, *Journey to the Northern Ocean*, 57.

[90] Williams, *Graham's Observations*, 176.

[91] Thomson's Journal, 19 Nov. 1798, p. 20.

[92] Masson, *Les Bourgeois* 2: 384–85. We are not told whether she also escaped being sold when the brigades arrived in the spring as the *bourgeois* intended.

[93] H.B.C. Arch., York Journal, 2 Dec. 1798, B.239/a/103, f. 14d.

[94] H.B.C. Arch. Pelican Lake Journal, 18 Jan. 1819, D.158/a/1, f. 7d.

[95] This account is derived from the Isle à la Crosse Journal, H.B.C. Arch., B.89/a/2, fos. 5–36d *passim*.

[96] Tyrrell, *Journals of Hearne and Turnor*, 446n, 449.

[97] Tyrrell, *Journals*, 449–50.

[98] Masson, *Les Bourgeois* 2: 387–88.

[99] Lamb, *Journals of Mackenzie*, 255; Rich, *Athabasca Journal*, 388.

[100] Masson Collection, Journal of Ferdinand Wentzel, 13 Jan. 1805, p. 41.

[101] Merk, *Fur Trade and Empire*, 127.

[102] Nelson Papers, Journal 1810–11, 41–42.

[103] W.S. Wallace, *Documents relating to the North West Company* (Toronto, Champlain Society, vol. 22, 1934), 211. This ruling was not enforced in outlying districts such as the Columbia. Even after the union in 1821, Governor Simpson continued to favour the formation of marital alliances in remote regions as the best way to secure friendly relations with the Indians. See Rich, *Athabasca Journal*, 392.

[104] For a discussion of the role played by mixed-blood women in fur trade society, see Van Kirk, "Role of Women in Fur Trade Society."

Indian Control of the Maritime Fur Trade and the Northwest Coast*

ROBIN FISHER

Historians have actually characterized the maritime fur trade on the northwest coast as a trade in which gullible Indians were exploited by

*Reprinted from *Approaches to Native History in Canada*, ed. D.A. Muise, National Museum of Man Mercury Series, History Division Paper no. 25. (Ottawa: National Museums of Canada, 1977), 65–86, by permission of the author and the publisher.

avaricious and unprincipled European traders. Stanley Ryerson has asserted that the maritime fur trade "depended on ruthless exploitation of Indian labour . . . backed wherever necessary by force or open threats of force."[1] Others, with less obvious ideological commitments, have made similar comments. H.H. Bancroft wrote of Captain James Cook buying furs from the "guileless savage,"[2] while F.W. Howay, the most meticulous student of the maritime fur trade, described it as a predatory affair, "merely a looting of the coast."[3] Like much historical writing on Indian–European relations, these conclusions are an attempt to pass judgment on European behaviour rather than to analyse Indian responses to the culture contact situation.

The first contact with the Indians of the area that was to become British Columbia was in July 1774 when the Spanish navigator, Juan Peréz, met a group of Haida off the northwest point of Langara Island. But this first fleeting contact between the two cultures was not renewed for four years[4] and a decade was to pass before the first fur trading expedition came to the coast. In 1778 James Cook, leading his third voyage to the Pacific, spent nearly a month refitting at Nootka Sound. While he was there his crews obtained a number of sea-otter skins from the Indians and the story has often been retold of how these pelts fetched fabulous prices in China. However, rumours of the profits to be made by selling sea-otter furs in China were not confirmed until the publication of the official account of Cook's third voyage in 1784, and Captain James King's revelation that some of the best skins had sold for $120.[5] In the following year the first fur trading vessel, appropriately named *Sea Otter*, under James Hanna, arrived at Nootka.

In the next few years, as explorers began to probe the sounds and circle the island, the continental foreshore was opened to the maritime fur trade. For the first three seasons all the trading ships were British, but in 1778 the first American ships arrived on the coast. In 1792 the maritime fur trade really began to burgeon. In that season there were twenty-one vessels engaged in the trade, nearly double the number of the previous year, and more than half of them were British. But in the following year the American outnumbered the English, and this trend was to continue until by 1801 the trade was dominated by American vessels, most of them out of Boston. The peak years of the maritime fur trade were from 1792 to about 1812. By 1825 the Hudson's Bay Company was becoming active on the northwest coast and the maritime fur trade had virtually ceased to exist as a separate entity.

During the very early years of the trade it was true that pelts were relatively easily acquired and some European traders made considerable profits. On 2 July 1787 Captain George Dixon was tacking into a bay that was later to become famous as Cloak Bay when some Haida approached in their canoes. As Peréz had found, curiosity was the initial reaction of the Indians. The Haida could not, at first, be tempted to trade; "their attention seemed entirely taken up with viewing the vessel, which they apparently did with marks of wonder and surprise."[6] Only after the Indians had satisfied their curiosity about the vessel could they be induced to trade. Later in the day Dixon ran his scow, the *Queen Charlotte*, further up the bay and a scene is described "which absolutely beggars all description." The crew was "so overjoyed, that we could scarcely believe the evidence of our senses," because the Indians were falling over each other to trade their cloaks and furs: "they fairly quarrelled with each other about which should sell his cloak first; and some actually threw their furs on board if nobody was at hand to receive them." In half an hour Dixon obtained three hundred furs.[7] A month later, when he left the islands that he had named the Queen Charlottes, his vessel had 1,821 furs in its hold.[8] In 1789, two years after Dixon's visit, the crew of the American ship *Columbia* emulated his example. John Kendrick, the master of the *Columbia*, made one of the best deals ever when, in a few minutes, he traded 200 pelts at the rate of one chisel each at the Indian village of Kiusta on the northern end of Graham Island.[9] In the first years of the trade these furs, so cheaply purchased, brought high prices in China. It was claimed that the 560 sea-otter pelts that Hanna collected on his first trip realized 20,600 dollars,[10] and that the Dixon and Portlock expeditions sold 2,552 furs for 54,875 Spanish dollars.[11] Prices such as these moved Dixon's associate, Nathaniel Portlock, to remark that this branch of commerce was perhaps "the most profitable and lucrative employ that the enterprising merchant can possibly engage in."[12]

Yet, even in these early years, the Indians were not passive objects of exploitation. Rather they vigorously asserted their demands. Northwest coast Indians were, for example, never very interested in baubles and beads as trade items. Cook noted in his journal that European beads could not supplant the Nootkans' own ornaments.[13] So the old stereotype of the avaricious trader stealing Indian furs for a few trinkets never applied to the maritime fur trade.

Furthermore, the comparatively easy trading and high profits of the first frantic years of the trade were not to continue. As vessels visited the coast with increased frequency the maritime fur trade settled into a more consistent pattern, and it was a pattern of trade over which the Indians exercised a great deal of control. It was, after all, Indian demands that had to be satisfied before sea otter pelts changed hands.

For one thing the Indians rapidly lost their curiosity about the Europeans and their vessels. A ship under full sail was an impressive sight, but to the trading Indians it became commonplace. In contrast to the curiosity with which the *Queen Charlotte* was received in 1787, the Indians of Cloak Bay wandered all over Jacinto Caamaño's ship, *Aranzazu*, in 1792 "without showing wonder at anything, nor was there any object of which they did not appear to know the use."[14] As in most contact

81

situations, the initial phase, when the white men were inexplicable and were perhaps even regarded as supernatural beings, soon passed. It quickly became apparent to the Indians that their visitors were quite human, and though some of their behaviour might be curious, many of their demands and desires were familiar.

As the Indians grew accustomed to the presence of the Europeans they also became shrewder in their trading with them. Even after his brief encounter with a group of Haida in 1774, Peréz declared that the Indians were expert and skilful traders.[15] The members of Cook's expedition reached similar conclusions. As one of them put it, "They are very keen traders getting as much as they could for everything they had; always asking for more, give them what you would."[16] The consequence of their astuteness was that the Indians of Nootka "got a greater middly and variety of things" from *Resolution* and *Discovery* than any other people that the vessels had visited.[17] When John Meares left on a trading expedition to the coast in 1787, he was warned that "it appears that the natives are such intelligent traders, that should you be in the least degree lavish, or inattentive in forming bargains, they will so enhance the value of their furs, as not only to exhaust your present stock, but also to injure, if not ruin, any future adventure."[18]

The Indian demand for metals, particularly iron, was recognized by most early traders. Cook's ships left Nootka with hardly any brass left on board, and his crews had also traded a considerable amount of iron.[19] Like the explorers, the early fur traders found that the coast Indians were most partial to iron. Members of the Spanish expedition led by Peréz had noted that the Indians particularly wanted large pieces with a cutting edge, and Dixon's staple medium of exchange was "toes," or iron chisels.[20] Early in 1789 the crew of the *Columbia*, trading in the Straits of Juan De Fuca, were mortified to see seventy pelts escape them "for want of Chizels to purchase them."[21]

Another indication of Indian control of the maritime fur trade was the rapid increase in the price of furs in the early 1790s. Traders in those years who hoped to follow the example of those who were first in the field and purchase large numbers of furs cheaply were often disappointed. John Boit returned to the coast in 1795 and found that the price of pelts at Dadens on Langara Island had increased 100 percent since 1792 when he had been there on the *Columbia*.[22] Archibald Menzies observed a similar rate of increase in Johnstone Strait when he returned there with Vancouver in 1792,[23] while another member of Vancouver's expedition claimed that prices generally had quadrupled since the earliest voyages.[24] At Nootka, where Meares had traded ten skins for one piece of copper in 1786, the asking rate six years later was one pelt for one piece of copper.[25] Price increases such as these led the Spaniard, Alejandro Malaspina, to conclude that the great profits of Cook's and Portlock's voyages should be forgotten as unattainable.[26] There were, of course, other factors that affected prices, including the growing scarcity of furs. However, the depletion of the sea otter was not as significant in the early 1790s as it was to be after the turn of the century. The Indians had learned to demand higher prices while furs were still relatively plentiful.

Not only did the Indians quickly learn to demand a greater quantity of goods for their furs, but they also became very discriminating about the nature of the goods they acquired. It is a commonly held view that the Indian taste in trade goods was "strangely whimsical and constantly variable."[27] By citing examples from widely differing points in time and place it is possible to create the impression that Indian demands were merely fickle,[28] and to obscure those patterns that their requests conformed to. Initially the Indians wanted articles that had meaning and use within pre-contact society. They possessed both iron and copper at the time of contact,[29] but these metals were not plentiful. For this reason iron and other metals were highly valued and in great demand in the early years of the maritime fur trade. The iron chisels brought by the traders were sufficiently similar to indigenous tools to be readily understood, hence the heavy initial demand for them. As the market became saturated with these items their value dropped, other needs began to operate, and new demands were made. The trade meant that the furs were not used as much for clothing as they had been prior to the arrival of the European. The need for an alternative arose, so the Indians turned their attention to trading cloth, clothing and blankets. The demand for blankets particularly remained fairly constant, and they became a staple in the trade. As a garment they served an important function for the Indians. But the blanket was also an article that could be easily counted and compared. It was, therefore, a useful medium of exchange both in the fur trade and for Indian potlatches. During the later years of the trade the Indians acquired some more exotic tastes. A liking for rum, smoking tobacco, and molasses gradually developed, and muskets also became an important trade item.[30]

Naturally, there were exception to this pattern, as the Indian market was as much subject to fads as any other. Yet most of these were also related to Indian usages. The popularity of the iron collars forged aboard the brigantine *Hope* has been seen as the height of Haida fadishness,[31] but this demand was consistent with the Haida taste in personal ornamentation. Copper bracelets, for example, were frequently worn and Joseph Ingraham made his collars from the pattern of one he had seen a Haida woman wearing.[32] The same point can be made about the ermine skins that William Sturgis sold with considerable profit at Kaigani.[33] Ermine pelts were an important wealth item among the coast Indians. But demand for this kind of article was temporary and the market quickly became glutted.

There were other factors that created the impression that the Indians would take a great variety of goods. At times they would receive as presents items, such as beads and trinkets, that they would not accept as trade.[34] Often when Indians accepted these baubles they were as an additional gift to facilitate trade and not as a part of the actual trading transaction. These presents added to the diversity of goods that changed hands but not to the number of articles that would buy furs.

Trading Indians not only paid great attention to the type of goods that they acquired, but they were also discriminating about the quality and trade articles were examined closely and carefully before bargains were struck.[35] Iron that contained flaws or was too brittle was of little value to the Indians because they worked it while it was cold.[36] Indians showed great "judgment and sagacity" when selecting firearms;[37] woolen goods of insufficient quality were turned down,[38] and porcelain imitations of dentalia shells were treated with contempt.[39] Usually the Indians knew what they wanted when they were trading and they were determined to get it.

Nor were Indian traders easily diverted from their purpose. One captain hoped that a few hours of conviviality in the house of the chief would bring him more furs, "but, no sooner was traffic mentioned, than from being the engaging master of the house, he became a Jew chapman and dealer."[40] There are numerous comments in the journals of trading expeditions to the northwest coast about the enterprise of Indian traders whose trading acumen meant that many captains "had the sorrow to see valuable furs escape us, the acquisition of which was the principal object of the expedition, for want of suitable objects to exchange."[41]

As vessels came in search of furs with increasing frequency the Indians became very tough-minded manipulators of competition. They forced prices upwards, particularly at places often visited by traders. As a consequence, in the early years furs were found to cost more at Nootka than at other places.[42] Later, harbours such as Newitty, Masset, and Kaigani became centres of trade and of high prices. At Kaigani John D'Wolf found in 1805 that the Indians were "so extravagant in their demands . . . that it was quite impossible to trade."[43] When more than one vessel was at anchor the Indians would move from one to another comparing prices and bargaining to force them upwards; and, as one trader observed, it was easy to increase one's price but always impossible to reduce it.[44] The American, Richard Cleveland, while on the northern coast in 1799, was told by another captain that he could expect ten other vessels from Boston to be trading in the area that year. He was, therefore, anxious to dispose of his "articles of traffic" before competition reduced their value, because, he said,

> . . . the Indians are sufficiently cunning to derive all possible advantage from competition, and will go from one vessel to another, and back again, with assertions of offers made to them, which have no foundation in truth, and showing themselves to be as well versed in the tricks of the trade as the greatest adepts.[45]

84

Even the captains of solitary vessels who felt that Indian prices were exorbitant were informed that other traders would soon follow who would be willing to pay what was asked.[46] Such exploitation of competition by the trading Indians was one of the reasons why, far from making a killing, many fur trading voyages were ruinous to the promoters.[47] As the Indians raised their prices captains were apt to overestimate the value of their cargo and, therefore, their margin of profit.

Indian traders were not above adding a few tricks to the trade. When Cook was at Nootka he found that the Indians were not quite as "guile-less" as Bancroft would have us believe. The explorer discovered that the Indians were deceiving his men by selling containers of oil that were partly filled with water. In fact "once or twice they had the address to impose upon us whole bladders of water without a drop of Oil in them."[48] Another captain found a Nootkan trying to pass off a land otter pelt as a sea otter in the dusk of evening.[49] Meares went as far as to claim that in their commercial transactions the Indians would play a thousand tricks. He was probably exaggerating when he added that Europeans were "more or less, the dupes of their cunning,"[50] but it is undeniable that Indians behaved with confidence when they were trading.

The Indians were able to assert their demands with such vigor that European captains had to modify their trading methods to accommodate them. In the early years of trade Dixon had largely coasted along the shore line and relied on the Indians to paddle out to him to trade. He was convinced "that this plan was attended with better and speedier success than our laying at anchor could possibly be."[51] Only four years later, in 1791, Ingraham collected 1,400 sea-otter skins off the Queen Charlotte Islands, and he attributed his success to the opposite tactic of remaining at one village until no further furs could be secured. The Indians preferred this approach to paddling out four or five miles to a moving vessel.[52] The tendency was for captains to have to spend more and more time in one place instead of moving about. It also became apparent that one season was insufficient time to gather a profitable cargo. Crews began to winter on the coast and, by 1806–1808, to trade all year round.[53] Initially most trading was conducted over the side of vessels with the Indians remaining in their canoes, but increasingly they had to be allowed to come on deck to display their wares.

Changes such as these resulted from the fact that the Indians preferred to trade at their leisure. They had plenty of time at their disposal and liked to use it to bargain over prices. Even though captains were invariably in a hurry to fill their holds, Indian concepts of time operated increasingly. Many "would wait alongside several hours — nay all day — to obtain their price."[54] D'Wolf complained that the Kaigani Indians would lie about the deck for days on end endeavouring to extort unreasonable prices for their furs, while affecting the utmost indifference as to whether they sold them or not.[55]

85

Other Indian usages had to be observed by captains hoping to acquire furs. The journals show that a considerable amount of Indian ceremonial accompanied trading contacts. One observer noted that it was a constant custom to begin and terminate commercial transactions with strangers with singing.[56] Although traders often found such ceremonies irritating and time consuming, they had to be patiently accepted before the exchange of goods began. However fixed European notions of the nature of trade might be, traders also had to accede to the custom of gift exchange with Indian leaders.[57] This ritual was observed in spite of the feeling on the part of some captains that furs exchanged as presents were sure to prove the dearest that they obtained.[58]

European traders were also adapting to the patterns of northwest coast Indian society by conducting most of their trading with Indian leaders rather than the general population. Some of the trading was done with individual families, but the people did not possess such an abundance of furs as their leaders.[59] Those chiefs who had the good fortune to be in the right place at the right time were able to exercise great control over the trade, and their wealth and, consequently, their prestige were greatly increased. Perhaps the most famous, if not the most powerful, was Maquinna, the leader of the Indians whose summer village was at Yuquot in Nootka Sound. Probably newly succeeded to chieftainship when the maritime fur trade began, Maquinna was able to tap the wealth of his own people as well as that of neighbouring groups. During the Nootka sound controversy he was feted by both the Spanish and the English, and European traders recognized him as the leading trading chief in the area. By manipulating the fur trade Maquinna became incredibly wealthy by Indian standards. In 1803, for example, it is reported that he gave a potlatch at which he dispensed 200 muskets, 200 yards of cloth, 100 chemises, 100 looking glasses and seven barrels of gunpowder.[60]

There were other Indian leaders whose power was comparable to that of Maquinna. It is possible that Wickaninish, the leader at Clayoquot Sound, was even more powerful.[61] On the northern Queen Charlottes, Cunneah, who resided at Kuista, was the first mentioned and best known chief. Also very important was Kow, who initially lived at Dadens, but during the 1790s moved across Dixon Entrance and established himself permanently at his summer village at Kaigani.[62] Like Maquinna, these leaders acquired great wealth. In 1799, when the author of the *Eliza* journal visited the house of Kow, the chief proudly displayed his wealth. The house was lined with boxes of goods acquired in the trade, but Kow drew particular attention to his hoard of ermine skins which were valued as gold or silver. By virtue of his collection of 120 of these pelts Kow claimed that, next to Cunneah, he was the wealthiest chief in the area.[63]

So great was the power and influence of some of these leaders that European leaders found it very much in their interest to cultivate their friendship and they had to be treated with much of the deference that they expected from their own people. Richard Cleveland was one trader who generally could not abide the presence of Indians on the deck of his ship. When he was at Kaigani, however, Kow had to be indulged with hospitality on board. It would, said Cleveland, "have been folly to have prevented him."[64] Indian leaders who were unwittingly insulted had to be mollified, while supposed insults from Indians were tolerated in the hope of driving a bargain.[65]

European traders were further subject to Indian trading patterns to the extent that those Indians who sold them furs were often middlemen who had their own mark-up. The first Europeans to arrive on the coast noticed how Indian traders made efforts to prevent other Indians from trading with them. While he was at Nootka, Cook, who by 1778 was an experienced observer of the behaviour of indigenous peoples, noted that the Indians that he first contacted attempted to monopolize the trade with the *Resolution* and the *Discovery*. Whenever strangers were allowed to trade with the ships, the transactions were managed by the people of Yuquot,[66] and in such a way as to increase their own prices while lowering the value of the English commodities.[67] On other occasions the local Indians used force to prevent outsiders from trading with the ships.[68] It was evident that these explorers had not arrived in a commercial desert, but that definite trading patterns already existed. Much is often made by European historians of the trading abilities of the Yankee captains out of Boston, but it is less frequently remembered that the Indians had a long tradition of trading among themselves.

87

Many, perhaps most, of the furs that changed hands during the period of the maritime fur trade were not captured by the Indians who traded them. When captains were exhorted, as they often were, to wait a day or two so that Indian traders could gather more furs, it did not mean that those Indians intended to hunt for them. Indian leaders on the outer coast collected furs from those who lived deeper inland, either as plunder or by trade. Some chiefs quite frankly told white traders that if they would wait they would go and fight for furs which they would then bring to sell.[69] No doubt this method of gathering pelts was not uncommon. It was well known that Maquinna controlled a trading network with the Indians who lived near the mouth of the Nimpkish River on the east coast of Vancouver Island. When European explorers established the insularity of Vancouver Island, they also found that the Indians who had villages along Johnstone and Queen Charlotte Straits were quite familiar with their merchandise. These Indians, in contrast to the Coast Salish to the south, had passed through the stage of high demand for iron and were also much sharper traders.[70] Maquinna nevertheless made considerable profit in his trade with these people.[71] Wickaninish, the chief of Clayoquot Sound, exercised a similar control over the trade of that area.[72] The Haida likewise traded with mainland groups. By 1799 it was considered that not half of the furs traded at the Queen Charlottes were collected there.[73] Indians on the outer coast exchanged European goods with inland Indians at two and three hundred percent profit margins,[74] and in this way furs were collected at the central locations of the trade with European vessels. Thus, one seaman observed, "we see the untutored Indian influenced by true Mercantile principles."[75] Certainly, if there was exploitation in the maritime fur trade, it was not confined to Europeans.

It has been argued that because trading captains seldom expected to return to a specific locality, they were frequently able to defraud Indian traders and regularly took violent action against them.[76] In fact there was more continuity in the trade than might be expected. There are records of some 300 fur trading vessels coming to the northwest coast during the forty years between 1785 and 1825. Of this total 40 percent spent more than one season trading on the coast, and about 23 percent made three or more visits.[77] Not only did many vessels and captains return to the coast more than once but also a large percentage of the trade was done with a few Indian leaders at a limited number of entrepots. So a European trader who made more than one voyage was very likely to return to the same place to trade, particularly if relations with the Indians had been amicable during the first visit. The possibility of a return trip militated against the indiscriminate use of fraud and violence.

During this early period of culture contact there was a certain amount of inter-racial violence but its extent should not be exaggerated. Such were the demands made by the Indians on European traders that it was considered that "a man ought to be endowed with an uncommon share of patience to trade with any of these people."[78] Of course, many trading captains lacked their fair share of patience and, caught in the squeeze between increasing costs on the northwest coast and declining prices in China, they were apt to become annoyed with Indians who made what they considered to be unreasonable demands. When the early method of coasting became unfruitful, vessels had to stay longer in one place to negotiate trading terms and the extended contact added to the possibility of friction. Given these circumstances, what is surprising is not that there were some outbreaks of violence, but that hostilities were not more frequent.

It is clear that the degree of mutual hostility between the two races during the maritime fur trading period has been exaggerated in European records. Captains came to the coast expecting the Indians to be hostile and often perceived hostility where it did not exist. Some captains tried to deter others from trading with the Indians by telling tales of their "Monstrous savage disposition."[79] Sometimes Indian leaders also tried to prevent traders from calling on neighbouring groups by emphasizing their uncooperative and warlike nature. In an effort to protect their trading interests, both races exaggerated the hostility of the other. The anticipation of violence occasionally brought its expected result, yet the number of violent incidents were still relatively few. A delicate balance of gains and losses had to be weighed up by those who contemplated an attack. The immediate advantage of plunder had to be assessed against the long term disadvantage of losing trade. Both races realized that trading possibilities were not enhanced by attacks on potential customers.

The Indians of the northwest coast, rather than feeling exploited by the European traders, became annoyed when opportunities to trade escaped them. If Europeans rejected offers to trade, particularly when furs were offered by the Indians in the form of reciprocal presents, the refusal could be, and sometimes was, taken as an insult.[80] Indian groups also became dissatisfied when the maritime fur trade passed them by. Sea otter were rare at Nootka Sound by the turn of the century, and vessels were neglecting the area in favour of visiting the more lucrative inner harbours. The Nootka resented this development and their resentment was part of the motivation behind their famous attack on the trading vessel *Boston* in 1803.

89

During the maritime fur trading period the Indians of the northwest coast were not, like some pre-Marxist proletariat, the passive objects of exploitation. Rather, they were part of a mutually beneficial trading relationship over which they exercised a good deal of control. Because the amount of overt coercion used against the Indians was limited they were involved in a process of non-directed culture change.[81] Within the trading relationship they selected those goods that they wanted and rejected those that they did not. The maritime fur trade was not "an unequal trade with a primitive people."[82] The overwhelming impression that emerges from the journals is that the Indians were intelligent and energetic traders, quite capable of driving a hard bargain. John Meares, after several months of trading with the northwest coast Indians, expressed the view of many European traders when he noted that "we learned to our cost, that these people, . . . possessed all the cunning necessary to the gains of mercantile file."[83]

NOTES

[1] Stanley B. Ryerson, *The Founding of Canada: Beginnings to 1815* (Toronto, 1963), 262.

[2] Hubert Howe Bancroft, *History of British Columbia* (San Francisco, 1890) 4.

[3] F.W. Howay, "An Outline Sketch of the Maritime Fur Trade," Canadian Historical Association, *Report* (1932), 14.

[4] In 1775 Juan Francisco de la Bodega y Quadra passed up the coast in the schooner *Sonora*. Although he discovered and named Bucareli Bay on the west coast of Prince of Wales Island he did not make a landfall between latitudes 49° and 54°40′ N.

[5] James Cook and James King, *A Voyage to the Pacific Ocean . . . Performed under the Direction of Captains Cook, Clerke, and Gore, in His Majesty's Ships the Resolution and the Discovery. In the years, 1776, 1777, 1778, 1779, and 1780* (London, 1784), 3: 437.

[6] George Dixon, *A Voyage Round the World; but more Particularly to the North-West Coast of America: Performed in 1785, 1786, 1787, and 1788, in the King George and Queen Charlotte, Captains Portlock and Dixon* (London, 1789), 199-200. Although Dixon's name appears on the title page of this work, it was actually written by William Beresford who was supercargo on the *Queen Charlotte*.

[7] Dixon, *A Voyage*, 201.

[8] Dixon, *A Voyage*, 228.

[9] Robert Haswell, Log [June 1789], in Frederick W. Howay, ed., *Voyages of the "Columbia" to the Northwest Coast, 1787-1790 and 1790-1793* (Boston, 1941), 96.

[10] Dixon, *A Voyage*, 315-16.

[11] George Dixon, *Remarks on the Voyages of John Meares, Esq. in a Letter to the Gentleman* (London, 1790), in F.W. Howay, ed., *The Dixon-Meares Controversy . . .* (Toronto, etc., [1929]), 30.

[12] Nathaniel Portlock, *A Voyage Round the World; but more Particularly to the Northwest Coast of America: Performed in 1785, 1786, 1787 and 1788 . . .* (London, 1789), 382.

[13] Juan Crespi, Diary, 21 July 1774, in Geo. Butler Griffen, ed., *Documents from the Sutro Collection, Publications of the Historical Society of Southern California* (Los Angeles, 1891), vol. 2, part 1, p. 192. Cook, Journal, 30 March and 26 April 1778, in J.C. Beaglehole, ed., *The Journals of Captain James Cook on his Voyages of Discovery; the Voyage of the "Resolution" and "Discovery," 1776-1780* (Cambridge, 1967), part 1, pp. 297, 302, and 314.

[14] Caamaño, Journal, 19 July 1792, Jacinto Caamaño, "The Journal of Jacinto Caamaño," *British Columbia Historical Quarterly* 2 (July 1938): 215. Cook had made similar remarks about most of the Nootka Indians as early as 1778. See Cook, Journal, 12 April 1778, in Beaglehole, ed., *Journals*, 301.

[15] Peréz, Diary, 20 July 1774, in Margaret Olive Johnson, "Spanish Exploration of the Pacific Coast by Juan Peréz in 1774," Master of Letters Thesis, University of California, Berkeley, 1911, p. 59.

[16] Beaglehole, ed., *Journals*, part 1, p. 302, fn. 2.

[17] Cook, Journal, 18 April 1778, in Beaglehole, ed., *Journals*, part 1, pp. 302-303.

[18] The Merchant Proprietors to Meares, 24 December 1787, in John Meares, *Voyages Made in the Years 1788 and 1789 from China to the North West Coast of America . . .* (London, 1790), appendix no. 1, unpaginated.

[19] Cook, Journal, 18 April and 29 March 1778, in Beaglehole, ed., *Journals*, part 1, pp. 302 and 296.

[20] Pena, Diary, 21 July 1774, in Griffen, ed., *Documents*, 123; Dixon, *A Voyage*, 200-201.

[21] Haswell, Log, 19 April 1789, in Howay, ed., *Voyages of the "Columbia,"* 81.

[22] Boit, Journal, 9 June 1795, in John Boit, "Journal of a Voyage Round the Globe, 1795 and 1796 [in the Union]," MS, Special Collections, University of British Columbia Library (hereafter cited as SC).

[23] George Vancouver, *A Voyage of Discovery to the North Pacific Ocean, and Round the World; . . . Performed in the Years 1790, 1791, 1792, 1793, 1794 and 1795 in the Discovery Sloop of War and Armed Tender Chatham under the Command of Captain George Vancouver* (London, 1798), 1: 348.

[24] Edmund S. Meany, ed., *A New Vancouver Journal on the Discovery of Puget Sound by a Member of the Chatham's Crew* (Seattle, 1915), 40.

[25] Cecil Jane, trans., *A Spanish Voyage to Vancouver and the North-West Coast of America being the Narrative of the Voyage made in the Year 1792 by the Schooners "Sutil" and "Mexicana" to Explore the Strait of Fuca* (London, 1930), 90. See also Vancouver, *A Voyage*, 1: 349.

[26] Alessandro Malaspina (*sic*), *Politico-Scientific Voyages Around the World . . . from 1789-1794*, typescript, SC 2: 244.

[27] F.W. Howay, "The Voyage of the Hope: 1790-1792," *Washington Historical Quarterly* 11 (January 1920): 28; Howay, "An Outline Sketch," 8; Paul Chrisler Phillips, *The Fur Trade* (Norman, 1961), 2: 54.

[28] See Hubert Howe Bancroft, *History of the Northwest Coast* (San Francisco, 1884), 1: 370-71.

[29] Pena, Diary, 20 July and 8 August 1774, in Griffen, ed., *Documents*, 121, 132. Cook noted that the Nootka had a word for iron and other metals, Cook, Journal, [April, 1778], in Beaglehole, ed., *Journals*, part 1, p. 328.

[30] This kind of pattern has been delineated for other areas of the Pacific, see Dorothy Shineberg, *They Came for Sandalwood: A Study of the Sandalwood Trade in the South-West Pacific* (Melbourne, 1967), 145, 150.

[31] Howay, "Voyage of the Hope," 10.

[32] Ingraham, Journal, 12 July 1791, Mark D. Kaplanoff, ed., *Joseph Ingraham's Journal of the Brigantine "Hope" on a Voyage to the Northwest Coast of North America* (Barre, Mass., 1971), 105.

[33] F.W. Howay, ed., "William Sturgis: The Northwest Fur Trade," *British Columbia Historical Quarterly* 8 (January 1971): 22.

[34] Vancouver, *A Voyage*, 1: 349.

[35] C.P. Claret Fleurieu, *A Voyage Round the World, Performed during the Years 1790, 1791 and 1792, by Etienne Marchand . . .* (London, 1801), 1: 449.

[36] Meares, *Voyages*, 368; Burney, Journal, 24 April 1778, "Journal of the Proceedings of His Majesty's Sloop Discovery — Chas. Clerke, Commander, 1776-1779," photocopy, Provincial Archives of British Columbia (hereafter cited as PABC).

[37] John D'Wolf, *Voyage to the North Pacific and a Journey through Siberia more than Half a Century Ago* (Cambridge, 1861), 19.

[38] M. Camille De Roquefeuil, *A Voyage Round the World, between the Years 1816-1819* (London, 1823), 87.

[39] G.H. Von Langsdorff, *Voyages and Travels in Various Parts of the World, during the Years 1803, 1804, 1805, 1806 and 1807* (Carlisle, 1817), 413.

[40] Fleurieu, *A Voyage*, 1: 422.

[41] Roquefeuil, *A Voyage*, 92.

[42] John Hoskins, Memorandum [August 1792], in Howay, ed., *Voyages of the "Columbia,"* 486; Puget, Log, 27 April 1793, Peter Puget, "Log of the Proceedings of His Majesty's Armed Tender Chatham Lieutenant Peter Puget Acting Commander 12 Day of January 1793," microfilm, University of British Columbia Library, p. 40.

[43] D'Wolf, *Voyage*, 18; for Newitty, see p. 17.

[44] Samuel Dorr to Ebenezer Dorr, 16 August 1801, in Ebenezer Dorr, Dorr Marine Collection, 1795-1820, MSS, PABC.

[45] Richard J. Cleveland, *Voyages and Commercial Enterprises of the Sons of New England* (New York, 1865), 94.

[46] Haswell, Log, 25 April 1792, in Howay, ed., *Voyages of the "Columbia,"* 323.

[47] Howay, ed., "William Sturgis," 20.

[48] Cook, Journal, 18 April 1778, in Beaglehole, ed., *Journals*, part I, p. 302; and cf. Bancroft, *History of British Columbia*, 4.

[49] Roquefeuil, *A Voyage*, 97.

[50] Meares, *Voyages*, 148.

[51] Dixon, *A Voyage*, 204.

[52] Ingraham, Journal, 2 September 1791, in Kaplanoff, ed., *Ingraham's Journal*, 146.

[53] Howay, "An Outline Sketch," 10.

[54] Ingraham, Journal, 2 September 1791, in Kaplanoff, ed., *Ingraham's Journal*, 147.

[55] D'Wolf, *Voyage*, 18.

[56] Fleurieu, *A Voyage*, 283.

[57] See for example Meares, *Voyages*, 120; and Ingraham, Journal, 5 August 1791, in Kaplanoff, ed., *Ingraham's Journal*, 126.

[58] Ingraham, Journal, 11 August 1791, in Kaplanoff, ed., *Ingraham's Journal*, 130; Hoskins, Narrative, January 1792, in Howay, ed., *Voyages of the "Columbia,"* 265.

[59] Suría, Journal, 13 August 1791, in Henry R. Wagner, ed., *Journal of Thomās de Suría of his Voyage with Malaspina to the Northwest Coast of America in 1791* (Glendale, 1936), 274.

[60] Jewitt, Journal, 24 November 1803, in John Jewitt, *A Journal Kept at Nootka Sound . . .* (Boston, 1807), 13.

[61] Puget, Log, 16 April 1793, in Puget, "Log of the Chatham," 39-40.

[62] Cf. Ingraham, Journal, 10 July 1791, in Kaplanoff, ed., *Ingraham's Journal*, 102, and *Eliza*, Journal, 27 March 1799. [*Eliza*], Journal of the *Eliza*, February-May 1799, photocopy, SC, 13.

[63] *Eliza*, Journal, 27 March 1799, p. 28. Kow owned these ermine skins before Sturgis glutted the Kaigani market with them in 1806, see Howay, ed., "William Sturgis," 22.

[64] Cleveland Log, 27 June 1799, R.J. Cleveland, Log Kept by Capt. Richard Cleveland, 10 January 1799 to 4 May 1804, MS, SC.

[65] Cleveland, Log, 17 June 1799; Meares, *Voyages*, 128; D'Wolf, *Voyage*, 18; and Hoskins, Narrative, July 1791, in Howay, ed., *Voyages of the "Columbia,"* 198.

[66] Cook did not anchor at Yuquot (called Friendly Cove by Europeans) but at Ship Cove (now called Resolute Cove) on the southwest tip of Bligh Island. But it seems likely that the people who had a summer village at Yuquot were the ones controlling the trade with the expedition.

[67] Cook, Journal, 18 April 1778, in Beaglehole, ed., *Journals*, part 1, p. 302.

[68] Cook, Journal, 1 April 1778, in Beaglehole, ed., *Journals*, part 1, p. 299. See also Charles Clerke, Journal, [April 1778], in Beaglehole, ed., *Journals*, part 2, p. 1326.

[69] Ingraham, Journal, 2 August 1791, in Kaplanoff, ed., *Ingraham's Journal*, 121.

[70] Vancouver, *A Voyage*, 1: 331-332, 346, 349; Jane, trans., *A Spanish Voyage*, 74-75; Menzies, Journal, 20 July 1792, in C.F. Newcombe, ed., *Menzies Journal of Vancouver's Voyage April to October 1792*, Archives of British Columbia Memoir no. 5 (Victoria, 1923), 88.

[71] Hoskins, Narrative, January 1792, in Howay, ed., *Voyages of the "Columbia,"* 265.

[72] Meares, *Voyages*, 142; Magee, Log, 31 May 1793, [Bernard Magee], "Log of the Jefferson," photocopy, SC.

[73] *Eliza*, Journal, 5 May 1799.

[74] *Eliza*, Journal, 4 March 1799, p. 13.

[75] Puget, "Log of the Chatham," 52.

[76] See Howay, "An Outline Sketch," 9; and Christon I. Archer, "The Transient Presence: A Re-Appraisal of Spanish Attitudes toward the Northwest Coast in the Eighteenth Century," *BC Studies* 18 (1973): 29.

[77] The figures are based on a series of articles by F.W. Howay, "A List of Trading Vessels in the Maritime Fur Trade, 1785-1794," *Transactions of the Royal Society of Canada* (hereafter cited as TRSC), 3rd series, 24, sec. 2 (1930): 111-34; "A List of Trading Vessels in the Maritime

Fur Trade, 1795–1804," *TRSC*, 3rd series, 25, sec. 2 (1931): 117–49; "A List of Trading Vessels in the Maritime Fur Trade, 1805–1814," *TRSC*, 3rd series, 26, sec. 2 (1932): 43–86; "A List of Trading Vessels in the Maritime Fur Trade, 1815–1819," *TRSC*, 3rd series, 27, sec. 2 (1933): 119–47; "A List of Trading Vessels in the Maritime Fur Trade, 1820–1825," *TRSC*, 3rd series, 28, sec. 2 (1934): 11–49. The percentages of vessels making more than one visit are probably a little conservative as the records for some of the single season voyages are of dubious authenticity. For the same reason the total figure is only approximate.

[78] Ingraham, Journal, 12 August 1791, in Kaplanoff, ed., *Ingraham's Journal*, 132.

[79] Haswell, Log, 16 September 1788, in Howay, ed., *Voyages of the "Columbia,"* 49.

[80] Puget, Log, 27 July 1793, Puget, "Log of the Chatham," 71; Edward Belcher, *Narrative of a Voyage Round the World Performed in Her Majesty's Ship Sulpher, during the Years 1836-1842* . . . (London, 1843) 1: 111.

[81] The distinction between "directed" and "non-directed" culture change is made by Ralph Linton, ed., *Acculturation in Seven American Indian Tribes* (Gloucester, Mass., 1963), 502.

[82] F.W. Howay, W.N. Sage, and H.F. Angus, *British Columbia and the United States, the North Pacific Slope from Fur Trade to Aviation* (Toronto, etc., 1942), 12.

[83] Meares, *Voyages*, 141–42.

The Society of New France

The population of New France grew extremely slowly due to the dominance of the fur trade, which required little manpower. In the autumn of 1608 only twenty-eight people lived at Quebec, and over thirty years later the population of New France still stood at less than three hundred. Only after the establishment of direct royal government in 1663 did the colony finally begin to expand.

Royal government helped the colony's growth in three specific ways. The Crown first established an effective political system. Second, the dispatch of a sizeable military force against the Iroquois led to an effective truce with the Confederacy, securing twenty years of peaceful development for the colony. Third, the French government sponsored the emigration of several thousand settlers, men and women, who helped to build a more diversified economy in New France. From 1663 to 1700 the colony's population grew from 2500 to 15 000. By the late seventeenth century the society of New France had taken on a definite form.

Who were these French Canadians of the New World? What was the nature of this new North American society? In what respects, if any, did New France differ from France? W.J. Eccles outlines the general characteristics of the French Canadian in New France in "Society and the Frontier," a chapter from his book *The Canadian Frontier, 1534-1760.* John F. Bosher reviews an important institution in the colony in "The Family in New France." And in "New France: Les femmes favorisées," Jan Noel examines in depth the role of women in the colony.

There are a number of excellent studies of the society of New France. One of the best, Louise Dechêne's study of Montreal in the late seventeenth century, *Habitants et Marchands de Montréal au XVII siècle* (Paris: Librairie Plon, 1974), is available only in French. In *The Beginnings of New France, 1524-1663* (Toronto: McClelland and Stewart, 1973), Marcel Trudel reviews several aspects of the society of New France in its early years. W.J. Eccles, in *Canada under Louis XIV, 1663-1701* (Toronto: McClelland and Stewart, 1964) and Dale Miquelon, in *New France, 1701-1744: "A Supplement to Europe"* (Toronto: McClelland and Stewart, 1987), study later periods. An overview of the seigneurial system is provided by the geographer Richard Colebrook Harris in *The Seigneurial System in Early Canada* (Madison: University of Wisconsin Press, 1966). Chapter 2 in Alison Prentice et al., *Canadian Women: A History* (Toronto:

Harcourt Brace Jovanovich, 1988), 41–64, entitled "French Women in the New World," examines the position of women in the French colony. Lilianne Plamondon writes of a very commercially minded woman in "A Businesswoman in New France: Marie-Anne Barbel, The Widow Fornel," in *Rethinking Canada: The Promise of Women's History*, ed. Veronica Strong-Boag and Anita Clair Fellman (Toronto: Copp Clark Pitman, 1986), 45–59. Cornelius Jaenen's *The Role of the Church in New France* (Toronto: McGraw-Hill Ryerson, 1976), reviews the work of this important institution in the colony. W.J. Eccles has also written a short book on *Canadian Society during the French Regime* (Montreal: Harvest House, 1968). Three important articles, by G. Frégault, J. Hamelin, and W.J. Eccles, are reprinted in *Society and Conquest*, ed. Dale Miquelon (Toronto: Copp Clark, 1977), 85–131, in the section entitled "The Debate on the Economy and Society of New France." A very readable summary of economic life in New France appears in "Doing Business in New France," a chapter in Michael Bliss' *Northern Enterprise: Five Centuries of Canadian Business* (Toronto: McClelland and Stewart, 1987), 55–77. Peter N. Moogk has written on an aspect of the popular culture of New France in "'Thieving Buggers' and 'Stupid Sluts': Insults and Popular Culture in New France," *William and Mary Quarterly*, 3rd series, 36 (1979): 524–47. An interesting article on a hitherto ignored aspect of the society of New France is Peter Moogk's "*Les Petits Sauvages:* The Children of Eighteenth-Century New France," in *Childhood and Family in Canadian History*, ed. Joy Parr (Toronto: McClelland and Stewart, 1982), 17–43, 192–95. As there were no newspapers in New France, historians have often underestimated the extent of popular discontent under the French regime. Terence Crowley presents the surviving evidence in " 'Thunder Gusts': Popular Disturbances in Early French Canada," Canadian Historical Association, *Historical Papers* (1982): 11–32.

For a first-hand account of New France in 1750, students might consult the English translation of Peter Kalm's *Travels in North America*, 2 vols. (New York: Dover Publications, 1964).

Society and the Frontier*

W.J. ECCLES

Of the more tangible factors that influenced Canadian society there can be no doubt that geography was very important. The St. Lawrence River and certain of its tributaries dominated life in the colony. The land suitable for agricultural settlement stretched in a narrow band along the

*Chapter 5 of *The Canadian Frontier, 1534-1760*, by W.J. Eccles. Copyright 1965 by University of New Mexico Press. Reprinted by permission.

St. Lawrence, wider on the south shore than on the north. Near Quebec the Laurentian Shield, scraped nearly bare long ago by an advancing ice age, meets the river. Below this point only small pockets of land at river mouths were suitable for agriculture. Above Quebec, on the north shore, the Shield draws away from the river to a distance of some forty miles at Montreal. On the south shore the belt of fertile land is quite wide between Quebec and Montreal but becomes a narrow ribbon along the river toward Gaspé. West of Montreal there is also good land but on both the St. Lawrence and Ottawa rivers, rapids make communications difficult. Consequently throughout the French regime land settlement was concentrated in the St. Lawrence Valley from a point a few miles west of Montreal to a little below Quebec, with pockets of settlement on both sides lower down the river.

Prior to 1663 the number of settlers and the amount of land cleared grew very slowly. In 1634 the first seigneurial grant was made to Robert Giffard by Richelieu's Company of New France. During the ensuing thirty years some seventy other seigneuries were granted. The company sent a few settlers to the colony but in the main let this responsibility fall to the seigneurs who, for the most part, lacked the means to engage in a large-scale immigration program. The religious orders did bring out a goodly number of servants, laborers, and settlers; and the crown from time to time sent detachments of soldiers to aid in the colony's defense. By these means the population slowly grew, and stretches of forest near the three areas of settlement, Quebec, Trois-Rivières, and Montreal, were cleared back from the shores of the river. In 1640 the total French population in the colony — settlers, soldiers, clergy, fur trade company employees — numbered only about 240; by 1663, largely as a result of the efforts of the religious orders, this number had increased to some 2500. After the latter date, under the stimulus of the crown, settlement increased very rapidly; by 1669 the population had increased by two thirds, and by the end of the century it was at approximately the 15,000 mark, doubling thereafter each generation to a total of some 70,000 at the Conquest.[1]   The St. Lawrence dictated the pattern of settlement in another way. It was the main means of communication in the colony, in summer by canoe or sailing barque, in winter by sleigh on the ice. The need for roads was thus obviated until the eighteenth century. Every settler desired land on the river, and the land holdings early took on the peculiar pattern that has endured to the present day, that of narrow strips running back from the river. Survey lines separating seigneuries ran at right angles to the river and as the generations succeeded each other the individual holdings became increasingly narrow. According to the law of the land, the *Coutume de Paris,* a seigneur's eldest son inherited the manor house and half the domain land; the rest was divided among the remaining children. The children of the humbler settlers, the *censitaires,* inherited equal parts of the parental land. After a few generations many of the individual holdings became too narrow to be worked efficiently, and in 1745 the intendant forbade anyone to build a house or barn on land narrower than one and a half arpents (approximately 100 yards) by thirty or forty linear arpents in depth. Those who contravened the *ordonnance* were fined 100 *livres* and their buildings were torn down at their expense.

By the eighteenth century the pattern was well established. Along both banks of the St. Lawrence from Quebec to Montreal the farms stretched back from the river, the houses and barns on the river bank spaced a few hundred yards apart. Every few miles there was a seigneurial manor house and a mill, and eventually a steep-roofed stone church. Later in the century concessions were taken up in the second range and another row of narrow strip farms stretched back from the rear of the first, with a roadway between the two. To anyone traveling by river up to Montreal nearly all of New France passed in review.

96

This pattern of land settlement was not without its disadvantages. Until the end of the seventeenth century the Iroquois were an almost constant menace, and with the homes spaced in this fashion mutual aid in times of attack was almost impossible. Individual farms and their occupants could be destroyed all too easily before aid could be mustered. While the Iroquois assaults were at their height stockaded forts had to be built in the exposed seigneuries where the people could take refuge

National Gallery of Canada, Ottawa.

Château-Richer. This painting by Thomas Davies (c. 1737–1812), completed in 1787, portrays typical habitant farm buildings on the shores of the St. Lawrence east of Quebec City.

with their livestock, abandoning their homes to the depredations of the enemy. Attempts by some of the royal officials to have the settlers live in villages, with their concessions radiating out like spokes of a wheel, were not very successful. The Canadians insisted on having river frontage and living apart, lords of their own little domains, with access to the wider world beyond by way of the river.

By the mid-eighteenth century the farm houses in the first range and the churches were nearly all of stone, thick-walled, substantial; steep Norman roofs were modified by a graceful curving wide eave, to afford shade in the hot Canadian summers. Peter Kalm, a Swedish professor of natural history who visited Canada in 1749, going by boat from Montreal to Quebec, remarked:

> The country on both sides was very delightful to-day, and the fine state of its cultivation added to the beauty of the scene. It could really be called a village, beginning at Montreal and ending at Quebec, which is a distance of more than one hundred and eighty miles, for the farmhouses are never above five arpents and sometimes but three apart, a few places excepted. The prospect is exceedingly beautiful when the river flows on for several miles in a straight line, because it then shortens the distance between the houses, and makes them form one continued village . . . . We sometimes saw *windmills* near the farms. They were generally built of stone, with a roof of boards, which together with its wings could be turned to the wind.[2]

The principal crop grown was wheat but the climate of the St. Lawrence Valley was not particularly suitable for this cereal. Heavy rains sometimes caused serious loss from smut; early frosts were a constant menace; and plagues of caterpillars occasionally destroyed everything growing. Yet crop failures appear to have been no more frequent than in France, where they were anticipated, on an average, once in five years.[3] In the early years the yield was high, the natural result of rich virgin soil. By the mid-eighteenth century it had declined considerably, despite the increase in the number of cattle and the consequent increased use of manure.

Peter Kalm was very critical of the inefficient agricultural methods he had observed in the English colonies. He was not less critical of those in New France; they both compared unfavorably with farming methods that he had studied in England, which he stated were the most advanced in Europe. One factor that militated against efficient agricultural production, in New France as in the English colonies, was the chronic shortage of labor. When able-bodied men could obtain land very cheaply, they were not inclined to work for others, except at excessively high wages. The wages paid skilled tradesmen were also high, resulting in a drift from the country to the three towns, which contained 25 percent of the colonial population. A much more important factor, however, was the large number of men, of necessity the young and physically fit, who were continually out of the colony on voyages to the west.

All the evidence indicates that the Canadian *habitants* and the laboring class in the towns enjoyed a higher standing of living and much more personal freedom than did their counterparts in Europe. This undoubtedly accounts, to some degree, for the difference in their attitudes and character that visitors from Europe all remarked on. But what seems to have had an even greater influence was their frequent contact, on terms of equality, with the Indian nations. Nor did they have to voyage far for this contact. Within the confines of the colony, or close by, were several resident Indian bands. Near Quebec, at Lorette, resided a band of Huron, survivors of the 1649 diaspora. A few miles south of Quebec was the Abenaki village of St. François, removed from Acadia to protect the colony's southern approaches from Anglo-American incursions up the Connecticut River. Near Montreal were two Indian settlements: the Mission Iroquois at Sault St. Louis and the Sulpician mission that had first been established on the lower slopes of Mount Royal, then, as the town grew, had been moved first to the north side of the island, later to the western tip, and finally across the Lake of Two Mountains to Oka. The Mission Iroquois at Sault St. Louis (Caugnawaga to the Iroquois) were originally Mohawks who had been converted to Christianity by the Jesuits and had then removed to New France the better to preserve their new faith.[4] Members of other of the Iroquois nations, after conversion, subsequently moved to Caugnawaga to spare themselves the constant taunts of their fellow tribesmen who had remained pagan.

Another reason for this Iroquois defection to Canada was the desire to avoid the Albany rum traders. Not all the Indians were incapable of resisting the temporary delights that intoxication brought; the authorities of both New France and New York were frequently asked by the chiefs of Iroquois and Algonkin nations to keep liquor away from their villages. The governors of New France, for the most part, did their best to comply and managed to curb the abuse to a considerable degree. The same could not be said of the authorities at Albany. There, rum and whiskey of such appalling quality that it was little better than poison was the main item of trade, used to get the Indians drunk before they traded their furs and then defraud them. This practice was so common that the Dutch traders at Albany were little more than Canada's secret weapon, for although many of the western Indians would bypass the French posts to go to Albany where they were given all the liquor they could drink,[5] they were not so besotted that they did not later realize the consequences. This is not to say that there were no Canadian traders willing to use liquor in the same way in their commercial dealings with the Indians. The Jesuit missionaries at Sault St. Louis waged a constant struggle to keep such traders away from their charges, and the Oka mission had removed to this site largely to keep the converts away from the taverns and unscrupulous purveyors.

The members of this latter mission were a mixture of Iroquois and northern Algonkin; the common factor was their conversion to Christianity. During the colonial wars these warriors, particularly those of Sault St. Louis, performed valiant service; indeed, the authorities at Albany were greatly concerned lest most of the Five Nations should remove to Canada. Had this occurred Albany and all the northern settlements would have had to be abandoned. Although in expeditions against the villages of the Five Nations the Mission Iroquois could not be depended on — they frequently gave their kinsmen warning — the devastating raids on the settlements of New England were carried out by war parties composed largely of these domiciled tribesmen, combined with Canadian militia, and led by officers in the colonial regulars, the Troupes de la Marine. Thus the Canadians were closely associated with the Indians, waging war after their fashion, using their techniques and becoming as adept in the harsh, cruel methods as any Iroquois or Abenaki. There was therefore a demonstrable degree of truth in the opinion of the Canadians expressed by one French officer: "They make war only by swift attacks and almost always with success against the English who are not as vigorous nor as adroit in the use of fire arms as they, nor as practiced in forest warfare."[6]

In peacetime, too, the Canadians were in constant association with the Indians. The Indians were frequent visitors to Montreal, and to prevent constant blood baths, the intendant had to set aside certain taverns for the Indian trade, allocated by nation, and strictly regulated. It is, therefore, hardly surprising that the Canadians early adopted much of the Indian way of life and became imbued with some of their character traits. Native foods such as corn, squash, and pumpkins found ready acceptance. Indian means of travel — the snowshoe, toboggan, and canoe — were quickly mastered. Many of the Canadians, who were inveterate pipe smokers, preferred to mix their locally grown tobacco with the inner bark of the cherry or dogwood tree, a custom borrowed from the Indians. In their mode of dress the *habitants* copied the Indians, with an effect rather startling to European eyes. The women, except when dressed up fine for Sunday mass, wore a short jacket or blouse and a short skirt which, Peter Kalm several times observed, "does not reach to the middle of their legs."

It was during their frequent trips to the west that the Canadians were most exposed to the Indian way of life. Immediately following the establishment of royal government in 1663 the population of the colony expanded rapidly, from approximately 2500 to an estimated 15,000 by the end of the century. Of the latter number as many as five hundred of the active males were always off in the west on trading expeditions. It was during these years that senior officials, newly arrived from France, began to comment on the striking difference between the Canadians and

99

their peers in France. Inevitably, these officials were first struck by what seemed to them the deleterious social and economic effects of the metamorphosis.

The Marquis de Denonville, governor general from 1685 to 1689, was appalled by certain attitudes and habits of the Canadians. Instead of laboring on the land, they preferred to spend their lives in the bush, trading with the Indians, where their parents, the *curés*, and the officials could not govern them, and where they lived like savages. Even when they returned to the colony these youths showed a shocking proclivity for going about half naked in the hot weather, as did the Indians. "I cannot emphasize enough, my lord, the attraction that this Indian way of life has for all these youths," Denonville wrote to the minister. But he then went on to say, "The Canadians are all big, well built, and firmly planted on their legs, accustomed when necessary to live on little, robust and vigorous, very self willed and inclined to dissoluteness; but they are witty and vivacious."[7] The intendant Jean Bochart de Champigny in 1691 wrote in much the same vein, stating, "It is most unfortunate that Canadian youths, who are vigorous and tough, have no inclination for anything but these voyages where they live in the forest like Indians for two or three years at a time, without benefit of any of the sacraments."[8] Peter Kalm in 1749 was also much impressed by the martial qualities of the Canadians, acquired through their frequent sojourns in the west. He noted that they were exceptional marksmen: "I have seldom seen any people shoot with such dexterity as these . . . . There was scarcely one of them who was not a clever marksman and who did not own a rifle." He then went on:

> It is inconceivable what hardships the people of Canada must undergo on their hunting journeys. Sometimes they must carry their goods a great way by land. Frequently they are abused by the Indians, and sometimes they are killed by them. They often suffer hunger, thirst, heat, and cold, and are bitten by gnats, and exposed to the bites of snakes and other dangerous animals and insects. These (hunting expeditions) [*sic*] destroy a great part of the youth in Canada, and prevent the people from growing old. By this means, however, they become such brave soldiers, and so inured to fatigue that none of them fears danger or hardships. Many of them settle among the Indians far from Canada, marry Indian women, and never come back again.[9]

Some of the Jesuit missionaries in the west took a much more jaundiced view of the effects of the close relations between the Canadians and the Indians. Fathers St. Cosme and Carheil at Michilimackinac made that post appear, from their description, a veritable Sodom or Gomorrah, where the only occupations of the Canadians, apart from trading furs, were drinking, gambling, and lechery. Things had come to such a pass that the *coureurs de bois* took Indian women with them rather than men

100

on their trading expeditions. The men claimed that these women worked for lower wages than men demanded, and were willing to perform such chores as cutting firewood and cooking. The missionaries refused to be persuaded that other fringe benefits were not involved.[10] The governor general Vaudreuil, although he did not support the Jesuit proposal to keep the Canadians and Indians as far apart as possible, was strongly opposed to mixed marriages. He claimed that the children of mixed blood incorporated the worst character traits of both races and were a constant source of trouble. He therefore issued orders forbidding such marriages at Detroit, the main French post in the west at that time (1709).[11]

These complaints on the part of the missionaries have to be taken with a pinch of salt. To them chastity, or failing this monogamy with the benefit of the marriage sacrament, was the ideal. They expected these *voyageurs* who, if married, had left their wives in the colony, to live like monks while in the west. The Indians had different moral values and chastity was not among them. Father Charlevoix, who was not a missionary, took a more tolerant view of Canadian society in the 1740s. He commented:

> Our Creoles are accused of great avidity in amassing, and indeed they do things with this in view, which could hardly be believed if they were not seen. The journeys they undertake; the fatigues they undergo; the dangers to which they expose themselves, and the efforts they make surpass all imagination. There are, however, few less interested, who dissipate with greater facility what has cost them so much pains to acquire, or who testify less regret at having lost it. Thus there is some room to imagine that they commonly undertake such painful and dangerous journeys out of a taste they have contracted for them. They love to breathe a free air, they are early accustomed to a wandering life; it has charms for them, which make them forget past dangers and fatigues, and they place their glory in encountering them often . . . . I know not whether I ought to reckon amongst the defects of our Canadians the good opinion they entertain of themselves. It is at least certain that it inspires them with confidence, which leads them to undertake and execute what would appear impossible to many others . . . . It is alleged they make bad servants, which is owing to their great haughtiness of spirit, and to their loving liberty too much to subject themselves willingly to servitude.[12]

These observations on the cupidity of the Canadians, coupled with their spendthrift attitude, are significant for these same traits were quite pronounced among the Indians. Like the Indian, the Canadian did not see any merit in storing up worldly goods; both looked down on those who did, and up to those who spent their money ostentiously on good living. The Canadians, too, became proud, independent, and improvident, glorying in their physical strength, their hardihood, and their contempt for

101

danger, caring little for the morrow. One French officer commented, in 1757:

"They are not thrifty and take no care for the future, being too fond of their freedom and their independence. They want to be well thought of and they know how to make the most of themselves. They endure hunger and thirst patiently, many of them having been trained from infancy to imitate the Indians, whom, with reason, they hold in high regard. They strive to gain their esteem and to please them. Many of them speak their language, having passed part of their life amongst them at the trading posts."[13]

It would seem an obvious conclusion that the Canadians had acquired this attitude from the Indians, and were able to do so because the necessities of life were relatively easily come by in Canada. In other words, this character trait was a product of relative affluence and the frontier environment. It was to no small degree the fact that the Canadians did come to share this attitude with the Indians that their individual relations with them were usually better than were those of the Anglo-Americans. Ruette D'Auteuil, the attorney general at Quebec, spoke the truth for his day when he claimed that, the price of trade goods being equal, the Indians preferred to have dealings with the French rather than with the English.[14] This view was later corroborated by a British commentator who stated that, "the French have found some secret of conciliating the affections of the savages, which our traders seem stranger to, or at least take no care to put it in practice."[15]   Not only did the Canadians travel to the far west, they also voyaged northeastward, serving as crews on fishing boats in the Gulf and in the seal- and whale-hunting expeditions along the coast of Labrador. There, too, they came in frequent contact with Indians, and also with the Eskimo. In wartime they served on privateers, preying on shipping along the New England coast. French privateer captains frequently called at Quebec to take on crews, Canadians being very highly regarded for their toughness and bellicosity.

Canadians in all sections of the colony were accustomed to make trips to distant parts of the continent and to live among peoples of an entirely different culture. The whole continent from Labrador and Hudson Bay to the Rocky Mountains and the Gulf of Mexico was their world. Unlike their counterparts in Europe who rarely moved beyond the confines of their native parish, there was nothing parochial about them; they were men of broad horizons and a continental outlook able to accommodate themselves to almost any conditions anywhere. Were life to become too restrictive in the settlements along the St. Lawrence or were a wife to nag too constantly, some of them at least could hire out as *voyageurs* for the west or as crew on a voyage to Labrador, France, or the West Indies. Even those who never made such a trip could feel that the opportunity was there, and this must have given them a sense of freedom.

102

They could not help but hear the tales of those who had voyaged far afield, of the strange peoples with stranger customs in these distant lands. They, too, shared the experience, vicariously.

Royal officials in the eighteenth century, upon first arriving in the colony, were quick to remark that the Canadians had become a distinct people with values and manners markedly at variance with those of the same class in the mother country. Usually they were quite taken aback by the attitudes and way of life of the Canadians. Only after they had been in the colony for a few years did they come to appreciate the positive side of what had at first seemed a society and people sadly in need of discipline and reform. It was the free and easy, seemingly dissolute, ways of the Canadians, their independent attitude, their insistence on being led not driven, that irked the officials, both civil and military. Other observers were struck by their profligacy, their feast or famine attitude, their recklessness. A Sulpician priest upon arrival in the colony in 1737 remarked that the bulk of the people — military officers, merchants, artisans, and *habitants* alike — were "as poor as artists and as vain as peacocks" and spent every sou they had on ostentatious living. He was shaken to see country girls who tended cows during the week, on Sundays bedecked in lace and hoop skirts, wearing their hair in the very elaborate, high-piled style known then as *à la Fontange*.[16]

103

Despite these shortcomings, all observers agreed that the Canadians were tough and hardy, gloried in feats of endurance that made Europeans blanch, could travel from one end of the continent to another while living off the land, and had no equal in forest warfare. It was also noted that these same men, when in their homes, were uncommonly courteous, with a natural air of gentility more usual among the nobility than the lower classes.[17] In this respect they compared very favorably with their counterparts, the peasants of France and the settlers in the English colonies. Peter Kalm was particularly struck by this and in his journal he noted that:

> The inhabitant of Canada, even the ordinary man, surpasses in politeness by far those people who live in these English provinces . . .
>
> On entering one of the peasant's houses, no matter where, and on beginning to talk with the men or women, one is quite amazed at the good breeding and courteous answers which are received, no matter what the question is . . . . Frenchmen who were born in Paris said themselves that one never finds in France among country people the courtesy and good breeding which one observes everywhere in this land. I heard many native Frenchmen assert this.[18]

It would, of course, be very easy to ascribe these peculiarities to the frontier environment of New France. There can be no doubt that the frontier had a good deal to do with this, but the changes that took place in Canadian society were very complex. It is therefore necessary to examine conditions in the colony closely to discover the various elements that differed from those of France and then decide which ones were occasioned by the frontier.

Perhaps the basic factor was the abundance of free, fertile land, and the peculiar terms of land tenure under the seigneurial regime. This meant that the Canadian *habitants* were assured of as much land as they could cultivate, and they paid for it only very modest seigneurial dues, if they paid any at all, amounting to less than 10 percent of their annual income from the land.[19] Apart from this obligation, and the tithe for the church, fixed by royal decree at one twenty-sixth of the wheat grown, the *habitants* paid no other taxes. Labor service for the seigneurs, in the form of *corvées*, was very rarely imposed and was, in fact, a violation of the *Coutume de Paris*. In the few seigneuries where it was imposed it consisted of one day's labor in March or an exemption payment of two *livres*. Parish and royal *corvées* for work on the seigneurial common land, roads, bridges, or fortifications were a form of taxation but they usually amounted to not more than three or four days of labor a year, and the seigneur was supposed to do his share, under the supervision of the militia captain.

Unlike the peasant in France who spent his life sweating, scrimping, cheating, and saving to put aside enough money to buy a small piece of land or to purchase exemption from manorial obligations, and who had to keep his little hoard well hidden, wearing rags, living in a hovel, giving every appearance of near starvation to prevent the tax collectors from seizing his savings, the Canadian could spend what he had earned without a care. He could buy land for his sons so as to have them near him and spare them the necessity of clearing virgin forest on a new seigneury, or he could spend his earnings on consumer goods and entertainment. Whereas the economics of the situation would tend to make the French peasant mean and grasping, the Canadian could afford to be openhanded, with little care for the morrow.

In 1699 the intendant Jean Bochart de Champigny commented that for the most part the *habitants* lived well, enjoying the right to hunt and fish, privileges that were stringently denied their European counterparts. In that age wood and leather were vital commodities; the Canadians had ample supplies of both. Canadians who moved to France complained bitterly of the shortage and high cost of firewood, and declared that they suffered far more from the damp winter cold there than they ever had in Canada. In the eighteenth century the intendant Gilles Hocquart remarked that no one starved in Canada. Of few lands in Europe could this have been said. The normal consumption of meat was half a pound per person a day, and of white wheat bread, two French pounds a day. Moreover, the climate allowed the Canadians to keep plentiful supplies of meat, fish, and game frozen hard for use throughout the winter; but a mid-winter thaw that lasted too long could be calamitous. At the town markets fish were sold frozen and cut with a saw.

Eels, taken at Quebec by the thousand, were a staple food; smoked or salted, they were described by Frontenac as the *"habitants'* manna." They were also a major export item to France, being considered far better than the European variety. Ice houses were common, making possible iced drinks and desserts all summer, not just for the wealthy as in France, but for the majority of the population. The colored ices served by the French in hot weather were a source of wonderment to visiting Indians when entertained by the governor, and their effect on the decayed teeth of certain elderly chiefs was electric.

The vitamin content of the Canadian diet, being much richer in protein, was considerably higher than that of the peasants and urban working class in France, who had to exist on coarse bread and vegetable stews with meat only on very rare occasions.[20] In Europe the bulk of the population went to bed hungry most nights. Such was rarely the case in Canada. Mme. Marie-Isabelle Bégon, widow of the governor of Trois-Rivières, who in 1749 moved from Montreal to the family estate near Rochefort, querulously asked, "Where are those good partridges we left for the servants? I would gladly eat them now."[21] It is not surprising that the fine physical stature of the Canadians occasioned frequent comment from persons recently come from France. In fact, the Canadians were better fed then than a sizable percentage of North Americans are today.

105

If the Canadians had been willing to work hard, they could all have been very prosperous. Some of the royal officials, charged with improving the colonial economy, declared that the men showed a marked distaste for hard work and that the unbridled vanity of their womenfolk kept them poor. In 1699 Champigny noted: "The men are all strong and vigorous but have no liking for work of any duration; the women love display and are excessively lazy."[22] Denonville, thirteen years earlier, had also remarked that the indolence of the men and the desire of the women to live like gentle ladies kept the people poor and the colony's economy backward. Such comments have to be considered in context.

The Canadian *habitant* could provide for his basic needs without too much effort, and he preferred to devote his extra time, not to produce an agricultural surplus to please the intendant or to add to his own store of worldly goods, but to the relaxed enjoyment of his leisure hours. He would grow enough flax or hemp to supply his own needs, but frequently declined to raise a surplus for export. Rather than raise more cattle, he raised horses; by the early eighteenth century all but the poorer families had a carriage and sleigh for social occasions, and every youth had his own horse, used not for the plow but for racing, or to pay calls on the neighborhood girls. During the War of the Spanish Succession the governor and intendant became concerned over this, claiming that in winter the men no longer used snowshoes because they always traveled by horse and sleigh. It was difficult, they stated, to find enough men who could use snowshoes when they were needed for war parties against New England. The question might well be asked; how many peasants in Europe owned horses and carriages, let alone used them for mere social purposes. The average horse cost forty *livres* (roughly $80.00 in today's money) and a good one a hundred *livres* or more,[23] thus the Canadian *habitants* were relatively affluent, and this could not help but have influenced their social attitudes.

Given these conditions it is hardly surprising that the Canadians were by no means as submissive or even respectful, on occasion, toward their social superiors as was thought fitting. As early as 1675 the members of the Sovereign Council were incensed by derogatory graffiti on walls in Quebec, and several years later the intendant had to threaten stern action against those who composed, distributed, or sang songs that he regarded as libelous and defamatory of certain prominent persons in the colony. This last, however, might be regarded as merely the continuance of an old French tradition that had flourished in the days of the *Mazarinades*. Thus, rather than the frontier environment, economic affluence and the French temperament were the more significant factors here.

Much is made of the prevalence of lawlessness on the Anglo-American frontier. To a limited degree this was also true of New France, and it is significant that it was at Montreal, the fur trade and military base, the main point of contact between European and Indian cultures, more than at Quebec, that respect for law and order was sometimes lacking. In 1711 the governor and intendant had to establish a police force in Montreal, consisting of one lieutenant and three archers, to make the citizens keep the peace and to control drunken Indians. An educated soldier in the colonial troops, newly arrived in Canada, remarked that the citizens of Montreal called those of Quebec "sheep," and that the character of the latter was gentler and less proud. The Quebecers reciprocated by calling the men of Montreal "wolves," a label that the soldier thought apt since the Montrealers spent much of their time in the forest among the Indians. In 1754 an officer recommended that Quebec men be employed to transport supplies to the Ohio forts because they were much "gentler" and almost as vigorous as those from the Montreal area.

Despite the frequent tavern brawls and duels, the incidence of crimes of violence was not great. But what is much more significant is that, given the nature of the populace, accustomed to the relatively unrestrained, wild, free life that the fur trade afforded, very rarely was there any overt resistance to authority. On the few occasions when the people protested openly and vigorously something done, or not done, the authorities were able to subdue them quickly without recourse to punitive measures. Most of these manifestations — some five in all — were occasioned by high prices charged for certain commodities, leading the people to believe that the merchants were profiteering and that the authorities were delinquent in not taking steps to stop them. The heaviest penalty inflicted on the leaders of these "seditious gatherings" appears to have been less than two months in jail.[24] The conclusion to be drawn from all this is that the Canadian people had little to complain about, but when they did complain too vigorously, order was maintained without the overt use of force.

The attitude of the Canadians toward the religious authorities makes it plain that their opinions had to be taken into account. When it was decided, immediately after the inauguration of royal government in 1663, to impose tithes on the people for the support of a secular clergy, the bishop stipulated that it be at the rate of one thirteenth of the produce of the land, payable in wheat. The people protested vigorously, claiming this to be more than they could afford. The bishop reduced his demand to one twentieth, but the *habitants* and seigneurs would agree to pay only one twenty-sixth of their wheat, not of all their produce, with a five year exemption for newly settled concessions. With this the clergy had to be satisfied. That it was not enough is made plain by the fact that the crown had to provide the clergy with an annual subsidy to make up the difference between what the tithe produced and what the *curés* needed. By the 1730s however, as more land came into production, many of the parish priests were relatively well off.

107

Further evidence that the Canadians were anything but subservient to clerical authority is provided by the frequent *ordonnances* of the intendant ordering the *habitants* of this or that parish to behave with more respect toward the cloth, to cease their practice of walking out of church as soon as the *curé* began his sermon; of standing in the lobby arguing, even brawling, during the service; of slipping out to a nearby tavern; of bringing their dogs into church and expostulating with the beadle who tried to chase them out. Frequently the bishop thundered from the pulpit against the women who attended mass wearing elaborate coiffures and low-cut gowns. But all to no avail; décolletage remained that of the Paris salons. When Bishop St. Vallier somehow learned that the female members of his flock wore nothing but petticoats under their gowns he was horrified. In a curiously phrased pastoral letter he demanded that they immediately cease to imperil their immortal souls in this manner.[25] What the response was is not known. And a practice that might be advanced in support of the thesis that the frontier bred initiative was the Canadian custom of *mariage à la gaumine,* a form of "do it yourself" marriage ceremony which both the clergy and the civil authorities frowned on severely.[26] At the upper end of the social scale, the most significant feature of this Canadian society was the aristocratic and military ethos that dominated it. This was not unique to Canada; it was part of the French old régime heritage. In the seventeenth century the aim of the rising, powerful bourgeois class was to gain entry into the ranks of the nobility, or at least to emulate the way of life of the aristocracy. Molière made this plain in *Le Bourgeois Gentilhomme*. Despite the fact that the Canadian economy was basically commercial and dependent largely on the fur trade, bourgeois commercial values did not dominate society; indeed, they were scorned. The ambitious Canadian merchant wished to be something more than prosperous. That was merely one rung on the ladder. The ultimate goal was entry into the ranks of the *noblesse* and receipt of the coveted Order of St. Louis for distinguished service. More than wealth, men wished to bequeath to their sons a higher social status and a name distinguished for military valor, some great achievement, or the holding of high office. The proverb, *"Bon renom vaut mieux que ceinture dorée,"* summed up the Canadian philosophy at all levels of society.[27] Wealth was, of course, desired, and ethics frequently went by the board in its pursuit. Men who might well have been ennobled for valiant service were denied if they lacked the means to live in a fitting manner. Wealth was sought, not for itself, but to enable men to live in the style of the class they sought to enter. Father Charlevoix, the Jesuit historian, writing in the 1740s commented on one aspect of this proclivity: "There is a great fondness for keeping up one's position, and nearly no one amuses himself by thrift. Good cheer is supplied, if its provision leaves means enough to be well clothed; if not, one cuts down on the table in order to be well dressed." He then went on to compare the Canadians with the English colonists to the south: "The English colonist amasses means and makes no superfluous expense; the French enjoys what he has and often parades what he has not. The former works for his heirs; the latter leaves his in the need in which he is himself to get along as best he can."[28] In Canada it was in some ways much easier than in France for ambitious men to adopt the values and attitudes of the nobility and even to become ennobled. Despite the fact that society was very much status ordered, it was relatively easy for a talented, ambitious man or woman to move up the social scale. Four factors help account for this: the availability of free land, the economic opportunities presented by the fur trade, the Royal edict of 1685 which permitted members of the nobility resident in Canada to engage directly in commerce and industry, something that, with a few notable exceptions such as the manufacture of glass and paper, was not permitted in France, and the presence of a large corps of regular troops in the colony in which Canadians could obtain commissions as officers.

It is rather ironic that when the king issued the edict of 1685 allowing nobles in Canada to engage in trade, he intended merely to stimulate the colonial economy.[29] It quickly came, however, to function in a way not anticipated by Louis XIV, for if those who were of noble status could engage in trade, there was nothing to prevent merchants and entrepreneurs who were not noble from aspiring to become so, provided they fulfilled the other requirements. Thus a Canadian of humble origin could make his fortune in the fur trade, acquire a seigneury, have his sons, if not himself, commissioned in the Troupes de la Marine, and hope that one day he, or his sons, would be ennobled for valiant service. Enough Canadians accomplished this feat to encourage a much larger number to govern their lives accordingly. It was the old story, few are chosen but many hear the call.

To be a seigneur, the first rung up the social ladder, was a distinct mark of social superiority, made manifest in a variety of ways; hence there was never any lack of applicants,[30] but it necessitated accepting rather onerous responsibilities and in the seventeenth century most seigneurs had a hard time making ends meet. Yet so eager were the Canadians to attach the coveted particle *de* to their names that by 1760 there were nearly 250 seigneuries in the colony. Even more significant, it is estimated that there were some 200 *arrière fiefs*, or sub-seigneuries, that is, small seigneuries granted by a seigneur within his own seigneury to a friend or relative whom he wished to see get on in the world. Another significant point is that many seigneurs, the majority of whom lived in the towns and not on their lands, did not bother to collect the stipulated dues, the *cens et rentes*, from their *censitaires*. Clearly, many seigneurs were not interested in the economic aspect of land holding. The only other motive would appear to be the social prestige attached to the title. In other words, Joseph Blondeau was undoubtedly a good name, but Joseph Blondeau de Grandarpents, or even de Petitarpents, was much better.

There were some who sought to gain entry into the *noblesse* through the back door, by simply assuming a title and claiming its privileges. In 1684 a royal edict was enacted levying a fine of 500 *livres* on any Canadian who falsely claimed noble status. A few years later the intendant Champigny stated that there were many such in the colony, but in time of war he thought it unwise to initiate an enquiry lest it cool their ardor for military campaigns. He also declared that several officers had requested to be ennobled, and although some of them merited it, he could not support their requests because they lacked the means to live as members of the *noblesse* should.[31] Although gaining entry into the ranks of the nobility was by no means easy, it was remarked in the mid-eighteenth century that there was a greater number of nobles in New France than in all the other French colonies combined. It was not the actual number of nobles that was important; rather it was the scale of values that they imparted to the whole of society, the tone that was set, and the influence it had on the way of life of the Canadian people.

Inextricably mingled with, and greatly strengthening, this aristocratic ethos was the military tradition of New France. In Europe wars were fought by professional armies, and civilians were not directly involved unless they happened to get in the way while a battle was being fought. This was more true of France and Britain than of other countries, since they both had sense enough to wage their wars on other nations' territory.

109

In Canada when war came, all the settled areas were a battlefield and everyone was obliged to be a combatant. The administration of the colony was organized along military lines. The entire male population was formed into militia companies, given military training, and employed in campaigns. In 1665 the Carignan Salières regiment arrived in the colony to quell the Iroquois; it comprised over a thousand officers and men, and many of them stayed on as settlers. This greatly enhanced the influence of the military, for at that time the total population was less than 3000. Twenty years later the Troupes de la Marine were permanently stationed in the colony, some 1300 men and 400 officers by the end of the century among a total population of 15,000.

In the campaigns against the Iroquois and the English colonies it was quickly discovered that Canadians made better officers in forest warfare than did regulars from France. Consequently this career was opened to the seigneurs and their sons. They seized on it eagerly. Youths in their teens were enrolled as cadets and served on campaigns with their fathers or elder brothers to gain experience, then were sent out in command of scouting and small raiding parties to capture prisoners for intelligence purposes. The minister, however, thought they were being enrolled at far too early an age, while still mere children, and suspected the practice was merely a means for their families to draw military pay and allowances. Mme. de Vaudreuil, wife of the governor general, declared, "It would be advantageous for the well-being of the colony to accept youths of good families as cadets in the troops at fifteen or sixteen; that would form their characters early, render them capable of serving well and becoming good officers." The minister and Louis XIV were not convinced; they ordered that cadets had to be seventeen before they could be enrolled.[32] The dominant values of Canadian society were clearly those of the soldier and the noble, the military virtues those held in highest regard.

The social circles of Montreal and Quebec, comprising the senior officials, the army officers, and seigneurs, were undoubtedly very urbane, reflecting the polish and social graces of the French *noblesse*. Certainly Peter Kalm found this society much more civilized than that which he encountered in the English colonies where few people thought of anything but making money and not spending it.[33] Some of the senior officials who came from France in the eighteenth century, men like the intendant Claude Thomas Dupuy and the Comte de la Galissonière, took a keen interest in natural science, as had earlier the doctor and surgeon Michel Sarrazan who was a corresponding member of the Académie Royale des Sciences, but few Canadians showed much interest in intellectual pursuits.

The parish schools provided a basic education for those who wished it, and the Jesuit college at Quebec offered facilities as good as those in the larger French provincial cities. The letters and dispatches of

Canadian-born officers and merchant traders in the mid-eighteenth century demonstrate that, with the rare exception of an officer such as Claude-Pierre Pécaudy de Contrecoeur who although a competent commandant had obviously had little schooling, they were all well-educated men. They expressed themselves succinctly and quite often felicitously: their syntax was good, the subjunctive employed where required; the literary style as well as the contents of their letters make them a pleasure to read. In fact, these men appear to have been as well educated as their counterparts in the French and British armies.

Yet the colony did not develop a literary tradition; the published journals depicting life in the colony were written by men from France and were intended for a metropolitan audience. But then, Canadians would see little merit in describing what was familiar to all their compatriots. Several Canadians had large private libraries, but there was no public library. Nor was there a printing press in the colony, hence no newspaper, not because of any sinister repression of thought by the clergy, but because there was no great need therefore no demand for one. In these realms of activity Canada lagged far behind the English colonies. In short, New France was the Sparta, not the Athens of North America.

111

NOTES

[1] *Chronological List of Canadian Censuses*, Bureau of Statistics, Demography Branch, Ottawa.

[2] Adolph B. Benson, ed., *Peter Kalm's Travels in North America*, 2 vols. (New York, 1966), 2: 416–17.

[3] Le Roi à Vaudreuil et Raudot, Versailles, 6 juillet 1709, *Rapport de l'Archiviste de la Province de Québec* (1942–43) (hereafter cited as *RAPQ*), 408.

[4] E.B. O'Callaghan and J.R. Brodhead, *Documents Relating to the Colonial History of New York*, 15 vols. (Albany, 1856–1883), 4: 693.

[5] Benson, ed., *Peter Kalm's Travels in North America*, 2: 600.

[6] Papiers La Pause. *RAPQ* (1931–32): 66–67.

[7] Denonville au Ministre, Que., 13 nov. 1685, Archives Nationales, Colonies, Series C11A, 7: 89–95.

[8] Memoire instructif sur le Canada, 10 mai 1691, *ibid.*, 11: 262–68.

[9] Benson, ed., *Peter Kalm's Travels in North America*, 2: 522, 563.

[10] Etienne de Carheil, S.J. à Champigny, Michilimackinac, 30 d'auest 1702, Public Archives of Canada, Series M, vol. 204, part 1, pp. 177–79; Fr. J.-F. St. Cosme, Michilimackinac, 13 sept. 1689, *RAPQ* (1965): 37.

[11] In a dispatch to the minister, Vaudreuil stated, "tous les françois qui ont épousé des sauvagesses sont devenus libertins feneans, et d'une independance insuportable, et que les enfans qu'ils ont esté d'une feneantise aussy grande que les sauvages mesmes, doit empescher qu'on ne permette ces sortes de mariages." Vaudreuil et Raudot au Ministre, Que., 14 nov. 1709, *RAPQ* (1942–43): 420.

[12] Charlevoix, *Histoire de la Nouvelle France*, vol.2, *Journal d'un voyage fait par order du Roi dans l'Amérique septentrionale adressé à Madame la Duchesse de Lesdiguières* (Paris, 1744), 247–49.

[13] Papiers La Pause, *RAPQ* (1931–32): 67. See also Fernand Ouellet, "La mentalité et l'outillage économique de l'habitant canadien 1760 . . ." *Bulletin des Recherches Historiques* (1956): 131–36.

[14] Memoire sur les affaires au Canada, Avril 1689, *RAPQ* (1922–23): 7.

[15] *The American Gazetteer*, 3 vols.(London, 1762), vol. 2, entry under Montreal.

[16] Relation d'un voyage de Paris à Montréal en Canadas en 1737. *RAPQ* (1947–48): 16–17.

[17] See Benson, ed., *Peter Kalm's Travels in North America*, 2: 446–47, 558; H.R. Casgrain, ed., *Voyage au Canada dans le nord de l'Amérique septentrionale fait depuis l'an 1751 à 1761 par J.C.B.* (Quebec, 1887), 169.

[18] Benson, ed., *Peter Kalm's Travels in North America*, 2: 558, 626.

[19] Richard Colebrook Harris, *The Seigneurial System in Early Canada* (Madison, Wis., 1966), 81.

[20] Robert Mandrou, *Introduction à la France moderne. Essai de psychologie historique 1500–1640* (Paris, 1961), 17–39.

[21] Mme Bégon à son gendre, Rochefort, 8 déc. 1750. *RAPQ* (1934–35): 129.

[22] Champigny au Ministre, Que., 20 oct. 1699. Archives Nationales, Colonies, Series C11A, 17: 106–110.

[23] Benson, ed., *Peter Kalm's Travels in North America*, 2: 536.

[24] For a revealing account of one such protestation, which could have become dangerous, and the cool way it was subdued without the *habitants* concerned being treated at all harshly, see Vaudreuil au Conseil de la Marine, Que., 17 oct. 1717, Archives Nationales, Colonies, Series C11A, 38: 123–24. It is interesting to note that in this dispatch Vaudreuil is justifying his having had the ten ringleaders summarily arrested and kept in cells for nearly two months without trial. He considered that the circumstances had warranted the use of his exceptional powers, which permitted arrest and imprisonment without trial only in cases of sedition and treason. The Council of Marine subsequently approved his action in this instance. The common sense attitude of the government toward the governed is illustrated in another incident, which at first appeared to be a seditious assembly but was treated as being much less serious. See Raudot au Ministre, Que, 11 nov. 1707, *ibid.*, 26: 202–203.

[25] Mandement de Jean éveque de Québec, 26 avril 1719 ("Trivia," Cameron Nish), *William and Mary Quarterly*, 3rd series, 23 (July 1966): 477–78.

[26] See Les Mariages à la Gaumine, *RAPQ* (1920–21): 366–407.

[27] Mme de Contrecoeur à son Mari, Montreal, 23 mai 1755. Fernand Grenier, ed., *Papiers Contrecoeur et autres documents concernant le conflit Anglo-Français sur l'Ohio de 1745 à 1756* (Quebec, 1952), 349. The context in which the proverb is cited is quite revealing.

[28] Pierre-François-Xavier de Charlevoix, S.J., *Histoire de la Nouvelle France*, vol. 3, *Journal d'un voyage fait par ordre du Roi dans l'Amérique septentrionale adressé à Madame la Duchesse de Lesdiguières* (Paris, 1744), 79.

[29] Arrest du Conseil d'Estat qui permet aux Gentilshommes de Canada de faire Commerce, du 10 mars 1685, Archives Nationales, Colonies, Series F3, 7: 214; Le Roy au Sr. de Meulles, Versailles, 10 mars 1685, *ibid.*, Series B, 11: 99

[30] Roland Mousnier, "L'évolution des institutions monarchiques en France et ses relations avec l'état social," *XVIIe Siècle*, 1963, nos. 58–59.

[31] Extrait des Registres du Conseil d'Estat, 10 avril 1684, Bibliothèque Nationale, Collection Clairambault, vol. 448, p. 369; Champigny au Ministre, Que., 10 mai 1691. Archives Nationales, Colonies, Series C11A, 11: 255; Memoire Instructif sur le Canada, *ibid.*, 265–67.

[32] Le Ministre à M. de Vaudreuil, Versailles, 30 juin 1707, *RAPQ* (1939–40): 375; Résumé d'une lettre de Mme de Vaudreuil au Ministre, Paris, 1709. *RAPQ* (1942–43): 416; Mémoire du Roy à MM de Vaudreuil et Raudot, à Marly, 10 mai 1710, *RAPQ* (1946–47): 376; Archives du Seminaire de Quebec, Fonds Verreau, carton 5, no. 62.

[33] Benson, ed., *Peter Kalm's Travels in North America*, 1: 343–46, 375–76, 392–93; 2: 446–47, 558, 626, 628.

The Family in New France*

JOHN F. BOSHER

One of the fundamental changes in Quebec since the 1940's is a marked decline in the birth rate which has lately become the lowest in Canada.[1] The large family is quickly disappearing, but until recently it was, as is well known, characteristic of French-Canadian society. Furthermore, if we go back to the history of that century and a half before 1763, when Quebec was a French colony, we find that the family, large or small, was a stronger and more prominent group than it is now. It was, indeed, one of the main institutions in New France. The study of it may help to explain how early Canadian civilization is so different from our own.

The typical family of New France may be described in figures drawn from statistical histories, making a sort of statistical portrait.[2] In the early eighteenth century, families had an average of five or six children, but this average includes families in which one of the parents had died and so stopped its growth. Those "arrested" families had, on the average,

*From *In Search of the Visible Past: History Lectures at Wilfrid Laurier University, 1973–1974*, ed. Barry M. Gough. Copyright 1975 by Wilfrid Laurier Press. Reprinted by permission.

four or five children, whereas the complete family, in which neither parent had died, had eight or nine. These averages conceal the variety, of course: some 16% of all families had from ten to fourteen children and 2.8% had no less than fifteen children. Death among the children also kept numbers down, and to a degree staggering in comparison with our present-day infant mortality. We now lose twenty or twenty-one babies out of every thousand; but in New France 246 out of every thousand died during the first year of life, and that was normal in the eighteenth century. What the figures suggest is that the small families at the bottom of the statistical scale were made so by the hazards of death, not by the habits or the wishes of the parents. If no parents or children had died, most families would have numbered a dozen or more children. These figures are for the early eighteenth century, it should be added, after the immigration from France had fallen off; and an analysis of the population in 1663 shows it at an earlier stage when four-fifths of all families had no more than from one to six children. But at every stage the family was enormous compared to the average Quebec family in 1951 which had only 2.2 children.

113

Taken by themselves, the statistical facts for New France may seem to confirm two common traditions about the family habits of all our ancestors: first, that women married very young; and secondly, that they tended to be eternally pregnant thereafter and to have a baby every year. Yet the facts for New France — as for Old France and England also — contradict both those traditions. The average age of women at their first marriage was nearly twenty-two in New France and about twenty-five in Old France. There are, of course, some well-known cases of girls being married at twelve, which was the youngest a girl might legally marry in New France. In 1637, the explorer, Jean Nicollet, set an extreme example by marrying an eleven-year-old girl, Marguerite Couillard, who was Champlain's god-daughter. Not many girls followed that example, it appears, because on 12 April 1670 the royal government ordered the Intendant to pay a premium — or a bounty, perhaps — to every girl under sixteen who found a husband, and to every man who married under twenty. The Crown thought it necessary to encourage people to marry younger. For the same purpose, the Crown also decided to help poor families with the dowries for their girls, and this brings to our notice one of the impediments to an early marriage: the dowry, often a struggle for a father to find for a numerous family of girls. For this and other reasons, too, no doubt, some 18% of women did not marry until they were thirty or more; 10% waited until they were thirty-five or over; and 6% until they were over forty. Women married later than tradition and a few famous examples have led us to believe that men, too, married older — on the average at nearly twenty-seven.

As for the frequency of births in a family, we learn that in New France women tended to have babies about every two years, not every year as legend has held. The demographic effects of such a difference were, of course, enormous; and one historian has concluded that the reason for this pause between babies, a pause of some twenty-three months from birth to birth or fourteen months plus nine months of pregnancy, was that women tended to remain temporarily sterile during the period of breast-feeding.[3]

To sum up, a typical "complete" family, which had not lost a parent, might consist of a father just over forty, a mother in her middle thirties and about eight children ranging from fourteen years of age down to a few weeks old. This may seem to be a very simple conclusion, disappointingly obvious, but it has the great merit of some basis in historical fact.

It leaves us wondering how to account for the phenomenal rate of the population's growth. In 1663, there were just over 3000 people in New France, and a century later there were perhaps 70,000.[4] The population had multiplied by more than twenty-three. During that century, it appears that less than 10,000 immigrants came from the mother country. The remaining 57,000 people had all been born to the 3000 Canadian families or to immigrant families as they came in, in less than five generations. If the French population had multiplied at that rate during the same century there might have been some 400 million Frenchmen by 1763, whereas there were, in fact, only twenty-two or twenty-three million. Lest we should be tempted to dismiss the figures for New France as improbable, we should glance at the increase during the two centuries after 1763 which amounts to an even more staggering rise of from 70,000 to 5½ million, or an eighty-fold increase. If the French had multiplied as quickly as the French Canadians since 1763 there would be nearly two billion Frenchmen by now, or more than half the population of the entire world. In this context, the figures for the twenty-three-fold increase in New France during the century before 1763 do not seem improbable. But they are nevertheless in need of explanation.

Leaving the mathematics of the problem to the demographers, we may sum up in general terms as follows: if women did not marry so young as we thought; if they had babies half as often as we thought; if nearly one-quarter of those babies died before they were a year old and nearly another fifth of them died before the age of ten; and if the annual crude death-rate for the country was somewhere between twenty and forty per thousand; then why did the population increase so quickly? Why was the crude birth-rate so much higher than the crude death-rate or from forty-eight to sixty-five per thousand? The answer (and the missing fact in the problem as I have posed it) is that the people of New France had a high propensity to marry. They were exceptionally fond of the married state.

People in Quebec today marry at an annual rate of about seven or eight per thousand, which is below our national average. The French during the eighteenth century used to marry at the rate of about 16.5 per thousand. But in the colony of New France, the marriage rate was

114

between 17.5 and 23.5 per thousand. The result of this high marriage rate was that from 30% to 40% of the total population were married or widowed, and this proportion seemed to be increasing in the first half of the eighteenth century.[5]

In addition to this, we find a marked tendency to re-marry. Nearly one-fifth of married men married twice, and nearly one-fifth of families had fathers who had been married before. Widows were not snapped up quite so quickly as Peter Kalm and other travellers like to think, but the average widow remarried after three years of widowhood. One way or another very few women reached the age of forty without having married and even re-married. The re-marriage rate was 163 per thousand or nearly twice as high as in 1948.

Another figure that may reflect the strong propensity to marry is the low rate of illegitimacy: it seems to have been not more than ten or twelve per thousand whereas in 1969 the average in Quebec was seventy-six per thousand. We are, I think, obliged to conclude from all the evidence that Canadians were fond of the married state and that this is one reason for the high birth rate. For all that the frontier, like any frontier, had large numbers of single young men, and for all that many Canadians were attracted by the adventurous life of the *coureur de bois*, the society as a whole consisted mainly of married people with families. After all, the *coureurs de bois* were not very numerous and not many girls went into religious orders. There were forty-one women in religious orders in 1663 and in 1763 all seven of the orders of nuns numbered only 190 women altogether, a large number of them from France.

The marriage ceremony which these early Canadians went through in such large numbers left people in no doubt about what their main duty was as a couple. Immediately after the couple had been blessed by the officiating priest, the marriage bed was blessed with the sprinkling of holy water, prayers, and exorcisms. The exorcisms were intended to ward off the evil effects of an especially dangerous curse which some enemy of the couple might put on the marriage to make it barren. This curse was known as the *nouage de l'aiguillette*, and on occasion the Church would dissolve a marriage which produced no children on the grounds that this evil magic had made it barren, so important was the procreation of children in that society. And yet the bed in which children were to be conceived and born was not supposed to be a place for pleasure, as the official ceremony for Quebec, *Le Rituel du diocèse de Québec*, made very clear. The priest was to say to the newly-weds,

> Remember that your wedding bed will some day be your death bed, from whence your souls will be taken to be sent before God's Tribunal . . .[6]

When we come to consider why the people of New France married so willingly and in such large numbers we may at first be tempted to think that the Church forced them into it. Marriage was, after all, a Christian institution, one of the seven sacraments of the Church. There was no civil marriage, nor any civil status at all, in New France. All marriages had to be Catholic marriages and priests were forbidden to marry anyone who was not a Catholic. Very few Canadians married Indians, baptized or not, and very few married Protestants. Priests had to make sure that people who wanted to marry were satisfied that God had called them to marriage; that they had been instructed of the duties and religious principles of marriage (for instance, that it was for having children and for no other purpose); that they had made a full and true confession and communion in their parishes; and that they intended to appear and to behave decently on their wedding day, not to give way to the Devil's temptation to dress vainly or to eat and drink too much. In 1682, Bishop Laval spoke out against women coming to church "in scandalous nakedness of the arms, of the shoulders and the throat or being satisfied to cover them with transparent cloth which often serves only to give more lustre to these shameful nudities."[7] We might be inclined to conclude that it was as good and faithful Catholics in a theocracy that the people of New France were drawn to marriage.

However, we do not have to look very far to see that marriage in that society was not only a religious sacrament, but much else besides. For one thing, weddings were one of the main social events, famous for celebrations lasting several days or even weeks together. That was why most marriages were held in November, January, or February, the idle months of the year between the labours of autumn and the labours of spring. Marriage was also set about with pagan customs like the *charivari*, a ritual gathering of young people who made a disturbance outside the house of a widow who had just been married soon after being widowed, or of people of very unequal ages who had married. The crowd shouted until the newly-weds came out and either explained their actions or else paid a fine.[8] Another folk custom, brought from France, like nearly all Quebec customs, was for young people who wished to marry without their parents' consent, or without a proper wedding, to attend a regular church service and announce at the end of it that they regarded themselves as married. This was called *mariage à la gaumine* and was based on a strict and (said the clergy) illegitimate interpretation of the Papal ruling that marriage required the Church's blessing. Although it died out in the eighteenth century, this custom showed that some people viewed the Church's rules as hindrances to marriage. But all these things are only small clues to the irreligious side of marriage. Much more importantly marriage was an act of the family as a business and social enterprise. It was only rarely an act of two free individuals.

In New France, and in Europe at the time, the family was truly the fundamental unit of society and not the frail and limited group we know today. But in New France, the family was particularly important because some of the other French social groups had not taken root here. The typical French peasant lived in a close-knit village with common lands, common taxes, and a collective or communal life reflected in the word "commune" still used in France more or less as a synonym for "village."[9] However, the *habitants* of New France were not peasants, for the most part, and they lived dispersed across the countryside without common lands or duties in a pattern of rural settlement known as *le rang*.[10] Again, tradesmen in France were organized in guilds or *corporations* which governed most aspects of their working lives, but in New France they worked in a much freer and more independent way. The family was therefore a relatively more important social unit.

In both France and New France, however, as Guy Frégault writes, "The ties of family relationship had extraordinary strength at that time."[11] Four of its basic features will show what I mean. First, the family tended to be a business or agricultural unit with every member expecting to live on the family wealth and in turn expected to take part in the family enterprise. It was also a social enterprise in which every member tried to assist in the advancement of the whole. Families climbed socially like ivy up a wall. The mentality of social advancement at the time may be glimpsed in, for instance, some statements by an eighteenth-century governor whose attitudes may be taken as exemplary in the colony. This is Vaudreuil, who wrote to the minister at Versailles on 15 November 1703: "We have chosen the Honourable Chevalier de Courcy to carry these letters . . . to you because he is the nephew of Monsieur de Callières. We have been pleased to give him this honour to let him know the respect we have for the memory of his late uncle." A year later, Vaudreuil wrote to the minister on behalf of his own children: "I have eight boys and a girl who need the honour of your protection. Three of them are ready for service. I entered the musketeers when I was as young as my oldest. I hope you will have the goodness to grant me for him the company of the Sieur de Maricourt who has died." He then discusses his wife's relations and concludes, "On my side [of the family] I have only one relation, to whom the late Sieur Chevalier de Callières gave a small office as ensign. I beg you to grant him a lieutenancy . . . "[12]

117

Of course patronage extended beyond the family, but the strongest claims were on blood relations and for them. We cannot read very far in any official correspondence of the time without encountering such claims, for there was almost no other way of getting ahead in life. The system of patronage is revealed in a vocabulary all its own, peculiar to the *ancien regime* whether in France or in Canada: *protection* meant patronage; *grâce* referred to a post, a promotion, a pension, or a title conferred by a patron or at his request; *estime* was the attitude of the patron towards his *créature* and it was the reason they both alleged for the *grâce*. And *crédit* was the power a friend or relation had to obtain a *grâce* from someone else; whereas *faveur* expressed the power he had to obtain something for himself.

A second feature of the family is that the act of marriage was in part a business event. In particular, the family had to find a dowry for a girl or else she would probably never find a husband. Trying to marry a girl off without a dowry would have been like fishing without bait on the hook. To use another image, the dowry was a sort of marriage "scholarship," and this metaphor seems all the more true when we remember that Talon gave the *filles du Roi* dowries of fifty *livres* in linen and other goods, and that in 1711 the government of New France set aside the sum of 3000 *livres* to be distributed as dowries among sixty girls. In New France, dowries varied a good deal and they reflect roughly the social level of the family. Here is an example of a modest dowry which Magdeleine Boucher brought to her husband, Urbain Baudry Lamarche:

118

> Two hundred *livres* in silver; four sheets; two table-cloths; six cloth and hemp napkins; a mattress and a blanket; two plates; six pewter spoons and six pewter plates; a pot and a cauldron; a table and two benches; a flour bin; a chest with a lock and key; one cow; two pigs, male and female. The parents gave the bride a suit of clothes and as much underwear as she wanted.[13]

This was an *habitant* family affair, of course. A rich shipping merchant's daughter, at the other end of the scale of commoners, might bring thousands of *livres* to her marriage: Denis Goguet, who retired to La Rochelle after making his fortune in Canada, put up dowries of 50,000 *livres* for his daughters.[14]

The main point about such dowries is that they were family property transferred by legal contract. At the time of the marriage a contract was drawn up before a notary stating this transfer of property and other business terms pertaining to the marriage. Marriage thus had a business side to it and the business negotiations were usually between the families rather than the betrothed couple. As a rule, the families signed these contracts in large numbers; we find the signatures of uncles, aunts, cousins, and so on, scrawled on the last page. One of the interesting effects of this system is that the wife, represented by her family and bringing considerable property to the marriage, tended to have a greater material equality with her husband than most wives in our time.

Needless to say, therefore, both families were very much interested in arranging the marriage in the first place, and this brings up my third point about the family as enterprise: marriage was a major theatre of the family struggle for social advancement or for security. To marry above the family station was a triumph, a step upward for the entire family. The new link with a grander or more noble family was a source of benefit through the influence if afforded. If the daughter of a successful merchant married a government official or his son, the assumption was likely to be that henceforth they were allies in a common struggle for advancement.

Why, we may wonder, would a family ever allow a marriage with a lesser family? The answer is that wealth attracted the poor but respectable; and respectability attracted the rich but low-born. Or else a powerful merchant or clerical family might be glad to marry into a large family of military officers with strong connections in the army. The benefit would still be mutual. Professor Cameron Nish has shown with many examples how the various social spheres intermarried in New France, there being only one ruling class and no such thing as purely military, purely seigneurial, or purely administrative families."[15]

The fourth feature of the family was its hierarchy with the father in command, captain of the family enterprise. It is all too easy these days to imagine that paternal authority was merely a rank injustice or a quaint superstition. Far from it. Every enterprise in a competitive world must be under the command of someone or some group with authority to make decisions: a manager, a president, a ship's captain, a general in the army, a board in a company, and so on. The family enterprise in New France and Old France was nearly always under the father, though there were no impediments to a widow taking over her husband's family firm. In France, especially, there were many firms with "widow" in their titles: *La Veuve Charly* of La Rochelle, *La Veuve Augier et fils aîné* of Tonnay-Charente; *La Veuve Courre-jolles et fils* of Bayonne, and so on.

It has been said that circumstances in Canada tended to put women and children much higher in the social scheme of things than French women and children and to make them more equal with the husband and father.[16] Yet such a difference was not sanctioned either by custom or by law, and normally the father's authority extended to most things, unless he died in which case his widow might assume some, though by no means all, of his authority. Parental authority over children may be seen very clearly in the field of marriage. No child could marry without his father's or widowed mother's consent until the age of twenty-five for girls and thirty for men. Until those ages, the children were considered minors. And in a world where life was shorter than it is now, we must add several years to those ages in order to appreciate the significance of that law. Marriage was primarily the family's business and by law as well as by custom the children were expected to make their marriages according to the best interests of the family.

French law provided that if a son, for example, wanted to marry a girl of whom his father did not approve, he might draw up three "respectful applications" (*sommations respectueuses*) at a notary's office, one after the other at a few weeks' intervals. Let me read to you the first

119

respectful application that a certain Jean-Claude Louet made to his father in January 1733. He was then thirty years old and wanted to marry a shoemaker's daughter, but the father did not approve of the marriage.[17]

My Very Dear Father,

I am in the throes of misery at finding myself deprived of the kindness that I was used to receiving from you. I am extremely pained that your tender impulses which have moved me so often and so deeply are entirely extinct. However, dear father, if I withdraw the obedience and submission that I owe you it is out of an indispensable obligation to restore the reputation of the one whom I have lost, without which there is no salvation for me.

Finally, dear father, I entreat you in your paternal love, and by all that is dearest to you of your own blood, to let yourself be touched and persuaded by the pitiable fate of the poor girl and the lamentable state to which I have been reduced for so long. You have spoken; I have obeyed. You have sent me away to a place where I have nothing but tears and sighs to console me and keep me company.

I believe, however, that today you will be moved by my woes and will grant me the favour I am asking of you.

From he who is,
My Dear Father,
Your most humble and submissive son,
C. Louet

After the third such letter, the son was then legally entitled to marry because he was thirty years old. Under thirty, if his father still refused to consent the son would have had to wait.

We see in all this that the family was engaged in a collective struggle for survival or advancement, and children could not usually please themselves as individuals but had to act as members of the family team. This state of affairs was not merely a quaint custom, but enforced by the law of the kingdom. The law in New France, as in Old France, was prepared to punish children who disobeyed and defied their fathers; for the government, the Church, and the society saw the family in that age as though it were itself a tiny kingdom in which the father, like a king, had almost total authority to rule, reward, and punish. In other words, in that society the family appeared as the smallest political cell in the kingdom, modelled on the kingdom itself.

This metaphor is, however, reversible, and if we reverse it we find that the family in that eighteenth-century society served as a general pattern of organization and authority. The Church, for example, appeared to the people as a sort of family because God was presented as a father to be obeyed as one obeyed one's own father. The letter of Claude Louet above reads a little like a prayer. And not only was God a fatherlike figure, but beneath him there was a whole hierarchy of fathers in authority: the archbishops, the bishops, and the priests. Catholic priests were addressed as "father" while the lay brothers were "brothers." The head of an order of nuns was, of course, a "mother superior," and the nuns were either "mother" or "sister." Girls first entering religious orders were expected to bring dowries as though they were being married, and a nun's dowry was not merely a symbol but a substantial sum of money, a piece of land, or a parcel of goods. Records of dowries brought to Quebec orders are a useful guide to the wealth of the girls' families: some brought several thousand *livres* in cash, others came with a dowry of annuities or planks, barrels of wine, linen, furniture, wheat, and so on.[18] When a Canadian girl chose to go into a monastery, she and her family prepared for the event in somewhat the same way as if she were going to be married, for they saw her as marrying into the Church. She joined the Church just as she might have joined a husband's family. Of course there were differences, but the similarities are striking.

121

Listen to the following ecstasies of love written by a woman who spent most of her life in New France: "Oh, beloved of my soul! Where are you and when shall I possess you? When shall I have you for myself and entirely for myself? Ah, I want you, but I do not want only half of you. I want all of you, my Love and my Life. . . . Come, then, come Oh my Love! The door of my heart is open to you . . . " and so on. Now who was this passionate woman? And who was the fortunate man to whom she was so passionately drawn? She was none other than Marie de l'Incarnation, a nun in the seventeenth century and now a saint in the Canadian Catholic calendar; and all these emotional outpourings were addressed to God. She was expressing her vocation, her call to a life in New France in God's service to which she devoted herself passionately. The point is that as these and other such passages show she saw herself as in some sense married to God or to Jesus and in her writings often referred to him as "my dear Husband."[19]

The image of the family was also present in the army. When a soldier wanted to marry, he needed the consent of his captain or other senior officer and of the Governor of New France. These two consents, which were not merely perfunctory, were duly registered by the officiating clergy. Military authority was thus in some measure paternal authority. But all authority which is not defined by clear regulations must inevitably appear as paternal in the sense that it has no limits and may extend, like a father's authority, into personal and family matters.

The political hierarchy, too, was organized on the family plan. What was the King in the Bourbon kingdom but a great father with paternal care for his subjects and paternal authority over them? Under him, the Governor and Intendant were also father figures expected to enforce not the law, but the King's paternal will. They themselves had paternal rights and duties; and this explains why they used their authority in many matters great and small which astonish us. Paternal authority had very different limits from those of men in authority in our world. "You must maintain good order and peace in families," the minister at Versailles wrote to one Canadian Governor, "refrain from joining in private discussions except to bring them to an end and not join in them if you cannot settle them, never listen to women's talk, never allow anyone to speak ill of someone else in front of you and never do so yourself. . . . " As the Intendant Raudot said, the colony was supposed to be managed "as a good father of a family would manage his estate."[20] When, for instance, the minister happened to hear of an officer who was not supporting his impoverished mother, he arranged to have the officer punished and part of his pay withheld for the mother.[21]

There were, then, a number of hierarchies of authority in Canada all patterned on the family and all helping to reinforce one another in the Canadian mind. To introduce the rule of law into such a society, as the British tried to do after 1763, was a difficult task. How could it be introduced in a society where all authority was regarded as personal and paternal? Still, under British rule, the change began in New France a quarter of a century before it began in Old France during the French Revolution. Since then the French have reverted frequently to the paternal authority of a father figure such as the Bonaparte emperors and General de Gaulle, not to mention Marechal Petain whose regime used the motto, *Famille, Patrie, Travail.* Let us hope that in Quebec the rule of law has taken a firmer hold on the minds of the people during the past two hundred years, and that the ancient vision of the polity as a family has faded away.

122

NOTES

[1] *The Canada Yearbook for 1972,* 241–42.

[2] Jacques Henripin, *La Population canadienne au début du XVIIIe siècle* (Paris, 1954); Henripin, "From Acceptance of Nature to Control: The Demography of the French Canadians since the Seventeenth Century," in M. Rioux and Y. Martin, *French-Canadian Society,* vol. 1 (Toronto, 1964), 204–216; Marcel Trudel, *La Population du Canada en 1663* (Montreal, 1973); J.N. Biraben, "Le Peuplement du Canada français," *Annales de démographie historiques* (Paris, 1966), 104–139.

[3] Jacques Henripin, "La Fécondité des ménages canadiens au début du XVIIIe siècle," *Population,* vol. 9 (Paris, 1954), 74–84.

[4] Trudel, *La Population du Canada en 1663,* 11. Professor Trudel lists 3035 people, but admits that he is not sure of 221 of them. On immigrants, see Biraben, "Le Peuplement du Canada français," and Henripin, *La Population canadienne,* Ch.2, quoting Georges Langlois, *Histoire de la population canadienne française de Montréal* (1934).

[5] Trudel finds that in 1663, the proportion was nearly 50% (*La Population du Canada en 1663,* 74).

[6] Robert-Lionel Seguin, *La Vie libertine en Nouvelle-France au XVIIe siècle,* vol. 2 (Ottawa, 1972), 365–66.

[7] Paul-André Leclerc, "Le Mariage sous le régime français," *Revue d'Histoire de l'Amérique française* 13 (1959): 525.

[8] Leclerc, "Le Mariage," 229ff. On "mariage à la gaumine," see *Le Rapport de l'Archiviste de la Province de Québec* (1920–21): 366–407 (henceforth cited as *RAPQ*).

[9] Marc Bloch, *Les Caracteres originaux de l'Histoire rurale française* (Paris, 1952; first published in 1931), Ch.5.

[10] Pierre Deffontaines, "The *Rang* — Pattern of Rural Settlement in French Canada," in Rioux and Martin, *French-Canadian Society,* 3–18.

[11] Guy Frégault, *Le XVIIIe siècle canadien* (Montreal, 1968), 179.

[12] *RAPQ* (1938–39): 21–22, 49–50.

[13] Leclerc, "Le Mariage," 59.

[14] Archives départementales de la Charente maritime (La Rochelle), minutes of the notary Delavergne, 10 December 1760 and 4 June 1770.

[15] Cameron Nish, *Les Bourgeois-Gentilshommes de la Nouvelle-France, 1729-1748* (Montreal and Paris, 1968), Ch.10, "La Bourgeoisie et le mariage."

[16] Philippe Garigue, *La Vie familiale des canadiens français* (Montreal and Paris, 1962), 16-17.

[17] *RAPQ* (1921-22): 60-63.

[18] Micheline d'Allaire, "L'Origine social des religieuses de l'Hôpital-général de Québec," *La Revue d'Histoire de l'Amérique française* 23 (March 1970): 559-83.

[19] Dom Albert Jamet, ed., *Le Témiognage de Marie de l'Incarnation, Ursuline de Tours et de Québec* (Paris, 1932), 70-72.

[20] Guy Frégault, *Le XVIIIᵉ siècle canadien,* 162-63.

[21] Frégault, *Le XVIIIᵉ siècle,* 163-64.

New France: Les femmes favorisées*

JAN NOEL

You constantly behold, with renewed astonishment, women in the very depths of indigence and want, perfectly instructed in their religion, ignorant of nothing that they should know to employ themselves usefully in their families and who, by their manners, their manner of expressing themselves and their politeness, are not inferior to the most carefully educated among us.[1]

123

Les femmes l'emportent sur les hommes par la beauté, la vivacité, la gaité [*sic*] et l'enjouement; elles sont coquettes et galantes, préfèrent les Européens aux gens du pays. Les manières douces et polies sont communes, même dans les campagnes.[2]

. . . les femmes y sont fort aimables, mais extrêmement fières.[3]

. . . elles sont spirituelles, ce qui leur donne de la supériorité sur les hommes dans presque tous les états.[4]

Many a man, observing the women of New France, was struck by the advantages they possessed in education, cultivation, and that quality called *esprit* or wit. Even an unsympathetic observer of colonial society, such as the French military officer Franquet, who visited New France in 1752-53, admitted that its women "l'emportent sur les hommes pour l'esprit, généralement elles en ont toutes beaucoup, parlant un français épuré, n'ont pas le moindre accent, aiment aussi la parure, sont jolies, généreuses et même maniérées."[5] He notes, albeit with disapproval, that women very commonly aspired to stations above those to which they were born.[6] The Swedish naturalist Peter Kalm, who deplored the inadequate housekeeping of Canadian women, nevertheless admired their refinement.[7]

*Revised from *Atlantis: A Women's Studies Journal,* vol. 6, No. 2 (Spring/printemps 1981): 80-98. Reprinted by permission.
For translation of all French passages in this article, please see page 146.

Those for whom history is an exercise in statistics have taught us caution in accepting the accounts of travellers, which are often highly subjective. However, the consensus (particularly that of seasoned observers such as Charlevoix and Kalm) on the superior education and wit of women in New France suggests that their views are founded on something more than natural male proclivity toward *la différence*. Moreover, historians' accounts of society in New France offer considerable evidence that women did indeed enjoy an unusually privileged position in that colony. It is difficult to think of another colony or country in which women founders showed such important leadership — not just in the usual tending of families and farms but in arranging financing, immigration, and defences that played a major role in the colony's survival. It is unusual for girls to receive a primary education better than that of the boys — as many evidently did in New France. One is also struck by the initiative of *Canadiennes* in business and commerce. In sum, with respect to their education, their range and freedom of action, women in New France seem in many ways to compare favourably with their contemporaries in France and New England, and certainly with the Victorians who came after them.

124

Two cautions are in order. First, to arrive at a full appreciation of the position of women in New France would require detailed comparisons with their contemporaries in other Western countries and colonies. The study of *ancien régime* businesswomen, in particular, is a nascent enterprise. In this paper some twenty outstanding figures in business and politics will be examined and hypotheses put forward about what facilitated their rise to positions of influence. To what degree these women were outstanding in the context of their times one cannot yet say with precision. Second, it is not intended to portray New France as some sort of utopia for women. Women, like men, suffered from disease, privation, class inequalities, and the perennial scourge of war. There were also women's particular hardships, such as the dangers of childbirth and the difficulties of assuming double duty when the men were away. A definitive study of women in New France, which will plumb the primary sources and range the continents for useful comparisons, remains to be made. The purpose of this paper is to marshal the fairly extensive evidence that can be found in published works on New France in support of the thesis that women there enjoyed a relatively privileged position, and to discuss why they might have done so.

Why did the women of New France assume leadership positions? How did they acquire a superior education? How did they come to be involved in commerce? There is no single answer. Three separate elements help account for the situation. First, as studies of Western Europe under the *ancien régime* have indicated, ideas about women's roles were surprisingly flexible and varied at the time New France was founded. Second, the particular demographic configuration of the colony gave female immigrants a number of advantages not available to their counterparts in Europe. Third, the colonial economy, with its heavy emphasis on war and the fur trade, seems to have presented women with a special set of opportunities. Thus, as we shall see, the French cultural heritage and demographic and economic conditions in the colony combined to create the situation that so impressed contemporary observers.

Women and the Family under the *Ancien Régime*

The notion of "woman's place" or "women's role," popular with nineteenth-century commentators, suggests a degree of homogeneity inappropriate to the seventeenth century. It is true that on a formal ideological level men enjoyed the dominant position. This can be seen in the marriage laws, which everywhere made it a wife's duty to follow her husband to whatever dwelling place he chose.[8] In 1650, the men *125* of Montreal were advised by Governor Maisonneuve that they were in fact responsible for the misdemeanours of their wives since "la loi les établit seigneurs de leurs femmes."[9] Under ordinary circumstances the father was captain of the family hierarchy.[10] Yet, it is clear that this formal male authority in both economic and domestic life was not always exercised. Of early seventeenth-century France we are told that

> si la prééminence masculine n'a rien perdu de son prestige, si elle n'a eu à se défendre contre aucune revendication théorique . . . elle a dû . . . souvent se contenter des apparences et abandonner devant les convenances et les exigences du public l'intérêt positif qu'elle défendait.[11]

The idea of separate male and female spheres lacked the clear definition it later acquired. This is in part related to the lack of communication and standardization characteristic of the *ancien régime* — along sexual lines or any other. Generalizations about women are riddled with exceptions. Contradicting the idea of female inferiority, for example, were the semi-matriarchal system in the Basque country and the linen workers' guild, in which a 1645 statute prevented a worker's husband from engaging in occupations unrelated to his wife's business, for which he often served as salesman or partner. More important, because it affected a larger group, was the fact that noblewomen were frequently exempt from legal handicaps affecting other women.[12]

One generalization, however, applies to all women of the *ancien régime*. They were not relegated to the private, domestic sphere of human activity because that sphere did not exist. Western Europeans had not yet learned to separate public and private life. As Philippe Ariès points out in his study of childhood, the private home, in which parents and children constitute a distinct unit, is a relatively recent development. In early modern Europe most of domestic life was lived in the company of all sorts of outsiders. Manor houses, where all the rooms interconnect with one another, show the lack of emphasis placed on privacy. Here, as in peasant dwellings, there were often no specialized rooms for sleeping, eating, working, or receiving visitors; all were more or less public activities performed with a throng of servants, children, relatives, clerics, apprentices, and clients in attendance. Molière's comedies illustrate the familiarity of servants with their masters. Masters, maids, and valets slept in the same room and servants discussed their masters' lives quite openly.[13]

Though familiar with their servants, people were less so with their children. They did not dote on infants to the extent that parents do today. It may have been, as some writers have suggested, that there was little point in growing attached to a fragile being so very apt, in those centuries, to be borne away by accident or disease. These unsentimental families of all ranks sent their children out to apprentice or serve in other people's homes. This was considered important as a basic education.[14] It has been estimated that the majority of Western European children passed part of their childhood living in some household other than their natal one.[15] Mothers of these children — reaching down, in the town, as far as the artisan class — might send their infants out to nursemaids and have very little to do with their physical maintenance.[16]

This lack of a clearly defined "private" realm relates vitally to the history of women, since this was precisely the sphere they later were to inhabit.[17] Therefore it is important to focus on their place in the pre-private world. To understand women in New France one first must pass through that antechamber which Peter Laslett appropriately calls "the world we have lost." Its notions of sexuality and of the family apply to France and New France alike.

In this public world people had not yet learned to be private about their bodily functions, especially about their sexuality. For aid with their toilette, noblewomen did not blush to employ *hommes de chambre* rather than maids. The door of the bedchamber stood ajar, if not absolutely open. Its inhabitants, proud of their fecundity, grinned out from under the bedclothes at their visitors. Newlyweds customarily received bedside guests.[18] The mother of Louis XIV held court and chatted with visitors while labouring to bring *le Roi Soleil* into light of day. Humbler village women kept lesser court among the little crowd of neighbours who attended the midwife's efforts.[19] On the other side of the ocean, Franquet, arriving at Trois-Rivières in 1753, enjoyed the hospitality of Madame Rigaud de Vaudreuil who, feeling poorly, apparently received her visitors at bedside; farther west, he shared a bedroom with a married couple at Fort St. Jean.[20] From the seventeenth century to the colony's last days, clerics thundered more or less futilely against the *décolletage* of the *élite*.[21] Lesser folk leaned toward short skirts[22] and boisterous public discussion of impotent husbands.[23] Rape cases also reveal a rather matter-of-fact attitude. Courts stressed monetary compensation for the victim (as if for trespass on private property) rather than wreaking vengeance on the lustful villain.[24] There was not the same uneasiness in relations between the sexes which later, more puritanical, centuries saw, and which, judging by the withdrawal of women from public life in many of these societies, probably worked to their detriment.

Part of the reason these unsqueamish, rather public people were not possessive about their bodies was that they did not see themselves so much as individuals but as part of a larger, more important unit — the family. In this world the family was the basic organization for most social and economic purposes.[25] As such it claimed the individual's first loyalty.[26] A much higher proportion of the population married than does today.[27] Studies of peasant societies suggest that, for most, marriage was an economic necessity:

127

> Le travail, particulièrement en milieu rural, était alors fondé sur une répartition des tâches entre les sexes: les marins et colporteurs sont absents plusieurs mois, leurs femmes font valoir les terres; les pêcheurs des marais vont au marché, les femmes à la pêche; le laboureur travaille aux champs, sa femme à la maison, c'est elle qui va au marché; dans le pays d'Auge, "les hommes s'occupent des bestiaux et les femmes aux fromages". Pour vivre il fallait donc être deux, un homme et une femme.[28]

The family was able to serve as the basic economic unit in pre-industrial societies because the business of earning a living generally occurred at home. Just as public and private life were undifferentiated, so too were home and workplace. Agricultural and commercial pursuits were all generally "domestic" industries. We see this both in France and in New France. Removal of the man from home for most of the working day, an event that Laslett describes as the single most important event in the history of the modern European family,[29] was only beginning. The idea of man as breadwinner and woman as homemaker was not clearly developed. Women's range of economic activity was still nearly as wide as that of their husbands. Seventeenth-century France saw women working as bonesetters, goldbeaters, bookbinders, doubletmakers, burnishers, laundresses, woolfullers, and wigmakers. Aside from their familiar role in the textile and clothing industries, women also entered heavy trades such as stoneworking and bricklaying. A master plumber, Barbe Legueux, maintained the drainage system for the fountains of Paris. In the commercial world, women worked as fishmongers, pedlars, greengrocers, publicans, money-lenders, and auctioneers.[30] In New France, wives of artisans took advantage of their urban situation to attract customers into the taverns they set up alongside the workshop.[31] It was in farm work, which occupied most of the population, that male and female tasks differed the least of all. *Habitantes* in New France toiled in the fields alongside the men, and they almost certainly — being better educated than their French sisters — took up the farm wife's customary role of keeping accounts and managing purchases and sales.[32] Studies of Bordeaux commercial families have revealed that women also took a large role in business operations.[33] Marie de l'Incarnation's background as manager of one of France's largest transport companies[34] shows that the phenomenon existed in other parts of France as well.

Given the economic importance of both spouses, it is not surprising to see marriage taking on some aspects of a business deal, with numerous relatives affixing their signatures to the contract. We see this in the provisions of the law that protected the property rights of both parties contracting a match. The fact that wives often brought considerable family property to the marriage, and retained rights to it, placed them in a better position than their nineteenth-century descendants were to enjoy.[35]

128

In New France the family's importance was intensified even beyond its usual economic importance in *ancien régime* societies. In the colony's early days, "all roads led to matrimony. The scarcity of women, the economic difficulties of existence, the danger, all tended to produce the same result: all girls became wives, all widows remarried."[36] Throughout the colony's history there was an exceptionally high annual marriage rate of eighteen to twenty-four per thousand.[37] The buildup of the family as a social institution perhaps came about because other social institutions, such as guilds and villages, were underdeveloped.[38] This heightened importance of the family probably enhanced women's position. In the family women tended to serve as equal partners with their husbands, whereas women were gradually losing their position in European guilds and professions.[39] We see this importance of the family in the government's great concern to regulate it. At that time, the state *did* have a place in Canadian bedrooms (whose inhabitants we have already seen to be rather unconcerned about their privacy). Public intervention in domestic life took two major forms: the operation of the legal system and governmental attempts at family planning.

The outstanding characteristic of the legal system in New France — the *Coutume de Paris* — is its concern to protect the rights of all members of the family. The *Coutume de Paris* is considered to have been a particularly benevolent regional variation of French law.[40] It was more egalitarian and less patriarchal than the laws of southern France, which were based on Roman tradition. The *Coutume* reinforced the family, for example, by the penalties it levied on those transferring family property to non-kin.[41] It took care to protect the property of children of a first marriage when a widow or widower remarried.[42] It protected a woman's rights by assuring that the husband did not have power to alienate the family property (in contrast to eighteenth-century British law).[43] The Canadians not only adopted the Parisian *Coutume* in preference to the

Norman *coutume*, which was harsher;[44] they also implemented the law in a way that maximized protection of all family members. Louise Dechêne, after examining the operation of the marriage and inheritance system, concludes that the Canadian application of the law was generous and egalitarian:

> Ces conventions matrimoniales ne nous apparaissent pas comme un marché, un affrontement entre deux lignées, mais comme un accord désintéressé entre les families, visant à créer une nouvelle communauté, à l'assister si possible, à dresser quelques barrières à l'entour pour la protéger. . . . [45]

The criminal law, too, served to buttress family life with its harsh punishments for mistreatment of children.[46]

The royal administration, as well as the law, treated the family as a matter of vital public concern. The state often intervened in matters that later generations left to the individual or to the operations of private charity. Most famous, of course, is the policy of encouraging a high birth rate with financial incentives. There were also attempts to withdraw trading privileges from voyageurs who showed reluctance to take immigrant women to wife.[47] Particularly in the seventeenth century, we see the state regulating what modern societies would consider intimate matters. However, in a colony starved for manpower, reproduction was considered a matter of particularly vital public concern — a concern well demonstrated in the extremely harsh punishments meted out to women who concealed pregnancy.[48] We see a more positive side of this intervention in the care the Crown took of foundlings, employing nurses at a handsome salary to care for them and making attempts to prevent children from bearing any stigma because of questionable origins.[49]

State regulation of the family was balanced by family regulation of the state. Families had an input into the political system, playing an important role in the running of the state. Indeed, it might be argued that the family was the basic political unit in New France. In an age when some members of the *noblesse* prided themselves on their illiteracy, attending the right college was hardly the key to political success. Marrying into the right family was much more important. Nepotism, or rewarding one's kin with emoluments, seemed a most acceptable and natural form of patronage for those in power.[50] In this sense, a good marriage was considered a step upward for the whole family, which helps to explain why choice of spouse was so often a family decision.[51] These family lines were particularly tightly drawn among the military élite in New France. Franquet remarked that "*tous les gens d'un certain ordre sont liés de parenté et d'amitié dans ce pays.*"[52] In fact, with top military positions passing down from generation to generation, by the eighteenth century this élite became a caste.[53]

In this situation, where the *nom de famille* was vastly more important than that of the individual, it was apparently almost as good for political (though not military) purposes to be an Agathe de Repentigny as a Le-Gardeur de Repentigny. Moreover, women's political participation was favoured by the large role of entertaining in political life. For the courtier's role, women were as well trained as men, and there seems to have been no stigma attached to the woman who participated independently of her husband. Six women, Mesdames Daine, Pean, Lotbinière, de Repentigny, Marin, and St. Simon, along with six male officers, were chosen by the Intendant to accompany him to Montreal in 1753.[54] Of the twelve only the de Repentignys were a couple. It is surprising to see women from the colony's first families also getting down to what we would today consider the "business" end of politics. Madame de la Forest, a member of the Juchereau family, took an active role in the political cliques that Guy Frégault describes.[55] Mme. de la Forest's trip to France to plead the cause of Governor de Ramezay was inconsequential, though, in comparison with that of Mme. de Vaudreuil to further Governor Vaudreuil's cause in 1709. *"Douée d'un sens politique très fin,"*[56] she soon gained the ear of the Minister of Marine. Not only did she secure the Governor's victory in the long conflict with the Intendants Raudot (father and son) and win promotion for his patrons; she appears to have gone on to upstage her husband by becoming the virtual director of colonial policy at Versailles for a few years. Vaudreuil's biographer discusses the influence Madame de Vaudreuil exerted with the Minister Pontchartrain who so regularly sought her comments on colonial patronage that supplicants began to apply directly to her rather than to the minister.[57] Contemporaries agreed that her influence was vast:

> Pontchartrain, rapporte Ruette d'Auteuil, ne lui refuse rien, "elle dispose de tous les emplois du Canada, elle écrit de toutes parts dans les ports de mer des lettres magnifiques du bien et du mal qu'elle peut faire après de lui," et le ministre "fait tout ce qu'il faut pour l'autoriser et justifier ses discours." Riverin confirme que . . . "ce n'est plus qu'une femme qui règne tant présente qu'absente."[58]

Governor Frontenac's wife (though not a *Canadienne*) also played an important role at court, dispelling some of the thunderclouds that threatened her husband's stormy career.[59]

As for the common folk, we know less about the political activity of women than that of men. That women participated in a form of popular assembly is hinted at in a report of a meeting held in 1713 (in present-day Boucherville), in which Catherine Guertin was sworn in as midwife after having been elected *"dans l'assemblée des femmes de cette paroisse, à la pluralité des suffrages, pour exercer l'office de sagefemme."*[60] Were these women's assemblies a general practice? If so, what other matters did they decide? This aspect of habitant politics remains a mystery. It is clear, though, that women were part of what historians have called the "pre-industrial crowd."[61] Along with their menfolk, they were full-fledged members of the old "moral economy" whose members rioted and took what was traditionally their rightful share (and no more) when prices were too high or when speculators were hoarding grain.[62] The women of Quebec and Montreal, who rioted against the horsemeat rations and the general hunger of 1757–58, illustrate this aspect of the old polity.[63]

In sum, women's position during the *ancien régime* was open-ended. Although conditions varied, a wide range of roles were available to women, to be taken up or not. This was so because the separate spheres of men and women in *ancien régime* societies were not so clearly developed as they later became. There was as yet no sharp distinction between public and private life: families were for most purposes the basic social, economic, and political unit. This situation was intensified in New France due to the underdevelopment of other institutions, such as the guild, the seigneurie, and the village. The activities of breadwinner and home-maker were not yet widely recognized as separate functions belonging to one sex or the other. All members of the family also often shared the same economic functions, or at least roles were interchangeable. Nor had the symbolic honorific aspects of government yet been separated from the business end of politics and administration. These conditions, typical of most of pre-industrial France, were also found in New France, where particular demographic and economic conditions would enable the colony's women to develop the freedoms and opportunities that this fluid situation allowed.

131

Demographic Advantages

Demography favoured the women of New France in two ways. First, the women who went there were a highly select group of immigrants. Second, women were in short supply in the early years of the colony's development, a situation that worked in their favour.

The bulk of the female immigrants to New France fall into one of two categories. The first was a group of extremely well-born, well-endowed, and highly dedicated religious figures. They began to arrive in 1639, and a trickle of French nuns continued to cross the ocean over the course of the next century. The second distinct group was *filles du roi*, government-sponsored female migrants who arrived between 1663 and 1673. These immigrants, though not as outstanding as the *dévotes*, were nevertheless privileged compared to the average immigrant to New France, who arrived more or less threadbare.[64] The vast majority of the women (and the men) came from the Île-de-France and the northwestern parts of France. The women of northern France enjoyed fuller legal rights and were better educated and more involved in commerce than those in southern France.[65] When they set foot on colonial soil with all this auspicious baggage, the immigrants found that they had yet another advantage. Women constituted a small percentage of the population. As a scarce resource they were highly prized and therefore in an excellent position to gain further advantages.

The first *religieuses* to arrive in New France were the Ursulines and Hospitallers who landed at Quebec in 1639. These were soon followed by women who helped establish Montreal in 1642. Their emigration was inspired by a religious revival in France, which is thought to have arisen in response to the widespread pauperism following the French civil wars of the sixteenth century. The seventeenth-century revival distinguished itself by tapping the energies of women in an unprecedented way.[66] Among its leaders were Anne of Austria and a number of the leading ladies at court.[67] In other parts of France, women of the provincial élite implemented the charity work inspired by Saint Vincent de Paul.[68] Occurring between 1600 and 1660, this religious revival coincided almost exactly with the period when the fledgling Canadian colony, besieged by English privateers and by the Iroquois, was most desperately in need of an injection of immigrants, money, and enthusiasm.[69] It was at this moment that the Jesuits in Quebec appealed to the French public for aid. Much to their surprise, they received not a donation but a half-dozen religious zealots, in person. Abandoning the centuries-old cloistered role of female religious figures these nuns undertook missionary work that gave them an active role in the life of the colony.[70] Thus the great religious revival of the seventeenth century endowed New France with several exceptionally capable, well-funded, determined leaders imbued with an activist approach to charity and with that particular mixture of spiritual ardour and worldly *savoir-faire* that typified the mystics of that period.[71] The praises of Marie de l'Incarnation, Jeanne Mance, and Marguerite Bourgeoys have been sung so often as to be tiresome. Perhaps, though, a useful vantage point is gained if one assesses them neither as saints nor heroines, but simply as leaders. In this capacity, the nuns supplied money, publicity, skills, and settlers, all of which were needed in the colony.

Marie de l'Incarnation, a competent businesswoman from Tours, founded the Ursuline Monastery at Quebec in 1639. Turning to the study of Indian languages, she and her colleagues helped implement the policy of assimilating the young Indians. Then, gradually abandoning that futile policy, they turned to the education of the French colonists. Marie de l'Incarnation developed the farm on the Ursuline seigneurie and served as an unofficial adviser to the colonial administrators. She also helped draw attention and money to the colony by writing some 12,000 letters between 1639 and her death in 1672.[72]

An even more prodigious fund-raiser in those straitened times was Jeanne Mance, who had a remarkable knack for making friends in high places.[73] They enabled her to supply money and colonists for the original French settlement on the island of Montreal, and to take a place beside Maisonneuve as co-founder of the town.[74] The hospital she established there had the legendary wealth of the de Bullion family — and the revenues of three Norman domains — behind it. From this endowment she made the crucial grant to Governor Maisonneuve in 1651 that secured vitally needed troops from France, thus saving Montreal.[75] Mance and her Montreal colleague Margeurite Bourgeoys both made several voyages to France to recruit settlers. They were particularly successful in securing the female immigrants necessary to establish a permanent colony, recruiting sizable groups in 1650, 1653, and 1659.[76]

Besides contributing to the colony's sheer physical survival, the nuns raised the living standards of the population materially. They conducted the schools attended by girls of all classes and from both of the colony's races. Bourgeoys provided housing for newly arrived immigrants and served in a capacity perhaps best described as an early social worker.[77] Other nuns established hospitals in each of the three towns. The colonists reaped fringe benefits in the institutions established by this exceptionally dedicated personnel. The hospitals, for example, provided high-quality care to both rich and poor, care that compared favourably with that of similar institutions in France.[78] Thus, the *dévotes* played an important role in supplying leadership, funding, publicity, recruits, and social services. They may even have tipped the balance toward survival in the 1650s, when retention of the colony was still in doubt.

In the longer run, they endowed the colony with an educational heritage, which survived and shaped social life long after the initial heroic piety had grown cold. The schools that the *dévotes* founded created a situation very different from that in France, where education of women in the seventeenth century lagged behind that of men.[79] The opinion-setters in France sought to justify this neglect in the eighteenth century and a controversy began over whether girls should be educated outside the home at all.[80] Girls in Montreal escaped all this. Indeed, in 1663 Montrealers had a school for their girls but none for their boys. The result was that for a time Montreal women surpassed men in literacy, a reversal of the usual *ancien régime* pattern.[81] The superior education of women that Charlevoix extolled in 1744 continued until the fall of New France (and beyond) — a tendency heightened by the large percentage of soldiers, generally illiterate, among the male population.[82] The Ursulines conducted schools for the élite at Quebec and Trois-Rivières. This order was traditionally rather weak in teaching housekeeping (which perhaps accounts for Kalm's famous castigation of Canadian housewif-

133

ery). Nevertheless they specialized in needlework, an important skill since articles of clothing were a major trade good sought by the Indians. Moreover, the Ursulines taught the daughters of the élite the requisite skills for administering a house and a fortune — skills which, as we shall see later, many were to exercise.[83]

More remarkable than the Ursuline education, however, was that of the *Soeurs de la Congrégation,* which reached the popular classes in the countryside.[84] Franquet was apparently shocked by the effect of this exceptional education on the colonial girls. He recommended that the *Soeurs'* schools be suppressed because they made it difficult to keep girls down on the farm:

134

> Ces Soeurs sont répandues le long des côtes, dans des seigneuries où elles ont été attirées pour l'éducation des jeunes filles; leur utilité semble être démontrée, mais le mal qu'en résulte est comme un poison lent qui tend à dépeupler les ᴗampagnes, d'autant qu'une fille instruite fait la demoiselle, qu'elle est maniérée, qu'elle veut prendre un établissement à la ville, qu'il lui faut un négociant et qu'elle regarde au dessous d'elle l'état dans lequel elle est née.[85]

The second distinct group of female immigrants to New France was the famous *filles du roi,* women sent out by the French government as brides in order to boost the colony's permanent settlement. Over 900 arrived between 1663 and 1673.[86] If less impressive than the *dévotes,* they, too, appear to have arrived with more than the average immigrant's store of education and capital. Like the nuns, they were the product of a particular historical moment that thrust them across the sea. The relevant event here is that brief interlude in the 1660s and 1670s when the King, his Minister Colbert, and the Intendant Talon applied an active hand to colonial development.[87]

There has been much historical controversy about whether the *filles du roi* were pure or not.[88] More relevant to our discussion than their morality are their money and their skills. On both these counts, this was a very selective immigration. First of all, the majority of the *filles du roi* (and for that matter, of seventeenth-century female immigrants generally) were urban dwellers, a group that enjoyed better access to education than the peasantry did.[89] Moreover, the *filles du roi* were particularly privileged urbanites. Over one-third, some 340 of them, were educated at the Paris Hôpital Général. Students at this institution learned writing and such a wide variety of skills that in France they were much sought after for service in the homes of the wealthy. Six per cent were of noble or bourgeois origin. Many of the *filles* brought with them a 50–100 *livres* dowry provided by the King;[90] some supplemented this with personal funds in the order of 200–300 *livres.* Sixty-five of the *filles* brought considerably larger holdings, in the range of 400 to 450 *livres*, to their marriages.[91] The Parisian origins of many *filles du roi*, and of the nuns who taught their children, probably account for the pure French accent that a number of travellers attributed to the colony's women.[92]

These two major immigrant groups, then, the nuns and the *filles du roi*, largely account for the superior education and "cultivation" attributed to the colony's women. Another demographic consideration also favoured the women of New France. As a result of light female emigration, men heavily outnumbered women in the colony's early days.[93] It might be expected that, as a scarce commodity, women would receive favoured treatment. The facility of marriage and remarriage, as well as the leniency of the courts and the administrators toward women, suggests that this hypothesis is correct.

Women had a wider choice in marriage than did men in the colony's early days. There were, for example, eight marriageable men for every marriageable woman in Montreal in 1663. Widows grieved, briefly, then remarried within an average of 8.8 months after their bereavement. In those early days the laws of supply and demand operated to women's economic advantage, as well. Rarely did these first Montreal women bother to match their husband's wedding present by offering a dowry.[94] The colony distinguished itself as "the country of the *douaire* not of the *dot*."[95]

135

In the social and legal realm we also find privileges that may have been attributable to the shortage of women. Perhaps it is due to the difficulties of replacing battered wives that jealous husbands in New France were willing to forgo the luxury of uncontrolled rage. Some of the intendants even charged that there were libertine wives in the colony who got away with taking a second husband while the first was away trading furs.[96] Recent indications that New France conformed rather closely to French traditions make it unlikely that this was common.[97] But the judgements of the Sovereign Council do offer evidence of peaceful reconciliations such as that of Marguerite Leboeuf, charged with adultery in 1667. The charge was dismissed when her husband pleaded before the Sovereign Council on her behalf. Also leaving vengeance largely to the Lord was Antoine Antorche, who withdrew his accusation against his wife even after the Council found her doubly guilty.[98] In this regard the men of New France differed from their Portuguese brothers in Brazil, who perpetrated a number of amorous murders each year; also from their English brethren in Massachusetts, who branded or otherwise mutilated their errant wives and daughters.[99] When such cases reached the courts in New France the judges, too, appear to have been lenient. Their punishments for adulterous women were considerably lighter than those imposed in New England. A further peculiarity of the legal system in New

France, which suggests that women were closer to being on an equal footing with men than in other times and places, was the unusual attempt to arrest not only prostitutes but their clients as well.[100]

Another indication of the lenient treatment Canadian women enjoyed is the level of insubordination the authorities were willing to accept from them. There was a distinct absence of timidity vis-à-vis the political authorities. In 1714, for example, the inhabitants of Côte St. Leonard violently objected to the Bishop's decision to cancel their membership in the familiar church and enrol them in the newly erected parish of Rivière-des-Prairies. A fracas ensued in which the consecrated altar breads were captured by the rebellious parishioners. An officer sent to restore order was assailed by angry women:

> L'huissier chargé d'aller assigner les séditieux, raconte que toutes les femmes l'attendaient "avec des roches et des perches dans leurs mains pour m'assassiner," qu'elles le poursuivirent en jurant: "arrête voleur, nous te voulons tuer et jeter dans le marais."[101]

136

Other women hurled insults at the Governor himself in the 1670s.[102] An even more outrageous case of insubordination was that of the two Desaulniers sisters, who by dint of various appeals, deceits, and stalling tactics continued to run an illegal trading post at Caughnawaga for some twenty-five years despite repeated orders from governors, intendants, and the ministry itself to close it down.[103]

A further indication of women's privileged position is the absence of witchcraft persecution in New France. The colony was founded in the seventeenth century when this persecution was at its peak in Western Europe. The New Englanders, too, were burning witches at Salem. Not a single *Canadienne* died for this offence.[104] It is not — as Marie de l'Incarnation's account of the 1663 earthquake makes clear[105] — that the Canadians were not a superstitious people. A scholar of crime in New France suggests that this surprising absence of witchcraft hysteria relates to the fact that "depuis le début de la colonie une femme était une rareté très estimée et de ce fait, protégée de la persécution en masse."[106]

Thus, on the marriage market, and in their protection from physical violence, women seem to have achieved a favourable position because of their small numbers. Their relatively high wages and lighter court sentences may also have related to the demographic imbalance. Moreover, the original female immigrants arrived in the colony with better than average education and capital, attributes that undoubtedly helped them to establish their privileged status.

Economic Opportunities

Even more than demographic forces, the colonial economy served to enhance the position of women. In relation to the varied activities found in many regions of France, New France possessed a primitive economy. Other than subsistence farming, the habitants engaged in two major pursuits. The first was military activity, which included not only actual fighting but building and maintaining the imperial forts and provisioning the troops. The second activity was the fur trade. Fighting and fur trading channelled men's ambitions and at times removed them physically from the colony. This helped open up the full range of opportunities to women, whom we have already seen to have had the possibility of assuming a wide variety of economic roles in *ancien régime* society. Many adapted themselves to life in a military society. A few actually fought. Others made a good living by providing goods and services to the ever-present armies. Still others left military activity aside and concentrated on civilian economic pursuits — pursuits that were often neglected by men. For many this simply meant managing the family farm as best as one could during the trading season, when husbands were away. Other women assumed direction of commercial enterprises, a neglected area in this society that preferred military honours to commercial prizes. Others acted as sort of home-office partners for fur-trading husbands working far afield. Still others, having lost husbands to raids, rapids, or other hazards of forest life, assumed a widow's position at the helm of the family business.

137

New France has been convincingly presented as a military society. The argument is based on the fact that a very large proportion of its population was under arms, its government had a semi-military character, its economy relied heavily on military expenditure and manpower, and a military ethos prevailed among the élite.[107] In some cases, women joined their menfolk in these martial pursuits. The seventeenth century sometimes saw them in direct combat. A number of Montrealers perished during an Iroquois raid in 1661 in which, Charlevoix tells us, "even the women fought to the death, and not one of them surrendered."[108] In Acadia, Madame de la Tour took command of the fort's forty-five soldiers and warded off her husband's arch-enemy, Menou D'Aulnay, for three days before finally capitulating.[109]

The most famous of these seventeenth-century *guerrières* was, of course, Madeleine de Verchères. At the age of fourteen she escaped from a band of Iroquois attackers, rushed back to the fort on her parents' seigneurie, and fired a cannon shot in time to warn all the surrounding settlers of the danger.[110] Legend and history have portrayed Madeleine as a lamb who was able, under siege, to summon up a lion's heart. Powdered and demure in a pink dress, she smiles very sweetly out at the world in a charming vignette in Arthur Doughty's *A Daughter of New France, being a story of the life and times of Magdelaine de Verchères*, published in 1916. Perhaps the late twentieth century is ready for her as she was: a swashbuckling, musket-toting braggart who extended the magnitude of her deeds with each successive telling, who boasted that she never in her life shed a tear, a contentious thorn in the side of the local curé (whom she slandered) and of her *censitaires* (whom she constantly battled in the courts).[111] She strutted through life for all the world like the boorish male officers of the *campagnard* nobility to which her family belonged.[112] One wonders how many more there were like her. Perhaps all trace of them has vanished into the wastebaskets of subsequent generations of historians who, with immovable ideas of female propriety, did not know what on earth to do with them — particularly after what must have been the exhausting effort of pinching Verchères' muscled frame into a corset and getting her to wear the pink dress.

By the eighteenth century, women had withdrawn from hand-to-hand combat, but many remained an integral part of the military élite as it closed in to become a caste. In this system, both sexes shared the responsibility of marrying properly and of maintaining those cohesive family ties which, Corvisier tells us, lay at the heart of military society. Both also appealed to the ministry for their sons' promotions.[113]

What is more surprising is that a number of women accompanied their husbands to military posts in the wilderness. Wives of officers, particularly of corporals, traditionally helped manage the canteens in the French armies.[114] Almost all Canadian officers were involved in some sort of trading activity, and a wife at the post could mind the store when the husband had to mind the war. Some were overzealous. When Franquet rode into Fort Saint Frédéric in 1752 he discovered a terrific row among its inhabitants. The post was in a virtual state of mutiny because a Madame Lusignan was monopolizing all the trade, both wholesale and retail, at the fort; and her husband, the Commandant, was enforcing the monopoly.[115] In fact, Franquet's inspection tour of the Canadian posts is remarkable for the number of women who greeted him at the military posts, which one might have expected to be a male preserve. Arriving at Fort Sault Saint Louis he was received very politely by M. de Merceau and his two daughters. He noted that Fort Saint Frédéric housed not only the redoubtable Madame Lusignan but also another officer's widow. At Fort Chambly he "spent the whole day with the ladies, and visited Madame de Beaulac, an officer's widow who has been given lodging in this fort."[116]

The nuns, too, marched in step with this military society. They were, quite literally, one of its lifelines, since they cared for its wounded. A majority of the invalids at the Montreal Hôtel-Dieu were soldiers, and the Ursuline institution at Trois-Rivières was referred to simply as a *hôpital militaire*.[117] Hospital service was so vital to the army that Frontenac personally intervened to speed construction of the Montreal Hôtel-Dieu in 1695, when he was planning a campaign against the Iroquois.[118] In the colony's first days, the Ursulines also made great efforts to help the Governor seal Indian alliances by attempting to secure Iroquois students who would serve as hostages, and by giving receptions for Iroquois chiefs.[119]

Humbler folk also played a part in military society. In the towns female publicans conducted a booming business with the thirsty troops. Other women served as laundresses, adjuncts so vital that they accompanied armies even on the campaigns where wives and other camp followers were ordered to stay home.[120] Seemingly indispensable, too, wherever armies march, are prostitutes. At Quebec City they plied their trade as early as 1667. Indian women at the missions also served in this capacity.[121] All told, women had more connections with the military economy than is generally noted.

While warfare provided a number of women with a living, it was in commerce that the *Canadiennes* really flourished. Here a number of women moved beyond supporting roles to occupy centre stage. This happened for several reasons. The first was that the military ethos diverted men from commercial activity. Second, many men who entered the woods to fight or trade were gone for years. Others, drowned or killed in battle, never returned.[122] This left many widows who had to earn a livelihood. This happened so often, in fact, that when women, around the turn of the eighteenth century, overcame their early numerical disadvantage, the tables turned quickly. They soon outnumbered the men and remained a majority through to the Conquest.[123] Generally speaking, life was more hazardous for men than for women[124] — so much so that the next revolution of the historiographic wheel may turn up the men of New France (at least in relation to its women) as an oppressed group.

139

At any rate, women often stepped in to take the place of their absent husbands or brothers. A surprising number of women traders emerge in the secondary literature on New France. In the colony's earliest days, the mere handful of women included two merchants at Trois-Rivières: Jeanne Enard (mother-in-law of Pierre Boucher), who "by her husband's own admission" was the head of the family as far as fur-trading was concerned; and Mathurine Poisson, who sold imported goods to the colonists.[125] At Montreal there was the wife of Artus de Sully, whose unspecified (but presumably commercial) activities won her the distinction of being Montreal's biggest debtor.[126] In Quebec City, Eleonore de Grandmaison was a member of a company formed to trade in the Ottawa country. She added to her wealth by renting her lands on the Île d'Orleans to Huron refugees after Huronia had been destroyed. Farther east, Madame de la Tour involved herself in shipping pelts to France. Another Acadian, Madame Joybert, traded furs on the Saint John River.[127]

With the onset of the less pious eighteenth century, we find several women at the centre of the illegal fur trade. Indian women, including "a cross-eyed squaw named Marie-Magdelaine," regularly carried contraband goods from the Caughnawaga reserve to Albany.[128] A Madame Couagne received Albany contraband at the other end, in Montreal.[129] But at the heart of this illegal trade were the Desaulniers sisters, who used their trading post on the Caughnawaga reserve as an *entrepôt* for the forbidden English strouds, fine textiles, pipes, boots, lace, gloves, silver tableware, chocolate, sugar, and oysters that the Indians brought regularly from Albany.[130] Franquet remarked on the power of these *marchandes*, who were able to persuade the Indians to refuse the government's request to build fortifications around their village.[131] The Desaulniers did not want the comings and goings of their employees too closely scrutinized.

These *commerçants*, honest and otherwise, continued to play their part until the Conquest. Marie-Anne Barbel (*Veuve* Fornel) farmed the Tadoussac fur trade and was involved in diverse enterprises including retail sales, brickmaking, and real estate.[132] On Franquet's tour in the 1750s he encountered other *marchandes* besides the controversial "Madame la Commandante" who had usurped the Fort Saint Frédéric trade. He enjoyed a restful night at the home of Madame de Lemothe, a *marchande* who had prospered so well that she was able to put up her guests in splendid beds that Franquet proclaimed "fit for a duchess."[133]

A number of writers have remarked on the shortage of entrepreneurial talent in New France.[134] This perhaps helps to account for the activities of Agathe de St. Père, who established the textile industry in Canada. She did so after the colonial administrators had repeatedly called for development of spinning and weaving, with no result.[135] Coming from the illustrious Le Moyne family, Agathe St. Père married the ensign Pierre Legardeur de Repentigny, a man who, we are told, had "an easy-going nature." St. Père, of another temperament, pursued the family business interests, investing in fur trade partnerships, real estate, and lending operations. Then in 1705, when the vessel bringing the yearly supply of French cloth to the colony was shipwrecked, she saw an opportunity to develop the textile industry in Montreal. She ransomed nine English weavers who had been captured by the Indians and arranged for apprentices to study the trade. Subsequently these apprentices taught the trade to other Montrealers on home looms that Madame de Repentigny built and distributed. Besides developing the manufacture of linen, drugget, and serge, she discovered new chemicals that made use of the native plants to dye and process them.[136]

Upon this foundation Madame Benoist built. Around the time of the Conquest, she was directing an operation in Montreal in which women turned out, among other things, shirts and petticoats for the fur trade.[137] This is a case of woman doing business while man did battle, for Madame Benoist's husband was commanding officer at Lac des Deux Montagnes.

The absence of male entrepreneurs may also explain the operation of a large Richelieu lumbering operation by Louise de Ramezay, the daughter of the Governor of Montreal. Louise, who remained single, lost her father in 1724. Her mother continued to operate the sawmill on the family's Chambly seigneury but suffered a disastrous reverse due

140

to a combination of flooding, theft, and shipwreck in 1725. The daughter, however, went into partnership with the Seigneuress de Rouville in 1745 and successfully developed the sawmill. She then opened a flour mill, a Montreal tannery, and another sawmill. By the 1750s the trade was flourishing: Louise de Ramezay was shipping 20,000-*livre* loads, and one merchant alone owed her 60,000 *livres*. In 1753 she began to expand her leather business, associating with a group of Montreal tanners to open new workshops.[138]

Louise de Ramezay's case is very clearly related to the fact that she lived in a military society. As Louise was growing up, one by one her brothers perished. Claude, an ensign in the French navy, died during an attack on Rio de Janeiro in 1711. Louis died during the 1715 campaign against the Fox Indians. La Gesse died ten years later in a shipwreck off Île Royale. That left only one son, Jean-Baptiste-Roch; and, almost inevitably, he chose a military career over management of the family business affairs.[139] It may be that similar situations accounted for the female entrepreneurs in ironforging, tilemaking, sturgeon-fishing, sealing, and contract building, all of whom operated in New France.[140]

141

The society's military preoccupations presented business opportunities to some women; for others, the stress on family ties was probably more important. Madame Benoist belonged to the Baby family, whose male members were out cultivating the western fur trade. Her production of shirts made to the Indians' specifications was the perfect complement. The secret of the Desaulniers' successful trade network may well be that they were related to so many of Montreal's leading merchants.[141] The fur trade generally required two or more bases of operation. We saw earlier in our discussion that this society not only placed great value on family connections but also accepted female commercial activity. It was therefore quite natural that female relatives would be recruited into business to cover one of the bases. Men who were heading for the west would delegate their powers of attorney and various business responsibilities to their wives, who were remaining in the colony.[142]

We find these husband-wife fur trade partnerships not only among "*Les Grandes Familles*" but permeating all classes of society. At Trois-Rivières women and girls manufactured the canoes that carried the fur trade provisions westward each summer. This was a large-scale operation that profited from fat government contracts.[143] In Montreal, wives kept the account-books while their husbands traded. Other women spent the winters sewing shirts and petticoats that would be bartered the following summer.[144]

The final reason for women's extensive business activity was the direct result of the hazards men faced in fighting and fur-trading. A high proportion of women were widowed; and as widows, they enjoyed special commercial privileges. In traditional French society, these privileges were so extensive that craftsmen's widows sometimes inherited full guild-master's rights. More generally, widows acquired the right to manage the family assets until the children reached the age of twenty-five (and sometimes beyond that time). In some instances they also received the right to choose which child would receive the succession.[145] In New France these rights frequently came into operation, and they had a major impact on the distribution of wealth and power in the society. In 1663, for example, women held the majority of the colony's seigneurial land. The *Veuve* Le Moyne numbered among the twelve Montreal merchants who, between 1642 and 1725, controlled assets of 50,000 *livres*. The *Veuve* Fornel acquired a similar importance later on in the regime. Some of the leading merchants at Louisbourg were also widows. The humbler commerce of tavernkeeping was also frequently a widow's lot.[146]

Thus, in New France, both military and commercial activities that required a great deal of travelling over vast distances were usually carried out by men. In their absence, their wives played a large role in the day-to-day economic direction of the colony. Even when the men remained in the colony, military ambitions often absorbed their energies, particularly among the upper class. In these situations, it was not uncommon for a wife to assume direction of the family interests.[147] Others waited to do so until their widowhood, which — given the fact that the average wife was considerably younger than her husband and that his activities were often more dangerous — frequently came early.[148]

142

Conclusion

New France had been founded at a time in Europe's history in which the roles of women were neither clearly nor rigidly defined. In this fluid situation, the colony received an exceptionally well-endowed group of female immigrants during its formative stage. There, where they long remained in short supply, they secured a number of special privileges at home, at school, in the courts, and in social and political life. They consolidated this favourable position by attaining a major role in the colonial economy, at both the popular and the directive levels. These circumstances enabled the women of New France to play many parts. *Dévotes* and traders, warriors and landowners, smugglers and politicians, industrialists and financiers: they thronged the stage in such numbers that they distinguish themselves as *femmes favorisées*.

NOTES

[1] F.-X. Charlevoix, *History and General Description of New France* (New York, 1900), 23: 28.
[2] Cited in R.-L. Séguin, "La Canadienne aux XVIIe et XVIIIe siècles," *Revue d'histoire de l'Amérique français* (hereafter RHAF), 13 (mars, 1960): 492.
[3] Séguin, "La Canadienne," 500.
[4] Séguin, "La Canadienne," 500.

5 L. Franquet, *Voyages et mémoires sur le Canada* (Montréal, 1974), 57, recording a tour in 1752-53.

6 Franquet, *Voyages*, 31.

7 Séguin, "La Canadienne," 492, 505.

8 G. Fagniez, *La Femme et la société française dans la première moitié du XVIIe siècle* (Paris, 1929), p.154.

9 Marcel Trudel, *Montréal, la formation d'une société* (Montréal, 1976): 216-17.

10 John F. Bosher, "The Family in New France," in Barry Gough, ed., *In Search of the Visible Past* (Waterloo, Ont., 1976), 7.

11 Fagniez, *Femme et société française*, 121.

12 Fagniez, *Femme et société française*, 149, 104, 193.

13 Philippe Ariès, *Centuries of Childhood* (New York, 1962), 392-406.

14 Ariès, *Centuries of Childhood*, 365-66.

15 Peter Laslett, "Characteristics of the Western Family Considered over Time," *Journal of Family History* 2 (Summer 1977): 89-115.

16 Richard Vann, "Women in Preindustrial Capitalism," in R. Bridenthal, ed., *Becoming Visible: Women in European History* (Boston, 1977), 206.

17 Vann, "Women in Preindustrial Capitalism," 206-08; Ariès, *Centuries of Childhood*, 397-406.

18 Fagniez, *Femme et société française*, 122-23, 179.

19 Vann, "Women in Preindustrial Capitalism," 206.

20 Franquet, *Voyages*, 135, 61.

21 Séguin, "La Canadienne," 499; R. Boyer, *Les Crimes et châtiments au Canada française du XVIIIe au XXe siècle* (Montréal, 1966), p.391.

22 Séguin, "La Canadienne," 506.

23 Boyer, *Crimes et châtiments*, 351.

24 Boyer, *Crimes et châtiments*, 344-46.

25 Laslett, "Western Family," 95.

26 I. Foulché-Delbosc, "Women of Three Rivers, 1651-1663," in A. Prentice and S. Trofimenkoff, eds., *The Neglected Majority* (Toronto, 1977), 26.

27 Bosher ("The Family," 3) found the marriage rate in New France to be about three times that of modern-day Quebec.

28 This information is taken from a study of Normandy, which was the birthplace of many of the Canadian colonists. J.M. Gouesse, "La Formation du couple en Basse-Normandie," *XVIIe Siècle* 102-3 (1974): 56.

29 Laslett, "Western Family," 106.

30 Fagniez, *Femme et société française*, 99-104, 108, 111, 114-16.

31 Louise Dechêne, *Habitants et marchands de Montréal au XVIIe siècle* (Paris, 1974), 393.

32 Fagniez, *Femme et société française* 101; Séguin, "La Canadienne," 503; also G. Lanctôt, *Filles de joie ou filles du roi* (Montréal, 1952), 210-13.

33 Cf. Paul Butel, "Comportements familiaux dans le négoce bordelais au XVIIIe siècle," *Annales du Midi* 88 (1976): 139-57.

34 M.E. Chabot, "Marie Guyart de l'Incarnation, 1599-1672," in M. Innis, ed., *The Clear Spirit* (Toronto, 1966), 28.

35 Bosher, "The Family," 7; H. Neatby, *Quebec, The Revolutionary Age* (Toronto, 1966), 46.

36 Foulché-Delbosc. "Women of Three Rivers," 15.

37 Bosher, "The Family," 3. I have rounded his figures.

38 Dechêne, *Habitants et marchands*, 434; Bosher, "The Family," 5.

39 Vann, "Women in Preindustrial Capitalism," 205; cf. also Alice Clark, *Working Life of Women in the Seventeenth Century* (London, 1968), Chs. 5,6; and Fagniez, *Femme et société française*, for the scarcity of women's guilds by the seventeenth century.

40 Fagniez, *Femme et société française*, 168ff.

41 Y. Zoltvany, "Esquisse de la Coutume de Paris," *RHAF* (décembre, 1971).

42 Foulché-Delbosc, "Women of Three Rivers," 19.

43 Neatby, *Quebec*, 46.

44 Fagniez, *Femme et société française*, 147.

45 Dechêne, *Habitants et marchands*, 423-24.

46 A. Morel, "Réflexions sur la justice criminelle canadienne au 18e siècle," *RHAF* 29 (septembre, 1975), 241-53.

47 Lanctôt, *Filles de joie*, 219.

48 Boyer, *Crimes et Châtiments*, 128-29.

49 W.J. Eccles, Social Welfare Measures and Policies in New France," *Congreso Internacional de Americanistas* 4 (1966), Seville, 9-19.

50 J. Bosher, "Government and Private Interests in New France," in J.M. Bumsted, ed., *Canadian History before Confederation* (Georgetown, Ontario, 1972), 122.

51 Bosher, "The Family," 5-7; Fagniez, *Femme et société française*, 182.

52 Franquet, *Voyages*, 148; cf. also Frégault, *Le XVIIIe siècle canadien* (Montréal, 1968), 292-93.

53 W.J. Eccles, "The Social, Economic and Political Significance of the Military Establishment in New France," *Canadian Historical Review* 52 (March 1971): 8-10.

54 Franquet, *Voyages*, 129-30. For another similar trip, see 140-42.

143

55 Frégault, *Le XVIIIe siècle*, 208–09, 216–21.

56 Frégault, *Le XVIIIe siècle*, 229–30.

57 Y. Zoltvany, *Philippe de Rigaud de Vaudreuil* (Toronto, 1974) 110, 217.

58 Frégault, *Le XVIIIe siècle*, 228–30.

59 W.J. Eccles, *Frontenanc: The Courtier Governor* (Toronto, 1959), 29.

60 *Rapport de l'archiviste de la province de Québec* (1922–23): 151.

61 For example, George Rudé, *The Crowd in the French Revolution* (New York, 1959).

62 Superbly described in E.P. Thompson, *The Making of the English Working Class* (London, 1976), Ch. 3.

63 Cited in T. Crowley, " 'Thunder Gusts': Popular Disturbances in Early French Canada," *CHAR* (1979): 19–20.

64 Jean Hamelin, "What Middle Class?" *Society and Conquest*, Miquelon, ed. (Toronto, 1977), 109–10); and Dechêne, *Habitants et marchands*, 44, who concludes that the largest contingents of male immigrants arriving in seventeenth-century Montreal were *engagés* and soldiers.

65 H. Charbonneau, *Vie et mort de nos ancêtres* (Montréal, 1975), 38; A. Burguière, "Le Rituel du mariage en France: Pratiques ecclésiastiques et pratiques populaires, (XVIe–XVIIIe siècle)," *Annales E.S.C.*, 33e année (mai–juin, 1978): 640; R. Mousnier, *La famille, l'enfant et l'éducation en France et en Grande-Bretagne du XVIe au XVIIIe siècle* (Paris, 1975); Fagniez, *Femme et société française*, 97. Commercial activities, however, also prevailed among the women of Bordeaux, an important port in the Canada trade. Fagniez, *Femme et société française*, 196.

66 Fagniez, *Femme et société française*, 267, 273–74, 311–12, 360–61.

67 Claude Lessard, "L'Aide financière de l'Eglise de France à l'Eglise naissante du Canada," in Pierre Savard, ed., *Mélanges d'histoire du Canada français offerts au professeur Marcel Trudel* (Ottawa, 1978), 175.

68 Fagniez, *Femme et société française*, 311–21.

69 Marcel Trudel, *The Beginnings of New France* (Toronto, 1973), for a gloomy assessment of the neglected colony during this period.

70 G. Brown et al., eds., *Dictionary of Canadian Biography* (herafter *DCB*) (Toronto, 1966–), 1: 118; J. Marshall, ed., *Word from New France* (Toronto, 1967), 2.

71 Fagniez, *Femme et société française*, 320–33, 358. Of course, not all *religieuses* were competent as leaders. Madame de la Peltrie, for example, patron of the Ursuline convent, appears to have been a rather unreliable benefactress. Despite her first-hand knowledge of the difficulties under which the Ursulines laboured, her "charity" was quixotic. In 1642, she suddenly withdrew her support from the Ursulines in order to join the colonists setting off to found Montreal. Later she again held back her funds in favour of a cherished chapel project, even though the Ursulines' lodgings had just burned to the ground.

72 Chabot, "Marie Guyart de l'Incarnation," 27, 37; *DCB* 1: 353; Lessard, "Aide financière," 169–70.

73 *DCB* 1: 483–87; also Lessard, "Aide financière," 175.

74 This is the interpretation given by G. Lanctôt in *Montreal under Maisonneuve* (Toronto, 1969), 20–24, 170.

75 Lanctôt, *Montreal under Maisonneuve*, 188.

76 Lanctôt, *Filles de joie*, 81; Trudel, *Montréal*, 21. The Hôtel-Dieu de Montréal also sponsored immigrants from 1655 to 1662 (Lanctôt, *Filles de joie*, 81.).

77 Trudel, *Montréal*, 84.

78 Eccles, "Social Welfare Measures," 19; F. Rousseau, "Hôpital et société en Nouvelle-France: l'Hôtel-Dieu de Québec à la fin du XVIIe siècle," *RHAF* 31 (juin, 1977): 47.

79 Mousnier, *La famille, l'enfant et l'éducation*, 319–31.

80 Vann, "Women in Preindustrial Capitalism," 208.

81 Trudel, *Montréal*, 276, 87; P. Goubert, *The Ancien Régime* (New York, 1974), 262.

82 Neatby, *Quebec*, 237; French soldiers had a literacy rate of three to four per cent. A Corvisier, *L'Armée française de la fin du XVIIe siècle ou ministère de Choiseul* (Paris, 1964), 862.

83 Fagniez, *Femme et société canadienne*, 191.

84 Séguin, "La Canadienne," 501, lists nine of these schools in addition to the original one in Montreal.

85 Franquet, *Voyages*, 31–32.

86 According to Lanctôt (*Filles de joie*, 121–30), there were 961. Silvio Dumas counts only 774 (*Les Filles du roi en Nouvelle France* [Québec, 1972] 164). Other estimates have ranged between 713 and 857.

87 J.-N. Fauteux, *Essai sur l'industrie au Canada sous le Régime Français* (Québec, 1927), "Introduction."

88 For the record, it now seems fairly well established that the females sent to New France, unlike those sent to the West Indies, were carefully screened, and any of questionable morality were returned by the authorities to France. Lanctôt (*Filles de joie*) and Dumas (*Filles du roi*) agree on this. See also Foulché-Delbosc, "Women of Three Rivers," 22–23.

89 Dechêne finds a majority of *Parisiennes* among the Montréal filles (*Habitants et marchands*, 96). Lanctôt states that one-half of the 1634–63 emigrants were urbanites and that two-thirds of the *filles* were from Île-de-France (*Filles de joie*, 76–79, 124). On education in France, see Mousnier, *La famille, l'enfant et l'éducation*, 319–25.

90 Lanctôt, *Filles de joie*, 110–30, 202.

[91] Dumas, *Filles du roi*, 39, 41, 51-54, 56, 59.

[92] Séguin, "La Canadienne," 492; Franquet, *Voyages*, 57.

[93] J. Henripin, *La population canadienne au début du XVIIIe Siècle* (Paris, 1954), 120. The overall population was 63 per cent male in 1663 (Trudel, *Beginnings*, 261), an imbalance that gradually declined.

[94] Trudel, *Montréal*, 45-47, 108, 113.

[95] Foulché-Delbosc, "Women of Three Rivers," 19.

[96] Cole Harris, *The Seigneurial System in Early Canada* (Québec, 1968), 163.

[97] The richest single source for evidence along these lines is Dechêne's *Habitants et marchands*.

[98] Boyer, *Crimes et châtiments*, 326.

[99] Toronto *Globe and Mail*, 29 October 1979, p. 1; Boyer, *Crimes et châtiments*, 329, 340. Cf. also N. Hawthorne's novel, *The Scarlet Letter*, based on an actual occurrence.

[100] Boyer, *Crimes et châtiments*, 329, 350, 361-62; also Morel, "Justice criminelle canadienne." See also the more recent discussions of women and crime by A. LaChance, "Women and Crime in Canada in the Early Eighteenth Century," in L. Knafla, ed., *Crime and Criminal Justice in Canada* (Calgary, 1981), 157-78.

[101] Dechêne, *Habitants et marchands*, 464.

[102] Séguin, "La Canadienne," 497-99.

[103] Jean Lunn, "The Illegal Fur Trade Out of New France 1713-60," Canadian Historial Association, *Report* (1939), 61-62.

[104] Boyer, *Crimes et châtiments*, 286-87.

[105] Marshall, *Word from New France*, 287-95.

[106] Boyer, *Crimes et châtiments*, 306.

[107] Eccles, "The Social, Economic and Political Significance of the Military."

[108] Charlevoix, *New France*, 3: 35.

[109] Ethel Bennett, "Madame de la Tour, 1602-1645," in M. Innis, ed., *The Clear Spirit* (Toronto, 1966), 21.

[110] *DCB* 3: 308-13.

[111] *DCB* 3: 308-13 Boyer, *Crimes et châtiments*, 338-39.

[112] For a splendid description of the attitudes and lifestyle of this class in France, see P. de Vaissière, *Gentilshommes campagnards de l'ancienne France* (Paris, 1903).

[113] G. Frégault, *Le Grand Marquis* (Montréal, 1952), 74-75; Corvisier, *L'Armée française*, 777.

[114] Corvisier, *L'Armée française*, 762-63, 826.

[115] Franquet, *Voyages* 56, 67-68, 200.

[116] Franquet, *Voyages*, 35, 76, 88.

[117] Dechêne, *Habitants et marchands*, 398; Franquet, *Voyages*, 16.

[118] *DCB* 2: 491.

[119] Marshall, *Word from New France*, 27, 213, 222-23, 233.

[120] Dechêne, *Habitants et marchands*, 393; Franquet, *Voyages*, 199; Foulché-Delbosc, "Women of Three Rivers," 25; Corvisier, *L'Armée française*, 760.

[121] Boyer, *Crimes et châtiments*, 349-51; Dechêne, *Habitants et marchands*, 41. Dechêne concludes that, considering Montreal was a garrison town with a shortage of marriageable women, the degree of prostitution was normal or, to use her term, *conformiste* (437-38).

[122] Eccles, "The Social, Economic and Political Significance of the Military," 11-17; Dechêne, *Habitants et marchands*, 121.

[123] J. Henripin, *Trends and Factors of Fertility in Canada* (Ottawa, 1972), 2; Séguin, "La Canadienne," 495, 503.

[124] Trudel, *Montréal*, 30-33; Charbonneau, *Vie et mort*, 135.

[125] Foulché-Delbosc, "Women of Three Rivers," 25.

[126] Trudel, *Montréal*, 163.

[127] Bennett, "Madame de la Tour," 16; Madame Joybert was the mother of the future Madame de Vaudreuil. *DCB* 1:399. For E. de Grandmaison, see *DCB* 1:345.

[128] Lunn, "Illegal Fur Trade," 62.

[129] Eccles, *Canadian Society*, 61.

[130] Lunn, "Illegal Fur Trade," 61-75.

[131] Franquet, *Voyages*, 120-21.

[132] Lilianne Plamondon, "Une femme d'affaires en Nouvelle-France: Marie-Anne Barbel, Veuve Fornel," *RHAF* 31 (septembre, 1977).

[133] Franquet, *Voyages*, 156-58.

[134] For example, Hamelin in "What Middle Class?" The absence of an indigenous bourgeoisie is also central to the interpretation of Dechêne in *Habitants et marchands*.

[135] Séguin, "La Canadienne," 494.

[136] For accounts of Agathe de Saint-Père, see *DCB* 3: 580-81; Fauteux, *Industrie au Canada*, 464-69; Massicote, *Bulletin des Recherches historiques* (hereafter *BRH*) (1944): 202-07.

[137] Neatby refers to this activity in the early post-Conquest era (*Quebec*, 72-73); Franquet encountered Madame Benoist in 1753 (*Voyages* 150).

[138] For discussion of the De Ramezay's business affairs, see Massicote, *BRH* (1931): 530; Fauteux, *Industrie au Canada*, 158-59, 204-15, 442.

145

[139] *DCB* 2: 548.

[140] Fauteux, *Industrie au Canada*, 158, 297, 420–21, 522; P. Moogk, *Building a House in New France* (Toronto, 1977), 60–64.

[141] Lunn, *Illegal Fur Trade*, 61.

[142] See Moogk (*Building a House*, 8) for one case of a husband's transfer of these powers.

[143] Franquet, *Voyages*, 17.

[144] Dechêne, *Habitants et marchands*, 151–53, 187, 391; Séguin, "La Canadienne," 494.

[145] Charbonneau, *Vie et mort*, 184; Fagniez, *Femme et société française*, 111, 182–84. A recent study by Butel ("Comportements familiaux") has documented the phenomenon of widows taking over the family business in eighteenth-century Bordeaux.

[146] Trudel, *Beginnings*, 250. This was largely due to the enormous holdings of Jean Lauzon's widow. Dechêne, *Habitants et marchands*, 209, 204–05, 393; Plamandon, "Femme d'affaires." W.S. MacNutt, *The Atlantic Provinces* (Toronto, 1965), 25.

[147] This happened on seigneuries as well as in town, as in the case M. de Lanouguère, "a soldier by preference," whose wife, Marguerite-Renée Denys, directed their seigneury (*DCB* 1: 418).

[148] The original version of this paper was written as the result of a stimulating graduate seminar conducted by Professor William J. Eccles at the University of Toronto. My thanks to him, and to others who have offered helpful comments and criticisms, particularly Professors Sylvia Van Kirk and Allan Greer at the University of Toronto. The revised version printed here has benefited from the detailed response of Professor Micheline Dumont to the original version published in the Spring 1981 volume of *Atlantis*. For Professor Dumont's critique of the article, and my reply, see *Atlantis*, 8, 1 (Spring 1982): 118–30.

146 TRANSLATIONS TO FRENCH PASSAGES IN *Les femmes favorisées*

Page 123

[2] Women surpass men in beauty, vivaciousness, cheerfulness and sprightliness; they are coquettish and elegant and prefer Europeans to the local folk. Gentle and polite manners are common, even in the countryside.

[3] . . . the women there are very pleasant but extremely proud.

[4] . . . they are witty, which affords them superiority over men in almost all circumstances.

[5] "surpass men in wit; generally they all have a great deal of it and speak in refined French, without the least accent. They also like finery, are pretty, generous and even genteel."

Page 125

[9] "the law establishes their dominion over their wives."

[11] if the masculine pre-eminence has lost none of its prestige, if it has not had to defend itself against any theoretical claim . . . it has often had to . . . be content with appearances and abandon, in the fact of expediency and public opinion, the substance of its claims.

Page 127

[28] Work, particularly in rural areas, was at that time, based on a division of labour between the sexes: sailors and pedlars were absent for several months, their wives worked the land; the fishermen of the marsh-lands went to the market, the women went fishing; the labourer worked in the fields, his wife worked in the home but it was she who went to market; in the Auge region "the men looked after the livestock and the women attended to the cheese". In order to live, therefore, they had to be a couple, a man and a woman.

Page 129

[45] These matrimonial conventions do not resemble a "marriage market" in which two groups confront each other, but rather an unbiased agreement between the families aiming to create a new community, to help it, if possible, to erect some barriers around it in order to protect it. . . .

[52] "all those of a certain class are linked by kinship and friendship in this country."

Page 130

[56] "Gifted with a very shrewd political sense,"

[58] Pontchartrain, Ruette d'Auteuil reports, refuses her nothing, "she has all the jobs in Canada at her disposal; she writes splendid letters from ports of call everywhere, about the good and the bad that she can do by using her influence with him", and the minister "does everything necessary to support her claims". Riverin confirms that . . . "there is no longer anyone but a woman in charge and she reigns whether she is present or absent."

[60] "in the assembly of the women in this parish, by a majority of votes, to practice as a midwife."

Page 134

[85] These sisters are spread out across the countryside, in seigneuries where they have gone to educate the girls; their usefulness seems to be evident, but the harm which results is like a slow poison which leads to a depopulation of the countryside, given that an educated girl becomes a young lady, puts on airs, wants to set herself up in the city, sets her sights on a merchant and looks upon the circumstances of her birth as beneath her.

Page 136

[101] The officer who was sent to put down the rebellion relates that all the women were waiting for him "with rocks and sticks in their hands to kill me" and that they chased him yelling "stop, thief, we want to kill you and throw you in the swamp."

[106] "in the early days of the colony, women were scarce, prized, protected from mass persecution."

Topic Four

The Early Society of Atlantic Canada

During the fifteenth century, Europe began an age of great expansion, one marked by the development of overseas commerce and the establishment of colonies. The English, the Portuguese, the Basques, and the French were among the earliest Europeans to harvest the rich Newfoundland fishery, and to travel to northeastern North America. Only one European group, as far as we know, had previously visited North America — the Norse, around 1000 A.D. Five centuries after the Norse voyages, European fishermen established a number of seasonal settlements on the Atlantic coast to prepare and dry their fish. One group, the Basques, from what is now the border country on the Bay of Biscay between Spain and France, arrived in the 1520s and '30s. The origins of English-speaking Canada date back to 1583 when Sir Humphrey Gilbert laid claim to Newfoundland. England's fishery off the island soon grew to rival that of France, Spain, and Portugal. Keith Matthews summarizes the first two centuries of English and French settlement in Newfoundland (and the struggle between these groups to control the fishery) in his two lectures, "The Nature of Newfoundland History" and "The Framework of Newfoundland History."

The French established their first permanent settlement on the Atlantic coast in 1604, naming it Acadia (later to become Nova Scotia). Its strategic location near the Gulf of St. Lawrence meant that England and France fought continually for its possession. The region changed hands frequently until 1713, when France ceded Acadia to England in the Treaty of Utrecht. For the next half-century Britain ruled over the colony with its predominantly French-speaking and Roman Catholic population.

The Acadians sought to remain neutral in conflicts between England and France. Initially this was possible, but with the construction of the large French fortress of Louisbourg during the 1720s on Cape Breton Island and the founding of Halifax in 1749, the situation changed. With the revival of hostility between France and England in 1755, Nova Scotia's Lieutenant-Governor, Charles Lawrence, and his council at Halifax insisted that the Acadians take an unconditional oath of allegiance to the British Crown. When they refused, Lawrence expelled approximately

10 000 French Acadians. Naomi Griffiths, in "The Golden Age: Acadian Life, 1713–1748," reviews Acadian society before the expulsion.

For an overview of European exploration in the North Atlantic, consult Samuel Eliot Morison, *The European Discovery of America: The Northern Voyages, A.D. 500–1600* (New York: Oxford University Press, 1971). The context of the Europeans' journeys around the world is given by Daniel J. Boorstin in *The Discoverers: A History of Man's Search to Know His World and Himself* (New York: Random House, 1983). A beautifully illustrated account of the Norse and their arrival in northeastern North America is *The Vikings and Their Predecessors*, by Kate Gordon, with a contribution by Robert McGhee (Ottawa: National Museum of Man, 1981). Three popular accounts of the Basques on the southern Labrador coast are James A. Tuck and Robert Grenier, "A 16th Century Basque Whaling Station in Labrador," *Scientific American* 245, 5 (November 1981): 180–90; Selma Barkham, "From Biscay to the Grand Bay," *Horizon Canada* 1, 1 (1984): 14–19; and the series of articles in the *National Geographic* 168, 1 (July 1985): 40–71, entitled "Discovery in Labrador: A 16th Century Basque Whaling Port and Its Sunken Fleet," with contributions by archaeologists James A. Tuck and Robert Grenier. D.W. Prowse, in *A History of Newfoundland* (London: Macmillan, 1895), and Frederick W. Rowe, in *A History of Newfoundland and Labrador* (Toronto: McGraw-Hill, 1980), deal with early settlement in Newfoundland. Several specialized articles on the early history of Newfoundland appear in *Early European Settlement and Exploration in Atlantic Canada*, ed. G.M. Story (St. John's: Memorial University, 1982). A short summary of Newfoundland's history is given by Gordon Rothney in his booklet *Newfoundland: A History*, Canadian Historical Association, Historial Booklet no. 10 (Ottawa: CHA, 1964).

An abundant literature exists on the Acadians; in fact, by the end of the nineteenth century two hundred books and pamphlets had been written on the subject of the Acadian expulsion alone. A short review of the major issues appears in C. Bruce Fergusson's "The Expulsion of the Acadians," *Dalhousie Review* 35 (1955): 127–35. Good introductions to Acadian society include Naomi Griffith's *The Acadians: Creation of a People* (Toronto: McGraw-Hill Ryerson, 1973); J.B. Brebner's earlier *New England's Outpost: Acadia before the British Conquest of Canada* (New York: Columbia University Press, 1927); and Andrew H. Clark's *Acadia: The Geography of Early Nova Scotia to 1760* (Madison: University of Wisconsin Press, 1968). For an award-winning account of life at Louisbourg, consult Christopher Moore's *Louisbourg Portraits: Five Dramatic True Tales of People Who Lived in an Eighteenth Century Garrison Town* (Toronto: Macmillan, 1982). Many valuable maps on early Atlantic Canada appear in the *Historical Atlas of Canada*, vol. 1, *From the Beginning to 1800*, ed. R. Cole Harris (Toronto: University of Toronto Press, 1987).

The Nature and the Framework of Newfoundland History*

KEITH MATTHEWS

The Nature of Newfoundland History

The basic factor in Newfoundland history is that which underlies many events in modern times — the expansion of Western Europe, which in the fifteenth century began to emerge from self-containment and comparative isolation to seek out and eventually to dominate vast areas in other parts of the world. This expansion took the form of overseas commerce and the establishment of colonies beyond the seas. From the very earliest days the Newfoundland fishery formed an important element in the development of European trans-oceanic commerce, and while the establishment of a settlement upon the Island occurred comparatively late when compared with those of the Spanish and Portuguese in South America, it was one of the first settlements to be attempted by the English who eventually possessed Newfoundland. Even more, it was through the "migratory" fishery wherein men from the west of England came annually to fish here that the English first acquired the seamanship interest in and knowledge of the North American world which enabled them to develop what eventually became a world-wide empire.

This brings us to a seeming paradox. This was the first part of North America to be visited by Englishmen and amongst the first areas to receive English settlers, and yet the Island's economic, social, and political development was painfully slow when compared to the West Indian colonies, or the thirteen British colonies in what is now the United States of America. This is one of the greatest puzzles of Newfoundland history, and in the lectures following we will try to find answers to it. We know that Newfoundland was not neglected because it was thought unimportant, for the Newfoundland fishery, the Grand Cod Fishery of the Universe as Pitt the Elder described it, was considered to be one of the most important foreign trades carried on from Western Europe. As early as 1620 it was said that without Newfoundland dried cod, Spain and Italy could hardly live, while France and England quarrelled, competed, and often fought over the right to control the fishery. If one thinks of the importance of the Grand Bank fishery to the fleets of many nations today, it is hardly surprising that ever since the discovery of the New World, it has been eagerly sought after by Europeans.

149

*From *Lectures on the History of Newfoundland: 1500-1830*, Newfoundland History Series, vol. 4. Copyright by M. Kathleen Matthews. Reprinted with the permission of Breakwater Press.

We can say therefore that the history of Newfoundland has been shaped by its fishery and by the international competition which arose around it.

The fishery alone attracted men to Newfoundland and in the competition for the fishery, the Island fell almost as a by-product into the hands of the English who won the struggle. The old west country fishermen of the seventeenth century had a rhyme; "If it were not for wood, water, and fish, Newfoundland were not worth a rush," and for the fishermen and for the nations they came from, that saying expressed almost all that was valued here. As can be seen today, the fishery could be carried on without necessarily occupying the land, but if you wanted to make the light salted "shore" fish for which Newfoundland became famous, then you needed "fishing rooms" in the harbours along the coast, and the first struggles over the Island, as distinct from the fishery, occurred as men quarrelled about who should take possession of the best fishing rooms. Yet the fact remained, the hopes and dreams of the first settlers notwithstanding, Newfoundland was valued only as a fishery and the Island as a great ship moored near the banks.

150

We know that the English won control over the Island of Newfoundland, but we should not assume that this was inevitable. Indeed until the last twenty years of the sixteenth century, her fishery at Newfoundland was puny when compared to that of France, Spain, or even Portugal. Why then did she emerge as the dominant nation? We will discuss this question quite often during the course of the series.

Newfoundland depended upon the fishery for its very life and that was established long before the first settlers came out to plant. The international fishery had developed its own rough laws and customs which took no account of the possibility of permanent settlement. In the rest of the New World, European settlers came out to virgin territory, unpopulated and unvisited by other Europeans, so that, able to ignore the native peoples as savages, they could do what they pleased. This was not true of Newfoundland for the first English settlers arrived to find thousands of English fishermen and many more of France, Portugal, and Spain who also claimed the right to use the Island for making fish. England claimed to own Newfoundland but France also laid claim to it and Spain could at least claim that she had anciently used the land for her fishing. Thus from the outset, colonisation in Newfoundland was radically different from that of the rest of the New World. Four nations claimed rights, thousands of men from different countries were established here, and settlement had to take account of this.

The experiences of the first settlers soon showed that they, as much as the visiting fishermen, must go a-fishing if they wanted to make a living for the land was infertile and our mining industry did not develop until the nineteenth century. Thus the settlers became completely dependent upon an uncertain industry which not even the merchants who bought their fish could control, for the fish had to be sold in foreign countries in Southern Europe. Unlike the settlers of the English mainland colonies, those in Newfoundland could not even hope to become self-sufficient, for the infertility of the soil, the shortness of the growing season, and (until the mid-eighteenth century) the lack of a hardy crop like the potato meant that almost all of the food they consumed had to be imported from abroad. If you kept a cow here in the seventeenth century, you might have to import hay from Boston to keep it alive during the winter. The fishing season lasted only during the summer so that a settler had to make enough money in three or four months to buy all that he needed to live for twelve and almost everything that he ate, wore, or used had to be imported and paid for with fish. It was a hard life and not many people wanted to emigrate here. However, for anyone who knew how to fish, a good living could be made, so that most of the early settlers were men from the west of England who, bred up to the trade by coming here annually to fish, decided for various reasons to settle down for a while at least and try the life of a "planter."

151

The origins of these early colonists made Newfoundland rather different from the English mainland colonies. There, men had come out from many different regions of Europe and for many different reasons, but most of them expected to "make a new life" and to leave the Old World behind forever. Those who came to Newfoundland, however, came out to fish and having relatives and friends back in the west of England (or later in Southern Ireland), could always return to their homes on a fishing ship anytime they wanted to. Many of our settlers were indeed indentured servants hired to come out and work here for two or three years before returning to Britain. This was in marked contrast to the rest of North America.

By 1800 the mainland colonies contained settlers from many different regions of Europe for the need to develop the land created a great demand for labour and called for skills which were widespread through much of Western Europe. In Newfoundland the demand was for skilled fishermen only — no one came to Newfoundland to go farming, and commerce and industry were only just beginning to develop. Only the French and the English knew anything about fishing in Newfoundland, and the French, after 1713, were not allowed to live here. This left the English and Irish as the only possible colonisers of our Province. In England, only the people living in the "West Country" counties of Devonshire, Dorset, Somerset, and Hampshire knew anything about the fishery, and most of the Irishmen came out via Waterford and Cork; two ports on the south coast of Ireland which had much contact with Newfoundland.

They were drawn mainly from four counties around those cities. Thus our population was remarkably homogeneous compared with North America as a whole, and of course it has largely remained so.

The fishery first drew men to Newfoundland; the fishery shaped the policies of the nations concerned in it; the fishery both created and limited the way of life of the colonists; and the fishery, through its fluctuating prosperity, its assumed value to Europe, and the conflicts it caused, determined when, where, in what numbers, and under what conditions the colonists should settle. By 1670 English settlement in Newfoundland had become firmly established, but England did not possess the entire Island. France had established settlements in Placentia Bay and at St. Mary's, and she and the Spanish monopolised the fishery north of Bonavista Bay. The English fishery in Newfoundland was confined to what is in some places still referred to as the "Old English Shore," a region stretching from Trepassey to Greenspond. Only in this area could English col-

onists find protection and here English settlement was confined until 1713. This was not a great handicap at the time for the area contained excellent fishing grounds and harbours for shipping and for making fish, but as the first region of English settlement, it continued to be the major region of population on the Island until the present century and contains the oldest settler families here. Expansion of settlement to the rest of Newfoundland had to await the evacuation of other nations and a growth in the population and fishery of Newfoundland which would make men want to exploit the other fishing areas, while the development of inland communities had to await this present century, for the population lived only by fishing. As a result, Newfoundland lacked a natural "centre" which could link together the many communities and regions into one whole "community." All communications were by sea, and each bay had its own major commercial centres which were independent of the others, importing and exporting goods and people directly from and to the outside world. The towns of the west of England which controlled the fishery at Newfoundland "divided up" the English shore, with particular parts of the west of England fishing only along particular parts of the Newfoundland coast. Thus the settlers who came to the various communities and bays chose their place of residence from the ports which their ship came to. Since the merchants of Poole, for example, controlled all the trade of Trinity and Bonavista Bays, most of the English settlers there came from the counties of Dorset, Hampshire, and Somerset. The "Southern Shore" from Torbay to Trepassey was fished by the fishermen and merchants of South Devon, so that most of the English settlers there came from the same region. It might be said that until the nineteenth century there was no "community" of Newfoundland, but a series of separate cultural and economic bays independent of and relatively indifferent to each other. This feeling exists even today in some forms.

Only with the rise of St. John's as the commercial and political capital of the Island did the feeling of distinctness and independence between the bays begin to decline, and this did not begin to happen until late in the eighteenth century.

These are some of the themes in Newfoundland history. Beginning as an international fishery, the Island became a largely British fishery carried on by a mixture of settlers and visiting fishermen, then an English colony, and finally a distinctive "community" with an identity and culture of its own.

The Framework of Newfoundland History

In the last lecture I mentioned that the main theme of our history was the manner in which Newfoundland changed from an international fishery to a largely British fishery and finally to a distinctive community on its own. This change took over 300 years and was caused by the ever changing pressures of events and the decisions and conflicts of men. To enable you to understand how these changes occurred I am devoting this lecture to a breakdown of that long period of time into seven distinct periods. With this chronology in mind the lectures which follow can be more easily understood.

153

The first period we will call the period of anarchy. It begins with the rediscovery of the Island by Europeans in the fifteenth century and ends in 1610 with the establishment of an English colony in Newfoundland. John Cabot claimed the Island for England by right of discovery, but this meant little, for England at this time was weak and backward, her naval and commercial strength were undeveloped and she was absorbed in the aftermath of the Wars of the Roses. Although English fishermen soon followed Cabot, they were few in number and the French and Portuguese nations soon outstripped the English in the Newfoundland fishery. By 1640 Spain, with her enormous wealth and power, had also become important in the fishery and all nations were soon competing to develop their interests at the expense of their neighbours. In Europe the shifting alliances of nations saw many wars and the fighting inevitably spread to the Newfoundland fishing fleets. Obsessed with these conflicts no nation attempted to establish a colony on the Island, although in the second half of the sixteenth century individuals in both France and England began to think of doing so. While Europe quarrelled, the international fishery in Newfoundland grew chaotically with no one to keep the peace either between the national groups or even within them. To solve this problem the fishermen gradually evolved a code of customs which, unrecognised by any government, at least attempted to control the anarchy and violence amongst the fishing fleets. As late as 1570 the

English still lagged far behind their competitors in the size of their fishery, yet the complex changes which occurred in Western Europe between then and 1600 created conditions in the Newfoundland trade which by 1700 had made England equal in importance to France while the fisheries of Spain and Portugal were in irreversible decline.

The next period in Newfoundland's history lasted between 1610 and 1660 and may be called the era of English settlement. With the end of the European conflict in 1604 nations turned to trade and colonisation, and both the French and English fisheries prospered well. By 1620 a de facto division of the land was taking place, each nation gradually confining its fishing operations to separate parts of the coast. The English fished along what became known as the "Old English Shore" stretching from Trepassey to Greenspond, while the French used the south coast and the area North of Bonavista Bay. This process was not the result of any international agreement and occurred only gradually and for a time; the Spanish and Portuguese continued to fish wherever they could find harbour room. England laid claim to most of Newfoundland but France too claimed sovereignty, and in practice each contented itself with what it could control. The English domination of the Avalon Peninsula turned men's thoughts towards the possibility of establishing colonies here which, paying their way by fishing, logging, agriculture, mining and even manufacturing, might become profitable to their promoters and help to secure the fishery for England. However, repeated attempts ended in failure for the settlements could not be made to return a profit. There was also conflict between the proprietors of some colonies and the already established English migratory fishery. The English Civil War brought chaos and ruin to the fishery, but although the Proprietary Colonies failed, groups of settlers had become firmly established on the Island.

The third period lasted from 1660 to 1713 and was the period of Anglo-French rivalry within the Island itself. Until 1659 France claimed sovereignty over parts of Newfoundland but, developing her colonies on the mainland and in the West Indies, did not formally plant here. In 1662 however she established a settlement in her main fishing area at Placentia and for a few years energetically promoted schemes to increase settlement. Simultaneously, the end of war in Europe saw a great revival in the French fishery which by 1675 was seriously affecting the fortunes of that of the English. The latter were in a state of decline, for the long wars and a series of disastrous fishing seasons in the 1660s had ruined the west of England merchants and captains. The old methods of fishing no longer sufficed and new ones were required. Both the settlers and visiting fishermen were ruined by the declining fishery and the latter attempted to have the settlers removed. The British government alone could decide upon this, and at first they agreed that settlement should be ended. However, they quickly changed their mind, but were unable to decide whether the Island should be formally recognised as a colony. For twenty years after 1680 the government followed a policy of having no policy and the Island was left to develop as best it could. In 1689 King William's War broke out and with an intermission between 1697 and 1701 the conflict lasted until 1713. The fighting both here and in Europe had drastic effects upon Newfoundland, and the government was forced to formulate some kind of policy towards her. That policy was unworkable, but the war obscured this to some degree. In 1713 by the Treaty of Utrecht France ceded her colony on the south coast to England and admitted English sovereignty over the entire Island. However, she obtained certain fishing rights along parts of the coast and the "French shore" problem began its wearying course. The war had also obscured fundamental changes within the fishery which were changing the old division between "settlers" and "migratory" fishermen, bringing them together under the west country merchants.

Newfoundland underwent a new series of adaptations in what I will call the era of integration within the English fishery between 1713 and 1763. English settlement expanded into the south coast and as far up as Fogo and Twillingate. The fishery continued to be poor until the

155

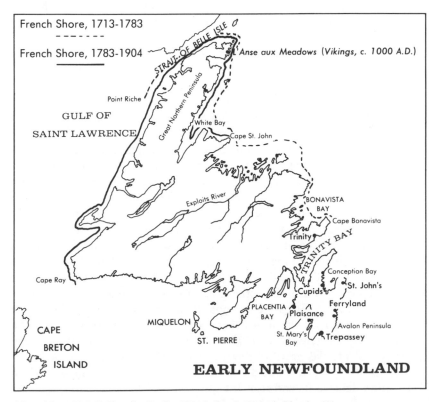

French Shore, 1713-1783
- - - - - - -
French Shore, 1783-1904

STRAIT OF BELLE ISLE

Anse aux Meadows (*Vikings, c. 1000 A.D.*)

Point Riche

GULF OF
SAINT LAWRENCE

Great Northern Peninsula

White Bay

Cape St. John

Exploits River

BONAVISTA BAY

Cape Bonavista

Trinity

TRINITY BAY

Conception Bay

Cape Ray

Cupids

St. John's

Ferryland

PLACENTIA BAY

Plaisance

Avalon Peninsula

MIQUELON

ST. PIERRE

St. Mary's Bay

Trepassey

CAPE BRETON ISLAND

EARLY NEWFOUNDLAND

Adapted from Cornell, Hamelin, Ouellet, Trudel, *Canada: Unity in Diversity*, 111.

late 1720s but the need for men to move into the newly ceded south coast resulted in the beginnings of large scale Irish emigration to Newfoundland with enormous effects upon its future history. Men found that the attempt to divide the Island into an area monopolised by the English and another shared between them and the French created much friction, but the French had lost their best fishing grounds, their competition in Europe gradually diminished and from 1730 onwards the English fishery began to prosper well. The English soon developed a thriving bank fishery which together with the bye boat keepers formed the backbone of the migratory English fishery causing not only its revival but a steady expansion by 1750.

It was an era when the merchants of London withdrew from the fishery which was now almost monopolised by merchants and fishermen of the west of England. After 1748 the population began to rise steadily and during the Seven Years' War (1756–1763) English fishermen for the first time learned of the rich fishing grounds along the Northern Peninsula and even more important on the Labrador. The British government was forced by increasing population to introduce a rudimentary civil government, and there was an end to discord between the settlers and the visiting fishermen. The Seven Years' War resulted in the English conquest of Canada and laid the conditions for an even larger expansion in Newfoundland after 1763.

Period five was short, lasting only from 1763 until 1775 when the outbreak of the American Revolution portended great changes for Newfoundland. However, it was a period of great prosperity and growth both in settlement and in the fortunes of the fishery. The Treaty of Paris in 1763, amongst other things, ceded the French possessions in Canada to Britain, and the English government decided to attach Labrador and the Magdalen Islands to Newfoundland. Thus began the Labrador fishery. In Europe the markets for Newfoundland fish continued to grow and for almost the entire period the fishery proved unusually successful. This created a great demand for ships, seamen, and fishermen, so that both the migratory and the sedentary fishery grew quickly and the population rose. However, after a long period of neglect the British government again looked at the question of how Newfoundland should be governed. Their first thought was to create a formal colony, but a change of government and the advent of Governor Palliser caused an abrupt change of mind. Alarmed by the growth of settlement the government sought to discourage it and to promote the migratory fishery. This policy was first adapted for the new fishery at Labrador, where it failed. The government persisted and in 1775 Palliser's Act was passed. It signalled a renewal of official hostility towards the settlers, but was viewed with intense hostility by the merchants, and the outbreak of the American Revolution delayed its enforcement.

The sixth period lasted from the beginning of the American Revolution in 1775 to the outbreak of the French Revolutionary Wars in 1793. Before 1775 America had been a great competitor to Newfoundland in the fishery, but it had also become almost the only supplier of shipping, foodstuffs, and rum without which the settlers could not live. The outbreak of war abruptly severed the supply routes between America and Newfoundland and caused great but temporary problems. The war itself had great effects on the fishery but even more important was the result. American independence took the United States out of the British Empire and her vessels could no longer bring supplies. Neither could fishermen and merchants buy American shipping and America could no longer supply the British West Indies with fish. In the years before 1775 anyone who wanted to leave Newfoundland during a time of depression could easily find a ship to take him to Boston. Now this was no longer possible and he would be forced to remain on the Island if he could not return to England or Ireland. The supply links with the American colonies were slowly replaced by links with the Maritimes of Canada and with Quebec. Newfoundland built its own ships and took over the West Indian markets for fish. From 1783 to 1789 there was a great post-war boom in the fishery which again caused a rapid increase in settlement. In 1789 the boom collapsed, but the population did not decline greatly as had been the case in past depressions. The migratory fishery began to decline and by 1793 it was becoming clear that Newfoundland now had a population which was too large to be moved, which could not even be discouraged from growing, and which was in desperate need of better government and laws. The British government was forced to abandon its policy of discouraging settlement and the future of the Island was assured.

157

Our last period commences with the outbreak of war in 1793 and lasts until 1832. It may be called the "era of Newfoundland's emergence as an independent community." The long and difficult wars killed the migratory fishery and made all dependent upon the resident fishermen. Until 1810 it was difficult to obtain labour from England or Ireland, but natural increase amongst the Newfoundland population kept it growing and restricted wartime markets meant that no more labour was required. From 1811 to 1815 the gradual re-opening of the European markets together with the temporary extinction of every fishing competitor with the exception of Canada created one of the greatest booms that Newfoundland had ever known. In response thousands of men poured into Newfoundland, especially from Southern Ireland. The Labrador seal and cod fisheries gave additional sources of employment, and there was a great boom in shipbuilding for the Labrador and the coastal trades. St. John's became truly the capital of Newfoundland, and the growth of a large more or less resident middle class led to the development of social and political consciousness which led to the formation of groups and institutions devoted to charitable, social, and eventually political ends. This middle class became the ruling elite of the Island and took the lead in the definition of a distinct Newfoundland consciousness, first expressed in the desire for internal self-government.

The Golden Age: Acadian Life, 1713–1748*

NAOMI GRIFFITHS

Until the 1950s Acadian history was most frequently written either as epic or as case study — as the drama of a people or as an example of the political and diplomatic struggles between great powers. The tragic nature of the deportation in 1755 seemed the obvious and fundamental starting point for all that the Acadians experienced since, and equally the culmination of everything that had occurred in their previous history. In the last thirty years, however, an ever-increasing number of scholarly works have been devoted to the examination of Acadian history from much more complex perspectives. These include attempts to analyze not merely 1755 as an event of major importance in the war between English and French for North America, but also works centred upon Acadian language,[1] folklore,[2] geography,[3] sociology,[4] as well as upon Acadian history as the history of a developing community.

Acadian studies have, in fact, come to an impressive maturity over the past thirty years. This maturity is magnificently documented in the work edited by Jean Daigle, *Les Acadians des Maritimes*, where some twenty scholars present complex essays outlining the problems, the work done, and the work to be done in every area of Acadian studies from history to folklore, from political science to material culture.[5] The result of all this publication is, of course, the temptation, if not the necessity, for present scholars to look at past syntheses of Acadian history, to discover where the new information demands new theories, and to build, if not entirely new interpretations of the Acadian past, at least interpretations which are more richly decorated and more densely structured.

This challenge is as dangerous as it is irresistible, for the amount of material is considerable indeed. As a result, this paper is a cautious one. Its main aim is to paint Acadian life between 1713 and 1748 in such a way that the reader may sense the complex nature of the Acadian community during these years. This was the period to be remembered by the community in exile after 1755. All those over the age of ten or eleven in 1755 would have had some knowledge of these years. It was the time that would be recalled in exile and the time which would form

*Griffiths, Naomi, "The Golden Age: Acadian Life, 1713-1748," *Social History* 17, 33 (May 1984): 21–34. Reprinted by permission.

the basis for the stories of past life as the Acadians once more established themselves in the Maritimes. It spanned the decades from the Treaty of Utrecht to that of Aix-la-Chapelle, during which years the lands on which the Acadians lived turned from being the border between two empires to the frontier between enemies.

The political geography of "Nova Scotia or Acadia," as the lands were called in the contemporary international treaties, had meant turmoil for its inhabitants from the outset of European colonization. As J.B. Brebner wrote, these lands were "the eastern outpost and flank for both French and English in North America." They made, in his words, a "continental cornice." Throughout the seventeenth century this cornice frequently changed hands between English and French. It became a true border, for whatever name it was given and whatever limits were claimed, it lay "inside the angle between the St. Lawrence route to French Canada

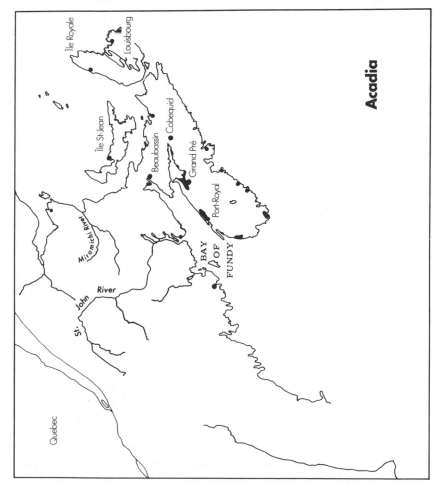

Adapted from Cornell, Hamelin, Ouellet, Trudel, *Canada: Unity in Diversity*, 121.

and the northern route to New England which branched off from it south of Newfoundland."[6] Those who settled there in the seventeenth century would quickly find their situation akin to such people as the Basques caught between France and Spain, the Alsatians moulded by French and German designs, and those who lived on the borders between England and Scotland or England and Wales.

It was the French who began the first permanent settlement in the area in 1604. Whatever the international designation of the colony over the next century, its non-Indian people would be called the Acadians. While predominantly French-speaking and Catholic, they were nevertheless a people who also absorbed English-speaking migrants such as the Melansons[7] and the Caisseys.[8] They also had a considerable knowledge of the Protestant religion, and it is very probable that some of the families who joined them from near Loudun in the 1630s were of the reform church.[9] By the end of the century the Acadians had known one lengthy and legitimate period of English rule, 1654–1668, as well as a number of much shorter periods of English control as a result of raids out of Massachusetts. By 1700 the Acadians were, as the detailed work of Professors Daigle and Reid has shown,[10] almost as accustomed to dealing with the officials of England as those of France. Thus the defeat of Subercase in 1710 and the subsequent transfer of the colony once more to English control by the treaty of Utrecht was for the Acadians yet one more step in a complicated ritual, an exchange of control over them from France to England, something which had happened before and would most probably be reversed in the not too distant future.

This fundamental belief in the mutability of power, this dominant sense of the probability of alternate French and English control of the colony, became the cornerstone of Acadian politics during the years 1713 to 1748. It was the basis for the Acadian action over requests made by the English officials that they swear an oath of allegiance to the King of England. From the Acadian viewpoint, it would have been folly indeed to engage in any action which would bind them irrevocably to one Great Power when the other was still not only obviously in the neighbourhood, but even more obviously still interested in the future status of the colony and its inhabitants. Thus the Acadians built a policy compounded of delay and compromise. The oath to George I was first rejected outright; among other reasons they presented for the refusal, the Acadians of Minas remarked that "pendant que nos ancetres ont étés sous la domination angloise on ne leur a jamais exigé de pareille Sermente. . . . "[11] Later on oaths were taken to George II, but in such circumstances as to enable the Acadians to believe that they had been granted the right to remain neutral. In fact, as Brebner pointed out, the practice of both English and French of referring to them from 1730 on as either "les français neutres" or "the Neutral French" indicates that this accommodation was generally tolerated, if not accepted, by those in power during these years.[12]

However it might have looked to outsiders, the question of neutrality was serious enough to the Acadians. It was in fact a consistent policy that was first enunciated in 1717 by the Acadians of Annapolis Royal and later adhered to by them, and others in time of war. On being asked for an oath of allegiance to George I, the response of Annapolis Royal Acadians was a refusal, the reasons given being that matters of religious freedom were not yet clarified and danger from Indians, who were bound to disapprove friendship between Acadian and English, led to fears for Acadian security. Nevertheless, the response continued, "we are ready to take an oath that we will take up arms neither against his Britannic Majesty, nor against France, nor against any of their subjects or allies."[13] In 1744 when hostilities broke out between English and French in North America, Mascerene, then the lieutenant-governor of the colony, wrote to his masters in London: "These latter [i.e., the French inhabitants] have given me assurances of their resolutions to keep in their fidelity to his Majesty".[14] Mascerene was convinced that had the Acadians not remained neutral during the hostilities, the colony would have fallen to the French.[15] Certainly there is more than enough evidence to show the Acadian dislike of the war, including a most strongly worded letter from those of Grand-Pré to the French, pointing out forcibly that the village preferred peace to war, tranquility and food to soldiers fighting across their farmlands.[16]

161

There is no doubt that between 1713 and 1748 the majority of the Acadians strove to live on their land truly as neutrals, giving loyalty to neither French nor English. This policy procured for their communities nearly thirty-five years of peace, but its final failure in 1755 has overshadowed its earlier success. It is worth emphasizing that it was a policy, not merely a series of inconsistent, unconnected reactions to the demands made by English and French. It was transmitted by delegates from the several Acadian communities to the English officials on a number of separate occasions and, as has been suggested, adhered to during a time of considerable pressure in the 1740s. It was a policy that produced peace and quiet for the Acadian communities, however catastrophic it finally proved to be. Its evolution and development gave the Acadians a knowledge of political action and a sense of their independent reality that would prove invaluable to them when they confronted the vicissitudes of the deportation.[17] Above all, it was the framework for the expansion and development of the Acadian communities between 1713 and 1748.

The demographic expansion of the Acadians during these years is a commonplace in one sense; in another it is something acknowledged rather than fully understood. As Gysa Hynes wrote in 1973, "the rapid natural increase of the population of the Acadians during the period from 1650 to 1750 . . . has long been recognised, but no historian has explored the demography of Acadia before the Dispersion."[18] As a result, while it is generally agreed that the Acadian population probably doubled every twenty years between 1713 and the early 1750s without the aid of any considerable immigration, there has been little real analysis of this development.[19] Gisa Hynes's excellent article was a pioneer study relating above all to Port Royal/Annapolis Royal and has not been followed by much else. Enough raw material does exist, however, to outline the tantalizing landscape waiting to be fully explored, a demographic territory which differs significantly from contemporary Europe and also, in some considerable measure, from that of other colonial settlements in North America.

It is a debatable point whether the longevity of the Acadians or their fertility should receive most comment. At a time when only 50 percent of the population reached the age of 21 in France, 75 percent reached adulthood in Port Royal.[20] Further, while mortality did take its toll during the middle years, death coming through accident and injury rather than epidemic, old age was a common enough phenomenon. In fact at the time of the Treaty of Utrecht, when the French were making every effort to withdraw the Acadians from land ceded to the English and to establish them on Isle Royal (Cape Breton), one of the priests noted that the Acadians refused to go because

162

> It would be to expose us manifestly [they say] to die of hunger burthened as we are with large families, to quit the dwelling places and clearances from which we derive our usual subsistence, without any other resource, to take rough, new lands, from which the standing wood must be removed. One fourth of our population consists of aged persons, unfit for the labour of breaking up new lands, and who, with great exertion, are able to cultivate the cleared ground which supplied subsistence for them and their families.[21]

The presence of an older generation in the community meant a rich heritage of memories of past politics. Any Acadian over forty-two in 1713 would have been born when the colony was controlled by the English, for the terms of the Treaty of Breda were not honoured by Temple until 10 January 1671. Any Acadian over twenty-five would have personal memories of the stormy raids by New Englanders on their villages and of the French counter-measures. The reality of life on a border would be a commonplace for Acadian reminiscences in a community whose people lived long enough to remember.

If Acadians could see relatively long life as a possibility, they could also see life itself as abundant. From the travelling French surgeon-poet Dièreville to the almost equally travelling English official, Governor Philipps, the observations were the same. In 1699 the Frenchman wrote that "the swarming of Brats is a sight to behold."[22] The Englishman commented in 1730 on the Acadians' ability to increase and spread "themselves over the face of the province . . . like Noah's progeny."[23] Present day research has confirmed the accuracy of these impressions.

Gisa Hynes discovered in her analysis of Port Royal that four out of five marriages were complete, that is "were not disrupted by the death of husband or wife before the onset of menopause."[24] In these marriages, if the women were under 20 on their wedding day, they had some ten or eleven children; those wedded between 20 and 24, nine children; and those married in their late 20s, seven or eight children.[25] For the population as a whole, it is probable that the average family in the colony had six or seven children.[26]

These bare statistical bones of Acadian family life can now be covered first with the skin of individual family genealogy and then clothed with the fabric of community life. As an example of the first, there is the life of Claude Landry, born in 1663, the youngest of some ten children of René Landry of Port Royal, who himself had arrived in the colony sometime in the 1640s from Loudun.[27] When he was about eighteen, Claude married Catherine Thibodeau, whose father had been an associate of Emmanuel LeBorgne and come to the colony from around Poitiers in the 1650s.[28] She was the fifth child in a family of sixteen, eleven of whom reached adulthood.[29] Catherine was apparently fifteen when married and bore her first child within the year. She had some ten children in all, eight of whom lived to maturity.

163

The young couple moved very early in their marriage to Grand-Pré where they brought up their family and watched their children's children flourish. When Claude Landry died in 1747, aged eighty-six, his grandchildren through the male line numbered forty-six and his great-grandchildren, also through the male line, eleven. Claude's last child, a son, had been born in 1708; his first grandson was born in 1710. Between 1717 and 1747 there was only one year in which no birth is recorded for his sons, and it is not unlikely that one of Claude's two daughters might have had a child that year. 1735 saw the birth of the first great-grandchild within the male line.[30]

The growth of such extended families was supported by a healthy mixed economy, based upon farming, hunting, and fishing with enough trade, both legal and illegal, to make life interesting. In Grand-Pré the Landry family was part of the flourishing development which Mascerene had described in 1730 as "a platt of Meadow, which stretches near four leagues, part of which is damn'd [sic] in from the tide, and produced very good wheat and pease."[31] Westward this great marsh is edged by the massive presence of Cape Blomidon, the tides of the Bay of Fundy curve across its northern shore, and wooded uplands circumscribe its other boundaries. Between 1710, when the first grandson was born, and 1747, when Claude died, the population of the area grew from well under a thousand to something more than four thousand.[32] The community lived in houses scattered across the landscape, not grouped close together in a village. Charles Morris, who was commissioned by Governor Shirley of Massachusetts to make a survey of the Bay of Fundy area in 1747, reported that the dwellings were "low Houses fram'd of timber and their

Chimney framed with the Building of wood and lined with Clay except the fireplace below. . . . "[33] Very often the houses sheltered a mixture of families, and the sheer work required to provide them necessities of life must have been considerable.[34]

The daily life of both men and women would be governed by the seasons, for the frame of the economy was what was grown and raised for food and clothing. Fishing, hunting, and trade could and did provide important additions to this base, but the standard of living of the majority of the Acadians depended upon the produce of their land-holdings. At the very least a household would possess a garden, and from the seventeenth century on travellers had noticed the variety and abundance of vegetables grown. Dièreville, whose evidence is of the close of the seventeenth century, remarked upon the wealth of cabbages and turnips,[35] and another report of the same period lists the gardens as including "choux, betteraves, oignons, carottes, cives, eschalottes, navets, panets et touttes sortes de salades."[36] Most families would have also an amount of land varying in size between that of a smallholding and a farm, depending on where the community was in the colony and what level of resources the family in question could command. A.H. Clark considered that the households of Grand-Pré and the surrounding area usually had five to ten acres of dyked and tilled farmland within the marsh, supplemented with an orchard situated on the upland slopes. Morris reported the marshlands to be "Naturally of a Fertile Soil . . . and . . . of so strong and lasting a Nature that their Crops are not Diminished in ten or twenty years Constant Tillage."[37] The crops sown included most of the grain crops common to western Europe: wheat, oats, rye, and barley, as well as peas, hemp, and flax. Writing in 1757 another traveller remarked on the abundance of fruit trees, apples, pears, "cherry and plumb trees," and noted that "finer flavoured apples and greater variety, cannot in any other country be produced."[38]

Working with the land, whether garden or farm, did not only imply digging and ploughing, weeding and gathering. There was also the care of livestock. Poultry was everywhere about, as much for feathers as for the eggs and meat. Down-filled mattresses and coverlets were a noted Acadian possession, and the export of feathers to Louisbourg a common item of trade.[39] Pigs rooting around the houses were so common that few surveyors interested in estimating Acadian wealth even bothered to count them. A number of observers, however, remarked on the Acadian liking for fat-back (*le lard*), which could be cooked with cabbage or fried and added to whatever vegetables were available.[40] Sheep were also numerous, raised for wool rather than for meat. Most households would also possess cows and a horse. The estimation of the total livestock in the colony varies widely since the Acadians, like most peasant populations, had no great wish to inform any official of the true extent of their possessions. Life must have been sustained at considerably more than bare subsistence, however, since extant records show that in the

1740s the Acadians, particularly those of Grand-Pré and of the Minas basin in general, were able to export cattle, sheep, pigs, and poultry to Louisbourg.[41] While the authorities at Annapolis Royal thundered against such trade, they also admitted that the Acadians were no worse than others, noting that "there is so great an illicit Trade carried on by the People of Massachusetts Bay and New Hampshire."[42] As has been suggested, the trade that existed was enough to make life for the Acadians interesting, and the goods imported included not only necessities such as "Spanish Iron, French Linnens, Sail Cloth Wollen cloths," but also "Rum, Molasses, Wine and Brandy."[43]

The sum of this evidence suggests an excellent standard of living among the Acadians, something which showed, of course, in the population increase of the first half of the eighteenth century. While there is little evidence of luxury, there is less of poverty. The staples of life, food, shelter, and clothing were abundant, even if the abundance was available only after hard work. Further, the absence of conspicuous consumption and the lack of development of towns and industry in no way meant an absence of specie. It is clear from the records of the deportation itself that Acadians took coinage with them into exile.[44] The Acadian community did not have the rate of economic growth that the New Englanders possessed, but it provided amply for the totality of individuals. Fishing and hunting added to the resources of the households. Charles Morris remarked that the population around Grand-Pré "had some shallops, in which they employed themselves in the catching of Fish just upon their Harbours, being out but a few days at a Time; This was rather for their Home Consumption than the foreign Market. . . . "[45] Clark remarked that the Acadians were "particularly interested in salmon, shad, gaspereau, and the like during their spring runs up the rivers and creeks. . . . "[46] As for hunting, it was less the meat that was immediately valued than the furs. Game was sought in order to sell it in Annapolis Royal,[47] but "avec les fourrures d'ours, de castor, de renard, de loutre, et de martre," they had material which gave them "non seulement le comfort, mais bien souvent de jolis vêtements."[48] Dièreville had also commented on the way in which the Acadians made shoes from sealskin and the hides of moose.[49]

Given the considerable work necessary to turn the resources of their environment into food and clothing for the family, it is extraordinary that the Acadians should have been criticized for being idle.[50] The tools they worked with were scarcely labour-saving devices and were basically of their own manufacture. Clark has listed the main implements available to them as "pickaxes, axes, hoes, sickles, scythes, flails, and wooden forks and rakes," as well, of course, as spades, essential for dyke-building.[51] They were known as competent carpenters and joiners, and the census made by the French during the seventeenth century reported the existence of blacksmiths, locksmiths, and nailmakers among them.[52] Working basically in wood, the Acadians built their own houses, barns, and

165

the occasional church, made their own furniture, including enclosed beds which must have provided considerable privacy in the crowded households, tables, chairs, chests, kegs, and barrels, as well as looms and spinning-wheels.[53] There was a remarkably fluid, though not entirely egalitarian social structure. Considerable importance was attached to the actual possession of land, and the recognition of proper boundaries.[54]

Specie did not serve as a major regulator of the internal economy. The available evidence shows that it was rare indeed for Acadian communities to pay one another, except in kind, for goods and services rendered. The gold gained through trade, or through wages from French and English officials, was kept for trade and most reluctantly handed over for any other purposes, especially rents and taxes.[55] Labour relations among the Acadians tended to be either barter-based (perhaps two days' digging or ploughing in exchange for some quantity of seed grain), co-operative (three or four people engaged in quilt-making or fishing, the resultant produce being divided equitably), or communal (several households joined together to build another dwelling and ready to be reconvened for such a purpose whenever the occasion warranted). The social ambiance produced by such labour relations encouraged the development of a community where family connections were as important as the particular attainments of an individual. Marriage would be seen as the connection between kin rather than the limited engagement of two individuals of particular social status. As Dièreville remarked, to his considerable surprise social barriers seemed to have no part to play in the regulation of marriage.[56]

In sum, Acadian life between 1713 and 1748 centred around the demands and rewards of family and land, although this did not mean isolation from a wider environment. During these decades the care and nurture of children must have been the dominating factor in the lives of most Acadians, male or female. A child born every two or three years on average in individual families meant the arrival of a child almost every year in multi-family households. Even with the importation of some yard goods, the provision of clothes and coverings for the children demanded continuous thought and activity. Records emphasize the extent to which the Acadians were self-sufficient in this area. Dièreville remarked on the way in which they made their own outfits, including caps and stockings.[57] Raynal, writing for Diderot's *Encyclopaedia* with information supplemented by the memorials of those Acadians exiled to France, asserted that they depended for their daily clothing on "leur lin, leur chanvre, la toison de leurs brebis."[58] From diapers to shawls, from shirts to shifts, with considerable liking for mixing black with red for ornament, and binding their skirts with ribbons,[59] the Acadians spun, wove, knitted, and sewed their garments. Even with every economy between one generation and the next, even with children fully accustomed to hand-me-downs, the sheer number of bonnets and mittens, stockings and shoes, cloaks, coats, and trousers, shirts, blouses, and jackets that would be needed is difficult to envisage.

Organizing the clothing was probably as much a year-round occupation for the women as the provision of meals was their daily chore. Grains were usually ground at grist-mills rather than within each household, although there is a tradition that most families possessed pestles and mortars capable of making coarse flour for porridge.[60] Bread would be baked in each household and was considered by Isaac Deschamps to have been the staple of Acadian diets.[61] Linguistic studies by Massignon show that doughnuts and pancakes were also common. She discovered references to documents dated 1744 referring to *croxsignoles*, a form of doughnut, as part of the Acadian diet.[62] It is also probable that those who came to the community from Normandy and Ile-et-Vilaine brought with them a taste for buckwheat pancakes, something that was certainly common among Acadians in northern New Brunswick at the close of the eighteenth century.[63] There is a strange debate about whether the Acadians grew potatoes before 1755, since a number of popular guides such as the *Guide Bleu de Bretagne* refer to them introducing the vegetable to France.[64] Again, it is certainly true that the potato was a staple of Acadian diets by the opening of the nineteenth century,[65] but more evidence is needed before one can accept that it was a common food for the Acadians fifty years earlier. Milk was abundant[66] and the Acadians found in exile that they had been particularly fortunate in this respect.[67] Its plenteousness must have been a great help in coping with what was known as the *pourginés d'enfants*.[68]

167

This charming word for a numerous family invites consideration of the emotional climate in which families grew and developed. The evidence here is, at present, somewhat sketchy. The extent to which the Acadians cared for one another during their exile, seeking news of brothers and sisters as well as advertising for husbands and wives, suggests the importance of family relations.[69] As to the actual treatment of children during these decades, one has very few concrete details. It is possible that the reputation the Acadians had for long and faithful marriages was not coupled with a bitterness against those whose lives followed other patterns. One of the few cases relating to children that reached the English officials at Annapolis Royal between 1720 and 1739 was one where grandparents fought for the privilege of raising an illegitimate child.[70] The folklore research of Jean-Claude Dupont reveals a considerable amount about children's toys and games current in the nineteenth century, and it is probable that some of these, at least, were also part of Acadian life during the eighteenth century. Certainly the early mobile-rattle, a dried pig's bladder filled with peas and hung so an infant could bat it about and watch it swing, listening to its noise, which Dupont has reported for the nineteenth century, would have been a useful toy to have in the house in the eighteenth century.[71]

There were, of course, the usual arguments and quarrels among the Acadians, the kinds of disputes common to any group of people. The court records of Annapolis show not only debates over landholdings and boundaries, but also slander actions, particularly between women, and at least one appeal for aid to control a nagging wife.[72] But the tenor of life was undoubtedly rendered easier by the ready supply of necessities, a supply which might depend on continuous hard work but one that was available. There was no major shortage of food for the Acadians between 1713 and 1748; shelter was readily available; clothing was adequate; and, above all, there were no major epidemics. Even when plague did reach the colony its ravages were confined, both in 1709 and 1751, almost exclusively to the garrisons.[73]

Quite how the Acadians escaped the general epidemics of the eighteenth century has yet to be fully determined. It is obvious from the mortality rates they suffered during the early years of exile that during the first half of the eighteenth century they had acquired no community levels of immunity to smallpox, yellow fever, or typhoid. When those diseases struck as the exiles reached Boston, Philadelphia, South Carolina, or the British seaports, a third or more of the Acadians died.[74] Yet the idea that this vulnerability developed because of the more or less complete isolation of the communities from outside contact is a theory which demands a great deal more examination. The Acadian tradition of trading-cum-smuggling which was established in the seventeenth century took at least some of the men regularly enough to Boston and probably to points south.[75] In the eighteenth century this activity was continued and Acadian connections with Louisbourg were also developed. The fact that between 1713 and 1748 no large body of immigrants came to the area has tended to overshadow both the trickle of newcomers to the settlements and the continuous nature of the relationships between this "continental cornice" and the wider world. The parish records of Grand-Pré examined by Clark show that of the 174 marriages for which detailed information is available almost exactly one-third involved partners either from elsewhere in the colony or from abroad, sixteen coming from France, eight from Quebec, and three from Cape Breton.[76] As for travellers, most of the settlements encountered them in the form of soldiers and traders as well as government and church officials. Given the normal rate of the spread of infections during these decades, it is extraordinary that no epidemics seem to have come to the settlements via contact with Boston or Quebec, Annapolis Royal, or Louisbourg.

If the life of the Acadian settlements was much more open to outside influences than has been generally thought, it was also much less controlled by religious devotion than has been generally supposed. There is no question that the Acadians cherished the Catholic faith. There is also no doubt that they were as much trouble to their priests as any other group of humanity might be. The immense political importance of the Catholic religion to the community has overshadowed questions about its social importance. Acadians' delight in litigation was not their only cross-grained trait. Quarrels that sprung up through their drinking were also matters that concerned their pastors. A report of the archdiocese of Quebec of 1742, which drew particular attention to this flaw, also inferred that bars (*cabarets*) were not only open on Sundays and feast-days, but also kept open during the celebration of Mass.[77] This same report also went on to condemn some of the Acadian communities that allowed men and women not only to dance together after sunset but even permitted the singing of "des chansons lascives." The lack of detail in the report is frustrating: was the alcohol spruce beer? Cider? Rum? Were the *cabarets* found in the front room of the local smuggler, or did Grand-Pré have something close to a village hostelry? Was the dancing anything more than square-dancing? Was the music played on flutes, whistles, and triangles only? Or were there also violins? And the songs — which of the presently known folklore airs might they have been: "Le petit Capucin"? "Le chevalier de la Tour ronde"?

169

Considerably more work needs to be done in the relevant archives before the nature of Acadian beliefs before 1755 can be fully described. The document just cited suggests only that the Acadian interpretation of Catholicism before 1755 owed very little to Jansenism. This would be scarcely surprising. There is little indication, even with the present evidence, that the Acadians indulged in major projects of ostensible devotion, either public or private. There are no stone churches built by them before 1755 nor are there any records of vocations among them before that date, either to the priesthood or to the religious life. Religion among the Acadians seems to have been a matter of necessity but not a question of sainthood, an important and vital ingredient in life, but not the sole shaping force of the social and cultural life of their communities.[78]

For, in sum, the life of the Acadians between 1713 and 1755 was above all the life of a people in fortunate circumstances, the very real foundation for the later myth of a "Golden Age." The ravages of the Four Horsemen of the Apocalypse were remarkably absent, for famine, disease, and war barely touched the Acadians during these years. There was sufficient food for the growing families and apparently enough land for the growing population. One's nearest and dearest might have been as aggravating as one's kin can often be, but circumstances not only did not add the burdens of scarcity to emotional life but in fact provided a fair abundance of the necessities. Certainly the daily round for both men and women must have been exhaustingly busy; but work did have its obvious rewards and, for both sexes, it would be varied enough and carried out with companionship and sociability. While the season would often have imposed harsh demands for immediate labour, for seeds must be sown, crops gathered, fish caught and fuel cut as and when the weather dictates, the year's turning would also have brought its own festivities and holidays. Massignon's work suggests that the Acadians kept the twelve days of Christmas, the customs of Candelmas as well as the celebrations common to Easter.[79] The long winter evenings knew card-playing, dancing, and pipe-smoking, as well as story-telling and sing-songs. The spring and summer months would see the celebrations of weddings and the most frequent new-births. Quarrels, scandals, politics, the visits of priests, the presence of Indians, people whose children occasionally married with the Acadians and who instructed the settlers in the use of local foods,[80] the presence of the English, now and again also marrying with the Acadians[81] — there is no doubt that Acadian life before 1755 was neither crisis-ridden nor lapped in the tranquility of a back-water. It was instead a life of considerable distinctiveness. It was a life rich enough to provide the sustenance for a continuing Acadian identity, based not only upon a complex social and cultural life, but also upon the development of a coherent political stance, maintained throughout the settlements over a considerable period of years. It is not surprising that, fragmented in exile, the Acadians remembered these years and that this remembrance would be built into their future lives.

NOTES

1 For example, Geneviève Massignon, *Les Parlers français d'Acadie*, 2 vols. (Paris: C. Klincksieck, n.d.).

2 For example, Antonine Maillet, *Rabelais et les traditions populaires en Acadie* (Québec: Presses de l'université Laval, 1971); Anselme Chiasson, *Chéticamp, histoire et traditions acadiennes* (Moncton: Éditions des Aboiteaux, 1962); Catherine Jolicoeur, *Les plus belles légendes acadiennes* (Montréal: Stanké, 1981).

3 A.H. Clark, *Acadia: The Geography of Early Nova Scotia to 1760* (Madison: University of Wisconsin Press, 1968), and J.C. Vernex, *Les Acadiens* (Paris: Éditions Entente, 1979).

4 Jean-Paul Hautecoeur, *L'Acadie du Discours* (Québec: Presses de l'université Laval, 1976).

5 Jean Daigle, ed., *Les Acadiens des Maritimes: Études thématiques* (Moncton: Centre d'Études Acadiennes, 1980). See my review in *Histoire social — Social History* 16 (May 1983): 192–94.

6 J.B. Brebner, *New England's Outpost* (New York: Columbia University Press, 1927), 15–16.

7 While there has been considerable debate about whether this family had Anglophone roots (for example, see Clark, *Acadia*, 101), there now seems no doubt of their origins. For details of their ancestry as recorded in declarations made by their descendants in Belle-Île-en-Mer after the deportation, see M.P. and N.P. Rieder, *The Acadians in France*, 3 vols. (Metairie, La.: M.P. & N. Rieder, 1972), 2, *passim*.

8 Bona Arsenault, *Histoire et Généalogie des Acadiens*, 2 vols. (Québec: Le Conseil de la vie française en Amérique, 1965), 2: 550.

9 This is suggested, in particular, in the reports of discussions with the second Mme La Tour, in Candide de Nantes, *Pages glorieuses de l'épopée Canadienne: une mission capucine en Acadie* (Montréal: Le Devoir, 1927), 150f.

10 Jean Daigle, "Nos amis les ennemis: relations commerciales de l'Acadie avec le Massachusetts, 1670–1711" (Ph.D. dissertation, University of Maine, 1975); and John Reid, *Acadia, Maine and New Scotland: Marginal Colonies in the Seventeenth Century* (Toronto: University of Toronto Press, 1981).

11 This document, headed "answer of several French inhabitants, 10 February 1717," is printed in the *Collection de documents inédits sur le Canada et l'Amérique publiés par le Canada français*, 3 vols. (Québec: Le Canada français, 1888–90), 2: 171. The collection was published anonymously, but its editor is known to be the abbé Casgrain. The original of the document is in the Public Records Office, London (hereafter PRO), CO/NS 2, as part of the Nova Scotia government documents.

12 Brebner, *New England's Outpost*, 97.

13 T.B. Akins, ed., *Selections from the Public Documents of the Province of Nova Scotia* (Halifax, 1869), 15–16.

14 Mascerene to the Lords of Trade, 9 June 1744, printed in *Collection de Documents inédits* 2: 80.

15 This was also the opinion of the French officer in charge of the attack on Grand-Pré, Duvivier. He defended himself at his court-martial on the charge of failure, by protesting that Acadian neutrality had rendered his task impossible. Robert Rumilly, *Histoire des Acadiens*, 2 vols. (Montréal: Fides, 1955), 1: 304.

16 Letter from the inhabitants of Minas, Rivière aux Canards, and Piziquid to Duvivier and de Gannes, 13 October 1744, printed in Rumilly, *Histoire des Acadiens* 1: 304–5.

17 The full story of the Acadian years in exile remains to be told, but some indication of the strength of the community is given in Naomi Griffiths, "Acadians in Exile: The Experience of the Acadians in the British Seaports," *Acadiensis* 4 (Autumn 1974): 67-84.

18 Gisa I. Hynes, "Some Aspects of the Demography of Port Royal, 1650-1755," *Acadiensis* 3 (Autumn 1973): 7-8.

19 For a good overview of what is available, see Muriel K. Roy, "Peuplement et croissance démographique en Acadie", in Daigle, *Acadiens des Maritimes*, 135-208.

20 Hynes, "Demography of Port Royal", pp. 10-11. In recent years scholarship about demography has been prolific. One of the most readable accounts of the French reality during the late seventeenth century is that of Pierre Goubert: "In 1969 the average expectation of life is something over seventy years. In 1661 it was probably under twenty-five. . . . Out of every hundred children born, twenty-five died before they were one year old, another twenty-five never reached twenty and a further twenty-five perished between the ages of twenty and forty-five. Only about ten ever made her sixties." Pierre Goubert, *Louis XIV and Twenty Million Frenchmen* (New York Random House, 1972), 21. On the demography of New England, see esp. James H. Cassedy, *Demography in Early America: Beginnings of the Statistical Mind, 1600-1800* (Cambridge, Mass.: Harvard University Press, 1969). Cassedy points out that the demographic scale was at first weighted towards mortality, but at a different time for each colony, "this precarious balance righted itself." The incidence of disease, malnutrition, and frontier warfare were demonstrably greater for New England than they were for Acadia. The conditions of life along the St. Lawrence were much closer to those along the Bay of Fundy. In the eighteenth century the population of Canada doubled every thirty years. In Acadia, however, the increase was even higher: it doubled every fifteen years between 1671 and 1714, and every twenty years between 1714 and 1755. Furthermore, migration was a minimal factor in Acadian demography after 1740. On Canada, see Jacques Henripin, *La population canadienne au début du XVIIIᵉ siècle* (Paris: Institut national d'études démographiques, 1954); on Acadia, see Roy, "Peuplement," 152.

21 Father Felix Pain to the governor of Isle Royale, September 1713, printed in Clark, *Acadia*, 187.

22 Sieur de Dièreville, *Relation of the Voyage to Port Royal in Acadia or New France*, ed. J.C. Webster (Toronto: Champlain Society, 1933), 93.

23 Public Archives of Canada (hereafter PAC), MG 11, CO 217, vol. 5, Phillipps to the Board of Trade, 2 September 1730 (PAC reel C-9120).

24 Hynes, "Demography of Port Royal," 10.

25 Hynes, "Demography of Port Royal," 10-11.

26 Clark, *Acadia*, 200f, arrived at somewhat different statistics, concluding that the average family size was closer to four or five.

27 Massignon, *Parlers français* 1:45; Arsenault, *Généalogie* 1: 432, 433; 2: 666.

28 Arsenault, *Généologie* 1: 518.

29 This calculation rests partly upon the assumption that the Acadians followed a common contemporary practice of using the name of a child that died for the next-born of the same sex.

30 Arsenault, *Généalogie* 1: 518; 2: 666, 667f.

31 PAC, MG 11, CO 217, vol. 2 (PAC reel C-9119).

32 These figures are my own estimations, based upon the work of Clark, *Acadia*, 216, and the overview by Roy, "Peuplement," 134-207.

33 "A Brief Survey of Nova Scotia" (MS in Library of the Royal Artillery Regiment, Woolwich, n.d.), 2: 25-26, cited in Clark, *Acadia*, 217.

34 There is considerable debate about the kin system of these households. Grandparents can only have lived in one home, and there is still debate on how siblings linked house-keeping arrangements.

35 Dièreville, *Relation*, 256.

36 PAC, MG 1, Series C 11 D, 3: 199-203, Villebon to the Minister, 27 October 1694.

37 Cited in Clark, *Acadia*, 237.

38 Captain John Knox, *An Historical Journal of the Campaigns in North America for the Years 1757, 1758, 1759 and 1760*, ed. A.B. Doughty, 3 vols. (Toronto, 1914-18), 1: 105.

39 PAC, AC 2B, 12, "Supplied from Acadia entering Louisbourg, 1740," printed in Clark, *Acadia*, 259.

40 L.U. Fontaine, *Voyage de Sieur de Dièreville en Acadia* (Québec, 1885), 56.

41 "Supplies from Acadia", in Clark, *Acadia*, 259; and "Report of custom collector Newton" (PAC, AC, NSA-26, 29-33), printed in A. Shortt, V.K. Johnston and F. Lanctot, eds. *Currency, Exchange and Finance in Nova Scotia, with Prefatory Documents, 1675-1758* (Ottawa, 1933), 223-24.

42 PAC, AC, NSA-26, 52, cited in Clark, *Acadia*, 258. See also the chart of Louisbourg trade on (324-25).

43 PAC, AC, NSA-26, 51, cited in Clark, *Acadia*, 258.

44 For example, the Acadians sent to Maryland and South Carolina were able to purchase ships. See PAC, NS A/60, "Circular to the governors on the continent, July 1st, 1756, Halifax."

45 Morris, "A Brief Survey," 2: 4, quoted in Clark, *Acadia*, 244.

46 Quoted in Clark, *Acadia*, 246.

47 Fontaine, *Voyage*, 56.

48 Observations made by Moise de Les Derniers shortly after 1755 and printed in Casgrain, *Un pèlerinage au pays d'Évangéline* (Paris, 1889), App. III, 115.

49 Dièreville, *Relations*, 96.

171

[50] It was Perrot who first commented upon this in 1686 (PAC, AC, C11D-2[1], 119, mémoires généraux); and many later observers, such as Dièreville and Phillipps, insinuated similar flaws.

[51] Clark, *Acadia*, 232.

[52] PAC, MG1, series C11D, 2: 96-106, report on Menneval, 10 September 1688.

[53] R. Hale, "Journal of a Voyage to Nova Scotia Made in 1731 by Robert Hale of Beverley," *The Essex Institute Historical Collections* 42 (July 1906): 233.

[54] Comments on the litigious nature of the Acadians span all regimes. See Clark, *Acadia*, 198, and Brebner, *New England Outpost*, 140.

[55] In particular, note the trouble that Subercase faced collecting taxes, in Shortt et al., *Currency*, 16.

[56] Dièreville, *Relation*, 93.

[57] Dièreville, *Relation*, 96.

[58] Guillaume Thomas François Raynal, *Histoire philosophique et politique des établissements et du commerce des Européens dans les deux Indes* (Paris, 1778), 6: 309.

[59] Moise de les Derniers, cited in Casgrain, *Un pèlerinage*, 155.

[60] Massignon, *Parlers français* 2: 548, 1316. The *bûche à pilon* is illustrated in Paul Doucet, *Vie de nos ancêtres en Acadie — l'alimentation* (Moncton: Éditions d'Acadie, 1980), 17.

[61] Deschamps, cited in Clark, *Acadia*, 237.

[62] Massignon, *Parlers français* 2: 550, 1320.

[63] Massignon, *Parlers français* 2: 551, 1322; Ph.F. Bourgeois, *Vie de l'Abbé François-Xavier LaFrance* (Montréal, 1925), 83.

[64] *Les Guides Bleus de Bretagne* (Paris, 1967), 662.

[65] Bourgeois, *Vie de l'abbé LaFrance*, 83.

[66] Dièreville, *Relation*, 266, 110.

[67] Records of the complaints of Acadians exiled to Brittany, described by Naomi Griffiths, "Petitions of Acadian Exiles, 1755-1785: A Neglected Source," *Histoire sociale — Social History* 11 (May 1978): 215-23.

[68] Massignon, *Parlers français* 2: 648, 1702.

[69] Griffiths, "Petitions of Acadian Exile," 218f.

[70] A.M. MacMechan, ed., *Nova Scotia Archives*, vol. 3, *Original Minutes of H.M. Council at Annapolis Royal, 1720-1739* (Halifax, 1908), 112, 122.

[71] Jean-Claude Dupont, *Héritage d'Acadie* (Québec: Leméac, 1977), 172, and *Histoire populaire de l'Acadie* (Montréal: Leméac, 1979).

[72] MacMechan, *Nova Scotia Archives* 3: 3, 17.

[73] W.P. Bell, *The "Foreign Protestants" and the Settlement of Nova Scotia: The History of a Piece of Arrested British Colonial Policy in the Eighteenth Century* (Toronto: University of Toronto Press, 1961), 44-45, 64-85, 328-35.

[74] Griffiths, "Petitions of Acadian Exiles," 216f.

[75] Jean Daigle, "Les Relations commerciales de l'Acadie avec le Massachusetts: le cas de Charles-Amador de Saint-Étienne de la Tour, 1695-1697", *Revue de l'Université de Moncton* 9 (1976): 353-61.

[76] Clark, *Acadia*, 203-4.

[77] Têtu et Gagnon, *Mandements, lettres pastorales et circulaires des évêques de Quebec, 1888*, 15-16, reprinted in E. de Grace, G. Desjardins, R.-A. Mallet, *Histoire d'Acadie par les Textes*, 4 fascicules (Fredericton: Ministère de l'éducation du Nouveau-Brunswick, 1976), 1 (1604-1760): 19.

[78] A most interesting question which needs further investigation and which reinforces the theory of Acadian respect for, but not subservience to, the Catholic church, is the matter of dispensations for marriage between second cousins accorded at Annapolis Royal between 1727 and 1755, the usual reason for such dispensations being pre-marital pregnancy. Cf. Clark, *Acadia*, 203-4, *passim*.

[79] Massignon, *Parlers français* 2: 691-99.

[80] Not only fiddle-heads but also *titines de souris (salicornia Europaia)* and *passe-pierre (saxifraga Virginiensis)*. See Massignon, *Parlers français* 1: 183.

[81] Knox, *Historical Journal* 1:94-96, quoted in A.G. Doughty, *The Acadian Exiles* (Toronto: Glasgow, Brook and Company, 1916), 40.

Imperial Conflict

The Seven Years' War in Europe, which set France, Austria, Sweden, and a few small German states against Britain and Prussia, might well be termed the First World War. Hostilities were waged from 1756 to 1763 over as large a portion of the world as in 1914–18. Britain engaged in naval campaigns against France (and later Spain) in the Atlantic, the Caribbean, the Mediterranean, and the Indian Ocean.

In North America the struggle between Britain and France had begun in 1754 with a clash between French troops and Virginia militia in the Ohio country, the result of an attempt by the American colonists to expel the French from the area immediately west of the Allegheny Mountains. The following year the British under General Braddock experienced a disastrous defeat at Monongahela (present-day Pittsburg, Pennsylvania). In 1756 this North American struggle merged into the Seven Years' War. Until 1757 New France, although outnumbered in population twenty to one by the American colonies, continued to hold the upper hand.

The whole character of the war changed in 1758, when William Pitt became England's prime minister. Pitt regarded the North American campaign as a primary, not secondary, theatre of the war. Instantly he redirected the emphasis of Britain's war effort to North America. The British fleet, which had twice as many ships as its French counterpart, blockaded the French navy, keeping it to its home ports and thus cutting off supplies and troop reinforcements to New France. Yet despite the extent of the British commitment, New France held out for another two years, until 1760. W.J. Eccles chronicles the final round of conflict for the control of northeastern North America in "The Preemptive Conquest, 1749–1763," a chapter from *France in America*. Military historian C.P. Stacey reviews the final two years of conflict in his "Generals and Generalship before Quebec, 1759–1760."

For a review of the nearly one-half century of armed conflict between the French and English in the New World, students should consult I.K. Steele's *Guerillas and Grenadiers* (Toronto: The Ryerson Press, 1969). For a more detailed examination of New France's final years, see George F.G. Stanley's *New France: The Last Phase, 1744–1760* (Toronto: McClelland and Stewart, 1968) and Guy Frégault's *La Guerre de la conquête* (1955), translated by Margaret Cameron as *Canada: The War of the Con-*

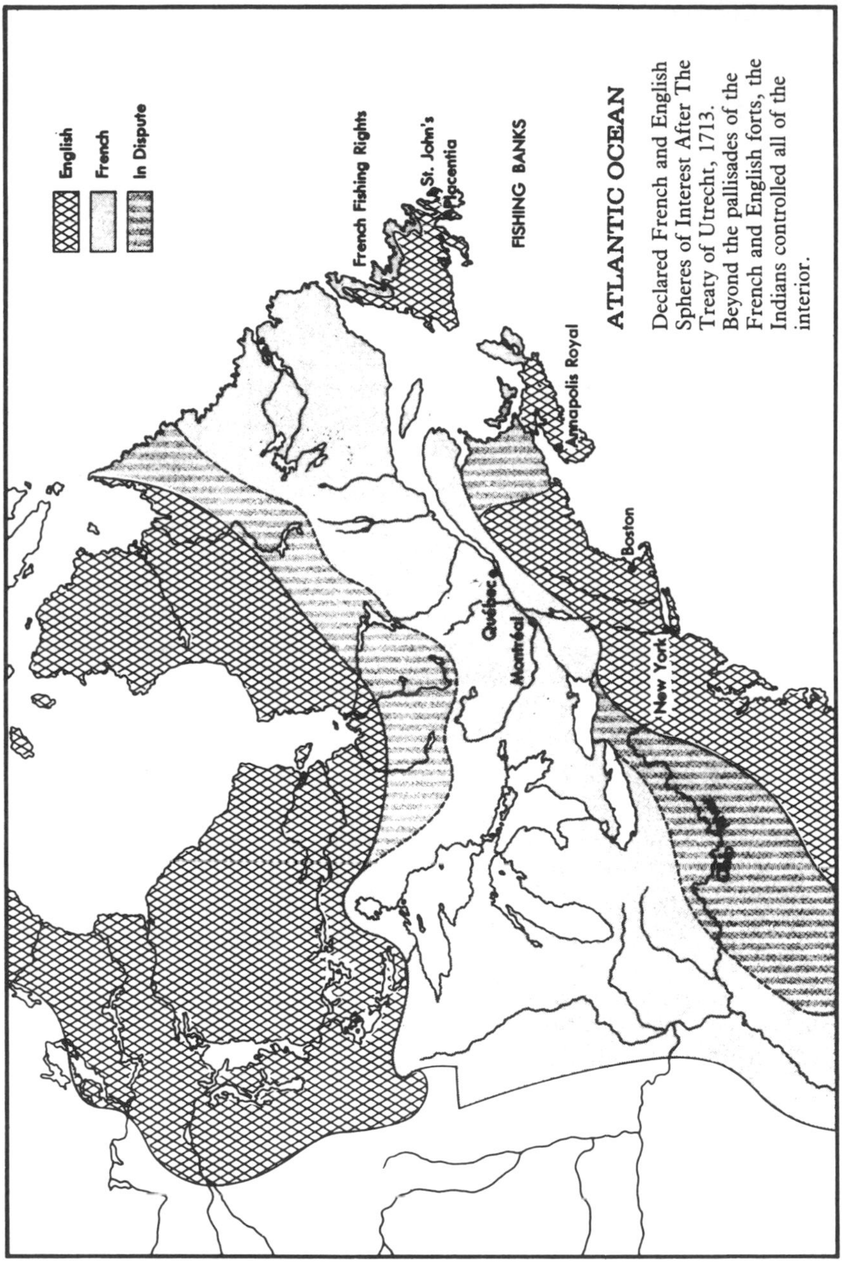

174

Map legend:

- English
- French
- In Dispute

French Fishing Rights

St. John's
Placentia

FISHING BANKS

Annapolis Royal

ATLANTIC OCEAN

Declared French and English Spheres of Interest After The Treaty of Utrecht, 1713. Beyond the pallisades of the French and English forts, the Indians controlled all of the interior.

Boston

Quebec

Montreal

New York

Cornell, Hamelin, Ouellet, Trudel, *Canada: Unity in Diversity*, 38.

Declared French and English spheres of interest after the Treaty of Utrecht, 1713.

quest (Toronto: Oxford University Press, 1969). C.P. Stacey's *Quebec, 1759: The Siege and the Battle* (Toronto: Macmillan, 1959) examines that crucial year in the struggle. The articles by W.J. Eccles, "The French Forces in North America during the Seven Years' War," and by C.P. Stacey, "The British Forces in North America during the Seven Years' War," in the *Dictionary of Canadian Biography*, vol. 3, *1741-1770*, xv–xxiii, xxiv–xxx, review the military strengths of the two opponents.

For a thorough discussion of the various interpretations of the Conquest, see Ramsay Cook, "The Historian and Nationalism," in *Canada and the French-Canadian Question* (Toronto: Macmillan, 1966), 119–42, and his essay "Conquêtisme," in *The Maple Leaf Forever* (Toronto: Macmillan, 1971), 99–113.

The Preemptive Conquest, 1749-1763*

175

W.J. ECCLES

In the Americas the War of the Austrian Succession had changed nothing and settled nothing. After 1748 France wanted an enduring peace to rebuild and restore, but the British commercial community wanted a renewal of the war at the earliest opportunity. The latter powerful group, with Newcastle and Pitt as its political agents, was convinced that peace was good for France, but bad for England. The struggle just ended had achieved sufficient success to demonstrate that were Britain to concentrate her resources on a commercial war, France as a competitor in world markets could be destroyed and British merchants could then pick up the pieces.[1] This aggressive policy found a counterpart in North America where the planters and land speculators of Virginia and Pennsylvania were now eyeing the rich lands of the Ohio Valley. Land companies were formed in both provinces to seize and parcel out these lands for settlement. Meanwhile, fur traders, who in some instances were also agents of the land companies, had established trading posts in the region and drawn the local tribes into a commercial alliance.[2]

The French in Canada were acutely aware of the danger posed by this encroachment on lands they claimed. Were it to go unchallenged the English colonials would not only threaten their hold on the northwest fur trade but, by expanding down the Ohio to the Mississippi, would eventually sever communications between Canada and Louisiana. Looking even further ahead, were the English to seize and settle the lands between the Alleghenies and the Mississippi their rapidly expanding population would grow immeasurably in numbers and wealth, and with that,

*From *France in America* by W.J. Eccles. Copyright © 1972 by W.J. Eccles. Reprinted by permission of Harper and Row, Publishers, Inc.

England's commerce. Since military power was determined to a considerable degree by the size of a country's population, by the number of trained men with muskets that could be put in the field, the much larger population of France compared to England's would eventually be offset by that of the English colonies. In America, therefore, English expansion had to be checked.

At Quebec the governor general, the comte de La Galissonière, took note of these dangers and recommended measures to circumvent them. He proposed that garrisoned forts be established in the Ohio Valley and the Indian tribes brought into the French alliance. In this way English expansion would be blocked. But more than that, from Canada and the proposed Ohio bases, the English colonies could be threatened by Canadian and Indian war parties. All that would be needed was a small force of French regulars to garrison the bases. In the previous wars the Canadians had more than held their own against the English colonials. In Britain's balance of trade those colonies were such an important item the English would have to respond to such a threat. They would have to send troops to aid the ineffectual colonial militia, and this would require the support of sizable elements of the Royal Navy which would then not be available for attacks on the French West Indies, or French maritime commerce, or to blockade the French ports as they had done so successfully in the past war. In other words, the role of the French in North America was to be that of a fortress, with a small garrison to tie down a much larger force of the enemy.[3]

With the approval of the Ministry of Marine, La Galissonière lost no time initiating this policy. In 1749 he dispatched an expedition, led by the veteran western commander Pierre-Joseph de Céloron de Blainville, to the Ohio to show the flag, claim the region for France, and drive out the Anglo-American traders. Céloron discovered that British infiltration of the region and influence over the Indian nations was far more serious than had been imagined. La Galissonière's successor, Pierre-Jacques de Taffanel, marquis de la Jonquière, strengthened the French forts in the Great Lakes area, but did little more. The governor of Louisiana, however, Canadian-born Pierre de Rigaud, marquis de Vaudreuil, showed a greater awareness of the need for action. He strengthened the garrisons at the posts in the Illinois country and began the construction of Fort Chartres, near Kaskaskia; but even after receiving reinforcements in 1751, he had only some two thousand indifferent regulars to hold the Mississippi Valley from New Orleans to the Illinois River. The French hold on this region had to depend on retaining the active allegiance of the Indian nations.[4]

On the Atlantic coast the French greatly strengthened the defenses of Louisbourg and sent out fifteen hundred garrison troops under officers who this time maintained discipline. Some of the Acadians of Nova Scotia were enticed to remove to Île Royale (Cape Breton); merchants and fish-

176

ermen, with their families, reestablished themselves there until by 1752 the population stood at 5845.[5] Other Acadians were persuaded to settle on Île St. Jean (Prince Edward Island), and at Beaubassin where the French had a fort. The swift economic recovery of Louisbourg fully justified the sacrifices made to regain it at the peace table. The fishery expanded rapidly, and the old trade with Canada, the West Indies, and New England throve. Yet in this region too the French had to count on the Indian tribes, the Micmacs and Abenaquis, and, hopefully, on the Acadians still resident in Nova Scotia. The English, however, were fully conscious of this revival of French power that threatened their North Atlantic trade. In 1749 they began the construction of a naval base and fortress at Halifax, which not only countered the menace to English shipping but precluded the possibility of the Acadians liberating Nova Scotia.

In the west the French seized the initiative.[6] Unlike the Anglo-Americans, the governor general of New France was able to mobilize the colony's entire military resources with no regard for cost. In 1753 he dispatched two thousand men to Lake Erie to construct a road from southeast of that lake to the headwaters of the Ohio and build a chain of forts at strategic points. The Indian nations, impressed by this show of strength, began to sever their trade connections with the Anglo-Americans. All that the latter could do to counter this erosion of their position was to send a major of militia, George Washington, with an escort of seven men and a letter from Governor Robert Dinwiddie of Virginia, protesting the French invasion of lands claimed by Great Britain and demanding their immediate withdrawal. Jacques Legardeur de Saint-Pierre, commandant at Fort Le Boeuf, a tough veteran of the west, received Washington politely, but contemptuously rejected his blustering ultimatum.

The following year a small force of Virginia militia attempted to establish a fort at the junction of the Ohio and the Monongahela. Before they were well begun a French force, five hundred strong, swept down the upper Ohio and forced them to retire over the crest of the Alleghenies, which the French claimed to be the border between their territory and that of the English colonies. The French now built Fort Duquesne on the site and thereby dominated the whole region. The Anglo-American response was to send George Washington back, at the head of a motley collection of militia, to drive the French out. They ambushed a small French party sent to order them to retire. The officer in command, Ensign Joseph Coulon de Villiers de Jumonville, and nine of his men were killed, twenty-one taken prisoner. This was the first clash of arms in what was to become a global war. Significantly, it began while both powers were at peace. It also began under very dubious circumstances.[7]

The French reacted swiftly. Washington, with some 350 undisciplined colonial militia, made a stand at Great Meadows, where 500 French, after a short engagement, compelled them to surrender. Washington

177

signed the capitulation terms without taking the trouble to inquire too closely into their meaning and subsequently dishonored them, then fled precipitately with his men back to Virginia. In his haste he abandoned his baggage containing his journal. The contents of that journal were to be used by the French government to brand the English as perfidious throughout Europe.[8] Washington's ignominious defeat brought the last of the wavering Indian nations to the French cause. From that point on, the English had not a single Indian ally in the west, while the strength of the French was enhanced immeasurably. At every turn of events the French had overreached the Anglo-Americans. They were securely in possession of the Ohio country, from its upper reaches to the Mississippi, and from their advanced forts war parties could fall on the rear of the English colonies at any time. For the time being, however, they kept their Indian allies securely on leash, determined on no account to give the enemy an excuse for attack.

178   The English colonies, with the exception of New York, which had no desire to have its profitable contraband trade with the French colonies disrupted, clamored for war to drive the French out of North America once and for all. In the previous wars England had furnished scant aid to her American subjects. This time the war party, led by Cumberland, Henry Fox, and William Pitt, forced Newcastle to agree to full-scale hostilities against the French in America and on the seas without bothering with the formality of declaring war.[9]

In October, 1754, Major General Edward Braddock, commanding two battalions, eight hundred men, was ordered to North America with orders to capture Fort Duquesne, while the colonial forces attacked Fort Niagara, the French forts on Lake Champlain, and those on the Nova Scotia border. This force could not sail until the following April, and on the eve of its departure the French obtained a copy of Braddock's orders. Immediately, they raised six battalions, three thousand men from the better regiments of the *troupes de terre*.[10] In April they too were ready to sail. When the British cabinet learned of this they issued secret orders to Admiral Edward Boscawen with two squadrons composed of nineteen ships of the line and two frigates to intercept the French convoy, seize the ships, and if resistance were offered, give battle. A few days after he sailed, on April 27, the French ambassador to the Court of St. James's received word that Boscawen had orders to attack the French squadron. On May 10, however, two cabinet ministers dined at his house and cheerfully reassured him that such rumors were completely false, that no such orders had been issued.[11]

Off Newfoundland Boscawen succeeded in intercepting only three ships of the French convoy. When Captain Toussaint Hocquart hailed Captain Richard Howe, asking if they were at peace or war, the reply came, "At peace, at peace," followed by shattering broadsides.[12] Two of the French ships were captured; the third escaped to Louisbourg. The rest of the convoy, with all but eight companies of troops, and with the newly appointed governor general of New France, Pierre de Rigaud, marquis de Vaudreuil, on board, reached Louisbourg and Quebec safely.[13] Elsewhere the Royal Navy had better luck. More than three hundred French ships and eight thousand sailors were seized in English ports or on the high seas.[14] This was a serious blow to French maritime strength. Needless to say, the French lost no time proclaiming the English to have been guilty of the blackest treachery.[15]

On land in North America, now that hostilities had begun in earnest, but still without a declaration of war, the British did not fare so well. Braddock, at the head of 2,200 men, British regulars and colonial troops, got his army over the mountains and within a few miles of Fort Duquesne — by itself no mean feat. In an almost forlorn hope Captain Daniel de Beaujeu led 108 Troupes de la Marine, 146 Canadian militia, and 600 Indians to oppose him. The ensuing clash was a disaster for the British. The Canadian and Indian forces took cover on the forested flank of the enemy, encumbered by siege artillery and a vast wagon train. The measured British volleys had little effect against the concealed foe. The Canadians and Indians advanced close. Noting that the British ranks reloaded to ordered drumbeats, they picked off the officers and drummers.[16] Confusion, then panic, spread through the British ranks. The battle became a slaughter. The troops broke and fled. More than two-thirds of the British force were killed or captured, along with the cannon and a vast store of supplies. This, at a cost to the French and their allies of twenty-three killed and twenty wounded.[17]

179

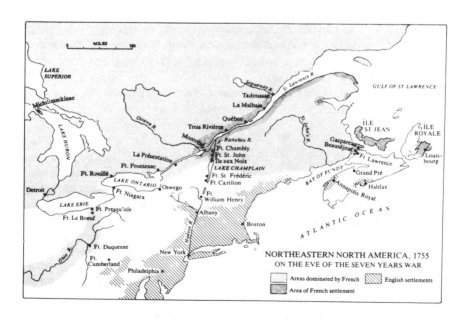

NORTHEASTERN NORTH AMERICA, 1755
ON THE EVE OF THE SEVEN YEARS WAR

Areas dominated by French   English settlements
Area of French settlement

In the mortally wounded Braddock's captured baggage the plans for the attacks on the other fronts were found. Thus, by the time the ill-organized colonial forces had mustered for an attack on Niagara, the French had moved reinforcements to oppose them. The acting commander in chief of the Anglo-Americans, William Shirley, governor of Massachusetts, after his 2,400 colonial troops had been reduced to 1,400 by sickness and desertion, abandoned the campaign. On the Lake Champlain front the Anglo-Americans failed to reach the lake, being forestalled by the French, led by the commander of the regular troops Jean-Armand, baron de Dieskau, who had the misfortune to be wounded and captured in the brief and inconclusive engagement that both sides claimed as a victory.

Only on the Acadian frontier did the British enjoy any success. Fort Beauséjour, at the foot of the Bay of Fundy, was captured and the threat to the English in Nova Scotia effectively removed. Then followed one of the most controversial acts of the war, the expulsion of the Acadians.[18] Not only were the Acadians, both those captured in arms and those who had sworn the oath to His Britannic Majesty, expelled in brutal fashion, but the Indians were likewise driven off their land to make way for New England settlers. Many of the Acadians managed to elude the New England troops sent to seize them, and made their way to Quebec. They constituted a warning to the Canadians of what they could expect should they be conquered. Nothing could have been better calculated to make them fight with a ferocity born of despair. The French authorities at Quebec made the most of this.

Although war had not been declared, and would not be until May, 1756, the British assaults on New France permitted Vaudreuil to take the offensive. Indian war parties led by Canadian officers ravaged the frontiers of Virginia and Pennsylvania; but Vaudreuil's strategy was defensive. His purpose was to use the advanced French bases in the west to hold the Indian nations in the French alliance, thereby offsetting the Anglo-American superiority in numbers. Thus small Canadian and Indian guerrilla detachments could force the British to maintain large defensive forces on their frontier. To take the offensive against these bases the British would require an army, have to build roads through the wilderness to move and supply it, and employ large bodies of men to maintain their supply lines. With their command of the rivers the French could move men and supplies much more easily than could the British. Moreover, the Anglo-American militia usually fled at the mere rumored approach of the enemy.[19]

On the New York frontier Vaudreuil's strategy was to block the Lake Champlain invasion route by maintaining a strong garrison at Fort St. Fréderic and by building an advanced fort at the head of the lake, Fort Carillon, later known as Ticonderoga. When the enemy attempted to attack Canada by this route, a relatively small force could delay them at Carillon and hold them at the narrows by Fort St. Fréderic while the Canadians and Indians harassed their supply lines. Carillon would also serve as an advance base to threaten Albany and the American frontier settlements, thereby containing sizable enemy forces. The main dangers to Canada were the threat of invasion from Lake Champlain, from Lake Ontario down the St. Lawrence, and a maritime assault up the river against Quebec. On the Lake Ontario front, the English fort at Oswego was the major threat, and Vaudreuil made plans in 1755 to destroy it. As for an assault on Quebec, the best that could be done there was to harass an invading fleet as it came up river, then rely on the natural defenses of the town to prevent its capture.

If necessary, the extended defense lines could be pulled back to Niagara, Fort Frontenac, and Fort St. Fréderic. The enemy's communications and supply lines would then be lengthened and more vulnerable to attack by the French irregulars. Thus the British would have to employ vastly superior forces, and their need to build roads through the forest to supply their armies on the periphery of New France, growing ever longer, would limit the number of troops they could bring into action.[20] The British could, of course, transport whole armies to America without much danger of attack from the smaller French fleet.[21] Moreover, Britain could use ports from Halifax to Charleston; Canada had only one. An English fleet in the St. Lawrence could isolate Canada completely. Without reinforcements and supplies from France, the colony could be starved into surrender. Yet, not until 1760 did the Royal Navy succeed in blocking the St. Lawrence. French supply ships reached Quebec every year until the city fell. Much, however, depended on the food the colony could itself provide, and this became crucial with all the additional mouths to feed, the army, the Acadians, and the allied Indians who had to be fed and provided with military supplies before they would take the field. When the crops failed in 1758 famine threatened, and inadequate food supplies, to some degree, dictated military tactics; yet food was never the major factor that it has sometimes been claimed. The people went hungry at times, but they did not starve. It was not a food shortage that caused the eventual fall of New France.

In 1756 a replacement for Dieskau arrived in the person of Louis-Joseph, marquis de Montcalm-Gozon de Saint-Véran, a battle-tried regimental commander. He had the rank of *maréchal de camp*, equivalent to major-general, and command over the *troupes de terre* only. He was subordinate to the governor general, Vaudreuil, who had overall command of all the military forces, *troupes de terre*, Troupes de la Marine, the naval detachments, and the Canadian militia; all told, some 16,000 men. In addition there were the Indian allies. One reason for Vaudreuil's appointment as governor general was his intimate knowledge of, and ability to control, these proud, independent, and unpredictable warriors. Although he had served in the Troupes de la Marine from childhood and in 1738 had been recommended by Governor General Beauharnais for the post of commander of the companies stationed in Canada, he had

181

served only briefly in one campaign in the west. Most of his experience had been administrative, lately as governor of Louisiana, where he had performed very creditably.[22]

Unfortunately, Montcalm and Vaudreuil quickly came to detest each other. Both were vain, each very jealous of his authority, each convinced of the other's incompetence and his own superior judgment. Vaudreuil did, however, know the country and what warfare in it entailed. He could, as much as anyone could, handle the Indians; and he was respected by both the Canadian militia and the Troupes de la Marine. He had contrived the strategy of extended defense lines and wanted to take full advantage of the differing capabilities of his motley forces. Montcalm rejected this strategic concept. He recommended that the French abandon the Ohio Valley and Lake Champlain, then concentrate the forces at the colony's inner defense line.[23] He wished the war to be conducted on European lines, sieges and set battles, in which superior discipline, training, and his leadership would bring victory. The sort of warfare that the Canadians excelled at he regarded with contempt, as accomplishing no worthwhile purpose. As for the Indian allies, he had no use for them at all.[24] But his greatest weakness was his confirmed defeatism. He quickly convinced himself that the French position was hopeless and devoted much of his time and energy to casting blame on Vaudreuil for the disasters he was sure would ensue. Nor did he make any attempt to hide his opinion of the governor general. He criticized Vaudreuil and all things Canadian before his officers, thereby fanning the latent hostility between the Canadian officers of the Troupes de la Marine and those newly come from France with the *troupes de terre* who looked down on the colonials. Naturally, the Canadian officers, with their much greater experience in forest warfare and their unblemished record of victory, resented the attitude of Montcalm and his staff. Montcalm's defeatism, and his attitude toward the Canadians, could not fail to sap the morale of both troops and militia.

Another factor that helped to lower morale, and to some degree to hinder the French war effort — although not to the extent that has been claimed — was the malversation of the intendant François Bigot. By a series of clever devices he and his associates mulcted the Crown of millions of livres. Supplies sent to the colony, or produced in the colony, were bought at low prices by Bigot's agents, then sold at upwards of thirty times as much to the Crown. That Bigot was able to organize this very lucrative looting operation and get away with it for so long was a measure of his cleverness and ability.[25] He was an extremely efficient administrator, and although a scoundrel, he did keep the army and the colony supplied. To what degree military operations were hindered by his activities is extremely difficult to discern.

Despite these internal problems, the French forces won a succession of victories during the first two years of hostilities. Before Montcalm's arrival Vaudreuil had made plans to destroy Oswego and remove that threat to French communications with the west. In February, 1756, he sent a war party which, by destroying Fort Bull, cut Oswego's supply route to Schenectady. Other detachments hovered about Oswego, cutting down the supply columns, keeping it blockaded. In July Montcalm, with many misgivings, took command of a three-thousand-man assault force which captured Oswego after a four-day siege. Thirty Americans were killed, seventeen hundred taken prisoner, and a vast store of boats, cannon, and supplies captured, with only thirty casualties among the French. This was stunning blow to the Anglo-Americans, opening up the northwest frontier of New York to invasion. The entire western frontier of the English colonies was now ravaged by Canadian and Indian war parties. The early confidence that Canada would quickly be destroyed was replaced by fear that the French would soon invade the English colonies in force. Pleas for aid, recriminations, fears of conquest were voiced in the middle colonies. Far from winning the war, they were losing it.

The following year Vaudreuil continued this strategy of forcing the Anglo-Americans onto the defensive in the west with his raiding parties, supplied and sent out from Fort Duquesne.[26] On the central front Vaudreuil had to expect the British to mass their forces for an assault on Lake Champlain to drive the French back and open the invasion route into Canada. To forfend this he sent Montcalm with 3,600 men and 1,500 Indian allies to destroy the advanced British fort, William Henry, and then press south to threaten Albany. Arriving at the fort on August 3, Montcalm went through all the motions of a siege in the accepted European style and mounted his batteries. On the ninth the garrison commander, Colonel George Monro, asked for terms. He, with his 2,331-man garrison, was granted the honors of war and freedom to withdraw on condition they did not serve in operations against the French for eighteen months. After they had surrendered and were marching off, Montcalm's Indian allies, enraged at seeing their hated foe walk away unharmed, and inflamed by the liquor with which the Americans had foolishly tried to appease them, fell on the straggling columns. The French then did everything they could to stop the massacre, but twenty-nine were killed, over a hundred taken prisoner.

Regardless of this nasty episode, which afforded the British an opportunity to brand the French as war criminals, Montcalm had dealt the Anglo-Americans a severe blow. Their forward base was destroyed, they were deprived of a large body of troops and large stores of arms and cannon, and some three thousand barrels of pork and other valuable food supplies were added to the French stores. All this at a cost of thirteen killed and forty wounded. The Anglo-American troops defending the northern front were completely demoralized; Montcalm's were ready for anything. At New York the Provincial Council waited to hear that the French had taken the next strongpoint, Fort Edward, and fully expected Albany to fall. They wrote to Lord Loudoun, the commander in chief, who was at Halifax, "We may fear New York also."[27] Yet although Montcalm knew the dispirited and disorganized state of the enemy, that Fort Edward was only sixteen miles away, that its capture would have created panic in Albany and further reduced the offensive spirit of the Anglo-Americans, he refused to follow up his victory. He claimed the road was bad, his men worn out, and the militia needed back on their farms for the harvest. Since the harvest in Canada did not usually begin until September, even if the militia could not have been kept in the field beyond the first week of that month, it still allowed the French more than a fortnight to take Fort Edward, and that would have been enough time as things stood. Montcalm here betrayed his grave weakness as a commander. He was not aggressive; he could not seize the initiative when the opportunity presented itself. He preferred to react to the enemy's moves rather than make the enemy react to his.

Vaudreuil, of course, was infuriated by Montcalm's failure to execute his orders to march on Fort Edward. Their latent animosity now surfaced, and they quarreled openly. Their dispatches to the minister made their attitude all too plain. For his part, Vaudreuil infuriated Montcalm by taking credit for the victories; first at Oswego, then at Fort William Henry, as though he had commanded the troops during the actions, from his desk at Quebec.

Despite these victories, Canada had to have continued support from France to withstand the assaults that had been delayed but were sure to come.[28] Vaudreuil sent one of his Canadian officers to Versailles to explain the strategic and tactical situation and outline the additional forces needed to defend New France. He also allowed Montcalm to send two of his officers, Colonel Louis-Antoine de Bougainville and the commissary Doreil, to add their pleas. They were listened to much more attentively than was Vaudreuil's emissary. The dispute between the governor general and Montcalm was resolved in the latter's favor. Montcalm was promoted to lieutenant-general and given overall command of all the military forces in the colony. Vaudreuil now had to defer to Montcalm's decisions in all military matters. In addition, the government ordered that Vaudreuil's extended lines defensive strategy be abandoned and Montcalm's instituted. The French forces were to fall back on the settlements in the St. Lawrence Valley as the enemy advanced and strive only to hold them on the doorstep of the colony proper. This meant that the enemy would be allowed to advance almost unopposed through the wilderness and consolidate their supply lines for a massed assault. Everything, therefore, would depend on the ability of the French forces to hold Quebec and defeat much larger enemy armies south and west of Montreal. The French were, in short, to conduct the war in Canada on European lines and strive to hold the rump of New France in the hope that some part of the territory could be retained until hostilities ceased. If France still had a foot-hold in North America it would be in a much stronger position when the bargaining began at the peace table. Montcalm, through his emissaries, had painted such a bleak picture of the military position that the King's council apparently decided it would be folly to commit large forces in a forlorn hope. Thus fewer than five hundred replacements for the army in Canada accompanied Bougainville on his return to Quebec, raising the effective strength of the regular troops to less than six thousand.

Ironically, the French government, although its armies in the field had won startling victories, reducing the authorities in some of the English colonies to plead for peace on any terms before further defeats rendered even those terms unobtainable, had adopted the defeatist attitude of Montcalm, whereas the British government, now dominated by Pitt, took determined measures to drive the French, not just out of the territory claimed by Britain but out of North America. More British regiments were shipped to the colonies until more than 20,000 regulars of an army now totaling 140,000 soldiers and marines were in the theater and one-quarter of the Royal Navy, in addition to 22,000 colonial troops and militia. The French army, on the other hand, had only twelve of its 395 battalions serving in Canada and Louisbourg plus 2,000 Troupes de la Marine.[20] To that degree, fortress Canada was fulfilling its intended role in French imperial strategy; with a handful of troops it was tying down a much larger enemy force, preventing its being employed in some other theater.

185

In 1758 Pitt, who dictated military strategy, planned three concerted campaigns against Louisbourg, Quebec, and Fort Duquesne. Louisbourg, without a strong naval detachment, withstood a sixty-day siege by 8,000 troops under Jeffrey Amherst, but under fierce bombardment had finally to capitulate. It had, however, held out long enough to force the abandonment of the intended maritime assault on Quebec for that year. Brigadier James Wolfe acidly commented: "If this force had been properly manag'd, there was an end of the French colony in North America in one Campaign."[30] The fall of Louisbourg, by removing that potential threat to British shipping in the North Atlantic, allowed Pitt to transfer a large naval force to the West Indies. The object there was to capture Martinique to exchange at the peace table for Minorca, taken by the French in June, 1756, and so avoid the necessity to give back Louisbourg. The French defenses of Martinique proving too strong, the assault was transferred to Guadeloupe. Not, however, until May 1, 1759, were that island's defenders forced to capitulate, but Pitt now had the gage his strategy required. The war had taken a new direction. Previously it had been waged for commercial aims. Now territorial conquest was the chief end.[31]

On the central Canadian front Major General James Abercromby massed an army of 15,000, 6,000 of them British regulars, to drive down Lake Champlain to the Richelieu and the heart of Canada. He got no farther than Ticonderoga, where Montcalm and 3,500 regulars and militia had hastily entrenched themselves behind a wall of logs and felled trees. Cannon would have blasted this breast-work asunder. Abercromby, however, chose to send his regulars against it in a frontal column attack. They suffered heavy losses, but returned again and again until even these disciplined troops could take no more. The British withdrew to Fort William Henry, their losses nearly 2,000 men. The French had lost only 527 killed and wounded. The demoralized British had suffered another stunning defeat. Their retreat was almost a rout. They abandoned boats, arms, and supplies, as though the devil had been after them. Although a large contingent of Canadians reached Montcalm immediately after his victory, he made no attempt to follow it up by pursuing the beaten foe. Vaudreuil pleaded with him to send raiding parties to harass the enemy and their supply lines, and hammer it home to them that the route to Canada was impregnable. Montcalm, however, appeared satisfied with what he had already accomplished. And certainly, he had put a stop to the drive on the colony for that year. But that was not enough.

186

In the west the British had better success. In August Lieutenant Colonel Bradstreet with nearly 3,000 men caught the French at Fort Frontenac off guard.[32] Although the fort was very poorly sited, its walls no protection against cannon fire, the commandant, Pierre-Jacques Payen de Noyan, conducted the defense very ineptly. With his armed sloops he could have intercepted the attackers in their bateaux and shot them out of the water. Instead they were allowed to land and bring up their cannon. Three days later the fort surrendered. After destroying the store of provisions, the small French fleet, and the fort itself, Bradstreet swiftly retired across the lake. It was not the destruction of the fort but the loss of the stores, and the boats to transport them to Niagara and the Ohio, that hurt the French.

Farther west the British slowly mounted a campaign to drive the French out of the Ohio Valley. Montcalm convinced himself that this was merely a feint to draw troops away from Lake Champlain. Unfortunately for the French, they were now deprived of their Indian allies in the midwest. In October the authorities of Pennsylvania had met with delegates of the war-weary Ohio tribes at Easton and there negotiated a peace, a principal condition of which was a renunciation by Pennsylvania of all claims to lands beyond the crest of the mountains. The Indians guilelessly assumed that the Americans would honor the treaty; thus having achieved their main objective, they withdrew from the war. When Brigadier-General John Forbes, whose forces had been badly mauled by small Canadian war parties, learned from a French prisoner that the garrison at Fort Duquesne was far less than the reputed thousand, and with the Indian menace removed, he pressed on against the fort. The commandant, François Le Marchand de Ligneris, his supplies almost exhausted, his men in like condition, stripped the fort of its cannon, blew it up, and retreated to Fort Machault, there to await reinforcements and supplies from Montreal. He fully intended, when they were received, to counterattack and drive the Anglo-Americans back over the mountains.

In Canada, that winter of 1758–1759, food supplies were again short. The mass of the population was reduced to bare subsistence rations. Not so their leaders. Bigot and his entourage wanted for nothing. Gambling for desperately high stakes was the principal amusement. Vaudreuil remained aloof. He knew that Bigot was protected by senior officials in the Ministry of Marine, and this likely explains why he did not use his authority to curb the excesses. Montcalm, in his journal and his correspondence, was bitterly critical, but felt that his presence was required at the constant round of dinners and balls with which the senior officials and his officers beguiled themselves during the long winter nights.

Another scourge, inflation, hit the junior officers hard.

They were no longer paid in specie, but in postdated letters of credit to be redeemed three years hence. The merchants in the colony accepted them at a mere quarter of their face value. Lieutenants were paid 1,330 to 1,500 livres a year, and it cost them more than 7,500 to live. Fortunately, the ordinary soldiers who were billeted on the *habitants* when not on campaign did not suffer. They received their rations and worked for inflated wages, earning up to a pistole a day sawing firewood. Many of them married Canadian girls and were determined to remain in Canada when hostilities ended.

187

With the regular troops dispersed among the civilian population in this fashion, discipline suffered and training proved impossible. The battalion commanders did not know how many men they had on strength, except at the beginning of the campaigns in the spring and again in the autumn when muster parades were held. The lack of regular training exercises was to prove fatal. The reinforcements sent from France in 1757 had been a particularly poor lot; as casualties thinned the ranks of the regulars, Montcalm pressed Canadian militia into the battalions to maintain them at full strength. For the type of set battle that he wished to fight, it required eighteen months of training on the drill ground to turn a civilian into a soldier, capable of maneuvering en masse, marching up to the enemy and firing in volleys on command, and standing fast in the face of the enemy's volley or bayonet charge. By 1759 Montcalm's troops were no longer capable of that style of warfare. Although he and his staff officers in their letters and dispatches expressed nothing but defeatism and the belief that the colony was doomed — indeed, Montcalm eventually proposed retiring to Louisiana with the army should the British break through his lines — yet his second in command, the Chevalier de Lévis, and some at least of the junior officers were more sanguine about the outcome.[33]

Fortunately for the French, twenty-two supply ships reached Quebec in May, 1759, bringing enough food to keep the army in the field until the harvest. Hard on their heels, however, came the Royal Navy, bringing an army of 8,000 seasoned troops commanded by Major General James Wolfe, for an assault on the bastion of New France. On the Lake Champlain front Jeffrey Amherst, the commander in chief of the British forces in America, had massed an army of 6,236 regulars and provincials to dislodge the French from their forts. It took him a month to get his army in motion. The French officers had orders to fight delaying actions only at Carillon and St. Fréderic, then retire on Fort Île aux Noix to make a stand. After Amherst had spent several days preparing trenches and gun emplacements at Carillon the French mined the fort, lighted the fuses, and slipped away. They did the same at Fort St. Fréderic, but Amherst made no move to pursue them. Instead he devoted the remainder of the summer to repairing the fort at Ticonderoga and building a massive new fort near where Fort St. Fréderic had stood. The only purpose these forts could serve was to block an army advancing south from Canada. Were Quebec to be taken there was no danger whatsoever of that. Obviously, Amherst did not expect Quebec to fall. This was a view shared by others in the British forces.

In the west, de Ligneris renewed his raids on the British supply lines to Fort Pitt, constructed near the ruins of Fort Duquesne. He was, however, forced to desist and rush to the aid of the small garrison at Niagara, under siege by an American provincial army 2,500 strong. De Ligneris never got there. His force was ambushed and cut to pieces by the Americans. On July 26 Fort Niagara capitulated. The Americans had finally achieved their original war aims. Their hold on the Ohio Valley and Lake Ontario was now secure. Moreover, the St. Lawrence was, at last, open for a descent on Montreal.

At Quebec, however, things were not going so well for the British. Although Montcalm had proposed siting batteries downriver at three spots which dominated the river channel and could have made the passage very costly for a fleet at the mercy of wind, current, and tide, nothing had been done. Admiral Charles Saunders was able to bring up the army and land it unopposed on Île d'Orléans on June 27. Only when the British fleet was in the river were measures taken to fortify the immediate approaches to Quebec. Entrenchments were dug on the Beauport flats, across the St. Charles River from Quebec. On the insistence of the Chevalier de Lévis they were extended to the Montmorency River, but, incredibly, Montcalm made no attempt to fortify the cliffs across the river from Quebec. To oppose the British, Montcalm had a total of nearly 16,000 men, regulars, militia, and Indians at his disposal, double the number that Wolfe commanded.

The French had prepared a flotilla of fire ships. On the night of June 28 they were sent down on the British fleet. The operation was a fiasco. Set alight too soon, British sailors in longboats were able to tow all seven clear before they reached their objective. The next day, on the insistence of Admiral Saunders, the British occupied Point Lévis and French attempts to drive them out failed miserably. The British were now able to mount heavy mortars to bombard the town across the mile-wide river. They were also able to get their ships upriver above Quebec and to threaten a landing on either side of the town. A landing above Quebec was particularly to be feared since Montcalm had established his main supply depot at Batiscan, some sixty miles upriver. Wolfe, however, stuck resolutely to his original plan to break the Beauport lines, but every assault was beaten back.[34]

Still convinced that if he could only force Montcalm to give battle on open ground he could defeat his foe, Wolfe, in his last letter to his mother, remarked, "The Marquis de Montcalm is at the head of a great number of bad soldiers, and I am at the head of a small number of good ones, that wish for nothing so much as to fight him — but the wary old fellow avoids an action doubtful of the behavior of his army." There was more than a little truth in his judgment, as events were to prove. Although Wolfe was a poor strategist, he had always been an excellent regimental officer, a great admirer of Prussian military methods.[35] The training, discipline, and morale of his troops was now vastly superior to that of Montcalm's regulars. The Canadians, however, could be counted on to fight with savage desperation to protect their homeland and avoid the fate meted out earlier to the Acadians.

189

As July became August, Wolfe, frustrated at every turn and suffering from poor health, quarreled with his brigadiers. They regarded his tactics to date inept and resented his secretive, arrogant manner. Unable to force the enemy to come out of his lines, Wolfe gave orders for the systematic destruction of the colony. The Canadian settlements were to receive the same treatment as had the Scottish Highlands after Culloden, in which Wolfe had played an active part. Upon first landing on the Île d'Orléans he had issued a manifesto ordering the Canadian people not to assist the "enemy," warning them that if they took up arms in defense of their homeland they would be punished with fire and sword, treated as Indians, who Wolfe had earlier declared merited extermination.[36] He took no account of the fact that every Canadian male between fifteen and sixty was a member of the militia, and thus had to obey the orders of his officers and fight the invader. To Wolfe war was the prerogative of regular uniformed troops; the civilian population had to stand aside and accept the outcome, regardless of its consequences for their lives and the lives of their descendants. At the end of July Wolfe repeated his proclamation, then turned loose the American Rangers, whom he had labeled "the worst soldiers in the universe," to burn the houses, buildings, and crops in all the parishes up and down the river. When any resistance was met, and prisoners taken, they were shot and scalped. At least fourteen hundred farms were destroyed, most of them fine stone buildings in the earlier-settled and more prosperous part of the colony. Bigot tersely commented: "M. Wolfe est cruel."

Wolfe claimed that this devastation was intended to force Montcalm to emerge and give battle. In this it failed. At the same time he increased the number of cannon bombarding Quebec from the Lévis side to forty pieces. Hardly a building in the city was left undamaged; 80 percent of Quebec was destroyed. It was the civilian population, not the army, that suffered. The bombardment served no useful military purpose. This whole policy of calculated destruction of Quebec and of the seigneuries about it made no military sense whatsoever, unless it had been concluded that Quebec could not be taken, and Canada not conquered. In his journal, under date of August 13, Major Patrick Mackellar noted that the bombardment of Quebec had been stepped up, and commented, "This was thought to be done either to favor a storm by water, or to do the town all possible damage if it could not be taken, which was now becoming doubtful, as there was little or no appearance of making good a landing upon that coast, it being so well fortified and defended by such Superior Numbers."[37] Wolfe himself, in his dispatch of September 2 to Pitt, in which he reviewed the course of the campaign, expressed profound pessimism as to the outcome, declaring: "In this situation, there is such a choice of difficulties, that I own myself at the loss how to determine." At that late date only a few weeks remained before the fleet

190

would be forced to withdraw, taking the army with it. Of his original troop strength of 8,500 barely half were fit for duty. Casualties had been heavy. The men were now on short rations, reduced to eating horse flesh. More than a thousand men were in sick bay. Dysentery and scurvy were taking a heavy toll. At the end of August, in a letter to Admiral Saunders, Wolfe stated, "Beyond the month of September I conclude our operations cannot go." He then made the revealing comment that Barré had prepared a list of where the troops would be quartered, "supposing (as I have very little hope of) they do not quarter here."[38] But Wolfe could not give up without making one last attempt to conquer Quebec.

He wanted to launch another attack on the Beauport lines below Quebec, but when he proposed three variants of this plan to his brigadiers they rejected the concept of any attack there. Instead they proposed a landing above Quebec between the city and the supply depot at Batiscan. Such a landing would, they pointed out, cut the road to Montreal. The brigadiers argued that there a landing in strength would force Montcalm to emerge from behind his defense works and give battle in the open. Ever since the fleet had forced a passage above Quebec, British raiding parties had landed above the town periodically. This had forced Montcalm to detach 3,000 of his better troops under Bougainville to march up and down abreast of the British ships to counter the threat.

Wolfe accepted the brigadiers' suggestion for a landing above Quebec; but whereas they had intended the landing to be made well above the city, he chose the Anse au Foulon, at the foot of the 175-foot cliff, less than two miles from Quebec. The operation required the troops to be transported above the city by the fleet, then, during the night, to embark in the landing craft, drift down with the tide, land, make their way up the steep path to the top of the cliff, overpower the French outpost stationed there, then assemble on the heights before the city walls and wait for the French reaction. It was a most desperate gamble, requiring the complete cooperation of the elements — and also of the French. Rear

Admiral Charles Holmes, who was in charge of the operation, afterward described it: "The most hazardous and difficult task I was ever engaged in: For the distance of the landing place; the darkness of the night; and the chance of exactly hitting the very spot intended, without discovery or alarm; made the whole extremely difficult."[39]

Everything depended on surprise. Were the French to have had a battalion of troops on the heights above the Anse au Foulon, the landing could never have succeeded. Montcalm was convinced that Wolfe would not lift the siege without one last assault, and reading his adversary's mind, he anticipated an attack on the right of the Beauport lines.[40] The fleet movements above Quebec he regarded as a diversion. He had moved a battalion to the heights near the Anse au Foulon on September 5 but recalled it the following day to the Beauport lines.[41] As it was, the small French detachment on top of the cliff was taken completely by surprise, routed by the first British troops to scale the heights. The way was open for the army to follow. When Wolfe himself landed, the situation still looked desperate. His comment reveals that he regarded the enterprise as a forlorn hope: "I don't think we can by any possible means get up here; but, however, we must use our best endeavour."[42] This they did, and the surprise of the French was complete. By daybreak Wolfe had more than 4,400 men on the Plains of Abraham, a thousand yards from the city walls. But they were in an extremely vulnerable position. Before them was Quebec, poorly fortified, but still protected by a wall that would have to be breached by heavy guns, brought up the cliff, before an assault could be made. In Quebec and the Beauport lines Montcalm had some 6,000 troops, and a few miles above Quebec was Bougainville with 3,000 more. Wolfe's army was between the two. Moreover, he had to win a complete victory. Few generals have burned their bridges more successfully than did Wolfe. Retreat was virtually impossible. The army would have had to withdraw down the steep cliff path, then wait to be taken off the narrow beach by the ships' long boats. Such an operation would have invited slaughter. The alternatives for the British would have been: be shot, be drowned, or surrender. It is doubtful that many would have escaped. The army most likely would have been destroyed, and the fleet would have had to sail back to England with the shattered remnants. But none of this happened. Yet the possibility must have been in the minds of the soldiers as they climbed the cliff. It speaks volumes for their morale and discipline.

191

Upon finding the British army on the heights, Montcalm had several courses of action open to him, and ample time to carry them out. He could have sent word immediately to Bougainville, ten miles away, to bring his forces up to attack the British in the rear while he launched a frontal assault. He could have marched his army around the British and joined up with Bougainville for a consolidated attack. He could have withdrawn his main force into the city and forced Wolfe to launch an assault while Bougainville and the Canadian militia harassed the British rear. Montcalm could afford to wait; Wolfe could not. Bringing up supplies for his army from the fleet would have been difficult, to say the least. A siege was out of the question. The British had only two or three weeks left in which to take Quebec or be forced to withdraw. In short, Montcalm could have forced Wolfe to fight on his terms. Instead, he chose to throw away all these advantages and fight on the ground and at the time chosen by the British, employing only half his available forces.

By nine o'clock he had some 4,500 men mustered on the plain in front of the walled city, facing the British. The Canadian militia, fighting from cover on the flanks in their traditional manner, had engaged the enemy and were inflicting casualties. Then Montcalm gave the order for a frontal attack. The French regiments, bolstered by untrained Canadian militia, advanced at a run, fired volleys at long range, then dropped to the ground to reload. Their lines quickly became ragged. The disciplined British lines held their fire until the French were close, fired measured volleys, reloaded, advanced out of the gunsmoke, then fired again. When the lines were thirty yards apart, volleys all down the British line shattered the reeling French ranks. The French turned and fled toward the city, the British in pursuit. All that saved the remnants of the army was the withering fire of the Canadian militia on the flanks that forced the British to turn and regroup. By noon Wolfe's men were in command of the field. The actual battle had lasted only fifteen minutes. Half of North America was lost and won in that short engagement.

When it was over, Vaudreuil, who had never thought Montcalm would attack so precipitately, arrived on the field with reinforcements. Bougainville appeared later still, then quickly retired. The British still held only the Plains of Abraham.[43] The French had more than twice as many effectives and held the town. Casualties on both sides had been very heavy: 658 for the British,[44] almost as many for the French. Among the killed was Wolfe, and among the dying, Montcalm. For the generals on both sides to be killed in a battle was indeed remarkable. True to form, Montcalm's last action before expiring was to address a letter to Brigadier General George Townshend, who had succeeded Wolfe in command, yielding up Quebec.

Vaudreuil, meanwhile, was struggling to rally the French forces to attack the British the following day, but the colonels of the *troupes de terre* had no stomach for it. Vaudreuil, therefore, gathered up all the troops and militia, then withdrew around the British to join Bougainville and regroup above the Jacques Cartier River, thirty-two miles from the city. In Quebec he had left the Chevalier de Ramesay with a token force and ill-conceived instructions to hold out as long as possible but not necessarily to wait for a British assault before surrendering. The Chevalier de Lévis, come posthaste from Montreal, now took command of the French army and prepared to counterattack. Before he could do so Ramesay surrendered Quebec and the British marched in. The French then fell back and established their forward outpost at Jacques Cartier, while the main forces retired to Montreal.

In Quebec, when the fleet finally sailed in October, Brigadier James Murray was left in command with the bulk of the army. He likely did not receive a letter until the following year written by Thomas Ainslie at Louisbourg and dated October 28: "I now congratulate you on your success at Quebec a thing little expected by any here, and posterity will hardly give credit to it, that such a handful of men should carry a point against such numbers, and with such advantages, thank God you have escaped, it is a miracle that you have."[45] After the British ships had sailed, the French got some of their ships past Quebec with dispatches for France pleading for a strong naval squadron to be sent early to block the St. Lawrence and prevent the British garrison at Quebec from being reinforced. Ten thousand troops, artillery, and supplies were also demanded to repel the British assaults that were sure to come the following year.

Murray's troops suffered cruelly during that winter in the city they had shattered. Sentries froze to death. Wood-cutting parties were savaged by the Canadians. Scurvy took a heavy toll.[46] In April Lévis gathered up his forces, 7,000 men, and marched back to try to retake Quebec. On the twenty-seventh he was at Ste. Foy, five miles from the city. Ironically, Murray committed the same tactical error as Montcalm had done. He marched his troops out, 3,866 strong, to give battle.[47] Lévis had 3,800 on the battlefield. Again the armies were evenly matched. But this time the British were routed. Abandoning their guns, they were pursued right to the city gates. Lévis then laid siege to the town while awaiting the relief ships from France. Those ships never came. Versailles had decided that Canada was irretrievably lost. The Duc de Choiseul sagely concluded that the British, by conquering New France, would merely strengthen their American colonies and their latent urge to strike out for independence. There was, therefore, no point in risking France's remaining naval strength, thousands of troops, and adding to the nation's hideous load of debt to achieve an end that the loss of Canada would achieve in due course at no cost to France. A token force was sent to Canada — five ships escorted by one frigate, bearing four hundred soldiers and some supplies. They sailed late. When they arrived in the Gulf of St. Lawrence a powerful British fleet was already in the Gulf. After putting up a gallant fight the French ships were sunk in Restigouche Bay.

By mid-May the British ships of the line were at Quebec. Lévis had to raise the siege and retire on Montreal, where he intended to make a last stand — not to save the colony, for that was clearly impossible, but to save the honor of the French army and his own reputation. Three British armies now moved in to crush what remained of Canada. Murray moved upriver, by-passing the French defense points, and pressed on toward Montreal. To quell the resistance of the Canadians the homes at Sorel along a four-mile stretch were put to the torch. Even though their situation was hopeless, the consequences of further resistance cruel, many of the Canadians kept on fighting. Many, however, gave up.

On the Lake Champlain front the French had to fall back before Brigadier William Haviland's army, abandoning the chain of forts on the Richelieu after a heavy artillery bombardment. To the west Amherst at long last put in an appearance, moving down the St. Lawrence from Oswego. On September 6 he landed at Lachine. Seventeen thousand British troops now confronted Lévis. His forces had shrunk to two thousand. More than fifteen hundred of his regulars had deserted.[48] On the seventh Vaudreuil asked Amherst for terms. With a conspicuous lack of gallantry Amherst refused to grant the honors of war. Lévis protested violently. He demanded that the regulars be allowed to make a final stand rather than accept such shameful conditions. Vaudreuil, fearing savage reprisals on the Canadian people and recognizing the futility of further resistance, ordered that Amherst's terms be accepted. That night Lévis ordered his regiments to burn their colors to avoid the dishonor and anguish of spirit of handing them over to Amherst. On September 9 the British marched into Montreal. What remained of the French and Canadian regulars stacked their arms on the Champ de Mars. Before the month was out, they and the administrative officials were transported to France.[49] According to the terms of the capitulation the troops could not serve again during the continuance of the war.

194

National Archives of Canada / C11043.

The capitulation of the French to the British, Montreal, September 1760. The Canadian artist, A.S. Scott, has re-created the scene as it might have looked, as the French turned their arms over to the British, and surrendered New France.

Canada had finally been conquered. Yet that conquest had, by no means, been inevitable. Had no regular troops been involved on either side it is highly unlikely that the Anglo-Americans could have conquered New France. Fifteen years later, on the eve of the American Revolution, Chief Justice Hey at Quebec remarked: "I believe it to be as true as anything can be that has not been reduced to absolute proof that the Colonies without the assistance of England, would have been reduced from North to south by this province in the last war. They thought so themselves. . . . "[50] And against Louisiana, where no British troops were engaged, the Indian allies of the French punished the American frontier so severely that no attempts were made to invade that province. Had Montcalm not employed such disastrous tactics at Quebec on September 13, 1759, the fortress city would not have fallen; instead the British army might well have been destroyed. Then, the wavering, war-weary British government would have been more inclined to seek an end to the war. Ineptitude in the French military command and government at home, and the fortunes of war, gave Britain dominion over the vast French territory. But what might have been was now of no account. All that mattered to the conquered Canadians was to restore their destroyed homes before the onset of winter. Beyond that their main concern was what their ultimate fate would be. They were all disarmed and obliged to swear an oath of allegiance to the British monarch. Over them all hung the terrible fear of deportation, not to be dispelled for three generations. Yet the war still raged in Europe. They could still hope that France might win victories elsewhere with which to purchase their liberation. Meanwhile they had to make the best they could of life under the military rule of their conquerors.

195

NOTES

[1] See Paul Vaucher, *Robert Walpole et la Politique de Fleury (1731-1742)* (Paris, 1924), 298-302; Sir Julian S. Corbett, *England in the Seven Years' War*, 2 vols. (London, 1918), 1: 23-29; E.E. Rich, ed., *The Cambridge Economic History of Europe* (Cambridge Univ. Press, 1967), 4: 536-37.

[2] It is not without significance that the furs of the Ohio Valley were considered by the Canadians to be of very little value. See the informed comments by D'Aigremont; Paris, Archives Nationales, Colonies, C11A, 29: 61. On Anglo-American aims and activities in the Ohio Valley see John Mitchell, *The Contest in America Between Great Britain and France with Its Consequences and Importance* (London, 1757), iii-xlix, 17-38; Alfred P. James, *The Ohio Company: Its Inner History* (Univ. of Pittsburgh Press, 1959).

[3] See W.J. Eccles, *The Canadian Frontier, 1534-1760* (New York, 1969), 157-60.

[4] Guy Frégault, *Le Grand Marquis: Pierre de Rigaud de Vaudreuil et la Louisiane* (Montréal, 1952), 163-77.

[5] George F.G. Stanley, *New France: The Last Phase, 1744-1760* (Toronto, 1968), 60.

[6] On the events, strategy, and tactics of the war see Stanley, *New France: The Last Phase*; Eccles, *The Canadian Frontier*, 157-85; Guy Frégault, *Canada: The War of the Conquest* (Toronto, 1969); Corbett, *England in the Seven Years' War*; Lawrence Henry Gipson, *The British Empire before the American Revolution*, vols. 4-8 (New York, 1939-54); Gerald S. Graham, *Empire of the North Atlantic: The Maritime Struggle for North America* (Toronto, 1950).

[7] This incident has long been a subject of controversy, American historians seeking to excuse Washington, while French and French-Canadian historians, for the most part, declare his act to have been that of a common assassin. See Stanley, *New France: The Last Phase*, 54-55.

[8] The journal was sent to Governor General Duquesne at Quebec, who predictably commented: "Rien de plus indigne et de plus bas Et meme de plus noir que les sentimens Et la facon de penser de

ce Washington, Il y auroit eu plaisir de luy Lire Sous le nez Son outrageant journal." He had a translation made, a copy of which is in the Archives du Séminaire de Québec. See Fernand Grenier, ed., *Papiers Contrecoeur et autres documents concernant le conflit anglo-français sur l'Ohio de 1745 à 1756* (Québec, 1952), 133–81, 251.

[9] Walter L. Dorn, *Competition for Empire, 1740–1763* (New York, 1963), 287–89.

[10] *Troupes de terre* were the regiments of the regular army, so designated because many of them took their nomenclature from the provinces where they were raised, e.g., Régiment de Languedoc, Régiment de Béarn.

[11] See Corbett, *England in the Seven Years' War* 1: 45–46; Richard Waddington, *Louis XV et le renversement des alliances* (Paris, 1896), 96–97.

[12] Waddington, *Louis XV et le renversement des alliances,* 104–110.

[13] The strength of the four battalions sent to Quebec, on arrival, was 108 officers, 1693 other ranks. See Paris, Archives Nationales, Colonies, D2C, 46: 254.

[14] See A.T. Mahan, *The Influence of Seapower upon History* (New York, 1890; paperback ed., New York, 1957), 1957 ed., p. 251. The strength of the French navy was depleted further by an epidemic of typhus that swept through the fleet and naval ports in 1757. It was this, rather than the greater strength or efficiency of the Royal Navy, that allowed the latter eventually to blockade the French ports and dominate the Atlantic. Seamen and dockyard workers fled the ports; ships could not be manned for lack of crews and sometimes had to go into action with a handful of seamen amid impressed landsmen. See Ruddock F. Mackay, *Admiral Hawke* (Oxford 1965), 204, 213, 227, 234, 249.

[15] For an example of the use made of these incidents by French diplomats abroad on instructions of the foreign minister see *Rapport de l'Archiviste de la Province de Québec* RAPQ (1949–51): 5, M. Durand d'Aubigny, Résident du Roi à Liège, au Ministre, Liège, 27 juillet 1755; RAPQ (1949–51): 9, D'Aubigny au Ministre, à Liège le 11 oct. 1755.

[16] See *RAPQ* (1931–32): 19, Mémoire du Chevalier de la Pause.

[17] The most detailed and frequently cited study of this action is Stanley M. Pargellis, "Braddock's Defeat," *American Historical Review* 41 (1936): 253–69. It is, however, dated; the limitations of the musket were not taken sufficiently into account, and the effectiveness of guerrilla tactics against regular troops untrained for such warfare had not been as clearly demonstrated in 1936 as it was to be in subsequent years.

[18] On this issue many historians have allowed national sentiment to weight their judgment. This is particularly true of Francis Parkman, *Montcalm and Wolfe* (London, 1964 ed.), 175–208, and Gipson, *The British Empire before the American Revolution* 6: 212–344. Waddington, *Louis XV et le renversement des alliances,* 372–417, gives a detailed account of events and roundly condemns the British. For a judicious view see Guy Frégault, *Canada: The War of the Conquest,* 164–200; "La déportation des Acadiens," *Revue d'Histoire de l'Amérique Française* 8, 3 (1954–55): 309–358.

[19] A contemporary American observer put the situation very succinctly: "Our colonies are all open and exposed, without any manner of security or defense. Theirs are protected and secured by numbers of forts and fortresses. Our men in America are scattered up and down the woods, upon their plantations, in remote and distant provinces. Theirs are collected together in forts and garrisons. Our people are nothing but a set of farmers and planters, used only to the axe or hoe. Theirs are not only well trained and disciplined but they are used to arms from their infancy among the Indians; and are reckoned equal, if not superior in that part of the world to veteran troops. Our people are not to be drawn together from so many different governments, views, and interests; are unable, unwilling, or remiss to march against an enemy, or dare not stir, for fear of being attacked at home. They are all under one government, subject to command like a military people. While we mind nothing but trade and planting. With these the French maintain numbers of Indians — We have none, — These are troops that fight without pay — maintain themselves in the woods without charges — march without baggage — and support themselves without stores and magazines — we are at immense charges for those purposes. By these means a few Indians do more execution, as we see, than four or five times their number of our men, and they have almost all the Indians of that continent to join them." Mitchell, *The Contest in America Between Great Britain and France,* 137–38. See also pp. 118–19, 125–26, and Charles Henry Lincoln, ed., *The Correspondence of William Shirley,* 2 vols. (New York, 1912), 2: 133–34, Shirley to James Delancey, Boston, Feb. 24, 1755.

[20] See Henri-Raymond Casgrain, ed., *Collection des manuscripts du maréchal de Lévis,* 12 vols. (Montréal and Québec, 1889–95), vol. 4, *Lettres et pièces militaires, instructions, ordres, mémoires, plans de campagne et de défense, 1756–1760* (Québec, 1891), 153.

[21] In 1756 France had 45 ships of the line ready for sea, 15 in dock being readied, several under construction (Waddington, *Louis XV et le renversement des alliances,* 246). England had 130 ships of the line, but they were inferior to the French; the reverse was true of the officers of the two navies. (Dorn, *Competition for Empire,* 105–121). In 1756, with war declared, the French government decided on an invasion of England. The American theater tied down a sizable part of the Royal Navy; a diversionary assault on Minorca would tie down more. Diversionary assaults were to be made on Scotland and Ireland, then the main invasion launched against England. It was anticipated that all the ships and troops in the latter assault would be lost, but not before they had caused worse panic than the Jacobite march on London in 1745, the collapse of the country's financial structure, and a consequent willingness of the ruling class to accept reasonable peace terms to avert worse losses. See Corbett, *England in the Seven Years' War* 1: 83–95; Dorn, *Competition for Empire,* 355.

[22] See Frégault, *Le grand marquis.*

[23] See Frégault, *Canada: The War of the Conquest,* 241–43.

[24] His attitude is revealed by a comment in his journal: "A quoi donc sont bons les sauvages? A ne pas les avoir contre soi." Casgrain, *Collection des manuscrits* 7: 591.

[25] Bigot's activities were regarded as criminal, and he later paid for them; but to a degree, he appears to have been used as a scapegoat. It is interesting to note the difference in attitude toward his malversations and the bland acceptance in England of Henry Fox's amassing of a fortune, perhaps as large as that acquired by Bigot, while serving as paymaster-general. See Lucy S. Sutherland and J. Binney, "Henry Fox as Paymaster-General of the Forces," *English Historical Review* 70 (Apr. 1955). For Bigot's checkered career see Guy Frégault, *François Bigot: Administrateur français,* 2 vols. (Montréal, 1948).

[26] For a brief contemporary description of the nature of this guerrilla warfare see RAPQ (1931–32): 43, Mémoire et observations sur mon voyage en Canada, Chevalier de la Pause.

[27] New York State Archives, Albany, Colonial Documents, 84: 149.

[28] Historians who accept — usually as an unstated, and likely unconscious, premise — that what happened had to happen, and therefore regard the conquest of New France as inevitable, always advance as a main argument the dependence of Canada on France for support. They thereby ignore that the English colonies were more dependent on England for military aid than Canada was on France.

[29] In 1758 the British army and marines numbered 140,000. Rex Whitworth, *Field Marshall Lord Ligonier: A Study of the British Army, 1702–1770* (Oxford, 1958), 208, 246. The French army at maximum strength, 1757–1762, was slightly under 330,000 men in line units. Lee Kennet, *The French Armies in the Seven Years' War* (Duke Univ. Press, 1967), 75–78.

[30] McCord Museum, McGill University, Wolfe Papers, No. 1288.

[31] On the West Indies campaign and Pitt's strategy see Corbett, *England in the Seven Years' War* 1: 371–95; Gipson, *The British Empire before the American Revolution,* vols. 5 and 8.

[32] Mr. James Turnbull, presently preparing a Ph.D. thesis on the role of Governor General Vaudreuil during the war, has advanced the proposition, on good evidence, that the French suffered a breakdown in the intelligence service provided them by the Five Nations. Previously the Iroquois had kept Vaudreuil well informed of English plans and preparations. On this occasion they conspicuously did not. It may be that they regarded it as in their interests to have the British destroy Fort Frontenac, located as it was on lands they claimed as theirs. When the French destroyed Oswego in 1756 the Iroquois pointedly thanked Vaudreuil for having thus "reestablished the Five Nations in possession of lands that belonged to them." See RAPQ (1932–33): 327.

[33] See Archives de la Guerre, Series A1, Vol. 3540, pt. 1, pp. 115, 138–39.

[34] On August 11 he wryly remarked: "We had a lively skirmish this morning — we are as usual victorious and yet I am afraid we lost more than the enemy owing to our original disposition and partly to the irregularity and folly of our men. . . . " Public Archives of Canada, James Murray Papers, Wolfe to Brig.-Gen. Murray, Aboard Sterling Castle, 11 Aug. 1759.

[35] See Wolfe to Captain Maitland, August 5, 1757: "I have ever entertained a profound admiration for the King of Prussia as the first soldier of this Age and our Master in the Art of War . . . . Some of H.M.'s manouvres are curious and the Deployments display uncommon ingenuity. They doubtless will be adopted by us if Occasion arises." McCord Museum, McGill University, Wolfe Papers, M1385. On Wolfe's generalship see E.R. Adair, "The Military Reputation of Major-General James Wolfe," Canadian Historical Association, *Report* (1936); C.P. Stacey, *Quebec, 1759* (Toronto, 1959), 170–78.

[36] For Wolfe's views on the Indians, see McCord Museum, McGill University, Wolfe Papers, No. 1288. His manifesto is printed in Casgrain, *Collection des manuscrits* 4: 273–76.

[37] Public Archives of Canada, MG23, GII-1, Series 2-7, P. Mackellar's short account of the expedition against Quebec, p. 20.

[38] Christopher Hibbert, *Wolfe at Quebec* (London, 1959), 165; Stacey, *Quebec, 1759,* 102.

[39] Stacey, *Quebec, 1759,* 132–33.

[40] C.P. Stacey, *Quebec, 1759,* 111–12, 168, opines that Montcalm lacked one essential quality of a good general, the ability to divine his antagonist's intentions, citing his failure to anticipate the landing above Quebec as an example. Montcalm gave abundant evidence of poor generalship, but in this particular case he cannot be faulted, for he had read Wolfe's mind very accurately. What he failed to divine was that Wolfe would defer to the tactics proposed by his brigadiers. He could not have been expected to know that this had transpired.

[41] For the confusion that this incident occasioned in the minds of Canadian historians see the intriguing critique by C.P. Stacey, "The Anse au Foulon, 1759: Montcalm and Vaudreuil," *Canadian Historical Review* 40, 4 (Mar. 1959): 27–37.

[42] See C.P. Stacey, "Quebec, 1759: Some New Documents,' *Canadian Historical Review* 47, 4 (Dec. 1966): 344–55; Frégault, *Canada: The War of the Conquest,* 253.

[43] In 1711 Governor General Philippe de Rigaud de Vaudreuil, father of the governor general of 1759, had prepared to repel an English seaborne assault on Quebec. He had entrenchments made and cut all the roads everywhere the enemy could effect a landing on both sides of the city, from Beauport to Cape Rouge. He stated that even should the enemy break through these defenses, which they could not do without suffering heavy losses, "they would still hold nothing." RAPQ (1946–47): 433–34.

[44] The total British casualties in the Quebec campaign were 21 officers killed, 93 wounded, 1,384 other ranks killed, wounded, and missing. McCord Museum, McGill University, No. 824, A Return of

the Kill'd & Wounded etc. of H.M. Forces up the River St. Lawrence from the 27th June to the Reduction of Quebec 10 [sic] Sept. 1759.

45 Public Archives of Canada, James Murray Papers, vol. 1, pt. 3, pp. 8-9.

46 Vaudreuil proposed to detach 1,500 to 1,800 men to harass the British garrison continually and by preventing their obtaining firewood force Murray to surrender. The proposal was rejected owing to the shortage of food supplies for such a detachment and also because the French were sure that Murray would retaliate by burning the homes of all the Canadians within his reach. This might indicate that the British policy of schrechlichkeit had served a purpose. See RAPQ (1938-39): 2.

47 The best brief account of this battle to date is G.F.G. Stanley, New France: The Last Phase, 242-50.

48 Their officers reported that the majority of the regulars were resolved not to return to France. Many of them had married Canadian girls, with the consent of Montcalm, who had promised them that they could take their discharge and remain in the colony at the war's end. See Eccles, The Canadian Frontier, 176, 184. For a graphic contemporary account of the collapse of French resistance see RAPQ (1931-32): 120, Relation de M. Poularies.

49 A handful of officers in the Troupes de la Marine, six captains, three lieutenants, four enseignes, were granted permission in 1760 to remain in the colony either to recuperate from serious wounds or to attend to urgent family affairs. Only three Canadian merchants returned to France at the capitulation: Guillaume-Michel Perrault, d'Étienne Charest, Louis Charly de Saint Ange. See Claude Bonnault de Méry, "Les Canadiens en France et aux colonies après la cession (1760-1815)," Revue de l'Histoire des Colonies Françaises 17 (1924): 495-550.

50 Shortt and Doughty, Documents Relating to the Constitutional History of Canada, 1759-1791 2: 669.

Generals and Generalship before Quebec, 1759-1760*

C.P. STACEY

I

The two hundredth anniversary of the fall of Quebec is a good time for Canadian historians to take stock of the most famous series of events in Canadian history. After two centuries, these events are still, apparently, interesting to the public. At any rate, publishers seem to think so; for about half a dozen new books about them are being published in 1959.[1]

There is an enormous literature about the Seven Years' War in America, and the Quebec campaign of 1759 in particular. In spite of this, many aspects of the period remain controversial. I shall today attempt a review of some of the controversies. But as a preliminary it seems desirable to review also the work of the historians who have contributed to them. Both things I propose to do in the light of a re-examination of the primary sources of information.

If I may begin with a personal explanation, some time ago I set out to write a short book on the events at Quebec in 1759. With what seems to me now considerable simplicity, I assumed that so much work had been done on these events that I could avoid doing much tiresome research and concentrate on producing a leisured and gentlemanly commentary on the well-established facts. Before I had done much reading

*From the Canadian Historical Association Report (1959), 1-15. Reprinted by permission of the Canadian Historical Association and the author. Colonel Stacey was affiliated with the Historical Section of Army Headquarters in Ottawa at the time of this article's original publication.

I discovered that I had been too optimistic. I found myself driven on to start digging into the primary sources — a process rendered fatally easy by the fact that I was living in Ottawa, which possesses the greatest existing collection of such sources on the subject. In the end, I wrote, not the essay I had hoped for, but a documented history of the campaign, an attempt, however inadequate, at a new interpretation based on a new study of the contemporary evidence. I had come to feel, rightly or wrongly, that this was needed.

II

As a result of my reading I arrived at two disturbing conclusions. The first was that the history of the siege of Quebec had been, on the whole, rather badly written. The second, I am sorry to say, was that the worst of the bad writing had been done in Canada.

Whatever the political, social, or economic historian may say, military operations are not the easiest stuff of which to make history. The fog of war has a way of drifting into the historian's study and getting into his eyes; and when to the grey fog of war is added the golden haze of romance, visibility tends to fall close to zero. The haze of romance settled over the Quebec area within a few weeks of the Battle of the Plains of Abraham, and it has not lifted yet. A good deal of what has been scribbled in the resulting murk seems to me not much better than romantic nonsense.

Prejudice, of course, has played a great part in the result. The influence of national prejudice is obvious. But there has been much personal prejudice too. Historians have become devoted adherents or bitter opponents of the leading personalities of the time. Moreover, some of them have suffered woefully from lack of military knowledge. Finally, there has been a considerable amount of just plain inadequate investigation. Writers of high reputation have been guilty of surprising lapses. I offer one example.

Sir Julian Corbett's book *England in the Seven Years' War* is regarded, not without some reason, as a standard military study of the war. In discussing the appointment of Wolfe to command the Quebec expedition, Corbett asserts that the Army in America had asked for him. There is in the Record Office, he says, a "curious paper" in which three colonels (Monckton, Murray, and Burton) recommended to Pitt that he appoint Wolfe. This seemed decidedly "curious," even in the eighteenth century, and with the aid of Mr. Ormsby of the Public Archives I checked the source cited by Corbett. It turned out to be a document sent, not from America to England, but in the opposite direction; it is in fact the "Proposals for the Expedition to Quebec" sent by Pitt to General Amherst for his guidance.[2] It begins by noting that Colonel Wolfe is to command, with the rank of major general "for and during the Expedition to Quebec only"; it then goes on to list as "Brigadiers to Act under the same Re-

199

strictions" the names of Monckton, Murray, and Burton. Incredible as it may seem, there appears to be no doubt that Corbett read these three names as *signatures* to the document. This led him, not only to perpetrate an historical absurdity, but to miss a point of much interest. This is the fact that Ralph Burton was originally slated to be the third brigadier, but was displaced, in circumstances which remain rather obscure, by the better-connected George Townshend. Townshend was evidently forced upon Wolfe.[3] Here we have, one suspects, part of the background for the serious rift that developed between Wolfe and Townshend before Quebec.

This example at least serves to indicate that not all the historiographical crimes in connection with the 1759 campaign have been committed by Canadians. The Canadians, however, have been responsible for more than their fair share. It is particularly astonishing that they have failed to make better use of the plans of Quebec available in the Ottawa archives. Nothing of the slightest value has ever been done on the state of the Quebec fortifications in 1759, though ample material lies ready to hand. The late Sir Arthur Doughty gave currency to the legend that there are no defensive works at Quebec today which antedate 1820 — though a mere glance at the plans immediately establishes the fact that, basically, the city walls today are the same that stood there in 1759. Sir Arthur also accepted as an accurate account of the fortifications the plan drawn by Patrick Mackellar (Wolfe's Chief Engineer) after his captivity at Quebec in 1757. Yet the defences on the land side in Mackellar's plan are those shown on Charlevoix's map of 1744. These were in fact wholly altered beginning in 1745. Mackellar's plan was thus fourteen years out of date in 1759.[4] It was lucky for Wolfe that, thanks to the inefficiency of the engineers and administrators of New France, the new fortifications were about as bad as the old ones; and Mackellar's basic conclusion, that the best way to take the city was to attack its weak land side, remained sound, even though the information on which it was based was entirely inaccurate.

Of the individual historians who have written about the events of 1759 one could speak endlessly. Leaving earlier writers aside, we may begin with Parkman. It seems to me that *Montcalm and Wolfe*, published in 1884, has worn remarkably well. There is not much that his successors can teach the Bostonian; on the contrary, many of them could learn from him. It is true that he tells some stories (which incidentally have been repeated by virtually every writer since his time) which are probably unfounded. It is true that he takes liberties with documents[5] — though never, so far as I have seen, to the extent of altering the sense. Also, his account of the Quebec campaign is relatively brief, and much is left out. But on balance one can only salute him for his achievement.

Among the other writers who have dealt broadly with the Seven Years' War, and more incidentally with the Quebec campaign, Richard Waddington is an eminent figure. *La Guerre de sept ans*, so far as I can judge it, is a book impressive in research as well as monumental in scope. And it is pleasant to be able to say that North American scholarship in our own day has produced a work worthy to stand beside these triumphs of the past. Professor Gipson's book *The Great War for the Empire*, a part of his larger work, *The British Empire before the American Revolution*, is fine in its sweep and most admirable in its investigation of the sources. I would not agree with everything in it, but it is a splendid achievement of the historian's craft.

I turn now to the more specialized studies, and first to the group of Canadian historians who laboured in the field in the late Victorian period and early in the present century. Among the French-speaking scholars of this period the dominant figure was the Abbé H.-R. Casgrain. Following in the footsteps of Garneau, be interpreted the war of the conquest in terms of French-Canadian nationalism. This appears particularly in his championship of Vaudreuil, who, it may be recalled, was Canada's first native-born Governor General. The eighteenth-century division between the French of France and the French of Canada is reflected and paralleled in the nineteenth-century bickering between Casgrain and René de Kerallain, the biographer of Bougainville. De Kerallain observed, "L'abbé Casgrain appartient à la catégorie des écrivains patriotes; et, quand le patriote se double d'un Canadien, son patriotisme est deux fois plus nerveux."[6]

Casgrain's great achievement is, of course, his edition of the Lévis Papers, a vastly important group of documents.[7] Since the original manuscripts are now in the Public Archives of Canada, it is possible to assess the value of the published version. It is certainly a most useful contribution. The documents which Casgrain did not publish are relatively few and unimportant. The transcription does not meet the meticulous standards of modern scholarship, but it is broadly accurate. Occasionally, it is true, Casgrain's transcriber made a real howler. Again one example, from the account of the Battle of the Plains in the journal called Montcalm's. The author of this part of the journal, apparently the artillery officer Montbeillard, describes a conversation with Montcalm just before the fatal attack. The Casgrain version makes the general say, "If we give him time to establish himself, we shall never be able to attack him with the few troops we have (*le peu de troupes que nous avons*)." But the phrase in the manuscript is clearly not "le peu de troupes" but "L'Espèce de troupes" — *the kind of troops* we have.[8] Fortunately, errors as bad as this are not frequent, and I must say that I should hate to have to pick my way through the Lévis manuscripts without the guidance of Casgrain's printed edition.

The most famous monument of English-Canadian scholarship in this field is the six volumes of Doughty's *The Siege of Quebec and the Battle of the Plains of Abraham*, published in collaboration with G.W. Parmelee in 1901. This book is partly a history, partly a collection of documents. The documents are — with some reservations — invaluable. The history belongs in a lower category. Doughty was one of those whose vision was seriously affected by the golden haze. He had a romantic regard for both Wolfe and Montcalm, and even for that versatile but inefficient soldier Bougainville. His knowledge of the Casgrain documents — a comparatively recent publication in his time — seems to have been imperfect. He devotes some indignation to the purblind people who insist on suggesting that Bougainville was at Cap Rouge on the eventful night of the 12th-13th September 1759, and produces some second-hand evidence to indicate that he was not there.[9] Yet Casgrain had published the only letter by Bougainville himself describing that night. Bougainville wrote to Bourlamaque, "Un homme se laisse surprendre à l'anse des Mères; je suis au cap Rouge."[10] Doughty, like some other partisans of Wolfe, convinced himself, in spite of the absence of any real evidence whatever, that Wolfe had in mind from the beginning the landing at the Anse au Foulon which was finally executed on 13 September.[11]

Even the documents Doughty presents, invaluable as they are, have to be treated with some reserve. I was surprised to discover that two paragraphs which the British government censored out of Wolfe's famous dispatch to Pitt when it was first published in 1759 are still missing from Doughty's version, as they are from almost every version in print. I found also that part of Wolfe's almost equally famous and informative letter to Admiral Saunders written on 31 August 1759 is missing from Doughty's text.[12]

A writer at least as influential in Canada as Doughty was Colonel William Wood, author of *The Fight for Canada* and several volumes in the "Chronicles of Canada" series. Wood was a devoted worker in Canadian military history, and it is not pleasant to have to depreciate his writings; but his influence, so far as the Seven Years' War is concerned, has been most unfortunate. He was an amateur soldier and an amateur historian, but he has been regarded by the authors of general histories of Canada as a reliable guide through the complexities of the Quebec campaigns. The results have been regrettable. Wood's predilections and prejudices were much the same as Doughty's: a romantic regard for both Wolfe and Montcalm, a deep hostility to Vaudreuil. How far his interpretation was really based on documents can be judged from the fact that he changed it late in life and published an account of Wolfe far less favourable to the general than the eulogistic one presented in *The Fight for Canada* some twenty years before.[13]

The fact is that Wood's work abounds in errors, major and minor. It would be no trick to compile a very long list of them. Perhaps the most egregious was his attribution to Vaudreuil of the phrase, "There is no need to believe that the English have wings," which was actually written to Vaudreuil by Montcalm on 29 July.[14] In *The Passing of New*

202

France[15] Wood dramatically represents Vaudreuil as making this remark to Montcalm on 12 September, "Raising his voice so that the staff could hear him." An author who is capable of this is capable of practically anything. Wood popularized the story of Vaudreuil's countermanding Montcalm's order moving the Guyenne battalion to the site of Wolfe's landing the night before the Battle of the Plains, though as I have tried to show elsewhere the evidence for this is extraordinarily slight.[16] He did not even know Wolfe's actual rank in the Army — having apparently not discovered the *Army List*.[17] He asserts that books contain statements which, on inspection, turn out to be not there.[18]

Wood's works are less well known outside than inside Canada — and the writing done outside is none the worse for this, though it is worth remarking that British and American writers have neglected his useful compilation *The Logs of the Conquest of Canada* as much as his less valuable works. But Canadian writers have tended to swallow him whole. Evidence of his prestige is the fact that even so thorough and reliable an historian as Professor Creighton clearly relied on Wood as a basis for the pages on the 1759 campaign in *Dominion of the North*. The result is that he repeated a succession of unfounded tales, including the inherently impossible one (also in Parkman and many other books) of the Highland officer who answered the sentry's question about his regiment with the words "De La Reine,"[19] and the oft-printed detail of the Royal-Roussillon battalion marching on to the battlefield "in its distinctive blue," (Royal-Roussillon, like all the other French regiments in Canada, wore white.)[20]

203

Two Canadian biographies, both old books now, may be mentioned. Sir Thomas Chapais was devoted to his subject, as biographers tend to be; yet his life of Montcalm is distinguished by considerable objectivity as well as by careful research. W.T. Waugh's *James Wolfe, Man and Soldier*, on the other hand, is one of the romantic works, ready to take leave of the documents at any time to achieve an interpretation favourable to his hero. (Read his account of the correspondence between Wolfe and the brigadiers at the end of August 1759.)

A quite different approach to Wolfe, however, was that of Waugh's McGill colleague, Professor Adair, in his presidential address to this association in 1936.[21] This was a realistic re-interpretation based on careful examination of a wide range of sources. It may be called, in fact, the most thorough account that could be compiled within the city limits of Montreal. I find myself of the opinion that Mr. Adair somewhat overdid his onslaught on Wolfe's reputation; he was not without prejudice against Vaudreuil; but his paper was certainly the most significant Canadian contribution to the subject and, in spite of its exaggerations, possibly the best thing on Wolfe ever written anywhere. More recently an eminent French-Canadian scholar, Mr. Frégault, has given us a full-length book on the Seven Years' War in America.[22] Like so many earlier works written in Quebec, it presents a nationalistic view favourable to Vaudreuil. It is distinguished, however, by its careful use of primary sources in both French and English. On matters of fact, Professor Frégault's narrative is almost always firmly grounded; as to his interpretation of the facts, there is almost always room for discussion. Unfortunately, although he goes into great detail about the operations at Oswego in 1756, he has comparatively little to say about the much more important ones at Quebec three years later.

Finally, a general word about document collections. My initial assumption that everything important was in print turned out to be unjustified. I have spoken of Casgrain and Doughty. The other basic collection is that of Gertrude S. Kimball, *Correspondence of William Pitt . . . with Colonial Governors and Military and Naval Commanders in America.*[23] This has the virtue that the text of the letters is accurately transcribed from the original manuscripts. But unfortunately none of the enclosures is printed; and often they are more important than the letter itself. The Kimball notes, moreover, have very little value.

Even at this late date, there are still significant documents that are not in print at all. A particularly striking example is Vaudreuil's long dispatch dated 5 October 1759 which is his description of the campaign and his *apologia* for the loss of Quebec.[24] A large number of very valuable papers are attached to it as appendices. I can only attribute the failure to print this document to the hostility to Vaudreuil, which has been so evident among certain historians, including Doughty. Apparently it was considered that the governor was so prejudiced that it was unnecessary or undesirable to allow his views to go before the court.

III

With this background, we may pass on to discuss the much-controverted campaign of 1759.

To me, after a long period spent studying the documents, it seems that there was no really first-class military figure among the men present at Quebec on that famous occasion. The claims to genius made on behalf of both Wolfe and Montcalm have been advanced by writers unduly influenced by the romantic circumstances in which they fought and died. Both possessed military talents. Neither deserves to rank among the great captains of history. Montcalm's reputation has been gilded by a glorious failure and a gallant death, while Wolfe's has reflected the splendour of a famous victory which he apparently did not expect and probably did not deserve.

Pitt took a considerable chance when he appointed Wolfe to the Quebec expedition, for the young general had had no experience in independent command. And the campaign which he conducted during the summer of 1759, in spite of the success which finally crowned it, suggests that

Wolfe was in fact unfitted for such command. Our knowledge of the development of his plans, though incomplete, is considerably improved by his letters to Monckton in the Northcliffe Collection at Ottawa,[25] which have not been used by his biographers or by any historian of the campaign. They serve further to document Wolfe's vacillations and uncertainties, which are already familiar to students and were emphasized by Adair. According to my calculation — and another person would probably arrive at another figure — Wolfe adopted and rejected seven different operational plans before finally settling upon the one which gave him his victory. To drag this audience through all the detail would be extreme cruelty; but I feel that I must at least attempt an outline.

Knowing before he reached Quebec that his basic problem was to get at the weak land side of the fortress, Wolfe's main idea was to seize and fortify the Beauport shore below the city, with a view to advancing thence across the St. Charles.[26] But when he landed on the Isle of Orleans on 27 June he at once discovered that Montcalm had anticipated him and had himself fortified that area. Wolfe's first plan was thus defeated. His second one, adopted on 3 July after consultation with Admiral Saunders, was to "get ashore if possible above the town."[27] To assist this scheme he proposed to bombard Quebec from the south shore of the St. Lawrence, and to make a landing below the Montmorency as a diversion. But by the 10th he had clearly abandoned this plan — probably partly because the Navy did not yet fully control the waters about Quebec, partly because of French military counter-moves — and had converted the Montmorency diversion into his main operation. On 16 July he outlined to Monckton in some detail a scheme for a frontal attack on the French entrenchments here.[28] This was his third plan. But on the night of 18-19 July a division of the fleet for the first time passed Quebec and got into upper river. Wolfe now, probably very wisely, switched back to that flank, abandoning the Montmorency scheme in favour of an enterprise above the town.

Early on the morning of 20 July he wrote Monckton[29] at Point Lévis ordering him to cooperate in an attack that evening which was apparently to be directed at St. Michel, a short distance above the Anse au Foulon. Preparations went forward actively; but at 1 p.m. the same day Wolfe postponed the operation, apparently because the French, alarmed by the movement of the ships, were moving men and guns. He kept this hopeful fourth plan alive for some days, but by 25-6 July he had abandoned it and was back to the eastern flank, reconnoitring the crossings of the Montmorency. Getting no encouragement here, on the 28th he announced that he had decided on an attack on an outwork of the French Beauport position. A small redoubt on the beach, which Wolfe calculated was out of musket-shot of the French entrenchments, was to be captured and strengthened. The hope was that Montcalm would attack it and allow the British to fight a defensive action. Wolfe wrote, "I take it to

205

be better that the Marquis shou'd attack a firm Corps of ours w^h superiority of numbers, than that we should attack his whole Army entrenched, w^h what we can put on shoar at one landing. . . . "[30]

This was his fifth plan. He tried to carry it out on the eventful 31st of July. The first stage was to run a couple of armed vessels ashore close to the redoubt. Wolfe boarded one of them to reconnoitre, and at once saw that his calculations had been at fault. The redoubt was closer to the entrenchments than he had believed, and would not be tenable under their fire. With the French shot flying about him, Wolfe made a reappraisal. He decided to go on with the operation; but now it took the form he had rejected a couple of days before — a frontal attack on the French army in its entrenchments, the circumstances in which the Canadian militia were most formidable. This was so fundamental a change that it deserves to be called his sixth plan. And the attack was a bloody failure.

A pause followed, during which Wolfe continued his incendiary bombardment of Quebec, and began systematically devastating the farming communities above and below the city. He hoped that this might goad Montcalm into coming out of his inaccessible entrenchments and attacking him; but "the Marquis" refused to be drawn. Then Wolfe fell ill; and in a famous memorandum he sought, belatedly, the advice of his three able brigadiers. He asked them to consider three possible plans of operations, all simply variants of the Montmorency attack that had failed on 31 July. In their forceful reply the brigadiers politely rejected all three and put their collective finger on the dominant fact of the strategic situation — the fact that there was virtually no food in Quebec, and that the garrison and the inhabitants were entirely dependent upon supplies brought in from the west. Cut that line of communication, and Montcalm would have to come out and fight. Their advice accordingly was, abandon the Montmorency position and concentrate the hitherto divided army for action above the town. It was excellent advice, and Wolfe took it.

By 7 September, accordingly, the main body of the army was embarked in the ships above Quebec. The brigadiers recommended a landing above Cap Rouge, in the St. Augustin–Pointe-aux-Trembles area, a dozen or more miles west of the city. Orders were issued for this operation, which we may term the seventh plan; and it came close to being executed on 8 September. But the weather broke; and before the rain stopped Wolfe changed his mind again. He had adopted, and kept to, the most vital features of the brigadiers' plan (a point which Doughty did not understand or appreciate); but on the important matter of choice of a landing-place he now took leave of it. What drew his attention to the Anse au Foulon we simply do not know;[31] but he decided to land there, less than three miles from Quebec, at a point where the steepness of the cliffs would make an opposed landing impossible, and where the main French

206

force was close at hand. The brigadiers' scheme offered the same strategic advantage — the cutting of the supply line from the west — with much less risk and better hope of a decisive result; for an army defeated near Pointe-aux-Trembles would have had fewer facilities for a withdrawal towards Montreal than one defeated on the Plains of Abraham. But fortune, which is said to favour the brave, favoured Wolfe; every break went his way; a plan whose success depended entirely upon luck was blessed with that commodity in unlimited quantities. To the last, indeed, Wolfe himself seems to have found it difficult to believe in his own good fortune. There is a fairly well authenticated story that after reaching the top of the cliff he sent Isaac Barré back to stop the landing until he could be quite certain that the French were not in the area in strength. Barré, finding that the "second flight" of troops were already offshore ready to land, simply refrained from delivering the order and allowed the landing to proceed.[32]

These are not the actions of a great commander. As a strategist — a big word for such small operations, but it seems to be the only one — Wolfe was painfully inadequate. There is no military figure so ineffective as a general who cannot make up his mind. Wolfe was the last man who should have been trusted with an independent command. Moreover, he had defects of personality which made it difficult for him to work effectively with his senior subordinates. Two of his brigadiers came to detest him, and while we know little about his relations with the third, Monckton, we do know that the general wrote Monckton two letters apologizing for some slight and begging him not to turn against him.[33] Wolfe's journal contains strictures on the Navy which suggest that he was a difficult colleague; Admiral Saunders' opinion of him unfortunately seems not to have been recorded. Add to this the policy of deliberate terror which Wolfe applied against the city of Quebec and the neighbouring parishes, a policy which did little or nothing to advance his campaign, and we get a total picture which is not impressive.

Nevertheless, Wolfe was not without valuable military qualities. He was an uncommonly fine fighting officer, at his best under fire; and this accounts for his great reputation among the junior ranks of his army, who knew nothing of his deficiencies as a planner. Once the army was ashore at the Anse au Foulon no mistakes were made. Wolfe was as decisive on the battlefield as he had been indecisive through the long weeks when he was fumbling with his strategic problem. To say that he was no more than "a good regimental officer" is I think to underrate him. It would be truer to say that he had it in him to be a good tactician, capable of vigorous and effective leadership and control in action. Working under a higher commander who could prescribe his tasks, he would have been a very valuable officer. He could win a battle, though he could not plan a campaign.

IV

Let us turn to Montcalm. As a strategist be seems to me to have been superior to Wolfe. French-Canadian writers, including Professor Frégault, have criticized him for adopting so exclusively defensive a policy; but this was the policy suited to his means and his circumstances, and therefore it was right. He had more men than Wolfe, but they were largely amateurs, confronting an army of professionals. Under these conditions, it was in Wolfe's interest to bring on a battle in the open field, and in Montcalm's to avoid one. And time was on Montcalm's side. If he could only hold his position and avoid a disaster, the approach of winter would drive the British out of the St. Lawrence. The best tribute to the soundness of Montcalm's policy is Wolfe's letters and dispatches, which testify repeatedly to the manner in which he was frustrated by the French defences and Montcalm's determination to remain within them. Yet Montcalm had made a fundamental strategic error in keeping the French food supplies in depots up the river, and thereby rendering his force dependent from day to day on an exposed line of communication. The object was to enable the field army to retire westward, and still be fed, in case of the loss of Quebec; and it is apparent that it was almost an article of belief among the French that major units of the British fleet could not get past the city. But when this happened, and the British cut the line of communication, Montcalm's whole defensive policy fell to the ground and he had to risk a battle.

Montcalm lacked one invaluable ability which some fortunate generals have possessed. He had no flair for penetrating his adversary's intentions. To him, as apparently to everybody else in authority on the French side, the landing at the Foulon was a thunderbolt out of a clear sky. All the evidence indicates that to the last he thought Wolfe's most probable course was a blow at Beauport, with a landing far up the river as second choice. And it is not to Montcalm's credit as a commander that he failed to observe the possibilities of the Foulon track — which offered a perfectly good means of moving cannon up from the river to the heights west of the city.

Montcalm, as has often been recognized, committed a serious tactical error on the battlefield. He certainly had to attack, to clear his line of communication; but he did not have to attack at ten o'clock in the morning instead of a few hours later. As I already mentioned, he feared that the British would soon establish themselves too firmly to be evicted; and with what seems to have been characteristic impulsiveness he launched his assault without waiting for Colonel de Bougainville, who was only a few miles away and had the best troops in the French army with him. He thus threw away his best hope of victory.

Like Wolfe, Montcalm had defects of temperament which affected his military usefulness. His feud with Vaudreuil is well known. The pompous

Governor undoubtedly gave him provocation, but Montcalm's own journal provides evidence that the general had a rather low boiling-point. I suspect that the same nervous impatience that drove him on to the premature attack on 13 September made it difficult for him to bear with Vaudreuil. The discord between the two men was a misfortune for New France, though its military effects have probably been somewhat exaggerated. The French Court ought to have removed one or the other. A proposal was in fact made at the end of 1758 to relieve Montcalm, replacing him with the Chevalier de Lévis; but the King seems to have decided against it. The decision was probably unfortunate, for it was important to restore concord to the colony, and Lévis, certainly a soldier of ability, would doubtless have conducted the defence as well as Montcalm did.

V

209

The more one considers the campaign of 1759, the more the conclusion emerges that the decisive factor in the result was not superior British generalship but the superior efficiency of the British forces. The professionals beat the amateurs, as they usually do. British sea power was of course the basic strategic determinant, but in addition the presence of a large and efficient British fleet before Quebec had enormous influence on the tactical operations. As for the military forces, the British superiority in quality, evident throughout the campaign, appears with special clarity in the final crisis of 13 September. The British tactical plan for the approach and landing at the Anse au Foulon, excellent in itself, was executed by the Navy with a skill which it requires some study of combined operations to appreciate. The same boats landed three flights of troops in rapid succession. The one hitch — the fact that the tide carried the first flight some distance below the intended point of landing — was offset by the resourcefulness of Lt.-Col. William Howe, who led his light infantrymen straight up the cliff before them, an athletic feat which was I believe no part of Wolfe's plan.

By comparison, the picture on the French side is one of extreme disorganization, beginning with the extraordinary fact that after ordering a movement of provision boats, and warning their posts to pass them through, the French authorities cancelled the movement without informing the posts. Everything else was of a piece with this. Control, communication, and vigilance were all lacking, with the result that at dawn, when the British army was pouring ashore at the Foulon, the French army, having manned its Beauport entrenchments much of the night, was retiring to its tents. In the actual encounter on the Plains, the result was clearly due to superior British discipline and training. The weak French regular battalions had been heavily diluted with militia, and the attackers were falling into hopeless disorder long before the British fired a musket-shot at them.[34] Wolfe had assumed with the utmost confidence that his highly trained professional soldiers would have an easy victory if the French could only be brought to action in the open; and the result justified his calculations.

VI

The Battle of the Plains was only half a victory: partly because of the plan Wolfe had adopted, which gave the French the chance of retiring behind the St. Charles River and getting away to the west by way of Charlesbourg and the Lorettes, and partly perhaps because of Wolfe's own death, which deprived the British of effective higher leading at a moment when a skilful and energetic tactician might possibly have made the triumph really complete. The result was that the British got Quebec, but the French field army remained in being, and another year's campaign was needed to destroy that army and end the war in Canada. About the 1760 campaign I propose to say only a few words.

The French position this year was hopeless, first because the Court of Versailles sent inadequate assistance, and secondly because the assistance it sent never reached its destination — since in 1760 the British fleet got into the St. Lawrence first. But the campaign conducted by Lévis and Vaudreuil in the hope of large-scale help from France was both a valiant adventure and a skilful strategic performance. The popular French-Canadian legend of this campaign and in particular of its chief incident, the defeat of Murray in the so-called Battle of Ste. Foy on 28 April, seems to be that it was an improvised effort carried out with inadequate means largely by the Canadian militia. The material means available to Lévis were certainly pitifully inadequate, but it would be an error to assume that at Ste. Foy the British regulars were defeated by the Canadian amateurs. In this battle, as in the one in the previous September, the professional soldier was the essential figure. Montcalm in the Battle of the Plains had five battalions of the *troupes de terre*. Lévis at Ste. Foy had eight (less detachments spared for Lake Champlain), three of them having been virtually unengaged in 1759. The total force collected for his expedition was just under 7,000 men, including 3,889 regulars, while Murray reports that he himself had 3,866 officers and men in the battle.[35] Thus Lévis had almost exactly the same number of regulars as Murray, plus his 3000 militiamen as a bonus. Taking a "calculated risk" with respect to other fronts, he had effected a powerful concentration before Quebec.

Murray has been criticized for abandoning his excellent defensive position outside the walls of Quebec in order to attack Lévis. The criticism is probably just, for in the presence of so superior an enemy a defensive battle was Murray's best chance for a victory. Nevertheless, he came closer to winning than has been generally recognized. He explains that,

210

reconnoitring the French, he "preceiv'd their Van busy throwing up Redoubts while their Main body was yet on their march"; and he attempted "to attack them before they could have time to Form."[36] Snow and mud-hindered the movement of his guns. Yet it was a very near thing — so near that Lévis momentarily lost his nerve, decided that his troops were not going to succeed in forming and ordered the abandonment of a vital position on the left flank. The day was saved for the French by Lt.-Col. Dalquier, commanding the La Sarre brigade in this sector. Estimating the situation more accurately than Lévis, he took it on himself to countermand the general's order and led his men to the attack. Subsequently Lévis thanked him for this timely disobedience.[37] Since both the opposing commanders made serious miscalculations, the level of generalship at Ste. Foy cannot be said to have been particularly high.

* * *

What can one say in conclusion? Reviewing these great events of two centuries ago, and what has been written about them, it is hard to take much pride in our historiography. To a large extent, the chief actors have been interpreted in the light of prejudice and sentimentality. They have been made romantic heroes or villains rather than human beings to be studied on the basis of the records. Historians have approached the men and events of the time with their minds already made up, and have looked to the documents for evidence to bolster up their preconceptions rather than for facts to enable them to arrive at an objective appraisal. In his presidential address last year Dr. Lamb quietly made the devasting remark, "Real accuracy in Canadian historical writing is rare." Many of the histories of the conquest of Canada illustrate this observation only too forcibly. Much remains to be done in Canadian history. Unfortunately also, it appears that a good deal is going to have to be done over again.

NOTES

[1] This paper is a by-product of a book by the author entitled *Quebec, 1759: The Siege and the Battle*, published in September 1959 by The Macmillan Company of Canada Limited. Since the book is fully documented, some documentation which would otherwise have been necessary has been dispensed with here.

[2] Corbett, *England in the Seven Years' War*, 2 vols. (London, 1907), 1: 398. Public Record Office, London, C.O. 5/213 (transcript, Public Archives of Canada [PAC]).

[3] See Wolfe to Townshend, 6 Jan. 1759, in Beckles Willson, *The Life and Letters of James Wolfe* (London, 1909), 414. Cf. Rex Whitworth, *Field-Marshal Lord Ligonier* (London, 1958), 278-80. Von Ruville in his *William Pitt, Earl of Chatham*, 3 vols. (London, 1907) notes that Burton was passed over; but his comment is not perceptive (2: 262n.).

[4] It is reproduced in A.G. Doughty's edition of Knox's *Historical Journal of the Campaigns in North America*, 3 vols. (Toronto, 1914-16), vol. 3, opposite p. 150. It should be compared with the subsequent *Plan of the Town of Quebec . . .* , also signed by Mackellar (PAC).

[5] *Eg.*, the version of Vaudreuil's letter to Bourlamaque, 6 Aug. 1759 (Bourlamaque Papers, PAC) printed in *Montcalm and Wolfe* (ed. 1910, 3: 75) in inverted commas, is not a quotation but a very free paraphrase.

[6] See De Kerallain's *La Jeunesse de Bougainville et la guerre de sept ans* (Paris, 1896), 7.

[7] *Collection des Manuscrits du Maréchal de Lévis*, 12 vols. (Montreal and Quebec, 1889-95).

[8] *Collections des Manuscrits du Maréchal de Lévis* 7: 612. MS of Montcalm journal, Lévis Papers, PAC.

[9] *The Siege of Quebec* 3: 107.

[10] *Collection des Manuscrits du Maréchal de Lévis* 5: 357 (18 Sept. 1759).

[11] *The Siege of Quebec* 3: 301.

[12] The dispatch to Pitt is published in full in Kimball. The letter to Saunders was published in *Gentleman's Magazine*, June 1801. For Doughty's version, published he says "in full," see *The Siege of Quebec* 2: 151–54.

[13] *Unique Quebec* (Literary and Historical Society of Quebec, 1924).

[14] Letter of 29 July 1759, appended to Vaudreuil to the Minister, 5 Oct. 1759, PAC, F3, vol. 15.

[15] Toronto, 1920 (Chronicles of Canada), 128.

[16] "The Anse au Foulon, 1759: Montcalm and Vaudreuil," *Canadian Historical Review* (March 1959).

[17] *The Fight for Canada* (ed. Boston, 1906), 142–43, 145. Wood calls Wolfe "a regimental lieutenant-colonel," but he had been Colonel of the 67th Foot since 1757.

[18] *The Fight for Canada*, 334, re Robert Stobo's *Memoirs*.

[19] This battalion was with Bourlamaque on Lake Champlain. And no French sentry would have asked such a question. Transport was no task for regular troops.

[20] *Etat Militaire de France, pour l'année 1759* . . . (Paris, 1759), 228.

[21] "The Military Reputation of Major-General James Wolfe," Canadian Historical Association, *Report* (1936).

[22] *La Guerre de la conquête* (Montréal, 1955).

[23] 2 vols., New York, 1906.

[24] Above, note 14.

[25] Monckton Papers, vol. 22.

[26] Letter to Major Walter Wolfe, 19 May 1759, Willson, 427–29. This letter also refers to the possibility of entrenching a detachment *above* the town.

[27] Wolfe's Journal, McGill University version.

[28] Monckton Papers, vol. 22.

[29] Monckton Papers, vol. 22.

[30] To Monckton, n.d. (29 July ?), Monckton Papers, vol. 22.

[31] The statements of Doughty and Wood that Robert Stobo cannot have suggested it because he left Quebec on 7 September with dispatches for Amherst have no validity — for it was on the very next day that Wolfe (according to Townshend) "went a reconoitring down the river" and may have first observed the Foulon path. Stobo might well have made the suggestion in a final interview. But there is no evidence for this.

[32] Henry Caldwell to James Murray, 1 Nov. 1772, Amherst Papers, Packet 28 (transcript, PAC).

[33] 15 and 16 Aug. 1759, Monckton Papers, vol. 22.

[34] See, eg., Malartic to Bourlamaque, 28 Sept. 1759, Bourlamaque Papers, *Variarum*, PAC.

[35] Lévis' Journal, April 1760, *Collection des Manuscrits*, vol. 1; strength return, *Collection des Monuscrits* 1: 257. Murray's dispatch to Pitt, 25 May 1760, C.O. 5/64.

[36] Murray's Journal, 28 Apr. 1760 (photostat, PAC).

[37] Lt.-Gen. le Comte de Maurès de Malartic, *Journal des Campagnes au Canada de 1755 à 1760* (Paris, 1890), 317. Cf. Bourlamaque to Bougainville, 3 May 1760, de Kerallain, *La Jeunesse de Bougainville*, 167.

Topic Six

The American Revolution and the Maritime Colonies

Ironically, Britain's success in expelling France from North America contributed to its own expulsion from the Thirteen Colonies only fifteen years later. The removal of the French threat from Quebec and Louisbourg had, in the minds of many American colonists, ended the need for Britain. This realization, in addition to a growing sense of nationalism among the Thirteen Colonies, led to the demand for greater self-government. Britain's attempt to tax the colonies finally led to open rebellion. The first armed clash at Lexington, Massachusetts, in mid-April 1775, officially began the American Revolution.

The Nova Scotians had to make a difficult decision: to support Britain, to join the American cause, or to remain neutral. As James Candow explains in "The New England Planters in Nova Scotia," three-quarters of Nova Scotia's roughly 20 000 settlers in 1775 were New Englanders with strong economic and family ties with the New England colonies. This being the case, why did they choose to stay loyal to the Crown? George Rawlyk offers an explanation of their loyalty in "The American Revolution and Nova Scotia Reconsidered."

During the Revolutionary War thousands of farmers, craftsmen, and small merchants, as well as large landowners and government officials, had sided with the Crown. After Britain's defeat about 80 000 of these United Empire Loyalists chose, or were forced, to depart with the British garrisons, over half of them settling in two of the remaining British colonies to the north, Nova Scotia and Quebec. Approximately 30 000 went to Nova Scotia, almost doubling the size of the existing population; about 5000 came to the St. Lawrence Valley, doubling, perhaps even tripling, the English-speaking population there, from four or five percent to ten or fifteen percent of the total population; and nearly 10 000 settled in the western portion of the Province of Quebec, which became Upper Canada in 1791. The Loyalist migration led to the founding of two new colonies, New Brunswick and Upper Canada. In "The United Empire Loyalists: A Reconsideration," W.G. Shelton outlines the importance of the Loyalists in Canadian history.

The classic account of Nova Scotia's response to the revolutionary struggle in the Thirteen Colonies is John Bartlet Brebner's *Neutral Yankees of Nova Scotia* (Toronto: McClelland and Stewart, 1969; first published in 1937). For a recent history of Nova Scotia–New England relations see George Rawlyk, *Nova Scotia's Massachusetts: A Study of Massachusetts–Nova Scotia Relations, 1630 to 1784* (Montreal: McGill-Queen's University Press, 1973). *Revolution Rejected, 1775–1776*, ed. George Rawlyk (Scarborough, Ontario: Prentice-Hall, 1968) and W.S. MacNutt's chapter, "Revolution and Reorganization, 1775–1785," in *The Atlantic Provinces, 1712–1857* (Toronto: McClelland and Stewart, 1965) are also useful. J.M. Bumsted's *Henry Alline* (Toronto: University of Toronto Press, 1971) reviews the career of the leader of an important religious revival in Nova Scotia during the years of the American Revolution.

The anthology *The United Empire Loyalists*, ed. L.S.F. Upton (Toronto: Copp Clark, 1967) provides a general overview. Neil MacKinnon reviews the impact of the Loyalists on Nova Scotia in *The Unfriendly Soil: The Loyalist Experience in Nova Scotia, 1783–1791* (Kingston and Montreal: McGill-Queen's University Press, 1986). On the background of the American Loyalists see W.H. Nelson, *The American Tory* (Toronto: Oxford, 1961). A very helpful study remains *Loyalist Narratives from Upper Canada*, ed. J.J. Talman (Toronto: Champlain Society, 1946).

Three new studies of the Loyalists are Wallace Brown and Hereward Senior, *Victorious in Defeat: The Loyalists in Canada* (Toronto: Methuen, 1984); Christopher Moore, *The Loyalists: Revolution, Exile, Settlement* (Toronto: Macmillan, 1984); and Ann Gorman Condon, *The Envy of the American States: The Loyalist Dream for New Brunswick* (Fredericton: New Ireland Press, 1984).

Robert S. Allen has compiled a useful bibliography, *Loyalist Literature: An Annotated Bibliographical Guide to the Writings on the Loyalists of the American Revolution* (Toronto: Dundurn Press, 1982). For books and articles produced after 1981, consult Bruce Bowden, "The Bicentennial Legacy — A Second Loyalist Revival," *Ontario History* 77 (1985): 65–74.

The New England Planters in Nova Scotia*

JAMES E. CANDOW

Background

The New England Planters (an Elizabethan term for colonists) have played an important role in the history of Nova Scotia, but their story is often overshadowed by that of the Acadians and the Loyalists. Their

*From the Environment Canada, Parks, publication, *The New England Planters in Nova Scotia*, by James E. Candow. Reprinted by permission of the Minister of Supply and Services, Canada.

migration to Nova Scotia in the period 1760–68 marked the introduction of the first sizeable English-speaking population into the colony. They brought with them their own culture, forged in America. Yet, when their relatives to the south revolted against Great Britain, the Planters, with one minor exception, did not follow suit. Instead, the revolutionary years produced among the Planters a profound state of confusion, from which they emerged with a new sense of identity.

By the Treaty of Utrecht in 1713, Nova Scotia, formerly part of French Acadia, was ceded to Great Britain. When fighting erupted again between Britain and France in the Ohio Valley in 1754, it marked the beginning of the final struggle between the two powers for control of North America. Lieutenant-Governor Charles Lawrence of Nova Scotia and Governor William Shirley of Massachusetts organized a New England expeditionary force that captured Fort Beauséjour on the Isthmus of Chignecto in June 1755. Lawrence viewed the Acadian population of Nova Scotia as a liability in time of war, and initiated their deportation to the Thirteen Colonies, commencing in the fall of 1755. He hoped that their place would soon be taken by British subjects, and he looked to New England to supply them.

215

Despite an offer of land from the Nova Scotian government, the New England troops at Beauséjour left for home in April 1756. They knew that the capture of Beauséjour and the expulsion of the Acadians had not secured Nova Scotia. Many Acadians were still at large, and with their Indian allies were waging guerilla warfare. Moreover, the French still held Louisbourg. With the formal declaration of war (Seven Years' War) in May 1756, enthusiasm for immigration was further dampened. Just as important to New Englanders was the quasi-military government that prevailed in Nova Scotia, consisting of Lawrence (named Governor in 1756) and an appointed Council. New Englanders wanted the representative government they possessed at home. Pressured by the New Englanders on Council, and by the Lords of Trade and Plantations (Board of Trade), overseers of the British colonial empire, Lawrence began to see the need for representative government as a prerequisite for settlement from New England.

Proclamations

Early in 1758, the Board of Trade advised Lawrence to distribute in New England a physical description of the Nova Scotian lands. At the same time, the Board gave Lawrence an ultimatum to call an Assembly. On 12 October, ten days after the first Assembly met, Lawrence issued a proclamation, published in the *Boston Gazette*, describing the Acadian lands and soliciting proposals for their settlement. This prompted a series of questions from prospective settlers, which Lawrence answered in a second proclamation dated 11 January 1759. Grants were to be made in the form of 100,000 acre townships. Individual settlers would receive land in proportion to their ability to enclose and cultivate it, to a maximum of 1,000 acres. Each head of family was entitled to at least 100 acres of wild woodland and an additional 50 acres for each member of the household. The grantee was obligated to plant, cultivate, improve, or enclose one-third of his land every ten years for 30 years. No rent was to be charged during the first ten years, after which it would be charged at the rate of a shilling a year for every 50 acres. Freedom of religion was guaranteed to all Protestants, and prospective settlers were assured that the form of government in Nova Scotia was the same as in New England. Each township of 50 families or more could send two representatives to the Assembly. For security, each township would have its own fort, garrisoned by British troops.

The second proclamation was warmly received in New England, where it was known that Louisbourg had been captured. There were other reasons, originating within New England, that made immigration to Nova Scotia so attractive. After 120 years of settlement, most of the best land in New England had been claimed. In the 17th century, there had been a pronounced population movement out of Massachusetts into nearby Connecticut and Rhode Island. By the mid-18th century, people were moving north into New Hampshire, Vermont, and Maine, since the British forbade settlement beyond the Appalachians. With the availability of the Acadian lands, Nova Scotia now emerged as a viable outlet for land-hungry New Englanders.

On 18 April 1759, the first agents representing prospective settlers appeared before Council at Halifax. In the company of Charles Morris, Surveyor-General of Nova Scotia, they were taken in an armed vessel to examine potential sites. As a result of this inspection, the agents informed Council that they were willing to settle two townships, Horton and Cornwallis, bordering on Minas Basin. Meanwhile, more agents continued to pour into Halifax, and before the year was out grants had been issued for Falmouth, Onslow, Granville, Annapolis, Cumberland, Amherst, Sackville, Tinmouth (New Dublin), Liverpool, Barrington, and Yarmouth townships.

Settlement

In spite of this activity, there was a delay in actual settlement. As long as Quebec held out, the Acadians and Indians in Nova Scotia kept up their guerilla warfare. A group of prospective settlers was fired upon near Cape Sable in 1759, and attacks were also recorded at Lunenburg, Dartmouth, Windsor, Canso, and Sackville. Council therefore decided that all grants issued for 1759 would not become operative until the following spring. The Planters began to arrive in 1760. By 1768 there were approximately 8,000 of them in Nova Scotia, by far the largest single component of the colony's 13,000 residents. Of Nova Scotia's 27 townships, 16 possessed New England majorities. In 1768, the Treaty of Fort Stanwix opened up the Ohio country and potential New England immigrants abandoned Nova Scotia for the west.

Although the Planters were a diverse group, most were farmers or fishermen. The Minas townships of Horton, Cornwallis, Falmouth, and Newport (1761) were the leading agricultural townships, containing the largest concentration of people and the best land. Most of the settlers in Horton and Cornwallis came from eastern Connecticut, with a few from Massachusetts and Rhode Island. Rhode Island was the main source for Falmouth and Newport. Aylesford township was created in 1770 as the original Horton and Cornwallis grantees expanded westward down the valley. At the other end of the valley, Annapolis township also had a strong Massachusetts flavour, as did Granville, although here there was also a New Hampshire component. Some families at Annapolis moved up the valley, leading to the creation of Wilmot township in 1764.

217

In the agricultural townships, land was theoretically parcelled out in the following way. The town plot consisted of one-half acre family lots arranged in squares around two or more central parades, usually in line. This allowed people to assemble conveniently for town meetings or, more importantly, for defence. The town plot also contained lots for a church, minister's house, and a school. In addition to his town lot, each Planter received a farm lot, dyke lot, and uncleared woodland totalling 500 acres or more, depending on the township. Each township had its own peculiarities. In Horton, each Planter received a 4–6 acre island lot on Long, Butte, or Oak Island to enable fishing in Minas Basin. Since there were not enough island lots, others received additional land lots instead. The actual settlement pattern did not rigidly follow these models. The town plots were never developed, and the Planters quickly consolidated their scattered holdings.

The leading fisheries townships of Yarmouth, Barrington, Liverpool, New Dublin, and Chester were concentrated on Nova Scotia's south shore. Most had been visited since early in the century by New England bank fishermen, who now sought to establish an inshore fishery to produce a better cure of fish. Lumbering, shipbuilding, and boatbuilding emerged as important related industries in these townships. Most of the Planters in the fisheries townships came from Massachusetts, particularly Cape Cod.

Although the soil along the Atlantic coast was poor, permitting only subsistence farming, this mattered little to the fisherman. His chief requirements were a house, space on shore to dry his fish, and perhaps a mill site on a nearby river. Thus the intricate lot system found in the agricultural townships was absent. In spite of the fact that more people settled in the agricultural townships, the fisheries townships were of greater economic importance since fish was the crucial item in Nova Scotia's foreign trade. Also, the provision of bait and supplies to the New England bank fleet that still worked the offshore formed the chief source of revenue in the colonial economy.

Politics

The Planters brought with them two great cultural trade-marks: their religion and their form of government. In New England, the township, through the instruments of the town meeting and local election of officials, was the key element of political life. Despite Lawrence's assurance in his second proclamation that the Planters could expect to find the same form of government in Nova Scotia, they encountered instead a central government anxious to extend its influence. At first, the townships did indeed have real power. They selected some local officials, allotted land, and provided for the poor. However, in 1765 the government at Halifax introduced "An Act for the Choice of Town Officers and regulating Townships," which set the form of local government for over a century. It empowered the Grand Jury to nominate people for local offices, with the final selection to be made by the Court of Quarter Sessions. This effectively gave the power of selection to the central government. In 1767, that government further extended its control by assuming responsibility for granting land in the townships. All that remained of township powers was responsibility for the poor.

Religion

The emphasis on local control in New England was also evident in religion. Most Planters were scattered, so it proved difficult to support churches and ministers. There were only eight Congregational Churches in Nova Scotia by 1770 and these were often supported by financial contributions from New England. The meagre church leadership was lost during the American Revolution (1775–83). Church ministers were sympathetic to the republican cause and most returned to New England. Weakened, the church was influenced by the Great Awakening, a religious movement that carried over to Nova Scotia from New England and which was led by Henry Alline of Falmouth. Alline's Newlights benefited from an organizational flexibility that was lacking in the Congregational Church. There was no formal ordination process; the ministers were itinerant; and services were held any day of the week a preacher visited.

218

By the end of the American Revolution, the Newlights had made serious inroads on Congregationalism.

The Planters and the American Revolution

The American Revolution was perhaps the central phenomenon in the history of the New England Planters. Three-quarters of Nova Scotia's approximately 20,000 inhabitants in 1775 were of New England origin. Yet, except for Jonathan Eddy's unsuccessful attacks on Fort Cumberland (formerly Beauséjour), they did not take up arms against Great Britain. The Planters embraced not one but several positions, including pro-revolutionary sympathies, neutrality, pro-British sympathies, and outright retreat in the form of religious revival. Economic recession and geographical isolation were undoubtedly important factors, but so too was the Great Awakening. It touched the life of every Planter and, whether they became converts or not, the Planters were preoccupied with spiritual matters. In that spiritual realm, they effected a revolution of their own, rejecting the formalism of Congregationalism for the emotionalism of the revival meeting.

219

The Planters' Legacy

After the American Revolution, the Planters continued to play a vital role in Nova Scotia society. After the death of Henry Alline in 1784, the Newlights merged mostly with the Baptist Church. Under that guise, Planter descendants were active in the establishment of Acadia College (now Acadia University) in 1838. The more conservative Congregationalists who withstood Newlight influence moved to Presbyterianism, although some Congregational churches survived until 1925 when they joined the United Church of Canada.

In the political sphere, the Planters also underwent a conversion of sorts. In 1843, when Joseph Howe and the reformers sought to withdraw provincial support for sectarian educational institutions, Planter leadership rallied around the Halifax Tories in order to save Acadia College. Politically, the Planters had come full circle. They had started out opposed to Halifax and jealous of conserving township powers; they ended up supporting the Halifax oligarchy against the forces of reform.

Prominent politicians of Planter ancestry included Sir Charles Tupper and Sir Robert Borden, both Canadian prime ministers. The Planters represent the first significant Anglophone population in Canada. Their North American values of self-government and religious autonomy have left an indelible stamp on Nova Scotia.

The American Revolution and Nova Scotia Reconsidered*

GEORGE A. RAWLYK

On the eve of the American Revolution, Nova Scotia was little more than a political expression for a number of widely scattered and isolated communities. These stretched from Halifax to Maugerville on the St. John River and to the tiny outpost of Passamaquoddy on the St. Croix. At the end of the Seven Years' War many land-hungry settlers from Rhode Island, New Hampshire, Massachusetts, and Connecticut pushed up into the fertile regions bordering the Bay of Fundy which had been abandoned by the Acadians when they were expelled from the peninsula in 1755. In 1775 Nova Scotia had a population of only approximately 20,000 inhabitants,[1] three-quarters of whom were New Englanders with strong economic, cultural, and family ties with their former homeland.[2]

In spite of the fact that Nova Scotia was virtually New England's north-eastern frontier and was peopled by a majority of recently arrived New Englanders,[3] the colony refused in 1775 and 1776 to join in attempting to shatter the framework of the British colonial system. Instead, most of the inhabitants, especially the New Englanders, endeavoured to pursue a policy of neutrality, even though their moral support was firmly behind the "rebels." It is interesting to note that this policy of neutrality was exactly the same policy that the New Englanders severely condemned when it had been adopted by the Acadians two decades earlier. However, toward the end of the Revolution, the sympathies of the neutral New Englanders, largely as the result of serious depredations committed by American privateers throughout Nova Scotia from 1777 to 1782, shifted towards Great Britain.[4]

Why did Nova Scotia not join the Thirteen Colonies in attempting to break away from Britain in 1775 and 1776? Three distinct schools of thought have emerged in the effort to answer this question. First, the proponents of the "Halifax-merchant" school have stressed that the influential Halifax merchants were directly responsible for keeping Nova Scotia loyal to the Crown.[5] The merchants, believing that the Revolution was a Heaven-sent opportunity to supplant the New England colonies in the West Indian trade, and also that in the long run their colony would gain more than it would lose in retaining political and economic ties with Britain, were able to impose their will upon the other inhabitants. This is indeed an interesting interpretation, but one without any real foundation, since in 1775 the population of Halifax was only 1800

220

*Originally published in the *Dalhousie Review* 43,3 (Autumn 1963): 379–94. Reprinted by permission.

and the influence of the Halifax merchants was largely confined chiefly to the area of the Bedford Basin.[6] It is clear that their economic ties with Britain were strong, but it is just as clear that they were in no effective position to impose their will upon the other Nova Scotians, who in actual fact reacted violently to the merchant clique that was attempting to manipulate the economic and political life of the colony.

Second, W.B. Kerr, who has written far more about Nova Scotia during the Revolutionary period than any other historian, has strongly argued that as early as 1765 it was inevitable that Nova Scotia would remain loyal to George III. Kerr maintains that there was an almost total absence of "national sentiment"[7] among the New Englanders of Nova Scotia and that, because of this lack of "nationalism,"[8] there was very little popular support for the Revolutionary cause in Nova Scotia.[9] It appears that Kerr has clearly underestimated the general significance of the widespread sympathy for Revolutionary principles. This feeling was prevalent throughout Nova Scotia, with the notable exception of Halifax, in 1775 and 1776. Moreover, he has failed to draw sufficient attention to the profound impact that the isolation of most of the Nova Scotian settlements and the British control of the North Atlantic had upon seriously weakening the indigenous Revolutionary movement.

221

Third, J.B. Brebner, in his excellent work, *The Neutral Yankees of Nova Scotia*, has asserted that the Revolutionary movement failed in Nova Scotia because "the sympathizers with rebellion among the outlying populace could make no headway because their friends in the rebellious Colonies had no navy and because they themselves could not assemble from the scattered settlements an effective force for unassisted revolt."[10] Brebner's is certainly the most satisfactory answer to the original question regarding Nova Scotia and the Revolution. A careful and critical examination of events in the Chignecto region of Nova Scotia in the years 1775 and 1776 will not only serve to prove the validity of Brebner's thesis, but will also cast a considerable amount of light upon the relations between Nova Scotia and the colonies to the south during a most critical period.

The Isthmus of Chignecto provided the stage upon which a somewhat inconsequential scene from the American Revolutionary drama was played. The Eddy Rebellion of 1776 had most of the characteristics of a tragic comedy; a glorious failure, it was nevertheless accompanied by death and destruction.

The Chignecto Isthmus is a narrow neck of land joining the peninsula of Nova Scotia to the North American mainland. Roughly ten miles in width and twenty in length, the Isthmus is bordered on the north-east by Baie Verte, on the south-west by the Cumberland Basin, and on the north-west and south-east by the Sackville and Amherst Ridges respectively. J.C. Webster, one of New Brunswick's outstanding historians, has asserted that "no area of its [Chignecto's] size anywhere in America has a greater or more varied wealth of historical memories and traditions."[11] There is much evidence to support Webster's sweeping generalization.

The vacuum created by the expulsion of the majority of the Acadians from the fertile Isthmus in 1755 was quickly filled at the end of the Seven Years' War by settlers from New England.[12] Unlike the Acadians, these men energetically began to clear and to cultivate the ridge lands which had a heavy forest cover.[13] Only after many frustrating failures were the New Englanders able to master marsh agriculture.[14] From 1772 to 1775 they sullenly observed the arrival of over 500 Yorkshire immigrants seeking "a better livelihood"[15] in the New World. These newcomers had been recruited by the aggressive Lieutenant-Governor of Nova Scotia, Michael Francklin.[16]

Thus in 1775 the general Chignecto Isthmus region contained three important elements within its population. The New Englanders were

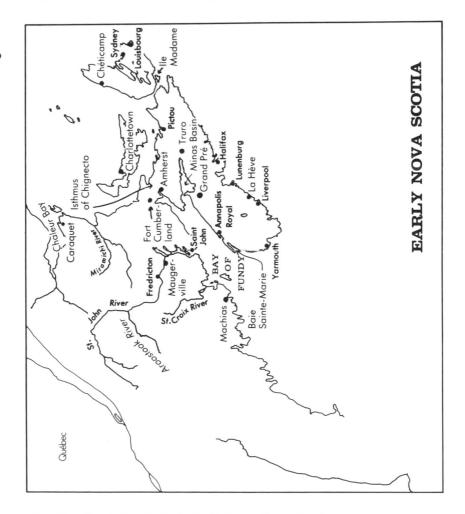

EARLY NOVA SCOTIA

Adapted from Cornell, Hamelin, Ouellet, Trudel, *Canada: Unity in Diversity*, 121.

the most numerous, but the Yorkshiremen were not too far behind. Together these two groups numbered 220 families.[17] The third element was the Acadian; there were thirty Acadian families, most of the members of which worked on the land belonging to the English-speaking farmers.[18]

There was considerable friction and ill-feeling between the New Englanders and the newcomers from the north of England on the one hand, and between the former and the Halifax government on the other. Most of the New Englanders detested their new neighbours, not only because the Yorkshiremen had settled on land that the New Englanders had long coveted and considered to be rightfully theirs, but also because the outlook of the Englishmen was almost diametrically opposite to that of the Americans. The Yorkshiremen were Methodists closely tied to the Mother Country and all she represented, while the New Englanders were Congregationalists who had been greatly influenced by the North American environment and whose ties with the Mother Country were extremely tenuous. The Old World was in conflict with the New on this narrow neck of land.

223

The New Englanders, moreover, were greatly dissatisfied with the Halifax government. Had not Francklin encouraged the Yorkshiremen to settle in the Isthmus? Furthermore, the New Englanders reacted violently to the fact that a small clique of Halifax merchants controlled the legislative and executive functions of government,[19] stubbornly refusing to grant to the New Englanders the right of "township form of government," which Governor Lawrence had promised them in 1758 and 1759.[20]

A spark was needed to set the kindling discontent ablaze. The American Revolution provided the spark, but the fire was quickly and easily extinguished before it could spread and result in any serious damage.

The centre of organized activity against Nova Scotia during the first years of the Revolution was the tiny lumbering outpost of Machias, a few miles west of the St. Croix River.[21] Most of the inhabitants wanted to grow rich by sacking the prosperous Nova Scotian settlements, particularly Halifax. These freebooters, these eighteenth-century filibusters, unsuccessfully endeavoured to hide their real selfish motive beneath a veneer of concern for Revolutionary principles.

In the summer of 1775 they proposed to General Washington to invade Nova Scotia if supported by a force of 1000 soldiers and four armed vessels.[22] When Washington was asked to act upon this bold plan in August, he tactfully refused; all available men and supplies were needed for the proposed Quebec invasion. His reasoned arguments justifying his refusal are of considerable consequence since they explain why Washington refused to mount any kind of offensive against Nova Scotia in 1775 and 1776:

As to the Expedition proposed against Nova Scotia by the Inhabitants of Machias, I cannot but applaud their Spirit and Zeal; but, after considering the Reasons offered for it, there are Several objections . . . which seem to me unanswerable. I apprehend such an Enterprise inconsistent with the General Principal upon which the Colonies have proceeded. That Province has not acceded, it is true, to the Measures of Congress; and therefore, they have been excluded from all Commercial Intercourse with the other Colonies; But they have not Commenced Hostilities against them, nor are any to be apprehended. To attack *them*, therefore, is a Measure of Conquest, rather than Defence, and may be attended with very dangerous consequences. It might, perhaps, be easy, with the force proposed, to make an Incursion into the Province and overawe those of the Inhabitants who are Inimical to our cause; and, for a short time prevent the Supplying the Enemy with Provisions; but the same Force must continue to produce any lasting Effects. As to the furnishing Vessels of Force, you, Gentlemen, will anticipate me, in pointing out our weakness and the Enemy's Strength at Sea. There would be great Danger that, with the best preparation we could make, they would fall an easy prey either to the Men of War of that Station [Halifax] or some who would be detach'd from Boston.[23]

Washington was no doubt right in the long run, but the inhabitants of Machias almost intuitively realized that in the summer of 1775 Nova Scotia was ripe for plucking from the British colonial tree. American economic pressure had resulted in a serious recession,[24] Governor Legge was alienating leading elements of the population, and the exploits of the Revolution had captured the imagination of the New Englanders.[25] In addition, there were only thirty-six British regulars guarding Halifax,[26] and Legge, who seriously believed that the New Englanders "were rebels to the man," sadly observed that "the fortifications [of Halifax] were in a dilapidated state, the batteries . . . dismantled, the gun-carriages decayed, the guns on the ground."[27] If the men from Machias had had their way, the invading force would have been enthusiastically welcomed and openly supported by the vast majority of "Yankees" and would have easily gained control of the colony. However, the lack of suitable land communications between the various settlements in Nova Scotia, as well as between Nova Scotia and the other colonies, together with the British control of the Atlantic, would have probably forced the American troops to abandon Nova Scotia after a brief occupation. Washington's refusal to attack Nova Scotia when it was ripe for conquest and the arrival of military reinforcements in Halifax in October[28] virtually made certain that the Colony would remain within the framework of the British colonial system during the war years.

In the summer months an indigenous revolutionary movement came into being in the Chignecto region.[29] It was led by John Allan, a Scot who had been won over to the American revolutionary cause, and Jonathan Eddy, who had left Massachusetts to settle in the Isthmus after the Seven Years' War. Sam Rogers, Zebulon Rowe, Obadiah Ayer, and William Howe, among others, all respected and prosperous New Englanders, supported Allan and Eddy. These men were greatly encouraged by the successful sacking in August of Fort Frederick, a tiny British military outpost at the mouth of the Saint John River, by a small Machias force,[30] and also by the bold pronouncement of the inhabitants of Maugerville in favour of the Revolution. The Maugerville settlers declared that they were willing "to submit ourselves to the government of the Massachusetts Bay and that we are ready with our lives and fortunes to share with them the event of the present struggle for liberty, however, God in his providence may order it."[31]

Towards the end of November, Allan, Eddy, and their not insignificant following were given an excellent opportunity to precipitate a crisis that could have conceivably led to a successful rebellion. The long-simmering discontent with the government authorities finally boiled over when the assembly, controlled by the small Halifax merchant clique with strong commercial ties with Britain, passed two acts, one to call out a fifth of the militia, the other to impose a tax for its support.[32] Almost immediately the two bills were loudly denounced throughout the colony, but especially in the Chignecto region. Allan and Eddy, instead of quickly harnessing the deep dissatisfaction within the framework of armed rebellion, decided to widen first the popular basis of their support by sending a rather mildly worded yet firm protest against the two bills to Governor Legge. In the protest, which was eventually signed by almost 250 inhabitants including many Yorkshiremen, the Chignecto settlers objected to the new tax and to the possibility of being forced to "march into different parts in arms against their friends and relations."[33] Allan and Eddy had succeeded in gaining much popular support for their attack upon the Halifax government, but at the moment when they attempted to use this support to emulate the example of the colonies in revolt, Legge suddenly pulled the rug from under their unsuspecting feet. Realizing the seriousness of the discontent as reflected in the Chignecto petition, the governor promptly suspended the two contentious acts. In so doing, Legge had removed the catalyst from the potential revolutionary situation not only in the Isthmus but throughout Nova Scotia.

Failing to grasp the significance of Legge's clever manoeuvre, Allan and Eddy decided during the first weeks of January, 1776, that the time was propitious for fomenting an insurrection. Nothing could have been further from the truth. Having won the support of the Acadians, but the equally enthusiastic disapprobation of the Yorkshiremen, Allan and Eddy decided that before taking any further steps on the road to rebellion it was first imperative to sound out carefully the general feeling of the mass of New Englanders towards the proposed vague plan. The two leaders were genuinely shocked to discover that the vast majority of New Englanders, even though they "would have welcomed an army of invasion,"[34] stubbornly refused to support the planned insurrection. Ground between the millstones of contending forces, most of the Chignecto New Englanders, as well as those throughout the colony, had decided to walk the tightrope of neutrality until it was clear that a strong rebel invading force would be able to gain effective control of Nova Scotia. Allan and Eddy were forced to alter drastically their proposed policy; they decided to petition General Washington and the Continental Congress to send an "army of liberation" to Nova Scotia. The Machias plan of August 1775 had been resurrected.

Jonathan Eddy, with a band of fourteen men, had set out in February from Chignecto to persuade Washington and the Continental Congress to invade Nova Scotia. On March 27, Eddy met with the American general at Cambridge.[35] Washington carefully considered Eddy's often illogical arguments, but believing that the British forces that had abandoned Boston[36] ten days earlier were now in Halifax, the General informed the ambassador that "in the present uncertain state of things . . . a much more considerable force [than Eddy had even requested] would be of no avail."[37] Washington reaffirmed the policy he had first enunciated on hearing of the Machias plan in August of the preceding year.[38] The disillusioned Eddy next went to the Continental Congress in Philadelphia, but as he expected, here too his urgent appeal fell on unresponsive ears.[39] After his return to the Isthmus in May it was decided that, as a last resort, the government of Massachusetts should be approached for military aid. The persistent Eddy, accompanied by Howe, Rogers, and Rowe, immediately set sail for Boston.

During the months of January and February the Halifax government had been strangely indifferent to developments in the Chignecto Isthmus. The loyalist leaders, Charles Dixon and the Rev. John Eagleson, had bombarded the Governor and his Executive Council with frantic letters.[40] A delegation had been sent to General Washington by the New Englanders;[41] and on hearing a rumour that the American army had captured Bunker Hill, the supporters of Allan and Eddy had procured "a chaise and six horses, postillion and a flag of liberty, and drove about the isthmus, proclaiming the news and blessings of liberty."[42] Dixon and Eagleson demanded immediate government action. In March the Executive Council resolved "that the lieutenant-governor [Francklin] be desired to proceed, as soon as possible to [Chignecto] . . . and there make a strict inquiry into the behavior and conduct of the inhabitants, and to make report thereof to the governor; also, that he will apprehend all persons, who, on due proof, shall be found guilty of any rebellious and treasonable transactions."[43] Francklin, however, was able to accomplish absolutely nothing. It was not until June that the government exerted some semblance of authority on the troubled Isthmus. This delay was

226

at least partly the result of the recall of Legge in May and his replacement by Lieutenant-Colonel Arbuthnot.[44] In June, 200 Royal Fencibles[45] under the command of Lieutenant-Colonel Joseph Gorham were sent to occupy Fort Cumberland, which had been abandoned by the British eight years earlier.[46] Fort Cumberland, the reconstructed French Fort Beauséjour, was strategically located at the extreme southern tip of the Fort Cumberland Ridge which, together with the Fort Lawrence Ridge, cuts through the Chignecto marshlands until it almost touches the waters of the Bay of Fundy. Gorham found the fort in a state of serious disrepair. He reported that "the face of the Bastions, Curtains, etc., by being so long exposed to the heavy rains and frost were bent down to such a slope that one might with ease ascend any part of the fort."[47] Gorham set about repairing the fort, and he went out of his way to overlook what he considered to be the harmless activities of the energetic American sympathizers. He hoped that a simple show of strength would completely undermine the position held by the Eddy-Allan faction.

227

It was not until July that the Halifax authorities, at last convinced of the seriousness of the revolutionary movement in the Isthmus, considered it necessary to strike against the leaders of the "American Party." A proclamation was issued offering a reward of 200 for the capture of Eddy and 100 for Allan, Howe, and Rogers.[48] On hearing that he was a man with a price on his head, Allan decided to join his friends in Massachusetts and left a committee in charge of "the revolutionary interests."[49]

Eddy was unsuccessful in his attempt to persuade the General Court of Massachusetts to send a military expedition "supplied with some necessaries, as provisions and ammunition . . . [to] destroy those [Nova Scotian] forts and relieve our brethren and friends."[50] Nevertheless, he had not entirely failed. He was promised sufficient ammunition and supplies to equip properly whatever force he himself could muster. Eddy immediately rushed off to Machias, where he knew there was a group of men still vitally interested in attacking Nova Scotia. By carefully playing upon their cupidity Eddy was able to recruit twenty-eight men from Machias.[51] On August 11, just as the invading army was embarking, Allan arrived. Fully aware of the weakness of the revolutionary movement on the Isthmus, Allan endeavoured in vain to dissuade Eddy from carrying out his rash and hopeless plan. Eddy refused to come to grips with the hard facts of reality; he hoped that his force would build up like a giant snowball at Passamaquoddy and Maugerville and that the Chignecto New Englanders would eagerly rally to his banner. He seemed to believe that it would be only a matter of time before his liberating army would force the British to abandon "New England's Outpost."[52]

At Passamaquoddy, a few miles to the east of Machias, Eddy added seven new recruits and then sailed to Maugerville in three whale boats.[53] At the settlement on the upper Saint John River he found the inhabitants "almost universally to be hearty in the cause,"[54] but was able to enlist only twenty-seven settlers and sixteen Indians.[55] Eddy's liberating army, now numbering some eighty men, returned to the mouth of the Saint John River to await the arrival of the promised ammunition and supplies from Boston.[56] There was an unexpected prolonged delay, and the force was unable to move eastwards until the last week of October. On October 29, Eddy's men easily captured fourteen of Gorham's troops who were stationed at the military outpost of Shepody, to the south of present-day Moncton.[57] The invaders[58] then swung sharply to the north and made their way up the Petitcodiac and Memramcook rivers to the Acadian settlement of Memramcook, where Eddy had no trouble whatsoever in persuading a number of Acadians to support him.[59] From Memramcook, on November 5, Eddy and his men marched eastwards towards their immediate objective — Fort Cumberland.[60]

The supporters of Allan and Eddy on the Isthmus loudly "expressed their Uneasiness at seeing so few [invaders] . . . and those unprovided with Artillery."[61] They vehemently argued that, taking everything into consideration, there was no possible chance of success. Even if Fort Cumberland were captured, and this was highly unlikely, British reinforcements would readily rout Eddy's motley collection of undisciplined freebooters, Indians, and Acadians. Eddy was forced to resort to outright intimidation and to false promises in order to win the unenthusiastic support of his friends. His policy was objectively described by his associate Allan:

> That they [Chignecto New Englanders] had supply'd the Enemys of America which had much displeased the States. That the Congress doubted their integrity, that if they would not rouse themselves and oppose the British power in that province [Nova Scotia] they would be looked upon as enemys and should the country be reduced by the States they would be treated as conquered people and that if they did not Incline to do something he [Eddy] would return and report them to the States. But if they would now assert their rights publickly against the King's Govt, he was then Come to help them and in Fifteen days Expected a reinforcement of a large body of men.[62]

These reinforcements existed only in Eddy's active imagination.

Only fifty New Englanders, against their better judgment, rallied to Eddy's banner, and they were joined a short time later by twenty-seven men from the Cobequid region of Nova Scotia.[63] The invading army now numbered roughly 180 men.[64] Eddy must be given a considerable amount of credit for using his relatively small force to gain virtual control of the entire Chignecto Isthmus, except, of course, for Fort Cumberland. Most of the Yorkshiremen, fearing the destruction of their property if they supported Gorham, quickly surrendered their guns and ammunition to the invaders.[65] It should be noted that well over half of the New Englanders supported neither Eddy nor Gorham, but instead carefully pursued a policy of neutrality.

Eddy was not a demagogue, nor was he a megalomaniac. He was convinced that all ties with Britain should be severed, and his fanatical enthusiasm for the Revolutionary cause seriously dulled his already undeveloped sense of military strategy. In spite of fantastic rumours regarding the size of Eddy's invading force which spread like wildfire throughout Nova Scotia during the months of October and November, the inhabitants could not be aroused from their lethargic neutrality.

As early as August, Gorham had heard of Eddy's invasion plans, but it was not until the beginning of November that he learned that Eddy was in the Chignecto region.[66] With fewer than 200 troops at his command[67] and believing that Eddy had at least 500 men,[68] Gorham was of the opinion that he was in no position to attack the invaders.[69] Therefore he felt that the only alternative was to adopt a defensive policy and to wait for reinforcements from Halifax. This was the right policy at the right time.[70]

During the early morning hours of November 7, Eddy's forces experienced their only real victory in the futile Chignecto campaign. Taking advantage of a thick fog which had settled over the coastal region, Zebulon Rowe and a handful of men thirsting for excitement and possible loot set out to capture a sloop filled with supplies for the Fort Cumberland troops.[71] Because of the low tide the sloop lay on the broad mud flats to the south-west of the fort. Eddy's description of this most humorous incident of the rebellion makes fascinating reading:

> After a Difficult March, they arrived opposite the Sloop; on board of which was a Guard of 1 Sergt and 12 men, who had they fir'd at our People, must have alarmed the Garrison in such a Manner as to have brought them on their Backs. However, our men rushed Resolutely towards the sloop up to their Knees in Mud, which made such a Noise as to alarm the Centry, who hailed them and immediately called the Sergt of the Guard. The Sergt on coming up, Ordered his Men to fire, but was immediately told by Mr. Row[e] that if they fired one Gun, Every Man of Them should be put to Death; which so frightened the poor Devils that they surrendered without firing a Shot, although our People Could not board her without the Assistance of the Conquered, who let down Ropes to our Men to get up by.[72]

As the working parties from the fort arrived to unload the sloop, they too were easily captured.[73] Altogether thirty-four of Gorham's troops, including Captain Barron, Engineer of the Garrison, and the Chaplain, the bibulous Rev. Eagleson, were seized by Rowe's detachment.[74] The captured sloop was sailed away at high tide in the direction of the Missiquash River, but not before the Royal Fencibles "fired several cannon shots"[75] at the brazen enemy.

Only two attempts were made to capture Fort Cumberland, one on November 13[76] and the other nine days later.[77] Both were miserable failures. Before Eddy could organize a third attempt, British reinforcements arrived.

On November 27 and November 28, the British relieving force, consisting of two companies of Marines and one company of the Royal Highlanders, finally landed at Fort Cumberland.[78] The relieving force had sailed from Halifax and Windsor.[79] On the 28th Gorham ordered Major Batt, an officer who had acompanied the reinforcements, to lead an attack on Eddy's camp, one mile north of the fort.[80] At five-thirty in the morning of the 29th, Batt marched out of Fort Cumberland with 170 troops, hoping to surprise the "rebels."[81] If it had not been for an alert young Negro drummer who furiously beat the alarm when he sighted the enemy,[82] Eddy's men would have been slaughtered in their sleep. Wiping sleep from their eyes, Eddy's confused followers ran into the neighbouring woods in search of cover.[83] In the skirmish that followed only seven "rebels" and four British soldiers were killed.[84] Seeing the hopelessness of the situation, Eddy ordered his men to retreat westwards "to the St. John River . . . and there make a stand."[85] Batt refused to pursue the "rebels"; instead he had his men put to the torch every home and barn belonging to those inhabitants of the Isthmus who had openly supported Eddy.[86] The billowing dark clouds of smoke could be seen by the defeated invaders as they fled in panic towards Memramcook.[87]

Eddy's rash attempt to capture Fort Cumberland failed not only because he lacked artillery, but also because his men were poorly trained, undisciplined, and badly led. With British control of the North Atlantic firmly established, with Washington's refusal to support the invasion, and with the great majority of Nova Scotians desperately trying to be neutral, Eddy's task was hopeless. Even though the Eddy Rebellion, by any broad strategic standards, was quite insignificant in the larger Revolutionary context, it is of some importance as an illustration of the fact that in 1775 and 1776, under their superficial neutrality, the New Englanders tacitly supported the Revolutionary movement. Moreover, the Eddy Rebellion helps to indicate how effectively British naval power and the isolated nature of the settlements of Nova Scotia had "neutralized the New England migrants."[88]

From 1777 to 1782 almost every Nova Scotian coastal settlement (with the notable exception of Halifax) from Tatamagouche on Northumberland Strait to the Saint John River was ravaged by American privateers.[89] As a result of these freebooting forays many New Englanders in Nova Scotia, who had originally been rather sympathetic to the Revolution, became increasingly hostile to their brethren to the south. In 1775 and 1776 most of the Nova Scotians "divided betwixt natural affection to our nearest relations, and good Faith and Friendship to our King and Country,"[90] had decided to walk the tightrope of neutrality even though they appeared to lean precariously in the direction of their "nearest relations." By the closing years of the conflict, however, as the "Neutral Yankees" reached the end of their hazardous journey, they had begun to lean towards the opposite extreme, towards the King.

What real impact did the Revolution have upon the inhabitants of Nova Scotia? Of course most of them resolved to adopt a policy of neutrality; many suffered because of the depredations of the American privateers; while a few, especially the Halifax merchants, grew rich from the usual profits of war. But was there nothing else? M.W. Armstrong has convincingly argued that probably the most important impact of the Revolution upon Nova Scotia was in precipitating the "Great Awakening of Nova Scotia."[91] In addition, Armstrong has emphasized that the "Great Awakening" encouraged the development of neutrality:

> Indeed, the Great Awakening itself may be considered to have been a retreat from the grim realities of the world to the safety and pleasantly exciting warmth of the revival meeting, and to profits and rewards of another character . . . an escape from fear and divided loyalties . . . an assertion of democratic ideals and a determination to maintain them, the Great Awakening gave self respect and satisfaction to people whose economic and political position was both humiliating and distressing.[92]

231

The prophet and evangelist of the spiritual awakening was Henry Alline who, when he was twelve, had moved from Rhode Island to Falmouth, Nova Scotia.[93] An uneducated farmer, Alline had experienced an unusual "Conversion,"[94] and in 1776 he began to preach an emotional Christian message that has been described as being a combination of "Calvinism, Antinomianism, and Enthusiasm."[95] The flames of religious revival[96] swept up the Minas Basin in 1777, across the Bay of Fundy in 1779, and to the South Shore in 1781.[97] All Protestant Churches in Nova Scotia were in one way or another affected by the "Great Awakening," and largely as a direct result the evangelical wing of the various Protestant Churches was able to dominate Maritime religious life throughout the nineteenth century.

British sea power, the isolated nature of the settlements, the refusal of Washington to mount an offensive against Nova Scotia, and perhaps the religious revival, all combined to keep the "Yankees" neutral during the Revolution.

NOTES

[1] W.B. Kerr, "Nova Scotia in the Critical Years, 1775–6", *Dalhousie Review* (April 1932), 97.

[2] S.D. Clarke, *Movements of Political Protest in Canada, 1640–1840* (Toronto, 1959), 63.

[3] It should be borne in mind that there was a significant German-speaking population in the Lunenburg region and that there were pockets of Highland Scots, Yorkshiremen, Acadians, and Scots-Irish scat-

tered throughout the peninsula of Nova Scotia. Most of these settlers (a few Acadians and Scots-Irish are the exception to the rule) also remained neutral during the Revolution even though their sympathies lay with the Crown.

4 J.B. Brebner, *The Neutral Yankees of Nova Scotia* (New York, 1937), 329–37.

5 V. Barnes, "Francis Legge, Governor of Loyalist Nova Scotia, 1773–1776," *New England Quarterly* (July 1931), 420–47. See also a convincing criticism of this view in W.B. Kerr, "The Merchants of Nova Scotia and the American Revolution," *Canadian Historical Review* (March 1932), 21–34.

6 A.L. Burt, *The United States, Great Britain, and British North America* (Toronto, 1940), 13.

7 W.B. Kerr, *The Maritime Provinces of British North America and the American Revolution* (Sackville, n.d.), 59.

8 Kerr, *The Maritime Provinces*, 60.

9 Kerr, *The Maritime Provinces*, 53–60.

10 Brebner, *Neutral Yankees of Nova Scotia*, 352.

11 J.C. Webster, *The Forts of Chignecto* (Sackville, 1930), 5.

12 W.C. Milner, *History of Sackville, New Brunswick* (Sackville, 1955), 14–21.

13 B.J. Bird, "Settlement Patterns in Maritime Canada, 1687–1876," *The Geographic Review* (July 1955), 398–99.

14 Bird, "Settlement Patterns," 398–99.

15 W.C. Milner, "Records of Chignecto," *Collections of the Nova Scotia Historical Society*, vol. 15 (Halifax, 1911), 41–45.

16 Milner, "Records of Chignecto," 40.

17 Kerr, *The Maritime Provinces*, 68.

18 Kerr, *The Maritime Provinces*, 68.

19 J.M. Beck, *The Government of Nova Scotia* (Toronto, 1957), 22–25.

20 D.C. Harvey, "The Struggle for the New England Form of Township Government in Nova Scotia," Canadian Historical Association, *Report* (1933), 18 [hereafter *CHAR*].

21 D.C. Harvey, "Machias and the Invasion of Nova Scotia," *CHAR* (1932), 17.

22 J.C. Fitzpatrick, ed., *The Writings of George Washington* (Washington, 1931), 3: 415.

23 Fitzpatrick, ed., *Writings of George Washington* 3: 415–16.

24 The Petition of the Chignecto Inhabitants, December 23, 1775, *Nova Scotia Archives*, A94, 330–38.

25 Kerr, "Nova Scotia in the Critical Years 1775-6," 98.

26 Governor Legge to the Secretary of State, July 31, 1775, *Canadian Archives Report for 1894* (Ottawa, 1895), 334 [hereafter *CAR*, 1894].

27 E.P. Weaver, "Nova Scotia and New England during the Revolution," *American Historical Review* (October 1904), 63.

28 B. Murdoch, *A History of Nova Scotia* (Halifax, 1860), 2: 554.

29 Kerr, *The Maritime Provinces*, 69.

30 Kerr, *The Maritime Provinces*, 63.

31 Quoted in F. Kidder, *Military Operations in Eastern Maine and Nova Scotia During the Revolution* (Albany, 1867), 64.

32 Kerr, *The Maritime Provinces*, 70.

33 The Petition of Chignecto Inhabitants, *Nova Scotia Archives*, A94, 330–38.

34 Quoted in Kerr, *The Maritime Provinces*, 73.

35 Fitzpatrick, ed., *Writings of George Washington* 4: 437.

36 H. Peckham, *The War for Independence* (Chicago, 1959), 32.

37 Fitzpatrick, ed., *Writings of George Washington* 4: 438.

38 Fitzpatrick, ed., *Writings of George Washington* 4: 438.

39 Kerr, *The Maritime Provinces*, 73.

40 See *CAR*, *1894*, 345.

41 *CAR*, *1894*, 345.

42 Kerr, *The Maritime Provinces*, 74.

43 Quoted in Murdoch, *History of Nova Scotia* 2: 568.

44 In the administrative shuffle Francklin was demoted to Indian Agent.

45 The Royal Fencibles were mostly recruited from the Loyalists in the Thirteen Colonies.

46 W.B. Kerr, "The American Invasion of Nova Scotia, 1776-7," *Canadian Defense Quarterly* (July 1936), 434.

47 Gorham's Journal, *CAR*, *1894*, 360.

48 Kerr, *The Maritime Provinces*, 78.

49 Kidder, *Military Operations*, 12.

50 Petition of Jonathan Eddy, Aug. 28, 1776, in P. Force, ed., *American Archives*, 5th series (Washington, 1851), 2: 734.

51 *American Archives* 2: 734

52 Kidder, *Military Operations*, 12.

53 Gorham's Journal, 355.

54 Quoted in Harvey, "Machias and the Invasion of Nova Scotia," 21.

55 Kerr, "The American Invasion," 434.

56 Kerr, "The American Invasion," 435.

[57] Kerr, "The American Invasion," 435.

[58] The description of the Rebellion is to be found in Gorham's Journal, *CAR, 1894*, 355-57, 359-65, and in Eddy's Journal, in Harvey, "Machias and the Invasion of Nova Scotia," 22-24.

[59] Eddy's Journal, 22.

[60] Eddy's Journal, 22.

[61] Eddy's Journal, 22.

[62] Allan's Journal, in Harvey, "Machias and the Invasion of Nova Scotia," 24.

[63] Kerr, "The American Invasion," 435.

[64] Eddy's Journal, 23.

[65] Kerr, "The American Invasion," 436.

[66] Gorham's Journal, 355.

[67] Gorham's Journal, 360.

[68] Gorham's Journal, 356.

[69] Gorham's Journal, 360.

[70] For the opposite point of view see Kerr, "The American Invasion," 441: "A well-directed sortie could at any time have broken up Eddy's camp."

[71] Eddy's Journal, 22.

[72] Eddy's Journal, 22.

[73] Eddy's Journal, 22-23.

[74] Eddy's Journal, 22-23.

[75] Eddy's Journal, 23; Gorham's Journal, 356.

[76] Gorham's Journal, 361-62.

[77] Gorham's Journal, 361-62.

[78] Gorham's Journal, 362.

[79] Gorham's Journal, 362. This point must be emphasized especially, after examining Stanley's inaccurate reference to an overland march. See G.F.G. Stanley, *Canada's Soldiers, 1605-1954* (Toronto, 1954), 118.

[80] Gorham's Journal, 362.

[81] Gorham's Journal, 362.

[82] C.E. Kemp, "Folk-Lore About Old Fort Beauséjour", *Acadiensis* (October 1908), 301-302. Also see Kerr, "The American Invasion," 440.

[83] Gorham's Journal, 362.

[84] Kerr, "The American Invasion," 441.

[85] Eddy's Journal, 23.

[86] Gorham's Journal, 362.

[87] The contest for present-day western New Brunswick continued until the end of the Revolutionary War. In the summer of 1777 Allan's invading force of some 100 men from Machias was compelled to retreat overland from the St. John Valley towards the St. Croix when confronted by a strong British military expedition led by Major Gilford Studholme and Francklin. For the remainder of the war Allan unsuccessfully attempted to persuade the St. John River Indians to join the Revolutionary cause.

[88] Brebner, *The Neutral Yankees*, 353.

[89] Brebner, *The Neutral Yankees*, 324-35.

[90] Petition of the Inhabitants of Yarmouth, Dec. 8, 1775. Quoted in Brebner, *The Neutral Yankees*, 291.

[91] M.W. Armstrong, "Neutrality and Religion in Revolutionary Nova Scotia," *New England Quarterly* (Mar. 1946), 50-61.

[92] Armstrong, "Neutrality and Religion," 57, 58, 60.

[93] Armstrong, "Neutrality and Religion," 55.

[94] See W. James, *The Varieties of Religious Experience* (New York, 1958), 134-35: "My sins seemed to be laid open; so that I thought that every one I saw knew them, and sometimes I was almost ready to acknowledge many things, which I thought they knew; yea sometimes it seemed to me as if every one was pointing me out as the most guilty wretch upon earth."

[95] Quoted in Armstrong, "Neutrality and Religion," 58.

[96] The following is Alline's description of the Liverpool revival of 1776: "We had blessed days, the Lord was reviving his work of grace. Many under a load of sin cried out, what shall we do to be saved? and the saints seemed much revived, came out and witnessed for God. In a short time some more souls were born to Christ, they came out and declared what God had done for their souls and what a blessed change had taken place in that town." Quoted in Armstrong, "Neutrality and Religion," 55-56.

[97] Armstrong, "Neutrality and Religion," 55.

233

The United Empire Loyalists: A Reconsideration*

W.G. SHELTON

The United Empire Loyalists occupy a strangely equivocal place in Canadian history. Although regarded with honour by some Canadians for having saved part of North America for the British connection, they are suspected by others of being not quite respectable political ancestors in this democratic age. As a result, especially since this country has become more independent of Great Britain, the Loyalists have received little attention from serious historians, and their role in the founding of Canada has been de-emphasized to the point where they appear as just another group of immigrants making their contribution to our cultural mosaic.[1]

A search through standard histories of Canada fails to reveal much agreement on the significance of the Loyalists. Edgar McInnis implies that they were a conservative group accustomed to a privileged position in society, many of whom were expelled from the United States for their opinions.[2] The motives of the Loyalists are not discussed by Donald Creighton, although he does mention that many of those who settled in Ontario were poor and illiterate.[3] D.C.C. Masters agrees that they came from all walks of life, but adds that they brought to Canada "a liking for an aristocratic society of privilege with themselves as the privileged group."[4] J.B. Brebner feels that the emigration of American settlers to Ontario was part of a general westward movement unrelated to principle. He, too, emphasizes the conservatism of the Loyalists which, interacting with British Toryism, consolidated an "anti-republican, anti-democratic, politico-economic system in Britain and America."[5] For J.M.S. Careless, also, they were conservative in outlook, but he recognizes that they "represented a declaration of independence against the United States," and that "they helped to create not only a new province, but a new nation."[6] W.L. Morton says that they were "for the most part" conservative, although the largest number was "like the revolutionaries, Whiggish by persuasion."[7] G.M. Craig, in his recent study of Upper Canada, sees the Loyalists as "a large and varied group" which "opposed the resort to force against British authority."[8]

Almost alone among Canadian historians, A.R.M. Lower thinks that the Loyalists are worth more than a passing mention. Like Careless, he sees Canada as a "by-product" of the American Revolution, which was "the great tragedy of history, the breaking of the unity of race,

234

*Originally published in the *Dalhousie Review* 45, 1 (Spring 1965): 5–16. Reprinted by permission.

the drawing of those of like blood apart." Canadians have since regarded it as a "foul and treasonable occurrence," and there has been "little understanding of the essential nature of the Revolution — still less sympathy with the fine generosity of the ideals that had inspired it and which it in turn inspired." Canada was the offshoot of the losing and conservative side of a great radical upheaval — a struggle between classes and masses in a "frankly anti-democratic" society, with the classes retreating to Canada after their defeat. Others who joined the trek north had merely put their money on the wrong horse and were repudiated by the victors. He does find it difficult to understand why so many Loyalists were non-British in origin but explains it on the basis that "those with whom tradition is an acquired one are often apt to be more tenacious of it than those with whom it originated, to whom it is familiar and perhaps threadbare."[9]

From these opinions, three conclusions seem to emerge. The first is that, considering their importance, surprisingly little attention is paid to the Loyalists in Canadian histories. Secondly, what is said about them is often contradictory, or at least confusing. For example, they did not want to break the unity of the race, but many were of different racial backgrounds; or they hoped to establish an aristocratic society on the frontier, but many could not read or write. Thirdly, to the extent that a consistent picture emerges, it is unfavourable: words such as "privilege," "anti-democratic," and "conservative" in a pejorative sense occur most often.

235

Why are the Loyalists handled in this way? Two possible reasons come to mind. One is their association, for many people, with the Family Compact and other self-perpetuating ruling cliques in British North America. It is assumed that the Loyalists would naturally dominate the social and political life in the colonies where they settled. This may have been true in New Brunswick but, since practically the entire population was composed of refugees from the American colonies, the inhabitants who were outside the charmed circle of authority and patronage were just as much Loyalists as those on the inside.

In Upper Canada, where the influx of immigrants soon made the genuine Loyalists a minority, we find that studies of the personnel of the legislative and executive councils show that between 1791 and 1841 there were only 22 Loyalists out of 105 appointees, and that many of these owed their position to Bishop Strachan rather than to their Loyalism. That Loyalists were not unduly prominent in the Family Compact is further indicated by the absence of such well-known Loyalist names as Johnson, Grass, Butler, and Van Alstine.[10]

A second factor probably responsible for the treatment meted out to the Loyalists is that they were on the wrong side in the American Revolution. The singularly unattractive portrait of the American Tories painted by earlier American historians has been to some extent corrected by more recent research. On the whole, American historians have been extremely generous in their reappraisal, but the fact remains that the Loyalists were on the losing side, and the victors went on to make a huge success of the American republic. This outcome cannot help being reflected in the writings of Americans on this subject.

The Loyalists have had their supporters in Canada, but the nature of this support has often done them more harm than good. They have been used by some of their descendants to reinforce claims of social superiority which do not sit well in a democratic society, and the emphasis on the purity of their Britishness has been an embarrassment in a country where other races now form a majority.

The main reason, however, why more attention has not been devoted to the Loyalists in Canadian history is that the formative period of their lives was spent in the American colonies and is therefore officially part of American history. Although true in a strict geographic sense, this fact has had the unfortunate effect of depriving the Loyalists of their past and much of their meaningfulness. The result is a strange impression of one group called American Tories vanishing into well-deserved oblivion, and another group known as United Empire Loyalists suddenly appearing in the Canadian wilderness clutching their Union Jacks.

236

Only a study of the American Revolution from a Loyalist rather than an American or British point of view can give an insight into their motivation and a fair evaluation of their role. It is too easy to assume, because the revolutionaries were fighting for self-government, equality, democracy, and liberty, that the Loyalists who opposed them also opposed these honourable ideals. This conclusion is not always drawn, but it certainly lurks in the background.

If we are permitted then to trespass on American territory for a moment, the first thing we should note is that, whether American grievances against Britain were completely justified or not, most Loyalists objected just as strongly as did the Whigs to British attempts to impose new taxes on the colonies. Furthermore, even the most extreme Tory admitted that some change was necessary in the constitutional relations between the colonies and the mother country. In other words, most Loyalists were not blind supporters of the British government — they were just as American in outlook as their opponents. Some of the Loyalists were recent arrivals, it is true, but so were Tom Paine and many of the recruits in Washington's army.

The major difference between the two sides was in their opinion of the seriousness of the British threat to American liberties and what action should be taken. The Loyalists believed that the Patriots were exaggerating their grievances out of all relation to fact — that in reality the American colonists were fortunate in living under laws that were about as mild and just as one could expect in an imperfect world. As T.B. Chandler, a Connecticut Congregationalist turned Anglican minister, put it, "A small degree of reflection would convince us, that the grievances in question, supposing them to be real, are, at most, no more than just grounds for decent remonstrance, but not a sufficient reason for forcible resistance."[11]

Many Tory pamphleteers were led to question the sincerity of the revolutionary leaders, who, they felt, were really seeking independence from the beginning. The fate of Joseph Galloway's Plan of Union seemed convincing evidence. Galloway, a leading Pennsylvania politician, provided in his scheme for a Grand Council representing all the colonies and possessing a large measure of autonomy. Although the moderate leaders of the first Continental Congress praised it warmly, and it was "tabled" by a vote of only 6 to 5, all reference to it was later expunged from the record, and the radical Whigs moved on quickly to uncompromising measures which led to eight years of war. Despite public denials, many of them admitted privately that they were seeking complete independence, and in any case, the demands they were making on Great Britain amounted in fact to independence. Their reluctance to bring their real intentions out into the open seems to indicate that they were afraid public opinion did not support independence at that time and that it was necessary to build up anti-British feeling by provoking violence and avoiding conciliation. For example, although Congress began secret negotiations to obtain help from France as early as the fall of 1775, Tories still ran the risk of being tarred and feathered in the spring of 1776 for accusing Whigs of advocating independence.

237

In response to protests in the past, Britain had given way in practically everything except a token tax on tea. The Loyalists felt that it was reasonable to expect that peaceful negotiations would result in a redress of the latest grievances without recourse to violence. If the colonists were truly united, passive resistance alone could accomplish a great deal, as it had in the past. Americans already possessed a large degree of self-rule — it was just a matter of solving a number of questions relating to the constitutional link with Britain. The cautious New York lawyer Peter Van Schaack knew his Locke as well as any of his fellow Whigs, but he questioned whether there was enough tyranny on the part of the British to warrant a repetition of 1688.

> From all the proofs I had, I could not, on a fair estimate, think them sufficient to establish the fact of an intention to destroy the liberties of the colonies. I saw irregularities, but I thought time would work out our deliverance, and it appeared to me, that, balancing conveniences and inconveniences, we were, upon the whole, a happy people. The idea of a civil war appeared to me to involve the greatest of human calamities, — I thought policy should make that in us the *last* resort.[12]

If, then, British tyranny was not the real reason for the revolution, what was? Hector St. John Crevecoeur, a Huguenot farmer and author of well-known sketches of colonial life, answered this question for many Loyalists:

> Ambition, we well know, an exorbitant love of power and thirst of riches, a certain impatience of government, by some people called liberty, — all these motives, clad under the garb of patriotism and even of constitutional reason, have been the secret but true foundations of this, as well as many other revolutions. But what art, what insidious measures, what deep-laid policy, what masses of intricate, captious delusions were not necessary to persuade a people happy beyond any on earth, in the zenith of political felicity, receiving from Nature every benefit she could confer, that they were miserable, oppressed, and aggrieved, that slavery and tyranny would rush upon them from the very sources which before had conveyed them so many blessings.[13]

238

With the revolutionary Whigs occupying the high ground of liberty, equality, and self-government, those who opposed them were outmanoeuvred. Many could not accept their arguments but, finding it dangerous to antagonize the Whig mobs, hoped to remain quiet. However, this became increasingly difficult as the situation deteriorated into outright war, and the Patriots began taking the attitude that those who were not with them were against them. At this point many Americans who did not support independence gave in to the threats and intimidation of the revolutionaries and switched their allegiance. How many times did something similar to the following take place? In the spring of 1776, a Pennsylvanian, Thomas Smith, is reported to have said,

> that the Measures of Congress had already enslaved America and done more damage than all the Acts of Parliament ever intended to lay upon us, that the whole was nothing but a scheme of a parcel of hot-headed Presbyterians and that he believed the Devil was at the bottom of the whole; that the taking up Arms was the most scandalous thing a man could be guilty of and more heinous than an hundred of the grossest offences against moral law, etc., etc., etc., etc.[14]

The Bucks County Committee of Safety decided that he be "considered an Enemy of the Rights of British America and that all persons break off every kind of dealing with him until he shall make proper satisfaction to this Committee for his conduct." By the time this appeared in the press, Smith had already decided to recant and make his peace. Some put up a stouter resistance than he did, but in most areas life became extremely difficult, even unbearable, for those who refused to conform, and they were eventually forced to make a choice between acquiescing or fleeing behind the British lines.

Those who chose the latter course were as varied in background as the Revolutionaries themselves. Occupational lists show that the Loyalists formed a cross-section of the population of the Thirteen Colonies in every respect. Some were rich and socially prominent, but so were the Washingtons, the Livingstons, and the Hancocks of the Patriot party. Many were so poor that they made no claim for compensation from the British government because they had owned no property which could be confiscated by the victors. There is no doubt that some of the Loyalists were anti-democratic, but for every statement which could be interpreted in this way by a Tory, one can probably find a dozen from the mouths of the Whigs. It is a waste of time to attempt to differentiate the Loyalists from the Patriots on the basis of conservatism, regardless of how one defines it, since the American Revolution is widely recognized as an essentially conservative movement.

One thing, however, many of the Loyalists did have in common, as W.H. Nelson points out in his recent book, *The American Tory*.[15] A study of their ethnic, religious, and economic composition indicates that most of them came from groups which were minorities in the localities where they lived, such as Anglicans in the north, Presbyterians in the south, Quakers and Mennonites from Pennsylvania, Highlanders from North Carolina, Lowlanders from New York, seaboard merchants in some colonies and frontiersmen in others, Indians, and of course Negroes. These people felt that they had more to fear from the unrestricted power of those around them than they did from the distant British government, which had often protected them by disallowing discriminatory colonial legislation.

239

This is a very useful approach but it is not completely adequate, since only a portion of each minority became active Loyalists. Families often split over the issues at stake, so that generalisations about types and categories do not really do justice to the individual human being. It must be remembered that each person had to make a decision, often an agonizing one, involving the loss of friends as well as property, and long periods of separation from wife and children as well as physical hardship and perhaps even death. For many this decision was made on the basis of conscience, self-respect, integrity, call it what you will. Social upheavals like the American Revolution force many people to make a choice between what seems safe, sensible, and expedient and what they feel to be right. Even for those not politically minded many painful dilemmas were created.

Here are several examples. The Anglican clergyman who was ordered to abjure the king would have to violate an oath taken at his ordination. The merchant who had undertaken to ship goods to a firm in England which had advanced him credit might very well drive old business friends into bankruptcy if he agreed to the export embargo called for by Congress. Officeholders are often looked upon as men who were Loyalists out of self-interest, but in most cases their personal welfare would have been better served by forgetting their oaths of office and throwing in their lot with the revolutionaries. This was especially true in New England, where the patriots formed an overwhelming majority. Typical of New England Loyalists was Colonel William Browne of Salem, who had extensive properties in Massachusetts and Connecticut. Fourteen valuable farms in the latter colony alone were later confiscated. He was so highly respected by the inhabitants that he was offered the governorship by the Committee of Safety, and a delegation which included Elbridge Gerry (whose idea of democracy is preserved in the term "gerrymander") pleaded with him to join them. He refused, saying that neither persuasion nor threats could make him do anything derogatory to the character of his office, and he ultimately went into exile.[16]

It was the very pressures by which the Whigs attempted to coerce the rest of the population into conformity with their wishes, however, which aroused the opposition of countless ordinary people and turned them into active Loyalists. Lorenzo Sabine, an early American student of the Loyalists, pointed out over a century ago that persecution made half the "king's friends."[17]

240

This contradiction between Whig theory and Whig practice was a source of never-ending amazement to their opponents. At the time of an earlier non-importation agreement, a Boston storekeeper published the following statement in a local paper:

> Upon the whole, I cannot help saying — although I never have entered far into the mysteries of government, having applied myself to my shop and my business — that it always seemed strange to me that people who contend so much for civil and religious liberty should be so ready to deprive others of their natural liberty; that men who are guarding against being subject to laws [to] which they never gave their consent in person or by their representative should at the same time make laws, and in the most effectual manner execute them upon me and others, to which laws I am sure I never gave my consent either in person or by my representative.[18]

This perplexity was echoed many times in Loyalist pamphlets during the Revolution. It seemed perfectly evident to them that the tyranny of Congress was much more severe and all-embracing than anything known under British rule.

Although originally in favour of avoiding bloodshed and arriving at a negotiated settlement with the home government, the active Loyalists eventually realised, especially after the Declaration of Independence, that the issue would be decided by force. As a result they volunteered for service with the British in such large numbers that it has been estimated that about half as many Americans enlisted on the British side as did in the Continental Army. Their aim was not to reimpose harsh foreign rule, as the Whigs would have it, but to liberate their homeland from the usurped authority of a ruthless faction claiming without justification to be acting for all Americans, and to restore the civil liberties guaranteed by the British constitution. They were fighting, in other words, for their own conception of freedom.

There was more, however, to the Loyalist position than mere response to the actions of the Whigs. For those Loyalists, at least, who published their ideas in contemporary pamphlets and newspapers and in memoirs and histories, there was fundamental disagreement with the political theory of the revolutionaries. They had, of course, to assume that the Whigs were sincere in their use of the vocabulary of freedom, since self-determination, in the words of Alfred Cobban, is "the usual demand of those who want to oppose others." However, whether these ideas were believed in or not by those who advocated them, they were obviously expected to influence public opinion by their self-evident rightness. The basis for revolt was found originally in the British constitution; but as that would hardly serve for independence, natural law became the final authority. Although other writers may have been cited more often by the revolutionaries than John Locke, it was his name which lent respectability to their cause. As interpreted by them, Locke sanctioned a rebellion such as the Glorious Revolution of 1688, if the sovereign violated certain natural rights, especially that of property. All that the revolutionaries had to do, according to this formula, was to demonstrate the tyranny of King George III, declare him deposed, and provide a substitute administration. This they did by the Declaration of Independence.

However, the Loyalists did not accept the analogy of 1688. In that case the country changed rulers but remained united, whereas in the 1770s the issue was nullification and secession. What the patriots did was to nullify certain laws which they did not like and then to secede when they were not allowed what amounted to *de facto* independence. Today, in Canada, it would be called separatism. The Loyalists objected that any argument which could be used against British tyranny would be just as effective against the tyranny of Congress: if pushed too far, the contract theory could lead to anarchy. Daniel Leonard, a lawyer who carried on a pamphlet debate with John Adams, put it this way:

> Admitting that the collective body of the people, that are subject to the British Empire, have an inherent right to change their form of government, or race of kings, it does not follow that the inhabitants of a single province, or of a number of provinces, or any given part under a majority of the whole empire, have such a right. By admitting that the less may rule or sequester themselves from the greater, we unhinge all government.[19]

The argument for separation against which Leonard wrote came home to roost 85 years later, with the side which adopted the Loyalist position, the North, emerging the victor at that time. In fact, Abraham Lincoln's arguments against secession in his First Inaugural address are strikingly

241

similar to those of Leonard. Another Loyalist, Galloway, forecast a civil war should independence come, in which the North would fight the South over control of the West, with the "ruthless and cunning Yankees" emerging triumphant.[20]

Today, of course, the right of a people to govern themselves is taken for granted; it is even made explicit in the United Nations Charter. But, as the Loyalists were aware, there are difficulties. The only way the Patriots could justify the break with Great Britain was on the grounds of their favourite Latin adage, *vox populi, vox dei*. It is indeed difficult to find a more obvious authority for legitimizing power, but the question immediately arises: Who are the people? "Popular demagogues," wrote Leonard, "always call themselves the people, and when their own measures are censured, cry out, the people, the people are abused and insulted."[21] However, the Loyalists objected not only to discontented politicians claiming to speak for everyone but also to the idea that the raw will of the "people" as exemplified in mobs, or the arbitrary actions of self-constituted committees and irregularly elected congresses, could ever be a substitute for the justice and order provided by a government which, though responsive to the people, must be to some extent above their momentary passions. They feared that public opinion was being deified at the expense of all other standards of morality, as in a Loyalist's portrait of *The Factious Demagogue*:

> As for his Religion, he could mix,
> And blend it well with politics,
> For 'twas his favourite opinion
> In mobs was seated all dominion:
> All pow'r and might he understood
> Rose from the sov'reign multitude:
> That right and wrong, that good and ill,
> Were nothing but the rabble's will:
> Tho' they renounce the truth for fiction,
> In nonsense trust, and contradiction;
> And tho' they change ten times a day
> As fear or interest leads the way;
> And what this hour is law and reason,
> Declare, the next, revolt and treason;
> Yet we each doctrine must receive,
> And with a pious grin believe,
> In ev'rything the people's choice
> As true as God Almighty's voice.[22]

The Loyalists thus anticipate some of the judgments of Alexis de Tocqueville and others who have been critics of the tyranny of the majority, or what is sometimes called "totalitarian democracy."

In sum, then, the case presented here is that the Loyalist was no more reactionary than the Whig, that he believed the dispute with Britain could be settled peacefully, that he felt he had more to lose than to gain by giving up the protection of British laws for the unlimited sovereignty of public opinion, that the actions of the revolutionaries very often put him in a position where there was no alternative to taking the British side if he wanted to preserve his self-respect, that he fought not to defend tyranny but to free his country from what he regarded as tyranny, and that he was aware of some flaws in the overoptimistic and sometimes hypocritical slogans of the Whigs.

It is not necessary to pretend either that independence was wrong or that it would not have come very soon in order to justify the stand taken by the Loyalists. Such a justification is particularly desirable from the standpoint of Canadian history because that preference for evolution rather than revolution, for patient negotiation rather than impatient violence, which is supposed to be a characteristic of the Canadian temper, can be traced directly back to the United Empire Loyalists. As the chief point of differentiation between the Canadian and American forms of democracy, it is surely worth emphasizing.

243

NOTES

[1] For example, not one of the papers presented at the annual meetings of the Canadian Historical Association since it was founded in 1922 has had the Loyalists as its subject, except in connection with land allotment.

[2] Edgar McInnis, *Canada* (New York, 1960), 160–65.

[3] D.G. Creighton, *Dimension of the North* (Boston, 1944), 177, 172.

[4] D.C.C. Masters, *A Short History of Canada* (Princeton, 1958), 22-23.

[5] J.B. Brebner, *Canada: A Modern History* (Ann Arbor, 1960), 106-107.

[6] J.M.S. Careless, *Canada: A Story of Challenge* (Cambridge, 1953), 113.

[7] W.L. Morton, *The Kingdom of Canada* (Toronto, 1963), 174-75.

[8] G.M. Craig, *Upper Canada — The Formative Years* (Toronto, 1963), 2-3.

[9] R.M. Lower, *Colony to Nation* (Toronto, 1959), 77, 84, 113-20.

[10] James J. Talman, ed., *Loyalist Narratives from Upper Canada* (Toronto, 1946), lxiii. The figures are from Alison Ewart and Julia Jarvis, "The Personnel of the Family Compact, 1791-1841," *Canadian Historical Review* 7: 209-221.

[11] [Thomas Bradbury Chandler], *A Friendly Warning to All Reasonable Americans* (New York, 1774).

[12] H.C. Van Schaack, *Life of Peter Van Schaack* (New York, 1842), 261.

[13] Hector St. John Crevecoeur, *Sketches of Eighteenth Century America* (New Haven, 1925), 251.

[14] Quoted in W.H. Siebert, *The Loyalists of Pennsylvania* (Columbus, Ohio, 1920), 26.

[15] W.H. Nelson, *The American Tory* (Oxford, 1961), 91.

[16] James H. Stark, *The Loyalists of Massachusetts and the Other Side of the American Revolution* (Boston, 1910), 450.

[17] Lorenzo Sabine, *Biographical Sketches of the Loyalists of the American Revolution*, 2 vols. (Boston, 1864), 1: 78.

[18] Sabine, *Biographical Sketches* 1: 311.

[19] John Adams and Daniel Leonard, *Novanglus and Massachusettensis* (Boston, 1819), 225.

[20] [Joseph Galloway], *A Candid Examination of the Mutual Claims of Great Britain and the Colonies* (New York, 1775), 59.

[21] Adams and Leonard, *Novanglus and Massachusettensis*, 225.

[22] Winthrop Sargent, ed., *The Loyalist Poetry of the Revolution* (Philadelphia, 1857), 129. *The Factious Demagogue* was dated at Halifax, May 13, 1780, and was probably written by the Rev. Jacob Bailey, the frontier missionary.

The Economy and Society of Post-Conquest Quebec

In the Treaty of Paris of 1763 France ceded New France to England. The British now faced the difficult task of formulating a policy to govern a colony whose population was different in language, culture, and religion from their own. That policy, as outlined in the Proclamation of 1763, limited New France, now renamed the Province of Quebec, to the St. Lawrence Valley. It was designed to transform the former French colony into a British one through the establishment of British institutions and laws; in short, it was designed to assimilate the French-Canadian population.

The policy failed, however. Very few English-speaking immigrants came to Quebec, preferring to settle in the more fertile Ohio Valley rather than in the colder region to the north (amidst an alien French-speaking population). Furthermore, the first two governors of Quebec, James Murray and Guy Carleton, sided with the French-speaking seigneurs against the aggressive, English-speaking merchants in the colony. Realizing that there was little likelihood of the colony becoming anglicized, Governor Carleton recommended the reinstatement of French civil law, the seigneurial system of holding land, and the right of the Roman Catholic Church to collect the tithe. London accepted his proposals and thus completely reversed its earlier policy of 1763, in the Quebec Act of 1774.

Although the old French civil law — the seigneurial system and the tithe — had been restored, the basic economic structure of the colony had changed. The few English-speaking colonists who had settled in Quebec had taken a prominent role in the economic life of the colony. While limited in numbers, this Anglo-American commercial class had obtained enormous influence — enough to lead to the recall of James Murray, the first governor, in 1766. In terms of economic power they even commanded (by 1777) a majority of the investments in the fur trade. How had this tiny English-speaking group prospered so? Was it because of the return to France of the commercial class of New France, the superior abilities of the English-speaking merchants, or the favouritism of the British administrators? Dale Standen reviews the various leading interpretations in "The Debate on the Social and Economic Consequences of the Conquest: A Summary." One of the most satisfactory of these interpretations is provided by José Igartua in "A Change in Climate: The Conquest and the *Marchands* of Montreal," which examines the rise of the English-speaking merchants in the fur trade.

For an overview of the period, see A.L. Burt's *The Old Province of Quebec*, 2 vols. (Toronto: McClelland and Stewart, 1968; first published in 1933) and Hilda Neatby's more recent *Quebec: The Revolutionary Age, 1760–1791* (Toronto: McClelland and Stewart, 1966). Fernand Ouellet has fully developed his argument in *Histoire économique et sociale du*

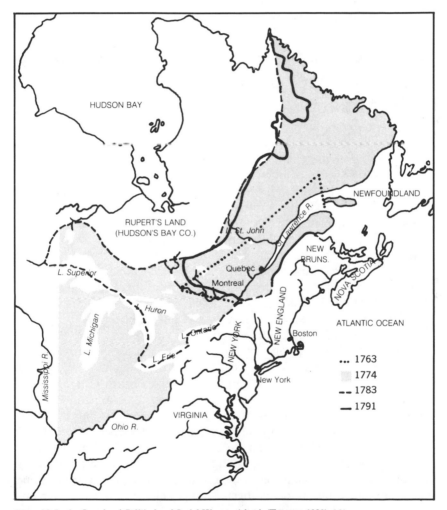

Edgar McInnis, *Canada: A Political and Social History*, 4th ed. (Toronto, 1982), 161.

The old province of Quebec, 1763–1791.

Québec, 1760–1850 (Montreal: Fides, 1966), translated in English as *Economic and Social History of Quebec, 1760–1850* (Toronto: Macmillan, 1980), while Michel Brunet presents his case in *Les Canadiens après la Conquête, 1759–1775* (Montreal: Fides, 1969). Dale Miquelon's *Society and Conquest* (Toronto: Copp Clark, 1977) contains a very useful collection of texts on the effect of the Conquest on French-Canadian society. A good introduction to the early English-speaking population in the Province of Quebec is provided by Ronald Rudin in *The Forgotten Quebecers: A History of English-Speaking Quebec, 1759–1980* (Québec: Institut québécois de la recherche sur la culture, 1985).

The Debate on the Social and Economic Consequences of the Conquest: A Summary*

246

S. DALE STANDEN

The debate over the Conquest of Canada in 1760 began with its consequences, then widened into a debate over the nature of society in New France and into a controversy over crisis in Lower Canada in the early nineteenth century. In its primitive stages the debate focussed upon the magnitude of immediate consequences, and whether or not these did irrevocable damage to the long-term social, political, and economic development of French Canada. The controversy acquired sophistication as further research raised more complex questions about the historical process at work in the St. Lawrence Valley from the seventeenth to the nineteenth centuries. Interest in the single event of the Conquest, however important, yielded to interest in the longer historical continuum in which the Conquest, like other events, was situated.

Even with this expansion, however, one pre-occupation dominates: it is to demonstrate one way or the other whether the economic development of Quebec and Lower Canada, and in particular French Canadian participation in that development, was retarded on the one hand by some circumstantial *force majeure* — the Conquest, imperial subjugation, geography, markets — or on the other hand by rooted social and cultural traits that led French Canadians to eschew business and material progress. It is notable that many participants in the debate on both sides assume Quebec's economic development to have been backward to some extent. Recently this notion has been seriously challenged. Cultural mentality or irresistible circumstance: these are the poles that inform the largest part of Quebec historiography.

*From the *Proceedings of the Tenth Meeting of the French Colonial Historical Society*, April 12–14, 1984, ed. Phillip P. Boucher. Copyright 1985 by the University Press of America. Reprinted by permission.

Debate over the effects of the Conquest dates from shortly after the event itself, and for long concentrated on the issue of whether Canadian society was deprived of its leadership by an exodus following the Conquest. In 1899 Louis Baby demonstrated from his research that emigration had not deprived Canadians of their social leadership, or at least nowhere near the degree that historians like F.-X. Garneau had claimed. The recent debate over the effects of the Conquest developed in the generation following the Second World War. Industrial and urban expansion since the end of the nineteenth century was accompanied as elsewhere by increased secularization. It was among the new, secular, Quebecois nationalists that the idea of the Conquest as the prime impediment to French Canadian development found its warmest adherents. By the 1950s in Quebec the ethnic division among occupations and corporate ownership was stark: Anglophones monopolized financial services and the managerial echelons of large corporations; and Anglophones, domestic or foreign, owned the lion's share of these corporations. How did this come to be?

247

In seeking an explanation the new nationalists were understandably reluctant to accept the notion that values inherent in their nationality might be responsible. This was quite unlike their clerical nationalist forebears who glorified the myth that the French Canadian's vocation was spiritual and moral, not mundane and material. The new nationalists, having embraced modernity and materialism, were drawn to explanations of their so-called "economic backwardness" that did not compromise their secular national self-image. If French Canadians were absent from the ranks of big business, it could not be due to a cultural deficiency in entrepreneurship or capitalist spirit. The Conquest, which for generations of nationalists had been a dark event in their history, became the object of reinterpretation. The result was to darken it even more.

Three historians of the University of Montreal — Maurice Séguin, Guy Frégault and Michel Brunet — are associated most closely with developing the hypothesis that the Conquest was responsible for the inferior economic position of French Canadians. Séguin originated the new hypothesis, and Brunet was the most enthusiastic of its developers. Reflecting a current sociological interest in the roots of modern capitalism and the role of the bourgeoisie, the Montreal historians predicated their hypothesis upon the assumption that for a colonial society to develop "normally" it required the achievements of a capitalist bourgeoisie. Prior to the Conquest, New France was developing as a normal French colony, replete with capitalist bourgeoisie that controlled wealth, power, and politics in the colony. Into this group were lumped seigneurs, nobles, military officers, administrators, as well as their entrepreneurial agents. By precipitating the exodus of this capitalist elite, the Conquest deprived *Canadien* society of its vital bourgeoisie and hence normal development in future. Into the vacuum jumped British entrepreneurs so that the

French Canadian collectivity never recovered its place. Thus, the new nationalists accepted in modified form the decapitation hypothesis that had been challenged half a century earlier.

Brunet found the effects of decapitation compounded by other consequences of the Conquest. British governors from Murray to Dorchester excluded French Canadians from their councils, except for a handful of cyphers chosen from among seigneurs hungry for favours, and for the clergy who collaborated to protect the interests of the Church. In the realm of commerce and military contracts, it was British merchants who benefited from patronage and favouritism. The small-scale *Canadien* merchants who did remain were greatly disadvantaged by having lost their familiar suppliers in France and suffered heavy war losses for which they had only worthless or discounted government promissory notes to show. The only vocations left for *Canadiens* were the Church, the professions, and most of all, agriculture. Thus began the clerical domination of French Canadian national ideology, planting the myth that the destiny of French Canadians was to perfect a Catholic, agricultural society. The Conquest had set in place conditions which, through an inexorable historical process, quickly led to social and economic distortion within the French Canadian community.

This so-called "bourgeoisie hypothesis" left little hope for "normal" development of French Canadian society in Quebec, particularly French Canadian participation in the highest echelons of business, unless the Conquest could be undone. Many could not accept this conclusion and challenged the hypothesis' basic assumptions. It was from among the Social Science Faculty at Laval University that the strongest criticism came, notably from Fernand Ouellet and Jean Hamelin.

In his thesis presented to l'Ecole Pratique des Hautes Etudes in Paris, published in 1960 as *Economie et Société en Nouvelle-France*, Jean Hamelin questioned the existence of a *grande bourgeoisie capitaliste* in new France. If there was no entrepreneurial bourgeoisie to be decapitated or otherwise destroyed, then there would have to be some other explanation than the Conquest for the disproportionately small number of French Canadians in large-scale business over the years. By employing quantitative methods, though only in part and to incomplete data, Hamelin examined aspects of the economy of New France, in particular skilled labour, agriculture, and the fur trade. He concluded that the colony had inadequate skilled labour to sustain any but small-scale manufactures; that agriculture was essentially subsistance; and that only the fur trade generated a respectable return on capital. However, since the returns from the fur trade went largely to investors in France, little profit was left to create a colonial *grande bourgeoisie capitaliste*. His conclusion is consistent with what intendants had been writing all along.

In the course of his work Hamelin offered as one explanation for the shortage of skilled labour the habitant's psychological disinclination for occupations that tied him down for lengthy periods. The source of this attitude he attributed to the quality of immigrants to New France, reinforced by their experience of seasonal labour in the colony, usually in the fur trade. Here we are offered as partial explanation for the weaknesses in the economy of New France a factor of mentality, culture, social value.

Professor Fernand Ouellet was particularly forthright in his dismissal of the bourgeoisie hypothesis and has rested his case more explicitly upon arguments of social mentality. In an article written in 1956 to answer Michel Brunet, Ouellet denied the existence of a Golden Age of bourgeois enterprise in New France. Furthermore, he rejected Brunet's description of a capitalist bourgeoisie as simplistic and meaningless because of its inclusiveness of numerous social groups. Citing the work of Werner Sombart and the *Annales*, he noted that pluralism within social groupings made broad definitions virtually impossible. There are, however, certain attributes and values necessary for successful entrepreneurship: dynamism, productivity, precision, calculation, foresight, opportunism, orderliness, frugality, and a penchant for reinvestment. Although there were some in New France who possessed these attributes, their efforts for the most part were frustrated, if not overwhelmed, by a dominant contrary mentality, that of the *noblesse*. The values of the nobility included recklessness, haughtiness, lack of system or diligence, improvidence, and a taste for consumption and lavish display that bore no relationship to income. That many colonial bourgeois and members of the lower orders assumed the values of the *noblesse*, rather than the other way around, is supported by the work of Professor William Eccles on the aristocratic ethos which pervaded colonial society and which was reinforced by its military establishment.

It is worth noting that Eccles in no way implied, as did other critics of the bourgeoisie hypothesis, that the values of society in New France inhibited its economic development. On the contrary, a peculiar combination of bureaucratic enterprise, paternalistic order, and military ingenuity served to develop the colony's resources more than they might otherwise have been. With the Conquest, new laissez-faire rules of economic exploitation introduced by the British were completely alien to the ordered, state-regulated environment of New France. The implication is that one ought not to be surprised if following the Conquest those accustomed to the new, though by no means superior, values should eventually subplant the *Canadiens* in directing the economic life of the colony.

The fundamental debate, however, was enjoined between the advocates of a deterministic Conquest and the advocates of a hostile social mentality, with their opposing explanations of subsequent failures in the Quebec economy and failures of French Canadians to participate proportionately in the business life of the colony.

Much research has been done on eighteenth century Canada, some directly inspired by the controversy over the Conquest and bourgeoisie hypotheses, but much in pursuit of answers to other questions which

249

nevertheless have illuminated the debate. Attempts to reconcile bourgeois and aristocratic characteristics by defining a new social class unique to the elite of New France were not long pursued. The synthetic *bourgeois-gentilhomme*, proposed by Cameron Nish as typical of such a class, was in the final analysis an exceptional case: that of François-Etienne Cugnet. The attempt at synthesis through sociological redefinition of class foundered in the sea of social particularities. One study by José Igartua of the immediate effects of the Conquest upon the community of Montreal merchants was more successful at clarifying some issues. We learn that British speculators may have been disadvantaged as much as *Canadien* merchants by holding discounted French government promissory notes. Where there was a will, *Canadiens* found financial backing and suppliers in London with little difficulty. There is evidence of British officials and military officers discriminating for security reasons in favour of British merchants in some military contracts, and in the issuing of licences to trade in the far west. At the same time there were ways, notably through partnerships, that *Canadiens* could and did neutralize this discrimination. Their expertise in local markets was a notable advantage in their favour. *Canadien* merchants did tend to withdraw from investing in the fur trade, but the question is whether this was by preference or necessity. Accustomed to a well-regulated trade environment during the French Regime, where the volume of business was in balance with the number of merchants engaged in it, the *Canadiens* were, Igartua suggests, disinclined to enter the murderous, unethical competition which accompanied the laissez-faire trade policy of the British. The "change in climate" to which Igartua alludes might be seen as a variant of the contrasting social values observed by William Eccles between the French and British regimes. Here the question of "mentality" once again comes into play.

Numerous articles and monographs on business, economic and social history betray an increasing interest in understanding how things worked. The work of historians such as Dale Miquelon, Louise Dechêne, and Peter Moogk, to mention only three, show that the tendency has been to qualify many generalizations made from scanty evidence. By exploring sources that are more likely to give answers to particular questions — notarial and business records — we are learning a great deal about how businesses were organized and managed, how colonial trade was financed, how investments were patterned, how colonial merchants made their livings, how farmers and tradesmen made theirs. The hundreds of case studies recently provided by the *Dictionary of Canadian Biography* have also contributed to our understanding of complexity in colonial society and economy.

The result of this research is probably to discredit the more exaggerated claims of the new nationalists concerning the disastrous effects of the Conquest on French Canadian society. If there was no *grande bourgeoisie capitaliste* in New France to be decapitated, there was nevertheless a viable colonial economy with adequate communities of businessmen and skilled labourers. But it is also true that these continued on in Canada after the Conquest, making their livings as before. If there were some disadvantages faced by *Canadien* merchants after 1763 in the fur trade and import-export sector, they also had the advantage of expertise and situation in the local market, and many demonstrated that their problems were not insurmountable. The inclination of many not to lose their shirts in the cut-throat fur trade may be seen as lack of enterprise, or just as easily as good business sense. I have yet to see a tally of the number of British merchants who went bankrupt in the fur trade in these years, or the number who responded, as did apparently the French Canadians, by leaving it to the hands of those more ruthless than they. The jury is still out on the issue of whether cultural mentality is the independent variable, or the dependent variable, in determining the course of the Quebec economy and the participation of French Canadians in it immediately following the Conquest.

251

The fact that the Conquest and its effects have receded lately in the historiography of early French Canada, and that attention has focussed upon long-term developments converging in Lower Canada, is perhaps evidence that the initiative passed to the critics of the bourgeoisie hypothesis. If so, the force of Fernand Ouellet's work is largely responsible.

Employing quantitative methods of social and economic history Ouellet, by scrutinizing price trends, demographic trends, commodity production, and other basic economic structures, found widespread continuities throughout the eighteenth century. These continuities were momentarily disrupted by the Seven Years' War but otherwise little affected by the Conquest. It was to structural changes in the early nineteenth century, coinciding with and in some cases responding to events in the larger Atlantic world, that Ouellet pointed as having significant consequences. In a series of articles he propounded his thesis that agricultural production in Lower Canada entered a phase of chronic crisis in the first decade of the nineteenth century. The thesis was elaborated upon and placed in the context of *histoire totale* in 1966 with the publication of his *Histoire Economique et sociale du Bas-Canada, 1760–1850*. It was a powerful argument that the watershed in French Canadian history was not 1760, but 1802.

Although Ouellet's work undertook to integrate economic development with social change, political response, and ideological development in Lower Canada, the major controversy has focussed upon whether or not the condition of the agricultural economy can properly be described as a crisis. It is probably fair to say that the "crisis" hypothesis has been increasingly challenged, largely by economic historians — two notable ones sitting on this panel, Gilles Paquet and Marvin McInnis. Their criticism aims to cast doubt upon claims that cultural factors had a notable effect upon the development of the agricultural economy in Lower Canada.

The belief that the agricultural economy of Lower Canada was unhealthy has existed since contemporary observers condemned it as such. It became widely accepted that the cultural attributes of the French Canadian farmer were largely responsible for this state of affairs — he was portrayed as being backward, unproductive, inefficient, and tenaciously clinging to ruinous, primitive, extensive farming techniques and technology. Even by mid-twentieth century when Lower Canadian agriculture fell beneath the scrutiny of scholarship, earlier impressions persisted. R.L. Jones, although he noted important circumstantial factors such as the absence of proximate markets and a series of natural disasters — wheat midge and potato failure in the 1830s and 1840s — still attributed the backwardness of agriculture to the French Canadian farmer's peculiar culture. Maurice Séguin, though he ascribed the primary cause to a lack of strong markets to which the French Canadian farmer would have responded by modernizing (as farmers elsewhere did), nevertheless accepted the "backwardness" assumption. He ultimately blamed the failure to modernize on the Conquest, since the exterior market for Lower Canadian wheat was Britain where producers from Upper Canada and elsewhere somehow had an advantage, and squeezed out the Lower Canadian producer.

The thesis of Fernand Ouellet sustains most vigorously the cultural argument for the failure of Lower Canadian agriculture to modernize, which produced a crisis condition. Although the *paysan* after 1760 showed some signs of responding positively to the opening of an imperial market for his wheat, the structural changes at the beginning of the nineteenth century proved too great a challenge for him. Ouellet contends that there was no shortage of markets: the same external markets were available to the Lower Canadian farmer as to the Upper Canadian, and there were local markets — Montreal, Quebec, and the lumber industry — which the Lower Canadian producer proved unable to take advantage of. The problem was supply, not demand. It was not the wheat midge in the 1830s that forced Lower Canadian farmers to abandon wheat as a crop: production began to fail seriously twenty years earlier, due largely to soil exhaustion from poor farming methods. A high rural birth rate and the unavailability of new cultivable land by the early nineteenth century led to rural overpopulation. Since little high-yield virgin land came into production, per capita agricultural output declined.

Thus, we have in the agricultural sector an apparent cultural deficiency that prevented French Canadian farmers from getting ahead, similar to the cultural deficiency among other orders of society that prevented French Canadians from assuming a role in business and many trades proportionate to their overall numbers in the province.

Every element of the "Agricultural Crisis" thesis has been assailed. Gilles Paquet and Jean-Pierre Wallot denied that a production problem

252

occurred as early in the century as Ouellet located it. The methodology they applied to the scarce statistical evidence available embroiled them in a secondary argument with Terry LeGoff, which served at least to underscore the ambiguity of evidence in this matter. However, the timing of production difficulties is important, for if there was no faltering of production until the 1830s, then insects and disease might be sufficient explanation. Paquet and Wallot drew attention to the significant point raised by Séguin and credited by most other critics as well, that the farming methods of Lower Canadians were similar to those elsewhere in North America until at least the 1840s. If this is so then it would make little sense to brand the Lower Canadian farmer as inefficient: what is the standard of efficiency? Paquet and Wallot further argue that there was no reliable external demand for wheat, and therefore the farmer was making a rational choice to avoid the risks of the wheat export market by diversifying into other products for which a growing market existed in Lower Canada. In other words, he was responding within the constraints imposed upon him as one would expect.

253

In a comparison of economic development in Ontario and Quebec before 1870, John McCallum reinforces and extends the argument that Lower Canadian agriculture did not lag behind other regions in North America. Extensive farming was common everywhere and he found no evidence of differences due to cultural factors. If there was a difference from New England, it was that Lower Canada lacked nearby markets for alternate crops such that substituting them for wheat gave less relief. McCallum judged the markets of Montreal, Quebec, and the lumber camps to be of insufficient size to invite large-scale modernization or specialization of agricultural production. Again, given the constraints facing the Lower Canadian farmer, there was no profit in intensive farming methods, and to expect him to have adjusted more rapidly than he did is to demand of him a higher efficiency than demonstrated by other North American farmers at the time. The Quebec farmer, McCallum concludes, "lived in the worst of all worlds," flooded by western produce from frontier areas and without large internal markets as substitutes. If there was evidence of any unique cultural response, it might be sought in the failure of Lower Canadian farmers to emigrate in larger numbers than they did.

The most recent and probably inclusive critique of the cultural-influence argument is that of Marvin McInnis. In fact, McInnis spares no one in his determination to expose the lack of empirical evidence behind most historians' assumptions about the nature of Lower Canadian agriculture — like the skeptic Pierre Bayle ferreting out the errors and inconsistencies in the Old Testament upon which Christian theology in his day depended. Nothing is sacred: the backwardness of the peasant farmer; the exhausted state of the soil; over-population; the shortage of cultivable land; the deficiency of markets; among others. All are scrutinized in light of new evidence and reinterpretation. He concludes that the case for the occurrence of an "agricultural crisis," "of a longer-term fall in the level of material well-being in Lower Canada," is not proven.

It should be noted that these issues are very much alive and that the adherents of the cultural argument have not been persuaded by their critics, though revisions have been made on several sides as is to be expected in the best of serious scholarly debates. The finality of statistical data lies in the interpretation put on it and there is clearly room for debate. One should keep in mind that the agricultural economy is only one element in the history of Lower Canada and that no matter what was happening to agriculture — crisis or healthy modernization — the social and political leaders within the colony could be expected to read events according to their own script in any case. The same might be said of contemporary perceptions of emerging ethnic divisions among occupations.

254

Thus, political, social, and ethnic tensions, such as those which Ouellet finds exacerbated, if not caused, in the early nineteenth century by the agricultural "crisis," and which he sees as precipitating the first French Canadian nationalist reaction, can arguably be anticipated in a period of severe structural change. Did agricultural crisis have to take place in order for a political elite to prey upon the imagined fears of the peasantry? If they had the *impression* that they were stagnating compared with outsiders, Lower Canadian farmers might have been susceptible to a nationalist adventure even if the impression were wrong.

The attractiveness of the circumstantial argument is that it relegates culture to the status of a dependent variable where it can be easily ignored. Perhaps too easily. One then need not deal with historical forces that are often obscure and always difficult to measure. Only the most rigid materialist would argue that wars and revolutions are an inevitable and direct consequence of particular economic circumstances. Political and social structures with their attendant ideologies play some role in constraining, or not, the fears, ambitions, and other responses of people confronted with social stress. These must be cultural atavisms. If they are in some way connected with material circumstances, they are not wholly dependent upon them. Or at least, over time, they have gained some independence. And if we are to understand the relationships between all variables, then some attempt must be made to assign weights to them all.

Of course, the economic historian may not be interested in undertaking this task, content to limit himself, as most of us do, to examining the particular historical processes that interest him. Skepticism is essential in a discipline where theology often passes for history. The debate over the consequences of the Conquest is, like all historical debates, an exercise in identifying what is theology and what is history. Along the way, one hopes, we have learned something about the historical process.

SELECTED BIBLIOGRAPHY

Baby, L.F.G. *L'Exode des classes dirigeantes à la cession du Canada*. Montréal, 1899.

Brunet, Michel. *French Canada and the Early Decades of British Rule 1760-1791*. Ottawa: Canadian Historical Association, 1963.

Brunet, Michel. "La Conquête anglaise et la déchéance de la bourgeoisie canadienne (1760-1793)." In *La Présence anglaise et les Canadiens*, 49-109. Montréal: Beauchemin, 1958.

Dechêne, Louise. *Habitants et Marchands de Montréal au XVIIe siècle*. Montréal, Paris: Plon, 1974.

Eccles, W.J. *The Canadian Frontier, 1534-1760*. New York: Holt, Rinehart and Winston, 1969.

Eccles, W.J. *Canadian Society during the French Regime*. Montreal: Harvest House, 1968.

Frégault, G. *Canadian Society in the French Regime*. Ottawa: Canadian Historical Association, 1956.

Hamelin, Jean. *Economie et société en Nouvelle-France*. Québec: Presses de l'Université Laval, 1961.

Igartua, José. "A Change in Climate: The Conquest and the *Marchands* of Montreal." *Historical Papers*, Canadian Historical Association, 1974.

Jones, R.L. "French Canadian Agriculture in the St. Lawrence Valley, 1815-1851." *Agricultural History* 16 (1942): 137-48.

Jones, R.L. "The Agricultural Development of Lower Canada, 1850-67." *Agricultural History* 19 (1945): 212-24.

Jones, R.L. "Agriculture in Lower Canada, 1792-1815," *Canadian Historical Review* 27 (1946): 33-51.

LeGoff, T.J.A. "The Agricultural Crisis in Lower Canada, 1802-12: A Review of a Controversy." *Canadian Historical Review* 55 (March 1974): 1-31.

LeGoff, T.J.A. "A Reply." *Canadian Historical Review* 56 (June 1975): 162-68.

McCallum, John. *Unequal Beginnings: Agriculture and Economic Development in Quebec and Ontario until 1870*. Toronto: University of Toronto Press, 1980.

McInnis, R.M. "A Reconsideration of the State of Agriculture in Lower Canada in the First Half of the Nineteenth Century." In D.H. Akenson, ed. *Canadian Papers in Rural History*, vol. 3. Gananoque: Langdale Press, 1982.

Miquelon, D., ed. *Society and Conquest: The Debate on the Bourgeoisie and Social Change in French Canada, 1700-1850*. Toronto: Copp Clark, 1977.

Miquelon, D. "Havy and Lefebvre of Quebec: A Case Study of Metropolitan Participation in Canadian Trade, 1730-60." *Canadian Historical Review* 56 (March 1975): 1-24.

Moogk, P.N. "Rank in New France: Reconstructing a Society from Notarial Documents." *Histoire Sociale/Social History* 8 (mai/May 1975): 34-53.

Nish, C. *Les Bourgeois-Gentilshommes de la Nouvelle-France*. Montréal: Fides, 1968.

Ouellet, Fernand. "M. Michel Brunet et la problème de la Conquête," *Bulletin de Recherches Historiques* 62 (1956): 92-101.

Ouellet, Fernand. *Histoire Economique et sociale du Québec, 1760-1850: Structures et conjonctures*. Montréal: Fides, 1966.

Ouellet, Fernand. "Le Mythe de L'Habitant sensible au marché" *Recherches Sociographiques* 17 (1976): 115-32.

Paquet, Gilles, and J.-P. Wallot. "The Agricultural Crisis in Lower Canada, 1802-1812: *mise au point*. A Response to T.J.A. LeGoff." *Canadian Historical Review* 56 (June 1975): 133-61.

Paquet, Gilles, and J.-P. Wallot. "Crise agricole et tensions socio-ethniques dans le Bas-Canada, 1802-1821." *Revue d'histoire de L'Amérique française* 26 (September 1972): 185-237.

Séguin, M. "La Conquête et la vie économique des Canadiens." *Action nationale* 28 (1947): 308-326.

Séguin, M. *La Nation "canadienne" et l'agriculture (1760-1850)*. Trois Rivières: Boréal Express, 1970.

A Change in Climate: The Conquest and the *Marchands* of Montreal*

JOSÉ IGARTUA

When the British government issued the Royal Proclamation of 1763, it assumed that the promised establishment of "British institutions" in the "Province of Quebec" would be sufficient to entice American settlers

*From the Canadian Historical Association, *Historical Papers* (1974):115-34. Copyright by the Canadian Historical Association. Reprinted by permission.

to move north and overwhelm the indigenous French-speaking and Papist population. These were naive hopes. Until the outbreak of the American Revolution, British newcomers merely trickled into Quebec, leading Governor Carleton to prophesy in 1767 that "barring a catastrophe shocking to think of, this Country must, to the end of Time, be peopled by the Canadian Race. . . ."[1] But the British newcomers, few though they were, had to be reckoned with. By 1765 they were powerful enough to have Governor Murray recalled and by 1777 they would be strong enough to command the majority of investments in the fur trade.[2] Did their success stem from superior abilities? Did the British take advantage of the situation of submission and dependence into which the Canadians had been driven by the Conquest? Did the newcomers gain their predominance from previous experience with the sort of political and economic conditions created in post-Conquest Quebec?

Historians of Quebec have chosen various ways to answer these questions. Francis Parkman was fond of exhibiting the superiority of the Anglo-Saxon race over the "French Celt."[3] More recently the studies of W.S. Wallace, E.E. Rich, and D.G. Creighton took similar, if less overt, positions.[4] One of the best students of the North West fur trade, Wayne E. Stevens, concluded: "The British merchants . . . were men of great enterprise and ability and they began gradually to crowd out the French traders who had been their predecessors in the field."[5]

The French-Canadian historian, Fernand Ouellet, attributed the rise of the British merchants to the weaknesses of the Canadian trading bourgeoisie: "Son attachement à la petite entreprise individuelle, sa réponse à la concentration, son goût du luxe de même que son attrait irrésistible pour les placements assurés étaient des principaux handicaps." No evidence is given for this characterization and the author hastens to concede that before 1775 "le problème de la concentration ne se pose pas avec acuité," but for him it is clear that the economic displacement of the Canadians resulted from their conservative, "ancien Régime" frame of mind, bred into them by the clergy and the nobility.[6] Ouellet painted British merchants in a more flattering light as the agents of economic progress.[7]

Michel Brunet has depicted the commercial competition between the British newcomers and the Canadian merchants as an uneven contest between two national groups, one of which had been deprived of the nourishing blood of its metropolis while the other was being assiduously nurtured. For Brunet the normal and natural outcome of that inequality was the domination of the conqueror, a situation which he sees as prevailing to the present day.[8]

Dale B. Miquelon's study of one merchant family, the Babys, shed new light on the question of British penetration of Canadian trade. It outlined the growth of British investments in the fur trade and the increasing concentration of British capital. The author concluded:

The French Canadians dominated the Canadian fur trade until the upheaval of the American Revolution. At that time they were overwhelmed by an influx of capital and trading personnel. English investment in the top ranks of investors jumped by 679% and was never significantly to decline. Even without explanations involving the difference between the French and English commercial mentalities, it is difficult to believe that any body of merchants could recover from an inundation of such size and swiftness.[9]

This conclusion had the obvious merit of staying out of the murky waters of psychological interpretations. But Miquelon's own evidence suggests that the "flood theory" is not sufficient to account for the Canadians' effacement; even before the inundation of 1775–1783, British investment in the fur trade was growing more rapidly than Canadian. By 1772, to quote Miquelon, the "English [had] made more impressive increases in the size of their investments than [had] the French, and for the first time [had] larger average investments in all categories."[10]

257

It is difficult not to note the ascendancy of the British in the fur trade of Canada even before the American Revolution. The success of the British merchants, therefore, was rooted in something more than mere numbers. It was not simply the outcome of an ethnic struggle between two nationalities of a similar nature; it was not only the natural consequence of the Canadians' conservative frame of mind. It arose out of a more complex series of causes, some of them a product of the animosities between Canadians and British, others inherent to the differences in the socioeconomic structures of the French and British Empires; together, they amounted to a radical transformation of the societal climate of the colony.

The aim of this paper is to gauge the impact of the Conquest upon a well-defined segment of that elusive group called the "bourgeoisie" of New France. It focuses on Montreal and its Canadian merchants. Montreal was the centre of the fur trade and its merchants managed it. Historians of New France have traditionally seen the fur trade as the most dynamic sector of the colony's economy; by implication it is generally believed that the fur trade provided the likeliest opportunities for getting rich quickly and maintaining a "bourgeois" standard of living.[11] It is not yet possible to evaluate the validity of this notion with any precision, for too little is known about other sectors of the economy which, in the eighteenth century at least, may have generated as much or more profit. Research on the merchants of Quebec should provide new information on the wealth to be made from the fisheries, from wholesale merchandising, and from trade with Louisbourg and the West Indies. But if one is concerned with the fate of Canadian merchants after the Conquest, one should examine the fate of men involved in the sector of the economy of Quebec which was the most dynamic *after* the Conquest, the fur trade. The paper examines the impact of the arrival of (relatively) large numbers of merchants on the Montreal mercantile community, the attitude of British officials towards the Canadians, and the changing political climate of the colony. It is suggested that it was the simultaneous conjunction of these changes to the "world" of the Montreal merchants, rather than the effect of any one of them, which doomed the Canadian merchants of Montreal.[12]

The Montreal Merchants at the End of the French Regime

In 1752 a French Royal engineer passing through Montreal remarked that "la plupart des habitants y sont adonnés au commerce principalement à celui connu sous le nom des pays d'en haut."[13] It was only a slight exaggeration. By the last year of the French regime one could count over one hundred *négociants*, merchants, outfitters, traders, and shopkeepers in Montreal. The overwhelming majority of them had been in business for some years and would remain in business after the Conquest. Over half were outfitters for the fur trade at some time or other between 1750 and 1775; these men comprised the body of the merchant community of Montreal. Above them in wealth and stature stood a handful of import merchants who did a comfortable business of importing merchandise from France and selling it in Montreal to other merchants or directly to customers in their retail stores. Below the outfitters a motley group of independent fur traders, shopkeepers, and artisans managed to subsist without leaving more than a trace of their existence for posterity.[14]

258

The fur trade, as it was conducted by the merchants of Montreal before 1760, had little to do with the glamorous picture it sometimes calls to mind. For the outfitter who remained in Montreal, it was not physically a risky occupation; its management was fairly simple and the profits which it produced quite meager. For the last years of the French regime the fur trade followed a three-tier system. Fort Frontenac (present-day Kingston) and Fort Niagara were King's posts; they were not lucrative and had to be subsidized to meet English competition. The trade of Detroit and Michilimackinac, as well as that of the posts to the South West, was open to licencees whose numbers were limited. Some *coureurs de bois* (traders without a licence) also roamed in the area. The richest posts, Green Bay and the posts to the northwest past Sault Sainte-Marie, were monopolies leased by the Crown to merchants or military officers.[15] The export of beaver was undertaken by the French *Compagnie des Indes*, which had the monopoly of beaver sales on the home market. Other furs were on the open market.

The system worked tolerably well in peace time: there was a stable supply of furs, prices paid to the Indians had been set by custom, the prices paid by the *Compagnie des Indes* were regulated by the Crown, and the prices of trade goods imported from France were fairly steady. There was competition from the Americans at Albany and from the English on the Hudson Bay, to be sure, but it appeared to be a competition heavily influenced by military considerations and compliance with Indian customs.[16]

The system faltered in war time. Beaver shipments to France and the importation of trade goods became risky because of British naval power. Shipping and insurance costs raised the Canadian traders' overhead, but the Indians refused to have the increase passed on to them. This was the most obvious effect of war, but it also produced general economic and administrative dislocations which led H.A. Innis to conclude that it " . . . seriously weakened the position of the French in the fur trade and contributed to the downfall of the French *régime* in Canada."[17]

Nevertheless, outside of war-time crises, the fur trade of New France was conducted with a fair dose of traditionalism. This traditionalism resulted from two concurrent impulses: Indian attitudes towards trade, which were untouched by the mechanism of supply and demand and by distinctions between commercial, military, political, or religious activities; and the mercantilist policies of France, which tried to control the supply of furs by limiting the number of traders and regulating beaver prices on the French market. While the fur trade structure of New France had an inherent tendency towards geographic expansion, as Innis argued, it also had to be oligopolistic in nature, if investments in Indian alliances, explorations, and military support were to be maximized. Open competition could not be allowed because it would lead to the collapse of the structure.[18]

It is not surprising, therefore, that most outfitters dabbled in the fur trade only occasionally. On the average, between 1750 and 1775, the Canadian merchants of Montreal invested in the trade only four times and signed up about eleven *engagés* each time, not quite enough to man two canoes. Few merchants outfitted fur trade ventures with any regularity and only six men hired an average of twelve or more *engagés*, more than twice before 1761 (See Table 1). Three of these were unquestionably wealthy: Louis Saint-Ange Charly, an import merchant who, unlike his colleagues, had a large stake in the fur trade, realized 100 000 livres on his land holdings alone when he left the colony for France in 1764; Thomas-Ignace Trotier Desauniers "Dufy," who in a will drawn up in 1760 bequeathed 28 000 livres to the Sulpicians; the illiterate Dominique Godet, who in a similar document of 1768 mentioned 5000 livres in cash in hand, land in three parishes in the vicinity of Montreal, "Batiment & Bateaux qui en dependent," around 5000 livres in active debts, and two black slaves.[19] Two other large outfitters left relatively few belongings at the time of their death: Alexis Lemoine Monière left less than 1000 livres, all of it in household goods, and Fran-

TABLE 1   Largest Canadian Fur Trade Outfitters in Montreal, 1750–1760

Name	Total No. of Years	Total No. of Hirings	Yearly Average
Charly, Louis Saint-Ange	6	85	14.1
Godet, Dominique	5	85	17.0
Léchelle, Jean	4	130	32.5
Lemoine Monière, Alexis	7	300	42.8
L'Huillier Chevalier, François	7	90	12.6
Trotier Desauniers, Thomas-Ignace "Dufy"	5	129	25.8

Source: "Répertoire des engagements pour l'ouest conservés dans les Archives judiciaires de Montréal," *Rapport de l'Archiviste de la province de Québec* (1930–31):353–453; (1931–32):242–365; (1932–33):245–304.

çois L'Huillier Chevalier just slightly more.[20] Little is known about the sixth man, Jean Léchelle.

If the fur trade made few wealthy men among those who invested heavily in it, it would be hard to argue that less considerable investors were more successful. It is not unreasonable to conclude that the fur trade was not very profitable for the overwhelming majority of outfitters and that it only sustained a very limited number of them each year. Yet the French had reduced costly competition to a minimum and had few worries about price fluctuations. How would Canadian outfitters fare under a different system?

The Advent of the British Merchants

With the arrival in Montreal of British traders, the workings of the fur trade were disrupted. At first, the licensing system was maintained and some areas were left to the exclusive trade of particular traders.[21] But from the very beginning the trade was said to be open to all who wanted to secure a licence, and the result could only be price competition. With individual traders going into the fur trade, the organization of the trade regressed. The previous division of labour between the *Compagnie des Indes*, the import merchants and outfitters, the traders, the voyageurs, and the *engagés* was abandoned and during the first years of British rule the individual trader filled all of the functions previously spread among many "specialists."

The story of Alexander Henry, one of the first British merchants to venture into the upper country, illustrates the new pattern of trade. A young man from New Jersey, Alexander Henry came to Canada in 1760 with General Amherst's troops.[22] With the fall of Montreal Henry saw the opening of a "new market" and became acquainted with the prospects of the fur trade. The following year, he set out for Michilimackinac with a Montreal outfitter, Etienne Campion, whom he called his "assistant," and who took charge of the routine aspects of the trip.[23] Henry wintered at Michilimackinac. There he was urged by the local inhabitants to go back to Detroit as soon as possible for they claimed to fear for his safety. Their fears were not without foundation, but Henry stayed on. His partner Campion reassured him: " . . . the Canadian inhabitants of the fort were more hostile than the Indians, as being jealous of British traders, who . . . were penetrating into the country."[24] At least some of the Canadians resented the British traders from the outset and a few tried to use the Indians to frighten them away.[25]

Henry proceeded to Sault Sainte-Marie the following year. In the spring of 1763, he returned to Michilimackinac and witnessed the massacre of the British garrison during Pontiac's revolt.[26] He was eventually captured by the Indians and adopted into an Indian family with whom he lived, in the Indian style, until late June 1764. Undaunted, Henry set out for the fur trade again, exploring the Lake Superior area. He was on the Saskatchewan River in 1776, tapping fur resources which the French had seldom reached.[27] Finally he settled down in Montreal in 1781 and while he did join the North West Company after its formation, he seldom returned to the upper country himself.[28]

Henry was not the first British merchant to reach the upper country. Henry Bostwick had obtained a licence from General Gage before him in 1761,[29] and the traders Goddard and Solomons had followed Henry into Michilimackinac in 1761. By early 1763 there were at least two more British merchants in the area.[30] In Montreal alone there were close to fifty new merchants by 1765. Governor Murray's list of the Protestants in the district of Montreal gives the names, the origins, and the "former callings" of forty-five.[31] Over half of them came from England and Scotland and 20 per cent were from Ireland. Only 13 per cent came from the American colonies and an equal number came from various countries (Switzerland, Germany, France, Guernsey). In the proportion of more than three to one, the newcomers had been merchants in their "former calling." The others had been soldiers and clerks. Many of the newcomers were men of experience and enterprise. Among them were Isaac Todd, Thomas Walker, Lawrence Ermatinger, Richard Dobie, Edward Chinn, John Porteous, William Grant, Benjamin Frobisher, James Finlay, Alexander Paterson, Forrest Oakes, and the Jewish merchants Ezekiel and Levy Solomons, all of whom became substantial traders.[32]

The arrival of so many merchants could only mean one thing: strenuous competition in the fur trade. Competition ruthlessly drove out those with less secure financial resources or with no taste for sharp practices. Among the British as among the French, few resisted the pressures. The story of the trader Hamback is not untypical. Out on the Miami River in

1766 and 1767, he found that competition left him with few returns to make to his creditor William Edgar of Detroit. "I live the life of a downright exile," he complained, "no company but a Barrel of drunken infamous fugitives, and no other Comfort of Life."[33]

The Canadian merchants of Montreal had competition not only from British merchants in their town, but also from American merchants moving into Detroit and Michilimackinac. William Edgar, a New York merchant, was at Niagara in late 1761.[34] In 1763 he was established at Detroit, where he conducted a brisk trade supplying individual traders at Michilimackinac and in the South West District.[35] From Schenectady, the partnership of Phyn and Ellice also carried on a profitable supply trade for the fur traders of the interior.[36]

Competition also came from the French on the Mississippi, who were trading in the Illinois country and the Lake Superior region. These French traders could all too easily link up with French-speaking traders from Canada, whose help, it was feared, they could enlist in subverting the Indians against British rule.[37] This always troubled Sir William Johnson, the Superintendent for Indian Affairs, who refused to abandon his suspicions of the French-speaking traders from Canada.

This many-sided competition produced a climate to which the Canadian merchants were not accustomed. The increased numbers of fur traders led to frictions with the Indians, smaller returns for some of the traders, and unsavory trade practices.[38] Even the retail trade was affected. Merchants from England flooded the market at Quebec "with their manufactures, so much so that they are daily sold here at Vendue Twenty per Cent. below prime Cost."[39] In 1760 alone, the first year of British occupation, £60 000 worth of trade goods had been brought into Canada.[40] From 1765 to 1768 the pages of the *Quebec Gazette* were filled with notices of auctions by merchants returning to England and disposing of their wares after unsuccessful attempts to establish themselves in the trade of the colony.[41]

By 1768 some thought the Canadians still had the advantage in the fur trade, even though there was "Competition" and a "strong jealousy" between Canadian and English. The Canadians' "long Connections with those Indians," wrote General Gage, "and their better Knowledge of their Language and Customs, must naturaly for a long time give the Canadians an Advantage over the English. . . ."[42] Sir William Johnson had expressed a similar opinion the previous year and had deplored the British merchants' tactics: "The English were compelled to make use of Low, Selfish Agents, French, or English as Factors, who at the Expence of honesty and sound policy, took care of themselves whatever became of their employers."[43]

Another observer, the Hudson's Bay Company trader at Moose Factory, complained of "Interlopers who will be more Destructive to our trade than the French was." The French had conducted a less aggressive trade: they "were in a manner Settled, their Trade fixed, their Standards moderate and Themselves under particular regulations and restrictions, which I doubt is not the Case now."[44] Competition was forcing the British merchants in Montreal into ruthless tactics, a development which upset the Hudson's Bay Company man and which would unsettle the Canadians.

The pattern of British domination of the fur trade began to emerge as early as 1767. Trading ventures out of Michilimackinac into the North West were conducted by Canadians, but British merchants supplied the financial backing. The North West expeditions demanded the lengthiest periods of capital outlay, lasting two or three years. British merchants, it seems, had better resources. Of the fifteen outfitters at Michilimackinac who sent canoes to the North West in 1767, nine were British and six were Canadian; the total value of canoes outfitted by the British came to £10 812.17 while the Canadian's canoes were worth only £3061.10. The British outfitters — most notably Alexander Henry, Isaac Todd, James McGill, Benjamin Frobisher, Forrest Oakes — invested on the average £1351.12 and the Canadians only £510.5. The average value of goods invested in each canoe stood at £415.17 for the British and £278.6 for the Canadians.[45] The Canadians' investment per canoe was only two-thirds that of the British and the Canadians were already outnumbered as outfitters in what would become the most important region of the fur trade.[46]

263

Open competition was not conducive to the expansion of the fur trade and an oligopolistic structure reminiscent of the French system soon reappeared as the only solution.[47] This led to the formation of the North West Company in the 1780's but already in 1775, those Montreal merchants who had extended their operations as far as the Saskatchewan felt the need for collaboration rather than competition. Again developments in the more remote frontiers of the fur trade foretold of events to occur later in the whole of the trade: the traders on the Saskatchewan were almost all of British origin.[48] The fur trade was returning to the structures developed by the French, but during the period of competition which followed the Conquest the Canadians were gradually crowded out. There was some irony in that. Why had the Canadians fared so badly?

The Attitude of Government Officials

Much has been made of the natural sympathies of Murray and Carleton towards the Canadians and their antipathies towards the traders of their own nation. Yet for all their ideological inclinations there is no evidence that the governors turned their sentiments into policies of benevolence for Canadians in trade matters. Rather, it is easier to discover, among the lesser officials and some of the more important ones as well, an understandable patronizing of British rather than Canadian merchants. Colonial administrators may not have set a deliberate pattern of preference in favor of British merchants. But the Canadian merchants of Montreal, who put great store by official patronage, cared not whether the policy was deliberate or accidental; the result was the same.

Official preferences played against the Canadian traders in many ways. First, the lucrative trade of supplying the military posts was given to British and American merchants as a matter of course, and this occasion for profit was lost to the Canadians. Under the French regime some of the Montreal merchants, notably the Monières and the Gamelins, had profited from that trade.[49] Now it fell out of Canadian hands. This advantage did not shift to the sole favor of the British merchants of Quebec. New York and Pennsylvania traders were also awarded their share of the trade. The firms of Phyn, Ellice of Schenectady and Baynton, Wharton, and Morgan of Philadelphia received the lion's share of that business while the upper country was under the jurisdiction of Sir William Johnson.[50] But this was of little comfort to the Canadians.

Less tangible by-products of the British occupation of the former fur trading areas of New France are more difficult to assess than the loss of the supply trade; they were, however, quite real. One was the British military's attitude towards Canadians. The military were wary of French-speaking traders in Illinois and on the Mississippi. Although the French from Canada had been vanquished, French traders in the interior could still deal with France through New Orleans. No regulations, no boundaries could restrain French traders operating out of Louisiana from dealing with the Indians, and the Canadians who were confined to the posts protested against the advantage held by the French traders.[51] But who were these French traders? Did they not include Canadian *coureurs de bois* and wintering merchants? How could one really tell a French-speaking trader from Canada from a French-speaking trader out of New Orleans? Were not all of them suspect of exciting the Indians against the British, promising and perhaps hoping for France's return to America?[52] As late as 1768, when Indian discontent in the West threatened another uprising, General Gage failed to see any difference between French-speaking Canadians and the French from New Orleans:

> There is the greatest reason to suspect that the French are Endeavoring to engross the Trade, and that the Indians have acted thro' their Instigation, in the Murders they have committed, and the Resolutions we are told they have taken, to suffer no Englishman to trade with them. And in this they have rather been Assisted by the English Traders, who having no Consideration but that of a present gain, have thro' fear of exposing their own Persons, or hopes

of obtaining greater influence with the Indians, continually employed French Commissarys or Agents, whom they have trusted with Goods for them to Sell at an Advanced price in the Indian Villages.[53]

Gage's suspicions of the French traders were nurtured by Sir William Johnson, who had to keep the Indians on peaceful terms with one another and with the British. It was part of Johnson's function, of course, to worry about possible uprisings and about subversive individuals. His job would be made easier if he could confine all traders to military posts where they could be kept under surveillance. But the traders had little concern for Sir William's preoccupations. If British traders were irresponsible in their desires of "present gain," the Canadian traders' vices were compounded by the uncertainty of their allegiance to the British Crown:

> Since the Reduction of that Country [Canada], we have seen so many Instances of their [the Canadian traders'] Perfidy false Stories & C[a]. Interested Views in Trade that prudence forbids us to suffer them or any others to range at Will without being under the Inspection of the proper Officers agreeable to His Majesty's Appointment. . . . [54]

265

Johnson's attitude spread to the officers under him, even though Carleton had found nothing reprehensible in the Canadians' behavior.[55] Johnson's deputy, George Croghan, believed there was collusion between the French from Canada and the French from Louisiana.[56] In 1763 the commandant at Michilimackinac, Major Etherington, had displayed a similar mistrust of the Canadians.[57] Major Robert Rogers, a later commandant at Michilimackinac, checked the Canadians by trading on his own account.[58]

The British military's mistrust of the French traders from Canada was understandable. Before 1760, one of the major reasons for the American colonials' antagonism towards New France had been the French ability to press the Indians into their service to terrorize the western fringes of American settlement. Thus there was a historical as well as a tactical basis for the military's attitude towards the Canadians. But British officers failed to recognize that not all Canadian traders were potential troublemakers and that there was indeed very little tangible evidence, as Carleton had reminded Johnson, of any mischief on their part. The military's attitude was directed as much by ethnic prejudice as by military necessity.

The Canadian traders could not fail to perceive this prejudice, and it dampened their spirits. Perhaps the military's attitude, as much as competition, forced the Canadians into partnerships with British merchants. (The express purpose of the bonds required for the fur trade was to ensure loyal conduct; what better token of loyalty could there be for a Canadian trader than a bond taken out in his name by a British partner?) The military's mistrust of the Canadian traders did not lessen with time. The advantage which this prejudice gave British traders would continue for some twenty years after the Conquest, as the American Revolution rekindled the military's fears of treasonable conduct by the Canadians.

Other patronage relationships between British military officials and British traders also deprived the Canadians of an equal chance in the competition for furs. It is hard to evaluate precisely the effect of such patronage; only glimpses of it may be caught. Late in 1763 a Philadelphia merchant who had lost heavily because of Pontiac's uprising wrote to William Edgar in Detroit that Croghan was in England where he was to "represent the Case of the Traders to his Majesty" and that General Amherst had "given us his faithful promise that he will do everything in his power in our behalf."[59] In 1765 Alexander Henry was granted the exclusive trade of Lake Superior by Major Howard, the military commandant at Michilimackinac. Nine years later Henry received the support of such patrons as the Duke of Gloucester, the consul of the Empress of Russia in England, and of Sir William Johnson in an ill-fated attempt to mine the iron ore of the Lake Superior area.[60]

These were obvious examples of patronage; other forms of cooperation were less visible. Another correspondent of William Edgar, Thomas Shipboy, asked Edgar to represent him in settling the affairs of a correspondent at Detroit and at Michilimackinac where, he added, "if you find any Difficulty in procuring his effects I dare say the Commanding officer will be of Service to you if you inform him in whose [sic] behalf you are acting. . . . "[61] Benjamin Frobisher also asked Edgar to "use your Interest with Capt. Robinson" to put a shipment of corn aboard the government vessel which sailed from Detroit to Michilimackinac.[62] Such shipping space was scarce and was only available through the courtesy of military officers or the ships' captains. Here again British traders put their social connections to good use. A last resort was sheer military force. Out on the Miami River, the trader Hamback saw "little hope of getting any thing from [Fort]St. Joseph at all, if I don't get protected, by the Commanding Officer, who might easily get those [Canadian] rascals fetch'd down to Detroit if He would. . . . "[63]

None of this patronage appears to have been available to Canadians. It is impossible to ascertain the degree to which military suspicions and patronage lessened the Canadians' chances in the fur trade. But more important, perhaps, than the actual loss of opportunities was the psychological handicap imposed upon the Canadians. What heart could they put in the game when the dice were so obviously loaded?

The Merchants' Political Activities

The enmity between British merchants and the military, the merchants' growing agitation in favour of "British liberties," and their sentiments of political self-importance have been ably told by others and need not be retold here.[64] What needs to be underlined is that political agitation was unfamiliar to the Canadians. They had had no experience in these matters under French rule. Only on rare occasions during the pre-Conquest years had the Canadian merchants engaged in collective political representations; such representations were elicited by the governor or the intendant to obtain the merchants' advice on specific issues.[65] As French subjects, the Canadian merchants of Montreal had lacked the power to foster their economic interests through collective political action.

After 1760, the Canadian merchants would gradually lose their political innocence under the influence of the British merchants. During the thirty years which followed the Conquest they would make "l'apprentissage des libertés anglaises" and in 1792 they would take their place in the newly created legislative assembly more cognizant of the workings of the British constitution than the British had expected.[66] But that is beyond the concern here. In the years preceding the American Revolution the Montreal merchants were still looking for bearings. They showed their growing political awareness by following in the *Quebec Gazette* the political and constitutional debates which were rocking the British Empire. The merchants also began to voice their concerns in petitions and memorials to the authorities in the colony and in London.

The *Quebec Gazette* was the province's official gazette and its only newspaper before 1778. The paper published public notices for the Montreal district and occasional advertisements sent in by Montrealers as well as matters of concern to Quebec residents. It also made an effort to publish Canadian news of a general character. It closely followed the debates raging across the Atlantic over the Stamp Act and the general issues of colonial taxation. It reported on changes in the Imperial government and on contemporary political issues in England, notably the Wilkes affair.[67]

The pages of the *Gazette* also served on occasion as a forum for political discussion. In September 1765 a "Civis Canadiensis" declared his puzzlement at all the talk of "British liberties" and asked for enlightenment. The following year, a Quebec resident wrote a series of letters arguing that the colony should not be taxed.[68] In 1767, a debate arose on the British laws relating to bankruptcy and their applicability in Quebec.[69] Because of the pressures of Governor Carleton the *Gazette* stifled its reporting of controversial issues after 1770 and thereafter had little to print about American affairs.[70] In 1775 the *Gazette*'s political outpourings

267

were directed against the American rebels and towards securing the loyalty of those Canadians who might be seduced by revolutionary propaganda.[71] The paper had become more conservative in its selection of the news but those Canadians who read the *Gazette* had been made familiar with the concepts of personal liberty, of "no taxation without representation," of the limited powers of the sovereign, and of the rights of the people. The *Gazette*'s readers most probably included the leading merchants of Montreal.

The *Gazette* was not the only instrument for the learning of British liberties. Anxious to give the appearance of a unanimous disposition among all merchants in Montreal, the British merchants often called on their Canadian confreres to add their names to various memorials and petitions dealing with the political and the economic state of the colony. The Canadian merchants who signed these petitions and memorials represented the top layer of the Canadian mercantile group in Montreal. Those who signed most often were the import merchants and the busy outfitters.

These Canadian merchants followed the political leadership of the British merchants. From 1763 to 1772 their petitions were either literal translations or paraphrased equivalents of petitions drafted by British merchants. It was only in December 1773 that they asserted views different from those of their British counterparts.[72] They petitioned the King that their "ancient laws, privileges, and customs" be restored, that the province be extended to its "former boundaries," that some Canadians be taken into the King's service, and that "the rights and privileges of citizens of England" be granted to all.[73]

The Canadians were becoming aware of their own position and were seeking to consolidate it against the attacks of the British element. The demand for the maintenance of the "ancient laws" was designed to counter British demands for British laws and representative institutions. The Canadians opposed the latter since, in their view, the colony was "not as yet in a condition to defray the expences of its own civil government, and consequently not in a condition to admit of a general assembly."[74] The demand for "a share of the civil and military employments under his majesty's government" came naturally to those who had lived under the French system of patronage. The Canadians had been accustomed to seek official patronage as the main avenue of upward mobility. The prospect of being denied such patronage was "frightful" to them, since they had little familiarity with alternate patterns of social promotion.[75]

In style as well as in content the Canadian merchants' petitions and memorials revealed differences in attitudes between Canadians and British. British memorials and petitions were rarely prefaced by more than the customary "Humbly showeth" and went directly to the point. In their own memorials and petitions, the Canadians first took "the liberty to prostrate themselves at the foot" of the royal throne and surrendered themselves to the "paternal care" of their sovereign. They often appealed to the wisdom, justice, and magnanimity of the King.[76] Their formal posture of meekness contrasted sharply with the self-assertion of the British. The Canadians' "Habits of Respect and Submission," as one British official put it,[77] may well have endeared them to Murray and Carleton, but those habits constituted a psychological obstacle against their making full use of their new-found "British liberties" to foster their own economic interest.

Conclusion

With the fall of Montreal to British arms in September 1760 something was irrevocably lost to the Canadian merchants of that city. More than the evil effects of the war or the post-war commercial readjustments, the most unsettling consequence of the Conquest was the disappearance of a familiar business climate. As New France passed into the British Empire, the Montreal outfitters were thrown into a new system of business competition, brought about by the very numbers of newly arrived merchants, unloading goods in the conquered French colony and going after its enticing fur trade. In opening up the trade of the colony to competition, the British presence transformed Canadian commercial practices. The change negated the Canadian merchants' initial advantage of experience in the fur trade and created a novel business climate around them.

269

Competition in trade, the new political regime, the Canadian merchants' inability to obtain the favors of the military, all these created a mood of uncertainty and pessimism among the Montreal merchants. The merchants could only conclude from what was happening around them that the new business climate of the post-Conquest period favored British traders at their expense. They can be understood if they were not eager to adapt their ways to the new situation.

It may be argued, of course, that the changes which produced the new situation are subsumed under the notion of "Conquest" and that the previous pages only make more explicit the "decapitation" interpretation advanced by the historians of the "Montreal school."[78] It is true enough that the new business climate described here may not have been created after the Seven Years' War had Canada remained a French possession. But there is no guarantee that other changes would not have affected the Montreal merchants. During the last years of the French regime they had reaped few profits from the fur trade. After the Conquest they continued in the fur trade much on the same scale as before. The Montreal merchants were not "decapitated" by the Conquest; rather, they were faced in very short succession with a series of transformations in the socioeconomic structure of the colony to which they might have been able to adapt had these transformations been spread over a longer period of time.

This paper has attempted to show that the fate of the Canadian merchants of Montreal after the Conquest followed from the nature of trade before the Conquest and from the rate at which new circumstances required the merchants to alter their business behavior. But it should be remembered that the decapitation hypothesis still remains to be tested in the area of the colony's economy which was most heavily dependent upon the control of the metropolis, the import-export trade of the Quebec merchants. Only a detailed examination of the role and the activities of the Quebec merchants, both before and after the Conquest, will fully put the decapitation hypothesis to the test.

270 NOTES

1 Public Archives of Canada [hereafter PAC], C.O.42, vol. 27, f. 66, Carleton to Shelburne, Quebec, 25 November 1767; quoted in A.L. Burt, *The Old Province of Quebec*, 2 vols. (Toronto, 1968), 1:142.

2 See Burt, *Old Province*, vol. 1, ch. 6; Dale B. Miquelon, "The Baby Family in the Trade of Canada, 1750–1820" (Unpublished Master's thesis, Carleton University, 1966), 145–46.

3 Francis Parkman, *The Old Regime in Canada* (27th ed., Boston, 1892), ch. 21, especially 397–98.

4 W. Stewart Wallace, ed., *Documents Relating to the North West Company* (Toronto, 1934); Wallace, *The Pedlars from Quebec and Other Papers on the Nor'Westers* (Toronto, 1954); E.E. Rich, *The Fur Trade and the Northwest to 1857* (Toronto, 1967); Rich, *The History of the Hudson's Bay Company*, vol. 2 (London, 1959); D.G. Creighton, *The Empire of the St. Lawrence* (Toronto, 1956).

5 Wayne E. Stevens, *The Northwest Fur Trade, 1763–1800* (Urbana, Ill., 1928), 25.

6 Fernand Ouellet, *Histoire économique et sociale du Québec, 1760–1850* (Montreal, 1966), 77.

7 Ouellet, *Histoire économique*, 104–106.

8 Michel Brunet, *Les Canadiens après la Conquête, 1759–1775* (Montreal, 1969), 173–74, 177–80.

9 Miquelon, "The Baby Family," 158.

10 Miquelon, "The Baby Family," 142.

11 The implication is unwarranted. A given economic sector can be dynamic and even produce the largest share of marketable commodities and still provide individual entrepreneurs with meager profits. The macro-economic level of analysis should not be confused with the micro-economic level. Jean Hamelin showed that only around 28 percent of the profits from the beaver trade remained in Canada. Since the Canadians had an assured market for beaver, one can wonder how much more profitable it was for them to deal in other peltries. See Hamelin, *Economie et Société en Nouvelle-France* (Quebec, 1960), 54–56.

12 The obvious economic explanation for the downfall of the Canadian merchants after the Conquest has to be dismissed. The liquidation of Canadian paper money by France hurt most of all those British merchants who bought it from Canadians for speculation. Canadian merchants had already compensated in part for the anticipated liquidation by raising prices during the last years of the Seven Years' War. Those Montreal merchants who had the greatest quantity of French paper were not driven out of business; on the contrary the most prominent merchants were able to open accounts with British suppliers soon after the Conquest without too much difficulty. See José E. Igartua, "The Merchants and *Négociants* of Montreal, 1750–1775: A Study in Socio-Economic History" (Unpublished Ph.D. thesis, Michigan State University, 1974), ch. 6.

13 Franquet, *Voyages et mémoires sur le Canada en 1752–1753* (Toronto, 1968), 56.

14 For a more elaborate description of the size and the socioeconomic characteristics of the Montreal merchant community at this time, see Igartua, "The Merchants and *Négociants* of Montreal," ch. 2.

15 See H.A. Innis, *The Fur Trade in Canada* (Rev. ed., Toronto, 1956), 107–113.

16 See Abraham Rotstein, "Fur Trade and Empire: An Institutional Analysis" (Unpublished Ph.D. thesis, University of Toronto, 1967), 72.

17 Innis, *Fur Trade*, 117. For his discussion of the impact of war on the fur trade and on New France, see 114–18.

18 In theory, the French licensing system set up to restrict the trade remained in operation from its re-establishment in 1728 to the end of the French regime; only twenty-five *congés* were to be sold each year. In practice, military officers in the upper country could also acquire for a modest

fee exclusive trade privileges for their particular area. With some care, concluded one author, they could make an easy fortune. See Emile Salone, *La Colonisation de la Nouvelle-France* (Trois-Rivières, 1970), 390, 392–93. No clear official description of the licensing system was found for the period from 1750 to 1760, but the precise way in which the fur trade was restricted matters less than the fact of restriction.

[19] On Charly see PAC, RG 4 B58, vol. 15, 19 September 1764, pass by Governor Murray to "Monsr. Louis Saint-Ange Charly [and his family] to London, in their way to France agreeable to the Treaty of Peace . . . "; Archives Nationales du Québec à Montréal [formerly Archives judiciaires de Montréal; hereafter ANQ-M], Greffe de Pierre Panet, 16 août 1764, no. 2190. Trotier Desauniers "Dufy"'s will is in ANQ-M, 29 juillet 1760, no. 1168, and Godet's will is in ANQ-M, 28 décembre 1768, no. 3140.

[20] The inventory of Monière's estate is in ANQ-M, 28 décembre 1768, no. 3141; that of L'Huillier Chevalier's in ANQ-M, 15 [?] juin 1772, no. 3867.

[21] See Alexander Henry, *Travels and Adventures in Canada* (Ann Arbor, University Microfilms, 1966), 191–92.

[22] W.S. Wallace, *Documents Relating to the North West Company*, Appendix A ("A Biographical Dictionary of the Nor'Westers"), 456.

[23] See Henry, *Travels*, 1–11, 34.

[24] Henry, *Travels*, 39.

[25] Henry, *Travels*, 50. Cf. the rosier picture by Creighton, *The Empire of the St. Lawrence*, 33.

[26] Henry, *Travels*, 77–84. The Indians killed the British soldiers but ransomed the British traders, giving to each according to his profession.

[27] Henry, *Travels*, 264–92.

[28] See Wallace, *Documents*, 456; Milo M. Quaife, ed, *Alexander Henry's Travels and Adventures in the Years 1760–1776* (Chicago, 1921), xvi–xvii.

[29] Henry, *Travels*, 11; Quaife, *Henry's Travels*, 12 n. 6.

[30] Rich, *History of the Hudson's Bay Company*, 2: 9.

[31] See PAC, C.O.42, vol. 5, ff. 30–31, Murray's "List of Protestants in the District of Montreal," dated Quebec, 7 November 1765.

[32] See Miquelon, "The Baby Family," 181–87.

[33] PAC, MG 19 A1, 1, William Edgar Papers, 1: 97, F. Hamback to W. Edgar, 2 November 1766. See also 1: 95, Hamback to D. Edgar, 29 October 1766, and 1: 104–106, same to Edgar, 23 March 1767.

[34] William Edgar Papers, 1: 12.

[35] See William Edgar Papers, vols. 1 and 2.

[36] R.H. Fleming, "Phyn, Ellice and Company of Schenectady," *Contributions to Canadian Economics* 4 (1932): 7–41.

[37] See Marjorie G. Jackson, "The Beginnings of British Trade at Michilimackinac," *Minnesota History* 11 (September 1930): 252; C.W. Alvord and C.E. Carter, eds., *The New Regime, 1765–1767* (Collections of the Illinois State Historical Library, vol. 11), 300–301; Alvord and Carter, eds., *Trade and Politics, 1767–1769* (Collections of the Illinois State Historical Library, vol. 16), 382–453.

[38] See "Extract of a Letter from Michilimackinac, to a Gentleman in this City, dated 30th June," in *Quebec Gazette*, 18 August 1768; see also Rich, *History of the Hudson's Bay Company* 2: 26: "The suspicions between the Pedlars [from Quebec], and their encouragements of the Indians to trick and defraud their trade rivals, especially by defaulting on payments of debt, were widespread and continuous."

[39] *Quebec Gazette*, 7 January 1768.

[40] Burt, *Old Province*, 1: 92.

[41] The flooding of the Quebec market by British merchants was part of a larger invasion of the colonial trade in North America. See Mark Egnal and Joseph A. Ernst, "An Economic Interpretation of the American Revolution," *William and Mary Quarterly*, 3rd series, 29 (1972): 3–32.

[42] Quoted in Alvord and Carter, eds., *Trade and Politics*, 288.

[43] Alvord and Carter, eds., *Trade and Politics*, 38.

[44] Quoted in E.E. Rich, *Montreal and the Fur Trade* (Montreal, 1966), 44.

[45] These figures are somewhat distorted by the inclusion of a single large British investor, Alexander Henry, who outfitted seven canoes worth £3400 in all. See Charles E. Lart, ed., "Fur-Trade Returns, 1767," *Canadian Historical Review* 3 (December 1922): 351–58. The definition of the North West as including Lake Huron, Lake Superior, and "the northwest by way of Lake Superior" given in Rich, *Montreal and the Fur Trade*, 36–37, was used in making these compilations. The French traders were "Deriviere," "Chenville," St. Clair, Laselle, "Guillaid [Guillet]," and "Outlass [Houtelas]."

[46] See Rich, *Montreal and the Fur Trade*, 36–37.

[47] Jackson, *Minnesota History*, 11: 268–69.

[48] Rich, *History of the Hudson's Bay Company* 2: 68.

[49] On the Monières, see Igartua, "The Merchants and *Négociants* of Montreal," ch. 2. On the Gamelins, see Antoine Champagne, *Les La Vérendrye et les postes de l'ouest* (Quebec, 1968), passim.

[50] See R.H. Fleming, *Contributions to Canadians Economics* 4: 13; on Baynton, Wharton and Morgan, see *The Papers of Sir William Johnson* [hereafter *Johnson Papers*], 14 vols. (Albany, 1921–1965), vols. 5, 6, 12, passim.

[51] PAC, C.O.42, vol. 2, ff. 277–80, petition of the "Merchants and Traders of Montreal" to Murray and the Council, Montreal, 20 February 1765; *Johnson Papers* 5: 807–15, memorial and petition of Detroit traders to Johnson, 22 November 1767; 12: 409–414, 1768 trade regulations with the merchants' objections.

[52] See Alvord and Carter, eds., *The New Regime*, 118–19, and *Trade and Politics*, 39, 287; see also Stevens, *The Northwest Fur Trade*, 44.

[53] Johnson Papers, 12: 517, Thomas Gage to Guy Johnson, New York, 29 May 1768.

[54] *Johnson Papers* 5: 481. See also Alvord and Carter, eds., *The New Regime*, 118–19; *Johnson Papers* 5: 362; Alvord and Carter, eds., *Trade and Politics*, 39; *Johnson Papers* 5: 762–64; 12: 486–87; Stevens, *The Northwest Fur Trade*, 28.

[55] PAC, C.O.42, vol. 27, ff. 81–85, Carleton to Johnson, Quebec, 27 March 1767.

[56] *Johnson Papers* 12: 372–75, Croghan to Johnson, 18 October 1767.

[57] Henry, *Travels*, 71–72.

[58] See PAC, C.O.42, vol. 26, f. 13, Court of St. James, Conway [Secretary of State] to the Commandants of Detroit and Michilimackinac, 27 March 1766. See also Alvord and Carter, eds., *Trade and Politics*, 207–208, Gage to Shelburne, 12 March 1768; 239, Johnson to Gage, 8 April 1768; 375, Gage to Johnson, 14 August 1768; 378, Gage to Hillsborough, 17 August 1768; 384, Johnson to Gage, 24 August 1768; 599, Gage to Hillsborough, 9 September 1769. More than trading on his own account, Rogers was suspected of setting up an independent Illinois territory. He was eventually cleared. See "Robert Rogers," *Dictionary of American Biography*, vol. 16 (New York, 1935), 108–109, and *Johnson Papers*, vols. 5, 6, 12, 13, *passim*.

[59] PAC, William Edgar Papers, 1: 43–44, Callender to Edgar n.p., 31 December 1763.

[60] Henry, *Travels*, 191–92, 235.

[61] PAC, William Edgar Papers, 1: 90, Thos. Shipboy to Rankin and Edgar, Albany, 21 August 1766.

[62] William Edgar Papers, 1: 201, Benjamin Frobisher to Rankin and Edgar, Michilimackinac, 23 June 1769.

[63] William Edgar Papers, 1: 104–106, F. Hamback to Edgar, 23 March 1767.

[64] The most detailed account is given in Burt, *Old Province*, vol. 1, ch. 6 and 7. See also Creighton, *Empire of the St. Lawrence*, 40–48.

[65] See for instance E.-Z. Massicotte, "La Bourse de Montréal sous le régime français," *The Canadian Antiquarian and Numismatic Journal*, 3rd series, 12 (1915): 26–32.

[66] See Pierre Tousignant, "La Genèse et l'avènement de la Constitution de 1791" (Unpublished Ph.D. thesis, Université de Montréal, 1971).

[67] See *Quebec Gazette*, 15 September 1766 and the issues from June to September 1768.

[68] See *Quebec Gazette*, 26 September 1765. Tousignant, "La Genèse," pp. 21–39, points out the political significance of this letter.

[69] See texts by "A MERCHANT" in the 10 and 17 December 1767 issues, and rebuttals in the 24 and 31 December 1767 and 7 and 21 January 1768 issues.

[70] Tousignant, "La Genèse," 39.

[71] See issues of 13 and 27 July, and 5 October 1775.

[72] Canadian notables of Quebec broke with the "Old Subjects" earlier: a petition, thought to date from 1770 and signed by leading Canadians of that city, asked for the restoration of Canadian institutions. See Adam Shortt and Arthur G. Doughty, *Documents Relating to the Constitutional History of Canada* (2nd. ed., Ottawa, 1918) [hereafter *Docs. Const. Hist. Can.*], 1: 419–21.

[73] The petition and the memorial are reproduced in *Docs. Const. Hist. Can.* 1:504–506, 508–510.

[74] *Docs. Const. Hist. Can.* 1: 511. The British merchants of Montreal signed a counter-petition in January 1774, requesting the introduction of an assembly and of the laws of England. See 1: 501–502.

[75] Recent historians have highlighted the influence of the military and civil administrations as sources of economic and social betterment in New France. See Guy Frégault, *Le XVIIIe siècle canadien* (Montreal, 1968), 382–84; W.J. Eccles, "The Social, Economic, and Political Significance of the Military Establishment in New France," *Canadian Historical Review* 52 (March 1971): 17–19; and Cameron Nish, *Les Bourgeois-Gentilshommes de la Nouvelle-France* (Montreal, 1968), *passim*.

[76] See PAC, C.O.42, vol. 24. ff. 72–73v.; ff. 95–95v; vol. 3, f. 262; *Docs. Const. Hist. Can.* 1: 504–508.

[77] See *Docs. Const. Hist. Can.* 1: 504.

[78] Maurice Séguin, of the History Department of the Université de Montréal, was the first to present a systematic interpretation of the Conquest as societal decapitation. His book, *L'Idée d'indépendance au Québec: genèse et historique* (Trois-Rivières, 1968), which contains a summary of his thought, was published twenty years after its author first sketched out his thesis. Guy Frégault's *Histoire de la Nouvelle-France*, vol. 9, *La guerre de la Conquête, 1754–1760* (Montreal, 1955) is a masterful rendition of that conflict, cast as the *affrontement* of two civilizations. Michel Brunet, the most voluble of the "Montreal school" historians, has assumed the task of popularizing Séguin's thought. See Brunet, "La Conquête anglaise et la déchéance de la bourgeoisie canadienne (1760–1793)," in his *La Présence anglaise et les Canadiens* (Montreal, 1964), 48–112. Brunet developed the point further in *Les Canadiens après la Conquête*, vol. 1, *1759–1775* (Montreal, 1969). An abridged version of Brunet's position is provided in his *French Canada and the Early Decades of British Rule, 1760–1791* (Ottawa, 1963). For a review of French-Canadian historiography on the Conquest up to 1966, see Ramsay Cook, "Some French-Canadian Interpretations of the British Conquest: une quatrième dominante de la pensée canadienne-française," Canadian Historical Association, *Historical Papers* (1966): 70–83.

The Society of British North America, 1780–1820

The social history of settlement in British North America in the late eighteenth and early nineteenth centuries is really a collection of separate regional stories. Two French-speaking populations existed — the French Canadians in the St. Lawrence valley and the Acadians in New Brunswick. As well, English-speaking communities had been established on Prince Edward Island, in New Brunswick, on Cape Breton Island (a separate colony from 1784 to 1820), and in Upper Canada. English-speaking migration had, in addition, strengthened the existing anglophone communities in the St. Lawrence valley, Newfoundland, and Nova Scotia. The following readings review developments in the St. Lawrence valley and southern New Brunswick.

From 1791 to 1815 the population of Lower Canada nearly doubled, to more than 300 000. As a result, as Jean-Pierre Wallot explains in "Culture Shock," the colony experienced important economic changes that contributed to competition among the various social groups in the colony for a redistribution of power and income. Since the bureaucratic, military, and business elites came essentially from the British community, the struggle had an ethnic quality.

In 1791 Upper Canada emerged as a new British colony, composed largely of Loyalists escaping from the newly independent thirteen colonies. The Loyalists had also created the province of New Brunswick. In "The Envy of the American States," a chapter from her book-length study by the same title, Ann Gorman Condon uses letters, diaries, and accounts of leading members of the Loyalist elite to review the Loyalists' dreams for New Brunswick. The Loyalist leaders had, she explains, a desire to create an ideal province which the Americans would want to emulate.

Numerous studies exist on French-Canadian society in the late eighteenth and early nineteenth centuries. See, in particular, Fernand Ouellet's monumental accounts, entitled (in their English translations) *Lower Canada, 1791–1840: Social Change and Nationalism* (Toronto: McClelland and Stewart, 1979) and *Economic and Social History of Quebec, 1760–1850* (Toronto: McClelland and Stewart, 1980). Two other studies, with conclusions different from Ouellet's, are Allan Greer's *Peasant, Lord, and*

Merchant: Rural Society in Three Quebec Parishes, 1740–1840 (Toronto: University of Toronto Press, 1985) and Gilles Paquet and Jean-Pierre Wallot's *Lower Canada at the Turn of the Nineteenth Century: Restructuring and Modernization*, Canadian Historical Association, Historical Booklet no. 45 (Ottawa: CHA, 1988). In "Religion and French-Canadian Mores in the Early Nineteenth Century," *Canadian Historical Review* 52 (1971): 51–91, Jean-Pierre Wallot discusses the role of religion in Lower Canada. David T. Ruddel's *Quebec City, 1765–1832: The Evolution of a Colonial Town* (Ottawa: Canadian Museum of Civilization, 1987) is a social history of the largest city in British North America in the late eighteenth and early nineteenth centuries.

On English-speaking British North American society in this time period see, in particular, Chapter three ("Carders of Wool, Drawers of Water: Women's Work in British North America") in Alison Prentice et al., *Canadian Women: A History* (Toronto: Harcourt Brace Jovanovich, 1988), 65–84. References to books and articles on the Maritimes can be found in the bibliographical entries included for Topic Six, "The American Revolution and the Maritime Colonies." A recent collection of articles has been edited by P.A. Buckner and David Frank: *Atlantic Canada before Confederation*, vol. 1, *The Acadiensis Reader* (Fredericton: Acadiensis Press, 1985). Two useful studies on town life in Atlantic Canada are the early sections of T.W. Acheson's *Saint John: The Making of a Colonial Urban Community* (Toronto: University of Toronto Press, 1985) and Judith Fingard, *Jack in Port: Sailortowns of Eastern Canada* (Toronto: University of Toronto Press, 1982). For an overview of developments in Newfoundland see Frederick W. Rowe's *A History of Newfoundland and Labrador* (Toronto: McGraw-Hill, 1980). The bibliography for Topic Eleven, "The Society of Upper Canada (Canada West)," contains numerous references for Upper Canada.

In "Patriarchy and Paternalism: The Case of the Eastern Ontario Loyalist Women," *Ontario History 81*, 1 (March 1989): 3–24, Janice Potter examines the experience of female Loyalists during the American Revolution and later in Upper Canada.

For sketches of the lives of leading British North Americans in the late eighteenth and early nineteenth centuries consult the multivolume *Dictionary of Canadian Biography* (Toronto: University of Toronto Press, 1966–   ), particularly volumes 4 to 8.

274

Culture Shock*

JEAN-PIERRE WALLOT

The period 1791 to 1812 was one of widespread upheaval and social change in the western world. The new, revolutionary ideas of the En-

*From *Horizon Canada* 21 (1985): 481–487. Reprinted by permission.

lightenment, the American Revolution, European wars, and the birth of democratic aspirations all had profound repercussions in North America. In Lower Canada these international events were mirrored by important local changes: the creation of new political institutions, the division of Quebec into two colonies, Upper and Lower Canada, and the emergence of new economic opportunities.

In the years following the division of Quebec into two colonies by the Constitutional Act of 1791, Lower Canada was reconstructed and modernized. From a sparsely populated colony relying on a single export, fur, and struggling with an agriculture hardly above the subsistence level, Lower Canada developed an expanded and diversified pre-industrial economy. With the emergence of new international markets, especially for timber, certain sectors of the economy prospered, offering opportunities for business people to accumulate capital and establish successful enterprises.

The population climbed from 165,000 in 1791 to more than 300,000 in 1815, with the towns growing at a faster rate than the countryside after 1805. The fur trade collapsed; exports of furs fell from 50 percent of total exports in 1790 to just 10 percent by 1810. However, wood products picked up the slack, beginning with a sudden boom in 1807. By 1810 wood exports amounted to 75 percent of the total. Finally, agriculture was stimulated by new international markets and growing home consumption. As a result, the value of Lower Canadian exports rose from £300,000 in the early 1790s to £1,221,000 in 1811, more than a fourfold increase in two decades.

275

Despite inflation this new economic activity led to a marked increase in income at all levels of society, the appearance of new economic sectors (for example, naval construction and many local factories), the development of new social groups (small business people, the liberal professions, rural merchants, large-scale farmers), and new institutions (insurance companies, corporations, and soon, banks).

Good Living

Social differences accelerated quickly, both between social groups and within them. Merchants diversified their activities and came to occupy positions of dominance in society, along with senior civil servants, while seigneurs who kept to the countryside and did not engage in other activities were becoming a dying breed. Members of the liberal professions (medicine and law) earned a good living and their numbers increased rapidly. In 1790 Lower Canadian society was pretty much an undifferentiated mass, with most members having a similar standard of living; by about 1810 artisans and *habitants* exhibited a great variety of incomes and lifestyles and the standard of living was on the whole much higher.

As economic prospects improved, individuals specialized much more in one line of work. Production was increasingly mechanized and luxury goods began to appear along with basic commodities. To take just one small example: after 1800 sofas appeared in the homes of *habitants*. Mirrors, cutlery and various utensils, and manufactured clothing all became readily available in this period. Stoves were another important innovation in the home, allowing houses to be partitioned into several rooms, each with its own source of heat. These commodities were, among other things, signs of a better way of life for all social classes.

Authorities worried about the morals of the people as the wave of prosperity gave rise to increased alcohol sales and an alarming growth in prostitution, transiency, and crime. The majority of the population was law-abiding of course; however, *Canadiens* continued to display a love of pleasure — eating, drinking, dancing, and partying — despite the disapproving frowns of the clergy and civil authorities.

276

Apart from a small minority of freethinkers (mostly members of the liberal professions and merchants), Canadians were practising Catholics. Nevertheless, they made a clear distinction between religious and secular matters, and did not recognize clerical authority over the latter. Unruly and independent, Canadians were not generous in their support of priest and parish and scandalized the clergy with their merrymaking. Monsignor Plessis, bishop of Quebec in 1817, went so far as to abolish parish feasts because of the scenes of "debauchery" which they generated.

The Catholic Church Besieged

There is nothing surprising about the quality of Christian observance at this time. Vocations were rare. Clerics were few, badly trained, and ordained at too young an age. In 1790, 75 parishes did not have a resident priest. In 1805, 186 parish priests were in charge of more than 200,000 faithful scattered across a vast territory.

For the most part, the British government prohibited the immigration of French priests. Considering the church an instrument of power and public order to be controlled by the state, the colonial government under governors Robert Shore Milnes (1799–1805) and James Craig (1807–1811) tried hard to subjugate the church to the "Royal Prerogative." The government wanted the power to appoint clerics, choose bishops, supervise seminaries, and also wished to see a greater influx of Irish priests. In fact, British authorities suspected the clergy were at the root of the resistance of French Canadians to assimilation. For its part, the *Canadien* middle class, with a majority in the assembly, tried hard to control the clergy by means of various laws, though they were thwarted in the end by the legislative council.

The Catholic Church managed to weather this storm of opposition. Its critics were divided amongst themselves and during the War of 1812 the clergy were a loyal and effective force for keeping the Canadian population loyal to the British cause. However, it was not for several decades that the church in Lower Canada gained the strength and power it would hold at the beginning of the 20th century.

Sources of Conflict

Before 1791, British and *Canadien* populations were relatively isolated; only their leaders had much to do with each other, forming temporary coalitions for mutual benefit. After 1791, however, the two groups were constantly at odds over a variety of issues in which their interests conflicted. During the War of 1812 the groups made a temporary alliance against the common enemy, the Americans, but this served only to delay the violent confrontation which took place in the post-war years.

277

One source of conflict, common to all British colonies, was the nature of the political system, which called for legislative and executive councils, with members named by authorities in Great Britain; and the newly formed elected assembly, with members chosen locally. The Canadian system was strongly democratic since almost all heads of families had the right to vote, whereas in England at the time less than three percent of the population had the vote. Naturally enough, the assembly promoted local interests and sought to increase its own authority and autonomy, while the councils and the governor represented metropolitan interests and attempted to restrict the assembly.

At the social level, members of the high bureaucracy and owners of large businesses, whose political power depended on links with the appointed councils and to Great Britain, found themselves confronted by the "people" and their leaders who dominated the assembly. Each group interpreted the constitution differently. The first emphasized the aristocratic nature of the English constitution and the importance of the legislative council, while the second supported the pre-eminence of the assembly.

An ethnic dimension also emerged. The aristocratic and wealthy group was comprised mostly of British subjects. The latter clashed with the small business people and popular masses, which were mostly *Canadien*. These ethnic confrontations also manifested themselves as clashes between different cultures and values.

And finally, at the economic level, members of the aristocratic "compact" controlled foreign trade, were the major landowners, and operated most of the colony's businesses, large and small. Their interests were often opposed to those of the small farmer, shopkeeper, and worker.

278

The first parliament. From the first session of its brand new elected assembly, Lower Canada was divided by the language issue. This painting depicts assembly members in January 1793 arguing which language would be used in debate. The assembly met in the chapel of the Bishop's Palace in Quebec City, which the government rented for the purpose.

The Confederation Life Collection.

The Language Issue

At the very first session of the assembly in 1793 the two main parties disagreed over the choice of speaker (Jean-Antoine Panet, who had said he would "flog the English to their feet," was eventually appointed), and then on the language of debates and laws. The arguments which were to be heard over and over again for the next 20 years were voiced. *Canadiens*, the British felt, should show their gratitude by adopting the English language and English laws, which were better suited to commerce; in short, they should become British. On the other hand, *Canadien* leaders retorted that the British should recognize the language and customs of the majority of the colony's population, who had the right to be ruled by laws in their own language.

The British party was not always united. Under governors Lord Dorchester (1786–1796) and Robert Prescott (1796–1799), for example, the British were divided over the sharing of land in the townships south of the St. Lawrence. But during the tenure of R.S. Milnes the first coherent policy was developed to increase the influence of the government and the "compact" over the people, and to make possible the gradual assimilation of the *Canadiens*. This policy provided for, among other things, the abolition of the seigniorial system, the opening of the Royal Institution for teaching English to *Canadiens* free of charge, and a motion for the subjugation of the clergy to the crown.

279

Craig and the *Canadiens*

Milnes' patient approach did not satisfy the impatience of the British. English-language newspapers, especially the *Quebec Mercury*, raged against the language, laws, morals, customs, and religion of *Canadiens*. They challenged their loyalty and called for their "anglicization." These attacks prompted the Canadian party in 1806 to create its own mouthpiece, *Le Canadien*. This newspaper set out to define and defend the *Canadien* nationality, rallying the majority of the francophone population to the views of the elite of professionals and small business people.

Despite his failing health, James Craig accepted the post of governor of the Canadas in 1807 because of the imminent danger of war between the United States and England. Unlike his predecessors, and even though he was without any apparent prejudice against the *Canadiens* when he took over, Craig quickly abandoned any pretence of neutrality and took the lead of the British party. He resented the nationalist, populist tone of the *Canadien* party, which dissolved the assembly twice, in 1809 and 1810, after sessions that were as brief as they were tempestuous. The governor even embarked on an electoral tour in the summer of 1809.

This initiative, together with the already troubled relations between the two parties, only served to polarize the debate even more.

The *Canadien* party proposed constitutional changes which, by giving the colonial assembly the same "sovereignty" as the House of Commons in Great Britain, would have made it *the* power in the colony. The British party, led by Gov. Craig, vigorously denounced the dangerous principles espoused by the *Canadiens*. Despite the best efforts of the governor, the high civil servants, and the British merchants, the *Canadiens*, because of their numerical majority, continued to win one election after another. Craig and his allies, who believed that *Canadiens* were French at heart and hated the English, proposed radical corrective measures in London. The objective was assimilation of the *Canadiens*. The means to accomplish

Conspiracy in Montreal

In March 1810, Governor Craig had the presses of the newspaper *Le Canadien* seized and its chief editors and distributors imprisoned. This sudden gesture was made just before an election and was intended to decapitate the leadership of the *Canadien* party. Quebec newspapers had been circulating rumours of a conspiracy involving the journalists and the French consul in Washington. Craig had his chief executive councillors in Montreal approach the editor of *La Gazette de Montreal* to suggest that he publish a completely fraudulent article on the situation. In it the editors of *Le Canadien* were accused of yielding to the lure of power and the desire to destabilize the colony, and of pocketing money from the French minister in Washington. Besides the people arrested, eminent *Canadien* leaders like Denis-Benjamin Viger and Louis Bourdages were also implicated. The editor of the *Gazette*, James Brown, refused to go along with this "infamous production" and conserved the text, in case of government reprisals. Thus, Craig was not able to carry out massive arrests around Montreal, the main bastion of the *Canadien* party. This incident did not change the results of the election. The Canadian party triumphed and the British party was reduced to 12 representatives. The governor released the prisoners one by one, on the condition that they were sufficiently repentant. The printer Charles Le François died shortly after his release. Pierre Bédard, the main leader of the *Canadien* party, vainly sought a trial and remained in prison until the session of 1811, oblivious to the government's pressure and sure of his innocence.

this end were various. They included: union of Upper and Lower Canada, which would give the British a majority in the legislature; suppression of the assembly, and the creation of a strongly British legislative council; abolition of the seigniorial system; increased British immigration; and strict control over all levels of education. Herman Ryland, the governor's secretary, went to London to promote this program. However, even if the British Prime Minister recognized the urgency of these problems, he did not dare tackle them while he had his hands full with the war in Europe and the threat of war with the United States.

James Craig returned to England in 1811 because of illness and was replaced as governor by another military man, Sir George Prevost. From the beginning, the latter made peace with the *Canadiens*; he needed them to fight the Americans, who once again posed a threat. The policies for assimilating and subjugating the French would have to wait.

Debate Suspended

The years 1791 to 1812 constitute a period of upheaval, uncertainty, and conflict. Out of the noisy confusion of political debate two "national" programs emerged. The majority of the representatives in the assembly wanted a more independent parliament, an objective which was opposed by British authorities who held to the markedly aristocratic nature of

281

No Seat for Mr. Hart

Besides the issue of judges sitting in the legislative assembly, another problem preoccupied Craig and members of the legislature in 1808. It was the case of Ezekiel Hart.

A rich merchant from Trois-Rivières, Hart had been elected in April 1807. His election provoked an outcry — while members of the legislature had to take their oath on the Bible, Hart was a practising Jew. Even if he could bring himself to swear on the Bible, was it not a fact that Jews were barred from sitting in the British Parliament? After lengthy debate, a vote was taken and Hart's seat was declared vacant.

In fact, Hart did take the obligatory oath. But the *Canadien* members, determined to hold on to their majority and all worked up against the English administration, denied him his seat. Despite Craig's personal intervention, the British government approved the assembly's decision.

English parliamentary government. The *Canadien* party, under the direction of members of the liberal professions and of small merchants, dreamed of a free and democratic Canadian nation, yet one that was necessarily loyal to Britain as an ally and buffer against its powerful next door neighbour, the United States. On the other hand, the British party endorsed a firm "anglicizing" policy for the French population of Canada.

The war of 1812 briefly stilled the debate as it brought the two adversaries together in an alliance against their common enemy, the Americans.

The Envy of the American States*

ANN GORMAN CONDON

282

> If I was to be transformed into an instrument of musick and to make choice for myself I wou'd chuse to be a fiddle, because it wou'd require some skill & taste to play upon me, and if I sounded well some little credit wou'd redound to myself. But if I was a band-organ and turn'd with a Wench — its a mere mechanical operation and neither the musician or the instrument gain much credit.

Edward Winslow[1]

The original Loyalist leaders of New Brunswick were intensely proud, self-conscious men. Although born in an apparently safe, secure world where the path to distinction was illuminated by a series of well-placed markers, their lives had in fact been characterized by flux, by a series of abrupt reversals and successes, over which they themselves had little control. Chance, caprice, bad luck, good fortune had played a far larger role in determining their fate than the anticipated tests of ability, hard work, good taste, and good connections. Instead of being able to exercise their talents in a satisfying and socially constructive manner, these men were haunted by the conviction that their "prime of life" had been spent fighting a fruitless war, coping with an unfamiliar wilderness, and striving to provide the rudiments of a decent existence for themselves and their families.

In short, the Loyalist leaders feared their lives might prove a waste. All the bright promises of their youth, the high standards they had set for themselves, the skills they had mastered, and the dreams they harbored of being prominent, productive members of their community were repeatedly subjected to frustration and failure. The Revolution had deprived them of their rightful place in the world, the aftermath had thrown

*From *The Envy of the American States: The Loyalist Dream for New Brunswick*, by Ann Gorman Condon. Copyright 1984 by Ann Gorman Condon. Reprinted by permission.

them into an unwelcome dependence on the British patronage system, and finally the northern frontier threatened to sap their energies and their talents without yielding any commensurate sense of achievement.

In establishing the society of New Brunswick, these Loyalist leaders strove to reverse the downward course of their lives. With an impetuosity that sometimes bordered on frenzy, they tried to reproduce the social customs and the set of religious and educational institutions which they had known before the war. These extensive cultural efforts can only be understood in terms of the Loyalist leaders' determination to defy fate, to retrieve the world they had lost, and to pass on to their children the social standards, the educational advantages, and the political and moral values which they esteemed so highly.

The goal of the Loyalist leaders was summed up by the phrase, "the envy of the American states." By envy was not just meant simply spite, although there certainly was an element of that in their motives. But even more importantly, the Loyalist leaders were determined to set up a society which would be envied because it was in fact better, finer — or, to use their favorite term, more respectable — than the rival republic to the south. Their goal was not merely to establish a viable community, but one that was characterized by dignity and cultural achievement as well. It must be a society that conformed to the elitist standards of their Tory background and that was a worthy home for themselves and their families.

283

The efforts of the Loyalist leaders to establish such a highly civilized society in New Brunswick were inspired by a profound sense of mission. For, if their province did in fact become "the envy of the American states," its distinguished character would justify the Loyalists' choices during the American Revolution — both to themselves and to posterity. Given the importance of this goal, the Loyalist leaders naturally placed an extremely high value on the internal social development of New Brunswick. They also tended to be quite exclusive and self-righteous in choosing which social and cultural institutions should be encouraged. And the standards which they set for the new province had a rigid quality which often did not make sufficient allowance for the character of the general population or the ruggedness of the northern frontier.

Finally, and perhaps most significantly, the Loyalists' sense of cultural mission was reflected in their relationships with their children. Much of their zealous haste to establish rich cultural institutions in New Brunswick, and to maintain a dignified style of life there, grew out of their determination that their children should not suffer from the effects of the American Revolution, that they should receive all the advantages which the Loyalist leaders had themselves enjoyed in their youth, and that they should have access to respectable, rewarding careers. With enormous love, and often at great personal cost, these men gave their children the best educations they could afford, they exposed them to the graces of civilized life, and they exerted all their influence to launch them upon profitable careers and suitable marriages. As the infirmities of age began to take their toll, the Loyalist leaders became increasingly anxious to pass on the torch, to transfer to their children both their personal and their political hopes. In the process, they imbued these children with their own civil and moral code, with their distinctive standards of public duty and private conduct, and with an unforgettable sense of the sacrifices their fathers had made to preserve the empire and to uphold a community ideal which permitted law, culture, and personal liberty to flourish together.

Style of Life

284

As the Loyalist leaders took up residence in the province of New Brunswick, they did so in a style befitting their status as members of the gentry and as public officials. Ward Chipman built an architectural gem of a town house in Saint John, which he decorated with English wallpaper and furniture. George Leonard's farm in Sussex was described by Bishop Charles Inglis as "exceedingly neat and in good taste, and resembles a gentleman's villa in Europe." Many travellers commented favorably on the "elegant pile" of private and public buildings which dotted Fredericton, although Inglis himself felt the Loyalists had gone too far when they designed the Anglican Church there: "Portland Chapel in London was absurdly taken for a model to build this Church," and the cost of construction proved excessive. Many of the Loyalist leaders lived on spacious farms overlooking the St. John River, in houses of "noble appearance," which were stocked with mahogany furniture that had either been brought up from their former homes or purchased from England. The hard-headed Scottish traveller, Patrick Campbell, deplored the Loyalists' preference for mahogany imports, and he noted approvingly that Chief Justice George Ludlow's tastes ran to the beautiful native woods: "I have not seen a bit of mahogony in his elegant and commodious new house, but he is a man of very enlightened understanding. . . . " For most of the Loyalist leaders, however, furnishings and clothes from England were considered marks of gentility. When Jonathan Bliss wished to buy a present for his wife, he wrote away to London and asked Mrs. Benedict Arnold to "once more display her elegant Taste in a Bonnet or Hat, or whichever is fashionable, for *Mrs.* Bliss."[2]

The high points of social intercourse in the province were the numerous balls. These were launched even before the province was founded and provided the main focal point for exchanging gossip, for matchmaking, and for displaying the prized ball gowns and military dress uniforms of the assemblage. The pride which the Loyalist gentry took in these moments of elegance was evidenced by Edward Winslow's whimsical challenge to Sir John Wentworth of Nova Scotia: "I am determined to figure at the Assemblies . . . 'tis say'd they are already very brilliant. — You men of Halifax must look out — We shall so far exceed you in our Society & our amusements will probably be so much more rational that those of your Ladies who have great sensibility and true taste must incline to our side of the Bay." In 1802, the American visitor Charles Turner was amazed and amused to discover how faithfully the social customs of New England had been preserved in the backwoods of New Brunswick. While travelling in a remote, northeastern corner of the province, Turner encountered "a collection of young folks, — nine young ladies and one widow, and six young gentlemen, who were prepared to spend the evening in dancing, after quilting. The ladies all dressed in white, and all performed their parts in the style and taste of Boston, where eighteen years ago, Satan's seat was. . . . "[3] Col. Joseph Gubbins, a senior British military officer had a more acid reaction to the social airs of the Saint John elite:

> The amusements at this place, like those at Fredericton, are same and tiresome. At evening parties, which are here denominated Gregories from the name of the person who first introduced them, the ladies sit round the room and entertain one another with whispers. . . . This is succeeded by a substantial supper, an hour after which is generally devoted to songs too bad to even laugh at. The ridiculous delicacy of their expressions are very diverting. A New Brunswick lady conceives it indecorous to call a male bird a cock, for which they substitute rooster, even to the weather rooster; knees they denominate benders, and so on.[4]

285

The frequent mustering of the troops provided another chance for color and conviviality, as did Governor Carleton's visits to various parts of the province. The governor's entry into the City of Saint John was marked with great formality: "On his arrival at the Kennebeckasis ferry, he was met and escorted thence by the Company of Light-Horse . . . to the Government House. — Many of the most respectable inhabitants went out on horseback to receive his EXCELLENCY; and he was welcomed to this City under a discharge of cannon from the Artillery Park. . . . " News of British military victories against either the French or the Americans occasioned elaborate displays of fireworks and celebratory balls. A special poem entitled "On the shore of the Potomack in Washington City" was sung at the ball after Hull's invasion of the American capital. Similar "rejoicing and mirth were 'the order of the day'" each time the British navy triumphed over the French fleets. Prominent citizens would illuminate their houses to demonstrate their patriotism. And the Loyalist ladies frequently chose blue as the predominant color in their ball gowns in order to honor the British navy.[5]

The moment of greatest pomp and circumstance in early New Brunswick history occurred in 1794 when Prince Edward, the Duke of Kent, visited the province. Mayor Gabriel G. Ludlow delivered the welcoming address for the citizens of Saint John, and he stressed the peculiar significance which they, as Loyalists, attached to this royal visit:

> We contemplate with Admiration and heartfelt Pleasure an event so little to be expected in this remote corner of His Majesty's Dominion, as the presence of one of the Sons of our Most Gracious Sovereign . . . our Loyalty and attachment to whose Person and Government induced us with chearfulness to sacrifice the Comforts of our former Situations, and seek an Asylum under the British constitution in this lately uncultivated wilderness. . . . [6]

Ward Chipman served as the Prince's host during his stay, and the experience was easily the most gratifying public moment in Chipman's long career. Although not normally given to hyperbole, Chipman was simply transported by the demeanor of his royal guest: "He is without exception the most accomplished character I have ever seen, his manners are so dignified & at the same time marked with so much affability & condescension, he discovers so much good sense, sound understanding & so improved a mind, that I can find no bounds to my admiration for him. . . . " On a more personal level, Chipman was profoundly moved by "the enjoyment of so distinguished an honor as that of entertaining a Son of our beloved Sovereign. I confess the circumstance has been peculiarly flattering to my feelings . . . his Royal Highness was pleased to express himself in very obliging terms respecting his accommodations while with us." Chipman's Loyalist friends congratulated him on this unique privilege, but his Yankee sister, who never relented in her campaign to lure her brother back to the land of his birth, was decidedly less impressed: "I congratulate Mrs. C. and yourself on the departure of your Royal guest — you would be freed from these cares if you would dwell in our Country where all are Princes alike."[7]

Two weekly newspapers helped to keep this isolated Loyalist community in contact with the world at large. The principal items of interest were news from England and from the United States, though provincial politics were given due attention in moments of dispute. The health of the King and the progress of British military efforts were the principal subjects reported from London, although occasionally New Brunswickers were treated to more gossipy matters, such as the mounting debts of the Prince of Wales or the political trials of Warren Hastings and George Gordon. American news consisted primarily of political reports, garnered almost exclusively from New York and Boston papers of a decidedly pro-Federalist, pro-British line. Ordinarily the New Brunswick papers simply reprinted items of interest published in the American journals. In 1801, however, *The Royal Gazette* broke its traditional silence in order to lament the political defeat of President John Adams: " . . . there is every reason to apprehend that a new administration will produce very different measures from those pursued under the mild and equitable system for which Mr. Adams has been so highly and justly distinguished. . . . "[8]

The more lurid events of the French Revolution were also noted by the two papers. Judging from the frequency of articles on the "'Crimes committed during the French Revolution,'" replete with details of blood-letting, the Loyalists must have derived a certain morbid satisfaction from the collapse of that experiment in republicanism.[9] Equally popular was the work of the great Tory satirist, William Cobbett. As an outspoken champion of the pastoral, semi-feudal life of the English countryside and an implacable foe of republicanism, Cobbett's views were obviously very congenial to the New Brunswick Loyalists — for both provincial newspapers carried his "Letters of Peter Porcupine." Cobbett had actually served as a British soldier in New Brunswick, and he may have acquired some of his prejudices against republicanism from the Loyalists. He certainly enjoyed his years there, albeit he seemed astonished by the inflated titles and pretensions of the Loyalist gentry: "Thousands of captains . . . without soldiers, and of squires without shares." This phenomenon would persist well into the nineteenth century, as Col. Gubbins noted:

287

> Militia titles do not convey great ideas of rank or respectability in this quarter of the world. . . . General Coffin on the British halfpay was fined for selling rum without a license and was in the act of retailing cabbages at St. John's market slip when he received the information of his promotion.[10]

New Brunswickers followed Cobbett's subsequent misadventures in the United States through their newspapers, and Jonathan Odell, for one, expressed great resentment at "the Wanton cruelty and democratic oppression" which the Americans inflicted on the "Poor Fellow."[11]

At least one New Brunswicker sought to maintain a more personal relationship with the English literary world. This was Jonathan Odell, the poet-intellectual among the Loyalist leaders, who continued to write verses of a heavily religious and royalist slant during his years in New Brunswick. He also contributed occasional articles on syntax and Hebrew punctuation to English literary journals and sought desperately to maintain some toehold in the world of ideas. Odell particularly mourned the death of Jonathan Boucher in 1804: "Thus I have lost the only friend of literary eminence that was remaining in the Circle of Friends in England," he confided to his main intellectual companion in the province, Ward Chipman.[12] The only other Loyalist leader to have a literary turn of mind was Edward Winslow, who occasionally wrote political satires for the amusement of his friends. Although Winslow's light pieces were far earthier and less formal than Odell's, they possessed a flair and an ironic, warmhearted acceptance of the human condition that was notably lacking in Odell's highly fragile, obsequious efforts. Unfortunately Winslow's straitened financial circumstances, as well as the lack of a large reading public in New Brunswick, prevented him from developing his satirical talents more extensively. For one can well imagine that, under more encouraging conditions, Winslow's "Tammany" might have joined company with T.C. Haliburton's "Sam Slick" to provide the world with two distinctive examples of Tory wit in the Maritimes.[13]

* * *

Travellers to New Brunswick confirmed the success of the Loyalists in taming the wilderness. All early accounts of the province portray a society blessed with fertility, affluence, and refinement. For some, the highly stylized manners of the Loyalist leaders seemed a bit excessive. The American Charles Turner noted that Gabriel Ludlow, the "Lord Mayor" of Saint John greeted his party "with as much Politeness as we could expect from a Provincial official aping the hauteur of the British." And even Winslow felt compelled to protest against the elegant incompetence of Jonathan Odell: "His Habits and manners are such as in the days of superstition might have suited a High priest of the order of Melchisedec, but are ill calculated for a civil department. His hauteur is so disgusting that he has become completely obnoxious. . . . " Yet for all their pretensions, the Loyalist leaders did establish a high standard for public service. Education, involvement in the community, and dignified personal behavior were held up as prerequisites for public leadership.[14]

288

This standard was difficult, if not impossible to maintain in a frontier community. As time passed the Loyalist leaders themselves grew old and increasingly weary of their missionary task. The hardships of the circuit ride on horseback, the rigors of attending Council meetings in wintertime, the time-consuming effort needed to manage a farm or maintain even a small law practice, the afflictions of the gout — all sapped their energies for public service until the records of these men in performing their duties became a matter of public concern. They were accused of clinging to their offices beyond their time, just to keep the title and the salary.

There was in fact a dark side to the Loyalist leaders' record of public service. For these men brought to New Brunswick many of the poorer political practices of the eighteenth century, such as nepotism and multiple-office holding, as well as many of the good ones. Jonathan Bliss, for example, sought to be mayor of the city of Saint John as well as attorney general of the province — despite the fact that his duties as attorney general required him to be in Fredericton, while the mayor was, of course, expected to be seventy miles away in Saint John. And Jonathan Odell was accused in the public prints of manipulating public offices so as to reserve a clerkship for "his Billy."[15] The most relentless office-seeker of them all, however, was Edward Winslow. During his years in New Brunswick, Winslow sought, or was appointed to, the following public posts: secretary of the province, member of the Council, surrogate general of the province, commanding officer of a regiment of New Brunswick Fencibles, justice of the peace, deputy paymaster of His Majesty's

Troops in New Brunswick, secretary to the Boundary Commission, receiver general of the quit rents, deputy surveyor of the King's Woods, collector of the customs, justice of the Supreme Court, and president of the Council.

The most egregious display of Winslow's ambition occurred in connection with the quit rents. When the Loyalists were given their original land grants, they were excused from paying quit rents for a period of ten years in recognition of their wartime services. When these fees finally became due in the 1790s, neither the provincial nor the imperial government regarded them of sufficient importance to press for payment. Suddenly, however, in 1800 Winslow sent an impassioned letter to Edward G. Lutwyche, an influential Loyalist living in London, urging that the quit-rent provision should be enforced in New Brunswick in order to support the British war effort. He claimed that the system of voluntary contributions to the Patriotic Fund was not working fairly: "The loyal and ambitious were making sacrifices beyond their means and . . . the factious and mercenary part of the community avoided all connection with the subscriptions." By contrast, a quit rent would, Winslow maintained, tax people according to the extent of their property holdings and would thus be much more equitable. Winslow reinforced this argument by suggesting to Lutwyche that "the instability and ill-timed indulgences of the Mother Country — contributed more to the establishment of American independence than all their severities and restrictions . . . It appears to me essential to the tranquility and happiness of this province That the inhabitants of it should realize and (on all occasions) acknowledge their *dependence upon Great Britain*." The quit rent, he concluded, was the most "rational" means for citizens to demonstrate their allegiance.[16]

Although he emphatically denied that "any consideration of personal benefit" prompted him to make this proposal, Winslow did allow that he would be willing to serve as receiver general of the quit rents. His proposal was seconded by his close friend, George Leonard, who explicitly nominated Winslow to be receiver general. At first, the British authorities reacted negatively to the proposal on the grounds that "the amount is too trifling in their estimation to risque exciting any discontent." Prompted, however, by the urgings of Governor Carleton and other provincial officials, Great Britain finally agreed to let New Brunswick collect her quit rents — provided the House of Assembly formally approved of the measure. This proviso completely unravelled Winslow's grand design — for both he and the governor well knew the Assembly would never willingly establish a fund over which it had no control. The New Brunswick leaders had, therefore, to reverse their position completely and work to dissuade Great Britain from insisting upon quit rent collection — a measure which might provoke a new political confrontation with the Assembly. Winslow was actually in England in 1806 when the new land regulations for New Brunswick were finally settled, and he proudly reported home that he had been "instrumental" in relieving New Brunswick "from the shameful oppression of Quit-rents. . . . " This last phrase leaves little doubt that Winslow's original arguments in favor of patriotism and equity were simply an elaborate device to get himself a good job.[17]

In the end, Winslow did get the well-paying post he had courted so assiduously for twenty years, but the particular appointment seemed to mock the Loyalists' high standards of public service. For through his English connections, particularly Lord Sheffield and the Duke of Northumberland, Winslow managed to get himself appointed to the Supreme Court of New Brunswick in 1806 — despite the fact that he was not a lawyer. Governor Carleton protested that "nothing can be more absurd or more injurious to the King's Service" than to appoint a nonprofessional man to such a high legal post, and the lawyers of New Brunswick wholly agreed. Even Ward Chipman, Winslow's dearest friend, felt mortified by this affront to the profession. Chipman had served as solicitor general of New Brunswick for twenty years without pay, and had in numerous other ways exerted himself to establish high standards for the provincial Bar. All these efforts seemed worthless, he confessed in a despondent letter to Jonathan Sewell, Jr., "when men, without any professional education, as in the late instance of our friend Winslow, are thrust in." Winslow, however, dismissed these criticisms out of hand. He felt his long record of service to the province had earned him the right to any post which opened up. As for the lawyers' professional quibbles, he refused to take them seriously, noting that this was "An objection which has never been considered of much weight in the appointment of puisne Judges in the colonies. . . . "[18]

Not only were the Loyalist leaders greedy in seeking public office, but they could on occasion be faulted for failure to perform their duties conscientiously. Governor Carleton's constant complaints about the difficulties of getting a quorum to attend Council meetings were one evidence of this neglect — particularly in view of the fact that only five of the twelve members were needed to make a quorum. At one point Carleton became so exasperated that he requested permission to reduce the quorum number to three. The depth of his difficulties may be illustrated by the fact that some of the Council members never attended even one meeting of the Board. Beverley Robinson, Sr., was the most flagrant example. For although Robinson accepted an appointment to the Council and held on to it until 1790, he never in fact left England to go to New Brunswick, and only gave up his post when he could safely pass it on to his son.[19] Jonathan Sewell, Sr., did come out to New Brunswick and strove desperately to cling to his remaining appointments as judge of the Vice-Admiralty Court and member of the Council. Yet Sewell spent his final days in New Brunswick as a virtual recluse and never

290

participated in any public business.[20] Even Christopher Billopp, a much younger, more active man, attended the Council meetings only six times during his entire term of twenty-seven years.[21]

The record of the Supreme Court was vulnerable to similar criticism. . . . [T]here was deep public resentment of the Court's unwillingness to sit anywhere but in Fredericton — a refusal which was criticized regularly in the press for being self-serving and detrimental to the public interest. John Saunders provided another insight into the Court when he applied for the chief justiceship in 1808. Although he was the most junior member of the Court, Saunders maintained that he should be preferred over his colleagues because the other judges were all too ill or too feeble to perform their duties.[22]

At the level of the House of Assembly, the Loyalist leaders' professed standards for public service also proved difficult to maintain in practice. Although members of the Loyalist gentry stood for election to the first Assembly, the duties were apparently so arduous and inconvenient that they declined to run again. As a result, the qualifications of the members dropped sharply, and it soon became apparent that many members sought Assembly seats only in order to get their hands on some ready cash. This, of course, was completely inconsistent with the Loyalists' ideals of public service. An anonymous letter writer was shocked in 1795 to find "That men destitute of Talents, without even the advantage of a common School Education, should aspire to a Trust of this Nature. . . . " And Edward Winslow as well lamented that "Our gentlemen have all become potato farmers — & our Shoemakers are preparing to legislate." Yet it was clear that this deterioration in the public service was due as much to the withdrawal of the gentlemen as it was to the ambition of the shoemakers.[23]

291

* * *

How can the Loyalist leaders' high standards of public service be reconciled with these obvious lapses? In the first place, it should be stressed that the Loyalist leaders regarded nepotism and plural officeholding as legitimate rewards for public service, rather than as corrupt practices. Thus Edward Winslow fought vigorously to retain his office of surrogate general after he was named to the Supreme Court on the grounds that both Mr. Cushing and Mr. Hutchinson had held the two posts simultaneously in colonial Massachusetts. Likewise, Jonathan Odell considered it part of his parental duty to facilitate the entry of his son — and many of his friends' sons — into the public service, and he simply ignored criticism to the contrary. In the second place, it can be said that the failures of the Loyalist leaders to live up to their own standards of public service were due much more to human frailty than to any lack of commitment on their part. The burdens of increasing age afflicted them all. And many had to bear heavy financial burdens as well. Edward Winslow, for example, never extricated himself from the debts he had accumulated during the American Revolution. His frantic office-seeking was, therefore, amply justified in his own eyes by the demands of his creditors and the needs of his large family.[24] Joshua Upham was nearly as badly off. In fact, both men died heavily in debt. And the New Brunswick House of Assembly, in a wholly unprecedented action, made substantial grants of money to the distressed families in recognition of the many meritorious services the two men had contributed to the province.[25] Even those who brought capital to New Brunswick found it difficult to live up to their own personal standards. Ward Chipman, who had made money during the Revolution and who received a substantial fee for his work as the British agent to the Boundary Commission, confessed in 1804 that he never dreamed life in New Brunswick would be so arduous and so unrewarding. "If I could have anticipated that so little advantage and emolument would have been reaped from a continuance in it, I should most certainly have quitted it many years ago, for after toiling here nearly twenty years, I find my circumstances in no degree bettered, and am now not only without an income sufficient to support me tho living in the most frugal manner consistent with a decent appearance, but have no prospect of any alterations for the better."[26]

292

* * *

Whatever their failure in performance, the Loyalist leaders never gave up their ideal of creating a respectable society in New Brunswick. When Gabriel Ludlow succeeded to the presidency of the province after Carleton's departure, he recommended to the Assembly that a heavy tax should be placed on rum, so as to raise the moral fibre of the community. Similarly, when Ward Chipman was raised to the Council Board in 1806, he viewed his appointment as an opportunity to revitalize the original Loyalist standards. "I think there is an Augean Stable to be cleaned . . . as our lot is cast here, at least while it so remains, it behooves us all to make the community as respectable as we can."[27]

Religion

The efforts to root the Church of England in New Brunswick's soil exhibited the same combination of interest and ennui which characterized other Loyalist undertakings. All the Loyalist leaders were members of the established Church, and they were theoretically eager to see it flourish in the province. In addition to the religious succour it offered, the leadership regarded the Church as a primary agent for inculcating habits of respect and obedience, and they welcomed the well-educated Anglican ministers as cultural assets. They even hoped and worked for the appointment of a bishop of New Brunswick, who would help kindle religious devotion and who, by his mere presence, would add to the dignity of the province.[28]

Despite this high level of theoretical commitment, the Anglican Church was an ineffective institution in the early history of New Brunswick. Several factors contributed to its weakness, which can only be fully understood in terms of the specific spiritual environment of the province. Despite the Loyalists' efforts at cultivation and civilization, New Brunswick remained a rugged frontier area until well after 1815. The pockets of settlement were small in comparison with the vast stretches of forest and the large amounts of uncultivated wilderness. There was, of course, an abundance of natural resources which men could exploit. Yet long, harsh winters and the lack of any transportation system other than the rivers created a sense of isolation among the inhabitants. Whether they were engaged in fishing, farming, lumbering, or commerce, most of the people spent their lives in a lonely, physically exhausting struggle with this tough natural environment. And whether their efforts were ultimately successful or not, they all soon became acquainted with the particular perils posed by the northern wilderness. The dread effects of getting lost in wintertime or in the forest, the havoc which a sudden Spring freshet could cause, the destructive fury of the winds and the tides in the Bay of Fundy — such were the commonplace experiences of the people of New Brunswick. Given this intimate, awesome contact with the powers of the physical universe, many of these people sought in religion a form of solace or reassurance or justification that matched their brutal encounters with nature. These early New Brunswickers wanted religion to provide them with a spiritual experience which corresponded in intensity to the physical and emotional rigors of their daily lives, so that it could calm their fears and make their efforts meaningful.

293

The longing for a highly emotional form of religious worship was, of course, a familiar phenomenon in the various frontier communities of North America. Unfortunately, however, the Anglican Church in New Brunswick was singularly unsuited to meet the spiritual cravings of many in its supposed "flock." The personal qualifications of its ministers, its institutional arrangements, and its operating philosophy were scarcely adequate for the needs of the population at large. Its first ministers, for example, were the aged, infirm survivors of the American Revolution. Although often men of eminence, they were physically ill equipped to spread the Gospel in the wilderness. Many of them had spent the years between their exile from New York and their appointment to parishes in New Brunswick in a "destitute Situation," without financial support, and they tended as a result to be excessively concerned with salary matters and physically comfortable accommodations at the expense of their spiritual responsibilities.[29]

The organization of the Church in New Brunswick further tended to dissociate it from the general population. The Church of England was formally established by law in 1786. At the same time, religious toleration was extended to all dissenting Protestant sects, although both the Loyalist leadership and the British imperial government hoped the Church of England would become the primary religious force in the province. In support of this goal, the British government agreed to finance the construction of the first Anglican churches in New Brunswick and to pay the ministers' salaries during the initial settlement period. Britain clearly meant this financial aid to be only temporary, but in fact the Anglican clergy remained financially dependent on British grants until well after 1815. At first this aid was continued because both Governor Carleton and Bishop Charles Inglis convinced the government that the province was too poor to support the Church. Later, it remained a habit. Inglis himself grew increasingly acid in his complaints about the "backwardness of the people in contributing to their support . . . now when their circumstances have become easy and comfortable. . . . " Although this British aid unquestionably enabled the Church to develop physically at an accelerated rate, at the same time it tended to isolate the clergy psy-

chologically from the daily concerns of the New Brunswick population. The sense of community which might have sprung up from a common effort to build a church and support a minister did not develop among the members of the Church in New Brunswick. For example, in 1814, a year of high wartime inflation in New Brunswick, the vestry of the Anglican Church in Saint John wrote Inglis begging for financial assistance because their own funds were "so much embarrassed" that they would have difficulty paying the salary of their new minister and could by no means afford to support an assistant. Yet in the very next sentence of their letter, they admitted that both the Methodist and Baptist societies were expanding their congregations, and the Kirk of Scotland was building a new church in the city — all without outside aid. It was clear that the dissenting churches, which depended on their members for support and spoke to them out of a common frame of reference, were much more effective in stirring the zeal and devotion of the New Brunswickers.[30]

A final obstacle which tended to separate the Church from the people was the highly formal, materialistic policies of the Anglican hierarchy. The New Brunswick clergy was under the jurisdiction of two church authorities — Charles Inglis, the first Bishop of Nova Scotia, and William Morice, the British Secretary of the Society for the Propagation of the Gospel in Foreign Parts (S.P.G.). Both men were rigidly conservative in their outlook, distrustful particularly of innovation in matters of ritual, and prone to equate religious enthusiasm with fanaticism or (in the case of Inglis) republicanism. As a result, both Inglis and Morice sought to extend the influence of the Church through building programs rather than through the development of more meaningful rituals. During the first twenty years of the Church's activity in New Brunswick, primary attention was given to such matters as the erection of churches, the acquisition of glebe lands, the definition of the respective powers of the governor, the bishop, and the vestry in Church government, the establishment of proper Anglican rituals, and the assignment of pew spaces. In 1809, for example, Inglis was distressed to learn that the pews in the Church at Kingston, New Brunswick, were held in common rather than being assigned individually, and he severely reprimanded the local vestry:

> I never knew an instance before this, in Europe or America, where pews were thus held . . . and where men — perhaps of the worst character — might come and set themselves down by the most religious and respectable characters in the parish. This must ultimately produce disorder and confusion. . . . What could occasion such an innovation — such a departure from the usage of the Church of England I am unable to conceive.[31]

Such preoccupations were far removed from the needs of the population at large. Although there has not been sufficient study of religion in early New Brunswick to permit quantitative comparisons, it does appear that the Anglican Church drew its members from the more static elements in New Brunswick society: the official and propertied classes plus the more stable agricultural communities. A larger percentage of the population preferred the more humanitarian, meliorist approach to life and to God which the dissenting churches, particularly the Baptists and Methodists, offered. And a growing number turned for comfort to the highly emotional "New Light" preachers, who were not necessarily attached to any congregation or rule, and whom Inglis denounced in 1809 as "Fanatical Itinerant Preachers who obtrude themselves in every district. The People," he fulminated, " . . . are insensibly alienated from the national Church and its worship."[32] Col. Gubbins reached the same conclusions about the power of the sects and the "pernicious" nature of their doctrines:

> The most importantly mischievous of their tenets is that a thorough convert to their faith can never sin in what they call spirit. After this spiritual regeneration, the soul they affirm is no longer accountable for the actions of the body even though it was to violate every law of the Decalogue.

Or, as Gubbins, was to put it more humorously on another occasion, the New Light preachers held "that there is no sin in man below his heart."[33]

On the whole, the Loyalist leaders accepted the limited effectiveness of the Anglican Church with a curious indifference. Jonathan Odell was really the only member of the leadership group to take strong exception to the rising influence of evangelical religion in New Brunswick. Odell

295

was, of course, an ordained Anglican minister, and although he never held a clerical post in New Brunswick, he did feel compelled periodically to go into the pulpit and protest against "the self appointed teachers" who were leading the Christians of the province away "from the Voice of Truth and that ancient apostolical form of worship which remain in primitive purity in the National Church." Yet most of the Loyalist leaders were at heart good eighteenth-century gentlemen: philosophical in their own religious outlook and quite tolerant of dissent. Although they personally disdained the more extreme forms of religious enthusiasm, most would have agreed with Edward Winslow that no legal sanctions should be invoked against the itinerant preachers — because persecution would simply increase their popularity. Winslow himself condemned the itinerants as unscrupulous "harpies," but he felt that only time and the example of a correct, righteous clergy could redeem the common people from such extravagances.[34]

296

The lukewarm attitude of the Loyalist leaders was particularly evident in their policy regarding marriage. The only real privilege of the "established church" in New Brunswick was that its clergy had the exclusive right to perform the marriage ceremony, although justices of the peace were permitted to marry people according to the Anglican rite when no minister was available. This privilege was a definite grievance for many devout New Brunswickers, who resented the fact that they could not be married by their own ministers according to their own forms of worship. At virtually every session of the Assembly a bill would be passed enabling dissenting ministers to perform the marriage ceremony — a bill which the Council invariably rejected because it violated the royal instructions as well as the firm policy of Bishop Inglis. In 1795 resentment over the marriage restrictions ran so deep that James Glenie was able to get through the House a "Declaratory Act" which effectively disestablished the Anglican Church. The Loyalist leadership managed to patch over this highly divisive issue by means of a compromise which reflected their basic apathy. On the one hand, they regularly rejected the Assembly's attempts to invade the privileges of the established Church, and they never even suggested to the imperial government that some change in the marriage regulations would relieve a source of deep distress in New Brunswick. On the other hand, they made it known that they were willing to bend the law a bit in practice, by offering the more respectable dissenting ministers commissions as justices of the peace, which would at least enable them to marry according to the Anglican rite. For better or for worse, the Loyalist leaders were simply not zealots on religious matters. They would not impose their religious convictions on the general population, nor were they willing to wave the flag of religious liberty in order to serve these people more effectively.[35]

New England Company

The lack of religious zeal among the Loyalist leaders also contributed to the tragic failure of the New England Company in New Brunswick. The New England Company was an English missionary society, dedicated to converting the North American Indians to both the Christian religion and the more sedentary Christian way of life. It was founded in 1649, under the inspiration of the powerful Puritan missionary, John Eliot of Massachusetts, and until the American Revolution its work among the Indians was confined to the New England area. When the thirteen American colonies achieved their political independence, the British directors of the Company decided to transfer its operations to British territory so as to insure adequate control. Thus in 1786, the New England Company appeared, much like manna from heaven, on New Brunswick's doorstep. As might be expected, the provincial government was delighted to welcome such a well endowed, highly distinguished British charitable institution, and a blue-ribbon committee of Loyalist leaders was appointed to the local Board of Commissioners: Isaac Allen, George Ludlow, Jonathan Odell, George Leonard, Jonathan Bliss, Ward Chipman, John Coffin, and Edward Winslow.[36]

297

Despite this warm official reception, the Company's program for Indian education never really found a home in the hearts or plans of the New Brunswick population. Over the course of the next thirty years a series of educational experiments were undertaken in order to find some means of assimilating the Indians into the provincial way of life. Roving schools, consolidated schools, agricultural programs, apprentice systems were all tried and then discarded. In support of these endeavors, the Company expended over $140,000, and some of the Loyalist leaders — particularly George Leonard — also made generous contributions of time and money.[37] Yet the project was a failure from start to finish. When two S.P.G. missionaries inspected the Indian School at Sussex Vale during the 1820s, they were appalled to find that the few Indians enrolled in the program were being ruthlessly exploited by local white farmers and that a great deal of the Company's money was being used to educate white children. An unseemly amount was also being pocketed by the director of the school, the Rev. Oliver Arnold. Both missionaries recommended that the Company should close down its operations in New Brunswick, and this judgment was confirmed by the findings of the new governor of the province, Sir Howard Douglas.[38]

The reasons for the failure of this extensive effort to convert the Indians were many. Certainly the most fundamental problems arose from the Indians' deep distrust of Protestant missionaries and the equally strong hostility of the average white settler toward the native people. The Indians much preferred the ministrations of Roman Catholic priests, who were willing to learn their language and adapt themselves to the native way of life — instead of insisting that the Indians conform to the white pattern.[39] As for the attitude of the New Brunswickers in general, this was well expressed in a letter to the local Board of Commissioners urging them to use their funds to provide schools for white children rather than the Indians: " . . . as we are . . . poor families in this new settlement, low in Circumstances, unable to help one another — as much in need of the means of Useful Knowledge as the aboriginal Natives of these Provinces (For these are already . . . Converted to Roman Catholicism)."[40]

It has also been argued that the failure of the Company's efforts in New Brunswick was due in large measure to "the board's composition of prominent, rapacious American Loyalists," whose "indifference to the aims of the New England Company" was matched by "their superabundance of interest in its funds." The charge has some validity, particularly in the case of the superintendent of the school, John Coffin, who did divert Company funds to his own uses. Yet Coffin's behavior was censured by other Loyalist leaders, and the group as a whole was demonstrably scrupulous in handling Company money, as well as occasionally generous in their own contributions. The problem was not that the Loyalist leaders were "rapacious," but that they were "lukewarm" (to use Inglis's favorite pejorative). They did not merely lack the spiritual commitment of a John Eliot — they positively disdained that kind of religious zeal. The Loyalist leaders did, of course, have their own special missionary goal, which they pursued assiduously. This goal was to create a civilized, respectable society in New Brunswick. If the Indian population could be integrated into this society, well and good. But the Loyalist leaders were not willing to abandon their goal and accept the Indians' way of life simply because the New England Company decided to move to New Brunswick. Indeed Ward Chipman candidly told the S.P.G. missionary, John West, that the Indian schools had never worked effectively in New Brunswick and that, in his opinion, the only feasible way to civilize the Indians was to give them land in remote areas and then get missionaries to live among them and train them. It was clear, however, that none of the Loyalist leaders ever saw themselves performing such a task. The fact that they were willing to arrange for "a French royalist priest to come as a missionary to the Indians" while the New England Company was trying to counteract such Catholic influence demonstrates their very limited involvement in the proselytizing side of the Company's program. It seems dubious, therefore, to judge these men by Eliot's standards — when they did not share his ambitions. Surely the record of the Loyalist leaders can only be legitimately assessed in terms of their professed goals. It would seem much more meaningful, for example, to compare the efforts of Ward Chipman to establish a respectable legal profession in New Brunswick with Eliot's work among the Indians. In pursuing his objective, the Loyalist lawyer displayed an intensity, a personal dedication, and a certain self-righteous idealism that was reminiscent of the Puritan missionary.[41]

Black Loyalists

The treatment accorded the Black Loyalists by the New Brunswick leaders — and indeed by the overwhelming majority of white Loyalists — underlines even more dramatically the limits which historical circumstances placed on the Loyalists' social outlook. The Black Loyalists were the very special offspring of the American Revolution. They originally were slaves who had been encouraged by the British military to run away from their masters and enlist in the British Army in return for their personal freedom. During the war they had served in various paramilitary capacities, and at war's end nearly 3000 free Blacks were dispatched by Sir Guy Carleton to the Maritimes, including about 300 who eventually settled in New Brunswick. They had been promised equal treatment with the white Loyalists in terms of land grants, food, and provisions.[42]

Theoretically the Loyalist leaders should have felt some special sense of obligation towards these comrades in arms. Both the wartime commitments of the British government and the Loyalists' own Anglican faith and their aristocratic code of *noblesse oblige* should have produced a paternalistic, protective policy toward such peculiarly vulnerable members of their community. And indeed, in dealing with the similarly placed Acadian population, Governor Carleton and his Loyalist Council proved admirably sensitive to the religious and material needs of a defenceless minority.[43] With the Black Loyalists, however, the case was quite the reverse.

The problem was, of course, the Black's historic position as slaves. The Loyalists had known them in this status in the American colonies and had brought over 500 Black slaves with them to New Brunswick. A majority of the Loyalist Council were themselves slaveowners: Edward Winslow, Isaac Allen, Joshua Upham, Jonathan Odell, Beverley Robinson, Jr., and both Gabriel C. and George Duncan Ludlow. As well, at least two ministers of the established Church, Odell and Rev. James Scovil, owned slaves, and the local newspapers carried frequent advertisements announcing slave auctions or seeking runaways.[44]

Given this clear acceptance by most white Loyalists of slavery and of the Black man as an inferior being, destined to serve whites, discriminatory treatment of the free Black Loyalists was probably inevitable. At no time were these Loyalists treated as gallant comrades in arms. Instead they were given smaller land grants, fewer provisions, and subjected to conditions not demanded of their white counterparts. In the

299

political sphere, they were not eligible to vote for representatives in the House of Assembly, or to enjoy the important privileges of freedom of the City of Saint John, or to fish in the Saint John River. Even in the religious sphere, while they were welcomed as members of the Anglican Church, they were assigned separate seating places. The Baptists too split off the Blacks into separate congregations. Only the Quakers and the Wesleyan Methodists accepted them fully as human beings.[45]

The Blacks of New Brunswick were, of course, profoundly discouraged by this kind of life. Not only was white discrimination the rule, but their own lack of inner resources drove them further into dependency and degradation. They had, after all, been born and raised in slavery. They were conditioned to accept dependence, to take direction, and look to others for necessities. Now they were suddenly expected to find the self-reliance and initiative systematically denied them for generations, to fend for themselves in a forbidding climate on wilderness lands. To have made this transition successfully, the Black Loyalists would have needed sustained special assistance from outside. Instead they got discrimination and commercial exploitation from a white community too preoccupied with its own problems of survival to lend anyone else a hand.

Many Blacks gave up. Some 200 completely lost faith in the promise of the New World and emigrated with British assistance to Sierra Leone, to begin their lives all over again on what they hoped would be more hospitable African soil.[46] Others formed their own separate Churches, where they received consolation from charismatic preachers like David George and Boston King, and baptised themselves exhuberantly in the Saint John River to the utter alarm of local authorities. George reported that on visits to Saint John and Fredericton, he was greeted by slaves "'so full of joy that they ran out from waiting at table on their masters, with knives and forks in their hands, to meet me at the water side.'"[47] Others retreated into the bottle, to dull the pain of their existence with New Brunswick's ubiquitous rum. Virtually all who remained slipped into a state of semi-dependency as servants or day labourers. This status would remain their fate long after slavery disappeared from New Brunswick.

Among the New Brunswick leadership, only Ward Chipman was conspicuous for his efforts to improve the condition of these people. In 1800 Chipman volunteered his services to the slave Nancy in order to test the legality of slavery in the New Brunswick Supreme Court. The Court's verdict was inconclusive but Chipman's action did induce several slaveholders to manumit their charges voluntarily. This trend continued until the New Brunswick government could report to Whitehall in 1822 that slavery no longer existed in the province. In part this rapid disappearance of slavery was inspired by the humanitarian impulses emanating from the Abolitionist movement in Great Britain, but in large part it must be attributed to the economy and topography of New Brunswick, which did not lend itself to large-scale, slave-based agriculture. Great Britain sent a new group of some 3000 Black refugees to New Brunswick in 1815. Chipman again took up their cause and sought to locate them "within a convenient distance from the city for them to carry home the earnings of their labour at such seasons as they find useful employment here." By this time, the importance of giving Blacks viable economic circumstances and preventing their becoming a "nuisance" was recognized by the Loyalist establishment.[48]

Among the Churches, only the local Quaker congregation in Beaver Harbor rejected slavery on principle, although in England such philanthropic groups as the Associates of Dr. Bray and the Wesleyan Methodists made practical efforts to raise Black levels of literacy. One school financed by the Associates of Dr. Bray was operated in Fredericton from 1798 to 1814 by the Rev. George Pidgeon, an Anglican. It proved discouraging work according to Pidgeon. For although the Blacks were "'exceedingly importunate'" to get the school, afterwards they proved "'negligent and indifferent'" about actually attending and applying themselves.[49]

301

* * *

The history of the Blacks and the Indians in New Brunswick was poignantly sad. It also seems intractable. Every modern historian who has studied the problem has absolved the Loyalist leadership of any violent prejudice, any conspiratorial purpose, any systematic exploitation. Rather their conclusions center on the deep-rooted nature of the cultural attitudes held by both the ethnic majority and the ethnic minorities, and the limited effectiveness of either political principles or religious ideals in counteracting them.[50] The white Loyalists felt they were fighting for their political and cultural survival, and they demanded every member of their community should accept and assimilate their goals. For their part, the Blacks and Indians simply could not follow the white way or accept white goals. So they either dropped out entirely or became peripheral. The Loyalist record towards both Blacks and Indians, in fact, compares favorably with other communities in North America. Yet one feels certain that if any of the bewildered Blacks, Micmacs, or Maliseets had learned the King's English well enough to comment on the Loyalists' record of stewardship, they would have condemned it unequivocally.

Education

In contrast to their attitude toward religion, there was no ambivalence whatsoever among the Loyalist leaders concerning the importance of educational institutions in New Brunswick. The need to pass on to their children the benefits of their cultural heritage and to protect them from the unrefined impulses of the frontier was given the highest possible priority. The original educational programs of the Loyalist leaders were designed primarily "for their own children, the leaders to be," and the responsibility for educating "plain folk" was delegated to "the traditional agencies of the Church and private initiative." Thus the Loyalist leaders effectively pursued a class policy in the educational area and worked to establish institutions which would serve the needs of the governing elite, rather than trying to develop a more comprehensive program which would benefit the entire population. Very soon after their arrival in New Brunswick, the Loyalist leaders tried to set up grammar schools, libraries, and even a college — academic institutions which would provide the necessary background for a professional or managerial career. No comparable effort was made on behalf of popular education. In fact, in 1793, the Council blocked the only early attempt by the House of Assembly to establish a parish school system.[51]

302   This narrow, exclusive educational policy was doubtless forced upon the Loyalist leaders by financial necessity. The letters of Charles Inglis demonstrate that the governing elite was quite sympathetic to the desire of "many poor families" to educate their children, and they hoped the S.P.G. would provide the necessary funds. The ability of the province itself to support any educational endeavor was, however, extremely limited, and the government leaders reserved the funds available for the education of the children of the more respectable classes. Even so, the minimal effort undertaken could not be sustained by the public purse. A high tuition fee and funds from the New England Company were needed to supplement the provincial grants, and the Loyalist leaders also tried, though without success, to get the imperial government to support their educational efforts. When the province's financial resources began to improve after the turn of the century, a local school system was begun — with the full support of the Council. In subsequent years, this system was extended as rapidly as public funds permitted. It would seem, therefore, that although the early educational efforts of the Loyalist leaders were definitely self-serving, they were more the product of necessity than of choice.[52]

The actual educational institutions established in New Brunswick before 1815 were few in number and inferior in quality. Although the Loyalist leaders aspired to a much better system, New Brunswick was simply too young, too remote, and too poor to meet their standards. As early as 1785, the Council approved a charter for a provincial college, but the British government declined to grant the necessary articles of incorporation. This refusal reflected British uncertainty as to how best to provide for higher education in the colonies — given the obvious limits of local support. Finally, in 1790, the Pitt government informed Governor Carleton that the King had decided to endow a college in Nova Scotia, which would serve students from all the North American colonies, and that in addition a fund would be set up at Oxford and Cambridge "for the maintenance of a certain Number of Young men, being natives of His North American Dominions. . . . " The scholarship fund was never actually established, so that in effect this policy decreed that New Brunswick was not to have her own college, but was to use King's College in Nova Scotia to educate her sons. In an eloquent letter describing the importance of a college to the New Brunswick Loyalists, Carleton pleaded with the British government to reconsider this decision:

> The inhabitants of this province are, with very few exceptions, in circumstances that cannot afford the expences of an Education at a distance from home; Yet many of the inhabitants have themselves had liberal Educations and covet the like advantages for their children; and it would be a great consolation to them to see this Institution cherished and encouraged by Government. . . . It would also be to them a pleasing proof that, in this respect, no preference has been given to the Elder province of Nova Scotia.[53]

303

Despite Carleton's strong advocacy, the British government was not willing to underwrite a second college in North America, and the New Brunswickers were forced to fend for themselves. A grammar school in Fredericton was the most they were able to establish before 1800. The council granted this "provincial seminary" a tract of 6000 acres, which produced a rental income of about £100 a year. The Assembly also made one grant of £100 to the school in 1792, but it specifically refused Governor Carleton's request to establish an annual allowance for the school, on the grounds that the revenues of "this infant province" were still too unstable to permit such long-term commitments. Tuition fees were another source of income for the school. Yet it evidently still had difficulty meeting its expenses, for in 1798 the Trustees of the Fredericton Academy "'found it necessary to annex the duties of Indian Missionary to the appointment of their president, of whose Salary a considerable part was paid by the Commissioners for Indian Schools. . . . '"[54] In 1800 this Academy was granted a provincial charter of incorporation as the College of New Brunswick. As the economic fortunes of the province improved, the House of Assembly was able to grant an annual allowance to this college, beginning with £100 per annum in 1805 and increasing periodically thereafter. Nonetheless, the college continued to be plagued by financial problems and the difficulty of inducing competent professors and administrators (who were required by the charter to be members of the Anglican Church) to accept appointments at this remote, frontier institution. It was not until 1828 that the college granted its first two degrees — a full forty-three years after the Loyalist leaders had begun their efforts to establish higher education in New Brunswick.[55]

The Loyalist leaders were truly distressed by the difficulties they encountered in trying to establish a respectable college in New Brunswick.

Although many sent their own children out of the province to complete their schooling, this did not lessen the desire of the leadership for good local educational institutions. George Leonard was a particularly active supporter of this cause. After it became clear that Great Britain would do nothing for education in New Brunswick, Leonard tried to persuade some private English philanthropists to become patrons of the Academy and to endow a provincial library. He feared, he confessed to Chipman, that unless such facilities soon became available, "the girls" would have no choice but to marry the "Common peasantry of the Country." When his English friends failed to provide any support, Leonard became despondent about the prospects for New Brunswick: "I begin to think that [Jonathan] Bliss is right respecting my madness about formal education in New Brunswick . . . and that it is more sense to give the Superiority to the women, leaving the rising tribe of men to be fools." Despite their profound commitment, the Loyalist leaders were unable to establish more than the rudiments of an educational system during their lifetime.[56]

Fathers and Sons

The narrow range of opportunities which New Brunswick offered to men of talent proved particularly frustrating to the Loyalist leaders as they contemplated the future of their sons. Loyalist life in New Brunswick centered around strong, affectionate family relations, and as the Loyalist leaders were forced to accept the limited possibilities of their own careers, they often transferred their ambitions to their sons. Considering the education offered by the college at Fredericton inadequate, many of them sent their sons out of the province for higher learning. Most of the boys went to King's College in Nova Scotia, although some fathers reached higher: Chipman and Upham sent their sons to Harvard, William Botsford, Jr., went to Yale, and the eldest Winslow boy and both Saunders children received their education in England. In addition, at least three Loyalist leaders — Ward Chipman, Munson Jarvis, and John Saunders — enabled their sons to read law at the English Inns of Court.

Even more difficult than the problem of education was the decision regarding a career. Perhaps New Brunswick offered a comfortable, peaceful area for the average settler, but was it good enough for the sons of the Loyalist leaders? Some, like Jonathan Odell and George Leonard, thought it was, and they proceeded to use every ounce of their political influence to insure that their sons would inherit their offices.[57] But many thought not. Jonathan Bliss, who never altered his opinion that New Brunswick was a "wretched country," trained one son to practice law in Nova Scotia, where he ultimately sat on the Supreme Court, and sent the other to England, where he became the New Brunswick agent. Winslow encouraged two of his boys to join the British Army and a third to pursue a merchant career with the East India Company.[58] Sometimes the young men made the choice for themselves. Gabriel V. Ludlow and Jonathan and Stephen Sewell all studied law under Ward Chipman and considered a New Brunswick career. But a short period of practice led to the acute observation (*circa* 1795) that all the profitable offices and clients in the province were taken up by the original Loyalist leaders, men still comparatively young in years, and that it would be decades before the second generation could expect to fill their shoes. Thus Ludlow took off for New York and the Sewell boys for their unusually distinguished careers in Lower Canada.[59]

Perhaps the two most revealing instances of father-son relationships among the Loyalist leaders occurred in the cases of Ward Chipman and John Saunders. Both men had but one son, and each had tender feelings for his heir. Chipman, the less affluent of the two, sent his son to grammar school in New England and then to Harvard College with the help of his brother-in-law, the wealthy merchant William Gray. Ward Chipman, Jr., proved to be such an outstanding student that he was asked to deliver the "English Oration" at his Commencement exercises, and his proud father informed Edward Winslow that "the great lawyer Sam Dexter pronounced it 'the best performance for matter & manner that he had ever heard in Cambridge.'" William Gray agreed that his nephew was a most impressive young man, and he offered either to take him into his merchant firm or to finance his legal education in the United States. But Chipman was adamant that his son should seek a career within the British empire, and Gray's largesse apparently did not extend to an English education.[60]

305

Since his own family could not afford to send him abroad for study, Ward, Jr., returned to New Brunswick after finishing Harvard and read law under his father's direction. While he pursued his studies, the elder Chipman wrote to such old Loyalist friends as Chief Justice Sampson Salter Blowers of Nova Scotia and Jonathan Sewell, Jr., then attorney general of Lower Canada, in order to ascertain the state of the legal profession in their provinces. "I see but little prospect," Chipman informed Blowers, "of his having sufficient business for his support in this Province in which I have so unprofitably sacrificed so great a part of my life. . . . I most certainly should prefer his living where I may have the best chance of sometimes seeing him and most frequently and easily hearing from him."[61]

After much deliberation, Chipman decided in 1808 to send his son to Quebec to begin his career under Sewell's guardianship. Although Chipman regarded Sewell "as dear to me as a Son or brother," the prospect of parting permanently with their only child filled both parents with intense agony. "Indeed," Chipman wrote, "when I think of his leaving me my heart fails me, but these feelings I must subdue and endeavour to reconcile his mother to the event. . . . " As the time of leave-taking drew near, Chipman declared that it was "one of the severest trials I have ever experienced. . . . But on the other hand when I consider how cruelly my own time has been sacrificed and the prime of my life thrown away in a place, where to this hour I am not able to obtain sufficient to *support me*, I start at the thought of being hereafter upbraided by him, for subjecting him to scenes of similar mortification if I should detain him here." In a final, desperate act of parental love, the Chipmans actively considered moving with their son to Montreal, and they begged Sewell for precise information on the cost of living in that city and the prospect of the elder Chipman's obtaining an official post there.[62]

One can only imagine the joy which filled the Chipman household when suddenly at this dark moment in their family life, Ward Chipman, Sr., was appointed to the Supreme Court of New Brunswick. The appointment opened up an entirely new, incomparably brighter prospect. For it meant that Ward, Sr., would have a secure, salaried post for the first time in his entire career, that Ward, Jr., could take over his father's law practice, and that money could be laid aside for further education. In 1810, enough had been saved to send young Ward to the Middle Temple. He spent three years there, rubbing off, as he informed his uncle William Ward, "a little of the college rust." Although he claimed to fear that "my fond father is probably expecting a second *Lord Mansfield*," the young man returned to New Brunswick with obvious joy. In succeeding years, he would chart the same course of public service which his father had pursued: recorder of the city of Saint John, solicitor general, attorney general, member of the Council, agent to the Boundary Commission, and Supreme Court justice. In 1834 Ward Chipman, Jr., was named Chief Justice of the New Brunswick Supreme Court, and two years later Harvard gave an honorary Doctor of Laws to its distinguished son. Unfortunately for the province, the Chipman tradition came to an end with his death in 1851, for Ward, Jr., was childless. Both father and son established in New Brunswick a record of public service that was marked by unusually high professional qualifications and a deep, sustained interest in the welfare of the province.[63]

Whereas the Chipmans found money to be the prime obstacle to their freedom of choice, John Saunders almost lost the company of his son through too lavish an education. John Simcoe Saunders was sent as a young lad to "one of the best public schools in England," according to his grandfather, James Chalmers. His classmates were the sons of "Admirals, Generals and Dignataries of Church & state," and his education included, in addition to the traditional academic subjects, instruction in dancing and fencing. He then went to Oxford and, after taking his degree in 1815, informed his father that he wished to study law under a special pleader in London. Although John Saunders had deliberately given his son this first-class English education, he had always intended that the young man should eventually return to New Brunswick

306

to practice law and manage the baronial estate he was trying to develop north of Fredericton. For young Saunders, however, the thought of returning to New Brunswick after living for ten years among the English upper classes was repugnant: "I can never bring down my own mind to the narrow sphere of prejudice and ignorance to which everyone there must accommodate himself . . . the society of New Brunswick is quite insulated. . . . Indeed after the exertions I have made I could never submit [to] lavish them on the woods & 'desert air.'"[64]

In fact, the younger Saunders was "astonished" that his father expected him to return to New Brunswick. "For I have always turned my thoughts either to the East or West Indies — Canada or Nova Scotia or the English bar; never allowing myself for a moment to degrade my prospect by thinking of the possibility of throwing away my views in life by practising in such a miserable place as New Brunswick." To drive his point home, the young man then compared his father's career with that of Jonathan Sewell, Jr., who was by then chief justice of the province of Lower Canada:

307

> At the time of your appointment to the [New Brunswick] bench Sewall set out a needy adventurer for the Canadian bar with a few shillings in his pocket and a few introductions to different gentlemen in Quebec. At that time you set out too — superior in talents, education, experience, friends & resources — but how wide is the difference at this moment — he after an active career retires to the highest post of honor with more than two thousand a year — you with four hundred & fifty still obliged to "bow the knee and bend the neck to Smyth" [the Lieutenant Governor of New Brunswick].[65]

The elder Saunders could be just as determined as his son, and the young man was apparently forced to come home because his father refused to underwrite his life in England any longer. From 1816 until 1822, young Saunders practiced law in New Brunswick, but it was not a happy experience, and he yearned to return to England and continue his legal studies. His father found it difficult to understand his son's feelings, for the elder Saunders himself frankly preferred "to be of some importance in the society where I might live." But rather than see his son unhappy, Saunders finally capitulated in 1823 and agreed to help the young man establish himself at the English Bar. He had concluded, in a moment of excruciating candor, that it was "through my want of judgment you were placed where you acquired habits perhaps impossible for you to overcome." Over the next six years, John Simcoe Saunders studied at Lincoln's Inn, was admitted to the English Bar, clerked under the distinguished London lawyer, Joseph Chitty, married an English bride, and published a legal text on "Pleading and Evidence" which would go through several editions. His father, true to his word, gave his son every possible support in these ventures. He not only supplied young Saunders with an annual income of £400, but offered to sell off part of the lands at his beloved "Barony" in order to provide him with a marriage settlement. He also informed him that he would be willing to resign his post as Chief Justice of New Brunswick in favor of his son — if this appeared desirable.[66]

Despite this solid parental support, young Saunders terminated his English career in 1830, and returned to New Brunswick where, like Ward Chipman, Jr., he became one of the government's most distinguished leaders. Although he never achieved his ambition to become chief justice of the province, he did hold many important posts, including provincial secretary, member of both the Executive and the Legislative Councils, surveyor general, and president of the Executive Council. The records do not reveal whether this second generation of Loyalist leaders (like their fathers) found that their early hopes and ambitions cast a shadow over the sense of fulfillment they derived from their service to the province.

308

* * *

The Loyalist leaders were determined to develop in New Brunswick a style of life which would make their province "the envy of the American states" and an "asylum of loyalty" within the empire. Yet these internal goals represent only one half of the challenge facing these pioneer community builders. Always confronting them from the outside was the unfolding example of the new republic to the south and the unpredictable, almost equally uncontrollable policies of the imperial politicians in London. To understand fully the challenge and accomplishment of New Brunswick under the Loyalist leadership, it is necessary to look at its external relations, both material and ideological, with the two great powers which impinged on its destiny.

NOTES

[1] Winslow to Chipman, 7 January 1784, Lawrence Collection of Chipman Papers, *Public Archives of Canada*.
[2] James Hannay, "The Loyalists," *The New England Magazine*, New Series, vol. 4, no. 3, 297–315; Diary of Bishop Charles Inglis, entries for 20 July 1792 and 9 August 1792, Inglis Papers, *Public Archives of Nova Scotia*, Charles Turner, "New Brunswick in 1802," in William O. Raymond, ed., *Acadiensis* 7 (1907): 132; Patrick Campbell, *Travels in the Interior Inhabited Parts of North America in the Years 1791 and 1792*, 40–42, 252; Jonathan Bliss to Benedict Arnold, 3 December 1798, Benedict Arnold Papers, *New Brunswick Museum*.
[3] Winslow to Wentworth, 27 November 1784,, Winslow Papers, *University of New Brunswick*. Charles Turner, "New Brunswick in 1802," 135.
[4] Howard Temperley, ed., *Gubbins' New Brunswick Journals 1811 and 1813* (Fredericton, 1980), 60.
[5] "New Brunswick," *Royal Gazette*, 26 August 1800; "Hull's Invasion," *Royal Gazette*, 21 September 1812; "St. Andrews," *Royal Gazette*, 30 October 1799; "Saint John," *Saint John Gazette*, 14 December 1798.
[6] "St. John," *Royal Gazette*, 24 June 1794.
[7] Chipman to Jonathan Sewell, Jr., 15 July 1794, Sewell Papers, *Public Archives of Canada*; Eliza Gray to Ward Chipman, n.d. [*circa* 1794], Chipman Papers.
[8] "New Brunswick . . . American Politics," *Royal Gazette*, 17 February 1801. George A. Rawlyk describes the remarkable congruence of political views held by the New England Federalists and the New Brunswick leaders in "The Federalist–Loyalist Alliance in New Brunswick, 1784–1815," *Humanities Association Review* 27 (1976): 147. Rawlyk's information is illuminating, although I find the New Brunswick leaders less arbitrary and conspiratorial than he (142–46).

9 "New York. Further Translations from the 'History of Crimes committed during the French Revolution,'" *Saint John Gazette*, 10 November 1797; "Important Documents," *Royal Gazette*, 30 July 1799.

10 Wallace Brown, "William cobbett in the Maritimes," *Dalhousie Review* 56 (1976-77): 452; Temperley, *Gubbins' Journals*, 84.

11 "Porcupine's Farewell to the People of the United States," *Royal Gazette*, 10 June 1800; Odell to Chipman, 20 March 1800, Chipman Papers.

12 Odell to Chipman, 10 May 1802, Papers of Jonathan Odell, *New Brunswick Museum*; Odell to Chipman, 8 November 1804, Lawrence Collection. Jonathan Odell, "The Agonizing Dilemma," in Thomas B. Vincent, ed., *Narrative Verse Satire in Maritime Canada, 1799-1814* (Ottawa, 1978), 173-86. For a description of the interest in lexicography shared by Odell and Boucher, see Anne Y. Zimmer, *Jonathan Boucher, Loyalist in Exile* (Detroit, 1978), 313-26.

13 The two most complete pieces written by Winslow were: (1) a satirical play written during the 1795 election, recently reprinted as Condon, "New Brunswick's First Political Play" and (2) the newspaper series by "Tammany" which he published in the *Royal Gazette* during 1802 to satirize the Loyalist half-pay officers who were returning to the United States (see Ch. 9 [in Condon, *The Envy of the American States*]). In addition his letters were filled with the vivid metaphors and similes which he fashioned to entertain his friends.

14 Turner, "New Brunswick in 1802," 131; Winslow to Daniel Lyman, 12 March 1800, Winslow Papers.

15 George Leonard to Ward Chipman, 11 March 1795, Chipman Papers; "Vth Letter of Alfred," *Saint John Gazette*, 16 October 1805.

16 Winslow to Lutwyche, 4 March 1800, Winslow Papers.

17 George Leonard to John King, 29 March 1799, C.O. 188/10; Carleton to Hobart, 21 June 1802, C.O. 188/11; Lutwyche to Winslow, 17 May 1800, Winslow Papers; Hobart to Carleton, 6 March 1802, C.O. 189/1; Winslow to James Fraser, 12 October 1806, Winslow Papers.

18 Lutwyche to Winslow, 5 January 1807, Winslow Papers; Thomas Carleton to John Saunders, 6 July 1809, Saunders Papers, *University of New Brunswick*; Chipman to Jonathan Sewell, Jr., 28 October 1808, Sewell Correspondence; Winslow to Lutwyche, 12 October 1806, Winslow Papers.

19 Carleton to Sydney, 5 December 1787, C.O. 188/4; Beverley Robinson, Sr., to Beverley Robinson, Jr., 15 March 1790, Robinson Papers, *New Brunswick Museum*.

20 Winslow to Jonathan Sewell, Jr., 14 January 1797, Sewell Papers.

21 Chipman to Lord Bathurst, 9 September 1823, C.O. 189/1.

22 Draft of letter, John Saunders to [Thomas Carleton], n.d., [*circa* 1808], Saunders Papers.

23 "To the FREEHOLDERS of the PROVINCE OF NEW BRUNSWICK," from "A Friend to the Province," 21 August 1795, *Saint John Gazette*.

24 Winslow to Chief Justice Ludlow, 22 July 1807, Winslow Papers.

25 *Journal of the House of Assembly* 2: 58 and 88.

26 Chipman to Stephen Kemble, 26 March 1806, Lawrence Collection of Chipman Papers.

27 *Journal of the House of Assembly* 2: 99 (30 January 1807); Chipman to Winslow, 29 July 1806, Winslow Papers.

28 George Leonard to Jonathan Odell, 24 October 1794, Papers relating to Church Matters (NBM); John S. Moir, *The Church in the British Era: From the British Conquest to Confederation* (Toronto, 1972), 22-23.

29 Rev. Samuel Cooke to Rev. Jacob Bailey, 6 May 1786, Papers of Jacob Bailey, *Public Archives of Nova Scotia*.

30 Inglis to William Morice, 25 August 1804, Inglis Papers; "W.S." and "A.T.," Church Wardens to Bishop Inglis, 24 May 1784, Chipman Papers.

31 Judith Fingard, *The Anglican Design in Loyalist Nova Scotia, 1783-1816* (London, 1972), 27-38, 182-83; Walter Bates, *Kingston and the Loyalists of the 'Spring Fleet'*, W.O. Raymond, ed. (Saint John, 1889), 17.

32 Samuel D. Clark, *Church and Sect in Canada* (Toronto, 1948), ch. 2; Goldwin French, *Parsons and Politics: The Role of the Methodists in Upper Canada and the Maritimes* (Toronto, 1962), 32-39; Inglis to Sir George Prevost; 22 June 1809, Inglis Papers. Lively sympathetic accounts of early Baptist congregations are in articles by George A. Rawlyk and Esther Clark Wright in Barry Moody, ed., *Repent and Believe: The Baptist Experience in Maritime Canada* (Hantsport, N.S., 1980), 1-26, 66-74. See also Thomas William Acheson, "Denominationalism in a Loyalist County: A Social History of Charlotte County, 1763-1940" (Unpublished M.A. thesis, UNB, 1964), 3-4, 16-17, 25, 29-31.

33 Temperley, *Gubbins' Journals*, 15-16, 83, 17.

34 Jonathan Odell, Sermon Preached in Fredericton, 9 August and 10 September, 1801, Odell Papers; Undated remarks of Edward Winslow on the Old Inhabitants and Itinerant Preachers [c. 1803], Winslow Papers, vol. 18.

35 Carleton to Inglis, 9 March 1791, Papers relating to Church Matters; "A Bill Declaratory of What Acts of Parliament are binding in this Province," C.O. 188/6; Hugh Mackay to Robert Watson, 26 April, 1803, Winslow Papers. Moir, *Church in the British Era*, 25.

36 William Kellaway, *The New England Company, 1649-1776* (London, 1961), 280; "Petition of the Company for the Propagation of the Gospel in New England and Parts Adjacent in North America," C.O. 188/2.

37 Leslie Francis S. Upton, *Micmacs and Colonists: Indian-White Relations in the Maritimes 1713-1867* (Vancouver, 1979) 160-63; Judith Fingard, "The New England Company and the New Brunswick

Indians, 1786-1826: A Comment on the Colonial Perversion of British Benevolence," *Acadiensis* 1 (Spring 1972): 28-43.

[38] "Report to New England Company by the Reverend Walter Bromley," 22 September 1822, Lawrence Collection; Report of John West on the Indian Academy at Sussex Vale to the New England Company, 20 September 1826, Lawrence Collection; Sir Howard Douglas to William Vaughan, 13 December 1824, Lawrence Collection.

[39] Upton, *Micmacs and Colonists*, xv, 101, 155-59.

[40] George Gillmore to George Leonard & Board, 22 January 1789, Lawrence Collection.

[41] Fingard, "The New England Company," 41; Extract of a letter from Governor Carleton to Henry Dundas, 14 June 1794, Papers of the New Brunswick House of Assembly. Col. Gubbins was as despairing as Chipman: "The Indians are so fond of a wandering life that I know of only one instance where an individual was weaned from it. (*Gubbins' Journals*, 11). The destructive impact of Loyalist culture on the Micmac way of life is described in Upton, *Micmacs and Colonists*, 127-41.

[42] Robin Winks, *The Blacks in Canada: A History* (Montreal, 1971), 29-31; William A. Spray, *The Blacks in New Brunswick* (Fredericton, 1972), 31.

[43] See Ch. 5 [in Condon, *The Envy of the American States*]. For a description of the contented, law-abiding state of the Acadians under Loyalist rule, see Temperley, *Gubbins' Journals*, 21-22, 72-74.

[44] Winks, *Blacks in Canada*, 44; Spray, *Blacks in New Brunswick*, 16-17, 20-21.

[45] James W. St. Gême Walker, *The Black Loyalists: The Search for a Promised Land in Nova Scotia and Sierra Leone, 1783-1870* (New York, 1976), 67-72.

[46] Winks, *Blacks in Canada*, 44; Walker, *Black Loyalists*, Ch. 5 ff.

[47] Walker, *Black Loyalists*, 71-79.

[48] Spray, *Blacks in New Brunswick*, 24; Chipman to William F. Odell, 2 November 1816, Lawrence Collection of Chipman Papers.

[49] Spray, *Blacks in New Brunswick*, 53; Winks, *Blacks in Canada*, 59.

[50] For examples, see Walker, *Black Loyalists*, 39, 45-46.

[51] Katherine B. MacNaughton, *The Development of the Theory and Practice of Education in New Brunswick, 1784-1900* (Fredericton, 1947), 41-42.

[52] Inglis to Dr. Morice, 28 September 1798, Inglis Papers.

[53] William Wyndham Grenville to Carleton, 3 June 1790, C.O. 188/4; Carleton to Grenville, 9 March 1793, Thomas Carleton Papers, *Public Archives of Canada*.

[54] Carleton to Grenville, 20 August 1790, C.O. 188/4; *Journal of the House of Assembly* 1:288; Inglis to Jonathan Odell, 18 October 1798, Papers relating to Church Matters.

[55] Carleton to Portland, 4 August 1800, C.O. 188/10; MacNaughton, *History of Education in New Brunswick*, 52; Thomas J. Condon, "Similar Origins: Effects of Isolation on the Early Development of the University of New Brunswick and Harvard University," *Atlantic Advocate* 55 (May 1965): 35-41.

[56] Leonard to Chipman, 28 October 1794, 6 November 1794, 13 November 1794, Hazen Collection of Chipman Papers, *New Brunswick Museum*.

[57] Memorial of Jonathan Odell to Lord Castlereagh, 5 September 1808, C.O. 188/14; George Leonard to J. Chapman in Lord Camden's Office, 30 November 1804, C.O. 188/12.

[58] Jonathan Bliss to Benedict Arnold, 12 July 1796, Benedict Arnold Papers (NBM); Joseph W. Lawrence, *The Judges of New Brunswick and Their Times* (Saint John, 1907), 180-84.

[59] Jonathan Sewell, Jr., successfully occupied every legal post in Lower Canada, until his career was capped by his appointment as Chief Justice of the Provincial Supreme Court in 1808. His brother Stephen confined himself mainly to private practice in Montreal, although he did serve for a brief period as Solicitor General of Lower Canada.

[60] Chipman to Winslow, 24 November 1804 and 5 October 1805, Winslow Papers; Chipman to Jonathan Sewell, Jr., 18 July 1800, Sewell Correspondence.

[61] Chipman to Blowers, 6 August 1808, Chipman Papers; Chipman to Jonathan Sewell, Jr., 16 November 1805, Sewell Correspondence.

[62] Chipman to Jonathan Sewell, Jr., 8 July 1808 and 28 October 1808, Sewell Correspondence.

[63] Ward Chipman, Jr., to William Ward, 1 August 1813, Thomas W. Ward Papers, *Massachusetts Historical Society*, Box No. 1; Lawrence, *Judges of New Brunswick*, 301-38.

[64] James Chalmers to John Saunders, 4 June 1806, Saunders Papers; G.H. Storie to John Saunders, 16 June 1815, Saunders Papers; John Simcoe Saunders to John Saunders, 4 September 1815, Saunders Papers.

[65] John Simcoe Saunders to John Saunders, 4 November 1814, Saunders Papers.

[66] John Saunders to his son, 27 June 1828 and 14 September 1824, Saunders Papers; Lawrence, *Judges of New Brunswick* 274-75.

Topic Nine

The Rebellions of 1837/1838 in Lower Canada

The rebellions in Lower Canada followed a long period of constitutional strife. The appointed Executive and Legislative Councils were almost exclusively English-speaking, while the Assembly was almost entirely French-speaking. In 1837 Louis-Joseph Papineau, an articulate bilingual lawyer, led a number of the Lower Canadian reformers into open rebellion against the entrenched Conservative elite who retained control of the provincial revenue.

After the first rebellions's failure in 1837 the British government sent Lord Durham to Canada to investigate the causes of the uprising. He issued his *Report* in late 1838, just after the suppression of the smaller uprising of that same year. To the joy of the Reformers, Durham recommended that responsible government be granted; henceforth the Executive Council and the upper house (the Legislative Council) were to be responsible to the elected Assembly. But he made a second recommendation that, for the Reformers of Lower Canada, initially negated the first. He proposed a union of the Canadas, for the purpose of assimilating the French Canadians. Gerald Craig places the *Report* and its famous author in their historical context in the following introduction to his abridgment of the document.

Britain, while rejecting Durham's recommendation of responsible government, favoured that of union and the assimilation of the French Canadians. In the proposed union the Colonial Office ruled that English would be the only official language and that Upper Canada (which still had a smaller population despite its faster growth rate) would obtain the same number of seats as Lower Canada. It was hoped that the Upper Canadian members would ally with the English-speaking members from Lower Canada (by 1840 the English-speaking minority constituted about twenty-five percent of Lower Canada's population) against the French Canadians.

In his short contribution, "The Insurrections," from *Canada: Unity in Diversity*, Fernand Ouellet introduces the economic as well as the political factors that contributed to the Rebellions of 1837/38. Elinor Kyte Senior adds the military dimension to the discussion of the revolutionaries' defeat in "Suppressing Rebellion in Lower Canada: British Military Policy and Practice, 1837–38."

Fernand Ouellet's *Lower Canada, 1791–1840* (Toronto: McClelland and Stewart, 1980) is essential for any understanding of the Lower Canadian rebellion. Helen Taft Manning's *The Revolt of French Canada, 1800–1835* (Toronto: Macmillan, 1962), an older study, covers the constitutional struggle. A popular account is Joseph Schull's *Rebellion* (Toronto: Macmillan, 1971). Ramsay Cook has edited a valuable collection of essays on the background to the rebellion, entitled *Constitutionalism and Nationalism in Lower Canada* (Toronto: University of Toronto Press, 1969). For the agricultural situation in the 1830s see R.M. McInnis, "A Reconsideration of the State of Agriculture in Lower Canada in the First Half of the Nineteenth Century," *Canadian Papers in Rural History*, ed. Donald H. Akenson, vol. 3 (1982), 9–49. In *Les Rebellions de Canada 1837–1838* (Montréal: Editions du Boréal Express, 1983), historian Jean-Paul Bernard includes a summary of the various interpretations of the Lower Canadian uprisings. Parallel developments in Upper Canada are reviewed by Colin Read in *The Rebellion of 1837 in Upper Canada*, Canadian Historical Association, Historical Booklet no. 46 (Ottawa: CHA, 1988).

312

For the impact of the rebellions see Jacques Monet, *The Last Cannon Shot: A Study of French-Canadian Nationalism, 1837–1850* (Toronto: University of Toronto Press, 1969), and Maurice Séguin, *L'idée d'indépendance au Québec: Génèse et historique* (Trois-Rivières: Le Boréal Express Limitée, 1968). Chester New's *Lord Durham's Mission to Canada* (Toronto: McClelland and Stewart, 1963; first published in 1929) continues to be useful. For an overview of subsequent developments in the 1840s, see J.M.S. Careless, *The Union of the Canadas: The Growth of Canadian Institutions, 1841–1857* (Toronto: McClelland and Stewart, 1967).

Lord Durham's Report*

GERALD M. CRAIG

Introduction

Lord Durham's *Report* has come to occupy such a central place in the history of the Commonwealth of Nations that no apology is needed for making it readily available to students and readers, both inside and outside the schools and universities. Indeed, so much praise has been showered on the famous *Report* that it may come as a surprise to some to learn that when it appeared, it was widely regarded as a partisan, opin-

*From the introduction to *Lord Durham's Report*, ed. Gerald M. Craig, published by McClelland and Stewart Limited, 1963. Reprinted by permission of the Estate of Gerald Craig.

ionated, and inaccurate document and that even now, after the smoke of contemporary controversy has long since lifted, we can easily find glaring weaknesses of fact and argument in this noted and notorious state paper. Nevertheless, it is true that no attempt to debunk or to deflate the great *Report* would be very successful. Despite all its shortcomings and defects it remains one of the most vigorous and perceptive expositions of the principles and practice of free government in the history of the English-speaking peoples.

Thus the *Report* has come to have a significance and a relevance that far transcend the circumstances of its immediate origins. Yet, if we are to understand both the strong and the weak features of the document we must look back, however briefly, to those circumstances, for Lord Durham was not only uttering a testament of his political faith that he thought to be universally valid; he was also prescribing for a particular political problem.

That problem existed in the two provinces of Upper and Lower Canada, and much more ominously and immediately in the latter, where the legislative assembly had been suspended following the outbreak of rebellion in 1837. This rebellion, which had a much less serious counterpart in Upper Canada, had in turn been only the last episode in a prolonged and increasingly acrimonious political conflict, a conflict that had seen the governor or lieutenant-governor and the appointed executive and legislative councils arrayed against the elected legislative assembly. In the upper province the conflict had been intermittent, since the assembly had as often been controlled by men in general sympathy with the government as by the opposition, and that had been especially true of the year or so before the rebellion. Moreover, that uprising had received support from only a fraction of the opposition. In the lower province, however, the confrontation had been turbulent and persistent: for more than fifteen years before 1837 a determined party of French-Canadian nationalists, joined by a few English-speaking associates, had controlled the Assembly and had announced their intention of controlling the whole government. The British government had sought to deflect these nationalists, led by Louis Joseph Papineau, from their purpose by following a policy of concession and conciliation, and had then abruptly replaced this policy with a tougher one in the spring of 1837. The upshot was the outbreak of a formidable uprising in the following November, which shook Lower Canada to its foundations and helped bring on the much smaller rising in the upper province.

These rebellions also shook the already wobbly Melbourne ministry in the mother country, and forced it to give Canadian affairs much more attention than they usually received. Lord Melbourne's answer to insistent demands that something be done about the Canadas was to renew his plea to Lord Durham to take on the government of these colonies and to make recommendations about their future. Although he had re-

313

fused this offer in the previous summer, Lord Durham now felt that the crisis left him no choice but to accept, especially since his commission would give him unprecedented powers and authority to meet his heavy responsibilities. He gathered his staff about him and reached Quebec at the end of May 1838.

Melbourne had turned to Durham because he needed a man of the front rank for the post, and Durham was easily the most important British political figure — often thought of as a possible prime minister — who had ever come out to Canada. Born in 1792 of one of the oldest and richest families in the north of England, John George Lambton from the start of his parliamentary career took his stand with the advanced Whigs, and had close ties with the Radicals. In 1830 "Radical Jack," who had become Baron Durham in 1828, entered the cabinet of his father-in-law, Lord Grey, and was at once in the thick of the fight for the Reform Bill. Indeed, he was its most pressing advocate in the government and shared with Lord John Russell the principal responsibility for drafting the measure. In 1833, however, ill-health forced this intense and ambitious man to resign from the cabinet, at which time he received an earldom. Two years later, he went to Russia as British ambassador, but a frail constitution again cut short his service.

The Melbourne government viewed Durham's return to England in 1837 with much trepidation. That government normally depended on the votes of a bloc of Radical members to maintain its precarious hold on office, yet the Radicals were both dissatisfied with Melbourne's failure to push for further reform and deeply alienated by the tough policy toward Lower Canada of the spring of 1837. If Durham joined the Radicals, and gave them a lead, the Whigs would almost certainly be turned out. Hence, it was essential for Melbourne to make overtures toward Durham. Yet the urbane and easy-going Melbourne shuddered at the thought of a cabinet colleague of such humourless intensity and so violent a temper. Thus Melbourne's urgent appeal to Durham, which would force the Radicals to hold their fire, arose much more out of the needs of British domestic politics than out of a concern to find the right man for Canada, although it happened to do just that.

The qualities that made Durham an uncomfortable colleague also made him an imperious governor who was quite prepared to stretch his already large powers. This aspect of his personality was revealed in many ways but most importantly in his decision to pardon the bulk of the prisoners accused of complicity in the rebellion, and to banish a few of the most serious offenders to Bermuda. There were sound political reasons for this decision, but it contained one or two legal flaws; in particular, Durham's commission did not extend to Bermuda. This flaw gave Durham's political opponents at home a stick with which to smite him, and they were quick to use it, especially Lord Brougham, once a close friend and now a bitter enemy. The din raised by the latter caused the Prime Minister to run for cover. Durham's ordinance was disallowed. To the Governor General in Canada this action made a mockery of Melbourne's promises of firm support and it came also as a vote of no-confidence. Durham decided at once that he had no choice but to resign, and after being in Canada just over five months he went home at the beginning of November. If communications had been faster his stay would presumably have been shorter. Contrary to the hopes and fears of many leading political figures, Durham made no effort to topple the Melbourne government upon his return. Instead, he and his staff devoted themselves without rest to the preparation of the *Report*, which was ready at the end of January 1839.

It was the crisis in Lower Canada, above all, that had brought Lord Durham across the Atlantic, and in his *Report* it was to this crisis that he turned at once after a brief introduction. His analysis of the problem was both trenchant and provocative. Before leaving home, he asserted, he had assumed that the contest was between a popular body contending for free government and an executive government upholding the Crown's prerogative. Instead, he found "two nations warring in the bosom of a single state . . . a struggle, not of principles, but of races," and he then proceeded upon a lengthy discussion of the "deadly animosity that now separates the inhabitants of Lower Canada into the hostile divisions of French and English." He found the French Canadians to be at fault at almost every turn. To be sure, they had certain amiable personal qualities; but as a people they were backward and illiterate, clinging to outworn customs and institutions, unresponsive to the progressive tendencies of the age, and easy victims of the irresponsible demagogues who sprouted in their midst. Their leaders used control of the Assembly, not for valid ends, but to protect French-Canadian nationality "against the progressive intrusion of the English race." By contrast, the English minority was forward-looking and practical in outlook, concerned to advance the material development of the province, and understandably exasperated by French-Canadian opposition to all progressive measures. This exasperation had reached an intense stage with the outbreak of rebellion. Any solution for Lower Canada must take account of the determination of the English minority never again to tolerate French-Canadian control of the Assembly.

After his lengthy discussion of Lower Canada, which takes up nearly half the text of the *Report*, Lord Durham moved on to consider the condition of Upper Canada. Here there was no racial animosity as in the lower province, yet there was a rebellion to be explained, even though it had been a small one. In his treatment of Upper Canada, Lord Durham was at a considerable disadvantage, for he had been in the province for only eleven days, mainly at Niagara Falls. Nevertheless, he had no doubt about the prime cause of the political discontent that had been visible there for many years. It lay in a defective constitutional system that

315

lodged irresponsible power in the hands of a small group of the lieutenant-governor's advisers, who were "linked together not only by common party interests, but by personalities." This "family compact" had a monopoly of offices, and it really ruled the province, for the lieutenant-governor usually yielded to it. Such a monopoly of power inevitably created an opposition, but this opposition, known as the reformers, discovered that even when they won a majority of the seats in the Assembly they could not implement their program. Hence the reformers, with a "practical good sense" that contrasted favourably with "the less prudent course of the French majority in the Assembly of Lower Canada," called for a change of constitutional practice that would make the executive council responsible to the Assembly. But the existing political discontent was greatly, and unnecessarily, heightened by the partisan administration of Sir Francis Bond Head, thus opening the way for the plot that led to rebellion.

316

The *Report*, after briefly examining affairs in the Atlantic provinces, proceeds to a thorough analysis of problems relating to land policy and immigration. Since this section reflected the views of a member of the staff, Edward Gibbon Wakefield, rather than of Lord Durham, and since the recommendations flowing from it were not acted upon, it might be argued that it could be omitted from an abridged edition of the *Report*. It has, in fact, been very considerably shortened in the text that follows, but many perceptive passages on the social and economic development of the provinces have been included.

Finally, after this lengthy discussion and analysis, Lord Durham came to his summing up and to his recommendations. British North America was afflicted with an "ill-contrived constitutional system" and suffered from "practical mismanagement" of its affairs at every turn. It was a condition that should not, and could not, continue; extensive and decisive measures were urgently needed. Urgency derived partly from the ingrained animosity of the races in Lower Canada, and partly from the proximity of the provinces to the United States. This latter factor was one to which reference is made on many pages of the *Report* and which affected its whole tone and direction. The English-speaking population of the provinces was acutely conscious of the material progress being made in the neighbouring states; unless they could see the prospect of an effective attack being made upon their own political and economic problems, they could not be expected to retain their British loyalty for an indefinite period. If things went on as they were, they might well find the American attraction too powerful to resist. As yet, however, their attachment to British allegiance continued to be strong, and there was still time for a solution that would bind them more closely to the mother country.

The solution was readily at hand — and here we come to the heart of Lord Durham's recommendations, and the reason for the enduring value of his *Report*. Like so many great ideas, it was extremely simple, not very original, indeed almost obvious. It lay in permitting the full and free operation of British institutions in the colonies, as at home. It lay in a constitutional reform that would establish "the foundation of an efficient and popular government, ensure harmony, in place of collision, between the various powers of the State, and bring the influence of a vigorous public opinion to bear on every detail of public opinion." Once this reform were made, colonial authorities could attack the many practical and concrete abuses and grievances; there was no need for Lord Durham or any other outsider to prescribe for these. In short, he argued that the British government must give up to the colonies the full authority to conduct their own internal affairs, and that it must be prepared to see those affairs administered by men in whom the representatives of the colonial electorate had confidence. Thus he argued for what has since become known as "responsible government," the cabinet system that was already in operation in Great Britain. In the colonies this principle would mean that the governor must draw his executive advisers from men who had the confidence of the majority in the Assembly, that he must be prepared to change his advisers when they lost the confidence of this majority, and that as long as they retained this confidence he must carry on the government, in all internal matters, according to their advice, despite differing views that he or the British government might have. If this principle were not accepted, wrote Durham, the colonies would surely be lost; if it were, their connection with the mother country would be permanent, and beneficial to both.

317

Responsible government was the dynamic idea in the *Report*, but it must not be forgotten how severely the idea was qualified by Lord Durham. It would apply to what he called internal legislation, and he would withhold only those matters that concerned the relations of the colonies with the mother country. These matters, he asserted, were very few: "the constitution of the form of government, — the regulation of foreign relations, and of trade with the mother country, the other British Colonies, and foreign nations, — and the disposal of the public lands." But these reserved areas, while only four in number, made up about three-quarters of the possible subjects for colonial legislation, and represented a more severe restriction on colonial legislative jurisdiction than the British government had been prepared to exact earlier in the decade. The grant of colonial self-government that Durham was prepared to make in 1839 was wholly genuine, but it was also extremely limited in scope. The limitations are not hard to explain. A broader grant of legislative competence would never have been accepted by the British government and parliament at this time. Nor would Durham have been in favour of it. As an ardent imperialist, he was concerned to avoid decentralization in the exercise of these vital legislative powers. Yet there is no reason to think that he would not have welcomed a gradual devolution as colonial legislatures and governments became more competent and more experienced under the schooling that responsible government would bring.

A second qualification was more fundamental, and more far-reaching in its implications and consequences. It was that the grant of responsible government could be made only to a legislature with an English-speaking majority. (Sometimes he spoke of the "English race," but apparently he considered it possible for other people to join this race, if English became their first language and if they became thoroughly imbued with an "English character.") Lord Durham has often been called a prophet of the modern Commonwealth, and with some reason; nevertheless, there is no warrant in his own utterances for believing that he would have favoured the grant of self-government to peoples who were not of British stock or who had not been thoroughly assimilated to British ways and institutions.

318

More particularly, of course, Lord Durham was not prepared to grant self-government to a legislature with a French-speaking majority. In the last section of the *Report* he continued and intensified the criticisms of the French Canadians that had marked the opening section on Lower Canada. This people was hopelessly inferior, and was doomed to be engulfed by the superior force and intelligence of the English-speaking majority in North America. Everything must be done to discourage the French Canadians from persisting in their "idle and narrow notion of a petty and visionary nationality." Any plan for the constitutional reform of the Canadian provinces must have imbedded in it the certainty that the French Canadians would be given an English character, that they would be amalgamated to the dominant race in North America. It should be noted that, according to his lights, Lord Durham did not seek to anglify the French Canadians out of harsh or vindictive motives. Considering the power and vigour of the English-speaking majority in North America, he did not believe that the French Canadians would ever be able to live on a level of equality with them. The French Canadians could not beat the majority; therefore, they should join it.

This line of reasoning led to the conclusion that the French Canadians must be subordinated to an English-speaking majority, in order that the process of assimilation and amalgamation might begin. This, in turn, meant intercolonial union. Lord Durham's strongest preference, for which he still had high hopes until he left Canada, was for a legislative union comprising the Canadas and the Maritime provinces, a union that would provide a very substantial English-speaking majority. But the Maritimes showed no enthusiasm for entering such a union, and Lord Durham realized that their consent would be gained, if at all, only after long and difficult negotiations. Yet the renewal of rebellion in Lower Canada in November 1838, as Durham returned home, showed the need for haste. Hence, the recommendation for union, as embodied in the *Report*, was for joining the two Canadas, leaving open the possibility of a broader legislative union at some time in the future. Dual union, although not an ideal answer, could be accomplished quickly and it would provide a working English-speaking majority, assuming that the English-speaking members all stuck together.

Responsible government and legislative union were the two outstanding recommendations in the *Report*, and they are the only two that can be reviewed in this brief introduction. But the reader of the text that follows will find that the *Report* contains many more striking and provocative observations and proposals on such matters as legislative procedure and administrative and judicial reform, municipal government, and the future relations of Canada and the United States. The passages on these and other subjects have helped to make the *Report* a document of enduring value and interest.

As was mentioned at the beginning, the *Report* was received by Lord Durham's contemporaries with more reservations than acclaim. Some doubted that it was his *Report* at all, and ascribed the bulk, if not all of it, to his staff, especially Wakefield and Charles Buller. (On this matter, see Chester New's biography of Lord Durham.) The same critics usually disliked its style; Lord Brougham said it read like a second-rate article in the *Edinburgh Review*; and it is true that it contained undiplomatic language that was needlessly offending, although this feature has enhanced its readability. Some Radicals were antagonized by the strictures on the French Canadians, while tories were incensed by criticisms of the Church of England's claims to the Clergy Reserves and by many other features of the *Report*. The Whig government, speaking through Lord John Russell, could not accept the doctrine of responsible government as set forth by Durham, although it was prepared to make certain piecemeal changes in colonial political practices. It did unite the two Canadas, although not in quite the form that Durham recommended, and it did adopt one or two of his practical and concrete suggestions.

The text of the *Report* reached Canada in the spring of 1839, and was soon widely reprinted in the newspapers. Here, too, the note of criticism was loud, and even strident. In Lower Canada the French Canadians were, of course, outraged by the low estimate placed upon their civilization and by the plan for lifting them to the level of the English race. The English-speaking minority in that province viewed these passages as ordinary common sense, and strongly approved the recommendation for union, which, after all, had been their own program for many years; but they were aghast at the proposal for responsible government, which would weaken and perhaps destroy their own political power. In Upper Canada conservatives and tories searched the *Report* in vain for anything with which they could agree. Committees of the Legislative Council and Assembly each submitted the *Report* to a severe and often telling review, stressing that the section on Upper Canada was full of factual inaccuracies and biased history, that the union would involve the people of the upper province in the bitter disputes of the lower, and that responsible government would allow the French-speaking majority of the one province to combine with the radical minority of the other to ride rough-shod over the loyal people of both. Only the reformers of Upper Canada were genuinely enthusiastic about the *Report*, for it gave powerful endorsement to their own program, responsible government, and the *Report* thus became a mighty weapon to be used against their conservative and tory opponents.

To carry the story further would be to recount the history of Canada for the following decade. Lord Durham himself died in 1840, and so did not live to see many things work out differently from his own hopes and expectations. Above all, he did not foresee, as the tories of Upper Canada did, that the French Canadians would join with the English-speaking reformers in an organized political party. It was this party that demonstrated that there was no alternative to responsible government, if Canada was to be governed peacefully and constitutionally within the British Empire, but it did it in such a way — by bi-racial co-operation — as to preclude the slightest movement toward Durham's other objective, the anglifying of the French Canadians. Thus, from the perspective of our own times, the sections on the French Canadians appear to be the faultiest and the most misguided in the whole *Report* — the one great blot in an otherwise admirable and enlightened analysis. Durham failed to see that Canadian development would have to be in the other direction: toward mutual respect and tolerance, towards the building of a nation based on a dual culture.

This adverse judgement on a major segment of the *Report* is now clear and irreversible, but we should also be concerned to understand as well as to judge. We should realize that no man of Lord Durham's time, who was as caught up as he was in the on-rushing material and political progress of the English-speaking peoples of the British Empire and the United States, could be expected to sympathize with an allegiance to conservative and traditional values. We should also note that Lord Durham could not know as clearly in 1839 what we know today, that it is foolhardy and naïve to speak of breaking down the customs of a well-established and organized ethnic and cultural community; in the last century we have seen many such attempts fail that were much harsher and more determined than anything Lord Durham had in mind. Finally, many French Canadians of our own time would be the first to agree that in large part Lord Durham's strictures were as true as they were hard; in particular, that there was a need for more education and a more practical education. French-Canadian zeal in this matter may owe something to the dash of cold water in the *Report*.

If we turn to other aspects of the *Report*, it would not be hard to maintain the proposition that what was sound was not very new, and what was new was not very sound. The great proposal for responsible government was planted in Lord Durham's mind by Robert Baldwin, and it was an idea that was also well understood by reformers in Nova Scotia and New Brunswick. Durham's own refinement, the distinction between local and imperial matters, was of tactical value in 1839, but it was not very generous, and it began to break down almost at once. In particular, the whole elaborate scheme for imperial supervision of the public lands proved to be still-born. Finally, although Lord Durham had a remarkable vision of a British-American nationality, it was a rather near-sighted one that did not reach out to the prairies and the Pacific.

Any careful evaluation of Lord Durham's *Report* has to take account of these and other limitations, but it must also explain why it is still alive and not a musty and forgotten official document. On this score one may confidently allow the *Report* to speak for itself. Its vibrant and eloquent argument for the self-government of free men rises through all faulty insights and is as compelling and as vital today as when it first appeared.

321

The first official publication of Durham's *Report* was in the Parliamentary Papers for 1839 (the "blue books"), where the appendices and relevant dispatches were also printed. Portions of the text of the *Report* first saw the light of day in *The Times* of London and in several Canadian newspapers. The full text of the *Report* was also published in London, Toronto, and Montreal in 1839. These versions sufficed until the imperial revival led the Methuen publishing house of London to bring out a new edition, with an introductory note, in 1902, followed by a cheaper edition in 1905. Renewed interest in the *Report* culminated in the publication of an elaborate three-volume edition in 1912 (Oxford, Clarendon Press). Under the editorship of Sir Charles Lucas, the edition provided an introductory volume, the full text of the *Report* along with extensive explanatory notes, and a third volume of appendices and related dispatches. This remains the standard edition of the *Report*, and is still indispensable for a thorough study of the *Report*. In 1945 the Clarendon Press brought out an abridged version of the *Report*, with an extensive introduction by Sir Reginald Coupland. A French translation was published at Quebec in 1948, with an introduction and bibliography prepared by Marcel-Pierre Hamel.

Like Coupland's edition in its day, the purpose of the present edition is to make the enduring features of the *Report* available to the student and general reader at a modest price. This edition provides about three-quarters of the full text, and is somewhat fuller than Coupland's version, although the principles of selection are basically the same. In the main, the omitted portions consist of illustrative material and amplifying detail, and are indicated by the usual ellipses. The essential analysis of the state of the provinces, and the recommendations, are given in full.

The Insurrections*

FERNAND OUELLET

The Origins of the Rebellions

To understand fully the nature and real repercussions of the rebellions of 1837–1838, it is not sufficient simply to cite the reactions to Russell's Resolutions, any more than it is to emphasize the preceding political conflicts. It is just as important to take into consideration the economic, social, demographic, and psychological aspects of this revolutionary attempt, since it is impossible to believe that the rural population with its low level of education and its traditions could have been aware of the constitutional principles involved in the debate. They were not trying to promote a democratic society by their action. The reaction of the habitant sprang from sources more intimately connected with his everyday existence and his mental outlook.

Nor is it correct to assume that the insurrection was in the hands of isolated individuals, drawn at random from all social strata. Rather, it was the activating of certain social groups and the reacting of others against them. This indicates that a certain amount of cooperation was taking place among individuals working to transform society to conform to their common ideals. A knowledge of this social background is indispensable to the understanding of the events that ushered in the establishment of a new order.

THE ECONOMIC INSTABILITY

The economic trends taking form at the turn of the century were thrown into sharper relief after 1815. As the decline of the fur trade gathered momentum, the agricultural situation of Lower Canada was becoming more critical. The lower prices which had prevailed for so long accentuated the problems facing the inhabitants of Lower Canada. This economic crisis was not, however, universal. The development of the lumbering industry and the expansion of agriculture in Upper Canada, in spite of violent fluctuations, did a great deal to alleviate the existing problems. Nevertheless, the economic situation remained, on the whole, unfavourable.

The decline in wheat production, in spite of occasional increases, continued without interruption after the War of 1812. Surpluses for export became progressively smaller, until after 1832 the deficits became

*Chapter 19 from *Canada: Unity in Diversity*, ed. P.G. Cornell et al. Copyright 1967 by Holt, Rinehart and Winston of Canada, Limited. Reprinted by permission.

chronic. At this stage the consumer in Lower Canada was obliged to import a large part of the grain necessary for subsistence either from Upper Canada or from the United States. The decline could not be attributed to a lesser demand from foreign markets, for as time went on these demands increased. Nor was its main cause the epidemic of wheat rust, since this did not occur in full force until 1835. It was owing, rather, to the continuance of outmoded techniques which inevitably caused an exhaustion of the land; however, it has a much greater significance for it was an expression of the deep agricultural crisis existent in Lower Canada during these times.

This decisive turn of events resulted in the restriction of agricultural production until it was aimed at mere subsistence. The habitant, in order to feed himself, was obliged to increase the number of his cattle and swine and resort to replacement crops, such as the potato, that had no foreign outlets. Furthermore, the impoverished farmer found it more difficult to obtain textiles and wools imported from Great Britain, and therefore was forced to devote more attention to the raising of sheep and the production of linen. In concentrating his efforts in this direction the habitant, instead of participating in the internal markets, was rather obeying a defence mechanism which led him to assert his agricultural independence. This reaction explains why Lower Canada remained a heavy importer of dairy products and butchered meats during this period. Technical progress did not keep pace with the increase in the quantities produced. Thus, after 1832, when the crisis forced the agricultural producer to substitute commodities, he was inevitably forced to watch a reduction in animal husbandry.

323

The extent of the crisis became more apparent as 1837 approached; it plunged the peasantry into debt, imperilled patrimonies, and engendered rancour and discontent. Instead of looking for a remedy to his problems through technical improvements, the French-Canadian farmer was led to look outward for the responsibility for his misfortunes. The political elite, although occasionally rather patronizing toward the agricultural groups, did help the farmers to find scapegoats in the capitalist, the immigrant, the local government, and, before long, in the British Government as well — in a word, the *English*.

THE DECLINE IN PRICES

After 1815, the habitant was faced with further difficulties — a universal fall in prices. This fall was consistent in spite of several vacillations and had a profound effect on the regional economics. It accented the seriousness of a problem already critical. The peasants' revenue tended to fluctuate in direct proportion to the general price vacillations, as did the salaries of city workers and agricultural labourers. The pressure affected even the seigneurs who reacted to it by demanding more from their tenants. Neither the business classes, nor the liberal professions escaped it. Profits were directly threatened by the economic situation, and this forced the merchants to look for solutions to the problems.

THE NEW IMAGE OF THE SEIGNEURIAL SYSTEM

During these years the seigneurial system acquired an image that was considerably less benevolent than before. The idea of profit had by this time penetrated deep into this stratum of society and became more and more a motivating force. The seigneurs, whether they were businessmen, descendants of the older families, lawyers, or ecclesiastics, were sensitive to the implications of the new definition of property. Property was becoming more mobile and took on a more personalized and intrinsic character. The new outlook and behaviour of the seigneurs is partly explained by the economic situation.

324   The new practices were most pronounced in the seigneuries owned by merchants where disposable land was more abundant. With a view to increasing the value of landed property and seigneurial rights, the holders of seigneuries restrained the rate of land concession. Not having the right to sell unsettled or uncleared land, the seigneurs did it indirectly. They demanded a gratuity (*pot-de-fin*) from those inhabitants desirous of obtaining a concession; or even transferred parcels of land to friends, retrieved them for non-clearance, and then sold them afterward. If, in the older seigneuries, whose rates had been fixed at a time of rising prices, the proprietors confined themselves to exercising their rights, other seigneurs did not hesitate to raise the rates of *cens et rentes*. They also redoubled their own privileged rights in contracts and restored privileges that had fallen out of use, even going so far as to establish new rights. In addition, the surge in the lumbering business led all seigneurs, whatever their initial origin, to reserve the wood on their lands for themselves.

The seigneurial regime, which the merchants, even those who owned seigneuries, wished to abolish, became an increasingly heavy burden for the habitants. But the political upper castes were watchful. Fearing that the peasants would turn their aggressiveness upon this institution, which they considered as being of ultimate national value, the French-Canadian political leaders tried to divert the rural discontent against the English merchants, the habitant's main creditors. In this manner they hoped to preserve French Civil Law.

LUMBERING

The preferential tariffs promoted considerable expansion in the exploitation of the forests during this period by supporting two sectors of the economy: naval construction, with its centre in Quebec, and the export of lumber which spread most of its benefits in the same area. At such a difficult time, lumbering had a profound significance. Not only did it sustain an important section of the middle classes, but it provided a wage to a large portion of the population, both urban and rural. This business tended, therefore, to temper the shock produced by the agricultural crisis and the drop in prices and to lessen the effect of the seigneurs' reaction to these events. It is of note that the political and social conflicts did not degenerate into a general crisis until the time when lumbering began to follow the other industries down the road of decline. These recessions, especially in the lumbering industry, never lasted more than a year or two. It might also be said that, in the circumstances, the British regime had been saved by the lumbering industry.

DEMOGRAPHIC PRESSURE

Astonishing as it may seem, the rate of increase of the French-Canadian population remained the same during this entire period. It is evident (taking into account the economy at this period) that the population as a whole tended to become poorer year by year. The land not only produced less, but it became scarcer throughout the entire seigneurial region. By about 1820 the majority of the seigneuries were overpopulated or nearly so. The habitant was no longer able to settle his sons around him and felt that he was witnessing the dissolution of the family.

It was at this stage that the migrations began. Some of the emigrants were content to leave the seigneurie and move to the townships where they might settle near their former parishes. Others left their original localities and went further afield in search of land. A final group began to emigrate to the United States, a trend that continued and expanded during the nineteenth century.

The habitant had become, naturally enough, extremely sensitive to the problem of land. He felt limited in his natural expansion by the borders of the townships; and since he was frequently in debt, he feared he would lose the small portion of soil that was his basis of security. He held the government responsible for the scarcity of seigneurial land and reproached it for not converting the townships into seigneuries, and so giving him access to all the land in Lower Canada. He reproached the capitalists for their desire to possess land which he regarded as his right.

This hostility toward the capitalists and the State expressed itself most forcibly in the attitude toward the English immigrant. Immigration after 1815, instead of being a modest flow as before, became an actual tidal wave; and in the eyes of the rural French Canadian the immigrant was a competitor for land and employment; therefore, he represented a vital danger both to the rural population and to the inhabitants of the towns. The pressure of overpopulation, then, as it was experienced by the rural groups, promoted the racial conflicts to the same degree as the agricultural crisis.

SOCIAL ILLS

The social misunderstandings were not solely the product of economic conditions, but were caused as well by purely social factors that in themselves implied conflicts of ideals and interest. The economic situation merely threw into bold relief the ambitions of the different groups composing the society.

Obviously the economic problem preoccupied the merchant classes most. The decline in the cultivation of wheat in Lower Canada affected the business groups, who tried to revive its traffic by encouraging the clearance of new lands. The merchants, therefore, attached considerable importance to the development of Upper Canada. Having lost all hope of a renewal of agriculture in the lower province, these merchants looked to the immigrants as the only future hope for economic improvement. But the drop in prices and the distances between the centres of production necessitated a lowering in transportation costs; especially at a time when the Erie Canal, finished in 1825, had strengthened American competition to the point where it was seriously threatening the leadership of Montreal.

The building of a road network the length of Lower Canada and the system of canals on the Saint Lawrence constituted the two essential measures needed to revive the economy of the two Canadas. These improvements were impossible to attain without government support and the cooperation of the French-Canadian members in the legislative assembly; for they implied a new concept in public finance and a reassessment of tax responsibility. In addition, the support of Upper Canada was of the essence in this mutually beneficial project.

It was not enough to agree to these reforms and organize credit. Since foreign competition was so strong, it was essential to firmly unite the efforts of the two provinces against the English free-trade movement that was battling with increasing success against the tariffs protecting Canadian wood and lumber on the English market. Finally, for economic and social reasons, the mercantile middle class demanded the dissolution of the institutions that were the basis of the old social regime, namely the *Coutume de Paris* and the seigneurial system. They were, however, content with an extensive revision of these structures. The proposed program encountered the determined resistance of the liberal professions and a large part of the French-Canadian rural population. In their discouragement, the merchant interests became more and more aggressive, and finally demanded, both in Canada and in London, the union of the two Canadas.

THE LIBERAL PROFESSIONS

The influence of the liberal professions, especially the French-Canadian elements, deteriorated during this period, partly as a result of economic difficulties. However, the excessive multiplication of professional practitioners as a result of the growth of the classical colleges was another aspect of the problem. The professional men were living for the most part in hardship, and therefore, tended to place a high value on the security of former times and to share the fears of the rural population.

The professional men came, more and more, to identify their own future with that of the French Canadians. Their mistrust of the merchant classes and the objectives they advocated became more extreme. They felt that the French-Canadian nation was disappearing as a result of the prevailing circumstances and the aims of the Anglo-Saxon group. The lumbering industry and the fur trade seemed opposed to their interests for they supported their political and social adversary. Their reaction was the same toward the banks and the preferential tariffs which the professional men saw as a gross attack upon individual liberty. The efforts of the merchants to modify the *Coutume de Paris* and to abolish the seigneurial system were regarded as aimed at depriving the French-Canadian nation of the institutions essential to the support of the social structure and its upper classes. The proposals to revamp the transportation system were regarded as the logical concomitants of this general program to undermine French-Canadian institutions. They believed that its only possible objective was to flood Lower Canada with English immigrants in order to achieve union of the two Canadas, and thereby to drown the French Canadians in an Anglo-Saxon sea. The aggressive attitude of the more militant-minded British simply seemed to confirm them in their convictions. Above all, they feared the domination of large capitalists, Anglo-Saxon for the most part, upon whom a mass of salaried workers would be forced to depend.

327

Goaded by these fears and by their class ambitions, the professional men intensified their efforts to attain a greater control of the political structure, since it was at this level they believed that they might succeed in solving their own problems and those of the nation. Of course there were many who refused to look at the situation in such a tragic light, and believed in policies founded on moderation and a spirit of compromise.

But the most influential factions moved deliberately toward intransigence and radicalism. An unstable rural population exerted an additional pressure on the decisions of the professionals.

THE CLERGY

The clergy did not remain unaffected by the trends that became evident after the turn of the nineteenth century. They were temporarily disconcerted by the rapidity of the changes, and did not hesitate in their reaction. The actions of the Anglican bishop, the State intervention in education, and the attraction of the new liberal ideas upon the upper-class laity contributed to the rise of new problems. Under Mgr. Plessis, the reaction of the clergy went no further than an opposition to new innovations. In addition, the clergy was deeply divided over the proposed establishing of a new episcopate at Montreal. But the founding of new classical colleges and schools, supervised by the curates, demonstrates that the episcopate had become aware of the need for positive action.

It was under Mgr. Lartigue that the counter-offensive of the clergy really began. Mgr. Lartigue, the first bishop of Montreal, a cousin of Papineau and a former lawyer, did not have the same prejudices as his predecessors toward nationalism. What he deplored most about this new ideology was its association with liberalism, that flower of the French Revolution. But once the idea of brotherhood had been excised, nationalism might well serve to build up a society respectful of tradition and, perhaps, even theocratic in nature. Mgr. Lartigue had been educated under the influence of the French theocratic school of De Maistre, De Bonald, and Lammenais, a school directly opposed to the Gallican school of which Mgr. Plessis was an advocate. Thus his hostility toward the French Revolution and to liberal and democratic ideas was even more pronounced.

Mgr. Lartigue was not content to confine his efforts to waging a fierce and desperate war against revolutionary ideas and their advocates, but worked diligently to restore the moral and temporal influence of the Church and to make the clergy the accepted dominant class. In struggling against the Royal Institution and the legislative assembly's scheme for public schools he hoped to restore the exclusive jurisdiction of the Church over education. He felt that education on all levels (primary, secondary, and university) was solely the responsibility of the Church. Mgr. Lartigue, in addition to planning a religious revival in the population, worked to extend the social radius of the Church. The counter-offensive begun in these years carried on during the course of the nineteenth century.

Thus, relations between the liberal professions, especially those elements of it engaged in the political struggle, and the clergy had become increasingly strained. The attitude of Mgr. Lartigue during the rebellions of 1837–1838 stemmed from these social and ideological controversies. Moreover the clerical influence had not been strong enough to prevent the *patriote* movement from exerting a large measure of influence over the rural population.

The Principal Actors

The critical economic situation, the pressures of overpopulation, and a society in which racial delineations tended to coincide with class boundaries, together formed the stage upon which the political drama was to unfold. The aims and policies of the emergent political parties remained consistent with the circumstances of the particular sectors of society from which they arose. It would be wrong, however, to underestimate the influence of the individual personalities in the foreground; for instance, the personalities and attitudes of the governors influenced public affairs according to their support of one group or another. Historians have frequently been misled by contemporary caricatures of the governors engaged in the conflicts of that time. "Francophile" or "Anglophile" were the most common descriptions, and these often obscured the real issues and occasionally led to errors in diagnosing causes.

Among the outstanding personalities, none stands out more clearly than Louis-Joseph Papineau, who was born in 1786 and was educated at the Quebec Seminary. His father was a notary who had been politically active since the establishment of parliamentary institutions. After leaving the Seminary the young Papineau decided to become a notary; dissatisfied by his studies there, he shortly thereafter chose law, which he also disliked. In 1818, he bought the seigneurie of Petite-Nation from his father. He would have liked very much to live there but his wife objected, and although he was attracted by the charm and solitude of country life, he was too much in need of an audience to enjoy himself fully in the country. In 1809, he entered politics which seemed to bring him the outlet he needed.

In reality, Papineau did not especially like politics. He constantly complained that he was engaged in a combat he was not suited for; and moreover, attributed his continuing this way of life to a sense of patriotic duty and an ardent desire to rescue his countrymen from the ills that threatened them. However he rationalized it, it is true that Papineau was not cut out for political life; he was a visionary and intransigent, and was disposed to take upon himself the perils threatening the French-Canadian group and to assume the ambitions and interests of the liberal professions.

At the outset of his career, he did not belong to the extremist wing of the *Parti Canadien,* but among the moderates; and when the question of a successor for Pierre Bédard and Antoine Panet arose, Papineau was the only deputy to finally poll the majority of his party's votes. It was only after 1818 that he adopted his extreme attitudes. He gradually became the natural leader of the French Canadians whose hopes he claimed to represent. A reformer until 1830, he subsequently came to desire independence and to wish for the establishment of a French-Canadian republic, with himself as president. His ineptitude in practical action, which drove him to specialize in verbal action, was the source of his setbacks. Despite his deficiencies, Papineau was nonetheless the most outstanding personality of the period upon which he left his mark.

329

The Political Conflicts

All these factors were transposed to the political level, where the fluctuations followed those of the economy and the society. Two political parties, representing different social and ethnic groups were locked in combat. The *Parti Canadien* drew its support mainly from the rural sector of the population and was led by an elite drawn from the liberal professions; the merchants' party was supported by the capitalists and landed interests, and rallied the British and the affluent. Until 1830, the clergy and the old seigneurial families supported or disapproved, more or less openly, the one or the other of the two parties, depending on the circumstances.

On the political scene there were as many irreconcilable views and opposing political ideas as there were in the social sphere. Each group wished to control the political structure in order to promote its own exclusive views on economic and social matters. Under these conditions, the constitutional issues were not, in themselves, very significant. If the legislature demanded "ministerial responsibility" and the control of finances, it was simply because they saw in these innovations a way to allow the liberal professions to assume not only political leadership, but also the social leadership, which would permit them to promote their concept of the future of the French-Canadian people. Until 1830, the French-Canadian political leaders were convinced that the mother country was not ill-disposed toward them; but the moment they believed that the latter did not favour the abolition of what they called the "reign of the oligarchy," they took the road toward political independence and the inauguration of a republican regime modelled upon the American political design. The *Parti Canadien* which had become the *Patriote* party in 1826, was not truly democratic; but was dominated by a nationalistic ideology, and thought it could attain its reactionary objectives by means of democratic institutions. On the other hand the Bureaucratic party, formerly the merchants' party, in spite of its urge for innovation in economic and social affairs, took the opposite course, putting its faith in a reactionary defensive policy executed with a measure of realism.

After 1830, the political atmosphere deteriorated more and more until the conflict between the legislative assembly and the councils, and between the lower house and the governors became so sharp that any compromise became extremely difficult, if not impossible. Elections were not only stormy, but they frequently gave rise to organized violence. During this period, associations were formed which merely aggravated the feeling of anarchy that reigned everywhere. The cholera epidemics and the acuteness of the economic crisis complicated the situation, and with the Ninety-Two Resolutions passed in 1834, the turbulence reached a peak. The extremists of both camps spoke of taking up arms, with the result that the slightest incident threatened to unleash an insurrection. The stage for revolution was set in the spring of 1837, when Lord John

330

Russell presented to the Parliament in London a series of resolutions which constituted a total rejection of the demands of the *Patriotes*.

Russell's Resolutions rejected the *Patriotes'* demands for an elective legislative council and granted power to dispose of government funds without permission from the legislative assembly. The adoption of these Resolutions took place at the most inopportune moment. The agricultural crisis reached a new low; for the general crop failure, after several years of deficits that were more or less universal in the colony, had accentuated the discontent among the farmers. The recession in the lumbering industry and in naval construction, and the effects of a contemporary English financial crisis reached country and town at the same time. This critical situation added to the social instability and to the privations already suffered by the most underprivileged groups in society. On the political level, the atmosphere was even more strained as a result. The explosive nature of the Resolutions is understandable in this light.

A challenge had been presented to the *Patriotes*, which left them no alternative but to surrender or to take up arms. The first alternative was impossible in such troubled times; they could only turn to insurrection. It could not, however, be a spontaneous uprising, for practical preparations had to be made and some supplementary agitation undertaken to rouse the populace. Although the extremists in the *Patriote* party had wanted an armed confrontation ever since 1830, they had taken no practical steps in this direction.

331

The Pre-Revolutionary Period: April 1837 to November 1837

It is difficult to ascertain with any degree of certainty the *Patriotes'* decisions following the divulgence of the contents of Russell's Resolutions, since they took care to destroy any documents likely to appear compromising. It is, however, obvious that they followed a precise program, whose general outlines can be traced both in their actions and through various sources of information.

The *Patriotes* were not unanimous in their aims. Some believed that the English Government would never stop at the stand taken by Russell, and that the only realistic solution was to organize the revolutionary forces as soon as possible and throw them into action. Others, nursing their illusions, continued to believe that systematic agitation would be sufficient to force England to revise her policy, and that recourse to armed rebellion would be unnecessary. Finally the two groups, the former one led by Dr. W. Nelson and the latter by Papineau, seemed to have agreed on a single plan.

The plan included two distinct phases. The first was constitutional agitation which was either to lead to the backing down of England, or to pave the way for revolutionary action should the English authorities refuse to yield to pressure. The armed uprising was projected for the beginning of December. The so-called constitutional agitation occurred on three levels. Firstly, a series of large public meetings were held to stir up the populace in both the urban and rural areas. A boycott of regular imports and the use of smuggling was also prescribed with a view to combating the merchant classes. Thirdly, a show of force was to be prepared either by enlisting volunteers or some other means.

During the summer of 1837, the campaign waged by the *Patriotes* throughout the province produced the desired results. From one assembly to the next the fever mounted, especially in the rural areas. Although the leaders tried, by and large, to remain within the legal limits, they did not always succeed, and were occasionally carried away by the atmosphere they created. After July, others, particularly the extremists, did not hesitate to incite the populace to revolt, and numerous incidents occurred throughout the countryside. The founding of the revolutionary *association des Fils de la liberté* ("Association of the Sons of Liberty") increased the unrest in the city of Montreal. It had its counterpart in the *Doric Club*, a society equally counter-revolutionary.

332

Tension reached the breaking point when the *Patriotes* organized the "Assembly of the Six Counties." The speeches were extremely violent, and the nature of the meetings indicated that the climax was fast approaching. A declaration of human rights was issued at the meeting, and measures that were plainly revolutionary were adopted. It was decided that officers of the militia and justices of the peace, previously named by the government, were to be replaced by officials elected by the populace. The new organization set itself up to a certain extent as independent. From this point on the actual revolutionary phase had begun.

The Revolt

The increasing tension, which spread in the rural areas and the city of Montreal, was expressed with new vigour after the formation of the Assembly of the Six Counties. The British minority became alarmed and demanded that the government intervene, but the latter continued to interpret the movement asa blackmailing operation until the beginning of November 1837. Monseigneur Lartigue, Bishop of Montreal, was the first to feel it necessary to intervene; and on October 24, at the time the *Patriotes* published the manifesto of the Assembly at St. Charles, he sent out a letter unequivocally condemning the actions of the French-Canadian leaders. He condemned their revolutionary intentions and the liberal ideas that bore them, and implicitly formulated the penalties the Church attached to actions intended to overthrow the established order. In spite of this clerical influence the revolutionary movement swept on.

It was November before the government finally decided to act and ordered the arrest of the principal *Patriote* leaders. Some of them hid in the parishes, one small group headed toward St. Eustache and St. Benoit, and others went to St. Charles or St. Denis. Camps were established in these places as rallying points for the peasant forces. After the incident at Longueuil between the police and the *Patriotes*, the government sent an expedition against St. Denis which was repulsed on November 23, 1837; but two days later the government forces captured St. Charles, at which point the resistance of the *Patriotes* collapsed. Colborne afterward succeeded in pacifying the parishes to the north of Montreal, and St. Eustache fell to him in spite of strong resistance from a small group of *Patriotes* commanded by Jean-Olivier Chénier.

The rapid collapse of the *Patriote* movement was not the result of a lack of planning of the revolt, but of weakness in the leadership. The *Patriote* chiefs, as far as the practical side of their venture was concerned, showed themselves to be very poor organizers; in combat, they were lamentable. Only Dr. Nelson, Charles-Ovide Perrault, and Chénier were equal to the task. Papineau, the commander-in-chief, left St. Denis just before the battle; moreover, his conduct during the entire revolutionary period was most inconsistent. His continual hesitation, his fear of responsibility and his physical cowardice explain his flight in disguise, and account for a large part of the climate of anarchy that existed. It is true that the government forces mobilized much more swiftly than the *Patriotes* expected, but this is hardly a sufficient explanation. The French-Canadian leaders undoubtedly put too much faith in the ability of the farmer to act alone. Without well-established leadership, the habitants were a disorganized and ineffective fighting force.

333

The Mission of Lord Durham in Lower Canada

The revolt in Lower Canada and the troubles in Upper Canada profoundly shocked public opinion in England. The problems could not be regarded lightly. English political leaders now became preoccupied with finding the source of the problems and the nature of the conflicts, and with formulating satisfactory solutions. Lord Durham's mission was the result of this desire to rectify these ills.

Durham arrived in Quebec in May 1838 with two types of responsibilities. He was to decide the future of the political prisoners and set up committees of inquiry to study the causes of the uprising. All this was not easy. The atmosphere was extremely strained and each group seemed bent on securing official validation and forwarding its own version of events. Therefore, the commissioner had to avoid compromising himself in the eyes of all the different elements of the population. In such circumstances, impartiality would not be easy.

The most pressing task was to decide the fate of the political prisoners. Many different solutions were possible, of course, but Durham was quick to realize that trial by jury was unthinkable. With emotions running high, justice could not have been dispensed fairly whatever the jury chosen. On the other hand, a trial without a jury would have resulted in a long series of particularly severe condemnations. The great volume of proof accumulated against the *Patriote* leaders guaranteed this. Wishing to avoid another popular uprising, Durham preferred another solution. He freed those prisoners who had played only a subordinate role in the insurrection, but showed more severity toward the principal instigators of the movement, exiling them to Bermuda. Those who had escaped to the United States he forbade to return under threat of punishment.

During this time, the committees formed by Durham were accumulating a large body of material dealing with all aspects of life in Lower Canada and in the other colonies. With the help of this material and his own personal observations, Durham was soon in a position to diagnose the problems of Lower Canada. Influenced by the European climate of ideas *Radical Jack* had thought he would find a genuine liberal conflict in Canada. He did discover traces of it, especially in Upper Canada, but to him it seemed that the conflict in Lower Canada had an entirely different character. The intensity of the racial conflict, which the liberal element masked but did not hide, seemed to him the most striking feature in the colony. "I found two nations warring in the bosom of a single State. . . . "

According to Durham, these two nations not only possessed different characteristics of language, race, and religion, but they differed in their degree of evolution as well. The French-Canadian society, he assumed, was essentially static and destined, as a result of its outlook, to remain so. The British, on the other hand, were sensitive to currents of progress in all their forms. Influenced by the atmosphere that existed in the society at the time of his stay, Durham finally concluded that the French sector was forever entrenched in inferiority and obstruction. He even saw in this element some organic and immutable tendency to be so. Hence the extreme nature of some of his recommendations.

Therefore, because he had observed the struggle at its greatest intensity, Durham saw no other solution to the ethnic problem except the assimilation of French Canadians into the English culture. For this reason he recommended the union of the Canadas and the undertaking of a policy aimed at absorbing the French group into the Anglo-Saxon. His *raciste* attitude was based on a distorted view of relations between the ethnic groups. Apart from the establishment of the union, necessary for other reasons, his solution was illusory. The future progress of Canada did not depend on the destruction of French culture, but on a change in attitude on the part of the French-Canadian population toward progress. In this sense, the French Canadians themselves held the key. By reversing their stand, they might prove Durham's conclusion unfounded. Instead of promoting assimilation, the union of the Canadas would prove to be no more than a means of achieving a number of economic and institutional reforms.

In his *Report*, which was published in the spring of 1839, Durham perceived another reform as indispensable as the union — the establishment of responsible government. His recommendation is not, of itself, startling. The commissioner had long been one of the main proponents of the English liberal movement, and even bore the reputation of being a radical. His background, together with a desire to find a solution to certain Canadian problems, explains Durham's proposal for ministerial responsibility. His recommendation seemed to him to be in tune with the natural evolution of the British Empire toward a thorough remoulding of its colonial structures. Ministerial responsibility, for Durham, was to be the political expression of this development, implying an increased autonomy of the colonies. It is from this point of view that the Durham Report marked a step toward the complete reform realized in 1848.

335

Fortunately, the enormous amount of work accomplished by his committees allowed Durham time to accumulate the information necessary to draw up his report, because his mission ended abruptly in 1838. He learned that the government in London had just overruled the decision he had made regarding the political prisoners. There was no other alternative under the circumstances but to tender his resignation.

The Second Outbreak: November 1838

A few days after Durham's departure another insurrection broke out in Lower Canada which was not, however, linked to the events surrounding his mission. It was, rather, a movement organized at long range by the Canadian refugees in the United States. After the setback of 1837, the *Patriotes* had never ceased to dream of avenging themselves; but deeply divided, they needed more than six months to recover and to agree on a new plan.

However, after July 1838, the *Patriote* leaders, having more or less rejected Papineau, succeeded in achieving a certain unanimity among themselves, and in establishing the *Société des Frères-Chasseurs*, a secret revolutionary organization drawing its adherents from the parishes of Lower Canada. The leaders counted on American aid in their insurrection planned for November 3. They hoped to capture St.-Jean, Chambly and Laprairie quickly, before marching on Montreal. Once Montreal was in their hands, they proposed to move on Quebec.

Events, however, did not occur as planned. On November 3, the *Frères-Chasseurs* agitated in all the parishes south of Montreal, and several thousand of them gathered at Napierville where independence for the country was once again proclaimed by two of their leaders, Robert Nelson and Côté. Anarchy prevailed everywhere. Once again the leaders were found incapable of commanding the movement and guiding it toward the desired objectives. A large mass of people gathered at Napierville but the majority dispersed before seeing any action, and government forces encountered no serious opposition.

This resounding failure, followed by severe repressive measures, was to have a profound influence upon the future course of the French Canadians. In 1840, the *Patriote* experiment had completely collapsed, and men with different objectives assumed the leadership of the French-Canadian group.

Suppressing Rebellion in Lower Canada: British Military Policy and Practice, 1837–1838*

336

ELINOR KYTE SENIOR

In the event of insurrection — whether in Ireland, in Jamaica, or in Canada — the usual British military practice in the early 1800s was to seize the papers of rebel chiefs, burn their homes, and imprison leaders when caught. Rank and file insurgents were less likely to have their homes burnt unless those buildings had been used by insurgents to fire upon Crown forces. "Free quartering" of troops was often imposed on a disaffected populace as part of the punitive measures, but exile or hanging of rebel leaders were measures of last resort. Imposition of martial law meant the suspension of civil government, a step contemplated with as much anxiety by loyal citizens as by disaffected elements. Government and military authorities clearly believed that rebels had to be punished, and that such punishment should be evident, not only to the loyal part of the population but to the neutral and wavering elements as well.

Most British officers and soldiers of this period who served abroad were familiar with coping with disturbed areas. It was then usual military practice to send regiments to Ireland prior to a posting overseas, as the Irish station was considered an excellent training ground both for use of troops in aid of civil power and for training in ceremonial procedures. Colonel George Cathcart of the 1st King's Dragoon Guards, for instance, had served in Ireland and then in Jamaica during the slave revolt there in the 1830s. When faced with insurrection in Lower Canada, he made use of his experience, particularly with regard to combined police-military operations. His expertise in these matters enabled him to

*From *Canadian Defence Quarterly* 17, 4 (Spring 1988): 50–55. Reprinted by permission.

exercise great influence in the reorganization of the Montreal police both during and after the rebellions.[1] Similarly, Colonel Charles Grey of the 71st Highland Light Infantry urged civil authorities to make use of the Irish Insurrection Act of 1798 to compel each Montreal householder to post on the front door a list of all residents and order them to be within the house by a certain hour each night.[2]

Outbreak of the First Rebellion

Even before the first actual battle of the 1837 rebellion occurred in Lower Canada, the British military command had formulated a policy of home burning as a punitive measure. This policy was instituted as a reaction to the rescue of arrested *Patriote* chiefs by a body of armed *Patriotes* under Bonaventure Viger. These insurgent leaders had been arrested in Saint Jean on 16 November 1837 by Montreal bailiffs, who were escorted by troopers of the Royal Mounted Cavalry under the command of Lieutenant Charles Oakes Ermatinger, an Ojibway chief. Lieutenant Ermatinger was hit by the first shot of the first rebellion, a shot fired by the insurgent son of a half-pay Scottish officer, Patrick Murray.[3] In the ensuing melée, the men of the Royal Montreal Cavalry were scattered, their prisoners freed, and authorities faced the first open defiance of government and military forces. The Commander of the British forces in Canada, Sir John Colborne, immediately sent a strong contingent of regulars back to the spot where the cavalry had been attacked, with orders to arrest the men who had fired on the troopers. "Should they resist the civil power or fire on the troops, you will fire on the rebels, also destroy any house from which they may fire".[4] On returning to Saint Jean, however, the troops found the houses deserted, the women and children hiding in the woods. The men had gone to Boucherville to reinforce insurgent ranks there under Bonaventure Viger. Some prisoners were taken, but no homes put to the torch.

337

Battles of Saint Denis and Saint Charles

This rescue of the Saint Jean *Patriote* chiefs was, however, the incident that triggered Sir John Colborne to move against the radical centres of Saint Denis and Saint Charles, on the Richelieu River, with some 800 troops, ostensibly as "an aid to civil power." The troops were to accompany magistrates with warrants to arrest the *Patriote* leaders Louis-Joseph Papineau, Doctor Wolfred Nelson, Thomas Storrow Brown, and others, who were then forming armed camps on the Richelieu.

Colborne's military policy was to move swiftly against the armed camps. In a two-pronged pincer movement, one brigade was to move

338

Adapted from Elinor Kyte Senior, *Redcoats and Patriotes*, Canada's Wings, Canadian War Museum.

south from Sorel toward Saint Denis, and a second would march from Chambly against the armed camp at Saint Charles. It was expected that the brigade headed to Saint Denis would pass through that small village with little opposition. When put into practice, however, this plan proved only partly successful. Bad weather and bad tactics on the part of Colonel Gore allowed rebel reinforcements to get to Saint Denis during the battle. The regular troops were exhausted after an all-night march in the frightful November weather, and victory ultimately went to the insurgents, who fought vigourously from a strong defensive position.

By contrast, two days later, good weather and effective military leadership enabled the Chambly brigade to move decisively against Saint Charles in a triumphant two-hour battle. Following this battle the first of the punitive military measures began — the burning of houses and barns from which rebels had fired on Crown forces. The armed camp at Saint Charles was destroyed, except for the manor house of Pierre-Dominique Debartzch, which the insurgents had used as their main headquarters.[5] Some twenty buildings were put to the torch immediately. Prisoners were rounded up and lodged in the parish church until sent to jail in Montreal, where they joined those *Patriote* chiefs from Montreal who had already been arrested since 16 November.

339

With the suppression of the rebel camp at Saint Charles, a brigade of some 500 regulars, with field artillery and a cornet's detachment of the Royal Montreal Cavalry, returned to Saint Denis on 1 December. They entered the village unopposed, and there was no sign of Doctor Wolfred Nelson, Papineau, or other rebel leaders. The officer commanding the regulars, Colonel Gore lost no time in putting the torch to the fortified stone building which a week earlier the rebel forces had defended so effectively that regular soldiers had been unable to storm it.

Home-Burning: A Policy of Punishment and Repression

In his first report to Colborne on 1 December 1837, Gore stated, "The fortified house has been burned and several others from which we were fired on." He added, "Wolfred Nelson's property will be destroyed tomorrow."[6] The destruction of Nelson's property and of other buildings was thus carried out as a punitive and as a repressive measure — to punish rebels and to prevent future uprisings. The British succeeded in the first, but failed in the second.

During and immediately after the first military engagements in Lower Canada, some 184 homes were burned. About 30 of these were disciplined military acts. The rest represented plunder and vengeance. After the battle of Saint Eustache, for instance, troops were ordered to "free quarters." This was a euphemism for plunder, as officers and soldiers fully understood. One regular officer described the pillaging at Saint Eustache as "equalling or surpassing that which followed the sack of Badajoz in Spain." Only two homes were ordered burned in Saint Eustache — those of the local *Patriote* leaders, the merchant William Henry Scott and Doctor Jean Chenier.[8]

When "unofficial" fires broke out after the battle, troops were ordered out to protect property, but without much effect, and some 60 houses were gutted.[9] There was probably a certain element of calculation on the part of the military authorities with regard to these unofficial burnings. Colborne had warned the men of nearby Saint Benoit that their village would be put to fire and the sword if a single shot was fired as the Crown forces approached the village. Not a shot was fired, but the village was gutted nonetheless. Colborne had ordered three homes burnt in Saint Benoit, those of the three principal *Patriote* leaders — Notary Jean-Joseph Girouard, Doctor Luc Masson, and J.B. Dumouchel. The rest were put to the torch by local volunteers and residents. The

340   church at Saint Benoit was set on fire three times; twice troops put out the flames, but the third time the church burned to the ground. Regular troops then marched through the disaffected area of the Lake of Two Mountains for three days. On orders, they burned two homes, took up surrendered arms and received the oath of allegiance from rural inhabitants. Their final duty was to escort to Montreal some of the 361 political prisoners that crowded the jails over that Winter.[10]

Terror and Persecution

Arrested rebels were expected to give depositions before magistrates about their part in the uprisings. Floggings and half-hangings, so much a part of the Irish rebellion scene in 1798, did not, however, form part of the repressive measures in Lower Canada in 1837. Rather, an atmosphere of terror was temporarily created by widespread police interrogation carried out under Pierre-Edouard Leclère, head of the newly-raised police. No one could know to what extent a neighbour's testimony might implicate one in treason, and there was thus a continual flight over the American border of rebels and their sympathizers. They were undoubtedly frightened, but they were not so terrorized that they refrained from engaging in border raids from their safe haven in the United States.

The military reaction to these first border raids was to order the Glengarry Highlanders to move from Upper Canada in the Spring of 1838 to police areas south of the Saint Lawrence, and regular officers were brought over from England on "particular duty," that is, to act as intelligence officers. They were scattered in a number of small towns south of the Saint Lawrence, with the task of reporting to Colborne any suspicious behaviour of the *habitants* and those suspected of disaffection.

It was no wonder that *Patriote* chiefs over the border spoke uneasily of "spies being sent throughout the agricultural districts."[11]

By May of 1838 additional troops from Great Britain were pouring into Lower Canada. The Grenadier Guards and the Coldstream Guards, along with two cavalry regiments, arrived under the command of Sir James Macdonell. In addition, three other regiments were brought in from the Maritime colonies. This brought Colborne's regular force up to a strength of 5,000 and, with his local volunteer troops numbering about 4,000, this combined military force exceeded the peacetime strength of the army of the United States.

In spite of the increasing size of the regular garrison, the *Patriotes* over the American line began preparations for a second uprising, this time through the agency of a secret society — *Les Frères Chasseurs*. Border raids were called off temporarily. With this lessening of border tension, Colborne released 200 of the lesser rebels from jail, a move that provoked considerable resentment on the part of the well-affected populace. Colborne went even farther. He agreed to a policy of general amnesty, expecting that such leniency would remove from the border the more turbulent spirits thought to be plotting another insurrection. Thus, six months after the first rebellion, all political prisoners had been released except for eight leaders who were sent into exile in Bermuda. Disaffected elements had accurately predicted this release of prisoners, and openly boasted that government dared not bring any of them to trial. Exile there was, then, for eight *Patriote* chiefs, but no executions. In fact, the only execution during the first rebellion in Lower Canada was that of a loyalist French-Canadian volunteer, executed by rebel forces who accused him of being a government spy.[12] This was in sharp contrast to what had happened in the upper province, where civil authorities promptly hanged two captured rebel leaders.

341

The Second Rebellion: The Scottish Suppression

When the second insurrection broke out in Lower Canada in November of 1838, if faced a well-prepared government which suppressed it within a week. The rebellion, and its suppression, had something of a Scottish tone about it. The leader of the *Chasseur* conspiracy in Montreal was John de Bélestre Macdonell, son of a half-pay Scottish officer who had settled in Glengarry County and married into the prominent de Bélestre family. It was out of Macdonell's law office in Montreal that the head lodge of the *Chasseurs* operated and funnelled money to Doctor Robert Nelson, leader of the insurgent forces south of the American line.

On the other side of the coin, the officer in charge of the harsh repressive measures after the second insurrection was Major-General Sir James Macdonell, brother of the late Highland Chieftain from Glengarry.

It was thus not surprising that Colborne had no hesitation in ordering Glengarry Regiments from Upper Canada to cross the provincial line and surround insurgent forces in the Beauharnois area. Numerous Macdonells and other volunteers from Glengarry were delighted to join forces with their kinsman as he moved west from Quebec City with a brigade of Guards, doubly indignant that a man by the name of Macdonell was numbered among the rebel leaders.

The insurgents' fear of the Scots was clearly stated by one of them — himself half-Scot. Pierre Reid claimed that the reason the insurgents tried to disarm the Caughnawaga Indians just prior to the second uprising was because they feared "the Indians were coming with the Scotch to massacre us."[13] Reid's fear contained some element of reality: Captain Edmund Thomas Campbell of the 7th Hussars was in charge of suppressing the insurgents at Chateauguay; Colonel George Cathcart of the 1st King's Dragoon Guards scoured the area around La Prairie; and still another Campbell, Major John Campbell, commanded the Huntingdon Volunteers as they moved down the Chateauguay River against a rebel encampment at Baker's Farm. It is no wonder then that the pipers of the Stormont Highlanders gaily played "The Campbells are Coming" as they marched into the Huntingdon camp, accompanied by 60 warriors from the Indian village of Saint Regis, just opposite Cornwall. The combination of the Scottish bagpipes and the Indian warcries proved to be too much for the insurgents a short distance away: they silently slipped away overnight.

On their march from Beauharnois towards the major rebel encampment at Napierville, the Glengarries boasted that they left a trail six miles wide as they came along "burning and pillaging."[14] The Scottish wife of Edward Ellice, *seigneur* of Beauharnois, described them as a "wild set of men — very like what one imagines the old Highlanders in Scotland and equally difficult to manage." She concluded that the rural *habitants* were less afraid of the Indians than of the Glengarries, and with reason. The Highlander who rowed her and her husband to safety at Lachine after they were rescued from the insurgents laconically told them "the houses they had spared in coming down the country, they would surely burn going back."[15]

A border raid on the windmill at Prescott sent the Highlanders scurrying back to defend their own province. Having come as infantry, most of them returned as cavalrymen, mounting, as they claimed, "stray French ponies they found on the wayside".[16] The horses were on the loose because the *habitants* had freed their animals, fearing that their properties would be burned as part of the repressive military measures. The use of the Glengarries and the Indians was part of a military policy of instilling terror amongst the rebel forces, a policy that succeeded, for fighting took place only briefly at Lacolle and Odelltown, on the frontier, and at Baker's Farm and Beauharnois. In none of the areas that rose during the previous Autumn was a shot fired, evidence of the efficacy of the repressive measures by the military in those areas.

A Harsher Policy: Fear of a Third Rebellion

This second revolt, coming so swiftly on the heels of the first, faced a harsher military policy. Colonel Charles Grey, son of a former British Prime Minister, expressed the common military attitude. "You certainly cannot allow people to give you all this trouble and to act as they have towards the loyal part of the population, and then go to their homes without any punishment."[17] Once the second insurrection was suppressed, a policy of "dragooning" was adopted, designed to check any possible attempt at a third uprising. The spectre of a third rebellion was indeed raised by Curé François-Xavier Bellamin Ricard of Ile Perrot. Identified as one "well acquainted with all the secret plans and designs of the late revolt," Curé Ricard visited Beauharnois in the wake of the troops on Sunday, 11 November 1838. He was horrified by what he saw, just as Jane Ellice was as she "stood watching the village in flames — an awful sight."[18]

343

As soon as Curé Ricard returned to his own parish from Beauharnois, he predicted that "they would revolt again next year and would be unsuccessful, but that in the year 1840, they would rise again in rebellion and be revenged for their injuries." Strangely, Ricard said this before a house full of people, among them two loyalist volunteer officers who immediately informed military headquarters of the priest's speech. "The prediction is the groundwork of a future insurrection."[19]

Military authorities did not need evidence of continuing disaffection in order to initiate a harsher policy. Having, as they believed, treated disaffection with great leniency the previous year — no executions, and all but eight of the prisoners freed — they concluded that their former policy had been interpreted as weakness. Many of the loyalists repeatedly insisted that a lenient policy would lead to fresh outbreaks of rebellion. Henceforth, troops were quartered south of the Saint Lawrence, some 3,000 regulars and 1,000 volunteers. Homes were searched for rebels and arms, arrests made and oaths of allegiance exacted. Houses of suspected insurgent leaders and of those thought to be still consorting with sympathizers across the American border were burnt.

Home-Burning Intensified

At Napierville, a village of about 80 houses, military authorities at first intended to burn all rebel homes. Non-commissioned officers from regular regiments were selected for the task, and had actually begun when the order was countermanded by Sir John Colborne. Colonel Charles Grey claimed that the countermand order arrived too late "to prevent several homes being burnt, among them Dr. Côté's which we saw in full blaze after we left the place."[20] Grey was heading towards Saint Edouard, accompanied by Captain Sydney Bellingham of the Royal Montreal Cavalry; their objective was to "burn the houses of the leaders of the insurgents." Bellingham described how the policy of burning had been adopted. It was largely the work of Attorney-General Charles Richard Ogden. "He (Ogden) discovered the authors of the outrages to which the loyal inhabitants had been exposed, and as the principal actors took refuge beyond the frontier, and secretly returned to excite the population, Mr. Ogden came to the conclusion that the best method of punishing them was to burn their homesteads. The officers in command of troops merely obeyed orders."[21]

344   A Montreal newspaper dolefully reported that not a single rebel home was left standing south of the Saint Lawrence. This was far from the case. At least 1,500 men took up arms in the second insurrection and there were as many as 7,500 among the disaffected, yet the number of homes burnt in the second uprising, even counting those burned at Beauharnois and Chateauguay immediately after military engagements, were probably under 100.[22]

Not all burnings were, however, authorized by the military.

At Beauharnois, for example, a village of about 45 homes, some 23 houses were burned by loyalists, who reasoned that it was the only punishment the rebels would receive.[23] The Lachine Volunteers were responsible for at least ten homes out of the 20 that were burned at Chateauguay. These were unauthorized burnings, and the Lachine Volunteers involved were put under military arrest.

In early 1839 the military burnings had ceased. But by then disaffected elements over the border had renewed raids and had started to burn properties themselves. In most cases, the border burnings were confined to barns, but in two cases homes of loyalist volunteers were set on fire. With regard to "free quarters," or pillaging, regulars and volunteers engaged in both with equal gusto, sometimes legitimately, as in the case of the church funds of Napierville, where insurgents had confiscated them from the local priest. In their haste to clear out of Napierville as regular troops neared, the rebels left the cart containing the funds behind. They took time out only to set fire to the house they used as their arms depot. Soldiers of the 71st Highland Light Infantry pulled the cart out of the way and, as they did so, it upset. The chest containing the "sacred silver" broke open, whereupon the delighted soldiers helped themselves. Colonel Grey regarded this as legitimate plunder, but he had harsh words for other incidents of pillage. "The sort of plunderers that the Guards, the Artillery and the 7th Hussars are, I think I never saw. There was this excuse for killing animals to eat, that no rations were issued to the men . . . but the slaughter of poultry of all sorts by the Guards and the Hussars in particular I never saw equalled."[24] His own regiment was not totally innocent, and pillaging ceased only after five men had been sentenced to twelve months imprisonment for plundering.

Effect of Persecution and Harsh Measures

The effect of this persecution, together with the courtsmartial of some 111 prisoners and the hanging of twelve insurgents in Montreal, drove at least 3,775 *Patriote* sympathizers over the border by 1839.[25] Some of these political refugees continued to think in terms of limited border raids, hoping to provoke war between Great Britain and the United States. But this new round of border outrages caused such negative reactions in the United States that *Chasseur* leaders as far away as Baltimore wrote to insurgent leaders on the border deploring the raids. "Tell our friends to cease these martial excursions," one wrote. "They do only harm to our cause."[26] Moreover, the firm stand against the raiders now being taken by the American Generals John Wool and Winfield Scott convinced military leaders in Montreal that the American government was anxious to avoid war.

By 1840 only a few desultory border raids were made. But the refugee communities were quick to denounce them as "individual private acts, not being pushed by the chiefs."[27] Many over the border were longing for home. Others had found work and established their families over the line, and were now anxious to raise the image of French Canadians in the eyes of their fellow American citizens.

By creating an atmosphere of terror, dragooning had done its job. Those disaffected elements who had sought safety across the American border soon learned that there was no chance of American military aid. And without such aid, they recognized the folly of continued resistance, for all hopes of a successful insurrection were predicated on an uprising *en masse* of the *habitants*, coupled with American aid. Thus, directly or indirectly, military policy and practice stamped out insurrection in Lower Canada.

345

NOTES

[1] Elinor Kyte Senior, *British Regulars in Montreal: An Imperial Garrison, 1832-1854* (Montreal, 1981), 28–30.
[2] Lt. Col. Charles Grey to his father, 5 November 1838, in William Ormsby, *Crisis in the Canadas, 1838-39* (Toronto, 1964), 155.
[3] Elinor Kyte Senior, *Redcoats and Patriotes: The Rebellions in Lower Canada 1837-38* (Stittsville, 1985), 54–55.

[4] Deputy Quarter Master General Sir Charles Gore to Lt.-Col. George Wetherall, 17 November 1837, PAC: MG11/Q239/2: 10.

[5] Wetherall to Gore, 28 November 1837, PAC: RG4/S390/A1/2: 147; Pierre Meunier, *L'Insurrection à Saint-Charles et le Seigneur Debartzch* (Quebec, 1986), 216.

[6] Gore to Major Goldie, 2 December 1837, PAC: Colborne Papers, MF24/A40/8043.

[7] Statement of Captain Joseph Swinburne in PAC: Wily Memoirs, PAC: MG29/E1/94.

[8] *Gazette*, Montreal, 16 December 1837.

[9] Lord Charles Beauclerk, *Lithographic Views of the Military Operations in Canada* (London, 1840), 12.

[10] *Transcript*, Montreal, 18 December 1837; Maitland to Gore, 16 December 1837, PAC: Q239/346–7; Colborne to Somerset, 22 December 1837, PAC: RG8/C1272/57.

[11] E.B. O'Callaghan to Thomas Falconer, 24 June 1838, PAC: Chapman Papers, MG24/B31/1: 37–44.

[12] For details see Senior, *Redcoats and Patriotes*, 101.

[13] Pierre Reid's testimony, in *Report of the State Trials* (Montreal, 1839), 1: 42–44.

[14] Grey to his father,13 November 1838, in PAC: Grey Papers, MG24/A10/2: 127.

[15] Ellice Diary, PAC: MG24/A2/50, see entry 14 November 1838.

[16] John Fraser, *Canadian Pen and Ink Sketches* (Montreal, 1890), 105.

[17] Grey to father, 11 November 1838, PAC: Grey Papers, MG24/A10/2: 124.

[18] Major J.A. Mathison's deposition, 12 November 1838, in Archives nationales de Québec: Documents relatifs aux événements de 1837–38, #2953; Ellice diary, PAC: MG24/A2/50, entry dated 10 November 1838.

[19] Captain Edward Jones' deposition, 23 November 1838, ANQ: Documents relatifs aux événements de 1837–38, #2951.

[20] Ormsby, *Crisis in the Canadas*, 147.

[21] Bellingham Memoirs, PAC: MG24/B25/2: 126.

[22] This figure is estimated from *First Report of Commissioners to enquire into losses occasioned by the troubles during the years 1837–38, Appendix to the Journal*, 1846, no. 2, app. X, see claims for over £100; see also Robert Sellar, *History of Huntingdon* (Huntingdon, 1888), 604; Fraser, *Pen and Ink Sketches*, 91; F.X. Prieur, *Notes of a Convict, 1838* (Australia, 1949), 49–55.

[23] Ormsby, *Crisis in the Canadas*, 150.

[24] Grey to father, 11 November 1838, PAC: Grey Papers,MG24/A10/2: 124.

[25] For figures see, Elinor Kyte Senior, "The Presence of French Canadians in American Towns bordering Lower Canada 1837–1840: Disaffection, Terror or Economic Pulls," in *Journal of the Northern New York American–Canadian Genealogical Society* (Plattsburgh, N.Y.) 4, 2 (Fall 1987): 17–30.

[26] Dr. Henri Gauvin to Louis Perrault, 5 April 1839, PAC: Duvernay Papers, MG24/C3/3: 1351.

[27] Assemblie de comité de l'association des Refugiés Canadiens d'état de Vermont, 29 août, 1840, PAC: Duvernay Papers, MG24/C3/3: 1860.

Urban and Commercial Development: 1840–1860

The colony of the United Canadas in the mid-nineteenth century was still predominantly rural and agricultural. Out of a population of roughly two million, only 135 000 — approximately eight percent — lived in the three major urban centres of Montreal (60 000), Quebec (45 000), and Toronto (roughly 30 000). Yet already these urban centres were emerging as focal points for the commercial and social life of the Canadas. John McCallum reviews developments to mid-century in "Urban and Commercial Development until 1850," a chapter from his *Unequal Beginnings: Agriculture and Economic Development in Quebec and Ontario until 1870.*

The British decision to abolish the old imperial preferences for Canadian flour and grain in the late 1840s forced British North Americans to look within North America for their trade and livelihood. This shift in emphasis necessitated in turn an extensive railway system that could link the urban centres of British North America with each other and with the prosperous American cities. The railways had decided advantages over the existing canal system for trade and communications: they were faster, more flexible in location, and operational year round. Together, the railways and the St. Lawrence canals held the potential to make the colony of the United Canadas one of the major centres of North American trade.

The 1850s was the great age of railway building in British North America. At the beginning of the decade, only 106 km of primitive track existed, but by the end, over 3000 km of new track had been laid. The construction of the Grand Trunk, which extended from Sarnia to Quebec City, developed into the most ambitious of all the projects. With 1800 km of track, it was, at the time, the longest railway system in the world.

One of the immediate effects of the railway industry was the rapid rise of towns and cities along the rail lines. Toronto in particular became an important trading centre, with rail lines extending into the northern part of the colony (the Georgian Bay area), into the American midwest, down to New York via Buffalo, and east along the St. Lawrence to Montreal and Quebec City. Railways also brought the industrial revolution to the Canadas: iron foundries, locomotive shops, and rolling mills were established in Toronto, Montreal, and other important Canadian towns.

In "Transportation Changes in the St. Lawrence–Great Lakes Region, 1828-1860," Gerald Tulchinsky reviews the impact of the development of canals, and later railways.

H.V. Nelles' introduction to T.C. Keefer's *Philosophy of Railroads* in the Social History Series edition (Toronto: University of Toronto Press, 1972) provides an introduction to the topic of railways in the Canadas. For a general history of railway development, the first volume of G.P. de T. Glazebrook's *A History of Transportation in Canada* (Toronto: McClelland and Stewart, 1964) merits examination. Peter Baskerville offers a useful summary of developments in present-day Ontario in "Americans in Britain's Back Yard: The Railway Era in Upper Canada, 1850-1880," *Business History Review* 55 (1981): 314-336. For a short review of the effect that the railway had on small towns, see J.J. Talman, "The Impact of the Railway on a Pioneer Community," Canadian Historical Association, *Report* (1955), 1-12. Jacob Spelt's *Urban Development in South-Central Ontario* (Toronto: McClelland and Stewart, 1972) reviews urbanization of the north shore of Lake Ontario.

348

The best short review of the growth of cities in the Canadas is J.M.S. Careless' *The Rise of Cities in Canada before 1914*, Canadian Historical Association, Historical Booklet no. 32 (Ottawa: CHA, 1978). *The Canadian City: Essays in Urban and Social History*, ed. G.A. Stelter and A.F.J. Artibise (Don Mills, Ontario: Oxford, 1984) contains articles on the early urban history of the Canadas. Three important studies of Canadian city life in the nineteenth century are David T. Ruddel's *Quebec City 1765-1832: The Evolution of a Colonial Town* (Ottawa: National Museums of Canada, 1987), J.M.S. Careless' *Toronto to 1918: An Illustrated History* (Toronto: Lorimer, 1984), and John C. Weaver's *Hamilton: An Illustrated History* (Toronto: Lorimer, 1982). For an overview of economic developments in British North America in the mid-nineteenth century, see the chapters entitled "Wood, Banks, and Wholesalers: New Specialties, 1800-1849" and "The Steam Revolution" in Michael Bliss' *Northern Enterprise: Five Centuries of Canadian Business* (Toronto: McClelland and Stewart, 1987), 129-92.

Urban and Commercial Development until 1850*

JOHN McCALLUM

Urban development in Quebec and Ontario is a study in contrasts. Between 1850 and 1870 the two largest cities of Quebec made up about

*Chapter 5 from John McCallum's *Unequal Beginnings: Agriculture and Economic Development in Quebec and Ontario until 1870*. Copyright 1980, by University of Toronto Press. Reprinted by permission of the University of Toronto Press.

three-quarters of the urban population of that province, while the equivalent figure for Ontario was between one-quarter and one-third. To arrive at the share of Quebec's urban population held by Montreal and Quebec City, one would have to include the fifteen largest towns of Ontario in 1850 and the thirty largest towns in 1870. Looking at the matter in a different way, dozens of urban centres filled the Ontario countryside, but outside Montreal and Quebec City the population of Quebec was overwhelmingly rural.

It is clear from Table 1 that these differences in urban structure had been firmly established by 1850 and that the differences merely intensified in the following two decades. Between 1850 and 1870 the number of towns increased faster in Ontario than in Quebec, and, while the share of Ontario's two largest cities in the urban population actually fell from one-third in 1850 to one-quarter in 1870, Montreal and Quebec City accounted for close to three-quarters of Quebec's urban population throughout the period. The causes of the basic differences in urban structure are therefore to be found in the years before 1850, and this chapter focuses on those years. Urban growth after 1850 cannot be separated from industrial and transportation developments.

349

Ontario

Regional patterns of wheat production and urban and industrial development may be seen at a glance in Figures 1 to 4. In mid-nineteenth

---

TABLE 1   Population in Quebec and Ontario, 1850–70

1. Number of towns:

Town size:	Quebec 1850	1860	1870	Ontario 1850	1860	1870
25,000+	2	2	2	1	1	2
5000–25,000	0	1	3	4	8	10
1000–5000	14	18	22	33	50	69
Total	16	21	27	38	59	81

2. Urban and rural population (thousands):

Town size:	Quebec 1850	1860	1870	Ontario 1850	1860	1870
25,000+	100	141	167	31	45	83
5000–25,000	0	6	20	41	83	95
1000–5000	31	39	42	67	108	149
Total urban	131	187	229	139	236	328
Total rural	759	925	962	813	1160	1293
Total population	890	1112	1192	952	1396	1621
Urban as percentage of total	14.7	16.8	19.2	14.6	16.9	20.2

Source: Census of Canada

Figure 1

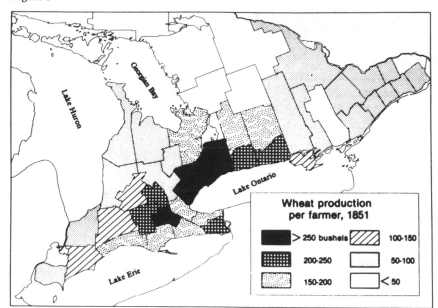

350

Figure 2

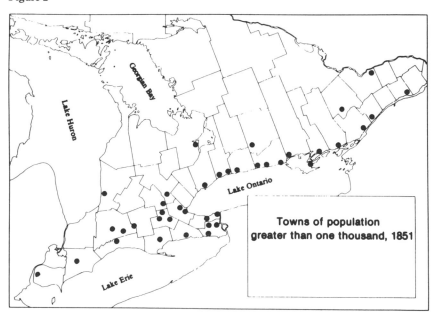

Source: Census of Canada.

Figure 3

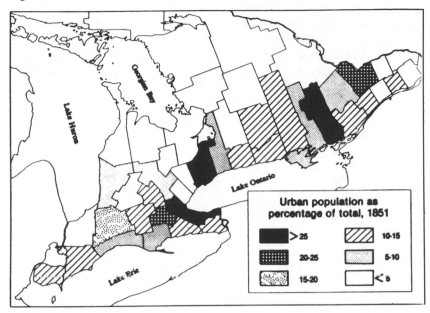

351

Figure 4

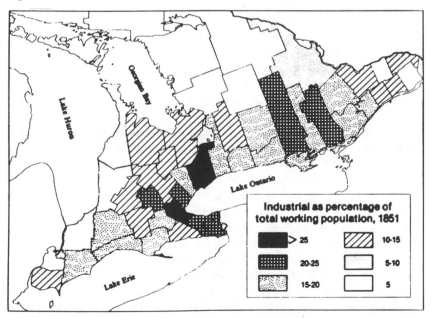

Source: Census of Canada.

century Ontario there was a striking concentration of activity in the triangle bounded roughly by York County, the Niagara River, and London. The region varies somewhat, sometimes extending further east along Lake Ontario and sometimes stopping short of London on the west; but as a snapshot of a rapidly changing scene the general outline is remarkably clear: the areas of highest wheat production tended also to be the areas of greatest urban and industrial development. This was so despite the very recent settlement of the western regions, which, at mid-century, were in the midst of their period of most rapid growth. This pattern suggests that wheat was at the root of urban development, a supposition that will be confirmed by an analysis of the growth of Ontario towns.

TORONTO

It was only by virtue of its position as provincial capital that the town of York, with its "very trifling"[1] trade and its undeveloped hinterland, had reached the grand total of 1700 inhabitants by 1824. Starting in the mid-1820s, settlers poured into the Home district, and the district population of 17,000 in 1824 increased at an annual rate of 8.6 per cent to reach 168,000 in 1851. York (or Toronto, as it became in 1834) grew with its agricultural hinterland, attaining a population of 9252 in 1834 and 30,800 in 1851.[2]

The driving force behind the growth of Toronto was the demand for goods and services from the immigrant and farm population. Financed initially by the savings of British immigrants, this demand was maintained by the farmers' cash income from wheat. In the earlier years of settlement, the demand from new arrivals was the major element. In the second half of the 1820s, according to T.W. Acheson, "the provision of housing, food, clothing, and tools for several hundred new family units each year created a demand which provided the economy with a dynamism otherwise inconceivable."[3] At the time of the peak immigration of 1831–32, immigrants deposited not less than £300,000 in the Bank of Upper Canada.[4] As exports of wheat and flour accelerated during the 1840s, the demand for goods and services from established farmers was felt with ever-increasing intensity. Throughout the period wheat and flour dominated the export trade of Toronto, accounting for more than three-quarters of exports at mid-century.[5]

As population and trade increased, the importance of the city's position as provincial capital declined correspondingly. Thus, in 1845 W.H. Smith, author of the *Canadian Gazetteer*, wrote: " . . . the seat of government was moved to Kingston in 1841. . . . Had this event taken place ten years sooner, it might have had a serious effect upon the prosperity of the town, but in 1841 Toronto had become a place of too great a commercial importance to feel much ill effect from the removal of the government offices, and the loss of the expenditure of a few thousand pounds per annum."[6]

Under these circumstances the primary functions of Toronto were to export flour and to import goods for sale to established and prospective farmers. Acheson described the operations of the retailers around 1830. About 90 per cent of the market of Toronto's retailers was in rural areas, and consequently the pattern of sales was determined by the farming seasons. Peak sales occurred in October following the harvest, and business remained fairly strong throughout most of the winter when the farmers transported their wheat and flour to the town. Demand fell off during the spring thaw, and it picked up again in July when there was a steady demand for tools and implements. The "struggling" patrons purchased cotton cloth and thread, glass, nails, scythes, and hardware supplies, while the more prosperous customers bought luxury articles such as Madeira, snuff, and silk. These prosperous customers, presumably mainly attached to government activities, were small in number, and it was the agricultural population which determined both the seasonal fluctuations and the principal commodity composition of retail sales.

353

Behind the retailers were the wholesalers. These were larger commercial enterprises which not only sold goods to the retailers but also purchased and exported flour. Manufacturing made modest progress in the years to 1850, and the goods supplied by the wholesalers were mainly imported. In the early years most imports were British goods purchased through Montreal, but after the opening of the Erie Canal in 1825 the wholesalers began to import more American goods. In the prosperous years of the late 1820s and early 1830s, larger and more specialized wholesalers established themselves, and to stay in business it became necessary to import goods directly from Britain.[7] In 1832 York had eight wholesalers; by 1850 this number had increased to twenty, fifteen of which had jettisoned retail activities altogether.[8]

Indeed, by mid-century a rising commercial group led by the wholesalers was challenging the position held by the old Toronto families. This group had arrived in the 1830s, and included such men as William McMaster (wholesaler and later banker) and F.C. Capreol (commercial salesroom operator and later railway promoter). Many of the old members of the Family Compact were still important in the economic life of the city, but by 1850 they were losing power to the newer group led by the wholesalers.[9]

While this commercial development based on settlement and wheat exports applied on a smaller scale to most other Ontario towns, a number of special factors favoured Toronto over other places. Between 1824 and 1829 York had the only bank in the province, but in the latter year the Bank of Montreal established a branch in York, and banks were established in Hamilton and Kingston in the first half of the 1830s. While the Bank of Upper Canada was sometimes credited with York's growing prosperity, it was remarked in 1831 that "the fine back Country does infinitely more for the advancement of York than the Bank can do."[10] To the advantages of an early lead in banking and an exceptionally large and fertile back country were added a good harbour, an early road, and the town's position as provincial capital, which made it a focal point for new arrivals to the province. It was only natural, then, that Toronto should be the main beneficiary of any trends in the direction of increased geographical concentration of economic activity.

In the years to 1850, such forces of concentration were limited. Toronto's export trade was not markedly higher than that of other lake ports, and according to Jacob Spelt its presence did not have any influence on the size or number of manufacturing establishments in York County. The one important sector of the economy in which forces of concentration had begun to assert themselves by mid-century was wholesale trade. In 1851 the value of direct imports to Toronto was $2.6 million, as compared with $2.2 million for Hamilton and $1 million for Kingston. The next largest importer was Chippewa at $318,000. By 1850 Toronto had established itself as the major distributing point for such ports as Oakville, Port Credit, and Whitby. There were economies to be gained in limiting the number of contacts with British and American suppliers, and "it was only natural that this trade should concentrate on the capital, the largest city and market with the biggest banks and one of the best ports."[11]

Furthermore, Toronto had started to invade the territory formerly held by Montreal. The city's direct imports (as opposed to goods imported through Montreal wholesalers) rose dramatically in the 1840s and imports from the United States more than doubled in the two years between 1849 and 1851. It has been seen that Toronto wholesalers began to import goods directly from the early 1830s, and in the same period they started to replace Montrealers as suppliers to merchants in smaller Ontario towns. Also, from the late 1840s a rising proportion of wheat and flour was shipped through the United States instead of through Montreal.

Toronto's development is therefore explained not only by the growth of its own hinterland but also by a start to its commercial penetration of other regions. In the process it began its escape from the control of Montreal. On the whole, however, the city's growth up to 1850 depended mainly on growth within its own territory, for, with the partial exception of wholesale trade, dispersion rather than concentration remained the hallmark of economic activity.

Finally, associated with all this was the accumulation of capital. Funds were derived first from the savings of immigrants and from the disposal of land held by the government and its associates, and then increasingly from the activities of the rising merchant class and its agricultural hinterland. Local governments, deriving their revenue directly from the wealth of the towns and countryside, were also important contributors. The point to be emphasized at present is that all these sources may be traced to the twin processes of settlement and wheat exports.

HAMILTON

Hamilton owed its early growth to its position at the head of Lake Ontario. According to W.H. Smith, "Hamilton is admirably suited for carrying on a large wholesale trade with the West, — being at the head of navigation of Lake Ontario, and in the heart of the best settled portion of the Province, it possesses peculiar advantages for receiving goods, and distributing them through the interior, while its central position makes it the depot of a large extent of grain and other produce."[12] The town's population reflected the course of settlement and the wheat trade. The Burlington Bay Canal, which connected Hamilton with Lake Ontario, was completed in 1825, and in 1831 it was said that "since the Burlington Canal started, Hamilton has increased from 3 to 18 stores. Its former trifling trade and its houses have doubled." Population rose from 1400 in 1833 to 3600 in 1837, 4300 in 1842, and 14,000 in 1851.[13]

As in the case of Toronto, this growth resulted from the rapid settlement of the city's back country and the acceleration of wheat exports during the 1840s. The population of the Gore district was 150,000 in 1851, or more than six times as high as in 1831. Exports of wheat and flour more than tripled between 1838 and 1844, and they had tripled again by 1850. By mid-century, Hamilton exported more wheat and flour than any Ontario town except Port Dalhousie, located at the mouth of the Welland Canal.

As Smith indicated, Hamilton was the major wholesale centre for points west of Lake Ontario. Douglas McCalla has produced a map that reveals, for the year 1857, the deep penetration into western Ontario by Hamilton's largest wholesaler, Buchanan, Harris and Company. Eighty centres from Niagara to Amherstburg and from Lake Erie to points north of Goderich contained one or more customers of this firm, and the most concentrated group of customers was located between London and Hamilton.[14]

Hamilton, then, was a commercial town. In his exhaustive study of the town in 1851 Michael B. Katz wrote that " . . . men in commerce, about a quarter of the workforce, controlled nearly 59% of the wealth, a figure which underscores the clear commercial basis of the city." As in Toronto, the industrial sector, operating overwhelmingly in local markets, played a passive role in the years up to 1850. The settlement and development of Hamilton's rich and rapidly growing agricultural hinterland was the basis not only of the town's growth but also of the wealth and capital accumulation of the commercial class. The export of wheat and flour, the importation and distribution of manufactured goods, land speculation, and personal profit derived from municipal funds[15] were all based directly or indirectly on the settler's supply of wheat and demand for land and other goods and services. This capital accumulation and general prosperity may be seen in a number of developments: the replacement of wooden structures with brick buildings and the 'vast improvement' in the character of the city's buildings in the last few years of the 1840s, the location of two bank headquarters and four branches in Hamilton, improvements such as the introduction of gas lighting in 1851, and the ambitious but misguided decision of the city to subscribe £100,000 for the construction of the Great Western Railway.[16]

This is not to paint a picture of general affluence and social harmony. As Katz demonstrated minutely, inequalities were enormous and individual business failures were commonplace. The large-scale Irish immigration brought problems of disease, riots, and violence. Nevertheless, during the last decade of the pre-railway age, Hamilton underwent a total transformation in its population, trade, social infrastructure, and wealth. It is impossible to attribute this transformation to anything other than agricultural settlement and the growth of wheat and flour exports.

356

OTHER ONTARIO TOWNS

The maps in Figures 1 to 4 indicate that the three westernmost counties of Ontario were not large-scale wheat producers and that they were relatively underdeveloped in terms of both urban and industrial growth. The only two towns of a thousand or more were Amherstburg (1880) and Chatham (2070). The former was a frontier post and naval depot during the War of 1812, and it continued to be a garrison town until after 1850. In 1850 and 1851 almost all enumerated exports consisted of wheat, but the quantities involved were not large. By Ontario standards Amherstburg was stagnant. Joseph Bouchette in 1831 gave the population as over 1200 and mentioned "the wealth and respectability of its inhabitants."[17] In the twenty years to 1851 population rose by only 50 per cent. The difficulties of wheat growing in the region and the correspondingly low production levels would seem to have limited the growth of the town. Chatham, on the other hand, was a product of the wheat boom. Its population rose from 812 in 1841 to 2070 in 1851, and, according to Smith, "Being situated in the midst of a fine agricultural country, it is a place of considerable business." Or in the words of F.C. Hamil, "The principal source of prosperity for the town was the prolific country about it, settled by industrious, intelligent, and thrifty farmers."[18] During the 1840s property values rose rapidly, bank branches were established, and brick houses began to replace less solid structures. In 1850 the town had two steam grist mills, two steam sawmills, two foundries and machine shops, a brewery, two tanneries, a woollen factory, and four distilleries.[19] Nevertheless, taken as a whole, the three counties of the Western District grew relatively little wheat, and difficulties in this area had led to an effort to expand tobacco production and in general to adopt a more diversified agriculture. Tobacco and other products were not good substitutes for large quantities of wheat, and the overall development of the district was meagre.

Moving eastwards, London, St Thomas, and Ingersoll were within about thirty miles of each other in Middlesex, Oxford, and Elgin counties. The maps indicate that in 1850 this area was more developed than the counties to the west and somewhat less developed than the counties along the shores of Lake Ontario. This was a newer region which at mid-century was in the middle of its period of most rapid growth: the population of the London District tripled during the 1840s, while the town of London grew from 1100 in 1834 to 2600 in 1842 and 7000 in 1851.[20] London became the district town in 1826, and in 1838 an imperial garrison was stationed in the town. These factors were the major non-agricultural influences on London's development, and, while they may explain the town's ascendancy over St Thomas, they were relatively unimportant in the urban development of the region as a whole. Some town in the region had to be the district centre, and, while the coming of the garrison in 1837 was a shot in the arm for the town's economy, its departure in 1853 was "almost unnoticed."[21]

After London was given the right to hold a public market in 1835, it quickly became the trade focus of a rich but very partially settled agricultural area. It was during the 1840s that London's economy became firmly based on wheat. In the words of Orlo Miller: "By the late 1840's, London's economy had become tied to a more stable commodity than either litigation or logistics [that is, district centre or garrison town]. That commodity was wheat. . . . By the middle of the nineteenth century Western Ontario had become one vast granary and London one of its principal market towns and shipping centres."[22]

As London grew, it attracted men with capital to invest and enriched those who were already there. Some of the town's leading citizens arrived with the settlers in the 1820s and early 1830s. This group included George Goodhue, merchant and land speculator, and Ellis Hyman and Simeon Morrill, both tanners. Men such as Elijah Leonard, iron founder and steam engine maker; John Birrell, dry goods wholesaler; and Thomas Carling, brewer, arrived soon after the Rebellion of 1837. John K. Labatt, brewer; Charles Hunt, miller; and the McClary brothers, warehousing, arrived in the late 1840s and early 1850s. These manufacturers and wholesalers served an area that "stretched west to Chatham, Windsor, and Sarnia, north to Goderich, St Mary's, and Stratford, east to Ingersoll and Woodstock, and south to St Thomas and Port Stanley." Strong commercial ties with Hamilton were developed from an early date. By 1850 London had four bank branches, two building societies, several insurance companies, three "extensive" foundries, one grist and sawmill, three breweries, two distilleries, two tanneries, and three newspapers. While provincial funds were spent generously on London roads because the position of public works commissioner was held by a London citizen, it was the local capital of such families as the Labatts and Carlings which paid for the road to the Huron Tract in 1849 and for the London–Port Stanley railroad in the 1840s.[23]

Ingersoll, Woodstock, and St Thomas were rivals of London in the 1820s and 1830s, but by 1850 they were clearly of secondary importance. To some extent they suffered from London's success, as in the case of Elijah Leonard's departure from St Thomas to London in 1838 on the conviction that London was "sooner or later to become the hub of Western Canada."[24] Nevertheless, the populations of Ingersoll and Woodstock grew extremely rapidly in the late 1840s, and it was not until the railway age that these towns suffered severely from the forces of concentration. At mid-century they were market centres surrounded by a booming agriculture, and each had its five to ten mills and manufactories. The same was true on a lesser scale for the fifteen to twenty smaller villages which dotted the countryside within a twenty-mile radius of London.

358

Goderich served as district town headquarters of the Canada Company and port for the surrounding country. Population rose from 300 in 1831[25] to about 1300 in 1851, and in the latter year the town had the usual assortment of mills, newspapers, and bank and insurance company agents. Exports were still very low, and the most important function in 1850 was to supply settlers bound for the northern sections of the Huron Tract.

In Norfolk County only the district town of Simcoe had as many as one thousand people. Lumber was more important in this county than elsewhere, and in 1850 Ports Dover, Ryerse, and Rowan exported mainly wood, although in the first of these, which was much the largest, wheat and flour made up close to half the total value of exports. None of these ports contained as many as a thousand residents. Simcoe, which had the usual quota of mills and other establishments, derived its existence from a combination of wood, wheat, and administrative functions.

We come now to the largest cluster of towns, those within about forty miles of Hamilton in Brant and Wentworth counties and in the Niagara Peninsula. A glance at Figure 1 shows that this region was second only to the neighbourhood of Toronto in its wheat production. In Brant County wheat production per farmer was the highest in the province in 1851 (370 bushels), and this county contained Paris and Brantford, with a combined population of 5800 or 23 per cent of total county population. Brantford, the largest of these towns, increased its population rapidly in the few years before 1850. It had the advantage of being located on the Grand River and on the Hamilton–London road. In 1850, 350,000 bushels of wheat and flour (just under three-quarters of the total value of shipments) were shipped from Brantford along the Grand River, and in addition "large quantities of flour, whisky and ashes are teamed down to Hamilton and shipped there." The manufacturing establishments seem to have been larger than average, for Smith lists "four grist mills, one of which is a large brick building; two foundries, doing a large business; a stone-ware manufactory, the only one yet in operation in the west of Canada . . . two tanneries, two breweries, four distilleries, a planing machine and a sash factory, &c. &c."[26]

The other towns on the Grand River had similar, if somewhat lesser manufacturing activities, and they too profited from their position on the river in the midst of highly productive wheat farming. Galt and Guelph had originated as supply centres for the Canada Company, but by mid-century most of the lands in the region had been settled. Dunnville was located at the mouth of the Grand River and was a point of trans-shipment of imports as well as an export point. In 1850 wheat and flour made up about three-quarters of the town's exports.

In Niagara District the largest town, St Catharines, benefited from its position on the Welland Canal and had six grist mills. Thorold was also on the Welland Canal, and it had grown rapidly in the few years prior to 1850, taking advantage of the hydraulic powers of the canal to establish a number of large grist mills and other enterprises. Niagara and Chippewa had declined somewhat with the opening of the Welland Canal: in 1851 they had a combined population of about 4500.

359

The Lake Ontario wheat ports east of Hamilton and west of Belleville were so similar that they may be described as a group. According to figures contained in Smith, for six of the eight ports in this region wheat and flour accounted for at least 80 per cent of total exports. The two exceptions were Port Hope and Cobourg, but these were also the only two towns (except Toronto) for which figures on exports to places other than the United States were not available. Most of the towns had wheat and flour exports between 175,000 and 300,000 bushels and total exports of $160,000 to $320,000, while the value of imports varied more widely. The ports competed for their respective back countries, and leading citizens were active in promoting and financing roads, and later railroads, to tap their agricultural hinterlands. Financial services and small-scale manufacturing of the type already described had developed in all of these towns by 1850.

This survey of towns in the wheat-producing areas of Ontario ends with Barrie and Peterborough, which were inland towns north of Lake Ontario. Barrie, with a population of 1007 in 1851, was the main supply centre for the settlers and farmers of Simcoe County, as well as the county town. Its growth had been moderate, and it contained a tannery, brewery, newspaper, and bank agency in 1850. Peterborough was more substantial, with a population of 2191 in 1851. Immigration and the settlement of the surrounding districts remained the town's most important function until about 1840, after which the export of wheat, flour, and lumber increased in importance. In 1850 wheat and flour exports were of about the same importance as exports of lumber and square timber.[27]

We come now to the towns in the part of the province which did not produce wheat as a staple product. From Hastings County eastwards there were in 1851 nine towns with population exceeding one thousand, of which the largest were Kingston (11,600), Bytown (7800), Belleville (4600), and Brockville (2200). For the region as a whole, the urban population made up 15.1 per cent of the total. This was a lower proportion than in the former districts of Niagara (19.1 per cent), Home (21 per cent), and Gore (18 per cent), but it was higher than in most counties west of Brant. Considering that this eastern section had been settled earliest, its urban development up to 1850 was not impressive.

In 1830 Kingston had a larger population than York and about four times as many people as Hamilton; by 1851 it had been surpassed by Hamilton and had less than 40 per cent of the population of Toronto. The economy of Kingston had traditionally been based on its position as entrepôt, together with civilian and military government establishments, the lumber trade through the Rideau Canal, and shipbuilding. The town's unproductive back country was said to have restrained its growth, and it suffered setbacks with the movement of the capital to Montreal in 1844 and the decline of its role as entrepôt. Smith wrote that "the Government establishments, naval and military, with the shipping interest, are the principal support of the City."[28]

Bytown (later Ottawa) was clearly a lumber town, and Belleville exported mainly wood in 1850, although wheat and flour were significant (28 per cent of exports). To a large extent, Prescott and Brockville were dependent on St Lawrence shipping, while Perth was originally the supply centre for local settlers and in later years had been connected to the Rideau Canal by private company. Cornwall lost population between 1845 and 1850, and the small towns of Napanee and Picton were market centres. Of the nine towns, only Belleville, Kingston, and Bytown had significant exports in 1850. Taken as a whole, the region from Belleville eastwards experienced slightly more than a doubling of its urban population between 1835 and 1850. West of Belleville, urban population rose by a factor of five over the same period.[29]

This analysis has covered the years up to 1850. In the next twenty years the number of towns increased from 38 to 81. Three-quarters of the newly established towns were located west of Trenton, and most of these were in the more recently settled inland counties which accounted for a rising proportion of wheat production as the older lands became exhausted. Dispersion remained the keynote of urban structure, as the share of the five largest cities in the urban population actually fell from 51 per cent in 1850 to 40 per cent in 1870.

Three sets of conclusions flow from this analysis. First, wheat was the driving force behind at least twenty-six of the twenty-nine towns

360

west of Belleville (Amherstburg, Simcoe, and Peterborough were partial exceptions). All of these towns were either export ports or inland transportation terminals for Ontario wheat, all were market centres for the agricultural population, most had been supply centres for settlers, and many were import ports or wholesale centres. Wood and garrisons had been of secondary or passing importance. In addition to the centres of over a thousand people, there were literally hundreds of lesser centres, concentrated in the most productive wheat-producing areas, which performed similar functions on a smaller scale. By producing the region's only major export and by providing the market for its imports, agriculture was the foundation of commercial activity. Also, it was this wheat-generated activity that attracted men of capital to the region's commercial and nascent industrial sectors, that provided the basis for further capital accumulation, and that provided the tax base and savings that financed the roads and other projects of the time.

Furthermore, by the standards of the day the wheat economy of 1850 was an economic success story. In the words of I.D. Andrews, the compiler of the most comprehensive statistics on the trade of the province, "The population of Toronto has doubled in the last 10 years, and is now 30,000. Hamilton, now containing 14,000, has been equally progressive. The imports show their commercial program to have been equally rapid; and there can be little doubt that in Upper Canada the export of produce, and the import and consumption of all the substantial and necessary products of civilization, are as high, per head, as in the best agricultural districts of the United States."[30]

361

The second conclusion is that wood had much weaker effects on urban growth than wheat. The eastern part of the province had been settled earlier, and the Ottawa Valley was the major contributor to Canada's very large exports of forest products. Yet urban growth in this region had been meagre. The reasons for this are discussed in a later chapter.

The final conclusion concerns the pattern of urban growth. Why was this growth so dispersed instead of highly concentrated in a single city, as in the case of Winnipeg in the prairie wheat economy? Why, indeed, was the commercial activity located in Ontario at all, when, for example, most of the commercial activity associated with southern cotton and much of that flowing from prairie wheat took place outside the staple-producing region? To these questions, so vital to the prospects of any staple-producing region, there are two basic answers. The technology of the mid-nineteenth century favoured dispersion. We have already mentioned the case of the tiny port of Oakville which transported the wheat to its warehouses, constructed the steam engines and flour mill machinery that converted the wheat to flour, and built and manned the ships that carried the finished commodity to Montreal.[31] In 1847 a small Peterborough foundry manufactured most of the threshing mills used in the district, as well as a wide variety of the agricultural implements.[32] Such examples could be multiplied, but, in general, technology in the areas of transportation and manufacturing favoured the very local retention of a very high proportion of the linkages flowing from the wheat staple.

This technological bias in favour of the local level naturally promoted the retention of commercial activity within the province. However, even in 1850 technology favoured a higher degree of concentration of imports and wholesalers, and in subsequent years technological changes promoted centralization of other activities. The question was whether these centralized activities would take place in Ontario or Quebec, and it was the availability of direct American imports and the American trade route that tipped the balance in favour of Ontario. By contrast, fifty years later the prairie wheat economy had no such escape from eastern control, for the high Canadian tariffs and the monopolistic American freight rates made it difficult to import goods or export wheat through the United States.[33] In the case of Ontario, the effective challenge to Montreal's monopoly position had permitted a growing independence on the part of Toronto wholesalers from the 1830s, and the story was to be repeated in banking, transportation, and industry. Nevertheless, this was a gradual and partial process, for it will be seen in the next section that Montreal derived much benefit from the Ontario wheat economy.

362

Quebec

MONTREAL

Much, if not most, of the literature on this period has concerned itself with the commercial empire of the St Lawrence, and there is no need to repeat the story of the Montreal merchants here.[34] Suffice it to say that a series of shocks in the 1840s destroyed both the old colonial system and Montreal's aspirations for the trade of the American west. Abandoned by Britain and excluded from American produce and markets, the Montreal merchants were driven to the Annexation Manifesto of 1849, in which they declared that the only solution to their problems lay in "going to prosperity, since prosperity will not come to us."[35]

Excluding for the moment its role as supplier of cheap labour, Quebec agriculture had little to do with the development of Montreal. The local farmers had made no significant contribution to exports since the early years of the century, their demand for imports was limited by their low and fluctuating incomes, and their role in capital formation was minimal. They supplied a portion of the city's livestock requirements, little of its wheat, and most of its limited requirements for other vegetable products.

On the other hand, Ontario agriculture was a major factor in the economy of Montreal. While Montreal never became the great emporium of the American mid-west, such shipments as it did receive came increasingly from Ontario rather than from the United States. Thus, wheat and flour shipments via the St Lawrence rose from 2.9 million bushels in 1840 to a peak of 5.8 million bushels in 1847, and by 1851 shipments were 4.3 million bushels. Ontario produce was less than half the total in 1840 and virtually all of it in 1850. In the latter year, wheat and flour made up 78 per cent of the total tonnage passing down the St Lawrence canals. This excludes lumber products which accounted for 10 per cent of the tolls collected.[36] Thus, by 1850 Ontario wheat and flour were of dominant importance in the shipments received at Montreal via the St Lawrence canals. The total tonnage, while not as great as had been anticipated, would have been almost negligible without the wheat and flour of the upper province.[37]

Montreal's imports were closely tied to conditions in Ontario. According to Fernand Ouellet, even by 1820 the incomes of Montreal importers were "directement fonction de l'agriculture haut-canadienne."[38] As indicated by the following figures, the volume of merchandise passing up the Lachine Canal to Ontario rose dramatically:[39]

363

1826	1,500 tons
1830	8,300 tons
1835	15,800 tons
1844	27,500 tons
1850	70,000 tons

In 1851 *direct* imports to Ontario towns via Montreal amounted to$3.0 million, as compared with $9.2 million entered as imports at Montreal.[40] A significant but unknown percentage of the latter figure would have been re-exported to Ontario.

Thus Ontario provided the great majority of Montreal's exports and absorbed perhaps one-half of the imports which reached the city. For Montreal, the upper province was the one bright spot in an otherwise gloomy decade. This is all the more remarkable in the light of Ontario's shift to the American route for both its imports and exports: the province's growth was so rapid that Montreal's declining share of the trade did not prevent the city's absolute level from growing at impressive rates.

There was little progress in manufacturing during the 1840s, and this, together with the commercial disappointments of the decade, led to the emigration of large numbers of workers. Referring to "Montreal and Quebec workmen" as the first class of emigrants, a Select Committee of the Legislative Assembly in 1849[41] described the causes of this emigration in the following terms:

— unsettled trade and industry for several years past
— want of manufactories for those previously in lumbering

— increase in U.S. wages and fall here
— lack of public works

It was not until the industrial growth of the 1850s and 1860s that Montreal began to call on the surplus labour of rural Quebec.

OTHER QUEBEC TOWNS

The timber trade and shipbuilding dominated the economic life of Quebec City. Local agriculture was of minor importance. Neither did Ontario agriculture exert much influence on Quebec, for while the city was a major exporter of wheat this trade was much less important than the trade in timber and ships.

In the rest of the province the major activity was agriculture, and Quebec agriculture was a miserable base for urban growth. Worse than this, the crisis in Quebec agriculture destroyed the economic base of established merchants and artisans, and rural artisans who were "réduits à la misère par l'effondrement du revenu de leurs clients" were forced to emigrate. The Select Committee of 1849 ascribed the emigration of "workmen who had settled in the villages and county parts" to the fact that the farmers "do themselves almost everything they might require from a tradesman," with the result that "the workmen . . . have little employment and lose courage." Also, the inability of the inhabitants to repay debt to "the fearful number of those who carry on trade in our country parts on a small scale" brought financial ruin to debtor and creditor alike.[42]

Outside Montreal and Quebec City the urban population made up 4 per cent of the total population in 1850 and 6 per cent in 1870. Even these figures understate the differential impact of agriculture in the two provinces. While the great majority of Ontario towns owed their existence to the wheat economy, most Quebec towns depended in large measure on activities other than agriculture. This has already been demonstrated for Montreal and Quebec City, and it was also the case for most of the remaining fourteen towns of mid-nineteenth-century Quebec.

The growth of Lachine was obviously not dependent on agricultural conditions, while Aylmer was an Ottawa Valley lumbering town. The economy of St Jean was based on its role as entrepôt for trade between Canada and the United States. Trois-Rivières was in the midst of a region of very poor soil and an agricultural back country which had little to buy or sell. Growth was based on the town's position as a half-way point between Quebec and Montreal, a minor administrative centre, and, from 1840, the exporter of wood from the country along the St Maurice. Laprairie was a commercial centre at the head of communication from Montreal to St Jean and the Richelieu, while Ste Thérèse was a lumbering centre.[43]

In Quebec the railway age began slightly before 1850. The Lon-gueuil–St Hyacinthe section of the St Lawrence and Atlantic Railway was completed in 1847, and these towns had become distribution points based on the railway.[44] Sherbrooke, which had 350 people in 1830, had 2998 in 1851, thanks in large part to the local railroad construction going on at the time of the census. Without the railroad, Sherbrooke "n'aurait jamais dépassé la taille d'un Lennoxville ou d'un Richmond."[45] Joliette, or Industrie as it was called before 1864, originated as a sawmill site in 1823. Under the energetic direction of its founder, the site acquired a flour mill in 1824, a wool factory and nail factory in 1825, a distillery in 1840, and an foundry in 1844. In 1850 a railway was constructed at a cost of $55,000, and at that time population doubled to about 2500. The towns of L'Assomption and Berthier were the two terminal points of this railway.[46]

Sorel and Berthier had been important centres of the wheat trade in earlier years, and the timber trade and shipbuilding were also important in the former. Population of both towns slightly more than doubled in the twenty years to 1850.[47] Finally, Montmagny, which with the exception of Quebec was the only town east of Trois-Rivières with as many as a thousand people, was dependent on local agriculture. Small manu-facturing enterprises were encouraged by water power, local raw ma-terials, river transport, and "l'emploi de l'abondante main-d'oeuvre d'or-igine agricole."[48] Thus, Quebec towns were only partly based on agriculture. The wood industry and entrepôt and administrative functions were also important, and in some cases railways provided stimuli un-related to local agriculture.

365

Consequently, the agricultural sector of mid-nineteenth-century Que-bec sustained less than 20,000 town-dwellers. By contrast, the great ma-jority of Ontario's 130,000 urban residents owed their livelihood to eco-nomic activity spawned by the wheat staple, and even Montreal, after its grander designs had been shattered during the 1840s, saw its fortunes tied increasingly to the Ontario wheat economy. On the other hand, the forestry sector, supporting a few small towns in both provinces as well as Bytown and Quebec City, had proven to be a much less potent gen-erator of urban growth.

NOTES

[1] This was the phrase of John Howison, *Sketches of Upper Canada* (1821; Toronto, 1965), 55.

[2] Population figures for Toronto are from Edith G. Firth, ed., *The Town of York, 1815–1834* (Toronto, 1966), xxvi; and Census of Canada, 1870, iv, 83, 131, 178. Unless otherwise stated, figures on town population are from the census.

[3] Acheson, "The Nature and Structure of York Commerce in the 1820's" (1969), in J.K. Johnson, ed., *Historical Essays on Upper Canada* (Carleton Library no. 82, 1975), 171.

[4] Jacob Spelt, *Urban Development in South-Central Ontario* (Carleton Library no. 57, 1972), 79.

[5] Unless otherwise stated, information on export and import values is from I.D. Andrews, *Report on the Trade, Commerce, and Resources of the British North American Colonies . . .* 31st Congress, 2nd Session, ex. doc. no. 23 (Washington, 1851), and Andrews, *Report on the Trade and Commerce of*

the British North American Colonies and upon the Trade of the Great Lakes and Rivers, 32nd Congress, 1st Session, ex. doc. no. 136 (Washington, 1853).

6 Smith cited in Spelt, *Urban Development*, 94.

7 Firth, *Town of York*, xxvi-xxviii.

8 Barry D. Dyster, "Toronto, 1840-1860: Making It in a British Protestant Town," unpublished Ph.D. thesis, University of Toronto, 1970; and Firth, *Town of York*, 75-76.

9 Donald C. Masters, *The Rise of Toronto, 1850-1890* (Toronto, 1947), 21-26; and Dyster, *"Toronto, 1840-1860,"* 293.

10 John Macauly, agent of the bank at Kingston, cited in Firth, *Town of York*, xxxi.

11 Spelt, *Urban Development*, 75-76, 79.

12 Smith, *Canada: Past, Present and Future*, 2 vols. (Toronto, 1851), 1: 223.

13 *Western Mercury*, cited in Marjorie Freeman Campbell, *A Mountain and a City: The Story of Hamilton* (Toronto, 1966), 65; population statistics, 62.

14 McCalla, "The Decline of Hamilton as a Wholesale Center," *Ontario History* 65 (1973): 253.

15 Katz, "The People of a Canadian City: 1851-2," *Canadian Historical Review*, 53 (1972): 411. Katz, in *The People of Hamilton, Canada West* (Cambridge, Mass., 1975), provides evidence that these were the primary sources of income of the "entrepreneurial" class.

16 Smith, *Canada* 1: 220-28; Campbell, *A Mountain and a City*, 76.

17 Bouchette, *The British Dominions in North America . . . and a Topographical Dictionary of Lower Canada*, 2 vols. (1831; New York, 1968), 1: 105-106.

18 Smith, *Canada* 1: 16; Fred Coyne Hamil, *The Valley of the Lower Thames, 1640 to 1850* (Toronto, 1951), 263.

19 Unless otherwise stated, information on the industrial and commercial establishments of each town in 1850 is from Smith, *Canada*.

20 The population figure for 1834 is from Frederick H. Armstrong and Daniel J. Brock, "The Rise of London: A Study of Urban Evolution in Nineteenth-Century Southwestern Ontario," in Armstrong et al., eds., *Aspects of Nineteenth-Century Ontario* (Toronto, 1974), 89.

21 Orlo Miller, "The Fat Years, and the Lean: London (Canada) in Boom and Depression," *Ontario History* 53 (1961): 76.

22 Miller, "The Fat Years," 74.

23 Armstrong and Brock, "Rise of London," 83-84, 91; Miller, "The Fat Years," 76.

24 Cited in Armstrong and Brock, "Rise of London," 91.

25 Bouchette, *British Dominions* 1: 118.

26 Smith, Canada 1: 237-39.

27 Thomas W. Poole, *A Sketch of the Early Settlement and Subsequent Progress of the Town of Peterborough* (Peterborough, 1867), 93-99. Estimate of price of square timber is from Smith, *Canada* 2: 229.

28 Smith, *Canada* 2: 278. Direct imports by Kingston were 74 per cent of direct imports of all Ontario ports in 1842. This ratio declined to an average of 30 per cent in 1844-46 and 10 per cent in 1848-51. Andrews, *Report on the Trade, Commerce, and Resources*, 198-99; *Report on the Trade and Commerce*, 457-58.

29 Estimates of urban population in 1835 are from Albert Faucher, *Québec en Amérique au XIXe siècle* (Montreal, 1973), 301.

30 Andrews, *Report on the Trade and Commerce*, 430.

31 Hazel C. Mathews, *Oakville and the Sixteen: The History of an Ontario Port* (Toronto, 1953), 204, 212.

32 Poole, *Sketch of the Early Settlement*, 62.

33 In comparison with mid-century Ontario, the prairies also faced more highly developed manufacturing and financial centres to the east, as well as a transportation network which denied to its nascent industry the "natural protection" enjoyed by Ontario in its early years of industrial growth. The comparison with the prairies is analysed further in Chapter 8 [McCallum, *Unequal Beginnings*].

34 Works in this area include D.G. Creighton, *The Commercial Empire of the St. Lawrence, 1760-1850* (Toronto, 1937); Gilbert N. Tucker, *The Canadian Commercial Revolution, 1845-1851* (New Haven 1936); and R.T. Naylor, "The Rise and Fall of the Third Commercial Empire of the St Lawrence," in Gary Teeple, ed., *Capitalism and the National Question in Canada* (Toronto, 1972).

35 Cited in Tucker, *Canadian Commercial Revolution*, 186.

36 Andrews, *Report on the Trade, Commerce, and Resources*, 276-77.

37 As noted above, the exclusion of shipments to Lower Canada and the Maritimes gives a false impression of the relative importance of the American route. This misleading impression is compounded by considering only wheat, in which case, according to Easterbrook and Aitken, as cited in Jean Hamelin and Yves Roby, *Histoire économique du Québec, 1851-1896* (Montreal, 1971), 47-48, the volume of Upper Canadian wheat exported by the American route was more than fifteen times that exported via the St Lawrence in 1850. The more meaningful figure, as given in Table S.2, includes flour shipments as well as shipments destined to Lower Canada and the Maritimes, and on this basis St Lawrence shipments were one-third greater than those via the United States in 1850 and 88 per cent greater in 1851.

38 Ouellet, *Histoire économique et sociale du Québec, 1760-1850* (Montreal, 1971), 265.

[39] 1826: *Journals of the Legislative Assembly of Lower Canada* (*JLALC*), 1830, app. D; 1830: *JLALC*, 1831, app. G; 1835: *JLALC*, 1835–36, app. Q; 1844: *Journals of the Legislative Assembly of Canada* (*JLAC*), 1844–45, app. AA; 1850: Andrews, *Report on the Trade, Commerce, and Resources*, 282–83. All figures refer to the Lachine Canal except in the year 1850, which refers to the St Lawrence canals. However, these would seem to be almost identical, since in 1844 shipments were 26,600 tons via the St Lawrence canals and 27,500 tons via the Lachine Canal.

[40] Andrews, *Report on the Trade and Commerce*, 454–55, 458.

[41] *JLAC*, 1849, app. AAAAA, 3.

[42] Ouellet, *Histoire économique et sociale*, 475; *JLAC*, 1849, app. AAAAA, 3, 11.

[43] Raoul Blanchard, *Le centre du Canada français* (Montreal, 1947), 153–56, 159–62, 166–68; *L'ouest du Canada français* (Montreal, 1953), 139, 145.

[44] Hamelin and Roby, *Histoire économique*, 122–23, 125.

[45] Blanchard, *Le centre du Canada français*, 320.

[46] Blanchard, *L'ouest du Canada français*, 144.

[47] Bouchette, *British Dominions* 1: 210, 305–306.

[48] Raoul Blanchard, *L'est du Canada français*, 2 vols. (Montreal, 1935), 1: 177.

Transportation Changes in the St. Lawrence–Great Lakes Region 1828–1860*

GERALD TULCHINSKY

Transportation has always been vital to Canadian economic life and was, in fact, the key to the movement of goods and people and to the expansion of various economic frontiers. The Canadian nation itself was realized when modern transportation systems joined scattered regions. In the short period from 1828–1860 creative and revolutionary transportation developments in the St. Lawrence–Great Lakes region laid the basis for the transportation system that eventually linked East and West. Steamboats came into general use; rivers were dredged; channels were marked; and major canals, docks, and lighthouses were built. There were early experiments in aerial transport by balloon, and the first railway networks were laid down.

These new and dramatic transportation developments in Canada during the mid-nineteenth century were stimulated by the ancient and continuing pattern of exploiting the country's agricultural and forest resources, a process which H.A. Innis called "staple economy." Another economic historian, H.G.J. Aitken, sees in these transportation developments an example of another long-standing Canadian tradition which he calls "defensive expansionism," or government-assisted growth of facilities which would prevent the United States from dominating British

*From the introduction to "Transportation Changes in the St. Lawrence–Great Lakes Region, 1828–1860," by Gerald Tulchinsky, *Canada's Visual History* 11: 1–5, published by National Museums of Canada and the National Film Board of Canada, 1974. Reprinted by permission.

368

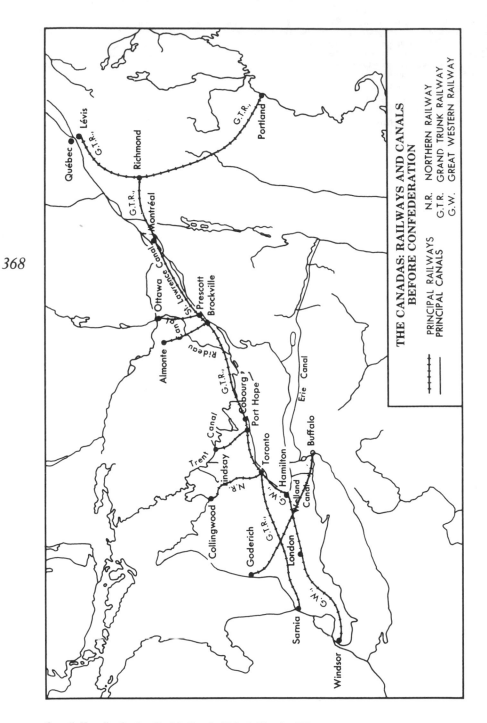

Cornell, Hamelin, Ouellet, Trudel, *Canada: Unity in Diversity*, 239.

North America. Both themes are highly important in understanding the connections between improved transportation facilities and Canada's place as an under-developed economy in the international trading system. They explain, too, the strategy of continental expansion in which government played a crucial role. Resource exploitation and "defensive expansionism" were carried out by the business class which promoted transportation innovations and also profited from them. The relationship between these businessmen and the politicians whose legislative measures largely shaped the climate of business enterprise is interesting and complex. Transportation developments touched other sectors of the economy as well. Perhaps the most profound effects were felt by the Canadian people in the course of their daily lives.

Canals

One of the major problems which arose during the settlement of Upper Canada was the high cost of transportation for goods coming from Montreal, the principal port of entry on the St. Lawrence River. These difficulties were more than just financial; there were very long delays and serious hazards in the movement of commercial goods and vital military supplies. In the aftermath of the War of 1812–14, the British government feared that these problems would hamper troops guarding the posts along the Upper Canadian frontier. It was this combination of commercial and military concern which prompted the construction of the earliest major canals built along the St. Lawrence–Great Lakes system in the 1820's and 1830's. These were the Lachine Canal, the Welland Canal (the first stage of which was completed in 1829 to by-pass Niagara Falls), and the Rideau Canal between Bytown and Kingston. The latter two were major feats of engineering, labour mobilization, and capital investment. Certainly these projects could not have been completed without the direct involvement of government.

After a weak and inadequate start under the auspices of a private company, the legislature of Lower Canada, despite a reputation for being anti-commercial, undertook financial responsibility for the construction of the Lachine Canal around the dangerous Lachine rapids above Montreal. The British government accepted a similar responsibility for the extremely costly (almost one million pounds) Rideau Canal which, in their view, would serve both military and economic strategies. Indeed, the Rideau was built under the supervision of British army engineers who employed local contractors to construct various portions of the work. Like the Lachine Canal, the Rideau was built mainly by Irish immigrants assisted by Scottish and French-Canadian artisans. A different engineering and financial influence can be seen in the earliest of the Welland canals where New York State had supplied capital, technical experts, and even a substantial number of the same working men who had only recently finished the Erie Canal. Yet, even here, large sums of Upper Canadian and smaller amounts of Lower Canadian government funds were invested, and when the first Welland Canal proved to be flimsy and inadequate, it was quickly taken over as a public work. This was a very common pattern throughout North America; in the neighbouring United States most of the major canal systems, including the immensely successful Erie, were state or local projects. Although entrepreneurs were not lacking, local capital was scarce; and there was no easy mechanism in Canada until later in the nineteenth century for drawing upon foreign, chiefly British, capital.

The importance to Canada of these canals of the 1820's and early 1830's was incalculable. Even though the canals did not succeed in drawing the vast trade of the entire mid-continental interior, they were highly important parts of a more efficient Canadian transportation system. Together with the competing Erie Canal, they perhaps aided in the extension of Upper Canada's agricultural frontier by greatly lessening transportation costs for imports, exports, and passengers. At the same time they opened up regions like the Rideau Lakes area which had been inaccessible. These projects provided brief employment for thousands of immigrants who often worked under hazardous conditions for low wages. Employers often used the truck system of payment by which men were paid in commodities, such as liquor, rather than in money. Canal labourers who organized to fight this situation (for example, the Lachine Canal strike of 1843) were among the first labour union agitators in Canada. Canal construction brought huge sums of money into the country and generally stimulated economic activity even though the funds filtered unevenly through the various regions and segments of the population. The demands for labour, food, supplies, hardware, and horses created expansion throughout the primitive economy of Canada.

Following the dramatic and significant burst of canal activity during the 1820's and early 1830's, nearly ten years intervened before a new era of significant waterway improvement was undertaken in the Canadas. Exhaustion of financial resources (the British government was furious at the huge cost of the Rideau Canal), economic stagnation, and political conflict deterred further activity until the union of the Canadas in 1840 introduced a new era of stability and optimism.

A vast and comprehensive new program was begun as a Canadian government public works project with the assistance of the British government who guaranteed the interest on the funds borrowed to build the canals. Planners aimed at improving the navigability of the St. Lawrence waterway between Montreal and Prescott where rapids and shallows had always impeded shipping. Canals were cut at Beauharnois, Cornwall and Williamsburg; and the Lachine and Welland canals were widened. When completed, at the huge expense of nearly two million pounds which the Province of Canada had borrowed in London, these canals provided an integrated, through-waterway from Montreal to Lake Erie for large vessels.

Although the canals succeeded only moderately as an outlet for the produce from the Canadian and United States regions bordering the Great Lakes, they constituted another important addition to the Canadian transportation network. It was cheaper to ship goods to the interior from Montreal than from New York City, but New York long continued to hold its advantage over Montreal as an ocean port because it did not freeze in winter. Furthermore at least one of the canals provided an important source of power for industrial use; during the late 1840's the Lachine Canal in Montreal became the site of dozens of new factories which manufactured flour, sugar, tools, lumber, clothing, steam engines, boats, and a substantial range of other goods. To encourage such industrialization, the government leased industrial sites at low rates. Consequently, manufacturers and speculators seized the opportunity to establish in Montreal and hence created a new aspect of economic life. Montreal had hitherto been principally a commercial city. By 1854, some twenty new factories employing approximately two thousand people had made Montreal the largest manufacturing centre in Canada.

371

Steamboats

The major canal building programs of the 1820's and 1830's as well as the several minor programs along the lower Ottawa, the Richelieu, and the St. Lawrence rivers were accompanied by a rapidly increased use of steamboats on Canadian waterways. While steamboats did not completely replace the bateaux, Durham boats, sloops, schooners, or rafts that were used to carry cargo and passengers, they were used increasingly for premium (high value) freight and passenger services. Starting in 1809, steamboats ran on the lower St. Lawrence River, and became common on the Great Lakes by the end of the following decade. During the next several years the "puffing billies," almost all of them built in Montreal shipyards, were to be found on inland waterways throughout the settled areas of British North America.

The building of steam engines for marine and stationary use developed into a major industry after the introduction of steamships. As early as 1818, a small foundry was set up by Americans in Montreal to build engines to meet the growing demand. This and similar factories established in Montreal and, later, in Kingston and Toronto formed the basis of the early Canadian engineering industry. A key link between the era of simple staple economy and the period known as the "age of steam and iron," they initiated Canada's transportation revolution. Both transportation and industrial activity were concentrated at the major commercial centres, and urban growth during these years was directly related to the growing connection between the two. This relationship became even clearer during the 1850's when railways encouraged the rapid growth and expansion of iron foundries and other industries.

Railroads

The age of steam and iron, which was foreshadowed in Canada by the launching of John Molson's steamship *Accommodation* in 1809, was to become an established fact of economic, social, and political life during the 1850's. Successful experiments in the use of steam engines on railroads in England during the 1820's inspired a flurry of railway construction in Britain and the United States during the next two decades. The enthusiasm for railways was at an extremely high pitch during the 1840's and, quite naturally, Canadians interested in improved transportation and profits readily took up the idea. In his famous pamphlet, *The Philosophy of Railroads*, published in 1850, Thomas Keefer, a distinguished Canadian engineer, extolled the virtues of railways in the following grandiloquent terms:

372

> The civilizing tendency of the locomotive is one of the modern anomalies, which, however inexplicable it may appear to some, is yet so fortunately patent to all, that it is admitted as readily as the action of steam, though the substance be invisible and its secret ways unknown to man. Poverty, indifference, the bigotry or jealousy of religious denominations, local dissensions or political demagogism, may stifle or neutralize the best intended efforts of an educational system; but that invisible power which has waged successful war with the material elements, will assuredly overcome the prejudices and mental weaknesses or the design of mental tyrants . . . it waits for no convenient season, but with a restless rushing, roaring assiduity, it keeps up a constant and unavoidable spirit of enquiry or comparison; and while ministering to the material wants, and appealing to the covetousness of the multitude, it unconsciously, irresistibly, impels them to a more intimate union with their fellow men.

Since the 1830's there lay strong interest in the possibility of building railways. Railways were discussed in the newspapers and in the Legislative Assemblies which would supply financial assistance to these projects; and the country's first railway, a fourteen mile portage line from Laprairie, near Montreal, to St. Jean, on the Richelieu River was completed in 1836. By the mid-forties, with general prosperity and the example of successful railway projects in Britain and the United States, lines were being planned to run between many Canadian towns and cities and there were visionary schemes of extending railways east to the other British North American provinces and west to the Pacific. At this relatively early date, the "philosophy of railroads" included estimates of social and economic benefits, and conceived of railways as instruments of policy, as means of better communications between existing communities and distant frontiers, and as aids to the strategy of British North American defense. Toronto and Montreal became the two major centres of Canadian railway promotion. Montreal entrepreneurs planned lines to winter ports on the Atlantic coast, and Toronto businessmen projected rail routes into new hinterlands to the north and west of the city.

It soon became apparent, however, that without strong government assistance, only a few short portage-type railways could be built; and, in 1849, the Canadian Legislature passed the Guarantee Act by which the payment of interest (up to 6%) on bonds issued by railways over 75 miles long would be guaranteed by the government once the railway was at least half-completed. This legislation was designed for big railway projects such as the Northern which was to connect Toronto and Georgian Bay, the St. Lawrence and Atlantic between Montreal and Portland, Maine, and the Great Western from Toronto to Windsor. Behind the protective skirts of this act, these projects went forward very rapidly and all were completed by 1854. There was a huge inflow of capital from Britain and the United States, but a considerable proportion was raised by private Canadian investors. More important, the granting of charters to these railways and many others (most of which were never built) reflected the rise of new groups of businessmen. There were the promoters of these lines, the speculators in railway stock issues or in land, the suppliers of building and operating equipment, the contractors, and a host of others. And there emerged, also, the entrepreneurs who often combined a number of these interests and who, by especially adroit manipulation, sometimes garnered huge profits. Although their actions are often extremely difficult to trace, those entrepreneurs who became wealthy through their railway interests often had close connections with politicians who sponsored and supported railway legislation. Sir Allan MacNab, leader of the Conservative party in Upper Canada, declared without hesitation, "my politics are railways." Few dissented and there are indications that huge numbers of politicians were obligated to the entrepreneur, Samuel Zimmerman, the key figure in the Great Western Railway.

The greatest railway project of this era was the Grand Trunk Railway, a Montreal to Toronto line begun in 1853, which was intended to be the Canadian section of an inter-colonial railway that would run through British North America from Halifax to Windsor. When Canadian railway promoters and politicians got through with this project, some had pocketed huge profits; and the public was saddled with a staggering debt of $26 million. This debt absorbed a large portion of government revenue

373

just to pay the interest on the loans (really outright gifts) that the government had extended to the company. The generous "legacy" the government allowed the Grand Trunk has been overshadowed by the even more generous grants of land, cash, railway lines, and other valuable benefits which were given to the Canadian Pacific Railway Company during the 1880's. Nevertheless, the Grand Trunk scheme was beset by waste, mismanagement, and some very dextrous sleight-of-hand. By 1853 the Grand Trunk company struggled under the ailing St. Lawrence and Atlantic Railway, the Quebec and Richmond line, a commitment to build the Victoria Bridge across the St. Lawrence River at Montreal, and the cost of constructing some two hundred additional and unnecessary miles of line from Toronto to Guelph and Sarnia, a region already served by the Great Western. Promoters A.T. Galt, Luther Holton, Casimir Gzowski, and David L. Macpherson were among the principal beneficiaries. British stock and bondholders and the Canadian people were left with an overly elaborate, expensive, debt-ridden, and unprofitable railway built on a gauge different from the western United States railways it was intended to join.

374

There were, however, some benefits to this extensive construction. The most substantial of them was probably the rapid acceleration of economic growth during the 1850's when capital formation, much of it for railway construction, ran up to a staggering $100 million. With the exception of a brief but serious business depression in 1857, this was a decade of significant economic expansion. Yet, it would be unwise to attribute all or even most of that expansion to the spin-off of railway construction. The rapid rise in the price of wheat during the Crimean War (1853–1856), the expansion of the American market for sawn lumber and other commodities, and the continuing expansion of Upper Canada were, in fact, the crucial elements in this prosperity. It is arguable, also, that the railways did not alone create the high rate of immigration or the general wide-spread industrial expansion in this era. Certainly some of the basic framework for the latter was clearly laid by 1850, before the railway age began in earnest. Nor can it be proven that railways were almost indispensable to the movement of commodities and to the expansion of the agricultural and lumbering frontier. For these, the lake, river, and canal systems were increasingly effective and, along with improvements to the road network, probably could have been extended with less cost than the amounts expended on railways. What the railways did accomplish, however, was to open the country to year-round transportation.

This did not mean, however, that commerce went on evenly twelve months of the year. The bulky cargoes of wheat, lumber, and timber moved mainly by water, still a far cheaper form of transportation than rail, and, railways notwithstanding, these staple industries remained seasonal. Even though the completion of the Victoria Bridge in 1859 made it possible to run trains from Sarnia and Windsor to Portland, Maine

(Montreal's winter port), a very small proportion of the staples went over that route. Indeed, very large quantities of Canadian exports were still carried to tide-water on American canals or railways. Still, it was the age of railways, and a healthy skepticism about the benefits commonly attributed to them should not blind one to the fact that practically everyone believed that railways were bound to bring prosperity in their wake.

Despite their questionable economic necessity, the railways became almost a sign of the times. Rail lines crossed the peaceful countryside and pushed into most of the major towns and cities; tracks were laid in the middle of streets; and locomotives spewed out smoke and noise, enraging concerned citizens. Railways considerably altered the areas in which they were built and deeply affected the lives of ordinary citizens by making relatively rapid transit available. Railway passage was cheap and fast. By reaching into the back townships where a less expensive right of way could be purchased, rail transportation served a broader segment of the population than steamboats had readily done. Although initially problem-ridden by derailments and other accidents, the railways soon became a very popular form of travel. Those who could afford it enjoyed comfortable sleeping and dining accommodations; there were upholstered chairs in second class and simple wooden benches in third class.

Railways gave rise to a whole new segment of the Canadian working class within a relatively short period. The railways were built by large gangs of labourers, among them immigrants who, not yet settled, were more mobile than earlier settlers. After the road beds were constructed, the tracks laid, and the bridges erected, the railroad still required regular maintenance. Often the road bed needed improvement, and large sections of most railways required a reduction in the grades. Men were needed to operate trains and repair equipment. The demand for locomotives and other railway stock created a broader market and stimulated expansion in the engine foundries and other metal working shops of Montreal. Railway-related factories arose in Kingston, Toronto, Hamilton, and London. The railway companies, in particular the Grand Trunk and the Great Western, erected what were, in those days, huge shops at their rail yards in Montreal and Hamilton. By 1860, Canadian railways employed a total of 6,600 men on their combined payrolls, and many more men worked in the factories that arose in several towns and cities to supply equipment.

Although one must concede that railways were just one part of the continuing transportation revolution, one should not underestimate their impact. The railways were a powerful engine of rapid change in the commercial and social fabric of the country. The railway was destined to expand. By 1860 the railway network in Ontario and Quebec extended along the more settled St. Lawrence-Great Lakes Valley, but promoters were now planning to build lines up the Ottawa Valley, east to Quebec,

375

and on into the Maritimes. There was the recurrent idea of building an east–west line to span the continent. Elsewhere in British North America, notably in the Maritime colonies where a highly ambitious, separate railway development program had been underway during the 1850's, there were several plans to connect cities and open new regions. Many of these schemes took decades to realize; yet with massive federal, provincial, and municipal government assistance, together with huge sums of foreign capital, many major railways were built. Indeed, one of the most important features of the railway era was the extent of government involvement in these schemes, many of them of questionable general utility. Growing sophistication in the ability to manipulate the financial structure of railway companies and to influence all levels of government created vast profits for an increasingly aggressive group of entrepreneurs. Notwithstanding the St. Lawrence–Great Lakes region had entered the railway age, it must be emphasized that the region still depended heavily on its maritime strength which, through canal developments, river improvements, and such important technological innovations as the screw propeller, grain loader, and iron hull, continued to grow during this period of rapid transition and diversification.

Topic Eleven

The Society of Upper Canada (Canada West)

On the eve of its creation by the Constitutional Act of 1791, Upper Canada had a population of roughly 20 000 (one-half white settlers and one-half Indians). By 1850 Canada West (as it came to be known after the Act of Union of 1841) had become the largest British North American colony, with a population of over one million white settlers (and still only approximately 10 000 Indians). Two groups, the Americans and the British, predominated. The Americans arrived in two waves — the United Empire Loyalists in the 1780s, settling mainly in the Niagara Peninsula and along the St. Lawrence River, and the later settlers, many with no Loyalist background, who arrived between 1791 and 1812. The British migrants came in great numbers between 1830 and 1860. Naturally, such rapid population growth created a society in transition. The following readings examine the nature of that society in the early nineteenth century.

The selections included here examine two aspects of the society of Upper Canada (Canada West) in the 1840s and 1850s. John Leslie's short article, "Buried Hatchet: The Origins of Indian Reserves in 19th Century Ontario," studies the native history of the province in mid-century. Michael Katz, in "The People of a Canadian City, 1851–1852," provides a look at life in the city of Hamilton during the same period.

The best surveys of Upper Canada are the two volumes in the Canadian Centenary Series: Gerald M. Craig's *Upper Canada: The Formative Years, 1784–1841* (Toronto: McClelland and Stewart, 1963) and J.M.S. Careless' *The Union of the Canadas: The Growth of Canadian Institutions, 1841–1857* (Toronto: McClelland and Stewart, 1967). Fred Landon's study, *Western Ontario and the American Frontier* (Toronto: McClelland and Stewart, 1967; first published in 1941) is still useful. R. Cole Harris, a historical geographer, provides a survey of Ontario in *Canada before Confederation: A Study in Historical Geography* (Toronto: Oxford University Press, 1974), 110–168. J.K. Johnson's *Historical Essays on Upper Canada* (Toronto: McClelland and Stewart, 1975) and his second collection of articles (edited with Bruce G. Wilson), *Historical Essays on Upper Canada*, vol. 2 (Ottawa: Carleton University Press, 1989) are very useful. The condition of the urban poor is treated by Patricia E. Malcolmson in "The Poor in Kingston, 1815-1850," in *To Preserve and Defend: Essays on Kingston in the Nineteenth Century*, ed. Gerald Tulchinsky (Montreal: McGill-Queen's University Press, 1976), 281–97. In "Class Conflict on the Canals of Upper Canada in the 1840s," *Labour/Le Travailleur* 7 (1981): 9–39, Ruth Bleasdale looks at the emerging working class in Upper Canada (Canada West).

Gerald Craig's edited work, *Early Travellers in the Canadas: Extracts from the Writings of Thirty Visitors to British North America, 1791-1867* (Toronto: Macmillan, 1955), is very helpful. Three of the most cited contemporary witnesses of early Upper Canada are women: Catharine Parr Traill, Susanna Moodie, and Anna Jameson. Catharine Parr Traill's *The Backwoods of Canada* (1836) and *The Canadian Settler's Guide* (1854), Susanna Moodie's *Roughing It in the Bush* (1852), and Anna Jameson's *Winter Studies and Summer Rambles in Canada* (1838) are available, in abridged editions, in McClelland and Stewart's New Canadian Library Series. Marian Fowler's *The Embroidered Tent: Five Gentlewomen in Early Canada* (Toronto: House of Anansi, 1982) contains sketches of these women's lives.

For a full review of the Iroquois residents of Upper Canada and their society in the early nineteenth century consult *The Valley of the Six Nations: A Collection of Documents on the Indian Lands of the Grand River*, ed. Charles M. Johnston (Toronto: The Champlain Society, 1964). Donald B. Smith tells the story of the Mississauga Indians in *Sacred Feathers: The Reverend Peter Jones (Kahkewaquonaby) and the Mississauga Indians* (Toronto: University of Toronto Press, 1987). A general review of the changes in Indian society is provided by Elizabeth Graham in *Medicine Man to Missionary: Missionaries as Agents of Change among the Indians of Southern Ontario, 1784-1867* (Toronto: Peter Martin Associates, 1975). Several chapters in Robin W. Winks' *The Blacks in Canada* (Montreal: McGill-Queen's University Press, 1971) deal with the arrival, and the lives, of Blacks in Upper Canada.

Recently two studies have examined the political loyalties of the early settlers in Upper Canada/Canada West: Jane Errington's *The Lion, The Eagle, and Upper Canada: A Developing Colonial Ideology* (Kingston and Montreal: McGill-Queen's University Press, 1987) and David Mills' *The Idea of Loyalty in Upper Canada, 1784-1850* (Toronto: University of Toronto Press, 1988).

David W.L. Earl's collection, *The Family Compact: Aristocracy or Oligarchy?* (Toronto: Copp Clark, 1967), contains a number of important essays on the conservative establishment, including excerpts from Robert E. Saunder's "What Was the Family Compact?" *Ontario History*, 49 (1957). A recent biography of a prominent member of the Family Compact is Patrick Brode's *Sir John Beverley Robinson: Bone and Sinew of the Compact* (Toronto: The Osgoode Society, 1984). William Kilbourn's biography of William Lyon Mackenzie, *The Firebrand* (Toronto: Clarke, Irwin and Co., 1956), offers a lively account of the radical reformer who led the rebellion of 1837 in Upper Canada. Two recent accounts of the Upper Canadian rebellion are Colin Read and Ronald J. Stagg, eds., *The Rebellion of 1837 in Upper Canada: A Collection of Documents* (Ottawa: Carleton University Press, 1985) and Colin Read, *The Rebellion of 1837 in Upper Canada*, Canadian Historical Association, Historical Booklet no. 46 (Ottawa: CHA, 1988).

Two of the best Canadian biographical studies are about the two leading political antagonists of the 1850s: D.G. Creighton's *John A. Macdonald*, vol. 1, *The Young Politician* (Toronto: Macmillan, 1952) and J.M.S. Careless' *Brown of the Globe*, vol. 1, *The Voice of Upper Canada, 1818–1859* (Toronto: Macmillan, 1959). J.M.S. Careless has also written the survey *The Union of the Canadas: The Growth of Canadian Institutions, 1841–1857* (Toronto: McClelland and Stewart, 1967).

Buried Hatchet: The Origins of Indian Reserves in 19th-Century Ontario*

379

JOHN LESLIE

Following the War of 1812, as relations with the United States improved, the strategic importance of Indian people as military allies to the British quickly declined. And in 1815 and 1816, two important developments occurred in British Indian policy. The Indian Department, established in 1755, was transferred from civil to military control, and the British government, which financed and directed Indian policy in British North America, embarked formally on a program to reduce departmental costs.

The reason for transferring the department to military control (until April 1830) was to keep the formulation of Indian policy out of the hands of local colonial legislatures which might be inclined to ignore Indian interests and seize Indian-occupied lands.

In terms of financial restraint, once proud Indian warriors, outfitted at British expense, were now to become self-reliant farmers as in 1821, the lieutenant governor of Upper Canada, Sir Peregrine Maitland, launched an experiment to promote Indian self-reliance. Indians would be established on reserves, converted to Christianity, and taught farming skills. The scheme would be financed from the sale of Indian lands to European settlers.

A Model Settlement

Maitland's efforts met with limited success. But as a result of discussions with the Rev. Peter Jones (Kahkewaquonaby or "Sacred Waving Feath-

*From *Horizon Canada* 40 (1985): 944–49. Reprinted by permission.

ers"), a Methodist minister of Welsh-Mississauga heritage, a model Indian village was established in 1826 at the mouth of the Credit River near present-day Toronto. Despite early difficulties, village life flourished under Jones' leadership. The model settlement was regularly visited by missionaries, educators, and government officials eager to see the future.

In July 1828, Gov. Gen. Lord Dalhousie received instructions from the British Colonial Office to prepare a report on Indian Department operations, taking into account that the service should soon be abolished. Both Dalhousie and Maitland were shocked at the tone and content of the colonial secretary's message.

Dalhousie's detailed response, forwarded in October 1828, stated that the Indian Department was still necessary to protect the rights and property of Indian people in the face of advancing European settlement. Indian people would eventually be able to manage their own affairs, he argued, but only after they had acquired the rights of other British subjects and obtained full citizenship.

380

The key to achieving Indian assimilation was to establish other settlements in Upper Canada on the Credit River model and under the supervision of the Indian Department. Otherwise, said Dalhousie, Indian people would remain totally dependent on the government, or they would soon starve in the streets and crowd the jails; worse still, they might become disillusioned and join forces with the Americans. Adoption of a formal program for Indian advancement would, in Dalhousie's view, replace the old military alliance and foster in Indian people "a love of the Country, of the soil on which they are settled and a respect for the Government which protects them."

After some discussion, Sir George Murray, the colonial secretary, accepted Dalhousie's Indian civilization plan and the British Treasury authorized £20,000 to finance it. To test the new approach and philosophy, two model Indian villages were established immediately at Coldwater (near present-day Orillia) and Sarnia.

Progress Reports

In 1835, the British government demanded progress reports on the new Indian settlements. In Lower Canada, a committee of the executive council conducted the investigation. In Upper Canada, Lt. Gov. Sir Francis Bond Head chose a different course. After a tour of Indian villages in Upper Canada in the summer of 1836, Bond Head concluded that Indian warriors would never become farmers; they were a "doomed race" incapable of ever attaining equality with their white neighbours. The best approach was to relocate them to the comparative isolation of Manitoulin Island where they would gradually die out. This would simultaneously solve the "Indian problem" and provide new land for settlers.

Bond Head's radical removal plan upset the tribes of Upper Canada and outraged the Methodist missionaries. In the midst of the resulting political uproar, the executive council of Lower Canada presented its findings, rejecting both Bond Head's philosophy and removal plans. Instead, the councillors urged that Indian villages be located close to non-Native settlements. The Indian Department, the distribution of annual presents, and the current civilization program should be continued without significant change.

The existing system was certainly not without fault, they acknowledged, observing that the "policy of Government has been to keep them [Indians] apart from the rest of Society, has trained in them an Aversion to Labour, and has in a measure incapacitated them from becoming useful members of Society." The key to progress was Indian education, and it was the duty of government to prepare the younger generation "for another and more useful mode of life."

The report of the executive council, printed in 1837, impressed Colonial Secretary Lord Glenelg, since it reflected his own views and offered him a way out of the Bond Head controversy. In August 1838, Glenelg asked for a similar report on Indian conditions in Upper Canada. The task was eventually assigned to Justice James B. Macaulay, a judge of the Court of King's Bench.

381

Macaulay's report reflected the findings of the executive council. He rejected Bond Head's philosophy, urged continuation of annual presents, and pleaded for patience and time to allow the Indian civilization program to work. In the meantime, officers of the Indian Department had a continuing responsibility for ensuring the well-being of Native people, protecting their lands and aboriginal rights.

The reports of the executive council and James Macaulay had little effect in changing Indian policy as they were soon overtaken by political events of greater importance — the rebellions of 1837, Lord Durham's report, and the union of Upper Canada and Lower Canada in 1840. The calmer political atmosphere that followed union permitted long-delayed plans for policy and administrative reforms to proceed. Once again, the plight of Canada's Indians came under scrutiny.

A Sorry Picture

This time the investigation was carried out by three royal commissioners appointed by Gov. Gen. Sir Charles Bagot. Their report, presented in 1844, painted a depressing picture of bungled departmental operations, deplorable Indian conditions, and unresolved policy questions. The civilization program set up in 1830 was condemned as too paternalistic for it had "a tendency to keep Indian people in a state of isolation and tutelage and materially to retard their progress."

382

INDIAN TREATIES AND PURCHASES
IN ONTARIO, 1781-1867

QUEBEC

LAKE SUPERIOR

LAKE HURON

LAKE MICHIGAN

UNITED STATES
OF AMERICA

LAKE ONTARIO

LAKE ERIE

A May 9, 1781
  - Mississauga and Chippewa
B Oct. 9, 1783
  - Algonquin and Iroquois
B₁ Oct. 9, 1783
  - Mississauga
B₂ 1784, 1787-88
  - Mississauga
A₂ 1785
  - Chippewa
C May 19, 1790
  - Ottawa, Chippewa,
    Potawatomi, Huron
D Dec. 2, 1792
  - Mississauga
E 1793
  - Iroquois
F 1793
  - Mohawk
G Oct. 24, 1794
  - Mohawk
H 1795
  - Chippewa
I Sept. 7, 1796
  - Chippewa
J Sept. 7, 1796
  - Chippewa
K June 30, 1798
  - Chippewa
L Aug. 1, 1805
  - Mississauga

M Aug. 2, 1805
  - Mississauga
N 1815
  - Chippewa
O Oct. 17, 1818
  - Chippewa
P Oct. 28, 1818
  - Chippewa
Q Nov. 5, 1818
  - Chippewa
R March 9, 1819
  - Chippewa
S May 31, 1819
  - Mississauga
T April 25, 1825
  - Ojibwa, Chippewa
U Aug. 13, 1833
  - Huron
V Aug. 9, 1836
  - Chippewa, Ottawa
W Aug. 9, 1836
  - Saugeens
X June 1, 1847
  - Iroquois
Y Sept. 7, 1850
  - Ojibwa
Z Sept. 9, 1850
  - Ojibwa
AA Oct. 30, 1854
  - Chippewa
AB Feb. 9, 1857
  - Chippewa

Land deals. Ontario was purchased from the Indians by the British. This map indicates the date and area of each land agreement made between 1781 and Confederation.

Dept. of Cartography, CEGEP de Limoilou, Que.

There were, said the commissioners, no racial barriers to Indian advancement, a process which could be accelerated by improvements in Indian education, legal protection of Indian land and resources, and a complete reorganization of the Indian Department. But the investigators were reluctant to recommend an expanded Indian service, or additional funding, because, in their view, Indian people were encountering the "incontrollable force of those natural laws of society to which every Government must bend," and eventually Indian people would simply be assimilated.

To reduce costs and the number of Indians under government supervision, the commissioners suggested two measures which still have some application to this day. First, Indian women who married white men would no longer receive presents; effectively, they would lose their Indian status. Second, any Indian who had received an education, and was able to support himself, would be granted title to his land, after which he would forfeit further claims to annuity payments of band property. This was the origin of the policy which came to be known as Indian enfranchisement, the attainment of full citizenship privileges indistinguishable from those of the general populace.

383

The commissioners failed to resolve the central problem facing the department which was a lack of administrative cohesion and focus. Too many government departments, both colonial and imperial, as well as various groups and vested interests, were involved in policy implementation. Proper coordination and unity of action was impossible.

British authorities reacted favourably to the report and recommended that the Canadian government implement its many proposals. Perhaps the most enduring legacy of the commission was a renewed commitment to Indian education based on a system of model farms and industrial schools. Thus by 1847 the civilization program had been redefined and set on a more optimistic course.

A Transfer of Power

By mid-century, however, Indian lands and resources were increasingly threatened by settlement and resource development. For the first time legislation was passed in Canada East (Quebec) and Canada West (Ontario) which protected Indian land and property from seizure or expropriation. As well, the term "Indian" was defined legally, based on principles of blood lineage, inter-marriage, or adoption. This legislation was the immediate forerunner of the 1857 Indian Civilization Act, which set down a procedure for the compulsory enfranchisement of Indian people, a virtual assault on the existing tribal structures. Later, these measures became the basis for the Indian Acts after Confederation.

About the same time that special Indian legislation was being enacted in the Canadas, a crisis in imperial financing led Britain to announce that it would stop funding the Indian Department in 1860. Canadian offers to pay part of the costs were unavailing. It was all or nothing.

So Canada assumed responsibility for Indian affairs in 1860. A civilization program, based on reserves and treaties, was in place for dealing with Native peoples on the frontier and a historic commitment had been often repeated that Canada would continue its funding and operation. At the time, of course, the Canadian government viewed both the reserve system and Native peoples as temporary features of the Canadian landscape which would eventually disappear as Indians took advantage of the 1857 Civilization Act and opted for enfranchisement.

More than a century later, however, Native peoples and Indian reserves still exist, as anomalous as ever, persistently and impatiently raising un-

One Last Look

The British government's cost-cutting policies and desire to drop its responsibilities for Indian affairs led to the last inquiry into Indian affairs before Confederation and set the stage for Canada to take over where Britain left off.

The 1858 inquiry report by Richard Pennefather, civil secretary to the governor general, concluded that 40 years of hard work had failed to raise "Indians as a body to the social or political level of their white neighbours." The Indians were partly to blame, but so were governments who had failed to act on the recommendations of previous inquiries.

Even before the report was published, the British government announced that funding for the Indian Department would be cut off in 1860. Canadian officials were dismayed. Pennefather had argued that the Indians, now totally dependent on the Crown, could not be abandoned. "The treaties made with several tribes, and the peculiar position of the people, require great care and consideration in securing their just rights whilst their lands are opened for settlements," he said.

Gov. Gen. Sir Edmund Walker Head agreed. In May 1858, he recommended that Canada assume total responsibility for Indian affairs and that the Indian Department be funded through the sale of Indian lands. The British eagerly accepted the proposal and on June 1, 1860, the final transfer of authority took place.

answered questions about their social conditions, reserved lands, treaty and aboriginal rights, self-government and tribal sovereignty. An Indian Affairs Department, too, remains, spending ever-increasing sums of money to come to grips with acute social problems which for more than a century it could not solve, and may have inadvertently created.

The People of a Canadian City: 1851–1852*

MICHAEL KATZ

On an average day in 1851 about 14,000 people awoke in Hamilton, Ontario. Most of them were quite unremarkable and thoroughly ordinary. In fact, there is no reason why the historian reading books, pamphlets, newspapers, or even diaries and letters should ever encounter more than seven hundred of them. The rest, at least ninety-five out of every hundred, remain invisible. Insofar as most written history is concerned, they might just as well have never lived.

385

One consequence of their invisibility has been that history, as it is usually written, represents the record of the articulate and prominent. We assume too easily, for example, that the speeches of politicians reflected the feelings and conditions of ordinary people. Another consequence is that we lack a foundation on which to construct historical interpretations. It was, after all, the activities, interactions, and movements of these invisible men and women that formed the very stuff of past societies. Without a knowledge of how they lived, worked, behaved, and arranged themselves in relation to each other our understanding of any place and point in time must be partial, to say the least. A third consequence is that we apply contemporary assumptions to past society. We use our everyday experience of modern social relationships to make models which we apply to the past. We believe, for instance, that we are more sophisticated than our ancestors about sex, marriage, and the spacing of children. As a result, we imagine that they must have married younger than we do today and reproduced as fast as nature would allow. Both of these assumptions, as it happens, are generally quite untrue.

The problem, of course, is evidence. How are we to write with meaning of the life of an ordinary labourer, shoemaker, or clerk in a nineteenth-century city? Or trace the most common patterns between important social features such as occupation, wealth, religion, ethnicity, family size, and school attendance? Those questions may be answered more directly and in a more straightforward manner than we have often imagined,

*From *Canadian Historical Review* 53 (1972): 402–426. Reprinted by permission of University of Toronto Press.

as I hope to make clear in the rest of this essay. My purpose is twofold: first, to show the range of questions about ordinary nineteenth-century people that may be asked and answered, and second, to sketch what, at this juncture, I take to be the primary social and demographic patterns within a mid-nineteenth-century Canadian city. The two great themes of nineteenth-century urban history, I shall argue, are transiency and inequality; I shall devote a section of this paper to each and, as well, to the nature of the family and household. For differences in family and household structure reflected, in part, the broad economic distinctions within urban society.

At the beginning two caveats are necessary: the quantitative information presented here is only partial; it is drawn from a great many detailed tables.[1] Second, figures given here are approximate. Such must be the case with all historical data. However, and this is the important point, the magnitudes, the differences between groups, may be taken, I believe, as a fair representation of the situation as it existed.

The manuscript census is the most valuable source of information about people within nineteenth-century cities. Its value is enhanced by its arrangement because it provides a list of features not only for each individual but for each household as well. For individuals the census from 1851 onward lists, among other items, name, age, birthplace, religion, occupation, school attendance, and birth or death within the year. It provides a residential location for each household and a description of the kind of house occupied; it permits the differentiation of relatives from non-relatives and the rough delineation of the relationships of household members to each other. In some cases it provides information about the business of the household head by listing other property, such as a store or shop owned, and number of people employed. Assessment rolls supplement the manuscript census with detailed economic information, usually about each adult member of the workforce. The assessment lists income over a certain level, real property, personal property, and some other economic characteristics. As well, it lists the occupation of each person assessed, the owner of the dwelling, and hence, whether the individual was an owner or renter of property. (In some instances a man who rents one house or store owns another; in other cases individuals own property around the city. These bits of information about individuals may be gathered together to present a more complete economic profile.) Published city directories corroborate the information from other sources and provide, additionally, the exact residential address of people and, in the case of proprietors, the address of their business if outside the home. Directories include, additionally, listings of people in various important political, financial, and voluntary positions within the city. Many other sources which list information about ordinary people supplement the census, assessment, and directory. Newspapers are the richest of these; mined systematically they yield an enormous load of information about the activities of people within the city. There are marriage records, church records, records of voluntary societies and educational institutions, cemetery records, and listings of other sorts as well. Each of these sources may be studied by itself and the patterns it presents analysed and compared with those found in other places. It is most exciting and rewarding, however, to join records together. By finding the same individuals listed in different records it is possible to build up rich and well-documented portraits of the lives of even the most ordinary of people.[2]

The project on which this essay rests uses all of the various records described above. Its most general purpose is to analyse the impact of industrialization on urban social structure and social mobility, using Hamilton, Ontario, as a case study. It deals with the years 1851 through, at the least, 1881; its basis is coded information about all, and not a sample, of the individuals listed in the kinds of sources described above, studied at differing intervals.

387

This essay discusses, primarily, the early 1850s. Its principal sources arc, specifically, the manuscript census of 1851, the assessment roll of 1852 (compiled three months after the census), the city directory of 1853 (the first published within the city), the marriage registers of 1842-69, and two local newspapers, one for both 1851 and 1852 and one for 1852.[3] In some instances the analysis rests on one source alone, in others on sources combined.

The sources for Hamilton as well as studies of American cities make clear that the first great theme of a nineteenth-century city is transiency. The most careful students of transiency to date, Stephen Thernstrom and Peter Knights, conclude from their study of Boston that far more people lived within the city in the course of a year than the census taker could find present at any point in time. The census of 1880 listed the population of Boston as 363,000; that of 1890 as 448,000. However, during those ten years they estimate that about one and one-half million different people actually lived within the city. Elsewhere Knights has estimated that twice as many artisans in some crafts plied their trade within the city in the course of a year as might be found there at any given moment. Eric Hobsbawm's tramping artisans, quite obviously, were a North American as well as a British phenomenon.[4]

The same transiency characterized the population of Hamilton. At this point it is not possible to provide exact figures or to say more than that transiency was a mass phenomenon. We do so on the following evidence. The assessment roll of 1852 listed 2552 people. Through careful linkage by hand (later replicated by computer) we have been able to join only 1955 of them to people listed on the census, which, as mentioned above, had been taken three months earlier. (There is no reason to assume that the intervening three months were unusual in any way.) Even with a generous allowance for error, large numbers of people could not be found because they had moved into the city during the intervening three months. In the same way a comparable percentage of household heads listed on the census could not be found three months later on the assessment. Most of them had left the city. Similarly, fewer than half the people on census or assessment could be found listed in the city directory compiled about a year and a half later, and there were a great many people listed on the directory and not on either census or assessment. Death records point to the same conclusion. Each household head was required to record on the census the name of any person within his household who had died during the preceding year. However, Hamilton cemetery and church records for both 1851 and 1861 reveal that the number of people who actually died within the city far exceeded the number recorded on the census. Only a few can be linked to families resident within the city at the time the census was taken.[5] In most instances the families apparently had left the city. It is difficult to estimate the number of deaths that fall into this category; certainly it is not less than a number half again as large as the number of deaths recorded on the census.

The population, this evidence suggests, contained two major groupings of people. The first consisted of relatively permanent residents who persisted within the city for at least several years. This group comprised between a third and two-fifths of the population. The remainder were transients, people passing through the city, remaining for periods lasting between a few months and a few years.

Many of the transients were heads of household, not, as we might suspect, primarily young men drifting around the countryside. The age distribution among the transient heads of household closely resembled that among the more permanent. If anything, the transients on the average were very slightly older. Nor, as one might expect, were the transients all people of little skill and low status. The percentage of labourers among the transients (15 per cent) was only slightly higher than among the more permanent residents. Indeed, there were many people with skilled or entrepreneurial jobs who moved from place to place; the transients included twenty-four merchants, fifty-eight clerks, seven lawyers, fifty-one shoemakers, twenty-eight tailors, and so on.

Although the transients approximated the rest of the population in age and occupation, they differed in one critical respect: wealth. Within every occupational category, the people who remained within the city were wealthier.[6] Thus, it was the *poorer* merchants, shoemakers, lawyers, and even the poorer labourers who migrated most frequently. All of this points to the coexistence of two social structures within nineteenth-century society: one relatively fixed, consisting of people successful at their work, even if that work was labouring; the other a floating social structure composed of failures, people poorer and less successful at their work, even if that work was professional, drifting from place to place in search of success.[7]

The significance of the existence of transiency as a key feature of social structure in both Boston, Massachusetts, and Hamilton, Ontario, becomes evident from considering the fundamental differences between the two cities. Late nineteenth-century Boston had become an industrial city; mid-century Hamilton remained a small, commercial, and pre-industrial one. Yet both were filled, in Knights' and Thernstrom's phrase, with "men in motion"; transiency formed an integral and international feature of nineteenth-century society and one not immediately altered by industrialization.

The relationship between workplace and residence underscores the pre-industrial nature of Hamilton. The separation of work and residence has been one of the most profound consequences of industrialization; the degree to which they remain united provides a rough guide to the extent of industrial development within a society. Contemporary sociologists contrast the organization of family and workplace by pointing to their basic structural differences in terms of authority relationships, criteria for rewards, and so on. They argue that people must play radically different roles in each setting. It becomes the task of the family and the school to teach the individual to make the transition between home and work and to learn to live with the sorts of internal switching required by a continual shifting from the personal and warm relations of the family to the impersonal, bureaucratic organization of work. This dichotomy in roles is a consequence of modern work organization. It came about as a result of the separation of residence and workplace. Its implication for the psychology of the individual person and for the functions of family and school are what make the shift of such profound significance.[8]

It is almost impossible to state precisely the proportion of men who were self-employed and the proportion who worked at their homes in Hamilton in the 1850s. What follows is a rough estimate of the minimum numbers in each category.[9] In 1851, 1142 male household heads were employees and 957 employers. Adding 1310 male adult boarders, almost all employees, gives a total male workforce of 3409 of which 2452 or 74 per cent were not self-employed and 26 per cent were. Given the approximate nature of the figures, it would be unwise to claim more than that between a quarter and a third of the men within the city worked for themselves. Certainly, this is evidence enough to point to a contrast with contemporary industrial society.

Of those men who were self-employed about 137 (comprising roughly half of the proprietors of businesses and attorneys) worked away from their homes. Interestingly, if the proportion had been based on the number of *businesses*, not the number of proprietors, the proportion uniting work and residence would have been much higher. For many businesses were partnerships in which one member lived at the place of business, the other elsewhere. On the basis of this estimate approximately 14 per cent of self-employed men worked away from their place of residence as did 72 per cent of all employed males or 60 per cent of household heads. Put another way, at least four out of ten households combined the function of place of work and place of residence for some of their members. That figure clearly demonstrates the pre-industrial character of life within the city.

Even though many people had to leave home each day to go to work, few spent their time in large, formal settings. Most people, regardless of where their job was done, worked in small groups. According to the census of 1851 (which is undoubtedly an underenumeration in this respect) there were within the city 282 artisan shops, stores, offices, and manufactories. The proprietors of over half of these (52 per cent) listed no employees. A further twenty-five listed one, and an additional sixty, between two and five employees. Only thirty places had between six and ten employees and but a handful had more than ten. This picture of smallness and informality is completed by the city government, which employed approximately fifteen people full-time, a few others part-time, and spent annually only about £18–20,000.[10]

The preceding discussion has described features of a nineteenth-century city that might be located almost anywhere in North America or Great Britain. There was, however, one feature of Hamilton that marked it as distinctively Canadian and, at the same time, adds more evidence to the theme of transiency; this was the birthplaces of its residents. Only about 9 per cent of Hamilton's workforce had been born in Canada West. The rest were immigrants, about 29 per cent from England and Wales, 18 per cent from Scotland, 32 per cent from Ireland, 8 per cent from the United States, and the rest from elsewhere. Hamilton in 1851 was an immigrant city and so it remained for at least a decade, as the figures for the birthplace of household heads in 1861 reveal. It was, thus, in a double sense that the people of Hamilton were "men in motion." At a very basic level, the origins of their people, early Canadian cities differed fundamentally from ones in the United States and Great Britain. The consequences of this demographic difference might provide a fruitful perspective from which to begin the comparative study of national development and of national character.

The immigrants to Hamilton did not gather themselves into ghettoes. On the basis of indexes of segregation used by both sociologists and historians, the degree of residential clustering by ethnicity, religion, and wealth appears slight, a feature apparently characteristic of Philadelphia and Boston in the same period as well. Nonetheless, there were some broad economic differences between regions of the city. It is possible to distinguish three zones: a core district, a district surrounding the core, and an outer district. The core zone had disproportionately few poor, 9 per cent, and disproportionately many well-to-do people, 45 per cent. In the outer district that situation was reversed: 32 per cent of the people there were poor and 24 per cent well-to-do. In the middle district over half the people were of average wealth and 18 per cent poor. This pattern reflects what other scholars have described as the typical residential patterns within a nineteenth-century city before the coming of urban transport systems, a pattern that changed when the well-to-do were able to move to the suburbs and the poor clustered in downtown ghettoes.[11]

Despite these trends, people of all degrees of wealth lived in close proximity to each other, the poor and the affluent intermingling on the same streets far more, probably, than they do at present. Indeed, it is clear already the extent to which the nineteenth-century city differed from the urban environment which we know today. The transiency, the newness, and the intermingling of its population, the small scale of its enterprise, the high degree of self-employment, and the continued unity of work and residence: all define a situation which our own experience of urban life prepares us poorly to comprehend, but which, as historians, we must try to recapture.

In fact, it is easy to be nostalgic about small pre-industrial cities. The absence of large-scale industry, the informality of government, and the lack of bureaucratic forms suggest an urban style both more cohesive and personal than that which we know today. We can imagine them, without too much difficulty, as filled with less tension and more warmth than contemporary cities, as stable, neighbourly, and easy places in which to live, as communities in a sense in which urban places have ceased to be. Unfortunately, the image just emerging from close, empirical study of nineteenth-century cities does not support the nostalgic vision. From one perspective it is partly contradicted by the facts of transiency, which we have already observed. The continual circulation of population prevented the formation of stable and closely integrated communities within nineteenth-century cities. At the same time, sharp inequalities in wealth and power reinforced the pressures of population mobility against cohesion and integration; together they made the nineteenth-century city, even before industrialization, a place at least as harsh, as insecure, and as overwhelming as urban environments today.

391

It is scarcely novel to assert that sharp inequalities existed within nineteenth-century cities or to posit a sharply graduated rank ordering of people. What should be stressed about that inequality is this: first, it may have been greater even than we have imagined; second, it underlay other social differences between people, such as household size and attitudes toward education; third, it shaped political patterns and processes. In short, the division of people on most social measures corresponded to the economic differences between them. Social, political, and economic power overlapped and interlocked, creating a sharply divided society in which a small percentage of the people retained a near monopoly on all the resources necessary to the well-being of the rest.

There are various ways with which to measure the division of wealth within a community, and each one, each scale that is adopted, yields a different result.[12] One division is property ownership: about one quarter of the population owned all the real property within the city. Roughly three-quarters of the people rented their living accommodations and owned no other real property whatsoever. The most affluent 10 per cent of the population held about 88 per cent of the wealth represented by the possession of property. From a slightly different perspective, people in the top 10 *income* percentiles (as reported on the assessment) earned nearly half the income within the city, and this figure, for a variety of reasons, is undoubtedly greatly understated. At the other extreme the poorest 40 per cent earned a little over 1 per cent of the income. Measured on a third scale, one designed to show economic ranking, the pattern of inequality is similar. On this scale "wealth" is a construct of different items and does not correspond exactly to either total income or assessed property; it is, however, the best available indicator of economic rank. On the basis of this measure, the wealthiest tenth of the people controlled about 60 per cent of the wealth within the city and the poorest two-fifths about 6 per cent.

The scale of economic ranking also reveals differences between the wealth of the various sectors of the city's economy. The people engaged in building, about 14 per cent of the workforce (indicating the rapid expansion of the city), held only about 7 per cent of the city's wealth; similarly, those engaged in some form of manufacturing (primarily artisans), about one-quarter of the workforce, had only 15 per cent of the wealth. Likewise, as might be expected, the unskilled and semi-skilled labourers, about 22 per cent of the workforce, had less than 5 per cent of the wealth. At the other extreme those engaged in professions, about 4 per cent of the workforce, held over 7 per cent of the wealth, and the men in commerce, about a quarter of the workforce, controlled nearly 59 per cent of the wealth, a figure which underscores the clear commercial basis of the city.

Religious and ethnic groups, like the various sectors of the economy, shared unequally in the city's wealth. Of the various immigrant and religious groups, the Irish and the Catholics fared worst. It is fair, I have argued elsewhere, to consider as poor the people in the lowest forty economic ranks. Using this criterion, 47 per cent of the working population born in Ireland were poor as were 54 per cent those who were Catholic. This, of course, is not a surprising finding. On the other hand it might be supposed that the English and the Anglicans were disproportionately wealthy, but this was not the case. Both groups formed a microcosm of the larger social structure, distributed quite normally among different economic categories.[13] The Free Church Presbyterians did rather better but the most affluent group, considering both numbers who were poor and numbers who were well-to-do, were the Wesleyan Methodists.[14] In terms of birthplace, the native Canadians and Americans fared best, a prosperity no doubt reflecting the problems of trans-Atlantic migration rather than inherent ethnic capacity or style. Of the Canadians 32 per cent were well-to-do as were 31 per cent of the Americans.[15]

It is difficult to associate economic rank with standard of living and to demarcate with precision the line separating the poor from the comfortable. To say that the fortieth economic rank marks the spot at which people ceased being poor means that it was the point at which they probably no longer had to struggle for and occasionally do without the necessities of life. Poverty in nineteenth-century cities did not mean the absence of luxuries, simple spartan living with good home-grown food and sturdy home-sewn clothes. Poverty meant absolute deprivation: hunger, cold, sickness, and misery, with almost no place to turn for relief. The poor within Hamilton, it is important to remember, remained quite at the mercy of the well-to-do, who controlled not only employment opportunity but dispensed what little welfare there was as a gift, not as a right. The Ladies Benevolent Society, a voluntary and paternalistic body, formed in effect the city welfare department. Financed by charitable donations and grants from the City Council, it assigned teams of gracious ladies to roam the streets, locate the worthy poor, and dispense loaves of bread, sometimes coal and groceries, even occasionally rent. The City Council coped with massive numbers of immigrants overcrowding the combination hospital and poorhouse by transporting newly arrived Irish people in wagonloads to country towns where they were summarily left. Clearly, they believed such widespread poverty was only a temporary problem, which could be solved by simple expedients that did not require the permanent and institutionalized extension of public responsibility for individual welfare.[16]

Aside from economic hardship, poverty in Hamilton meant powerlessness and invisibility. The lack of public provision for welfare reveals part of the powerlessness: the poor had no assistance on which they could draw as a right. Nor could they make their wants heard in any legal way, as the suffrage restrictions show. Less than half of the adult males in Hamilton owned or rented enough property to vote; 53 per cent of all adult men, or 43 per cent of household heads, could not meet the economic requirements for suffrage. Neither could 80 per cent of the labourers, 56 per cent of the artisans, or 59 per cent of the business employees (primarily clerks). No working class political protest could be expressed through the ballot in Hamilton; most of the working class simply lacked the vote. The invisibility that accompanied powerlessness is harder to demonstrate; its existence has come to light by comparing the records of the Ladies Benevolent Society with the manuscript census. The former contain a month by month listing of the recipients of welfare. Early checking to find these names on the census, even for the very month in which the census had been taken, located very few of them. Perhaps they were simply passed by, a blot on the city it was as well, if possible, to ignore.

393

Even within a relatively simple society like Hamilton's, the affluent had tangible means of demonstrating their degree of success. One was the employment of servants. It was at the 80th economic rank that a family became more likely than not to employ domestic help, and the likelihood increased with each higher rank on the scale. Overall, about one-quarter of the families in Hamilton had a servant living with them. If Hobsbawm's assertion that the possession of a servant defined middle-class status applies to Canada as well as England, then the percentage of households without servants indicates, again, the magnitude of the working class in Hamilton.[17] Most of the servants, 60 per cent, had been born in Ireland and 47 per cent were Catholic. They were by and large young girls: slightly more than half were under twenty years old, and three-quarters were under twenty-five. Nearly nine out of ten servants were females, 93 per cent unmarried, although some of the latter had children of their own. Families that employed servants were likely to live in a brick or stone house with two or more stories surrounded by an extra-large plot of land. The first two became, like the employment of servants, more likely than not at the 80th economic rank, the latter, size of plot attached to dwelling, increased most often at the 90th.

Household size also increased quite directly with wealth: to take one example, 15 per cent of the households in the 20–40th ranks were large (eight or more members), compared to 30 per cent of those in the 60–80th and 61 per cent of those in the top 1 per cent. There was, however, little relationship between wealth and number of children. Consequently, the presence of servants, boarders, and relatives accounted for the larger household size of the wealthy. In fact, servants, boarders, and relatives all lived more frequently with affluent than with poor families. School attendance also varied directly with economic standing. Families with no servants sent only slightly more than a third of their school age children to school; families with one servant sent just over half; families with more than one servant sent still larger proportions. Wealthier people also kept their children in school longer. Twenty-two per cent of the fourteen-year-old children from families with no servants had attended school compared to 42 per cent of those from families with one servant and 82 per cent of those from families with two servants. The employment of servants, the occupancy of a large brick or stone house, a spacious plot of land, a large household, the steady and prolonged attendance of one's children at school: these, then, were the principal means through which the affluent demonstrated their success to their neighbours.

The affluent of the city solidified their economic control with political power. First of all, as we have already observed, property qualifications excluded most of the poor from voting. Moreover, the wealthy monopolized local political offices. Despite the fact that nearly 30 per cent of elected city officials called themselves by an artisan title, most were wealthy. They were by no means workingmen as we usually employ that term. Of the elected officials, nearly 70 per cent were in the top ten economic ranks; 83 per cent were in the top twenty. In the two years 1851–52, 42 per cent of the wealthiest 1 per cent of the workforce held political office.

To understand the exercise of power within the city it is necessary to grasp the extent of overlap between membership in elite positions. Measured grossly from listings in the newspaper, the overlap between membership in three elites — people elected to city political offices, business officials, and officers of voluntary societies — is striking and, beyond question, statistically significant.[18] Of the forty-eight elected city officials, for instance, fifteen were business officials, twenty-one officers of voluntary societies, and eight jurors. Of the 130 business officials, fifteen were elected city officials, forty-one officers of voluntary societies, thirty-six petitioners (asking the city for favours), and twelve jurors. Among 196 officers of voluntary societies (a very high figure suggesting an extraordinarily important role for voluntary activity with this society), twenty-one were elected city officials, forty-one business officials, eight appointed city officials, six school trustees, and eighteen jurors. Of the seventy-four jurors who served during 1851 and 1852, eight were elected city officials, twelve were business officials, and one was an appointed city official. Ten people were elected city officials, business officials, and officers of voluntary societies simultaneously.

Measures designed to test statistical significance — to see whether or not the results described above could have occurred by chance — tell the same story. The relationships were strong and real. The unmistakable overlap between elites underlines the interconnections between economic, political, and social power within this nineteenth-century city. More than that, the relation of people in elite positions with petitioners and jurors is revealing. A poor or unimportant man in Hamilton, it is quite clear, lacked the temerity to ask the city for favours, and, in fact, if he incurred its displeasure he was not even tried by a jury of his peers.[19]

Just as poverty and powerlessness brought invisibility, so did affluence and power make a man visible. On the basis of their mention in local newspapers it is possible to divide the people of the city into three groups according to their "visibility": those "invisible" (not mentioned in the newspapers at all) or about 94 per cent of the population in 1851; those moderately "visible" (mentioned once or twice); and those highly "visible," mentioned five or more times, about 1 per cent of the population. Who then were the highly visible people? They were, as might be expected from the foregoing analysis, the members of the interlocking elites. Highly visible people comprised more than half of the following categories: city and county officials, appointed city and county officials, business officials, officers of voluntary societies, school trustees, petitioners, jurors, advertisers, union members (only six were mentioned in the newspapers at all), political committee members, and people publicly honoured. Interestingly, as with the case of overlap between various sorts of officeholders, jurors and petitioners interconnect with the most powerful men within the city.[20]

These interconnections between kinds of power within Hamilton pose important comparative questions. Did economic, social, and political power exist in a closer relationship at that time than they do at present? What impact did industrialization have upon their relationship to each other? Is the curve of inequality steady over time, or did it widen in the initial stages of industrialization and then diminish in the twentieth century? Whatever the answers to these questions turn out to be, the detailed examination of the distribution of income and power should help dispel any lingering nostalgia about the existence of equality and community in nineteenth-century cities.

396   Detailed examination of actual cases also dispels a number of common notions about families in pre-industrial society. It is often thought that the nuclear family emerged as a consequence of industrialization, that in early times people married at very young ages, and that the poor, especially, had very large families. None of these propositions are true. There were clear relations between transiency and inequality, the two great themes of the nineteenth-century city, and the domestic arrangements of its people. However, to some extent the family and household exhibited characteristics partially independent of wealth and related rather (sometimes at this stage of research inexplicably) to other measures. Thus, it is important to consider family and household structure by themselves.

We may begin with the formation of the family through marriage. The statistics are based upon the marriage registers for Wentworth County for the years 1842–69.[21] Marriage patterns within Wentworth County were endogamous. Of 5327 brides, 4443 resided in Wentworth County as did 4026 of the same number of grooms. It is to be expected that most brides would be from Wentworth County, since marriage customarily takes place at the bride's residence. What is more notable is the small proportion of local girls who married men from outside the county. Nevertheless, the majority of marriages throughout the period involved people who had both been born outside of Ontario and, indeed, outside of Canada.

For the most part the figures for age of marriage contradict our stereotypes of early marriage among the people of pre-industrial society. The mean age of marriage for men was 27.7, the median 25.7; 61 per cent of grooms were twenty-five years old or over; 25 per cent were over 30. Brides were considerably younger, about four years on the average. Their mean marriage age was 23.2 and the median 21.8. Just over one-quarter of the girls married before they were twenty and 72 per cent had married by the time they were twenty-five.[22] Both religion and birthplace influenced marriage age, though of the two, birthplace appeared strongest. Younger marriages were slightly more common among Baptists and "Protestants" and later marriages more common among Presbyterians. Similarly, the Scottish people married notably later than other groups.[23] People born in Canada West married youngest by far, and there were no unusual distributions of age among brides and grooms born in England, the United States, or, contrary to what might be expected, Ireland.[24]

Figures for births, like those for marriage, do not support common notions about Catholic families. From what we can tell at this point, the birth-rate among Catholics or Irish born people was no higher than among the population as a whole. What appears striking from an analysis of the births listed in the 1851 manuscript census is the congruence between the percentage of total births in the city occurring among a particular group and that group's percentage of the total population. Thus, Catholics aged 20–29 formed 18 per cent of the household heads of that age group within the city; to them occurred 18 per cent of the births among that age group. The poor form 26 per cent of the household heads; they had 27 per cent of the births. It would be tedious to continue to present these figures; with one exception they remain the same for ethnicity, religion, and wealth. That exception, and an interesting one, is the people born in French Canada, who formed a tiny 0.4 per cent of the 20–29-year-olds but accounted for 2 per cent of the births, a disproportion consistent with trends in French-Canadian demography.[25]

397

This initial survey of Hamilton's demography would be incomplete without some mention of death and death rates. At this juncture it is not possible to discuss the relations between death rate, age at death, and other social variables, such as religion, ethnicity, and wealth. We do know that the infant mortality rate was staggeringly high. Of 210 people recorded as having died on the census, 106 or 51 per cent were five years old or younger; all but twenty-one, or 10 per cent, were under the age of fifty.

Figures for the number of children within a household are generally, though not completely, consistent with the statistics of marriage and birth. Among the heads of households as a whole 55 per cent had small families (0–2 children); 36 per cent had medium sized families (3–5 children), and 10 per cent had large families (6 or more children). Any discussion of family size is affected by the age distribution of the population. In order that we may have a fair basis of comparison I shall restrict the following discussion to heads of household aged 40–49, those whose families were both complete and, to the largest extent, still living together. Of the 40–49-year-old household heads, 37 per cent had small families, 44 per cent medium sized ones, and 18 per cent large numbers of children.

First of all, as with births, family size among the 40–49-year-olds shows little relation to wealth.[26] The poor did not breed more quickly than the rest of the population. In fact the only discernible relation between wealth and number of children works in the other direction. Among the heads of household as a whole 0.3 per cent of the very poorest people, those in the bottom twenty economic percentiles, had a large number of children compared to 15 per cent of those in the 95–99th percentiles. Among the 40–49-year-old household heads the poorest men had no children about twice as often as most other groups; similarly, they had the smallest percentage of medium sized families of any group. Considering all ages together, the mean number of children among the poorest 20 per cent of household heads was 0.54 and, among the wealthiest 1 per cent, 3.32. In between, however, scores are quite similar. One other difference, which relates to economic standing, shows the same trend. Transients, who were poorer than those people we consider more permanent residents, had a slightly lower mean number of children despite their similarity in age.

398   An examination of the mean number of children among 40–49-year-old household heads highlights some ethnic and religious distinctions generally unrelated to wealth. North Americans, natives of Canada West and the United States, had small families. The lowest mean score, 2.40, was that of the Americans, followed by the Canadians, the English, the Irish, and the Scottish, in that order.[27] These figures reflect the late marriage age of Scottish people, which we observed earlier.[28] Among religious groups those with heavily Scottish membership rank high in mean number of children among 40–49-year-olds.[29] At the other end of the scale the denomination with the smallest mean family size, the Baptist, is heavily American in origin.[30] The mean size for the Catholics, it might be pointed out, was quite average for the 40–49-year-olds, although their mean for the 20–29-year-olds was the highest in that cohort, which indicates that Catholics had more of their children when they were younger, not, as is often thought, that they had a greater number in all than did other groups.[31]

The mean family size of different occupational groups reveals more systematic differences. The means for all merchants and clerks were 1.78 and 1.91. For bakers, blacksmiths, carpenters, shoemakers, tinsmiths, and labourers the means were: 2.69, 2.96, 2.78, 2.34, 2.89, and 2.89 respectively. Quite clearly, the entrepreneurial white collar groups had fewer children than men who worked with their hands. In this respect it is the line separating the people engaged in commerce from those following the trades that counts most. Distinctions between skilled and unskilled workers appear to matter but little. More than that, the difference in number of children appears more related to kind of work performed than it does to wealth. The mean number of children, as we have observed, varied but little with economic rank, and the relations between occupation and wealth were not as tidy as we might expect, as we have noticed in the case of elected city officials. In fact, there was usually a great variation in wealth between individuals in the same trades. Thus, on the basis of the evidence at hand, it is entirely reasonable to suppose that the aspiring business classes had begun to practice some form of family limitation.[32]

There were distinctions, it is critical to note, between the family size of people engaged in commerce and other non-manual workers. Relatively small family size remained more a hallmark of men with an entrepreneurial outlook than a badge separating white and blue collar workers in our modern sense. This becomes apparent from the mean family size of other, non-entrepreneurial and non-manual groups: the mean family size of teachers, for instance, 3.71, was the highest of any group; the mean for gentlemen was 2.89, the same as for labourers and tinsmiths; and the mean for lawyers fluctuated strangely with age. For lawyers in their forties it was 6.00. All of this suggests that limiting the number of his offspring had become linked in the mind of the aspiring entrepreneur with increasing his wealth. The source of that idea is particularly important to locate. For, if the facts that I have presented here are correct, he would not have learned it from the world around him where, in fact, the most successful men did not have small families.

399

As we have observed already, the mark of a wealthy man was the size of his household, not the number of his children. That household was composed of boarders, servants, relatives, and visitors in addition to husband, wife, and children. There were fewer extended families in this pre-industrial city than we might have expected; relatives other than husband, wife, and children lived in only 15 per cent of the households. Like the families Peter Laslett and his associates have studied in England over a period of four hundred years, the ones in Hamilton were overwhelmingly nuclear. As with servants, relatives lived most frequently in the households of the well-to-do; they were present in 4 per cent of the poorest 20 per cent of the households and in 24 per cent of those in the 95–99th economic ranks.[33]

The same is true of boarders, who were found in 28 per cent of the households. They lived, however, with 8 per cent and 15 per cent respectively of the families in the 0–20th and 20–40th economic ranks and with 46 per cent of those in the 90–95th. There were boarders, in fact, in more than four out of ten households in each group above the 80th economic rank. This finding is somewhat surprising. We might suppose, offhand, that boarders would be most likely to live with poorer families, who needed the extra income they could provide. But this was not the case. It prompts us to look closely at exactly who boarders were and at their place within the household.

The presence of boarders in so many households reflects an important characteristic of social life: it was extremely unusual for people to live alone; everyone was expected to live within a family grouping. Not much more than 1 per cent of the workforce lived by themselves. Large numbers of young unmarried people living alone is clearly a modern development. This pattern of residence, moreover, constituted an informal system of social control. For young men a close supervision and a constant scrutiny of their behaviour constituted the other side of the warmth of living in a family grouping. Boarding the young men of the town provided the affluent with a convenient means of keeping a close check on their behaviour.

Most of the boarders, 71 per cent, were men; 14 per cent were married. This accounts in large part for the women and children who were listed as boarders. Like the servants, boarders were young, though not quite so young: 34 per cent were under twenty and a further 52 per cent between twenty and twenty-four years old; 84 per cent were under thirty. They came more often from Ireland than from elsewhere in 43 per cent of the cases, but many, 19 per cent, had been born in Canada West, a disproportionately large number considering that men from Canada West made up only a bit more than 9 per cent of the workforce. These boarders were, perhaps, young migrants to the city from rural areas. A little over one-third of the boarders were Catholic, the largest single figure for any denomination, and the rest were scattered among other religious groups. Boarders followed a staggering variety of occupations. Many of them, about 54 per cent, were craftsmen of one sort or another; of the remainder, about 13 per cent were labourers and 8 per cent clerks. Spinsters, widows, and women following domestic occupations like dressmaking frequently boarded as did some young professionals, nine lawyers and seven physicians probably establishing themselves in practice.

It appeared likely, from these figures, that many boarders were young men living with their employers in households that combined work and residence. However, a close comparison of the occupations of boarders and their landlords demolished that hypothesis. It is extremely difficult to determine if a boarder and a household head might have worked together. Occupational terminology is vague and sometimes misleading. But in most cases it was clear that no reasonable connection could be made. Not only occupation but class seemed to make little difference. Labourers lived with judges, physicians, attorneys, and gentlemen, as well as with fellow labourers, moulders, and widows. Widows, in fact, took in many boarders, obviously a way to make a little money. Other than that, there seems little pattern in the distribution of boarders by occupation. Over all, slightly over 9 per cent of the boarders might have been living with their employers.

Other obvious principles on which boarders might have selected their residence are religion and ethnicity. Perhaps young men coming to the city looked for families of similar ethnic and religious backgrounds with whom to live, whatever their occupation might be. In most cases this did not happen. There was some tendency for Irish and for Catholic boarders to choose landlords of the same background, and a very slight tendency for the English and the Anglicans to do the same. But in no instance did those living with people of similar religious or ethnic backgrounds constitute a majority.

In short, it appears that other factors were more important in the choice of a lodging, probably convenience, price, and the presence of some friends already living there or nearby. The population of Hamilton, we must not forget, was expanding rapidly. The estimated growth between 1850 and 1852 was from ten to fourteen thousand. The practical implication of this must have been a severe strain on housing facilities. Perhaps rooms were in such short supply that people took whatever they could find. Perhaps, too, there was great pressure on anyone with a spare bed to take someone in. This is why so many of the more affluent, with larger houses, had boarders.

It is as important to discover the behavioural patterns associated with types of families and households as it is to determine their size and structure. There are, however, fewer indexes of behaviour than of structure on which to base systematic observations. One of the most readily available, and most interesting, is school attendance. The analysis of school attendance links parental attitudes to social, demographic, and economic measures and, as our data reveal, to family size as well. It thus provides a way of joining the family and household to the large social context in which they are embedded.[34]

401

Of all the children in the city aged 5–16 in 1851, 50 per cent attended school at some point during the year. Rather more boys than girls attended at each age level. Very few children entered school before the age of six. At the age of six a third began to attend, but the ages from 7–13 were the period of heaviest school attendance, the proportion attending exceeding 40 per cent only in each of those years. The peaks were reached between the ages of nine and eleven, the only time when more than half of the age group attended school.

Part of the variation in school attendance can be explained by family size. It is often thought that small families provide settings conducive to education. Indeed, twentieth-century studies have shown an inverse relation between school achievement, scores on intelligence tests, and family size. If our data have anything to contribute on this point, it is that the contemporary relationship did not hold within the nineteenth century. The percentage of school-age children attending school generally increased with the number of children in the family.[35] This relationship held even for the youngest and eldest children attending school: 3 per cent of children aged 3–5 from families with two children attended school compared to 10 per cent from families with five children; 18 per cent of 15–16-year-old children from families with two children attended school compared to 23 per cent from families with five children.

The birthplace of the head of household also affected school attendance. Irish fathers were least likely to send their children to school. The percentage of Irish children aged 5–16 attending school was under one-third. For two groups, however, it was over one-half; these were the Scottish and the native Canadians. The relations between religion and attendance reinforce these findings: fewer than 30 per cent of Catholic children attended schools, compared to over 50 per cent for Church of Scotland and Wesleyan Methodist and over 60 per cent for Free Church Presbyterians. Scottish Presbyterianism should obviously be added to family size as an important factor promoting school attendance.

So should wealth, as we observed earlier. Measuring wealth by the possession of servants, the relation with school attendance was striking. That relation supports the observations of school-promoters who perceived their problem as persuading poor families to school their children. Insofar as educational reform took its impetus from a perception of idle, vagrant children from poor homes wandering the streets, it was based on a very real situation.

402

The relations between occupation and school attendance spoil the neatness of the foregoing analysis, for they fail to adhere completely to the boundaries set by wealth, ethnicity, and religion. Lawyers, for instance, sent few of their children to school. It is entirely possible that they hired private tutors. Tinsmiths, on the other hand, were exceptionally conscious of schooling; 85 per cent of their school-age children attended school during 1851, a figure exceeded only by the children of teachers, 92 per cent of whom had attended. Labourers, as could be expected, were at the bottom; less than one-quarter of their school-age children went to school in 1851, compared, for instance, to 46 per cent of the children of merchants and 58 per cent of the children of physicians. Differences between artisan groups parallel those between professionals; 38 per cent of shoemakers' school-age children attended school, for instance, as did 54 per cent of the children of cabinet-makers. There are at present no explanations for most of these differences.

Although school attendance often followed economic lines, it is clear that cultural and social factors intervened to make the pattern that finally emerged quite complex. Two of these factors are noteworthy: North Americans kept their children in school somewhat longer than other groups, and the relationship between wealth, Catholicism, Irish origin, and low school attendance did not hold among the very youngest age groups. Perhaps school served as baby-sitting agencies for large, poor families, relieving the parents of pressure at home and permitting the mother to work. At the same time affluent parents of large families may have realized that they were unable to teach at home certain basic skills, which it was traditional for children to learn before they started school at age seven. They may have used the school to remedy what, given the size of their families, would have had to be accomplished by a private tutor if their children were not to lag educationally.

But all conclusions must remain tentative at best. The most we can say is this: the people who most frequently sent children to school were well-to-do, had larger than average families, and had been born in Scotland or North America. Those sending fewest were poor, Irish Catholic, and labourers. The same groups generally kept the most and the fewest children in school past the usual school leaving age. But the figures for early school attendance revealed slightly different rankings, which indicates that early schooling served important economic functions for some poor families and important psychological ones for large families. The relations between occupation and schooling are unclear, aside from the figures for labourers. Why did the lawyers send so few children? Why did the tinsmiths send so many? We cannot answer these questions at present; like so many of the findings discussed in this essay they remain beginnings, as much questions to be answered as conclusions.

Clearly family and household patterns in Hamilton were complex; they defy simple general descriptions. Equally clearly, they contradict many *403* commonly held assumptions about pre-industrial families. Men and women married relatively late, later probably than most people do today. In the vast majority of instances they formed nuclear families, the more wealthy adding a servant, a boarder, or, in comparatively few instances, a relative. Almost everybody lived in a family, whether they were married or not, young or old. Within families there was relatively little difference in the number of children born to parents of different economic conditions. Ethnicity and religion, in fact, were more influential than wealth in determining age of marriage and number of children. The traditional image of the frugal, self-denying, and ambitious Scot emerges intact; the picture of the indulgent, overbreeding Irish Catholic is shattered. In fact, there were at least two types of households within the city. At one extreme was the Irish Catholic labourer living with his wife and two or three children in a one and a half story frame house. At the other extreme, but perhaps on the same street, was the prosperous merchant living with his wife, two or three children, a servant, and a boarder in a three story stone house surrounded by a spacious plot of land. Most other families fell somewhere in between. It will take a good deal more analysis to isolate other widespread family types, and a good deal of imaginative research into other sorts of sources to explain the results that emerge; to answer, that is, questions such as why did American Baptists have small families?

It is also important to ask if the relations between family size and ethnicity that existed in Hamilton were present in other Canadian cities as well. That, in turn, is part of the larger issue of representativeness. How can one know that the findings from Hamilton have meaning for any other place? From one viewpoint the question is irrelevant. Every city's history is both unique and at the same time representative of larger trends and forces. More than that, the relationships we wish to study can be investigated only on the local level. Even if Hamilton turns out to be less "representative" than one might wish, the study is important because it provides a datum with which to begin an analysis of what is special and what is general within nineteenth-century cities in Canada and elsewhere.

Hamilton was not representative of some things, quite obviously: for instance, it was not like villages and rural areas. On the other hand, it should have had a number of similarities to pre-industrial cities in nineteenth-century Britain and the United States. Most of all, it was not too unlike other cities in Canada West. That is clear from studying published census figures for a number of Canadian cities. It is striking to observe the extent of similarity between Kingston, London, Toronto, and Hamilton with respect to the birthplace and religion of their residents; their age structures and sex ratios; their birth and death rates; and even their occupational structures. On the basis of these similarities it is obvious that Hamilton was structurally similar to other cities in Canada West. On that basis we may conclude with some general observations about the nature of a pre-industrial Canadian city.[36]

First, even in the mid-nineteenth century a relatively small commercial city was an enormously complex place. Simple general statements about its society, families, or households are inadequate to the richness of its structural patterns. Economically, even before industrialization, Canadian cities were highly differentiated. Socially, they were highly stratified.

Second, the pre-industrial family was a more rational and "modern" organization than we have often suspected. Even at this early date people clearly related decisions about marriage and often about the size of their families to other, undoubtedly economic, considerations. The difference between the pre-industrial and modern family does not rest in structure; both are nuclear. It lies, rather, in the number of children born to the average couple and in the structure of the household, which in terms of size has lost its clear relation to affluence.

Third, in no sense can we think of pre-industrial cities as communities defined by stability, integration, and egalitarianism. The problem of inequality we have touched on above; the facts of transiency destroy any further illusions about community. The population simply changed too rapidly.

Fourth, the articulation of various structures with each other produced a powerful concentration of interlocking forms of power in the hands of a very small group of people. Household structure, political power, school attendance — the privileges that this society had to offer — all related to wealth. The distribution of men by economic rank corresponded to their division on most other social measures. Looked at another way, the business elite, the political elite, and the voluntary elite overlapped to a striking and significant extent. We know already that the political elite overlapped with the top rungs of the scale of economic rank. There is every reason to believe that the others did so as well.

The group that controlled economic, political, and social power within Hamilton contained at most 10 per cent of the household heads. People within elite positions formed slightly more than 8 per cent of men aged twenty and older. This figure is quite close to the 10 per cent estimated elsewhere as wealthy. It is close, in fact, to the approximately 75 per cent of elected city officials who we know to have been within the top ten income percentiles. Hence we can conclude that about 8 or 10 per cent of the adult men, at the very maximum, controlled virtually all the resources necessary to the health, well-being, and prosperity of the rest.

In Hamilton the rulers, the owners, and the rich were by and large the same people. They clearly headed the stratification system. At the bottom the grouping was likewise clear: poor, propertyless, powerless men made up about 40 per cent of the workforce or between a fifth and a quarter of the household heads. In between fell the rest. About 40 per cent were marginal; they owned no property, they possessed no power, but they were prosperous enough to differentiate themselves from the poorest families. Their margin seems so slim and the consequences of falling so appalling, however, that these people must have lived always with great tension and great fear. Between them and the wealthy, comprising about a fifth of the families, was a qualitatively more affluent group. Most of them employed a servant and lived in a brick house, which they owned. They were likely to vote but still not very likely to hold political office.

405

These four groups existed within Hamilton in the middle of the nineteenth century. Using wealth, power, and ownership as dimensions on which to rank people, they form somewhat overlapping but nonetheless distinguishable clusters of people holding a similar position on each scale. Were they classes? That depends on the definition of class, which is a subject beyond the scope of this essay. Clearly, however, by whatever definition is followed it would seem difficult to deny that class was a fundamental fact of life in mid-nineteenth-century urban Canada.[37]

NOTES

The research on which this essay is based has been entirely supported by the Ontario Institute for Studies in Education. The project is officially titled "The Study and Teaching of Canadian Social History" (The Canadian Social History Project, for short).

[1] For detailed quantitative information see the first two interim reports of the project as well as subsequent working papers, all of which are available from the Department of History and Philosophy of Education of the Ontario Institute for Studies in Education. See also my essay, "Social Structure in Hamilton, Ontario" in Stephen Thernstrom and Richard Sennett, eds., *Nineteenth-Century Cities: Essays in the New Urban History* (New Haven and London, 1969), 209–44. I have rounded all percentages in this essay to whole numbers. Considering the inexactness of historical data, this seems quite appropriate, especially when it increases ease of reading.

2 Record-linkage is one of the central technical problems of all studies similar to the one described here. For a discussion of the problem, and of our approach to it, see Ian Winchester, "The Linkage of Historical Records by Man and Computer: Techniques and Problems," *Journal of Interdisciplinary History* 1,1 (Autumn 1970): 107-24. The hand-linkage of the 1851 census, 1852 assessment, and 1853 directory was done by Mr John Tiller, who also has done most of the coding of the 1851 census and assessment. I should like to acknowledge Mr. Tiller's continued and invaluable participation in this project.

3 The *Spectator* and the *Gazette*.

4 Stephen Thernstrom and Peter Knights, "Men in Motion: Some Data and Speculations about Urban Population Mobility in Nineteenth Century America," in Tamara K. Hareven, ed., *Anonymous Americans: Explorations in Nineteenth-Century Social History* (Englewood Cliffs, N.J., 1971), 17-47; Peter R. Knights, "Population Turnover, Persistence, and Residential Mobility in Boston, 1830–1860," in Thernstrom and Sennett, *Nineteenth-Century Cities*, 258-74; E.J. Hobsbawm, "The Tramping Artisan," in his *Laboring Men: Studies in the History of Labor* (London, 1964): 34-63.

5 Unpublished papers by Mrs. Judy Cooke and Mr. Dan Brock, OISE.

6 The mean assessed wealth of all the people engaged in commerce was £96; of the transients in commerce, £63; of resident professionals, £71; of transient ones, £21; of resident artisans, £25; of migrants, £13; of resident labourers, £9; of migrant ones, £7.

7 The existence of a similar phenomenon — a division of success within trades — is clearly revealed by Henry Mayhew's description of the organization of various trades in London in the middle of the nineteenth century. An example is the distinction between the "honorable" and "dishonorable" parts of the tailoring trade. See E.P. Thompson and Eileen Yeo, *The Unknown Mayhew* (London, 1971), 181-277, on tailors.

8 Robert Dreeben, *On What Is Learned in Schools* (Reading, Mass., 1968), 95, provides an example of this point. See also Talcott Parson and Robert F. Bales, *Family, Socialization and Interaction Processes* (Glencoe, Ill., 1955).

9 Not all employed men necessarily worked away from their homes. As Mayhew, [cited in] *The Unknown Mayhew*, points out, it was common for manufacturers of various sorts to give work to craftsmen to perform in their own homes.

10 See, for example, Proceedings of the Council of the City of Hamilton, 22 Jan. 1851, pp. 398-99; 19 Jan. 1850, pp. 128-29, available on microfilm in the Public Archives of Ontario.

11 For a discussion of calculating the Index of Segregation see Karl E. Taeuber and Alma F. Taeuber, *Negroes in Cities: Residential Segregation and Neighborhood Change* (Chicago, 1965), 195-245; for the application of the index, see Leo F. Schnore and Peter R. Knights, "Residence and Social Structure: Boston in the Ante-Bellum Period," in Thernstrom and Sennett, *Nineteenth-Century Cities*, 247-57, and Sam Bass Warner, Jr., *The Private City: Philadelphia in Three Periods of Its Growth* (Philadelphia, 1968), 13. For studies of residential patterns in nineteenth-century cities, see also two recent monographs, David Ward, *Cities and Immigrants: A Geography of Change in Nineteenth Century America* (New York, 1971), and Peter Goheen, *Victorian Toronto* (Chicago, 1970).

12 I have discussed the construction of these scales in working paper no. 21, "The Measurement of Economic Inequality."

13 Fifty-one per cent of the working population born in England and Wales were in the middle (40–80th) economic ranks as were 46 per cent of the Anglicans.

14 Of the Free Church Presbyterians 26 per cent were poor, compared to 16 per cent of the Wesleyan Methodists. At the same time 31 per cent of the Free Church Presbyterians were well-to-do (80–100th economic ranks) as were 29 per cent of the Wesleyan Methodists.

15 Of the other major ethnic and religious groups, briefly: The Scottish-born were predominantly middle-income, much like the English; the adherents of the Church of Scotland, and those who called themselves simply Presbyterians, were likewise middling in terms of wealth, except that the former had few wealthy adherents. The figures for Methodists were much like those for Presbyterians; and for Baptists, much like members of the Church of Scotland.

16 The records of the Ladies Benevolent Society are available in manuscript at the Hamilton Public Library. For the actions of the City Council with respect to immigrants see, eg., Proceedings of the Council, 20 Aug. 1849, p. 31; 10 Sept. 1849, pp. 149-50. On the institutionalization of poverty in the United States see the recent, provocative book by David Rothman, *The Discovery of the Asylum* (Boston, 1971).

17 E.J. Hobsbawm, *Industry and Empire* (London, 1969), 157.

18 Mrs. Anne-Marie Hodes coded the 1851 and 1852 newspapers for the project.

19 Only the top three-quarters of the assessed population were eligible to serve on the jury. I suspect that those actually chosen did not represent a cross-section of that group.

20 For the idea of constructing a scale of visibility I am indebted to the work of Professor Walter Glazer of Cincinnati.

21 The marriage registers were coded by Mrs. Margaret Zieman.

22 The figures are supported by those found for European countries. See, eg., Peter Laslett, "Size and Structure of the Household in England Over Three Centuries," *Population Studies* 33, 2 (July 1969): 199-223.

406

[23] Only 20 per cent of Scottish grooms were less than twenty-five years old compared to 39 per cent of all grooms, while 30 per cent of Scottish grooms were in their 30s compared to 18 per cent of all grooms.

[24] Among people born in Canada West, 51 per cent of the grooms, compared to 39 per cent of all grooms, had been married before the age of twenty-five; of the brides, 82 per cent, compared to 75 per cent of all brides, had been married before they were twenty-seven years old.

[25] For an overview of Canadian population history that makes this point, see Census of Canada, 1931, Chapters 2 and 3 of the excellent monograph on the family.

[26] Of the poor, 18 per cent had a large family; so did 20 per cent of the middle-income and 21 per cent of the well-to-do. Similarly 38 per cent of the poor had a small number of children, as did 35 per cent of the middle-rank and 38 per cent of the well-to-do.

[27] The means are: U.S. born, 2.40; Canadian, 3.18; English, 3.35; Irish, 3.52; Scottish, 4.01.

[28] The Scottish rank third in mean number of children among 20– 29-year-olds, fifth among 30–39, and first among the 40–49-year-old group.

[29] Thus the mean for members of the Church of Scotland is 4.39 and for Free Church Presbyterians, 4.62.

[30] The Baptist score is 2.17.

[31] In fairness to traditional ideas it should be pointed out that very preliminary inspection of the 1861 results indicates a larger than average family size for Catholics and Irish. At this point the change is inexplicable.

[32] For comparative figures on class and birth control, see E.A. Wrigley's excellent book, *Population and History* (New York, 1969), 186–87. On the method of studying birth control in past societies, see E.A. Wrigley, "Family Limitation in Pre-Industrial England," *Economic History Review*, 2nd Series, 19, 1 (1966): 82–109. For more on the relation between status and birth control in the nineteenth century, see J.A. Banks, *Prosperity and Parenthood: A Study of Family Planning Among the Victorian Middle Classes* (London, 1954) and D.E.C. Eversley, *Social Theories of Fertility and the Malthusian Debate* (Oxford, 1959).

[33] On general patterns of household size in England over four hundred years, see Laslett, "Size and Structure of the Household."

[34] There has been amazingly little written on the history of school attendance. The only monograph in English that I know to be specifically devoted to the topic is David Rubenstein, *School Attendance in London, 1870-1904: A Social History* (Hull, 1969). See also my article, "Who went to School," *History of Education Quarterly* 12, 3 (Fall 1972).

[35] For families with two children it was, for instance, 42 per cent; for families with five children, 61 per cent. Similarly, the percentage of families which sent more than half their school-age children to school rose from 24 per cent for families with one child to 35 per cent for families with two, to 58 per cent for families with five children and 67 per cent for families with seven.

[36] Tables comparing these cities are in the project working paper no. 23.

[37] I want to include a plea that more Canadian historians undertake empirical analyses of past social structures. Those who are interested but hesitant should gain some knowledge of how to proceed from two recent books: Edward Shorter, *The Historian and the Computer: A Practical Guide* (Englewood Cliffs, N.J., 1971), and Charles M. Dollar and Richard J. Jensen, *Historian's Guide to Statistics, Quantitative Analysis and Historical Research* (New York, 1971). Our team is continually developing a store of practical lore which we should be delighted to share with anyone venturing into related studies.

407

Topic Twelve

Economic Developments in the Maritime Colonies in the Mid-Nineteenth Century

Very few ties existed between the Atlantic colonies and the Canadas in the mid-nineteenth century. Halifax and Saint John, the leading ports of Nova Scotia and New Brunswick, lay much closer to the great American ports of Boston and New York than to the Canadian harbours on the St. Lawrence; moreover, in winter, ice completely severed what links they did have with Canada. Rather than westward to the interior, the Atlantic colonies — before the building of a rail link with the Canadas — looked eastward to Britain and southward to the American Atlantic seaboard and the West Indies.

Of the four Maritime colonies, Nova Scotia was the most significant in the mid-nineteenth century. It had the greatest strategic importance, being located at the entrance to the Gulf of St. Lawrence and on the shipping lanes of the North Atlantic. It had the most balanced economy of the four, with excellent fisheries, good lowland farmland, and supplies of iron and coal. In 1861 Nova Scotia's population of 330 000 exceeded that of any of the other three Atlantic colonies.

Not unlike Prince Edward Island, which depended largely on its agriculture, New Brunswick also really depended on a single staple industry. The colony had some good farmland in the Saint John River Valley, but lumbering remained the mainstay of its economy. The commercial ambitions of the merchants of the leading city in New Brunswick are examined by T.W. Acheson in "The Great Merchant and Economic Development in Saint John, 1820–1850." The economic situation in Prince Edward Island is reviewed by Ian Ross Robertson in his introduction to *The Prince Edward Island Commission of 1860*.

For an understanding of the Maritime region in the mid-nineteenth century students should consult W.S. MacNutt's *The Atlantic Provinces, 1712–1857* (Toronto: McClelland and Stewart, 1965). MacNutt has also written *New Brunswick, A History: 1784–1867* (Toronto: Macmillan, 1963). See also Graeme Wynn, *Timber Colony: A Historical Geography of Early Nineteenth Century New Brunswick* (Toronto: University of Toronto Press, 1981). William Menzie Whitelaw provides a general overview of all aspects of life in the Atlantic colonies in the mid-nineteenth century in "The Atlantic Provinces and Their Neighbors," a chapter in his book *The Maritimes and Canada before Confederation* (Toronto: Oxford University Press, 1966; first published in 1934), 9-37. Important essays on the Maritime colonies are contained in *Historical Essays on the Atlantic Provinces*, ed. G.A. Rawlyk (Toronto: McClelland and Stewart, 1967). Thomas H. Raddall's *Halifax, Warden of the North*, rev. ed. (Toronto: McClelland and Stewart, 1971) provides a readable account of that city's past. The metropolitan ambitions of the business community in Halifax are examined by David Sutherland in "Halifax Merchants and the Pursuit of Development, 1783-1850," *Canadian Historical Review*, 59, 1 (1978): 1-17. In "The Relief of the Unemployed Poor in Saint John, Halifax, and St. John's," *Acadiensis* 5, 1 (1975): 32-53, Judith Fingard reviews the early system of poor relief, a topic often ignored. T.W. Acheson has provided a model study of Saint John in his *Saint John: The Making of a Colonial Urban Community* (Toronto: University of Toronto Press, 1985).

409

Students should consult the volumes of *Acadiensis* (since 1970), which contain many important articles on Atlantic history. A volume of essays collected from back issues of *Acadiensis* is available under the title *The Atlantic Provinces before Confederation* (Fredericton: Acadiensis, 1985), edited by P.A. Buckner and David Frank.

The Great Merchant and Economic Development in Saint John, 1820-1850*

T.W. ACHESON

One of the liveliest debates in recent Canadian business history has centred on the role of the nineteenth-century merchant in promoting or retarding the development of a locally controlled British North American industrial base. Supporters of the retardation theory usually argue that the colonial merchant was nurtured in a system based upon the export of raw and semi-finished produce and the import of fully manufactured materials. Dominating the ports and the transportation systems of British North America, he became the principal defender of the economic *status quo*, viewing any substantial re-arrangement of economic relations as a threat to his world. Thus he remained the harbinger of a form of economic colonialism which bound the destiny of British North America and of the forming Dominion of Canada in a subservient re-

*Reprinted with permission from *Acadiensis: Journal of the History of the Atlantic Region* 8, 2 (Spring 1979): 3-27.

lationship to more advanced national economies, particularly those of the United Kingdom and the United States. Opponents of this theory have accepted the primacy of the merchant in the colonial economies but have argued that the gulf separating the merchant from other dynamic elements in the business community was less wide than the retardationists would have us believe. They maintain that the dramatic shift from commercial to industrial emphases and from external to internal markets in the last half of the nineteenth century occurred with the consent and participation of this dominant commercial element.[1]

There are several difficulties within this general argument. One of the most basic concerns the definition of "merchant." The meanest cordwainer in the mid-nineteenth century offered his shoes for sale to the general public; conversely, many important shippers and wholesalers owned, in whole or in part, the means to process the basic staple commodities of their region. Even a restricted use of the term leaves a group of businessmen involved in a variety of commercial, financial and transportation functions. In colonial Saint John, for example, "merchant" was a legal status conferred on certain men at the time of their admission to the freedom of the city. Within the hierarchy of occupations which were admissible as freemen, that of merchant was clearly the most important and this importance was reflected in the fees required of those admitted to the status. Although a merchant might also be a sawmill owner, a legal and social line was clearly drawn between merchants possessing a sawmill and sawmill owners by occupation whose status was lower. Moreover, there were a number of commercial functions characteristically performed by merchants, including the importing and wholesaling of produce, the export of fish and wood products, the trans-

410

Saint John and Portland, 1842.

port of other people's goods, the purchase of staples produce on other people's accounts, the sale and auction of other people's goods, private banking, and acting as agents or directors for chartered banks, fire, marine, and life insurance companies. In village business a single merchant might have exercised most of these functions; the most successful urban merchants were those who focussed their efforts on three or four. In time, the development of competing interests sharply limited the issues on which merchants were able to speak as a class or community. Indeed, on many issues, it is doubtful whether colonial boards of trade and chambers of commerce spoke for anything more than one of several elements within the business community.

Another important question raised by the retardation debate concerns the extent to which "normal" merchant behaviour was modified by the local environment. There can be little doubt but that all merchants in British North America responded to short-term opportunities and that only rarely were they willing to sacrifice these opportunities on the alter of national, colonial, or civic interest.[2] Yet, over time, a merchant became attached to the community in which he lived, his response to opportunity conditioned by the idiosyncracies of the local economy, the nature of the relationship between the local and metropolitan economies, and the impact of the economic cycle in reducing the short-term profitability of existing relationships. Any final assessment of the merchant's role in the economic development of British North America will therefore have to wait the completion of a number of case studies of individual communities and firms.[3] The paper which follows is an attempt to explore the role of the merchant in the economic development of colonial Saint John. The city affords an interesting case study both because of its size — in 1840 it was the third largest urban centre in British North America — and because of the central role played by the trade in timber and deals in its economic life.

Traditionally the central problem in the study of the economy of Saint John has been to explain the failure of the city to make the necessary adjustments to compensate for the dislocations occasioned by the stagnation of the wood trade following Confederation. Recently, Peter McClelland has put the date of that stagnation back to mid-century, arguing that the shipbuilding industry, the most dynamic element in the provincial economy after 1850, added little to the well-being or growth of that economy.[4] McClelland has highlighted the role of New Brunswick businessmen in this problem by demonstrating the tenacity with which they stood behind the wooden shipbuilding industry, investing perhaps $8 million between 1870 and 1879 in a technology which was effectively obsolete.[5] These businessmen failed to make the transition to metal ships or to establish backward linkages from the shipbuilding industry — particularly those relating to the outfitting of ships and the manufacture of chains and anchors — which could develop in time into significant

411

industries. McClelland has explained this failure in terms of "the absence of alternatives capable of giving to regional growth the sustaining force which timber was losing" after 1850.[6] But even if it is admitted that shipbuilding was unable to play this dynamic role — a thesis that is much more compelling in 1870 than in 1840 — McClelland offers scant evidence to prove that manufacturing and, to a lesser extent, fishing and agriculture, could not have contributed a dynamic element to the regional economy. To support his contention, he is forced to argue that they could not because they did not, an idea grounded in the assumption that by mid-century New Brunswick was backward relative to other colonial economies. To demonstrate this position McClelland offers an output analysis of New Brunswick and Ontario agriculture at the end of the nineteenth century, and points to the inability of some New Brunswick consumer goods producers to compete with central Canadian producers on the central Canadian market in the post-Confederation period. Much of this can be demonstrated for 1890, but it all presumes that what was true at that time must have been true a half-century earlier, and that the absence of a particular resource, say coal, must preclude the development of any industry which employed that resource.

412

The doubts raised by the ahistorical nature of this analysis are heightened by the persistence with which the provincial business community pursued and supported the wood trade and the wooden ship, even in the face of a technological obsolescence which by 1870 was obvious to all observers. This persistence suggests a commitment to a declining economic base understandable in the small resource-based village economies of much of the province, but more difficult to comprehend in the context of the complex, differentiated economy which existed in Saint John. Indeed, the continuance of these forms of activity and the failure of other kinds of development to occur may have been more the result of human factors than the absence of any particular material resource. Certainly Saint John in the colonial period possessed considerable potential. In 1840 the city was one of the largest urban centres in British North America, with a population of about 27,000. Its merchants possessed a monopoly of the commerce of the Saint John River Valley and its tributaries, a market of nearly 100,000 people. They also dominated the commercial life of the Bay of Fundy counties of New Brunswick and Nova Scotia, containing another 90,000 people.[7] The population of the Saint John River Valley exceeded that of the Home District of Upper Canada, while the city's whole market area compared favourably with that of the Quebec City District of Lower Canada.[8] Shipbuilding had been an important feature of the city's economy for two full generations by 1840 and the Saint John industry was clearly the most significant in British North America.[9] In addition, a substantial and diversified manufacturing sector designed to service both the timber trade and the growing consumer market of the area had emerged over the previous two decades, a development reflected in the strong labour movement which had become an important feature of city life in the years following the War of 1812.[10] By 1840 Saint John was marked as a growth centre with a distinct advantage over any other community in the Atlantic region. And this is of special significance because nineteenth-century manufacturing growth tended to be cumulative: early leaders generally improved their advantage over other communities as James Gilmour has demonstrated in his study of the spatial evolution of manufacturing in Ontario.[11]

In many ways the 1840s was the most critical decade of the colonial period. It witnessed the collapse of the preferences for colonial timber on the British market, a disaster which Saint John businessmen were able to overcome mainly by making the transition from the export of timber to the export of deals. Nonetheless, the trade in wood products reached its largest volume in that period and thereafter stagnated; the economy of the province grew increasingly dependent in the 1850s on the still further processing of wood into ships and their sale on the British market. The abrogation of the Old Colonial System was marked by several short-term economic downturns which severely mauled the wood trades and raised serious doubts about the viability of an economy based upon them. At this point in time any group which persisted in subordinating all other interests to the needs of an already failing industry, it could be argued, can be perceived as contributing to the retardation of the provincial economy at a critical juncture in its history. If, by virtue of their influence within the political framework of the colony and their control of the principal sources of capital, merchants were able to promote or to inhibit certain kinds of development, then their role in determining the economic destiny of the city and its hinterland and was as important as the presence or absence of any specific resource.

413

The study which follows will test this hypothesis in the context of merchant behaviour in the city of Saint John between 1820 and 1850. It will do so by examining the extent and nature of merchant wealth and the role of leading merchants in promoting or opposing development strategies in the first half of the nineteenth century. A major problem is the sheer size of the city's merchant community. During the colonial period about 800 men held the legal status of merchant and a number of others illegally participated in merchant functions. There were large numbers of transients whose residency in the city was confined to a few years, and even larger numbers of minor businessmen whose sole claim to the status of merchant seems to have been their role as small-scale importers. Their impact on the commercial life of the city was marginal and any attempt to include them in a study of this nature — even if sufficient information were available — could seriously distort its purpose. At the other extreme, the council of the Chamber of Commerce provides a definite group of the influential merchants but these might represent only one faction of important merchants. To overcome both of these difficulties an effort was made to determine which merchants played important roles in the commercial and public life of the city and province over a number of years. The criteria used in the selection included ownership of significant shipping, wharfing and waterfront facilities, directorships of important financial agencies, public esteem and influence as manifested in the press and in public documents, public service, and personal wealth. Although the final decision of who to include is both arbitrary and subjective, for the purpose of this study forty leading commercial figures have been identified as "great" merchants. Members of this group comprehended a variety of commercial interests, but all participated in vital shipping and financial concerns of the port and all possessed substantial personal resources. Their influence stemmed not only from this control over most of the city's financial resources, but also from their ability to create a climate of public opinion which identified their interests with the welfare of the community at large,[12] and from their access to the political institutions of the colony.[13] The group included 19 men who held the legal status of merchant, 4 mariners, 2 grocers, 1 fisherman, 1 clerk, and 3 who were not freemen of the City.[14]

414

The great merchants were drawn from all elements within the broader community, but the most numerous were those of Loyalist or pre-Loyalist origins. Several, notably Ezekiel and Thomas Barlow, Noah Disbrow, Ralph Jarvis, John Ward, Stephen Wiggins, and John M. and R.D. Wilmot, were scions of important Loyalist merchant families. Several others, such as Nehemiah Merritt, and Thomas and William Leavitt, were children of frugal Loyalist fishermen. Still a third group was the Simonds connection, the principal landed interest in the province, which included the pre-Loyalist, Charles Simonds, and the two fortunate young Loyalists who married his sisters, Thomas Millidge and Henry Gilbert. Equally as important as the natives were the British immigrants. By far the most significant were the Scots, Lauchlan Donaldson, John Duncan, James Kirk, Hugh Johnston, John Robertson, and John Wishart, who greatly outnumbered the Protestant Irishmen, John Kinnear and William Parks.[15] All of these immigrants were the offspring of prosperous families and came to the colony as young men of substance, bringing with them at least some capital resources. From positions of comparative advantage in the early nineteenth century, these merchants rode the crest of the timber trade to wealth by the 1840s. Virtually all were involved, to some degree, in the timber trade itself. Frequently they shipped timber which their crews had harvested. More often they bought timber or deals from the producer or took them in trade. Sometimes they would ship them on consignment to the British market. Rarely was the timber merchandising a single activity. Usually it was part of a pattern of business endeavour which included the wholesaling and retailing of British and American imports, coastal shipping, and the purchase, use, and sale of sailing vessels.[16]

Central to the business activity of all leading merchants was involvement in or ownership of one or more of the three vital elements in city commerce: the banking system, the wharves of the port, and the ships. Most sat on the directorates of at least one of the three local public banks or the local advisory committee of the Bank of British North America.[17] Indeed, given the centrality of credit to the commercial system of the province, it was unthinkable that any substantial local firm would not have easy access to the financial stability which the banks offered, an access ultimately controlled by the bank directors whose committees met twice weekly to approve all loans. Access to the city wharves and water lots on the east side of Saint John harbour, the most valuable mercantile property in the colony, was also critical. The water lots had been leased in perpetuity by the city in return for an annual rental of between £5 and £31, depending on location in the harbour, a merchant received the right to erect improvements on the wharf, to provide free wharfage for his ships and goods, and to charge the legal rates of wharfage to all ships choosing to load or unload at this landing.[18] Possession of this vital harbour resource provided the merchant with both the most geographically advantageous terminal for his sea and river commerce and a modest but continuous income.

The central feature of New Brunswick trade was its de-centralization. Most great merchants were not involved in the timber-harvest or the sawmilling industry. Similarly, although they bought, sold, and contracted for the construction of vessels, they rarely participated directly in the shipbuilding industry. The role of most merchants was that of entrepreneur closing the links between the harbours of Saint John and Liverpool. Their vehicle was the sailing vessel and by 1841 the port possessed nearly 90,000 tons of shipping, about equally divided between small coasting vessels and those designed for trans-Atlantic crossings.[19] There were great differences in patterns of ownership among the city's major mercantile firms. More than half of the port's tonnage was owned by its great merchants, several of whom possessed sizeable fleets. John Kirk owned 14 vessels totalling over 7,000 tons, Stephen Wiggins 10 vessels of nearly 7,000 tons, and John Wishart 9 vessels of 4,500 tons. At the other extreme, a number of merchants actually owned very little shipping, apparently preferring to ship through others. The large firm of Crookshank and Walker, for example, had only a single vessel in 1841. The different ownership patterns reflected the kinds of mercantile specialization that had developed by 1840. The large shipowners were heavily committed to the timber trade, both as merchants and as carriers; Crookshank and Walker were West Indies merchants with strong ties to the coasting trade and played the role of commission merchant and auctioneer. But whatever the area of specialized activity an individual firm might tend to follow, the collective control by the great merchants of the financial structure, harbour facilities, and shipping industry of Saint

415

John placed them in the position both to accumulate personal wealth and to play a significant role in determining the kind of economy which might emerge in the city and the colony.

Most great merchants built up sizeable fortunes at some point in their careers. And while time and fortune were not always kind to them, the great majority managed to avoid calamitous failures.[20] Any attempt to establish the extent of personal wealth of an individual over time is an exceedingly treacherous enterprise, but it is possible to get a glimpse of the collective resources of the merchant community and to establish with some accuracy the holdings of most merchants at one point in their lives. Something of the size of Saint John merchant capital can be glimpsed in the city's fleet. Assuming an average price of £5 a ton, a conservative estimate of the value of vessels registered in Saint John in 1841 would be £450,000, and the capital investment of firms such as those of James Kirk or Stephen Wiggins would have been in the order of £30–40,000.[21] All firms had a basic business investment in offices, stores, warehouses, and the harbour-area land or wharves on which they were located. While the size of this investment varied with the scope of the facilities, even a single store in the harbour area was worth £3,000 by mid-century and the larger facilities of many merchants plus the value of stock on hand could multiply that figure five or six times. Yet few merchants committed most of their assets to their mercantile activities. In 1826 the firm of Crookshank and Walker, one of the largest in the city, owned assets valued at more than £50,000 ($200,000). Of this total only 20 per cent was represented by vessels (the firm owned four) and less than 10 per cent by goods on hand.[22] The remainder consisted of investments in property and notes. Johnston withdrew from the firm in 1826 and received the sum of £25,000 from his partner. He also retained ownership of his own firm, H. Johnston & Co., and his total personal assets in that year amounted to over £40,000.[23] Similar stories of substantial capital investment outside the major mercantile operation can be constructed for other great merchants. Nehemiah Merritt died in 1843 possessed of an estate worth about £60,000 ($240,000) exclusive of ships and business stock.[24] In 1864 Stephen Wiggins left more than $700,000 to his heirs, about half of it composed of assets not connected with the firm.[25] And still later, in 1876, "The Lord of the North," John Robertson, passed on $454,000 for the benefit of his children.[26] By 1840 there may have been a dozen merchants each with assets exceeding a quarter of a million American dollars, and a large part of this capital was available for investment beyond the primary enterprises of their holders.

Not surprisingly the most important uses to which the great merchants of Saint John devoted their wealth were those designed to further the development strategies which the merchant community deemed essential to its economic well-being. While direction and emphasis of these strategies changed from time to time in response to external circumstances, the broad outline is clearly visible throughout the first half of the nineteenth century. Like their counterparts in most North American ports, Saint John merchants emphasized a combination of financial institutions, transportation links, resource exploitation, and urban development to enable them to facilitate trans-Atlantic trade and to dominate a hinterland extending for 200 miles around the city. By 1840 their dominance in shipping had turned the Bay of Fundy into a St. John lake and their location had made the entire St. John Valley a satrapy of the city. Their greatest concerns were the development of transportation facilities into the interior and to the north shore of the province and the exploitation of the natural resources found within this natural zone of control. To achieve the first, the merchants pressured for a canal system to open the Grand Lake, some 60 miles from the city. After 1835 they sought to extend the city's control to the North Shore by means of a combined ship–railroad system which would involve construction of short railway lines between Grand Lake and Richibucto and between Shediac and Moncton. To exploit the natural resources of the area, they proposed to develop the sources of water power at the mouth of the St. John River and at the Grand Lake, to mine the coal resources of the Grand Lake area, and to promote the Bay of Fundy and southern whale fisheries.[27]

417

The most important institutions necessary to the maintenance of this commercial system were financial organizations, notably banks and insurance companies. Banks facilitated the transfer of funds in transAtlantic trade and control of the province's major credit agencies gave the leading merchants considerable leverage in their dealings with other parts of New Brunswick society. The Council of New Brunswick had co-operated with the merchant community to charter the first bank in British North America in 1820.[28] But the conservative policies and limited capital resources of the Bank of New Brunswick could not keep pace with the financial needs of merchants in a rapidly expanding colony and by 1836 they had secured royal charters for two more banking institutions, the Commercial and the City banks, over the opposition of the Executive Council of the province.[29] By 1845 the three banks possessed a paid up capital of £250,000 ($1,000,000), most of which was probably held within the city by the merchant community.[30] Through the period 1830–50 banking stock never yielded less than 8 per cent a year and was viewed not only as an excellent security but also a first-class opportunity for speculation. Similar emphasis was placed on the city's two marine insurance companies, and on its fire insurance company. The £50,000 capital of the N.B. Marine Company, the largest of these firms, yielded an annual dividend of 10 to 60% in the 1840s,[31] and more than 80% of the stock of that company was held by city merchants in 1841.[32] The stock of these companies not only yielded an excellent dividend income, but provided the basis for a flourishing speculative trade in stocks.

Nonetheless, the most important single investment made by Saint John merchants was in land. It is interesting to speculate on the reasons behind this phenomenon. Land was clearly acquired both incidentally, in payment for debts owed, and because of the high degree of security which it offered. As well, many merchants saw an opportunity to achieve a certain status in the possession of well-known farms and favoured city residences. The nature of the acquisitions reveals several motives on the part of the purchasers: a desire to emulate a landed gentry, to create the security of rental income, to speculate on rising land prices and, in the case of purchases outside New Brunswick, to escape the consequences of the provincial bankruptcy laws in the event of commercial disaster. All merchants maintained one and sometimes two city residences. A large land-holder such as Noah Disbrow owned 12 city lots and 5 houses, [33] while John Robertson paid city taxes on real estate assessed at £25,000 ($100,000) — which almost certainly greatly underestimated its true market value — and held long-term leases, through his brother, on more than 100 city lots.[34] At his death in 1876 Robertson owned city real estate valued at $250,000.[35] Virtually all merchants owned several city lots and most possessed long-term leases on substantial tracts of city land in the harbour area.

Perhaps the most obvious case of land speculation on the part of leading merchants was the development of the suburban lands lying along the Marsh Road area directly north and west of the city. As early as 1819 most of this land had been acquired from the Hazen estate by several merchants — notably Nehemiah Merritt, Stephen Wiggins, Henry Gilbert, Hugh Johnston, and Walker Tisdale — as building lots and farms.[36] By mid-century most of the land remained in the hands of the merchant-buyers, who were in the process of subdividing it into township building lots. The same assumptions concerning the development of the interior of the province marked the merchant's land acquisition in the St. John River Valley. Instead of buying up timber land, most merchants deliberately set about to acquire land bordering on the river. Their holdings were marked by a high proportion of intervale land, working farms and tenants, and comprised some of the most valuable agricultural resources in the province. The estate of Hugh Johnston alone contained nearly 12,000 acres of Valley land in 25 separate holdings scattered through Queens, Sunbury, York, and Carleton counties in 1835.[37] A number of merchants also acquired extensive holdings in other areas, notably Nova Scotia, Maine, New York, and Upper Canada. Nehemiah Merritt, for example, owned three houses at Greenwich & Amos streets in New York City,[38] and he and Walker Tisdale each possessed more than 2,000 acres of land in Northumberland and Durham counties, Upper Canada.[39]

In addition to ownership of lands and financial institutions, the St. John merchant sought security through the public sector of the economy. The debt of the city and the province and the financing of public utilities within the city offered ample opportunity for investment. The city, in particular, had no agency through which it could carry long-term debt contracted for the construction of essential public works and from 1819 onward the merchant came to play an important role as city creditor.[40] By 1842 the municipal funded debt totalled £112,000 of which 40 per cent was held directly by merchants and their families and another 20 per cent by St. John banks and insurance companies.[41] The city's major public utilities were promoted and financed by its merchants. The water company was formed following the cholera epidemic of 1832 and by 1844 had expended £27,000 on the system.[42] The Gas Light Company and Reversing Falls Bridge Company were founded in the 1840s under the inspiration of the same group.[43]

Of all the potential investments in New Brunswick, the one that found least favour with the merchant community was secondary industry. Most merchant investment in this sector was related to the processing of natural resources produced in the province. In the wake of the growing English demand for deals in the mid-1830s several merchants acquired or constructed sawmills in conjunction with their shipping activities. Within the city John Robertson erected a large steam sawmill powered by sawdust and offal,[44] while less impressive operations were conducted by Robert Rankin & Co., Stephen Wiggins, R.D. Wilmot, Thomas and Ezekiel Barlow, and Nehemiah Merritt.[45] Outside the city the Kinnear brothers operated the Wales Stream mill.[46] Several others lent their support to the Portland Mills and Tunnel Company which proposed to cut tunnels through the Reversing Falls gorge to provide water power for a sawmill complex in Portland.[47] The most important industrial undertaking of any merchant before 1850 was the establishment of the Phoenix Foundry by the Barlow brothers in the 1820s. During the first two decades of its existence the firm introduced a number of technical innovations into the city, including construction of the first steamship manufactured entirely in the colony.[48] However, these examples were the exceptions rather than the rule. Most leading merchants had no financial involvement with secondary industry before 1840; those who did, with exception of Robertson and the Barlows, had a very limited investment in the undertakings. There was little investment in the city's major secondary industry — shipbuilding — and most lumber, even in the St. John area, was made in 49 sawmills owned by a different group of men.[49] Quite clearly, comprehensive industrial development stood low on the list of merchant priorities in the period.

In view of the rapid pace of industrial growth in the city between 1820 and 1840, the low level of merchant participation is surprising. In 1820, apart from a few shipyards, sawmills, and flour mills, St. John's secondary industry consisted of a wide variety of traditional crafts practiced in dozens of small workshops. Over the course of the next three decades, in response to the needs of a rapidly expanding provincial so-

419

ciety, the city and its environs was transformed into an important manufacturing centre. This development occurred along a broad front. Most obvious and most significant was the growth of the shipbuilding and sawmilling industries. But there was also a host of industries producing for provincial consumers. Apart from the enterprises of the master tailors and shoemakers, these included 24 tanneries, 16 flour mills, 4 iron foundries, 2 brass foundries, 12 furniture and 4 soap manufacturers, 8 carriage makers, 2 breweries, a paper mill, and a number of minor industries.[50] The capacity and resources of these firms is perhaps best illustrated in the flour industry which by 1840 represented a capital investment of over £50,000 in mills capable of annually producing more than 150,000 barrels of flour, enough to feed the entire population of the province.[51] The tanners — 4 of whom were capable of generating more than 60 horsepower from their steam engines — made a similar claim for their industry.[52] The Harris Foundry comprised a block of buildings in 1846 with a replacement value of more than £10,000.[53] Most of these firms were developed by local entrepreneurs using their own skills and either their own capital or that of their family or friends.

420

Before 1840 most merchants either held this development at arm's length or viewed it with outright hostility. Wood and fish processing and shipbuilding were regarded as important elements in the commercial system and some merchants were prepared to invest in these undertakings. When local grain and livestock production was expanding in the 1820s, several merchants indicated some support for the tanners in their efforts to exclude the cheap Canadian leather from the province, and even promoted the first steam flour mill to grind local wheat.[54] However, such support was rare. More common was a violent negative reaction. The special objects of the merchants' wrath were the millers and bakers. The latter had long protested because American flour entered the colony with 5 shilling-a-barrel duty while bread entered free.[55] The merchants' reply was to demand the removal of provincial tariffs on both.[56] A clearer indication of the merchants' view of early industrial development is seen in the issues on which they took no position. These included virtually every request for assistance, support, or tariff protection by every manufacturing industry and interest in the city between 1820 and 1840. Given the rapid growth of the manufacturing sector during this time, this lack of participation by the merchant community stood in sharp contrast to the support which the manufacturers were able to command in almost every other major segment of urban society.

The principal organization of the merchant community was the Chamber of Commerce and the world which the merchant sought to create and maintain before 1840 is clearly visible through its petitions to the municipal, provincial, and imperial governments. The central doctrine in these petitions was the reciprocity of mercantilism and imperial economic preference in return for colonial deference and loyalty in matters economic and political. The merchant identified the prosperity of the colony with his right to buy cheaply and sell dear. To do this he must not only be able to sell colonial produce in a protected imperial market, but to purchase that produce in as free a market as possible. The latter doctrine carried a special significance for colonial producers for the merchant was prepared to use American timber and foodstuffs to keep costs as low as possible in the timber trade. Indeed, on any issue deemed vital to the prosecution of the timber trade the ranks of the great merchants never broke in nearly half a century. Thus woods resources held by the crown and after 1836 by the province must be leased at nominal fees;[57] severe penalties must be imposed on those stealing timber or making lumber, timber, fish, and flour of inferior quality;[58] debtors must continue to be imprisoned lest British creditors lose confidence in the colony's will to protect them and cheap justice must be provided to permit the collection of debts;[59] no provincial duties could be imposed on timber, lumber, flour, bread, pork, or manufactured tobacco; and provincial tariffs must stand at no more than 5 per cent so that the merchant might keep control of the commerce of the Annapolis Valley of Nova Scotia.[60] Until 1843 imperial regulations permitted the merchant to treat the entire eastern seaboard of the United States and New Brunswick as a single commercial entity for the purposes of the timber trade,[61] and New Brunswick timber makers found their prices set by American competition. Even more significant, in terms of its implications for the fortunes of farmers and millers, was the merchants' bitter and continued opposition to any attempts by either provincial or imperial parliaments to establish or maintain duties on flour or salted provisions, an opposition which finally led lieutenant-governor Sir John Harvey to express doubts as to what extent the St. John Chamber of Commerce "represents the real commercial interests of the province."[62]

By 1840 there is some evidence to suggest that a minority of merchants were prepared to dissent from the Chamber on economic issues not directly related to the timber trade. The flour trade was a case in point. While most fleet owners strongly supported free trade in wheat and flour in order to assure the cheapest provisions for their crews, a number of other great merchants came to see the commercial possibilities of a high tariff on foreign wheat and flour which would enable them to ship wheat from England for processing in St. John mills. And the rapidly expanding domestic market had persuaded a few that not only could greater returns be obtained by importing wheat, rather than flour, but that flour mills offered the best return of all.[63] Nonetheless, until the 1840s the vast majority of merchants still believed that low tariffs were essential.

After 1841 the assumptions upon which the merchants' system had been built were undermined by external factors. The first major jolt was the dramatic recession of 1841 occasioned by the collapse of the British timber market. As the ripples of this unusually severe crisis spread

421

through the local economy, the layers of provincial society collapsed hierarchically, beginning with the ships labourers, passing into the minor shopkeepers and journeymen craftsmen, then into the ranks of the master craftsmen, shipbuilders, traders, contractors, small merchants, and lawyers,[64] finally claiming its victims among even the most stalwart with the bankruptcies of leading merchants such as James Hanford, Alex Yeats, and J. & H. Kinnear in 1843.[65] Just as the economy was recovering from the recession in 1843, the British Government began its gradual dismantlement of the mercantilist structure with the regulations prohibiting the import of Maine-produced timber into the United Kingdom under the preferential tariff.[66] In the short run the regulations produced no significant impact on the timber trade other than to limit the merchants' choice of producers. The long-run effect of the tariff declension between 1843 and 1849 was a sharp decline in the quantity and value of timber shipped from St. John, and a corresponding increase in the export of lumber and deals.[67]

422

The rapid change and threat of change in the early 1840s produced a crisis of confidence in the mercantile assumptions which had dominated the economy of New Brunswick since Napoleonic times. The producer, whether shoemaker, farmer, sawmill owner, or founder, had existed in a gray area of semi-protection since the creation of the colony. Although the combination of imperial protective tariffs and provincial revenue duties had been sufficient to keep most local produce competitive with that from the United States, British produce entered the colony burdened only by the small revenue tariff. Provincial duties on British manufactures, for example, were fixed at 2½ per cent while those levied on American were 10 per cent.[68] The proposed elimination of the imperial tariff threatened to visit further disaster on an already badly demoralized artisan community. Hundreds of St. John artisans and mechanics had abandoned the city during the recession of 1841–42 and the exodus continued through 1842 and 1843 as economic prospects for the colony dimmed. By 1843 the city was divided by acrimonious debate between those prepared to follow the mother country into free trade, and those who argued that the wealth of the colony was being dissipated on imported produce to the detriment of the producing classes. These protectionist views were strengthened by the emergence of a significant mechanics' revolt against what was perceived as the tyranny of the merchants. Out of the thriving mechanics community which had developed in the 1830s was formed, late in 1843, the Provincial Association, which brought together representatives of every major group of producers in the province.[69] The Association advocated protection and promotion of the interests of farmers, fishers, mechanics, and manufacturers, through the use of duties, bounties, model farms, and mechanics fairs. Among other things it urged the imposition of a substantial tariff on cordage and canvas, coupled with the payment of a bounty to farmers to grow hemp and flax.[70]

By 1844 the debate between free traders and protectionists had been transferred from the meeting hall to the Legislative Assembly, where the protectionists succeeded in imposing a compromise on the merchant interests after six close divisions in the House. Provincial duties were raised to 25 per cent on clocks, 20 per cent on wooden ware and chairs, 15 per cent on furniture and agricultural implements, 10 per cent on castings, cut nails, and brick, and specific duties were imposed on cattle, oxen, horses, and apples. At the same time any product required for the building of ships or the provisioning of crews, including flour, was placed on the free list. The debate over the most hotly contested duties, those on footwear and clothing, ended in a tie when a 10 per cent duty was imposed on footwear (a 5 per cent proposal was narrowly defeated) and clothing was admitted under a 4 per cent tariff.[71]

The compromise was only a temporary truce. Led by the St. John Chamber of Commerce, the free traders counterattacked at the 1845 sitting of the Assembly. Winning the support of several farmers who had voted with the protectionists the previous year, the free traders succeeded in reducing the tariff schedule to its 1843 levels, cutting some duties by as much as 60 per cent.[72] In response, one outraged protectionist leader vented his spleen in the columns of *The Morning News* on the "Free Trade Chamber of Commerce" of St. John, those "few selfish individuals" who were prepared to impose "this vicious system of one-sided free trade" on the "productive classes . . . the bone and sinew of the country."[73] However, this setback was temporary. Much to the chagrin of leading reformers like George Fenety, protection became a basic political issue during the 1840s and 50s, one that cut across the constitutional issues so dear to the hearts of reformers.[74] The Revenue Bill of the province was prepared each year by a select committee of the Assembly which acted on resolutions passed at each sitting of the Legislature. In 1847 the House, by a 21–10 majority, accepted the principle that "in enacting a Revenue Bill, the principle of protection to home industry, irrespective of revenue, should be recognized by levying duties on those productions and manufactures of foreign countries which the people of this province are capable of producing and manufacturing themselves."[75] The thrust of this resolution was directed against American produce and the Revenue Bill of that year introduced differential duties on British and foreign manufacturers. After 1850, however, the protectionists on the select committee were able to develop a policy of modest protection for a number of local industries. This included a 15 per cent tariff on footwear, leather, furniture, machinery, iron castings (stoves, ranges, boilers, furnaces, grates), most agricultural implements, wagons and sleighs, veneers, cigars, hats, and pianos.

423

The merchant community of St. John was ill-prepared to meet the threat posed by the rise of the Provincial Association. By 1843 it was still recovering from the blows dealt it by the collapse of 1841–42 and it perceived the major threat to its security among the British free traders rather than in a diverse group of local protectionists. While the Chamber of Commerce traditionally had been the principal vehicle of merchant views, by 1843 it had come to represent the great fleet owners in their struggle against the threats to the protected status of the colonial timber trade. The Chamber's initial reaction to the Provincial Association and its proposals to divert provincial resources from the timber trade into agriculture and manufacturing was negative. In strongly worded petitions to the provincial and imperial authorities it reiterated support for traditional mercantilist policies in the timber trade and for a maximum 5 per cent duty on all provincial imports.[76] Yet, while the majority apparently accepted the Chamber of Commerce position, a significant minority came out in support of the Provincial Association and its policies of economic diversification and protective tariffs.[77] Among the heretics were R.D. Wilmot, William Parks, the Jarvises, Henry Gilbert, John Walker, Noah Disbrow, Charles Ward, and Walker Tisdale.[78] The principal spokesman for the movement in St. John in the mid-1840s was R.D. Wilmot. When the Provincial Association entered the political arena with its platform of the "new New Brunswick," Wilmot was returned to the House of Assembly where he replaced his cousin, Lemuel Allan Wilmot, as the province's leading protectionist. Meanwhile, in an effort to restore a semblance of unity to the divided merchant community, the Chamber of Commerce was re-organized in the spring of 1845 and the membership of its new directorate reflected the attempts made to provide representation from a wide range of merchant opinions and interests.[79] At the final crisis of mercantilism, in 1849, the Chamber played an important part in the organization of the New Brunswick Colonial Association which brought together the city's most distinguished citizens in an effort to define the province's role in the new economic order.[80] The early programme of the Association clearly represented an attempt to reconcile all viewpoints and included a proposal urging the encouragement of home industry.[81] These efforts muted but could not entirely conceal the tensions between merchant free traders and protectionists.

By 1850 the Colonial Association had dropped its proposal for the encouragement of home industry and offered reciprocity in trade and navigation with the United States as the sole panacea for the province's economic ills.[82] And in the House of Assembly the merchants and their supporters were able to impose a compromise on the protectionists the effect of which was to create two economic systems. The artisan and manufacturer were granted a moderate tariff on material not required in the prosecution of the wood trades, while virtually everything necessary to the lumber industry, the timber trade, the building of wooden ships, and the victualling of crews was admitted free to the New Brunswick market. The latter included mill engines, anchors, chain, canvas, cordage, tackle, felt, sails, spikes, cotton ways, and iron bolts, bars, plates, and sheating, as well as rigging, tin and copper plate, sheathing paper, grain, flour, meal, bread, meats, fruit, and vegetables.[83] In effect, every backward linkage that the rapidly growing shipbuilding and shipping industry might have provided to the provincial economy was discouraged by provincial policy. Ship builders were encouraged to import all materials required in the building process, other than wood. Merchants were rewarded both with the transportation costs of the building materials and with cheap vessels which they sold in the United Kingdom. It was a policy which permitted the application of a limited range of skills and the use of a small capital to produce a product which was competitive on the British market. Unfortunately such a policy conferred only limited benefits on the provincial economy and did not provide the flexibility or profit margins that gave the ship builder either the capital resources or the incentive to undertake any extensive technological innovation. More important it did not allow the development of substantial industries, dependent on these backward linkages, which might have promoted these changes.

425

Nonetheless, the activities of the Provincial Association remained an important theme in city politics into the 1850s. Of the 37 great merchants still living in St. John after 1842, 16 lent their support to at least some significant part of the protectionist programme and 12 of these consistently supported its general objective.[84] Not surprisingly, the merchants split on the issue of protection in terms of the emphasis which their business activities gave to the timber trade. Those with the most significant trading concerns — like John Ward, John Wishart, and John Robertson — remained largely divorced from the concerns of other elements within the broader community. They were, as well, the major shipowners and their focus remained on the trans-Atlantic community. They did not, necessarily, oppose the protectionist impulse *per se*, but they did fear its emphasis on economic self-sufficiency, its inefficiencies, and, particularly, the stated goal of protectionists to transfer resources out of the timber industry and into manufacturing, agriculture, and fishing.[85] Yet, while leading merchants opposed protectionist policies where they threatened to make the New Brunswick shipping industry uncompetitive on international runs by imposing substantial tariffs on flour, bread, and pork, a number were prepared to accept the new order. Although it is difficult to generalize about them, they tended to include men whose principal activities had centred on the merchandising activities of the wholesaler and those whose interests were more concerned with New Brunswick than the trans-Atlantic community. While they were men of substance, none could match the personal fortunes amassed by the more substantial timber merchants, particularly those with heavy investments in ships. At his death in 1853, Noah Disbrow left over $80,000 (£20,800) to be divided among his 6 daughters and 2 sons,[86] and three years later Munson Jarvis' brother, William, a prominent dockside merchant, left $50,000.[87] The next year William Parks placed a value of £17,484 (about $70,000) on the assets of his firm.[88] By comparison, Stephen Wiggins' share of the firm of Stephen Wiggins & Son was valued at $389,000 in 1863, most of which would have been in shipping.[89] Over the course of the 1850s, however, a minority of the great merchants did play an increasingly important role in the industrial development of the city through promotion of enterprises as diverse as woollen mills and coal oil refineries. As their industrial interests grew, their involvement in the staples' trade became less significant. Several had been or became agents for the transfer of resources from the staples to the manufacturing sector of the provincial economy in an attempt to create a more balanced economy. The Barlow brothers have been mentioned already in connection with the secondary iron industry. The hardware merchant, William Henry Scovil, established his cut nail factory in the early 1840s, while the wholesale grocer, William Parks, ended his career in the 1860s as proprietor of one of the first cotton mills in British North America.

Those who identified most closely with the community were generally most willing to commit capital to its internal development; those with strong British ties and alternatives were usually much less willing to make this commitment. The former characteristic is reflected in the relatively high proportion of merchants of Loyalist origins who supported the Provincial Association and its objectives. In essence, they viewed St. John as the central element in a limited regional economy, in preference to its position in the larger metropolitan economy. It was merchants who had developed these more limited horizons and who saw their future in terms of local enterprise who came to the support of the manufacturers and artisans of the city, the group largely responsible for the not inconsiderable manufacturing development of the period from 1820 to 1850. The manufacturers and artisans were drawn from different origins, participated at different levels of civic society, and enjoyed a distinctly inferior status to their mercantile counterparts. Their special interests and ideas received serious consideration by the leaders of the community only during periods of economic crisis, such as the 1840s and 1870s. Even then the producers were able to achieve a position of influence only in alliance with a portion of the merchant community. When merchants closed ranks, they were able to establish the goals of the community at large and these goals were almost always designed to further the integration of the region into a larger trading complex in which the region was subordinated to the interests of a metropolitan community. So long as the imperial economic system was possible, the merchants used their capital and their great influence to maintain and further that system, largely ignoring the interests of farmers, manufac-

426

turers, and other producers in the province. Nowhere was this more evident than in the crucial area of credit. Not only did they use the financial
institutions in the city to direct the available credit to their own commercial purposes, but they successfully thwarted every effort by producers
to obtain their own banking facilities.

The great merchants certainly organized and financed the commercial
and financial super-structure needed for the conduct of the timber trade
in a major sea port and they played important roles in providing capital
for the exploitation of the natural resources of the region and for the
construction of public works and utilities within the city. A minority,
distinguished by their wholesaling concerns and native origins, began
to participate in some fashion in the development of a more diversified
urban economy. But the majority of great merchants retained a commitment to an unmodified staples economy. In the early nineteenth century it was this group which produced the dominant economic class,
the institutions, and myths — particularly that of commerce as the great
creator of prosperity — which formed the community of St. John.
Throughout the period they were able to mould the economy to their
essentially interregional export-oriented needs. In so doing, they exploited the province's natural resources of timber and stimulated the
development of major sawmilling and shipbuilding industries, both of
which produced significant short-term benefits for the economy. Ancillary benefits were derived from the provision of shipping, credit facilities, and insurance services.

427

The manufacturing sector of the New Brunswick economy did grow
rapidly in the 1850s and 60s. Gordon Bertram has demonstrated that
in 1871 the *per capita* output of the province's manufacturing industries
rivalled that of Ontario and Quebec and was nearly twice that of Nova
Scotia.[90] Nearly half of the industrial output of New Brunswick was produced in and around the city of St. John.[91] McClelland suggests that
there was an average annual growth of one per cent in New Brunswick's
deal and lumber exports during the period.[92] Not surprisingly, the largest
components of the province's industrial output were sawmill products
and wooden ships (44% for the province and 38%for the city).[93] Apart
from these traditional staples, however, virtually every industry which
had received even a modest degree of protection in the previous generation flourished. Foundry products, footwear, and clothing all exceeded
shipbuilding in value, while furniture and carriage making, boiler making,
saw and file manufacture, and tin and sheet iron output and leather
making all played significant roles in the local economy.[94] Some backward
linkages from shipbuilding, which earlier tariff policies had done so little
to encourage, were also able to develop by the later 1860s. The most
obvious example was the small rope making industry functioning in the
city and there can be little doubt that at least some of the foundry activity
was stimulated by the market created by the ship builders.[95]

Yet the outlines of the earlier emphases were still visible in the city's industrial structure. There was, apparently, no industry capable of producing the chain, anchors, and canvas used in the shipbuilding industry, nor to provide the machinery employed in the province's 565 sawmills.[96] Although steam engines had been constructed in St. John in the 1840s, there was no engine building firm in the province by 1870.[97] A similar situation existed in the basic food industries. The ancient flour industry had been virtually eliminated and only a miniscule meat curing industry survived.[98] There were no distilleries and only four small breweries.[99] The debate over the virtues of the ordered pastoral life as opposed to the disordered and transient nature of the timber industry was a recurring theme in nineteenth-century New Brunswick. The debate came to be couched in such explicit moral terms that it is difficult to make any assessment from it of the economic viability of provincial agriculture in the period, or to determine the extent to which the agricultural development of the province was affected by the timber trade.[100] The rapidity of agricultural development between 1840 and 1870 would seem to indicate that there was some truth to the charges of the timber critics; at the very least, the combination of rewards which the trade could offer to the rural inhabitants coupled with the refusal of the provincial legislature to provide any protection for the nascent colonial agriculture, severely retarded the development of a substantial agriculture in the early nineteenth century.[101]

428

The retardation was of vital importance to the health of the colonial economy. New Brunswick ran a perennial deficit in its current account and in most years the entire trade imbalance resulted from the substantial imports of foodstuffs for use within the province. The most prominent example of this phenomenon was American wheat and flour, but it was reflected, as well, in large imports of rye flour, Indian meal, pork, beef, lamb, butter, potatoes, vegetables, fruit, and even oats. The proportion of agricultural products ranged from just over 20% of the province's total imports in 1840 to just under 40% in 1855.[102] Wheat and flour imports alone exceeded the value of timber exports by 1852, and by 1855 the 170,000 barrels of flour and 110,000 bushels of wheat, worth £334,000 in all, rivalled the £380,000 in deals shipped from the province.[103] New Brunswick agricultural conditions were not particularly suited to the production of wheat, although the doubling of output following the National Policy of 1879 indicates that a much larger production than occurred up to Confederation was possible.[104] But it is more difficult to explain the import of most other foodstuffs which could be produced domestically. Given the fact that substantial quantities of these products were grown in the province in the 1840s, that the land for producing more was readily available, and that there was a substantial local demand for these foodstuffs which could not be met by local producers, it seems probable that the incentives offered by the timber trade, and the refusal of the province to afford even nominal protection to local producers were the major factors in inhibiting the growth of a more substantial agricultural sector before 1850.

In the final analysis there is no simple answer to the question of merchant responsibility for economic growth or retardation in St. John and New Brunswick. While they agreed on the validity of the concept of economic growth, merchants rarely spoke with a single voice when the subject of a specific development strategy was raised. Most were prepared to permit, and some to support a strategy which included the development of certain kinds of secondary industry. These efforts were generally successful although this success was due more to the efforts of the city's artisans than to its merchants. Merchant endeavours were particularly aimed at supporting and preserving the traditional timber staple and its milling, shipping, and shipbuilding ancillaries. The manufacture of producers' goods used in any of these activities, including mill engines and machinery, shipbuilding materials, and domestic foodstuffs needed for ship crews, woods workers, and mill labourers, were afforded no encouragement. In effect two economic systems based upon mutually exclusive values were the result of the synthesis which emerged from the conflict of the 1840s. The most obvious victim of that synthesis was the shipbuilding industry, potentially the most dynamic element in the provincial economy, which was locked into the more conservative timber-trade economy. Thus a city containing a number of secondary iron and steel firms, which for decades had possessed the capability of manufacturing complete steamships and engines, and a labour force skilled at working in both wood and iron was unable to manufacture metal ships or even to make any substantial adjustment in the face of technological changes which were gradually eroding this vital industry. In the course of the 1860s and 70s the ship builders built and the timber merchants bought and sold ships in the traditional way simply because they could not perceive the industry apart from the timber trade or from the lumber which was basic to both building and trade. While the timber merchants were not alone able to shape the provincial economy to their perceptions, they provided an effective and powerful leadership to substantial interests in the province which identified with the traditional timber trade. By 1871 the economy was becoming increasingly diversified and self-sufficient and the dynamic elements in this development were to be found in secondary industry and in agriculture, but the influence of the great merchants delayed this development by two critical decades. In this sense they contributed to the retardation of a viable industrial base in the city.

429

NOTES

[1] The literature of this debate has been explored by L.R. MacDonald in "Merchants against Industry: An Idea and Its Origins," *Canadian Historical Review* 56 (1975): 263–81 [hereafter *CHR*].

[2] A point most recently made by Professor Gerald Tulchinsky in *The River Barons* (Toronto, 1977), 234.

[3] Nonetheless, a good beginning has been made with Tulchinsky's examination of the Montreal business community at mid-century, and in David Sutherland's study of the business strategies of Halifax merchants in the colonial period. Tulchinsky, *The River Barons*; David Sutherland, "Halifax Merchants and the Pursuit of Development, 1783-1850," *CHR* 59 (1978): 1-17.

[4] Peter D. McClelland, "The New Brunswick Economy in the Nineteenth Century," Ph.D. thesis, Harvard University, 1966, 3-4. McClelland argues that shipbuilding may have added no more than 2.6% to the gross regional product (p. 189) and that it had few significant backward or forward linkages.

[5] McClelland, "New Brunswick Economy," 229-30.

[6] McClelland, "New Brunswick Economy," 4.

[7] New Brunswick, *Journal of the House of Assembly*, 1841, xvii-xxx; Canada, *Census of 1871* 4: 125.

[8] Canada, *Census of 1871* 4: 128.

[9] The early development of this industry is discussed by Lewis R. Fischer in "From Barques to Barges: Shipping Industry of Saint John, N.B., 1820-1914," unpublished paper read to the Atlantic Canada Studies Conference, Fredericton, 1978.

[10] Eugene A. Forsey, *The Canadian Labour Movement, 1812-1902* (Ottawa: Canadian Historical Association, 1974), 3-4; J. Richard Rice, "A History of Organized Labour in Saint John, New Brunswick, 1813-1890," M.A. thesis, U.N.B., 1968), ch. 1.

[11] James M. Gilmour, *Spatial Evolution of Manufacturing: Southern Ontario, 1851-1891* (Toronto, 1972).

[12] For the extent to which they succeeded in this goal see the testimonials to the merchants delivered by George Fenety and Henry Chubb, the city's most respected and influential newspaper editors in the 1840s. See *The Commercial News and General Advertiser* (St. John), 10 September 1839, and *The New Brunswick Courier* (St. John), 10 February 1843.

[13] This thesis is argued by Stewart MacNutt in his "Politics of the Timber Trade in Colonial New Brunswick, 1825-40," *CHR* 30 (1949): 47-65.

[14] This group includes L.H. Deveber, Thomas Barlow, Ezekiel Barlow, Jr., Issac Bedell, Robert W. Crookshank, Noah Disbrow, Jr., Lauchlan Donaldson, John Duncan, Henry Gilbert, James T. Hanford, John Hammond, David Hatfield, James Hendricks, Ralph M. Jarvis, Hugh Johnston, Sr., Hon. Hugh Johnston, Jr., John H. Kinnear, James Kirk, Thomas Leavitt, William H. Leavitt, Nehemiah Merritt, Thomas Millidge, D.L. McLaughlin, Thomas E. Millidge, William Parks, John Pollok, Robert Rankin, E.D.W. Ratchford, Hon. John Robertson, W.H. Scovil, Hon. Charles Simonds, Walker Tisdale, John V. Thurgar, John Walker, John Ward, Jr., Charles Ward, Stephen Wiggins, John M. Wilmot, R.D. Wilmot, John Wishart.

[15] David Macmillan explores the early development of the St. John Scottish community in "The New Men in Action: Scottish Mercantile and Shipping Operations in North American Colonies, 1760-1825," *Canadian Business History: Selected Studies, 1497-1971* (Toronto, 1972), 82-99.

[16] A good description of these activities is found in Graeme Wynn, "Industry, Entrepreneurship and Opportunity in the New Brunswick Timber Trade," in Lewis R. Fischer and Eric W Sager, eds., *The Enterprising Canadians: Entrepreneurs and Economic Development in Eastern Canada, 1820-1914* (St. John's: Memorial University of Newfoundland, 1979).

[17] Reports revealing the directors and the financial state of affairs of each bank were published annually in *Journal of the House of Assembly*.

[18] Schedule of Real Estate Belonging to St. John, Wharf Leases in Perpetuity, Records of the Executive Council, REX/PA, Miscellaneous, Provincial Archives of New Brunswick [hereafter PANB].

[19] This description of the St. John fleet, containing information on the date of acquisition, size, and ownership of each vessel, is found in "Customs House Account, Returns of Shipping, Port of Saint John, New Brunswick," *Journal of the House of Assembly*, 1842, cclvii-cclxvii.

[20] Two notable failures were the firms John M. Wilmot, in 1837, and James Hanford, Alex Yeats, and J. & H. Kinnear, in 1843. *The New Brunswick Courier*, 4 March, 18, 25 November 1843; A.R.M. Lower, *Great Britain's Woodyard* (Toronto, 1973), 151.

[21] Prices for New Brunswick-built vessels fluctuated between £5 and £12 a ton throughout the 1830s and 1840s.

[22] Account Book I, 5-10, Hugh Johnston Papers, New Brunswick Museum [hereafter NBM].

[23] Schedule of Real and Personal Effects, May 1826, Hugh Johnston Papers.

[24] Last will and testament of Nehemiah Merritt, Records of the Court of Probate, City and County of St. John, Book G, 131 ff., PANB. The totals include estimates of property values.

[25] Stephen Wiggins, 1864, RG 7, RS 71, PANB.

[26] John Robertson, 1876, RG 7, RS 71, PANB.

[27] New Brunswick, Records of the Legislative Assembly [RLE], 1834, Petitions, vol. 2, no. 41; 1836, Petitions, vol. 5, nos. 70, 75, 81; 1834, Petitions, vol. 6, no. 130, PANB.

[28] James Hannay, *History of New Brunswick* (St. John, 1909), 2: 428-29.

[29] NB, RLE, 1836, Petitions, vol. 5, no. 64, PANB; Hannay, *History of New Brunswick*, 430-32.

[30] These estimates are drawn from Bank of New Brunswick dividend payments, newspaper accounts of bank stock sales, and wills. There was no public statement disclosing the ownership of bank stock in colonial New Brunswick.

[31] The annual reports of the N.B. Marine Insurance Company between 1830 and 1850 may be found in the appendices of the journals of the New Brunswick House of Assembly.

[32] New Brunswick, *Journal of the House of Assembly*, 1842, Appendix — Returns of Incorporated Companies, The N.B. Marine Insurance Company.

[33] Records of the Court of Probate, City and County of St. John, Book H, 454 ff., PANB.

[34] John Robertson to Common Council, 10 October 1849, St. John Common Council Supporting Papers, vol. 20, St. John Manuscripts, PANB; Saint John Schedule (etc.), 1842, REX/PA, Miscellaneous, PANB.

[35] John Robertson, 1876, RG 7, RS 71, PANB.

[36] Extract of Cash Received for Land Sold 1814–1821, Hon. William F. Hazen Papers, Daybook and Journal 1814–34, NBM.

[37] Inventory of Estate of Hugh Johnston, 1 May 1835, Hugh Johnston Papers, Account Book I, NBM.

[38] Probate Records, Book G, 131, PANB.

[39] Probate Records, Book I, 267.

[40] The city debt rose from £4413 in 1822 to £115,366 in 1845. Minutes of the Common Council, vol. 5, 5 April 1822; vol. 17, 10 September 1845, Common Clerk's Office, Saint John City Hall.

[41] Common Council Supporting Papers, vol. 6, 7/8–12/13 September 1842, Saint John Manuscripts, PANB.

[42] NB, RLE, 1844, Petitions, vol. 7, no. 181, PANB.

[43] *The New Brunswick Courier*, 27 March 1843.

[44] *The New Brunswick Courier*, 11 September 1852.

[45] *The Morning News* (St. John), 23 April 1841.

[46] *The New Brunswick Courier*, 25 November 1843.

[47] NB, RLE, 1834, Petitions, vol. 2, no. 41; 1836, Petitions, vol. 5, no. 75; 1839, Petitions, vol. 2, no. 43, PANB.

[48] Common Council Minutes, vol. 15, 23 December 1840, 14 January 1841, Common Clerk's Office, St. John City Hall.

[49] The most important of these was probably George Bond who held the lease for the tidal-powered Carleton mills, the most significant power source in the St. John area.

[50] NB, RLE, 1840, Petitions, vol. 4, no. 122; 1843, Petitions, vol. 6, no. 149; 1850, Petitions, vol. 17, no. 357; 1850, Petitions, no. 414; 1836, Petitions, vol. 5, no. 112, PANB, *The New Brunswick Courier*, 12 October 1850, 5 July 1851.

[51] NB, RLE, 1840, Petitions, vol. 4, no. 122, PANB.

[52] NB, RLE, 1845, Petitions, vol. 9, no. 298.

[53] *The New Brunswick Courier*, 27 June 1846.

[54] NB, RLE, 1834, Petitions, vol. 4, no. 91; 1828, Petitions, vol. 2, no. 43, PANB.

[55] NB, RLE, 1835, Petitions, vol. 4, no. 124; 1842, Petitions, vol. 3, no. 54.

[56] NB, RLE, 1833, Petitions, vol. 3, no. 102; 1840, Petitions, vol. 4, no. 121; 1842, Petitions, vol. 12, no. 237; 1851, Petitions, vol. 15, no. 457; *The New Brunswick Courier*, 4 February 1843.

[57] W.S. MacNutt, "Politics of the Timber Trade in Colonial New Brunswick, 1825–40," 47–65; Graeme Wynn, "Administration in Adversity: The Deputy Surveyors and Control of the New Brunswick Crown Forests Before 1844," Acadiensis 7 (Autumn 1977): 49–65.

[58] NB, RLE, 1839, Petitions, vol. 3, no. 80; 1824, D, Petitions, no. 6, PANB.

[59] NB, RLE, 1831, F. Petitions, vol. 2, no. 10.

[60] NB, RLE, 1850, Petitions, vol. 6, no. 138; *The New Brunswick Courier*, 24 February 1849.

[61] *The New Brunswick Courier*, 20 January 1844.

[62] Sir John Harvey to Lord Glenelg, 15 May 1838, CO 188/59, ff. 733–42, but also see Petition of St.John Merchants, 17 February 1834, CO 188/49, ff. 169–71; Sir John Harvey to Lord John Russell, 4 September 1840, CO 188/69, ff. 152–53; Sir William Colebrooke to Stanley, 29 March 1842, CO 188/75, ff. 341–45. Both Harvey and Colebrooke feared the economic and social consequences of an over-specialized staples economy.

[63] NB, RLE, 1840, Petitions, vol. 4, no. 122, PANB. Among the dissenters were N. Merritt, R. Rankin, John Walker, D. Wilmot, I. Bedell, Wm. Parks.

[64] *The New Brunswick Courier*, 4 March, 3 June, 15 July, 7 October 1843.

[65] *The New Brunswick Courier*, 4 March, 18, 25, November 1843.

[66] NB, RLE, 1843, Petitions, vol. 9, no. 244, PANB.

[67] Between 1840 and 1849 the value of timber exports from New Brunswick declined from £271,000 to £179,000; that of deals and boards increased from £180,000 to £266,000. New Brunswick, *Journal of the House of Assembly*, 1841, 1850, Customs House Returns.

[68] *Journal of the House of Assembly*, 1842, Appendix, cclxxiv.

[69] *The New Brunswick Courier*, 4 January 1844.

[70] *The New Brunswick Courier*, 10 February 1844.

[71] New Brunswick, *Journal of the House of Assembly*, 1844, 152–57.

[72] *The Morning News*, 24 March 1845. The defectors included Barbarie from Restigouche, Earle from Queens, Hanington and Palmer from Westmorland. See New Brunswick, *Journal of the House of Assembly*, 1845, 219–21.

[73] *The Morning News*, 19 March 1845.

[74] Editor and publisher of *The Morning News* and later Queens Printer under the Liberals, Fenety was unsympathetic to the views of the protectionists. G.E. Fenety, *Political Notes and Observations* (Fredericton, 1867), vol. 1, chs. 5, 21. On the other hand both Lemual Allan Wilmot and Samuel Leonard Tilley supported the protectionist position.

431

[75] New Brunswick, *Journal of the House of Assembly*, 1847, 190–91.

[76] *The New Brunswick Courier*, 4 February 1844.

[77] *The New Brunswick Courier*, 10 February 1844.

[78] NB, RLE, 1843, Petitions, vol. 6, no. 143, PANB.

[79] *The Morning News*, 2 April, 16 April, 6 May, 7 May 1845; 25 February 1846.

[80] *The New Brunswick Courier*, 28 June, 4 August 1849.

[81] *The New Brunswick Courier*, 15 September 1849.

[82] *The New Brunswick Courier*, 8 June 1850.

[83] The evolution of New Brunswick policy between 1837 and 1860 is illustrated through the following commodities:

	1837		1842		1844	1845	1848		1855	1859
	Brit.	For.	Brit.	For.			Brit.	For.		
Wagons	2.5%	10%	2.5%	10%	10%	4%	4%	30%	15%	15%
Footwear	2.5%	5%	2.5%	10%	10%	7.5%	4%	30%	15%	15%
Agricultural Implements	Free	Free	Free	Free	10%	4%	4%	15%	15%	15%
Stoves	2.5%	10%	2.5%	10%	10%	7.5%	4%	15%	15%	15%
Chain	2.5%	10%	2.5%	10%	Free	Free	Free	Free	1%	1%
Canvas	Free	Free	Free	Free	Free	Free	Free	Free	1%	1%
Cordage	Free	Free	Free	Free	Free	Free	Free	Free	1%	1%
Mill Engines	Free	10%	Free	10%	Free	Free	Free	Free	10%	12.5%
Meat	Free	Free	Free	Free	Free	Free	Free	Free	Free	Free
Bread Flour	Free	Free	Free	Free	Free	4%	4%	10%	Free	Free

Source: Statutes of New Brunswick, 7 William IV, c.1.; 5 Victoria, c.1.; 7 Victoria, c.1.; 8 Victoria, c.2.; 11 Victoria, c.1.; 18 Victoria, c.1.

[84] NB, RLE, 1850, Petitions, vol. 6, no. 416, PANB.

[85] NB, RLE, 10 February 1843, 23 February 1850.

[86] Noah Disbrow, 1853, RG 7, RS 71, PANB.

[87] William Jarvis, 1856, RG 7, RS 71, PANB.

[88] Partnership Agreements, William Parks Papers, F #3, NBM. This figure does not include Park's personal estate.

[89] Stephen Wiggins, 1853, RG 7, RS 71, PNB.

[90] Gordon W. Bertram, "Historical Statistics on Growth and Structure in Manufacturing in Canada, 1870-1957," in J. Henripin and A. Asimakopulas, eds., *Canadian Political Science Association Conference on Statistics 1962 & 1963* (Toronto, 1964), 122. The figures for Ontario, Quebec, New Brunswick, and Nova Scotia were $69.60, $62.60, $59.80, $30.70.

[91] St. John County output totalled $8,312,627; that of the province was $17,367,687. Canada, *Census of 1871*, vol. 3, Table 54.

[92] McClelland, "The New Brunswick Economy," 124.

[93] McClelland, "The New Brunswick Economy," Tables 22, 39.

[94] The shipbuilding industry produced vessels to a value of $538,042 and employed 647 men. Foundry output, including fittings, nails, and tacks, was $786,000 (507 employees); clothing $826,660 (1033 employees); footwear $539,230 (565 employees). Canada, *Census of 1871*, vol. 3, Tables 21, 22, 23, 24, 36, 39, 45, 51, 52, 53.

[95] Canada, *Census of 1871*, Table 50.

[96] The number of sawmills in the province had declined in the 1860s. There were 609 Water-powered and 80 steam-powered sawmills in 1861. Canada, *Census of 1871*, vol. 4, 336–43.

[97] Canada, *Census of 1871*, vol. 3, Table 46.

[98] Canada, *Census of 1871*, Tables 21, 37.

[99] Canada, *Census of 1871*, Table 35.

[100] Soil maps would seem to indicate that the agricultural potential of the province is limited. However, since the arable area comprises several million acres of land, this source is only useful as an indicator of the upper limits of agricultural growth. In the short run the province possessed a considerable potential as the rapid growth of mid-century reveals.

[101] Acreage of cultivated land increased from 435,861 in 1840 to 1,171,157 in 1870 at a rate much more rapid than that of population growth. Consequently the number of cultivated acres *per capita* rose from 2.7 to 4.6. In the single decade of the 1860s the number of farmers in the province rose by nearly 30%; the population by 13%. Canada, *Census of 1871*, vol. 3, 90–91; vol. 4, 129, 336–43.

[102] New Brunswick, *Journal of the House of Assembly*, 1841, cclxxvi–cclxxvii; 1856, clxiii–clxvi.

[103] Flour and wheat to the value of £169,000 was imported in 1854. This compared with exports of 134,000 tons of timber valued at £165,000. Two years later the respective values of the two com-

modities were £286,000 and £160,000, and in 1855 imported flour and wheat totalled £377,000, a value rivalling that of the province's lumber output (£437,000). See New Brunswick, *Journal of the House of Assembly*, 1853, 1855, 1856, Customs House Returns.

[104] Canada, *Census of 1881*, vol. 3, 42–43, 120–21, 158–59. New Brunswick wheat output rose from 204,911 bushels in 1871 to 521,956 in 1881.

The Prince Edward Island Commission of 1860*

IAN ROSS ROBERTSON

Introduction

The distinguishing characteristic of the history of Prince Edward Island as a colony within British North America was the controversy over lease-hold tenure known as the land question. In 1860 the local government, the imperial government, and a group of proprietors selected a three-man commission to inquire into the problem, which reported in the following year. For the purposes of the historian the testimony before that "land commission," as it became known, constitutes the most important single document for understanding the leasehold system as it had evolved by the middle decades of the 19th century.

433

The roots of the issues associated with leasehold tenure in Prince Edward Island lay in the 18th century. On 23 July 1767 virtually all the land on the Island had been given away to favoured individuals and groups in townships or lots of approximately 20,000 acres, numbered consecutively from one to sixty-seven. The grants had been conditional upon the recipients satisfying a number of requirements. They were to settle each lot with at least one person per 200 acres within ten years; the settlers were to be Protestants from foreign countries or other parts of the British empire (not Britain itself); and the owners, or proprietors, were to pay annual quitrents, or fees for commutation of feudal services (set at 20, 40, or 60 pounds per township, depending upon the general quality of the land), to the crown. In 1769 a group of proprietors were able to persuade London to make the Island, which had been administered as part of Nova Scotia, into a separate colony, with one of their own, Walter Patterson, as governor. The quitrents were to supply the necessary revenue for the first several years of separate status (after that revenues could be generated locally), and thus the creation of the new colony would not cost the British treasury anything. These arrangements never worked as they were intended to, and perhaps they could not have worked. The actual story of the breakdown in the system as envisaged

*From the Introduction to *The Prince Edward Island Commission*, ed. Ian Ross Robertson, ix–xviii. Copyright 1988 by Acadiensis Press. Reprinted by permission.

in 1767 is complex, and much revolves around the impact of the American Revolutionary War in disrupting government, commerce, and settlement in the region. Settlers ceased arriving; some who had come in earlier years left as the lines of supply broke down in wartime; the proprietors, almost all residing in Britain, felt little obligation to pay quitrents on lands they could not develop owing to a war whose causes were unrelated to them; and by 1777 the British treasury was making an annual grant to help defray the expenses of local government. With only a small fraction of the quitrents being paid, local officials, including Patterson, did their best to despoil vulnerable proprietors of their lands on the Island. Apparently the officials hoped that through resale or development of the seized lands they could eventually receive what they believed was due to them in salary arrears and compensation for hardship and inconvenience.

One consequence of the very tangled events of the last third of the 18th century was deep and lasting reciprocal antagonism between the proprietors and the local government. Those proprietors who had made the most serious efforts to fulfill the conditions of their grants (except the limitations on the religion and geographic origin of settlers, which no one appears to have taken seriously) found that the Island and often the officers of the local government simply absorbed their money without yielding an accounting, let alone a return on their investment. The judicial system was under the control of the local elite, and thus it was futile to seek redress through the courts. By the beginning of the 19th century most proprietors were reluctant to spend any money on their Island properties and were far in arrears in quitrents. But although unwilling to invest in their estates, having witnessed the problems of those in the first generation of proprietors who had done so, they had no intention of simply abandoning title to their lands. Some saw their Island estates as a long-term proposition, and hoped that exertions by other proprietors or by common settlers would raise the value of their properties to the extent that they either would be lucrative to operate or could be sold at a profit.

There had been so many changes in ownership by the early 19th century that only a few of the original grantees, such as the Montgomery, Sulivan, and Townshend families, remained. Some proprietors, indeed, seem to have acquired their Island properties as speculative investments, and to have determined to risk as little as possible beyond the purchase price. Many, including some who owned several townships, did not even have local agents representing them in the colony. Hiring an agent would have cost a retainer plus expenses (and possibly a percentage of rents collected) — although, in fairness to the overseas proprietors, one of the most difficult problems for a landlord interested in developing his property was finding a competent, conscientious, and trustworthy resident agent. For many proprietors their experiences with their agents had been little better than their experiences with the Island government. This history of frustration on one side and unaccountability on the other suggested that acquiring a local agent was unlikely to be profitable, and could turn out to be expensive; perhaps, from the perspective of the overseas proprietors, it was more prudent to do nothing at all. Towards the end of the Napoleonic wars, one proprietor, who had inherited his estate as a minor many years earlier when serving in the Royal Navy and had had little time in the interim to think about it, began to make inquiries among long-time owners of Island lands. The responses could not have been encouraging. A Townshend "strongly" advised him to sell if he could get five shillings an acre; and by the Montgomerys he was informed that "Of the integrity of the Inhabitants Mr. [Robert] Montgomery does not speak very favorably, and he will not venture to recommend any one to you in particular."[1] After the first generation that was typical. In 1817 the same proprietor would learn from a Sulivan that the family had heard nothing from the Island for several years — partly because of laches on their part.[2] As historian J.M. Bumsted has written, "the lines of conflict had been plainly drawn between Islanders and proprietors. Islanders were scoundrels, proprietors were parasites."[3]

435

Thus Prince Edward Island and its settlers spent most of the 19th century wrestling with a land system which was unique in British North America and in which those who had been expected to provide leadership were content to be more or less passive. There can be no doubt concerning the grip which leasehold tenure had on the Island, and the minority position in which freeholders found themselves. The census of 1861, which can be seen as a sort of progress report ten years after the attainment of responsible government, revealed that 60 percent of the occupiers of land were tenants or squatters. Still more significantly, leasehold tenure was continuing to expand; since the previous census, in 1855, the number of leaseholders (although not their proportion of all occupiers of land) had risen.[4] Given that virtually all unoccupied land was owned by proprietors, there was little opportunity for the ordinary settler to become a freeholder. He was expected, by the norms of the system, to lease land from a proprietor and pay an annual rent. The usual rent was one shilling per acre per year, and the terms of the lease were almost certain to provide that the tenant was also responsible for paying the equivalent of the quitrents due, plus any land taxes levied; in other words, the terms of the lease, which were not often negotiable, allowed the landlord to pass on to the leaseholder the annual public charges on the land. These were in addition to such initial fees as "lease money" and "plan money," totalling perhaps two pounds or more, which the new tenant would probably be required to pay. The standard farm consisted of 100 acres (although there were many farms of other sizes) and thus, by the usual terms, the tenant would owe five pounds annual rent plus several odd shillings and pence for quitrents and taxes. Often the lease specified that the rent was one shilling *sterling*, as opposed to *currency*, which meant local currency. Sterling, or British money, was scarce on the Island, and hence it was customary for landlords or their agents to accept payment in currency, with a calculation being made for exchange. Here, custom, as it evolved in the 19th century, favoured the tenant over the landlord. For ordinary commercial and government transactions, that is for all transactions other than the payment of rent, it was accepted that there was a 50 percent rate of exchange; the tenant, however, was customarily allowed to pay his rent at a one-ninth rate of exchange. By mid-century it was rare for a landlord to insist upon the full 50 percent, although he retained the legal right to do so. The exercise of this right appears to have been capricious, and could usually be accounted for by the tyrannical disposition of an uncommonly harsh landlord or by a specific conflict with a particular tenant. In normal circumstances, for the tenant who was owing five pounds rent, if his lease stipulated "British sterling," it meant that he would be expected to pay five pounds, eleven shillings, and one and one-half pence "currency."

Regardless of the favourable rate of exchange allowed on "sterling" rents, many settlers resented paying any rent whatever. In the first place, most had paid their own passage to the Island, or at least had received little or no assistance from the landlord. Secondly, in most cases the settler had been faced with a dense forest which he had had to clear — again, with no assistance from the landlord. It would be years before he could clear enough land to generate sufficient income to pay his rent, years in which his main concern would be survival and provision of enough food for himself and his family. Some leases took account of this to a certain extent, allowing minimal or no rent to be paid for several years, with the amount slowly escalating until the full annual rent was due. Even so, it was difficult for a settler to avoid falling into arrears and remaining in arrears. It is reasonable to infer from available evidence generated over many years that virtually all tenants were in arrears at one time or other; that at any specific time a large number were in arrears, some being *several years* behind; and that some never escaped being in arrears. This situation tended to create a sense of insecurity in the tenant, since at any time he could be sued for back rent. If he could not pay the sum and the legal costs of the suit (the latter sometimes exceeding the former), he was ultimately liable to eviction. If evicted, there was no legal provision for compensation for his improvements, in effect for the results of years of labour. Although there was no systematic collection of statistics on eviction over the years, it must be emphasized that eviction and loss of all improvements were not mere theoretical possibilities. A researcher hired by the land commissioners of 1860 reported being told by "several persons" that "at least one half of the new settlers lose their farms, or hold them only until the landlord can get a tenant who will pay a part of the back rent."[5]

436

Yet it was quite possible that a farmer could avoid the troublesome issue of back rent for years since, as already noted, for a long period many landlords did not bother to retain local agents on the Island. Farmers settled on lands and remained there for several years without hearing from landlords or their agents. But as the population grew rapidly in the second quarter of the 19th century it became more important for proprietors to have at least some representation in the colony. In the eight years between the censuses of 1833 and 1841 the number of inhabitants increased from 32,292 to 47,034, or by 45.7 percent;[6] by the mid 1830s virtually all townships had significant numbers of settlers. If a settler could prove 20 years undisturbed possession of land it became his in freehold through the simple process of "squatting." Hence by the late 1830s demands for rent, which by their nature entailed acknowledgement of the proprietor's title, were being made with increasing frequency. In some cases agents or purported agents showed up, demanded rent, and once paid, were not seen again. There were reported cases of second agents or purported agents of the same landlord, or agents of a second landlord with a claim conflicting with that of the first, appearing, and making the same demand for rent, with results which were unpredictable. Often certain agents did not have proper written leases to offer the settlers, which left the tenant who paid with only a receipt and a verbal agreement for security of tenure. Significantly, those holding farms by verbal agreements were sometimes alluded to as "tenants at will." Given the general clamour over the issue of leasehold tenure, it has been easy to overlook the fact that a standard written lease, properly executed, provided the tenant who observed its terms with absolute security of tenure for its duration, which was usually set at 999 years, often referred to as "perpetual tenure." A grievance which occupiers of land voiced frequently in the 1830s and 1840s was the unavailability of leases from those who demanded rent. This complaint, of course, should not be construed to imply, in a back-handed way, endorsement of leasehold tenure in principle, or a preference for leasehold over freehold. It was rather a pragmatic response to the concrete situation in which many an Island farmer found himself: if expected to pay rent and threatened with dire consequences for failure to do so, the settler believed he should receive in return at least the protection which a written lease offered.

In addition to the specific grievances of individual tenants, such as lack of proper leases, by the 1830s there was a sense in which the farmers of the Island were questioning the legitimacy of the entire system. It is possible that they had always had their mental reservations, but in many instances they could live for years on "their" land without being challenged by landlord or agent; in effect, they were squatters, for they had neither freehold title nor written lease nor verbal agreement. When the demand for rent was eventually made, the settler often came to won-

437

der about the justice of his situation. After all, he was living in North America, the "New World," where the norm was freehold tenure, not leasehold. This assumption, that there was something about residence in the New World which made the payment of rent on agricultural land unnatural, would prove over the years to have enormous and increasing strength among Island farmers, and there can be no doubt that it was closely wedded to the sense that it was *they* who had made the land arable. Whereas in the Old World the tenant was presented with a farm ready for cultivation, in Prince Edward Island he was presented with the forest and invited to create a farm in the midst of it. Hence there was a rational basis for the insistence by so many Island farmers over several decades that the rules of the Old World should not apply.[7] In the 1830s the rejection of leasehold tenure took the form of the "escheat" movement. Escheat was a term derived from the feudal inheritance of the Old World. If a landlord who held his land from the crown on con-

438 dition of performing certain duties failed to meet his obligations, his land was liable to be *escheated*, or returned to the crown. The argument of the Escheat party which arose in Prince Edward Island in the 1830s was that the grantees of 1767 and their successors had not fulfilled the conditions of their grants, and that therefore their lands should be escheated; in effect, the advocates of Escheat sought to turn the logic of feudalism against the neo-feudal system which had been imposed on the Island in 1767. Once the crown had resumed title, the next prescribed step would be to regrant the land in freehold to the actual occupiers. It was a heady doctrine and, fuelled by the fears and experiences of Island farmers, it enjoyed widespread popularity in the 1830s. Indeed in 1838 the Escheat movement, the first organized agrarian protest movement in what is now Canada, won an astonishing eighteen to six victory in a general election for the Island's house of assembly.

The Escheat movement faded in popularity after it became clear that the British government would not consent to dispossess the proprietors of their lands. The refusal of the British to cooperate with the Prince Edward Island Escheators is not difficult to understand. In the first place, the proprietors included men with influence — such as Samuel Cunard, owner of one-sixth of all the land on the Island by the end of the 1830s. Cunard, a Nova Scotian who spent most of his time in London after the early 1840s, had founded Cunard steamship lines and, according to the author of the article on him in the *Dictionary of Canadian Biography*, was treated by the Colonial Office as an authority on the affairs of the Maritime colonies.[8] George F. Seymour, a proprietor on a much smaller scale but intensely interested in his Island estate, was sergeant at arms to the House of Lords from 1818 to 1841, King William IV's master of robes, and in the 1840s an admiralty lord; on the basis of a reading of his diaries and correspondence it is fair to say that he knew almost everyone who was anyone in the British political, court, and military establishments for more than a generation. Men like Cunard and Seymour enjoyed easy access to the corridors of power and were assured at the very least a courteous and respectful hearing. Seymour's papers record that a secretary of state for the colonies would even submit to be lectured by proprietors on the proper discharge of his duties.9 In contrast, William Cooper, the Escheat leader from Prince Edward Island who went to London in 1839 as speaker of the colonial assembly, representing the majority resulting from the recent general election, was denied an audience with the colonial secretary. Cooper had come, in effect, to negotiate a deal between the local assembly and the British government. But this was not to be. Although undoubtedly representing the will of the Island electorate, he was treated as a political leper.

Quite aside from the issue of "proprietary influence," which caused much dismay and outcry among Island tenants and politicians for decades, there was in the minds of British public men the broader question of the rights of property. All British governments of the era, Whig or Tory, included a substantial proportion of members who were in their private capacities (and often on weekends) agrarian landlords with large numbers of tenants paying rent to them in a system of feudal origin. Any move to dispossess Island landlords *en masse* for what seemed by the 1830s like ancient grievances could raise awkward questions closer to home. The British government was committed in principle to maintenance of the rights of property, and could turn away a William Cooper with an easy conscience. Unlike the typical Island pioneer clearing the land and creating a farm, the typical British cabinet minister saw nothing unnatural in the Island situation; indeed one could go further and state that he knew virtually nothing at all of the Island situation except what Cunard, Seymour, and other proprietors with access, plus the official correspondence with the lieutenant governor, told him. His own sense of what was right and wrong could supply the rest. To expect him to welcome Cooper and his doctrines would be akin, to use a modern metaphor, to expecting an astute chicken to welcome Colonel Sanders and his strange, not to say repugnant, notions.

The failure of Cooper's mission in 1839 complicated Island politics. The credibility of the Escheat leader, a former land agent and moreover a tenant who continued to pay his rent, thus avoiding legal problems, while counselling other tenants to withhold theirs, plummeted.[10] The Escheat movement declined in strength, and was gradually supplanted by the more moderate Reform party which took shape in the mid and late 1840s. The Reformers, particularly the brilliant young Irish-born journalist Edward Whelan, argued that responsible government was a necessary first step to land reform on the Island. With responsible government, the assembly could control the local executive, which in turn could pass progressive legislation which the British government would eventually accept. After winning responsible government in 1851 the Re-

439

formers, or Liberals, led by George Coles, were able to put their theory to the test.

The Reformers' land programme of the 1850s had two basic objectives: to soften the workings of the leasehold system through expansion of tenant rights, and to commence the gradual abolition of leasehold tenure through purchase of proprietary estates by the local government and resale of the farms to the actual occupiers. The proprietors would be given added incentive to sell through increased taxation. The programme had limited success. A bill to entrench legally the right of certain tenants to pay their sterling rents at an exchange rate of one-ninth was first refused by London, and later assented to in amended form. A narrowly circumscribed tenant compensation bill was refused royal assent. A bill imposing a tax of five percent on the nominal rentals of landlords,[11] known as the rent roll bill, was also refused royal assent. The centrepiece of the Reform strategy was the Land Purchase Act of 1853. Its terms were predicated on the assumption that the doctrine of Escheat had had two fatal flaws: it had offered no compensation to landlords and had been compulsory. Hence the Land Purchase Act provided for compensation, and was entirely voluntary in its operation. It authorized the Island government to negotiate purchases *en bloc* with consenting proprietors. There was to be no coercion. The British government allowed the statute, but by the end of the 1850s only one major estate had been purchased and resold to its occupiers. This was the property owned by Charles Worrell, who had left the colony in the 1840s after several decades of residence. Unfortunately for the Reform government, the Island treasury, and the proprietor, Worrell's local representatives were able to twist the sale in such a way as to make the purchase price more than 70 percent greater than the amount Worrell received, skimming off some £10,000 in a manner that amounted to breach of trust. The government paid the exorbitant price, probably because they believed they had little choice. In fact, they faced a cruel dilemma. To abandon the sale because of the impending swindle would undermine the credibility of their land reform programme, for no other large estates were on the market; and proceeding with the sale would compromise the same programme by identifying the Land Purchase Act with a scandal. In the end they were probably swayed by the belief that the piecemeal abolition of leasehold tenure had to be commenced, regardless of the embarrassment of having been victimized by the "Worrell Job."[12]

The Liberal government was defeated at the polls in 1859, largely because of a dispute over the role of religion in the district schools of the Island. Once in power, the Conservatives dealt with the "Bible question" essentially by giving a statutory basis to the status quo. But it would not be so simple to dispose of the land question, which had been a secondary issue in the campaign. The Conservative government, led by Edward Palmer, himself a landlord and land agent, had an unresolved and potentially explosive issue on its hands. Throughout the 1850s Palmer had argued that the Liberal land reform programme was ineffective, without explaining precisely what his party proposed to do. The years in opposition had provided him with opportunities for embarrassing the Liberals, and on one occasion when objecting to the Land Purchase Act he had even found himself allied with Cooper and other diehard Escheators, who had been absorbed into the Liberal caucus (but who were upset by the statute's implicit recognition of proprietary titles as legitimate). Once in office Palmer did not have the luxury of flirting with Escheators to score opportunistic political points; something more concrete was required. In effect, he was now on the spot, and it is clear that he did not have a comprehensive programme of land reform. Given his own conservatism and the make-up of his government, which included several landlords and land agents, it would have been unrealistic to expect drastic reforms from him. Thus, with little apparent sense of direction on the issue and perhaps with the idea of buying time, Palmer established the land commission of 1860.[13]

441

NOTES

[1] Lord James Townshend to George Francis Seymour, 1 December 1814; Julius Hutchinson to Seymour, 22 October 1814, both in Seymour of Ragley Papers, CR 114A/563/1, Correspondence, Warwick County Record Office (WCRO), Warwick, England.

[2] See Hutchinson to Seymour, 22 May 1817, Seymour of Ragley Papers, CR 114A/537/8, Correspondence, WCRO.

[3] J.M. Bumsted, *Land, Settlement, and Politics on Eighteenth-Century Prince Edward Island* (Kingston and Montreal, 1987), 195. Bumsted's book has provided a masterful scholarly account of the era from the mid 1760s to the detailed census of 1798.

[4] Calculations based on Censuses of 1855 and 1861, in Prince Edward Island, House of Assembly, *Journal*, 1856, Appendix D, and 1862, Appendix A. The "Number holding by lease or written agreement" and the "Total number of occupiers of land" are both incorrect in the column for 1855 in Andrew Hill Clark, *Three Centuries and the Island: A Historical Geography of Settlement and Agriculture in Prince Edward Island, Canada* (Toronto, 1959), 95, Table 3. The errors resulted from Clark's reliance on the census of 1861 for 1855 material, which had been copied by the census compiler of 1861 without taking into account a change in classification.

[5] P.E.I. House of Assembly, *Journal*, 1863, Appendix A. Several currencies are mentioned in the text. British sterling was, of course, the dominant medium of international exchange in this era. The dominant medium within Prince Edward Island was local or Prince Edward Island money, often identified simply as "currency"; but British money, Halifax or Nova Scotia currency, and apparently even Newfoundland money were also used. What were the relationships among these currencies? There is no perfectly neat explanation. For all purposes *except* the payment of rent on agricultural land it was accepted that there was a 50 percent rate of exchange between British sterling and local currency. Therefore, a pound sterling would fetch one pound and ten shillings "currency." It would also fetch five dollars; a pound in Halifax money or Newfoundland money would fetch four.

[6] Calculation based on the Censuses of 1833 and 1841, in P.E.I. House of Assembly, *Journal*, 1834, Appendix C, and 1842, Appendix N.

[7] Poet Milton Acorn captured well the spirit of defiance which this situation tended to breed in the tenant with stanzas 3 and 4 of the poem "The Figure in the Landscape Made the Landscape"; see Acorn, *The Island Means Minago: Poems from Prince Edward Island* (Toronto, 1975), 47. This poem was reprinted in Milton Acorn, *Dig Up My Heart: Selected Poems, 1952-83* (Toronto, 1983), 152.

[8] See Phyllis R. Blakeley, "Sir Samuel Cunard," *Dictionary of Canadian Biography* 9 (Toronto, 1976), 183.

[9] See particularly "Memo Mr. [E.G.] Stanley May 13[,] 1834," Seymour of Ragley Papers, CR 114A/565, Miscellaneous Lot 13 Papers, WCRO.

[10] On Cooper see Harry Baglole, "William Cooper," *Dictionary of Canadian Biography* 9: 155-58.

[11] The *actual* rental could be much less than the nominal rental derived from the landlord's rent roll, and therefore under the proposed legislation a landlord could be taxed on money he did not receive.

But by the same token the actual rental could also be greater if the landlord was able to collect arrears. An example of a landlord whose actual rental exceeded his nominal rental over the years 1863–1868 is cited in Ian Ross Robertson, "Political Realignment in Pre-Confederation Prince Edward Island, 1863–1870," *Acadiensis*, 15, 1 (Autumn 1985): 42, n. 28.

[12] On the leading Reformers, their land reform programme, and the Worrell swindle, see Ian Ross Robertson, "George Coles," *Dictionary of Canadian Biography*, 10 (Toronto, 1972), 182–88; "Edward Whelan," *Dictionary* 9: 828–35; "William Henry Pope," *Dictionary* 10: 593–94; M. Brook Taylor, "Charles Worrel," *Dictionary* 8 (Toronto, 1985), 954.

[13] On Palmer see Ian Ross Robertson, "Edward Palmer," *Dictionary of Canadian Biography* 11 (Toronto, 1982), 664–70.

The Northwest

By the mid-nineteenth century, a new and distinct society was evolving at the junction of the Red and Assiniboine rivers. The Red River colony had a population of over 5000 mixed-bloods and several hundred white settlers. Of the mixed-blood population, roughly half were English-speaking Métis, or "Country-Born," the descendants of the British fur traders and their native wives. The other half were French-speaking Métis, the descendants of the early French fur traders and their Indian wives. Until 1870 the Red River was the largest agricultural centre between Canada West (Ontario) and the Pacific coast.

In "Indian Views of the White Man prior to 1850: An Interpretation," John Ewers discusses the early history of the Europeans and Indians on the Northern Great Plains. D.N. Sprague provides an overview of the Red River colony in the mid-nineteenth century in his introduction to *The Genealogy of the First Métis Nation: The Development and Dispersal of the Red River Settlement, 1820–1900* compiled by D.N. Sprague and R.P. Frye.

Gerald Friesen's early chapters in *The Canadian Prairies: A History* (Toronto: University of Toronto Press, 1984) offer a good overview. Jim Miller reviews the secondary literature on the Red River colony in "From Riel to the Métis," *Canadian Historical Review*, 69 (1988): 1–20. This study complements Frits Pannekoek's "The Historiography of the Red River Settlement, 1830–1868," *Prairie Forum*, 6 (1981): 75–85. Other references are listed in the bibliographical section of Topic Two, "The Impact of the Fur Trade."

On the controversial question of the relationship between the Protestant English-speaking and Roman Catholic French-speaking mixed-bloods, see Frits Pannekoek's "The Anglican Church and the Disintegration of Red River Society, 1818–1870," in *The West and the Nation: Essays in Honour of W.L. Morton*, ed. Carl Berger and Ramsay Cook (Toronto: McClelland and Stewart, 1976), 72–90; and Irene M. Spry's "The Métis and Mixed-Bloods of Rupert's Land before 1870," in *The New Peoples: Being and Becoming Métis in North America*, ed. Jacqueline Peterson and Jennifer S.H. Brown (Winnipeg: The University of Manitoba Press, 1985), 95–118.

Hugh A. Dempsey's two biographies, *Crowfoot* (Edmonton: Hurtig, 1972) and *Big Bear* (Vancouver: Douglas and McIntyre, 1984), introduce the Plains Indians in the mid-nineteenth century. A recent study of Big

Bear's tribe is John S. Milloy's *The Plains Cree: Trade, Diplomacy and War, 1790 to 1870* (Winnipeg: The University of Manitoba Press, 1989).

A comparative description of two nineteenth-century families, one from the Red River colony and one from Prince Edward Island, is provided by J.M. Bumsted and Wendy Owen in "The Victorian Family in Canada in Historical Perspective: The Ross Family of Red River and the Jarvis Family of Prince Edward Island," *Manitoba History* 13 (1987): 12–18.

Indian Views of the White Man Prior to 1850: An Interpretation*

JOHN C. EWERS

444

I am calling this paper "an interpretation," because I recognize the difficulties of trying to walk in the moccasins and to think the thoughts of people who lived more than one and one-quarter centuries ago. I have been studying the Indians of the Northern Plains for more than 40 years, but I have never talked to an Indian who was old enough to recall what *he* was thinking and other members of his tribe were saying before 1850. How then am I to know what Assiniboine, Cree, and Dakota Indians who met Frenchmen before 1700, Mandans who saw French traders in their villages in 1738, or even Crows who observed the first white explorers in their country in 1805, thought of those palefaces?

Paradoxical as it may seem, any interpretation of Indian views of Whites prior to 1850 *must* rely heavily upon the writings of some of the people who were the *objects* of the Indians' appraisals — white men. I believe, however, that a number of white writers reported objectively and with candor the views expressed by the Indians they met, and that some of those views are confirmed by evidence from Indian languages, and by the Indians' own literature — picture writing. I believe also that Indian attitudes were reflected in their actions and that we do have a rich record of Indian behavior toward Whites on the Northern Great Plains before 1850.

It will simplify my problem some if I may confine my remarks to those tribes whose histories and cultures I have studied most intensively. These are the tribes who, in 1850, lived in the region my teacher, Clark Wissler, used to refer to as the Missouri–Saskatchewan area, which includes the valleys of the Saskatchewan River and its tributaries in present Canada and the valleys of the Upper Missouri and its tributaries in the United States. Many of the best-known tribes of the American West

*From *Red Men and Hat-Wearers: Viewpoints in Indian History*, ed. Daniel Tyler. Copyright 1976. Reprinted by permission of the author and editor.

lived in that region. They included the Arikara, Hidatsa, and Mandan, who were sedentary farmers; and the nomadic, buffalo-hunting Plains Cree, Plains Ojibwa, Assiniboine, the three Blackfoot tribes, Gros Ventres (Atsina), Crow, and Teton Dakota (or Western Sioux).

Throughout the historic period prior to 1850, the tribes of this region prided themselves upon their independence, their skill as hunters, their astuteness as traders, and their prowess as warriors. Archeological evidence of strongly fortified prehistoric villages on the Missouri in the Dakotas indicates that intertribal warfare existed in this region centuries before the arrival of Whites. It continued for more than three decades after 1850. For thousands of years, Indians hunted buffalo in this region, and this animal was still the staff of life for the nomadic tribes of this area in 1850. None of those tribes had ceded their hunting grounds to the Whites in 1850. It was not until 1851 that the boundaries of many of those tribes were first defined by treaty, and the Blackfoot tribes did not negotiate their first treaty with the United States until 1855.

445

Present-day Indians, convinced of the need for pan-Indian organizations to protect Indian rights and to seek solutions to pressing Indian problems, may find it hard to conceive of a time when "Indianness" was not of prime importance to Indians. There was no basis, however, for such an ethnocentric concept *before* the Whites arrived. Then all the Indians' friends and enemies were other Indians. Rather, Indians were then "tribo-centric," if I may coin a term. They tended to remain so throughout the period of White contact well beyond 1850. The Indian owed his allegiance not to his race but to his family, his band or village, and his tribe. A warrior was proud to be a Crow, a Mandan, a Cree, or a Dakota. Each tribe spoke its own dialect, and regarded its members as "the people." Members of others tribes were outsiders. Whether they were friends or enemies depended upon the extent to which their tribal interests were in harmony or conflict with one's own. Tribes in continual competition for hunting grounds became hereditary enemies — as Cree versus Dakota, or Blackfoot versus Crow. Some tribes became allies of neighboring tribes for their mutual protection against strong, common enemies — such as Cree and Assiniboine, Blackfoot and Gros Ventres, Mandan and Hidatsa. Trading with the enemy was not unknown, however. The Mandan and Dakota negotiated temporary truces in order to exchange garden produce for products of the chase to their mutual advantage.

Inasmuch as the very great majority of Whites known to Indians of this region prior to 1850 were traders, it is well to know that these Indians were experienced traders when they first met white men. Finds of marine shells from both the Pacific and Gulf coasts in prehistoric village sites on the Missouri indicate that extended trade routes led to and from these villages of farming tribes in pre-White times. Pre-eighteenth-century village sites also have yielded trade materials from less distant sources: obsidian, probably from present Yellowstone National Park in western Wyoming, and red pipestone from the famed catlinite quarry in southwestern Minnesota.[1]

Through intertribal trade northward from the Southwest, the European horse reached the Crow and Blackfoot tribes in the western part of this area *before* those Indians met white men. By the time the first Whites arrived in their country, members of those tribes were riding horses on the buffalo chase and to war and were using horses as burden-bearers in their camp movements. Horses had also become prized booty in warfare.

Through intertribal trade, also, limited quantities of European-made manufactured goods reached the tribes in the central and western portions of this area before they met Whites. These items were brought by Indian intermediaries who traded directly with Whites at distant trading posts. When Pierre La Verendrye accompanied an Assiniboine trading party to the Mandan villages in 1738, he observed that the Mandans were "sharp traders and clean the Assiniboine out of everything they have in the way of guns, powder, ball, knives, axes, and awls."[2]

The villages of the farming tribes were flourishing trading centers before the Whites arrived. By the time the Whites appeared, these and neighboring nomadic tribes had obtained enough articles of European manufacture to be sure of theirusefulness as weapons, tools, or utensils, or their attractiveness as luxuries, and to whet their desire for more of these goods. The Indians were experienced barterers, knew something of values and markups, and were prepared to pay for what they wanted. These Indians had become literally "horse traders" — with all of the keen bargaining sense that term implies.[3]

Another very important aspect of Indian culture in this region at the time of first contact with Whites conditioned Indian reactions to Whites during the early years of interracial relations. I refer to the Indians' world view — their belief in supernatural powers, or medicine in the religious sense. They envisioned the world around them — the sky, the land, and water — as the abode of powers which were stronger than their own, and which could help or harm them. They sought to placate malevolent powers, such as thunder and serpent-like underwater monsters; they sought the aid of benevolent ones, such as sun, birds, and animals. Any object that was unique or strange to them was looked upon as medicine that inspired both awe and reverence. The individual who owned such an object, professed to know its origin and function, and used it to his own advantage was thought to be blessed with supernatural power.

Given this prevailing Indian world view, or body of beliefs, it should not seem strange to us that the Indians of this region looked upon the white men's many technological inventions as awesome medicines, that they sought to obtain strange objects from the white man's culture for their own medicines, or that they regarded white men who appeared to be skillful users of these objects as possessors of very potent supernatural powers.

The literature of Indian–White contacts in this region is rich in white men's observations on these points. Among the many wonders of the white men's world which Indians once looked upon as medicine were the gun, iron pot, compass, telescope, burning glass, magnet, thermometer, sextant, music box, watch, steamboat, white artists' portraits of Indians, and any specimen of handwriting. Whites sometimes took advantage of the Indians' ignorance of some of these wonders which remained incomprehensible to them, even after many years of contact. At the end of our period, Edwin T. Denig, the factor at Fort Union, wrote that Indians in that neighborhood could "be made to believe almost any story, however absurd, if read in appearance from a book."[4]

Ingenious Indians were eager to adopt strange objects from the white man's world as personal war medicines. Francois Larocque, the first white man known to have visited the Crow Country, observed in 1805 that one Crow warrior had as his medicine a fragment of colored glass from a magic lantern; another wore the tail of a Spanish cow as a hair pendant.[5] Surely neither of these war medicines was more remarkable than was that of a Dakota chief to whom Father De Smet later gave a religious medal. That chief opened a box, unwrapped a buckskin covering, and unrolled a colored picture of General Diebitsch, a prominent Russian leader in the Napoleonic Wars, in full uniform and astride a beautiful horse. He explained to De Smet that for years this had been his war medicine. He offered his pipe to that general "before all his enterprises against his enemies, and attributed to him the many victories he had gained."[6]

447

Father Hennepin (in 1680) and the French trader Pierre-Charles Le Sueur (in 1700) knew the Dakota in Minnesota. Both claimed the Dakota called them "spirits."[7] James Kipp, regarded as the traders' best authority on the Mandan dialect of Siouan in 1833, translated their term for white man — wasschi — as "he who has everything, or everything good."[8]

Jean Baptiste Truteau, pioneer white trader among the Arikara, wrote of them in 1796: "They have a great respect and a great veneration for all white men in general, whom they put in the rank of divinity, and all that comes from them is regarded by these same people as miraculous. They do not know how to distinguish among civilized nations, English, French, Spanish, et cetera, whom they call indifferently white men or spirits."[9]

The persistence of the term Napikwan (old man person) for the white man among the Blackfoot shows that they likened him to an ambivalent wonder worker in their own mythology. Napi was also a clever trickster with very human frailties. Likewise the Algonquian-speaking Gros Ventres, Arapaho, and Cheyenne named the white man after their trickster, Spider or "the wise one."

So much has been written in recent years about the Indians' contributions to world medicine that we may tend to forget that in this region during the early decades of White contact Indians regarded the white man's remedies for physical ailments as superior to their own. Lewis and Clark were repeatedly beseeched by Indians to treat their sick. Alexander Henry, a trader among the Blackfoot, wrote in 1811: " . . . they are perpetually begging medicine from us, and place the greatest confidence in whatever we give them, imagining that everything medical which comes from the trader must be a sovereign remedy for all diseases."[10] In that same year, John Bradbury, an English botanist, made friends with an Arikara shaman while he was collecting plants near the villages of that tribe. The Indian looked upon Bradbury as a fellow practitioner and proudly revealed the contents of his deerskin medicine bag to him.[11]

Father Nicholas Point, the first Christian missionary among the Blackfoot on the Missouri in 1845–1846, found that these Indians looked upon him much as they did their own medicine men. They thought he could cause disease or make the thunder roll if he became angry. They believed he possessed the power to cure sickness and implored him to treat them. They thought that baptism, like the traditional Indian sweat-bath, would insure bodily health.[12] We know, too, that for several decades, beginning at least as early as the early 1830s, the Blackfoot, who were fearful of handling their own dead, brought the bodies of prominent chiefs to Fort Benton where the white traders prepared them for burial.[13]

As Indians became better acquainted with Whites, they became more impressed with their human qualities. Indeed, the Arikara appear to have removed Frenchmen from their pantheon of divinities by the year 1804. Pierre-Antoine Tabeau, who was trading with the Arikara when the Lewis and Clark Expeditionreached their villages on their upriver journey that fall, observed: "It is only a little while since the Ricara deified the French, who, unhappily, have only too well disabused them by their conduct and their talk. Thus they have passed today from one extreme to the other and we are indeed nothing in their eyes."[14]

He noted that the only member of the Lewis and Clark party whom the Ankara regarded with great awe was "a large, fine man, black as a bear." He referred to York, Clark's Negro servant, the first black man the Indians of the Upper Missouri tribes had seen.[15] Because Negroes entered their country in the company of Whites, they came to be known as "black white men" to those Indians.

The Mandans, near whom the Lewis and Clark party wintered in 1804–1805, retained a higher regard for the supernatural powers of Whites than did the Arikaras. In their buffalo-calling ceremony, it was the custom for younger married women to have sexual relations with older men of the tribe who were thought to possess very potent supernatural powers, so that the women in turn might transmit these powers to their husbands. They invited men of the Lewis and Clark party to play the roles of some of the older men in this religious ceremony.[16] Other writers on the Mandans around the turn of the century may have maligned their women by alluding to their easy virtue. These women also may have been interested in white men as sources of supernatural power.

As Indians became better acquainted with Whites, they came to believe that some white men had stronger powers than did others. During the winter that the Lewis and Clark party resided near the Mandan and Hidatsa villages, their blacksmiths were kept busy making and repairing metal articles for the Indians in exchange for corn. Indians looked upon the smiths' bellows as medicine. A Hidatsa chief offered his frank opinion of the men of the American expedition to a British trader who was in his village: "There are only two sensible men amongst them, the worker in iron and the mender of guns."[17]

449

White artists were another occupational group whom Indians thought were gifted with exceptional powers. The Indians of this region had both religious and secular art traditions in which human figures were depicted. Successful warriors portrayed their coups in battle. Some Indians made

Glenbow Museum, Calgary.

Indian Greeting White Man. "Real White Man" is still what the Blackfoot Indians of Alberta call the French, probably because the French were the first Europeans to make contact with them. The painting is by Frederic Remington, the famous American illustrator.

crude representations of their personal enemies so that they might destroy them through witchcraft. Indian art could serve good or evil ends.

In their own art, as in their gesture language, they distinguished the White from the Indian by representing the former as a hat-wearer. In their sign language, the white man was designated simply by passing the right hand across the brow, palm down, to convey the idea of a hat brim or visor. This was, of course, a purely descriptive gesture. Whether the white man was friend or enemy depended upon the larger context in which the gesture was used. In the winter counts of the Teton Dakota, white men were pictured as hat-wearers. Several winter counts picture the first white trader to establish a post in Dakota territory on the Missouri, and who supplied these Indians with guns. Known to the Dakotas as The Good White Man, he was probably Regis Loisel, a Frenchman from St. Louis, who built that trading post at the beginning of the 19th century.[18]

450   Indians had traditionally pictured humans with knob-like heads devoid of individual features. When white artists came among them who created life-like portraits in two dimensions, some Indians refused to sit for their portraits, fearing that the reproduction of their likenesses would deprive them of their power. George Catlin wrote of his difficulties in convincing the Mandans that they would not be harmed if he painted their portraits. On the other hand, a Blackfoot warrior, the following summer (1833), bragged that he had survived a battle with the Assiniboine and Cree outside Fort McKenzie without a wound *because* "Mr. Bodmer had taken his portrait." At the Hidatsa villages the next fall, Bodmer painted birds and animals for Indians, which they thought "would make them proof against musket balls." These were probably the birds and animals that were those warriors' guardian spirits.[19]

In the British possessions in 1848, Paul Kane apparently convinced the Cree that by sketching their sacred pipestems he was enhancing their potency as war medicines.[20] Yet Rudolph Kurz encountered violent opposition from the Hidatsa when a cholera epidemic broke out among them as he was beginning to picture those Indians in 1851. They recalled that a disastrous smallpox epidemic had occurred in 1837, after both Catlin and Bodmer had painted members of their tribe, and they threatened to kill Kurz if he continued to draw them. The Swiss artist was forced to move up river to Fort Union; he encountered no such resistance on the part of the Assiniboine, Cree, and Crow Indians who traded there.[21]

Whether Indians looked upon white artists' works as good or bad medicine appears to have depended upon the circumstances under which they were made. In any case, a common interest in art seems to have afforded a basis for close rapport between some Indian and white artists, and the more detailed and more realistic renderings of humans and horses that began to appear in the works of Indian artists *after* they had opportunities to observe closely how the white artists worked, and after they gained access to smooth paper and precise drawing instruments (pencils and crayons), must have been in part due to white influence.[22]

It appears clear to me from an examination of the written record that white traders' penetration deeper and deeper into this region, in order to profit from direct trade with more and more tribes, threatened the interests of many tribes and roused both ill feelings and open hostilities toward the Whites. Different tribes were affected in different ways and at different times as this movement progressed. This movement first threatened and then eliminated the profitable activities of the peripheral tribes in supplying manufactured goods to the more remote ones. It also upset the delicate balance of powers that had existed in the intertribal warfare of this region. Furthermore, the actions of these tribes indicate that they were fully aware of these threats to their interests.

In this region, the fur trade initially expanded from east to west. Those tribes on the eastern periphery of the region were the first to receive guns and other metal weapons. They were strengthened at the expense of their more remote Indian enemies who lacked those weapons. Surely the Assiniboine saw the advantage of gaining access to the flow of firearms from Hudson Bay when, even before 1700, they abandoned their Dakota allies and allied themselves with their former Cree enemies. By the early years of the 18th century, the Cree and Assiniboine also were receiving improved war materials from French traders operating from Montreal. As early as 1736, a Dakota war party wiped out a party of Frenchmen and mutilated their bodies. One of those Frenchmen was a son of La Verendrye. Two years earlier he had joined a Cree campaign against the Dakota. The message of that Dakota action was clear — Whites must not take sides in Indian warfare.[23]

There were early indications that the peripheral tribes were aware of the potential loss of profits to them if Whites extended their trade to the more remote tribes. In 1797, the Assiniboine traders tried to dissuade David Thompson from visiting the important Mandan trading center by telling him of the danger of meeting Dakota war parties en route. In 1805, Mandan and Hidatsa traders, in turn, sought to prevent Larocque from going on to the Crow Country by representing the Crows as thieves and liars and stressing the dangers of encountering hostile tribes. We know that the extension of the white man's trade did eliminate Assiniboine intermediaries from the trade with both the Mandans and the Blackfoot tribes, and the importance of the old Mandan trading center declined rapidly after Whites opened direct trade with the still more remote tribes who had traded there.

Those tribes who had established direct trade with Whites resented white traders' efforts to penetrate deeper into the Indian country to supply their enemies with war-making materials. Doubtless those Teton Dakota who sought to prevent the passage of Lewis and Clark's boats up the Missouri in 1804 looked upon those Whites as traders who would supply their Mandan and Hidatsa enemies. The Blackfoot tribes tried to prevent British traders from carrying arms and ammunition to enemy tribes west of the Rockies, although the traders circumvented the Blackfoot blockade by crossing the mountains farther north and outside Blackfoot territory.[24]

I have quoted Tabeau's observation that the Arikara were disenchanted with the Whites as early as 1804. By that time, his firm was already doing business with their enemies, the Teton, farther up the Missouri. Another factor helped to rouse the Arikara to open hostility. An Arikara chief died during a trip to Washington in 1805, and the Arikara thought the Whites had killed him.

Arikara hostility toward Whites continued until the smallpox epidemic of 1837 greatly reduced the population of that tribe. When Lieutenant Pryor tried to return the Mandan chief, Shahaka, who had been to Washington, to his people in 1807, the angry Arikara opened fire on his party and forced them to turn back to St. Louis. In 1823, Ashley's large party of trappers who were bound up river were stopped by the Arikara at their villages; in the ensuing battle, thirteen or fourteen of those Whites were killed or mortally wounded. This action precipitated the only U.S. Army campaign against a tribe of this region prior to 1850. Col. Henry Leavenworth's soldiers, augmented by mountain men and a large contingent of Dakota Indian allies, moved against the Arikara villages. The Dakota warriors were eager to attack, but Leavenworth delayed, and the Arikara slipped away in the middle of the night. A lasting result of this inaction was the contempt for the courage of white soldiers that persisted in the minds of aggressive Dakota warriors. Arikara–Dakota warfare continued for three generations. By the 1860s, Arikara chiefs were pleading for white soldiers to help defend their people against repeated Dakota attacks.[25]

The Blackfoot tribes and their Gros Ventres allies, who hunted on both sides of the international boundary, had traded with the British in the Saskatchewan Valley for a half-century before American mountain men roused their hostility — and with good reason. The Americans were supplying war materials to their Crow, Shoshoni, and Flathead enemies. The Blackfoot also profited by robbing the mountain men and taking their beaver pelts and other booty to friendly Whites in the north to exchange for arms, ammunition, and other desirable goods. During the quarter-century prior to 1831, numerous skirmishes took place between the Blackfoot (and/or Gros Ventres) and the trappers near the Missouri headwaters and in the mountains. Twice during that period (in 1811 and 1823) the Indians chased the trappers out of present-day Montana, leaving numbers of dead Whites in the field. Not until 1831 were Americans able to open peaceful trade with the Blackfoot tribes. By then it was clear that a major cause of Blackfoot resentment had been the trappers' exploitation of the rich fur resources of their hunting grounds from which the Indians derived no share of the profits. As a Blackfoot chief confided to Indian Agent Sanford in 1834, "If you will send Traders into our Country we will protect them and treat them well; but for Trappers — Never."[26]

Much has been written about the profits Whites made from the fur trade. It would be difficult to believe that Indians did not profit from that trade, also, before 1850. They offered furs, buffalo hides, and pemmican from animals which were abundant in exchange for manufactured goods which they wanted. Standards of value were established by agreement between Indians and Whites. The records of the trading companies contain many references to Indian refusals to accept articles they did not want, or ones of inferior quality. Firearms experts rate the popular Northwest trade gun as an efficient as well as a cheap weapon. The Crows and the Mandans (in the early 1830s) refused to accept liquor in their trade. Competition among white traders gave Indians a choice of markets, and it checked inflation of prices on manufactured goods. Indians employed metal tools and ornaments, cloth, twine, thread, beads, and other materials as replacements for aboriginal materials in ways that saved them labor and enriched their lives. At the same time, they became more and more dependent upon Whites for both luxuries and necessities other than food.[27]

453

The conduct of the trade brought some Indians into much closer relationships with Whites than it did others. In the beginning, white traders visited Indian villages where they were protected and their actions regulated by members of the tribal Soldier Societies. After white traders built posts surrounded with palisades to protect them from attacks by hostile Indians, prominent Indian warriors continued to play important roles in regulating trade. I refer especially to the "Soldiers of the Fort," Indians who were recognized as tribal leaders, but who also served the interests of the Whites. Not only did they encourage members of their tribes to trade at particular posts, but they kept their white employers informed of tribal wants and activities, and they served as policemen who kept order and prevented thefts of white men's property while other Indians were at the forts.

Two of the best-known Indians of this region in the 1830s were "Soldiers of the Fort" for the American Fur Company. One was Four Bears, second chief of the Mandans, who claimed the best war record of any man in his tribe, and who served as a director of his people's major annual religious ceremony, the Okipa. Another was The Light; he was the son of the prominent Assiniboine chief who selected the site for Fort Union, the principal trading post on the Upper Missouri for several decades after 1827. Both of these men were tragic figures. Four Bears died in the smallpox epidemic of 1837 that decimated his tribe. Shortly before his death, he cursed the Whites as black-hearted dogs for repaying his long and faithful friendship with this fatal pestilence. The Light was the first member of his tribe to visit Washington and the cities of the East, in 1831–1832. After his return, he was killed by a man of his own tribe who refused to believe his oft-repeated stories of the wonders of the white man's world.[28]

Many Indian women had even more intimate relations with Whites that were longer lasting and ended more happily. I refer to the hundreds of Indian women of all of the tribes of this area who married white men. There is no complete record of the total number of these interracial marriages before 1850. Some of the brides were members of chiefly families whose marriages to prominent traders enhanced the positions of their relatives. Most of these Indian women married Whites who held less important positions in the fur trade, clerks or laborers. White men were considered good catches because it was thought that their wives would not have to work so hard and that they would be better fed and dressed than were the wives of Indians.

Some of these interracial marriages did not last; others proved to be partnerships for life. In either case, we know that they were productive; there was a growing number of individuals of mixed Indian and White descent in the population of this region. Sons of Indian women and white traders themselves became employees in the fur trade as factors, clerks, guides, interpreters, hunters, and laborers. Well before 1850, large communities of Métis or Red River half-breeds were formed in the eastern portion of this region. They developed a way of life that was marginal to both Indian and white cultural traditions. They lived in log cabins, grew some crops, and took part in prolonged, semiannual buffalo hunting excursions, during which they killed large numbers of buffalo and carried tons of meat and hides homeward in their creaking, two-wheeled carts. Still other sons and daughters of mixed marriages became leaders in their mothers' tribes in later generations.[29]

It seems clear to me from my examination of the written record that Indian attitudes toward Whites changed over the years prior to 1850. If indeed Indians of this region tended to view Whites as divinities or supermen during the earliest years of contact between the races, Indians became increasingly aware of the white men's human qualities as they became better acquainted. It is also clear that different tribes and different individuals within those tribes held different opinions of Whites. The Cree warrior who benefited from the white man's war materials during the early years must have held a more favorable view of Whites than did the Dakota brave who believed the Whites were helping his Indian enemies. The Blackfoot warrior of the 1820s certainly distinguished between the Hudson's Bay Company trader and the American trapper who exploited his hunting grounds without any advantage to him. The chief who was acknowledged by the trader with gifts of a medal, a handsome suit of clothes, and kegs of liquor, must have had a more friendly feeling toward that White than did his younger rival for band or tribal leadership who had received no favors from the trader. The Indian woman married to a white man certainly understood white men's customs and values better than did her tribal age-mate whose husband was an Indian. Indian attitudes toward Whites probably varied as greatly as did white men's attitudes toward Indians prior to 1850.

This is not to say that misconceptions about Indians did not persist in the minds of white traders who lived in the Indian Country. Even so, those traders had better opportunities to gain an understanding of Indians than Indian traders had of understanding either that larger culture of which the White trader was a part or the many Whites outside the Indian Country who also had interests in the fur trade. The White trader in the Indian Country could visit every camp or village of a tribe — to estimate their numbers, to reckon their potential for trade or war. He knew their leaders, and he observed their customs at first hand. The Indian trader, on the other hand, met in the white trader only that tip of the white man's far-flung and complex civilization that protruded into the Indian Country. He never met the English gunsmith, the Venetian beadmaker, the New England textile weaver, the Brazilian tobacco grower, the New Jersey maker of shell hairpipes, the Missouri lead miner, or the London, New York, or St. Louis investor — all of whom had stakes in the Indian trade. Before 1850, few Indians of this region had ever seen a white woman. Nor could the stay-at-home Indians of this region believe the seemingly fantastic stories told by the few Indians who had visited St. Louis, Philadelphia, New York, and Washington of the white men's teeming cities, his many-storied houses, his vast industrial and war potential.

A few Indians of this region learned of the white men's concepts of the universe, which differed markedly from their own, and these Indians reacted differently. At Fort Clark during the winter of 1833–1834, the German scientist, Prince Maximilian of Wied-Neuwied, and his artist-companion, Karl Bodmer, exchanged ideas about the heavenly bodies and the origin of the universe with friendly Mandan Indians. The Prince reported: "They laughed outright when we affirmed that the earth was round and revolved about the sun. Others, however, would not reject our views, and were of the opinion that, as Whites could do so much that was incomprehensible to them, it was possible they might be right on this point also."[30]

By the mid-nineteenth century, most of the tribes of this region had known Whites for more than a century. They knew that Whites differed from Indians culturally as well as physically, and that cultural differences went well beyond the fact that Whites were hat-wearers. In their conceptions of these differences, they revealed something of their attitudes toward Whites. In 1854, a statement of an Indian viewpoint of these differences was written by Edwin T. Denig, who was probably the most knowledgeable white student of the tribes of the Upper Missouri at that time. The son of a Pennsylvania physician, he had traded with the tribes on the Missouri for more than two decades. He had married two Assiniboine women, and he fathered four children by them. Denig presented the Indian viewpoint in these words:

> Now this Supernatural Unknown Cause or Mystery created all things in the beginning. After the earth a few men and women of different colors were made, from whom descended all people. Different races were created for different purposes. They say that the whites were allotted education, knowledge of the mechanical arts, of machinery, etc., and therefore the whites are in many ways Wah-con. They were also made rich and clothed, or have the means of getting clothing,,and everything they want without hardship or exposure. The Indians, they say, were made naked and with such qualifications as to suit a hunter, knowledge enough to make his arms and use them at war or in the chase, a constitution to stand severe cold, long fasting, excessive fatigue, and watchfulness, and this was his portion. The position and pursuits of people were not defined by any laws, oral or otherwise delivered, but each with the powers granted to him was enabled to live.[31]

NOTES

[1] W. Raymond Wood, "Northern Plains Village Cultures Internal Stability and External Relationships," *Journal of Anthropological Research* (University of New Mexico, Albuquerque), 30, 1 (Spring 1974): 1–16.

[2] L. J. Burpee, ed., *Journals and Letters of Pierre Gaultier de Varennes de la Verendrye and his Sons* (Toronto, 1927), 332.

[3] John C. Ewers, "The Influence of the Fur Trade upon the Indians of the Northern Plains," in *People and Pelts: Selected Papers from the North American Fur Trade Conference*, ed. Malvina Bolus (Winnipeg, 1972).

[4] Edwin T. Denig, *Indian Tribes of the Upper Missouri*, 48th Annual Report, Bureau of American Ethnology (Washington, D.C., 1930), 528. John C. Ewers, "When Red and White Men Met," *The Western Historical Quarterly* 2, 2 (April 1971): 136–38.

[5] Francois Larocque, *Journal of Larocque from the Assiniboine to the Yellowstone*, Publication no. 3, Canadian Archives (Ottawa, 1910), 62–66.

[6] Pierre Jean De Smet, *Western Missions and Missionaries* (New York, 1862), 46.

[7] Louis Hennepin, *A New Discovery of the Vast Country in America*, ed. Reuben Gold Thwaites, 2 vols. (Chicago, 1903), 1: 292; Mildred Mott Wedel, "Le Sueur and the Dakota Sioux," in *Aspects of Upper Great Lakes Anthropology: Papers in Honor of Lloyd A. Wilford*, Minnesota Historical Society (St. Paul, 1974), 171.

[8] Maximilian, Prince of Wied-Neuwied, "Travels in the Interior of North America," in *Early Western Travels*, ed. Reuben Gold Thwaites, vols. 22–24 (Cleveland, 1906), 24:246.

[9] A. P. Nasatir, ed., *Before Lewis and Clark: Documents Illustrating the History of the Missouri, 1785–1804*, 2 vols. (St. Louis, 1952), 2: 382.

[10] Alexander Henry and David Thompson, *New Light on the Early History of the Greater Northwest*, ed. Elliott Coues, 3 vols. (New York, 1897), 2: 731.

[11] John Bradbury, "Travels in the Interior of America, in the years 1809, 1810, and 1811," in *Early Western Travels*, ed. Reuben Gold Thwaites, 5: 132–33.

[12] Pierre Jean De Smet, *Life, Letters, and Travels of Father Pierre Jean De Smet*, ed. H. M. Chittenden and A. T. Richardson, 4 vols. (New York, 1905), 3: 953–54.

[13] Maximilian, Prince of Wied-Neuwied, *Travels*, 23: 140–42. Testimony to author of *Richard Sanderville*, Piegan (1940s).

[14] Annie Heloise Abel, ed., *Tabeau's Narrative of Loisel's Expedition to the Upper Missouri* (Norman, Okla., 1939), 200–201.

[15] Abel, ed., *Tabeau's Narrative*, 201.

[16] Abel, ed., *Tabeau's Narrative*, 196–97. In 1833, Prince Maximilian was invited by an Hidatsa woman to assume the role of ceremonial father in that tribe's buffalo calling ceremony. See Maximilian, *Travels*, 24: 30.

[17] Charles Mackenzie, "The Missouri Indians, 1804–1805," in Louis R. Masson, *Les bourgeois de la Compagnie du Nord-Ouest*, 2 vols. (Quebec, 1889–1890), 1: 330.

[18] John C. Ewers, *Images of the White Man in 19th Century Plains Indian Art* (The Hague, Netherlands: Mouton Publishers, in press); Garrick Mallery, *Picture-Writing of the American Indians*, 10th Annual Report, Bureau of American Ethnology (Washington, D.C., 1893), 313, 653.

[19] George Catlin in *New York Commercial Advertiser*, Nov. 23, 1832. Maximilian, *Travels*, 23: 152, 319; 24: 35.

[20] J. Russell Harper, ed, *Paul Kane's Frontier* (Austin, Texas, 1971), 144.

[21] Rudolph Friederich Kurz, *Journal of Rudolph Friederich Kurz . . . 1846–1852*, trans. Myrtis Jarrell, ed. J.N.B. Hewitt. Bureau of American Ethnology Bulletin 115 (Washington, D.C., 1937), 76–77, 98, 215.

[22] John C. Ewers, "Plains Indian Painting: The History and Development of an American Art Form." *The American West* 5, 2 (March 1968): 4–10.

[23] L. J. Burpee, ed., *Journals and Letters of Pierre Gaultier de Varennes de la Verendrye and his Sons*, 262–64.

[24] Ewers, *The Influence of the Fur Trade*, 4.

[25] Edwin T. Denig, "Of the Arikaras," in *Five Indian Tribes of the Upper Missouri*, ed. John C. Ewers (Norman, Okla., 1961).

[26] John C. Ewers, *The Blackfeet, Raiders on the Northwestern Plains* (Norman, Okla., 1958), 45–57.

[27] John C. Ewers, *The Influence of the Fur Trade*, 7–11.

[28] For further biographical information on Four Bears and The Light see John C . Ewers, *Indian Life on the Upper Missouri* (Norman, Okla., 1968), 75–90, 103–109.

[29] Ewers, *Indian Life*, 57–67.

[30] Maximilian, *Travels*, 23: 288.

[31] Edwin T. Denig, *Indian Tribes of the Upper Missouri*, 486–87.

457

The Red River Settlement to 1869*

D.N. SPRAGUE

Origins

A native population unlike any of the others began to emerge in the context of the fur trade launched in the 1600s separately by Britain and France. The English found their access to the continent via Hudson Bay, the French found theirs by following the St. Lawrence River to the Great Lakes and beyond.[1]

In both cases, they established long-lasting business relationships with the Indians that extended to the sharing of gifts and other courtesies including women. The taking of an Indian wife was not a casual encounter, however. Normally the traders remained with such "country wives" for years, perhaps extending to the entire length of a trader's stay in Indian country because it was good for business. "While I had the Daughter I should not only have the Father's hunts but those of his relations also," one trader explained.[2] What emerged, then, was a form of marriage inspired by the profit motive, rather than casual re-

---

*"Historical Introduction" from *The Genealogy of the First Métis Nation*, compiled by D.N. Sprague and R.P. Frye, 11–24. Copyright by Pemmican Publications, 1983. Reprinted by permission.

lations for brief or promiscuous sexual gratification.[3] And since such marriages tended to be as durable as a trader's stay in North America, family units (including children) emerged.

But nearly all Hudson's Bay Company newcomers saw their posting to the wilderness as temporary (profitable) excursions to be followed by a return home and a rise in British society. More than 80 percent of the personnel recruited by the HBC before 1800 were taken from the impoverished Orkney Islands northeast of Scotland. Most of the Fletts, Taits, Spences, and Sutherlands recruited there were hired young (before age 21) and worked as contract labourers for periods as short as three or four years at 6 pounds per year. Some, remaining ten, fifteen, or more than twenty years had stayed long enough to father large families before leaving their native wives and children to return home with their savings for a comfortable retirement. In some cases, departure was preceded by provision of annuities or substitute fathers. But whether the returning fur trader made provision for his wife and children or simply abandoned them without support, the people left behind were "a breed of People easily distinguished from the real Indians. . . . "[4] Moreover, it was they who were most likely to provide the "country wives" for later newcomers who regarded such women as no less native than other aboriginal people as one James Spence made clear in referring to his "Indian wife Nostishio." But he identified her also as the "daughter of Isaac Batt" — another fur trader.[5] The comment is significant not only for the way the people were regarded as native but also because it shows a possible fondness of Batt for his daughter by what may have been an arranged marriage for her with the junior trader Spence. In return, Spence may have gained career advantages by accepting the patronage of Batt.[6]

A similar pattern of intermarriage first with leaders of Indian bands to secure their trade, then marriage of the daughters of older employees to junior colleagues was evident in the history of the Montreal-based company as well. The only important deviation from the pattern was a stronger tendency for the lower ranking employees to remain with their native families once their term of service was completed because the French *voyageur* seems to have regarded his familial responsibilities more seriously than did the upwardly mobile Orkney Scot who married and saved. The French Canadian servant of the North WestCompany more frequently married and stayed.

Another important difference was that the officers of the Montreal based company recognized that a population of retired employees and their families did not pose a serious threat of competition in the fur trade. Given the long lines of supply, the Bonneaus, Brelands, Ducharmes, Larocques, and the others performed indispensable work as provisioners, making it unnecessary to transport all the fur trader's food west or to divert Indians from their trapping activities to hunting roles.

Consequently, in sharp contrast to the region under the control of the Hudson's Bay Company, the Montreal based firm gave rise to literally dozens of small villages inhabited by people of mixed ancestry — the Métis.[7] But with the advance of white settlers many Métis retreated west and north, and gathered in largest concentration at Pembina on the Red River in the early 1800s. Large herds of buffalo were readily accessible in the area, and dried buffalo meat (pounded into bits and mixed with buffalo fat and berries) made a wholesome nonperishable food-concentrate called "pemmican" that was highly marketable to the North West Company once it began to operate west of Lake Winnipeg. The Nor'westers' Fort Gibraltar at the forks of the Red and Assiniboine rivers thus emerged as an important provisioning point. But just as the new Métis economy was becoming established, the Hudson's Bay Company decided to break the competition of its Montreal rivals.

Red River Colony versus the "New Nation"

459

The HBC pursued two strategies to defeat its competition. One was to establish new posts wherever the North West Company was also in operation. The other was to plant a settlement astride the Nor'westers' pemmican supply line. Incidentally, the settlement would also serve philanthropic purposes since the settlers were to be recruited from the growing ranks of impoverished Scots. Another source of potential settlers was the HBC itself to accommodate that minority who might find it preferable to retire on their savings with their native families to a Company colony rather than abandoning them and returning home in the usual manner.

The officer who took charge of the settlement scheme was Thomas Douglas, the Earl of Selkirk. But his efforts were frustrated from the start by North West Company directors who knew that the success of Selkirk's venture threatened their own. On this account, Simon McGillivray, one of the leading directors, launched a propaganda campaign in Scotland to convince prospective settlers that the promised farmland along the Red River was anything but the Garden of Eden described by Selkirk's agents. In McGillivray's version, the land was an arctic waste, sparsely treed, and filled with dangerous beasts and hostile Indians.[8] Perhaps because of the impact of the Nor'westers' negative advertisements, only 105 recruits had signed on by the date of the departure of the first contingent in 1811. Arriving on Hudson Bay too late to reach Lake Winnipeg before freeze-up they spent their first winter on the shore of the Bay in total misery. Then, in the spring of 1812 they fought their way through clouds of black flies and mosquitoes on their trek south to proclaim possession of a stretch of river front near the Nor'westers' Fort Gibraltar.[9] In 1813 a second group arrived on the scene and, looking to the future agricultural development of the colony, the company surveyor, Peter Fidler, laid out seven lots for farming. No crop had been planted in 1812; that of 1813 failed. But the colonists did not starve because of the generosity of the Métis who fed them over both winters.[10]

In January of 1814, the company-appointed leader of the settlers, Miles Macdonnell, rewarded their generosity by forbidding the natives from trading pemmican with anyone but the HBC. The Métis, for their part, ignored Macdonnell's bad manners and traded as usual but began to regard the Scot "gardeners" with increasing suspicion.[11]

Once the Nor'westers' learned of developments since 1813, they sent their own man, Duncan Cameran, to build on Métis suspicion by telling them that the HBC intended to take over the whole territory. At the same time, the Scot settlers were told that better land and a more hospitable climate awaited them in Canada. About three quarters (more than 140 persons) took advantage of the Nor'wester's offer of transportation to the alternate promised land in June.[12] The remaining part were harassed by the Métis who trampled their crops on horseback.

The stubbornly persistent group of about sixty remaining settlers were reinforced in November of 1815 with what proved to be the last contingent of Selkirk colonists. With a new leader, Robert Semple, and a fortified stronghold they called Fort Douglas (named after Selkirk), the Scots prepared to remain and to fight if necessary.

But the Métis had become equally determined to protect their prior claim that was apparently undisputed by the Indians of the area (perhaps because the Métis were allies in the continuing struggle against the Sioux).[13] The result of the Métis hostility to the Scots' invasion was intensified conflict in 1816. On June 19 a group of about 35 led by Cuthbert Grant approached Semple's fortress. Semple responded by riding out to meet them with twenty-six of his own men and attempted to address the natives like a schoolmaster shouting at a gang of unruly children. In the course of his speaking, he reached for someone's gun, a shot was fired, and the shooting became general. In the mêlée that followed, Semple himself and 21 of his fellows were struck dead, mutilated, and stripped naked.[14] Thus, the first manifestation of the political consciousness of the Métis resulted in bloodshed. They served notice to intruders that they were the people who owned the land and were prepared to back that claim by force if necessary. To the Métis, the "Battle of Seven Oaks" was an heroic moment of self-defence and self-affirmation. To the HBC, however, the action was an episode of brutal mass murder — a massacre.

Selkirk retaliated by raising a private army of Swiss mercenaries and taking his case to court in Canada. Eventually, in 1821, the two companies agreed to settle their dispute by a merger rather than by a continuation of the legal and military action. Since no fresh waves of farmers poured

460

into the territory from Scotland, and since one buyer of pemmican was as good as another, the Métis also gave up the fight, eventually agreeing to settle in the vicinity of the old Selkirk colony, led by none other than Cuthbert Grant.

A New Colony

The settlement that developed on the site of Selkirk's old colony continued to serve the purposes of the Hudson's Bay Company but without becoming the haven of Scot farmers that Selkirk had envisioned. In 1818, fewer than fifty of the families he had brought over still remained in the area.[15] A handful of his private army had also been persuaded to stay but increasingly through the 1820s, the colony emerged as a gathering-place for the two groups of native people that had developed along with the two companies before 1821.

After the merger, almost 1,300 employees lost their jobs since the single organization that emerged had no need for most of the *voyageurs* and many of the old HBC staff.[16] About 15 percent of the "retired" employees made their way to Red River in the 1820s.[17] Those headed by Orkney Scots tended to find river frontage just to the north of the tiny remnant of the Selkirk settlement. Those whose attachment was to the other company located south of the Scots, and below the mercenaries at the other end of the colony. To the west, yet another group appeared after 1824 because the HBC was afraid of Cuthbert Grant's Métis remaining at Pembina. Grant was given a title ("Warden of the Plains"), a salary, and orders to bring his people to a tract of river frontage west of the Red on the Assiniboine. Before the end of 1824, he had persuaded about 100 families to abandon Pembina and join him at Grant Town, also known as White Horse Plain.[18]

The colony that started afresh in the 1820s was thus overwhelmingly native in origin. That tendency became even more pronounced after a disastrous flood in the spring of 1826 so discouraged the Swiss that they abandoned the region for a less challenging climate and drier ground, but the colony continued to receive new infusions of native families — sometimes headed by a former servant of one of the two companies.

Maintaining the geographical and social separation of the several populations that was evident even before the flood were missionaries who indoctrinated the people in different versions of Christianity. At the same time, the Company granted land to the two groups of Christian natives, favouring Protestants over Catholics. The Scots and the "natives of Hudson Bay" were supposed to become Anglicans and good farmers. They received grants of 50 to 100 acres each. The others were granted 25

461

acres or less.[19] In this way, although the two populations born of the fur trade came into geographical proximity in the 1820s, they were kept separate in religion and expected social position.

The tiny remnant of the Selkirk colony was held up as the community of model colonists; they were Protestant and the most stubborn farmers despite agricultural practices that lead usually to failure or barest subsistence.[20] But they were the best colonists from the Company's standpoint. They had no influence with the Indians. They were orderly. They were no competition. Below the Selkirk Settlers were the natives descended from HBC paternal ancestors. Although not properly British, they were at least Protestant and believed to be more stable than the other native population because of their Scottish paternal ancestry. The last-place group were the Métis: Catholic, inclined to speak a native language as commonly as French, and believed to be totally uninterested in agriculture. Notwithstanding the HBC's low estimate of their worth, however, they were the most important group in the colony. They were the most numerous; and thanks to their work in the hunt, the colony did not starve. Normally, it was the produce of the plains that fed the Red River Settlement and provisioned the fur trade.[21]

462

The Pemmican Industry

By 1830 the Hudson's Bay Company stabilized at about 1,000 employees and remained at that level for the next several decades.[22] To operate the trading system from its streamlined network of posts, the Company needed more than 60 tons of pemmican per year.[23] With perhaps 40 million buffalo on the prairies, there was a seemingly unlimited supply of the raw material. The problem was processing and distributing the finished product. Consequently, the main line of the economic development of the native community at the forks of the Red and Assiniboine rivers from about 1830 to 1840 was in responding to that need.

From the mid 1820s, expeditions involving nearly the entire community left in mid-June to exploit the largest of the herds in the valley of the Missouri River.[24] Having located their quarry and slaughtered what could be processed and hauled home, the meat was transformed on the spot into pemmican and the produce of the hunt was loaded onto two-wheeled horse-drawn carts and the "wagon people" (as the Indians called them) made their way the hundreds of miles back to Red River.

The amount of pemmican that might be traded with the Company depended upon the labour supply for hunting and processing, and the supply of carts available for transport. Since it was not until about 1835 that the community had enough hunters, pemmican makers, and transportation to meet the colony's and the Company's needs, the production of plains provisions was a growth industry through the 1830s. By 1835, approximately 500 families with as many carts were available to rendezvous at Pembina for the spring hunt. If all went well, each cart would return by August with its full load of six ninety-pound bags of pemmican — more than 130 tolls of cured meat in total. Such a return would be enough to feed the settlement through the winter, and to satisfy the demand of the Company as well. That level of population assured security to the Company and prosperity for the producers. The Métis had their independence and also the wares of the HBC (since each family's summer haul of pemmican was worth about as much as the same season's wage to the Company's salaried employees who laboured the year round for 20 pounds per annum).[25] But the native population of the Red River settlement continued to grow at a rapid rate (doubling every fifteen to twenty years).[26] As a result, the much larger population of the 1840s had to find alternate lines of work or suffer a drop in its standard of living.

463

Native People and the HBC

The first alternative to pemmican production was wage labour for the Hudson's Bay Company. Since the HBC considered native people in general to be inferior to Europeans, and the natives with French Canadian backgrounds to be worse than those who were partly British, George Simpson, the on-site manager of operations after 1821 ("Governor of Rupert's Land"), decided that the "indolent and unsteady" Métis could become suitable replacements for the increasingly expensive Orkney Scots only with careful management.[27] Their qualities were that they knew the country, the languages, could be hired on a merely seasonal basis, and could be worked for wages that were about 25 percent less than what was needed to attract European labour.[28] Consequently, more and more natives became part of the seasonal and even the permanent labour force, accounting for about one third of the manpower by the end of the 1830s and roughly one half by 1850.[29]

The work for which native labour became most important was "voyaging" to Portage La Loche.[30] Beginning in June of 1831 (and continuing every June thereafter until 1870), a force of about 30 to 60 men, 8 men to a craft called York boats (each capable of carrying three or four tons freight) departed from Lower Fort Garry laden with "plains provisions" and headed for Norway House. There they collected "pieces" of trade goods (parcels weighing about 100 pounds each). Then, they proceeded out the Saskatchewan system travelling as far as Portage La Loche. Thus, it was they who provisioned the Mackenzie River district, and after reaching their ultimate northwestern destination, they of course retraced their route taking fur back to Norway House. (Sometimes another brigade linked that port with the HBC's main warehousing point on the Bay-

York Factory). But the Portage La Loche brigade was the main link in the overall system. They covered the most territory and were the most vital carriers of plains provisions, trade goods, and bales of fur, on their last leg transporting whatever was imported from Europe to Lower Fort Garry. Since the work of the "tripmen" was as hazardous as it was arduous, the job was distinctly second choice relative to pemmican production. But the Company was able to entice workers with advance payments of one third of their wages in December, another third before departure in May, and the final installment of 6 or 7 pounds after returning to Red River.[31] Thus, the men engaged in voyaging earned more than pemmican producers but after returning home in the Autumn they still had to hunt for their winter subsistence on fish, fowl, and buffalo.

Somewhat more attractive than lake freighting was land cartage because a man and a cart could be more independent than a lake freighter, and still earn the same wage.[32] But work by the job was somewhat unpredictable. Consequently, a growing number of natives became traders in their own right in the 1840s by re-establishing links with the Métis of the United States and exchanging fur or pemmican for imports as far away as St. Paul, Minnesota.[33]

A select few of the native people had the option of rising above voyaging roles and filled a special officer candidate position that was created by 1840 to suit the heirs of former "gentlemen" of the HBC.[34] Eventually, a group of about twenty native sons of former Chief Factors and Chief Traders were appointed "Apprentice Postmasters" in the 1840s and 50s and subsequently, a few rose to higher levels in the Company's service. But since such clerks in training were natives in every respect but paternal ancestry, their starting pay was set almost as low as a tripman's wage, and their apprenticeship was longer than that demanded of Europeans. On this account, one of their fathers complained that they suffered a "glaring injustice."[35] But those who did complete their eleven-year apprenticeship gained a large reward for suffering the Company's racism so long; their pay rose from less than 20 pounds per annum to more than 75 pounds.[36]

The discrimination inherent in the rank of Apprentice Post Master thus cut two ways. It showed the Company's bias towards Europeans for clerical-managerial positions; and the rank also showed that the Company believed that one segment of the native population was capable of such duties with special training. By preferring one native group over another, however, they further divided natives who were already separated by religious training. Consequently, the theoretical possibility of the emergence of one Métis nation continued to be an abstraction that was lost in day to day living. The first special favour accorded to the natives of Hudson Bay (the larger grants of land) and the later patronage (superior employment) set them further apart from the "inferior" Catholic Métis. Of course, the continuing discrimination of the HBC served further to sour relations between the Métis and the Company, a matter that reached crisis proportions in the 1840s when the HBC decided to restrict the independent trading activities of the more enterprising free traders.

The Disintegration of Company Rule

In 1844 the Hudson's Bay Company decided that the native people who traded independently posed a threat to their own profits. Theoretically, the Company enjoyed a complete monopoly of the fur trade by Royal Charter. The problem was enforcement. In the 1840s the only police or military force of any consequence in the area were the Métis horsemen, and they paid more allegiance to the free traders than to the HBC. Consequently, the Company did not take any serious steps to limit their activities until they had successfully persuaded the British to garrison the colony by telling them the Americans planned to take over the region south of Lake Winnipeg just as they had recently grabbed the southern half of British Columbia (renaming it "Oregon").[37] But the troops provided by Britain were no match for the Métis cavalry. As a result, when Guillaume Sayer was charged in 1849 with illegal trading a committee of other native smugglers called out the hunters and tripmen and together they broke the Company's authority. The judge, Adam Thom, defied what he called a half-breed rabble, tried Sayer in his absence, and an all-white jury brought in a verdict of guilty but the Company wisely decided not to proceed further. Once it became known that all charges were to be dropped, the Métis left the scene shouting that "the trade is free."[38]

465

The Sayer trail was thus a milestone in the history of the native people in the area — for two reasons. First, the committee included leaders from both groups, the Protestant as well as the Catholic. Second, they had shown that with the whole community united they could force outsiders to back down. Of course, the HBC continued to claim authority and also to pretend that they ruled Red River through their appointed Council of Assiniboia but that structure by-passed the real leaders of native society. The Council of Assiniboia consisted almost exclusively of retired fur traders and the clergy.[39] The persons who probably commanded more respect were the Métis entrepreneurial elite on whom the Company heaped nothing but scorn.

The HBC's failure to defer to the natural leaders of native society showed that the colony was forced into a dual existence between ideal and actual reality. On the level of fantasy, the Company's ideal was a "Little Britain" in the wilderness, a community of Christian farmers owing allegiance to none but the "Honourable Company" (and through them to the English Crown). On this account, the persons supposed to become the best farmers were pampered with a wide assortment of special favours and throughout the 1830s a number of weird and wonderful experiments were launched to nurture the agricultural development of the colony.[40] Since the agricultural experiments all failed, it was clear that the more rational lines of development ran toward pemmican and trade. But those who prospered outside the approved spheres of economic activity were never rewarded with political power. Consisting mainly of the relics of the Church and the HBC, the Council of Assiniboia never included the personnel who led in the real energy and growth of the colony.[41]

Naturally, the conflict between the two realities led to difficulty. Curiously, the group that was most outspokenly opposed to the HBC's petty tyranny was the population most favoured in the past because a new group of Protestant missionaries arriving in the colony in the 1850s persuaded the native English that the Company had erred in placing Romish priests on the Council.[42] The denunciation of the HBC in the form of complaints against "Popery" thus led to a controversy that drove Protestant further from Catholic. Already trained to seek their marriage partners exclusively from the population of their coreligionists,[43] a new element of animosity was added to their already wide separation. As a result, the remarkable cooperation of the two native groups in 1849 emerged as a passing phenomenon, an event that did not lead to a firmer alliance or assimilation before 1869. But at the end of the 1850s, the two communities faced a threat that was much greater than gratuitous discrimination or the supposed advancement of one branch of Christianity over another. In the 1850s, the native people of Red River witnessed the vanguard arrival of those who would displace them almost entirely.

Canada Discovers a Western Destiny

Separated from the old fur trade hinterland since 1821, Canadians looked westward with new interest in the late 1850s as hard times made them anxious to find "new lands to conquer."[44]

As with other episodes of expansion, exploration was to precede colonization. Henry Youle Hind, a Toronto geology professor, was hired in 1857 to tour the west and to report on its potential for agriculture. Reporting in 1860, Hind described the prairies around Red River as a "vast ocean [that] must be seen in its extraordinary aspects before it can be rightly valued. . . . "[45] Such unqualified praise was the kind of advertisement that discoverers had been making since the days of Christopher Columbus. So also was another of Hind's themes — the notion that the natives had not the slightest idea of the region's true value.

Everything Henry Hind wrote in description of the Red River colony was to suggest that no true settlement had yet occurred. He pointed out that the 7,000 inhabitants reported to be living in the area according to the HBC census of 1856 were almost all native and the colony was becoming less and less European each decade. He cited the same statistics to show that between 1843 and 1856 "the increase of native or half-breed families was 132," but the white population had actually declined by 102 families.[46] What remained were the Métis like Pierre Gladu whose house fronted on the Red River in St. Vital. Nearby was a cattle yard that Hind said also held pigs, horses, and poultry. In the stable in which the horses should have been kept Hind found a "neat, light, four wheeled carriage." But the most peculiar aspect of the Gladu farm (from Hind's point of view) was that Pierre was preparing to go off on an autumn buffalo hunt instead of looking after his numerous stacks of peas, wheat, and hay or splitting wood for the winter. In Hind's judgement, Gladu and the others were "improvident and . . . indolent, they prefer the wild life of the prairies to the tamer duties of a settled home."[47] Consequently, Canada's explorer of Red River looked forward to the day when Gladu and his neighbours would be succeeded by "an energetic and civilized race, able to improve its [the land's] vast [agricultural] capabilities and appreciate its marvellous beauties."[48]

467

Hind did not have long to wait. Encouraged by Hind's glowing report (but ready to move westward in any event) a vanguard of white newcomers from Ontario began arriving in the Red River region at the end of the 1850s.[49] At the same time, the Hudson's Bay Company started a steamer service on the Red River to bring trade goods into Rupert's Land by way of the United States, thus eliminating some of the growing labour cost associated with land freighting by cart or the utilization of the water route from York Factory.[50] Thus, native people along the Red faced the prospect of declining employment just as they also observed the first arrival of what was likely to be a future invasion. One other disturbing development was a realization that the vast — seemingly inexhaustible — herds of buffalo were in fact "dwindling."[51] No prospect of extinction was evident in 1860 but there was some sign that the population dependent upon buffalo might not continue to double every generation and still expect a comfortable subsistence. The result was a land rush in the 1860s — a definite, perceptible recognition that the economy was on the verge of major changes, and the realization that land was going to be critically important in establishing one's security in society.

The Council of Assiniboia responded by adopting an ordinance to legitimize what had already occurred since 1835 and was proceeding with new emphasis since the late 1850s. In 1860, the nominal government of the community adopted a rule to the effect that anyone could occupy vacant riverfront of up to twelve chains (about 800 feet) in width. Since the normal depth of a river front claim was two miles, the area of vacant

468

Strip farms of the Red River Settlement (c. 1870)

LAKE WINNIPEG

LAKE MANITOBA

RIDING MOUNTAIN

GOVERNMENT OF MANITOBA

DISTRICT OF ASSINIBOIA

PEMBINA HILLS

Winnipeg R.
Whitemouth R.
Seine R.
Roseau R.
Pembina R.
Whitemud R.
Minnedosa R.
Assiniboine R.
Souris R.
R. aux Islets de Bois

St. Peter's
St. Andrew's
St. Paul's (Middlechurch)
Kildonan
St. John's
Upper Port
St. Boniface
St. Vital
St. Norbert
Lower Port
Poplar Point
St. François Xavier
Headingley
St. James
St. Charles
Westbourne
High Bluff
Portage La Prairie
St. Laurent
Ste. Anne-des-Chênes
Pembina

Miles
0 10 20 30 40 50

100°

Adapted from Cornell, Hamelin, Ouellet, Trudel, *Canada: Unity in Diversity*, 277.

land that might be occupied by such squatter's rights was thus established at about 200 acres.[52] The new rule accommodated the first newcomers from Ontario (a group of more than forty families arriving in the 1860s).[53] At the same time, the ordinance also secured the occupancy of about 2,000 native families — passed over in the general distribution of 1835, or officially landless from the time of their appearance after that date. The land ordinance of 1860 was thus one of the few (perhaps the only) significant achievement of the Company's puppet government. But at the end of the 1860s, in the face of a horrible drought in which the produce of the hunt and the river front farms and gardens both failed,[54] the people of the colony learned that the Hudson's Bay Company had just completed an arrangement with the new federation of Canada that was to transfer the west to the Canadians with compensation to be paid only to the HBC and to the Indians. There was no indication in 1869 that anyone intended to consult or to recognize the rights of the "wagon people."

469

NOTES

[1] The differences attributable to the two native populations' attachments to the different companies are discussed briefly by John Foster, "Origins of the Mixed Bloods in the Canadian West," in Lewis H. Thomas, ed., *Essays in Western History in Honour of Lewis Gwynne Thomas* (Edmonton, 1975).

[2] Jennifer Brown, *Strangers in Blood: Fur Trade Company Families in Indian Country* (Vancouver, 1980), 105.

[3] Sylvia Van Kirk, *"Many Tender Ties": Women in Fur-Trade Society in Western Canada, 1670–1870* (Winnipeg, 1980), 4.

[4] William Falconer's "Remarks on the Natives" quoted in Brown, *Strangers*, 69.

[5] Spence's "Last Will and Testament" quoted in Brown, *Strangers*, 70.

[6] The issue of marriage for career advantage is discussed by Brown, *Strangers*, 74.

[7] Jacqueline Peterson, "Prelude to Red River: A Social Portrait of the Great Lakes Métis," *Ethnohistory* 25 (1978): 41–67.

[8] Article in *Inverness Journal* quoted by E.E. Rich, *The Fur Trade and the Northwest to 1857* (Toronto, 1967), 210.

[9] A brief account of the Selkirk venture is found in Rich, *The Fur Trade*, 209–235.

[10] Alexander Ross described their hospitality as "extreme kindness," in his mid-nineteenth century history of *The Red River Settlement: Its Rise, Progress, and Present State*, recently reprinted (Edmonton, 1972), 24.

[11] The "gardener" label is found in James Jackson, *The Centennial History of Manitoba* (Toronto, 1970), 49.

[12] Rich, *Fur Trade*, 220.

[13] M.A. Macleod and W.L. Morton, *Cuthbert Grant of Grantown: Warden of the Plains of Red River* (Toronto, 1963), ix, 112.

[14] Macleod and Morton, *Cuthbert Grant*, 48–51.

[15] A list of "Settlers at Red River" dated August, 1818, enumerates 45 "Scotch" families and 46 de Meurons, Swiss mercenaries (Public Archives of Canada [hereinafter abbreviated as PAC], Selkirk Papers, 5237–38.

[16] Figures established by Philip Goldring indicate that the HBC's labour force fell from 1,927 in 1821 to 694 by 1826, "Papers on the Labour System of the Hudson's Bay Company," in Parks Canada, Manuscript Report Series, no. 362, 32–33.

[17] The 15 percent value is derived from the genealogies of thenative people in the Archibald Census of 1870. In the "French Métis" line, 107 white forebears appear to have settled at Red River. In the "English Métis" line, the number is 74, for a total of 181 — roughly one seventh of the European labour force discharged between 1821 and 1826.

[18] Macleod and Morton, *Cuthbert Grant*, 94.

[19] Hudson's Bay Company Archives, Provincial Archives of Manitoba, Memoranda Respecting Grants of Land no. 1 and 2, E.6/7–8.

[20] A brilliant work by G.H. Sprenger develops the idea that insistence upon farming at Red River before the 1870s indicated more of stubbornness than rational development. His content analysis

of the settlers' own evaluations of their efforts in farming shows that crops were either "short" or outright "failures" in 31 of the 50 years between 1820 and 1870. See Sprenger, "An Analysis of Selective Aspects of Métis Society, 1810-1870," unpublished M.A. thesis, University of Manitoba, 1972, 79-86.

[21] W.L. Morton has described the attempts at farming in the colony as "slovenly, squatter agriculture, ancillary to the hunt" in "Agriculture in the Red River Colony" reprinted in A.B. McKillop, ed., *Contexts of Canada's Past* (Toronto, 1980), 81. Morton also suggests that "most of the meat eaten in the Settlement [not to mention the fur trade] was 'plains provisions,'" in his *Manitoba: History of a Province* (Toronto, 1957), 87.

[22] Goldring, "Papers on the Labour System," 33, 84.

[23] See Arthur Ray's "Table 9: Hudson's Bay Company Provision Orders for the Northern Department," in *Indians in the Fur Trade: Their Role as Hunters, Trappers, and Middlemen in the Lands Southwest of Hudson Bay, 1660-1870* (Toronto, 1974), 208-209.

[24] The classic description of the hunt is that of Alexander Ross, *Red River Settlement*, 243-300. But Ross emphasized waste more than productivity. More recent historians have a keener appreciation of the hunt as a light manufacturing process. In this regard, Irene Spry has denied that the hunt was wasteful until American skinners armed with repeating rifles went after the southern herd for hides alone. Buffalo hide drive belts in factories were good for American industrial development but the southern herd was totally decimated between 1871 and 1875. What followed were repercussions on the northern herd as more people began to hunt northward. See Spry, "The Great Transformation: The Disappearance of the Commons of Western Canada," in Richard Allen, ed., *Man and Nature on the Prairies* (Regina, 1976), 21-45. For more precise measures of native productivity see Sprenger, "Aspects of Native Society," 68, and Robert Gosman, "The Riel and Lagimodière Families in Métis Society" (unpublished report to Parks Canada, 1977). Gosman has found evidence that a group of about 50 families in 1849 slaughtered roughly 1,700 buffalo in the autumn of 1849. From that kill they obtained 1,213 bales of dried meat, 166 sacks of fat, and 556 bladders of bone marrow, with a market value of about 2,000 pounds sterling. Clearly, hunters did not chase buffalo simply for the thrill of the shoot, nor did they slaughter animals only for a few "choice bits" leaving the rest for the wolves (as Morton alleges in *Manitoba*, 81).

[25] According to Goldring, 20 pounds was an average wage for a low-ranking salaried employee from the 1830s to the 1850s ("Papers in the Labour System," 60). In the same period, top quality pemmican sold for 2 or 3 pence per pound according to Ross and Morton (Ross, *Red River Settlement*, 273; and Morton, "Agriculture in the Red River Colony," 81). At the higher price, a full cart load of six 90 pound bags was worth 6.75 pound sterling.

[26]

Years	1827	1840	1856	1870
Persons	1,100	4,700	7,000	12,000

Data for 1827-56 are from the HBC Censuses, the 1870 total is from the enumeration of population under Governor Archibald's auspices after the transfer to Canada. To convert *Persons* to *Families*, divide by 5.

[27] Quoted in Carol M. Judd, "Native Labour and Social Stratification in the Hudson's Bay Northern Department, 1770-1870," *Canadian Review of Sociology and Anthropology* 17 (1980): 310.

[28] 15 versus 20 pounds. Compare the wage scales in Goldring, "Papers on the Labour System," 60 and 103.

[29] Judd, "Native Labour," 310, 311, and John Nicks, "Orkneymen in the HBC, 1780-1821," in C.M. Judd and A.J. Ray, eds., *Old Trails and New Directions: Papers of the Third North American Fur Trade Conference* (Toronto, 1980), 123.

[30] See Goldring, "Papers on the Labour System," 98-107 and John Gunn, *Echoes of the Red* (Toronto, 1930), 24-58.

[31] Gunn, *Echoes*, 36; Goldring, "Papers on the Labour System," 103.

[32] Tripmen worked about 5 months for as little as 15 pounds or 300 shillings — 2 shillings per day (the same wage as day labourers). Goldring, "Papers on the Labour System," 112.

[33] Gosman, "Riel and Lagimodière Families," 16.

[34] Judd, "Native Labour," 312.

[35] James Anderson, quoted in Judd, "Native Labour," 312.

[36] Goldring, "Papers on the Labour System," 61; Judd, "Native Labour," 312.

[37] An excellent account of Simpson's use of imperial crises to further Company interests is found in J.S. Galbraith, *The Little Emperor: Governor Simpson of the Hudson's Bay Company* (Toronto, 1976).

[38] A brief but lucid account of the Sayer trial is found in Morton, *Manitoba*, 76-79.

[39] See Lionel Dorge, "The Métis and *Canadien* Councillors of Assiniboia," *Beaver* 305 (1974), 1: 12-19, 2: 39-45, 3: 51-58.

[40] See Ross, *Red River Settlement*.

[41] Interestingly, in the first elections in the history of the colony — the process for choosing delegates to the national convention late in 1869 — every Councilor but one was rejected (Dorge, "Councillors," Part 3, 56).

[42] The fullest account of the new religious division is found in F. Pannekoek, "The Churches and the Social Structure in the Red River Area, 1818-1870," unpublished Ph.D. thesis, Queen's University, 1973.

43 Marriages between Protestants and Roman Catholics did occur. Comparing the religions of the house-holders in Table 1 of this volume [*Genealogy of the First Métis Nation*] with the religions of their parents the following pattern emerges:

	Parents Protestant		Parents Catholic	
	Prot.	Cath.	Cath.	Prot.
Children as Householders	510	54	1,131	35

44 See Doug Owram, *Promise of Eden: The Canadian Expansionist Movement and the Idea of the West, 1856-1900* (Toronto, 1980).

45 Henry Youle Hind, *Narrative of the Canadian Red River Exploring Expedition of 1857 and of the Assiniboine and Saskatchewan Exploring Expeditions of 1858* (London, 1860), 1: 134-35.

46 Hind, *Narrative*, 1: 177.

47 Hind, *Narrative*, 1: 164-65, 179.

48 Hind, *Narrative*, 1: 134.

49 W.L. Morton, ed., *Alexander Begg's Red River Journal and Other Papers Relative to the Red River Resistance* (Toronto, 1956), Introduction, 13.

50 Morton, *Manitoba*, 101; see also Galbraith, *Little Emperor*, 188.

51 Contemporary observers warned that the numbers of buffalo were "falling off" as early as the 1850s. See Ross, *Red River Settlement*, 267; and Hind, *Narrative*, I: 180.

52 For the background to the regulation's adoption see Dorge, "Councillors," Part 2, 43. For the Government of Canada's careful study of the same see PAC, RG15, vol. 235, file 5537.

53 The Archibald Census of 1870 enumerated 38 white, male householders who were born in Ontario. Since a number of persons born in the United Kingdom emigrated to Manitoba in the 1860s (after having lived in Ontario for a number of years), it is safe to assume that the "Canadian Party" included considerably more than the 38 persons who are positively in that category.

54 B. Kaye, "Some Aspect of the Historical Geography of the Red River Settlement," unpublished M.A. thesis, University of Manitoba, 1966, 251.

Topic Fourteen

The Pacific Coast

In the early nineteenth century fur traders of the North West Company, operating out of Montreal, reached the Fraser and Columbia river-basins. Subsequently the Hudson's Bay Company, after its union with the North West Company in 1821, extended fur-trading operations all along the North Pacific Coast. Exactly a quarter of a century later, however, the boundary between British and American territory was extended along the 49th parallel to the Pacific Coast, which led the Hudson's Bay Company to leave the Oregon Territory, and to establish its new commercial headquarters on Vancouver Island. The economic history of Victoria, the commercial centre of Vancouver Island, is outlined in J.M.S. Careless' "The Business Community in the Early Development of Victoria, British Columbia."

In 1858 the discovery of gold on the Fraser River opened up the mainland, leading Britain to establish the separate colony of British Columbia that same year, to offset the domination of American prospectors. James Douglas, the governor of Vancouver Island, became governor of the new mainland colony as well, firmly planting British institutions there, and making New Westminster the new capital. In 1866 the two colonies were joined under the title of British Columbia. Barry Gough offers an interpretative sketch of British Columbia in his "The Character of the British Columbia Frontier."

Barry Gough's *Distant Dominion: Britain and the Northwest Coast of North America, 1579–1809* (Vancouver: University of British Columbia Press, 1980) discusses the maritime history of the Pacific Coast. W. Kaye Lamb has edited the journals of George Vancouver's expedition, 1791-95, in four volumes, *The Voyage of George Vancouver, 1791–1795* (London: The Hakluyt Society, 1984). For the later period see Barry Gough, *The Royal Navy and the Northwest Coast of North America, 1810–1914: A Study of British Maritime Ascendancy* (Vancouver: University of British Columbia Press, 1971) and his *Gunboat Frontier: British Maritime Authority and Northwest Coast Indians, 1846–90* (Vancouver: University of British Columbia Press, 1984).

Margaret A. Ormsby has written a valuable introduction to *Fort Victoria Letters, 1846–51* (Winnipeg: Hudson's Bay Record Society, 1979), edited by Hartwell Bowsfield. On the history of coal mining in the early settlement period, see Lynne Bowen's *Three Dollar Dreams* (Lantzville,

B.C.: Oolichan Books, 1987), and John Douglas Belshaw's "Mining Technique and Social Division on Vancouver Island, 1848–1900," *British Journal of Canadian Studies* 1, (1986): 45–65.

For an overview of developments on the mainland, see R. Cole Harris' "British Columbia" in *Canada before Confederation*, ed. R. Cole Harris and John Warkentin (Toronto: Oxford, 1974), 289–311. The standard, but now rather dated, history of the area is Margaret Ormsby's *British Columbia: A History* (Toronto: Macmillan, 1958). George Woodcock provides a readable sketch of an early British Columbian journalist and politician in *Amor de Cosmos: Journalist and Reformer* (Toronto: Oxford University Press, 1975). *British Columbia: Historical Readings*, ed. W. Peter Ward and Robert A.J. McDonald (Vancouver: Douglas and McIntyre, 1981) contains several valuable essays on early British Columbia history.

The Business Community in the Early Development of Victoria, British Columbia*   473

J.M.S. CARELESS

The rise of Victoria from the Hudson's Bay fort of the 1850's to the substantial commercial city of the later nineteenth century may be readily associated with striking events like the Fraser and Cariboo gold rushes, the political course of able Governor Douglas and the somewhat colourful officialdom about him — or the still more colourful doings of Amor de Cosmos, a kind of dedicated opportunist in politics, working toward the crucial decision of federal union with Canada. Far less likely is Victoria's growth to be associated with the more prosaic, lower-keyed activities of the city's businessmen. None the less, their quieter, continuing operations played an essential part in making the Vancouver Island community the chief entrepot of young British Columbia. Nor was the process lacking in colour or in noteworthy figures of its own. To trace that process, the development of the business community in conjunction with Victoria itself, is thus the object of the present study.[1]

Before 1858, and the onset of the gold rush to the Fraser on the neighbouring mainland, Victoria was a tranquil little hamlet of some three hundred inhabitants clustered about a fur trade depot. For Victoria, founded in 1843, did have the distinction, of course, of being the Hudson's Bay headquarters on the coast, as well as seat of government for the colony of Vancouver Island that had been erected in 1849, still in the keeping of the fur trade company. As a part of a great British com-

*From *Canadian Business History: Selected Studies, 1497–1971*, ed. David S. Macmillan. Used by permission of the Canadian Publishers, McClelland and Stewart, Toronto.

mercial and imperial enterprise, and on the open Pacific within the world reach of British seapower, Victoria was by no means wholly isolated or unchanging. Parties of colonists had arrived from the United Kingdom to settle among the Company's officers and employees. The mild climate and fertile soil of the adjacent districts produced good crops. The Company had opened valuable coal mines up the coast at Nanaimo in the early fifties, and the timber wealth of the Island's heavy forests was initially being tapped. Finally, there was an increasing trade southward in coal, lumber, and sometimes fish or potatoes to San Francisco, the bustling Californian gold metropolis, from where most of the colony's necessary imports were derived.

Nevertheless, Victoria had remained an outpost community of small endeavours and limited opportunities. It was not one to invite much business enterprise when the fur company dominated the major economic activities — not to mention political — and when markets were either local and scanty or far off and uncertain. True, the Hudson's Bay interests had worked at developing farms, mines, or sawmills, and had diversified their trading operations on the coast well beyond the traffic in furs. Yet problems of access to market and to sufficient shipping plagued them too, while the established, hierarchical ways of the old fur monopoly inevitably made new adjustments harder. Outside of the quasi-bureaucratic world of the Bay Company, moreover, there scarcely was a business community, other than well-to-do tavern-keepers like James Yates (a former Company employee), some artisans, and a few independent settlers engaged in trade.

John Muir, formerly a Company coal-miner, sent spars, piles, and lumber to Victoria from his small mill at Sooke, for shipment to the California market. Captain William Brotchie had pioneered in opening the spar trade, but found it hard to get adequate transport, and subsequently became Victoria's Harbourmaster. And Captain James Cooper, who had commanded Hudson's Bay supply vessels, had set up as an independent trader, bringing the little iron schooner, *Alice*, out from England in sections, then shipping cargoes like coal, cranberries, and spars to San Francisco and the Hawaiian Islands. The role of sea captains in early business development on Vancouver Island was notable, in fact. But shipmasters then had long been roving businessmen, used to trading where they could, seeking cargoes, and commissions in their own or others' service. They were particularly prominent in early lumbering on the Island. Of fourteen subscribers to the Vancouver Steam Saw Mill Company five were ship captains, the rest Hudson's Bay officials or associates.[2] The Company itself introduced the first steam saw mill machinery to Victoria in 1853, but the venture failed from lack of sufficient capital, and the mill did little before it was destroyed by fire in 1859.

This, then, was the restrictive climate for business enterprise in early Victoria: lack of funds outside the Company for any but the smallest scale of operations, and lack of stimulating demands generally. The San

474

Francisco market itself was far from satisfactory, when the products of Washington or Oregon were competitive and closer, and also did not face duties there. During the California boom that reached a peak in 1853, demands had been high enough to make the Vancouver Island lumber trade important; and of the nineteen lumber ships that left Victoria that year eighteen were bound for San Francisco.[3] When the boom faded, however, so did much of the Island's wood trade. Coal did better, earning a place in the California market as good steamer fuel; but again it could suffer from price fluctuations and the competition of coal from Britain, Australia, or the eastern United States. In short, down to 1858, Victoria had not yet found a trade pattern that could encourage much business growth. Then came gold, to change the picture almost overnight.

In the spring of 1858, news of gold strikes in British territory along the lower Thompson and Fraser valleys reached San Francisco. The mass hysteria that makes gold rushes surged within the city, and thousands prepared to leave for a new El Dorado. Some might make their way to Puget Sound or by rough overland trails up through the mountainous interior, but most chose the quickest, surest route by sea, the four-day passage to Victoria. For here was a port of entry to the British far western domains, the one place of settlement in all that wilderness. It offered a base of supply and a point of transhipment for the river journey up the treacherous Fraser, unnavigable by large ocean-going vessels. The importance of already existing patterns of transport in focussing this flow of traffic is fully evident here. The mass of shipping that was now swept into highly profitable runs to Victoria was simply following a recognized lane to an established harbour that lay beside the entrance to the Gulf of Georgia, from where the fur trade had long maintained contact with the mainland posts of the interior by way of the Fraser route.

For Victoria, however, the flow of ships brought golden inundation by waves of eager miners, who needed food and shelter, transport to the interior, supplies beyond what they had carried with them, and had money to spend for it all. The first four hundred and fifty arrived in April on the American steamer *Commodore*. They came in ever-mounting numbers through the summer, until, it was estimated, the town's population had climbed to seven thousand.[4] Most of the newcomers soon had to be housed under canvas; Victoria became a veritable tent city. But construction proceeded rapidly, brick as well as wooden buildings going up, while land values soared — rising for choice lots from an initial fifty dollars to three thousand dollars and more.[5] For with the miners had come entrepreneurs with capital, store and hotel keepers, commission merchants, and real estate buyers, who were ready to invest in the business which they envisaged would acrue to Victoria from its services to the gold fields.

Some, of course, were essentially speculators, planning to grab a quick return and move on. Others were agents of established San Francisco firms, seeking profitable new branches, and still others were more vaguely attracted by the thought of commercial opportunities in another California-like boom. Many would leave, especially after the initial enthusiasm of the rush ran out in disillusionment by the winter, and contraction and depression followed. But enough of the new commercial element remained, along with miners in the hinterland, to bring an enduring change to Victoria. And when the next year sufficient finds further up the Fraser kept the mining frontier going, then its main outlet continued to grow also as a town. Though Victoria's population had fallen back under three thousand by 1860,[6] it had indeed become an urban centre with a trading pattern of its own, supplying a considerable market on the mainland and exporting quantities of gold to San Francisco.

The pattern was strengthened in 1860, when Governor Douglas declared the town a free port. New Westminster, established near the mouth of the Fraser in 1858 as capital of the new mainland province of British Columbia, faced the burden of customs duties as well as the problems of Fraser navigation. It became little more than a river-steamboat halt, while Victoria remained the terminus for ocean shipping. The Vancouver Island town, indeed, had the best of both worlds: free external contact with an international, maritime traffic system, customs and licenses on the mainland to check encroachments on its inland trade from over the American border. Accordingly, although Victoria's business life, like its population, ebbed and flowed with the fortunes of gold mining, it nevertheless acquired substance and solidity as an entrepot, building a merchant group alongside the older Hudson's Bay and official elements that would steadily gain in stature.

Its business community grew particularly with the new rush to the Cariboo goldfields in 1862. Over the next two years, as Barkerville and other mining towns grew up far in the interior, as the Cariboo Road was opened to serve the fields, and as their deeper-driven mines increasingly needed capital and a greater volume of supplies, Victoria once more grew apace. But this time its business operations were necessarily on a bigger scale, in provisioning, transporting, and financing for the larger enterprises of the Cariboo — where, moreover, farming and ranching were soon widening the bases of hinterland activities. It was good evidence of growth when Victoria was incorporated as a city in 1862, and its Chamber of Commerce was organized in 1863. That year, indeed, *The British Columbian and Victoria Guide and Directory* could say of the new city, "Her true position as the center and headquarters of commerce north of the Columbia has been placed beyond a doubt."[7]

In these early years of growth, Victoria's business community of several hundreds had acquired some significant characteristics, as well as many individuals worthy of note. One frequently remarked feature was the high proportion of Americans in the rising merchant group; another, its strongly marked cosmopolitan flavour as well. The former was to be expected from the commercial ties that made Victoria an outpost of San Francisco. The latter reflected the multi-national nature of gold rush society, whether among miners or those who would mine the miners, and whether in California or the British possessions to the north. But if Victoria had become "in effect, San Francisco in miniature,"[8] it none the less had features of its own. There were the continuing elements of the older settler society and the Hudson's Bay–official elite. Some of their members did quite well by the Victoria boom, in hotels, stores, and real estate; James Yates, for instance, piling up sufficient fortune to retire. Besides, other businessmen of British or British North American background arrived to share in the town's expansion, and later more generally stayed on, when Americans tended to withdraw. Finally, some of the "American" business migrants were better included in the multi-national category, since a number of them had earlier been immigrants to the United States; and, having moved on temporarily to San Francisco, had now moved on again.

In this regard, it has been noted that of the first 450 newcomers who arrived in 1858 aboard the *Commodore* from San Francisco, only about 120 were either British or Americans (about equally divided), the rest being mainly German, French, or Italian.[9] There was also a notable Jewish admixture in the cosmopolitan influx of the gold-rush era, not to mention a significant contingent of American Negroes, and additional numbers of Slavs, Hawaiians, and Chinese. The commercial community that took shape in Victoria was more Anglo-American in its upper ranks, more varied on the level of small shopkeepers or skilled tradesmen. Yet French, German, and Jewish names figured prominently on the higher levels, while two Negroes, Mifflin Gibbs and Peter Lester, set up the first large general store to compete effectively with that of the Hudson's Bay Company.[10]

Adolph Sutro, a cultivated German Jew, arrived in 1858 to extend the wholesale and retail tobacco business he and his brothers had established in San Francisco. The Sutro warehouse in Victoria continued under brothers Gustav and Emil, though Adolph shortly afterward returned to San Francisco, to make a fortune in the Comstock Lode and became one of the Californian city's most lavish benefactors.[11] In similar fashion David and Isaac Oppenheimer, also German Jews, arrived from California to develop a wholesale dry goods business in Victoria. After flourishing for years, they were to move to the newly founded town of Vancouver, where they became two of its wealthiest citizens and David a celebrated mayor.[12]

And in the days of the rising Victoria business community there were, besides Sutros and Oppenheimers, men like Selim and Lumley Franklin, English-born Jews, who again came in the early wave from San Francisco. They were two of Victoria's first auctioneers, prospered in real estate and as commission agents, promoted shipping and cattle sales. Selim, moreover, sat for Victoria in the Vancouver Island legislature from 1860 to 1866, while Lumley was mayor of the city in 1865.[13] Still further, there were names like Ghiradelli and Antonovich, commission merchants, Jacob Sehl, furniture dealer from Coblentz, and P. Manciet, who kept the Hotel de France (a leading establishment in the sixties), all to demonstrate the variety of this new little urban business world.[14]

As for Americans, almost the most significant for the future was William Parsons Sayward, of New England origin. In 1858 he came up from a lumber business in San Francisco to found a similar one in Victoria. His wharf and yards grew over the years; but, more important, he went into sawmilling at Mill Bay in 1861, and ultimately became one of the chief figures in lumbering on the North Pacific coast.[15] Then, there was C. C. Pendergast who opened an office for Wells Fargo in Victoria in 1858. From the start, Wells Fargo played a major part in banking, in exporting gold to San Francisco, and for some time in handling mail for the business community: all of which made "Colonel" Pendergast a man of wide regard.[16] Equally well regarded was T.N. Hibben, a South Carolinian whose stationery and bookselling firm, begun in 1858, would have a long existence in Victoria. Still others prominent in the American segment of the community were Edgar Marvin, hardware and farm machinery importer (an 1862 arrival who became United States consul), and J.A. McCrea and P.M. Backus, both auctioneers.[17] Theirs was an important occupation at the time, when so many cargoes as well as properties inland were disposed of through auction sales.

There were also agents of San Francisco shipping lines, wholesalers, and forwarding houses in the Victoria trade; for example, Samuel Price and Company, Dickson, De Wolf and Company, or Green Brothers. Sometimes their local representatives were Americans, but often instead they were Victorians of British background, serving as local partners in their firm — which itself might reach back far beyond San Francisco in a chain of interlocking partnerships to New York, Liverpool, and London. Dickson De Wolf, for example (locally Dickson and Campbell), was based on H.N. Dickson's of London, and also had houses or correspondents in Liverpool, Boston, and Halifax.[18] Yet from the time of the Fraser gold rush, a good deal of Victoria's expanding wholesale trade was handled by local commission agents and general merchants, who of course had San Francisco correspondents. And in this field it seems evident that the British segment of the business community became particularly important.

The relative prominence of British wholesale merchants in the basic import trades no doubt related to the fact of operating in British territory, and the likelihood of their securing better contacts with colonial authorities or the still influential Hudson's Bay Company — not to mention the possibility of their having useful business ties back to Great Britain herself, where some of them returned to visit. A good illustration is that of J. J. Southgate, an Englishman who had been a commission merchant and ship-handler in San Francisco, but moved to Victoria in 1858 with a letter of introduction to Governor Douglas. Southgate soon prospered there, gaining, for example, a contract to provision His Majesty's warships lying in nearby Esquimalt harbour.[19] He built a fine brick store (still standing), with financial backing from Commander H.D. Lascelles, R.N., dealt in real estate, took the lead in organizing a Masonic Lodge, and was elected to the legislature in 1860.[20] Another example is that of the Lowe brothers, Thomas and James, two Scots commission merchants in San Francisco, who similarly transferred their business to Victoria in 1861–62. Thomas was an old Hudson's Bay man who had close links with the Company trading network along the coast, and in the fifties had pioneered in selling coal from the Company's Vancouver Island mines in the San Francisco market.[21] It was notable, incidentally, that the Lowe firm wrote the letter of introduction that Southgate carried to Douglas.[22] Subsequently the brothers took over the latter's wholesale business when he was absent in England; and James Lowe became President of the Chamber of Commerce in 1866, though he failed to win election to parliament in 1869.

479

Among many other leading early British businessmen one may mention R.C. Janion, with Liverpool and Honolulu connections, J. Robertson Stewart, Robert Burnaby, and G.M. Sproat — President of the local St. Andrew's Society in 1863. Born in Kirkcudbrightshire, Gilbert Sproat had come to Vancouver Island in 1860 in the service of Anderson and Company, a big London firm of shipowners and shipbrokers who were developing a large steam sawmill at Alberni on the west coast of the Island. He became manager of the mill himself when its initiator, Captain Edward Stamp, resigned; but he also built up his own importing and insurance business in Victoria.[23] Another Anderson employee was to become Sproat's partner, Andrew Welch, an Englishman with a distinguished business career ahead of him. And Thomas Harris, also from England, Victoria's first butcher, grew to be a well-to-do provisioner and the city's mayor in 1862.

The British element was also found in banking, for the wealthy London-based and chartered Bank of British North America had opened a Victoria branch in 1859. A few months previous, however, the town's first private bank had already been established by Alexander Macdonald, an enterprising Scotsman who had come up from California with the gold rush in hopes of living by it. He did well at first, making advances in gold dust for sale in San Francisco. But in 1864 his bank was burgled (through the roof) of well over $25,000, which ruined him, and sent him fleeing back to California.[24] The Bank of British Columbia, again London-based with a royal charter of 1862, proved more substantial and reliable, helping to finance wholesale operations, and soon, indeed, the government itself.

"British" at this period quite properly could cover subjects of the Queen who came to Victoria from the eastern colonies of British North America. It is of interest to note that there was some (prospective) Canadian content in contemporary Victoria business and professional circles, as evidenced by Thomas Earle, wholesale grocer and later member of parliament, an Upper Canadian who arrived in 1862.[25] Gradually more eastern British Americans did appear, usually still by way of California; but one of the earliest significant indications of their coming was in journalism. The first newspaper, the *Victoria Gazette*, established in June, 1858, may have been an extension of American press enterprise, but it is worth observing that its publisher, James W. Towne of California, was born in Nova Scotia.[26] And the far more important David Higgins, who arrived in 1860 and subsequently would edit Victoria's enduring *Colonist* for many years, was similarly of Nova Scotian birth, if American upbringing.[27] Above all, there was the founder and first editor of the *British Colonist* (begun late in 1858), Amor de Cosmos, also a native Nova Scotian, who also came via California. His vehement and erratic career in press and politics may not suggest too close an analogy with Joseph Howe; but at least there was some Nova Scotian ingredient added to early Victoria, through this transplanting of Bluenoses from one coast to another.

480

The character of this business community, strongly associated with the American Pacific metropolis but also with the older British metropolis of the Atlantic, did not greatly change for years the stamp it had received in the gold boom era of the early 1860's. New men were to come forward, additional interests to develop; but the men largely emerged out of older firms and partnerships, and the broader economic developments did not alter Victoria's basic role as a maritime commercial entrepot serving a simple extractive hinterland. Of course, declining gold production from the mid-sixties onward, the coming of Confederation with Canada in 1871, and the mounting influence of Canadian metropolitan power thereafter — signalized by the National Policy of 1878 and the building of the Canadian Pacific in the next decade — all brought significant changes that inevitably affected Victoria business more and more. Yet well into the 1880's, and perhaps even to the nineties, the patterns of Victorian commercial society set between 1858 and 1864 continued as a basis; even while American or continental European elements within it decreased or were assimilated, and British and Canadian elements were enlarged. This, then, is the general framework for the next two decades. It remains to discuss the newer activities and the newer men that did emerge inside it.

The falling output of the gold mines after 1864, and the failure to find rich, easily workable new fields, did not seriously harm Victoria at first, still living on the momentum, so to speak, of the expectations of more finds, and with some stimulus to trade derived from the American Civil War. Falling gold revenues and heavy colonial debt burdens, however, did lead in 1866 to the union of Vancouver Island and British Columbia as an urgent move of retrenchment. And this union sharply affected Victoria by removing its privileges as a free port. It was almost the hand-writing on the wall; continental costs of development and need for customs duties had defeated the interests of maritime free trade. At the public proclamation in Victoria of the new united province of British Columbia, so the Colonist noted, members of the crowd variously informed the sheriff that he was reading his death-warrant, warned a red-nosed bystander that port was no longer duty-free, and urged "a seedy-looking individual" to hurry up Government Street and buy a suit while he could still save fifteen per cent.[28] At least there was the consolation that Victoria remained provincial capital — to New Westminster's chagrin.

Activity in lumbering had offset in some degree the lessening role of gold. At Alberni, Gilbert Sproat's steam saw mill had reached a splen-did peak in 1863, producing over eleven million feet of lumber, until the rapid exhaustion of timber close to water, accessible to the hand or ox-logging of those days, forced its closing by 1865.[29] However, the saw mill that W.P. Sayward had opened in 1863 up the Island's east coast near Cowichan thrived on a more accessible timber supply. In 1864 his mill alone brought two million feet to Victoria, and by the close of the decade put him into the export trade.[30] At the time of the union of 1866, moreover, there were six Vancouver Island saw mills in operation, much of their produce being marketed by way of Victoria. Furthermore, during the depression of the later sixties, they and the Burrard Inlet mills, that had now appeared on the mainland at Moodyville and Hastings, ended the former dominance of American Puget Sound mills over the import market.[31] While for some years following, Island lumbering failed to grow markedly, an important productive basis had been laid for future development, in which the Sayward milling and lumbering interests would play full part.

481

Then there was coal. In 1858 the Hudson's Bay Company had returned control of Vancouver Island to the Crown, and the next year its trading rights on the mainland had ended. Thereafter the Company had sought to concentrate on its original concern, the fur trade, divesting itself of other complicating ventures, such as its coal mines in the Nanaimo area. Thus in 1862 it sold these holdings to the Vancouver Island Coal Mining and Land Company, which was based in England and backed by British capital. (It also seems to have had an oddly literary connection, since T.C. Haliburton was its first chairman and among its investors were Agnes Strickland and the father of John Galsworthy.)[32] In Victoria, the thriving firm of Dickson, Campbell and Company served as its agents, George Campbell being made a director. Much of the Vancouver Coal

Company's output went directly from Nanaimo to market, to San Francisco or the Royal Navy based at Esquimalt. But some as well went via Victoria, where Charles Wallace, also of Dickson and Campbell, managed the two ships that the Company bought for its trade in 1864.[33] The next year coal production rose to 32,000 tons; and to 44,000 in 1868.[34] But by 1870 it seemed to have reached a plateau, and in the following decade the Company ran into trouble, owing to lack of further capital to develop new mines, and competition not only in the American market but within Vancouver Island itself.

The latter competition came from Robert Dunsmuir, the son of a Scottish coal master, who had first been employed at Nanaimo in the Hudson's Bay Company mines, but had been engaged in his own independent workings there since 1855. In 1864 another English coal mining venture, the Harewood Company, was launched, backed by the Hon. H.D. Lascelles, commanding H.M.S. *Forward*, and Dunsmuir became its resident manager.[35] Though he drove his miners rigorously (which did not stop them entertaining him to a public tea that year),[36] he could not overcome the fact that the Harewood Mine, after starting well, began to peter out. Dunsmuir withdrew. In 1869, however, he discovered the truly rich Wellington Mine, and set up a company to work it, with financial aid from another naval officer, Lieutenant W.N. Diggle of the Grappler.[37] The Dunsmuir Company soon flourished, having one of the best coal seams on the coast and thus well able to stand the competition in the San Francisco market. Moreover, it undertook dock and railway developments at Nanaimo that ministered to that town's growth. And some of the benefit would redound to Victoria, since it kept much of the supply trade of the area. Hence, by the seventies, at least, growth in this coal hinterland could help balance decline in the older one of gold.

And then there was shipping. During the 1860's Victoria became the centre of shipping and shipbuilding interests of its own. It started, of course, with the rush of mining traffic to the Fraser. At the outset the Hudson's Bay Company had commanded the transport service; its pioneer steamers, the *Beaver* and *Otter*, would long be famous around the coasts and up the lower reaches of the river. But because of the demands for transport during the gold rush, Governor Douglas had recognized the need to allow American steamboat captains to enter the river navigation. A number of veterans of Puget Sound or Columbia River steamboating thus came in, and largely found it practicable to make Victoria their base of operations, as the main terminus of the Fraser trade. Captain William Irving became the most prominent and enduring of them — but here again the description of "American" is misleading, since he was a Scot, with much seagoing experience behind him before he pioneered with the first steamboat in Oregon.[38]

Irving joined with another Scottish steamboat pioneer from the Columbia, Alexander Murray, to build the stern-wheeler *Governor Douglas* at Victoria in 1858, her engine being brought from San Francisco.[39] This "first steamer built in the province for the inland trade" was soon joined by a sister ship, the *Colonel Moody*.[40] The previously mentioned merchants, Thomas and James Lowe, invested in the vessels; James for a time was an agent for the line, as were the also-mentioned Samuel Price and Company.[41] Irving built still more ships at Frahey's yard in Victoria, the *Reliance* in 1862 and the *Onward* in 1865.[42] The Hudson's Bay Company also acquired new craft to meet their competition and that from American steamboats. But the fall in gold-mining activity after 1864 led American captains to leave the Fraser, so that for the rest of the decade Irving's and the Bay Company's ships between them controlled the river.[43] Indeed, this situation virtually continued until Captain Irving's death in 1872, and afterwards his son, John Irving, built a still larger shipping domain.

Joseph Spratt was significant also, because the Albion Iron Works, the foundry and marine machinery works he established in Victoria in 1862, became central to the subsequent growth of the city's shipping activities. After having had some training as a marine engineer in England, Spratt had gone to San Francisco, where he had opened a foundry and reputedly built the first steam locomotive on the Pacific coast.[44] As well as running his iron works, he went into shipbuilding, later salmon-canning and whaling, and organized a shipping line up the island's east coast. In any case, by the end of the 1860's he had added the beginnings of industrial enterprise to Victoria. And by that time, too, nine of the seventeen steamers trading to British Columbia and eighteen of the twenty-eight schooners were Victoria-built.[45]

483

As the sixties drew to a close, however, the city was in a state of depression. The newer activities in lumber, coal, or shipbuilding had not yet hit full stride, and what was still far more apparent was the passing of the gold frontier, with its consequent effects on the wholesale trade, real estate, and financial interests of the Victoria entrepot. Business in the city in 1869 was so slow, in fact, that thistles grew in the gutters along Government Street, while the population was falling back again to little more than three thousand.[46] In this condition, it is not surprising that the business community was considerably despondent, or that, in the midst of continuing discussions on joining the new and far-off Canadian Confederation, some of its members might look to the simpler, sharper release of annexation to the United States. At any rate, the Annexation Petition of 1869 appeared in Victoria in November, signed with 104 names in all.

It is true that this was a limited number; that many of the signers were small men, not leading merchants; and that they included a large element of foreign born who had no strong political positions, either anti-British or pro-American, but voiced what was indeed "primarily an expression of economic discontent."[47] It is also true that the essential issue in Victoria was union with Canada or no union; that annexation was never a real alternative. Yet it is possible, besides, that doubts and fears expressed in anti-unionism among Victorians found a sharper focus in some of those businessmen who did subscribe to annexation: a matter of choosing the devil you knew at San Francisco to the distant unknown one at Ottawa, especially when the former so obviously commanded power and fortune. And certainly one might see concern for the wholesale trade or property values in such substantial signatories as Isaac Oppenheimer and David Shirpser, dry goods merchants, W.H. Oliver and W. Farron, heavy investors in Victoria real estate, or Emil Sutro, tobacco merchant, and T.N. Hibben, the prominent stationer.[48]

At all events, the flurry passed with little consequence; and within a few months Confederation was settled policy. By the time it took place in July, 1871, a brighter Victoria was ready to welcome it, hopeful indeed of the terms that had been agreed upon, including a railway to link East and West. For it well might be expected that a Pacific railway would have its terminus in or near Victoria, crossing to Vancouver Island over the narrows at its northern tip. Certainly the fact that a survey party for the projected Canadian Pacific were present in Victoria for the celebrations that accompanied the proclamation of British Columbia's entry into Confederation did not lessen the festivity.[49] And Victoria's businessmen could thus anticipate that change would also mean improvement for their community.

As the 1870's opened, it was a good thing that Victorians did have expectations from Confederation, for times continued slow in many respects: their city's population only passed 4,600 by 1874.[50] However, they could look to some federal relief from the provincial debt burden, some aid from a broader union in meeting the high costs of developing transport in the rugged hinterland. And there was the prospect of the railway, which raised new visions of Victoria as the San Francisco of the North, with its own transcontinental rail link like the newly opened Union Pacific, and its own Pacific oceanic empire of trade. Politically, at least, the city had been connected into a new continental system. Now it looked for the necessary communication network to be constructed also, to put it on the highroads of world development.

Gradually, moreover, its basic hinterland trades improved.

Gold production, after reaching a low point in 1870, went up in 1871, and up still further in 1874–75, although it never came near the scale of the early sixties.[51] Coal output also began a steady climb from 1873 to 1879, though bigger years of growth would come in the next decade.[52] And if lumbering on the Island experienced no great advance yet, a new hinterland enterprise of considerable export potential made its appearance: salmon-canning. The salmon-canning industry had reached the American Pacific coast in the 1860's, from earlier beginnings in Maine and New Brunswick; but it was first established on the lower Fraser

484

in 1870, independent of any American connection.[53] Victoria commission merchants effectively financed the Fraser river canneries and acted as agents in exporting their product directly to Great Britain.[54] For the canning process offered a means of overcoming the barrier of distance between a rich North Pacific food resource and a hungry industrial market. Furthermore, it produced a valuable trade that did not face the impediment of ever-rising American tariff barriers.

British Columbian salmon-canning grew slowly at first in the seventies, faster in the eighties, by which time the industry had spread northward to the Skeena (in 1877) and to the Nass and beyond. Victoria businessmen continued to play a major role in the enterprise: J.H. Todd provides a good example. Born in Brampton, Upper Canada, he had gone to Barkerville in 1863, speculated in mines and operated a successful merchandising business before moving to Victoria in 1872 to undertake another. Through profits from mining properties, and through acting as agent for canners on the Fraser, the Todd wholesaling firm was able to acquire two canneries there and another at Esquimalt. Subsequently it added a much larger one on the Skeena obtained from another prominent Victoria house of the day, Turner, Beeton and Company. Todd and Sons, in fact, continued to operate from Victoria as late as 1954, its fishing interests ultimately going to B.C. Packers.[55]

485

Furthermore, the redoubtable Joseph Spratt of the Albion Iron Works early entered the business. He developed the oilery (for pressing out herring oil) that he had opened on Burrard Inlet in 1868, at the site of the present city of Vancouver, into a floating salmon cannery.[56] Popularly termed "Spratt's Ark," it was a pioneer in the area's canning industry. More important in the long run, however, was R.P. Rithet, a Victoria wholesale merchant of widespread interests and enterprises. After acting as an agent for local Fraser river canners, he organized a number of them into the Victoria Canning Company in 1891, to meet the competition of two British-backed companies, British Columbia Canning and Anglo-British Columbia Packing, who had acquired virtually all the other canneries on the river.[57] That story, however, runs beyond this study, and it is more important here to examine the advancing career of Robert Paterson Rithet as an exemplification of Victoria business in itself.

Born in Scotland in 1844, he was in the Cariboo in 1862; but after a few years came to Victoria, still in his early twenties, to find employment in the wholesale trade. In 1868 he was working for Sproat and Company; indeed, was running its Victoria office, since Gilbert Sproat, a man of many parts — merchant, insurance agent, sawmill manager, lobbyist, author, and ethnologist — was then mainly in London, directing the Committee on the Affairs of British Columbia that he had organized.[58] The next year Rithet moved to San Francisco, to deal with the firm's interests there; evidently a promotion, for Sproat had sent him "kind words of confidence" by letter.[59] And here he came in close contact with Sproat's San Francisco partner, Andrew Welch. Welch, who had begun as a bookkeeper from England and worked with Sproat in the Alberni sawmill before entering into partnership in his wholesale business, was already emerging as a wealthy and prominent member of the San Francisco commercial elite. Before his death in 1889 he was to become a millionaire several times over, do much to develop the shipping trade between Victoria and that city, gain control of the Burrard Inlet mills at Moodyville, and thus build up a large-scale lumber export business.[60] Rithet could hardly have made a better connection. It resulted, eventually, in his own partnership with Welch.

Before that transpired, he returned to Victoria, still in Sproat's service; and there in 1870 had a stiff little encounter with a Mrs. Sutton, who did not approve of his attentions to her daughter. In fact, he broke his engagement to Miss Sutton by formal note to her mama — a Victorian touch in the wider sense of the term.[61] That year, moreover, Rithet left Sproat's firm to join that of J. Robertson Stewart, one of the old original British merchants in Victoria, who carried on insurance business for British and American companies, and helped direct the British Columbian Investment and Loan Society, as well as operating a large wholesale warehouse.[62] In May of 1871, Rithet was "at present managing his business" because of Stewart's illness.[63] The latter soon decided to dispose of his interests and retire to Scotland. Andrew Welch bought him out, with Rithet's cordial approval.[64] In fact, that August a new firm was announced in the press, Welch, Rithet and Company, successors to J. Robertson Stewart. "We began," wrote Rithet, "under very favorable auspices, when the colony seems to be about to enter an era of improvement and progress. . . . with houses in San Francisco and Liverpool we should be able to make a business, and our outside connections arc also tip-top."[65]

Thereafter through the seventies, and on into the eighties, Rithet's interests continued to grow: in wholesaling, shipping, insurance, lumbering, canning, grocery importing, and generally financial investment in a wide range of enterprises. With Welch, he became engaged in the sugar trade of the Hawaiian Islands; they acquired control of plantations there.[66] He invested in the mills at Moodyville, the Albion Iron Works, in sealing, whaling, and in farming. He became president of the Board of Trade and a justice of the peace in the 1870's, mayor of Victoria in 1885, then was elected to the legislature in the 1890's.[67] And on Welch's death he took over as head of both Welch and Company, San Francisco, and R.P. Rithet and Company, Victoria.[68] There is no space to deal with his later ventures in the mining and railway development of the British Columbia interior, nor in the building of deepwater dock facilities at Victoria through his Victoria Wharf and Warehouse Company. All that can be noted is his connection with the continued growth of the city's shipping interests through the founding of the Canadian Pacific Navigation Company in 1883. And this brings in another of the leading Victorian entrepreneurs of the era, John Irving.

Irving had assumed control of his father's steamship company in 1872, although only eighteen years of age. Gold discoveries in the Stikeen and Cassiar districts in the seventies revived the coastal shipping trade, and Irving moved vigorously into competition, adding new boats to his fleet. At the same time growing settlement on the mainland and its expanding needs produced more traffic to the Fraser, while soon plans for the Pacific railway's construction brought a further stimulus. In 1878 Irving obtained a contract to carry the first shipment of rails from Esquimalt to Yale, and from then on increasingly left all rivals behind.[69] His chief competitor was still the Hudson's Bay Company's fleet. In 1883 he successfully arranged to merge it with his own.

It might not be without significance that a year earlier John Irving had married the daughter of Alexander Munro, Chief Factor of the Company in Victoria — nor that two of the bride's brothers worked for R.P. Rithet, who himself had married one of the Munro girls in 1875.[70] At any rate, the Canadian Pacific Navigation Company that now emerged to combine the lines under his management had Rithet as one of its directors and chief shareholders, along with Munro and that other noted business figure, Robert Dunsmuir of colliery fame.[71] Understandably, one of the line's fast ships was the *R.P. Rithet*. Irving's shipping empire (a far cry from Captain Cooper's little schooner, *Alice*) took over minor companies at the end of the eighties, and increasingly went into inland navigation on the lakes of the interior. It was ultimately bought out by the Canadian Pacific Railway as its coastal service in 1900. That, in itself, marked the passing of Victoria's as well as Irving's steamboat hegemony; but it had been a very good run indeed.

487

Meanwhile Robert Dunsmuir's coal operations had grown steadily. In 1873 his one mine, the Wellington, had turned out 16,000 tons (just entering full production) to 45,000 for all those of the Vancouver Island Coal Company's.[72] In 1880, his holdings alone produced 189,000 tons, and three years later he bought out his partner for $600,000.[73] He was well on his way to being the province's outstanding industrial capitalist, with a fleet of cargo vessels, a mine railway, and a large part of the Albion Iron Works besides.[74] As if to fit the classic picture of the nineteenth-century capitalist, he had a hard reputation with labour. He faced strikes at the mines in 1877 and 1883, brought in strikebreakers, and on the former violent occasion, a gunboat and the militia also. Apart from this, Dunsmuir, now settled in Victoria, was also moving into railway promotions and construction. In 1883, the Esquimalt Railway Company of which he was president (it included the powerful figures, Leland Stanford and Charles Crocker of San Francisco, and C.P. Huntington of New York) obtained a contract from the federal government to build the Esquimalt and Nanaimo line, on terms that included a lavish grant of land.[75] Begun in 1884 under Dunsmuir's direction, it was finished in 1886, for the first time giving Victoria overland access to the coal hinterland.

Yet the seventy-mile Esquimalt and Nanaimo was a rather small consolation prize for Victoria not securing the Canadian Pacific — which was essentially what it had turned out to be. Through much of the seventies the city had envisioned and urged the transcontinental line by way of Bute Inlet and Seymour Narrows to Vancouver Island, and hotly protested proposals for a Fraser valley route to tidewater instead. In 1874 the railway on the Island was at least promised anew by the Mackenzie federal government, but the bill for it was defeated in the Senate, leaving Victoria bitterly disappointed, and much angry talk of secession in political and business circles. But though the dispute rose and fell in the ensuing years, with recurrent swells of separatism again, the fact was that the capital or the Island did not necessarily speak for the province as a whole; and the British Columbian mainland communities saw far more benefit to be gained from a Fraser valley rail route. Here was, indeed, still further indication that the island community of Victoria had been brought into a continental system, and now had little weight to bear against the whole thrust of Canadian metropolitan designs. The best that could be done was look for consolation prizes.

The Esquimalt dry dock and the E. & N. itself were two of these. And by the time that Dunsmuir undertook to build the latter (seeking truly magnificent consolation for himself and friends in terms for subsidies, coal fields, and lands), Victoria interests were ready to make the best of the inevitable. Hence, in 1884, when the C.P.R. was already well advanced in its building, both up the Fraser and into the Rockies from the east, a final settlement of terms was harmoniously achieved. Victoria still had a sizeable and prosperous maritime trading domain; its population stood at twelve thousand that year,[76] and the city was thriving and hopeful. For at least it would have its own Island railway now.

Not only was the Island railway opened in 1886, but the C.P.R. that year also carried its first through trains to the Pacific — to Burrard Inlet. And this really marked the ending of an era for Victoria, for now Vancouver's meteoric rise was under way, as the true beneficiary of the transcontinental railway, the National Policy, and the forces of Canadian metropolitanism in general. The little lumber settlement on the Inlet had been launched into its role as Canada's chief western outlet and Pacific port of entry. Not till 1898 did the import trade of the upstart city pass that of Victoria's; yet the trend was there before that was to make Vancouver the new British Columbian entrepot and distributing centre.[77] In the later eighties and nineties Victoria would further develop its coal, salmon, and lumber trades, along with new growth in deep-sea fishing, scaling, and also in grain exports. But a reorientation of commercial patterns from sea to land was in process, in which Victoria could not hope to dominate great new hinterlands of deep-rock mining in the interior ranges or of agriculture on the prairies. A phase was over for the maritime city; and the completion of the transcontinental railway signalized it better than anything else.

There had not been want of energy or initiative in the Victorian business community. Men like Rithet, Dunsmuir, and Irving demonstrated that fact, as did W.P. Sayward, who had built a large new lumber mill at Victoria in 1878 — which by 1890, was cutting nearly eleven million feet a year itself, while Sayward's logging camps were scattered up the Island, feeding his large-scale export trade.[78] Others, perhaps, in the community had showed less enterprise, being more content with things as they were, in a pleasantly civilized little world readily open to greater worlds in San Francisco or London, but remote from the harder, cruder surroundings of the continental interior. Yet it would be difficult to prove such a point; and in any case it was not so much lack of enterprise as lack of situation and economic leverage that had placed it beyond the power of Victoria's businessmen to deal with changing patterns of trade. They had responded successfully to various favourable factors in the climate of enterprise; there was not much that could be done when the unfavorable overtook them.

There are many other names that could be singled out in the period of the seventies and eighties that would show the general stability and substance of this business community. Many firms from gold rush days continued in being, carrying on names like Southgate, Hibben, Dickson and Campbell, Sehl, Pendergast, Heisterman, and others. Some early merchants indeed had died, retired or left, the Lowes going, one to Scotland, one to San Francisco, in the seventies; David Oppenheimer shrewdly moving to Vancouver in 1886, to become "the father of Vancouver's jobbing trade."[79] Yet there were still others who had known Victoria's earlier days actively on hand, like William Ward, manager of the Bank of British Columbia since 1867 and clerk before that, or A.H. Green of Garesche and Green, whose large private bank had taken over from Wells Fargo in 1873 but who had worked for that agency previously.[80] A notable feature of the Victoria commercial community, in short, was still its continuity; new leaders largely rose from within its own ranks. But no doubt this was a result of there having been no spectacular advances since the gold rush to bring new groups of entrepreneurs. Victoria was already an "old," settled, quietly growing town, after less than three decades of urban existence.

Its ties with San Francisco and Britain remained fully evident. In 1886, the bulk of its external trade was still directed to the former, though British goods continued to be of much significance as imports, and exports of salmon to Britain (and eastern Canada) were fast rising. Offsetting San Francisco influence, of course, was British influence through politics, capital investment, business personnel, and the very dealings with major firms in San Francisco that were themselves part of a London–Liverpool and Glasgow metropolitan network; like Welch and Company, Dickson, De Wolf, Falkner Bell, and several others.[81] Noticeable, too, was the growth of eastern Canadian agencies and imports in Victoria by this time, behind the national tariff wall; but nothing comparable to the change effected in a few years through the C.P.R. — to which one might ascribe the fact that advertisements for Canadian firms and products clearly began to displace those of San Francisco in Victoria directories by about 1890.

And thus, in a sense, passed the San Francisco of the North, gradually to be replaced with today's centre of tourism and retirement enterprises, and of that truly big modern growth-industry, provincial government. Yet the businessmen who had seen Victoria rise from a fort or a gold rush tent town to a flourishing port city in well under thirty years, had no cause to minimize the comfortable affluence they had acquired, and done much to give to their adopted home.

What had the business community done for Victoria? In the first place — without at all forgetting other factors, the role of politicians and bureaucrats, of the labour force, or simply, the citizenry of consumers — they had essentially shaped its economic functions, furnished the bulk of jobs and services that made it an operative centre of urban population. In the second place, they had considerably influenced its political, social, and cultural life, businessmen having widely entered into provincial and municipal politics, benevolent and religious societies, educational movements, literary and musical organizations, and the like. To deal with this would be to write another chapter. All that can be said here is that the record of early Victoria's business community in participating in primarily non-economic activities in their society seems as good as, or better than, the record of similar groups in comparable Canadian cities at similar stages of development. And this, again, is not to see this very human collectivity of fallible, self-interested individuals as peerless visionaries and altruists. It may have been more a result of Victoria's relative isolation, insularity, and small size, whereby the entrepreneurial element readily came to know, and feel committed to a fairly compact local society that did not soon become heterogeneous and amorphous through continued rapid growth.

In the third place, the business community marked Victoria's character in the broadest sense: in its identity, to use a not-unheard-of term. The city's affiliations with California that still exist surely relate not just to sea and sunshine (unlike the humidity of Vancouver and the northwest American coast) but to the historic communications and exchange that its merchants sustained with San Francisco. Victoria's oft-noted "British" attributes, also, may well be derived less from an obsolete Bay Company officialdom or a small emigrant English gentry than from the strongly British element in the dominant wholesale trades, which easily maintained the outlook and behaviour of the old gentry elite as it rose in wealth and social position. And finally, even the faint continuing touch of cosmopolitanism in an otherwise provincial city — which seems to give it a more mature ambiance than many an older Canadian town — assuredly may come from the original non-British, non-American component of the business community that largely persisted through Victoria's first formative decades. There is, then, much more in the early development of Victoria than the affairs of provincial governments or the vicissitudes of public men.

NOTES

[1] On the general significance of this theme, see D.T. Gallagher, "Bureaucrats or Businessmen? Historians and the Problem of Leadership in Colonial British Columbia," *Syesis* 3 (1970): 173–86.

[2] W.K. Lamb, "Early Lumbering on Vancouver Island," pt. 1, *British Columbia Historical Quarterly* (January 1938), 43.

[3] Lamb, "Early Lumbering," 46.

[4] *Gazette* (Victoria), December 25, 1858.

[5] Alfred Waddington, *The Frazer Mines Vindicated* (Victoria, 1858), 19.

[6] *British Colonist* (Victoria), June 12, 1860.

[7] *The British Columbian and Victoria Guide and Directory for 1863* (Victoria, 1863), 49.

[8] W. Ireland, "British Columbia's American Heritage," Canadian Historical Association, *Annual Report for 1948*, 68.

[9] Ireland, "British Columbia's American Heritage," 69.

[10] M. Ormsby, *British Columbia: A History* (Toronto, 1958), 141.

[11] R.E. and M.F. Stewart, *Adolph Sutro* (Berkeley, 1962), *passim*.

[12] "The Oppenheimers of Vancouver," typescript, British Columbia Archives (hereafter BCA).

[13] British Columbia Archives, Vertical Files (hereafter, BCAVF).

[14] Edgar Fawcett, *Some Reminiscences of Old Victoria* (Toronto, 1912), 60; British Columbia Miscellany, Bancroft Library, Berkeley.

[15] Lamb, "Early Lumbering," pt. 2, *British Columbia Historical Quarterly* (April 1938), 114.

[16] Fawcett, *Some Reminiscences*, 64.

[17] BCAVF.

[18] *Prices Current* (San Francisco). See advertisements from 1853 onward, also E. Mallandaine, *First Victoria Directory* (Victoria, 1860), 42. For Samuel Price, *Gazette*, January 25, 1858 — J.N. Thain was the local representative.

[19] *Colonist*, February 2, 1865.

[20] Fawcett, *Some Reminiscences*, 62; *British Columbian and Victoria Guide*, 137.

[21] On the Lowes, see J.M.S. Careless, "The Lowe Brothers, 1852–70: A Study in Business Relations on the North Pacific Coast," *B.C. Studies* 2 (1968–69): 1–18.

[22] Careless, "The Lowe Brothers," 10.

[23] I.M. Richard, "Gilbert Norman Sproat," *British Colonial History Quarterly* (January 1937), 22–23.

[24] BCAVF.

[25] British Columbia Miscellany, Bancroft.

[26] BCAVF.

[27] BCAVF.

[28] *Colonist*, November 20, 1866.

[29] Lamb, "Early Lumbering," pt. 2, 105.

[30] Lamb, "Early Lumbering," pt. 2, 114.

[31] Lamb, "Early Lumbering," pt. 2, 121.

[32] BCAVF.

[33] P.A. Phillips, "Confederation and the Economy of British Columbia," in W.G. Shelton, ed., *British Columbia and Confederation* (Victoria, 1967), 51, BCAVF.

[34] Phillips, "Confederation," 51.

[35] Ormsby, *British Columbia*, 215.

[36] J. Audain, *From Coal Mine to Castle* (New York, 1955), 36.

[37] Audain, *From Coal Mine to Castle*, 51.

[38] M.A. Cox, *Saga of a Seafarer* (New Westminster, 1966), 8.

[39] E.W. Wright, ed., *Marine History of the Pacific North West*, by Lewis and Dryden (New York, 1961), 81.

491

[40] Wright, ed., *Marine History*, 81.
[41] Careless, "The Lowe Brothers," 10. Lowe Papers, BCA, T. Lowe to A.C. Anderson, July 2, 1859.
[42] Wright, ed., *Marine History*, 140.
[43] Wright, ed., *Marine History*, 82.
[44] BCAVF.
[45] Phillips, "Confederation," 57.
[46] S. Higgins, "British Columbia and the Confederation Era," in Shelton, ed., *British Columbia and Confederation*, 28.
[47] Ireland, "British Columbia's American Heritage," 71.
[48] BCAVF.
[49] *British Colonist*, July 20, 1871.
[50] *City of Victoria Directory for 1890* (Victoria, 1890), 122.
[51] *Annual Report of the Minister of Mines* (Victoria, 1900), chart, n.p.
[52] *Annual Report of the Minister of Mines* (Victoria, 1900), chart, n.p.
[53] Phillips, "Confederation," 55.
[54] K. Ralston, "Patterns of Trade and Investment on the Pacific Coast, 1867–1892: The Case of the British Columbia Salmon Canning Industry," *B.C. Studies* 1 (1968–69): 42.
[55] BCAVF.
[56] J.M. Grant, "British Columbia in Early Times," *British Columbia Magazine* (June 1911), 494.
[57] Ralston, "Patterns of Trade and Investment," 42–43.
[58] Richard, "Gilbert Norman Sproat," 22–29.
[59] BCA, *R.P. Rithet Letterbook* 1, Rithet to G. Sproat, December 11, 1868. BCAVF.
[60] *Rithet Letterbook* 1, Rithet to Mrs. Sutton, April 16, 1870.
[61] *British Colonist*, November 11, 1869.
[62] *Rithet Letterbook* 1, Rithet to R.P.D. Duff, May 9, 1871.
[63] *Rithet Letterbook* 1, Rithet to A. Welch, August 24, 1871.
[64] *Rithet Letterbook* 1, August 25, 1871.
[65] *Colonist*, July 26, 1889.
[66] BCAVF. See also *Victoria Illustrated* (Victoria, 1891), 77–78.
[67] BCAVF.
[68] BCAVF.
[69] BCAVF.
[70] *Colonist*, April 17, 1889.
[71] Wright, ed., *Marine History*, 303.
[72] Audain, *From Coal Mine to Castle*, 52.
[73] Audain, *From Coal Mine to Castle*, 65, 73.
[74] *Colonist*, April 13, 1889.
[75] Audain, *From Coal Mine to Castle*, 79.
[76] *City of Victoria Directory for 1890*, 122.
[77] *Annual Reports of the British Columbia Board of Trade, 1887–1900* (Victoria, 1900), tables, n.p.
[78] *Victoria Illustrated*, 50.
[79] L. Makovski, "Rise of the Merchant Princes," *British Columbia Magazine* (June 1911), 57.
[80] BCAVF. Francis Garesche was drowned in 1874, but the firm continued in both names.
[81] See directory and newspaper advertisements of period for indications of operations of these firms. On all three, for example, see *San Francisco Directory for 1873*, M.G. Langley (San Francisco, 1873), and on Falkner Bell specifically, W.T. Jackson, *The Enterprising Scot* (Edinburgh, 1968), 222, 374, *passim*. Falkner Bell also appears in the Lowe and Rithet letters — and Jackson's work notes that the Scottish American Investment Company, for and with which they dealt, bought extensive California ranch property on the recommendation of John Clay (who had been George Brown's estate manager in Ontario), as well as involving Thomas Nelson, the leading Edinburgh publisher in its investments. Nelson was Brown's brother-in-law, who with Clay succeeded in restoring Brown's Bow Park estate to financial health after the latter's death. One can see many ramifications here worth tracing out!

492

The Character of the British Columbia Frontier*

BARRY M. GOUGH

Chief among the concerns of historians studying the founding of new societies has been the concept of the frontier, and in the writing of the

*From B.C. Studies, 32 (1976/77): 28–40. Reprinted by permission.

history of Canada, the United States, South Africa, Australia, and New Zealand, among others, the frontier has been a substantial theme.[1] "Frontier" itself has been variously defined — from the outer fringe of metropolitan influence, to the actual geographical area of control, to a zone to be occupied, to a border between states.[2] Usually such definitions tend to be Eurocentric and agrarian, describing the process of the founding of the new society in question in terms of the expanding society's change in new conditions, its occupations of lands suitable for agriculture, and its evolving legal systems. Often such historical inquiry neglects two essential ingredients: the contact of cultures and races within the zone of influence and the geographical features of the zone itself. By doing so, such studies frequently do violence to the important result of how the aboriginal society already occupying the land and exploiting its resources responded and changed in the face of new circumstances. And such research neglects the role of environment in the historical process.

Our study of the formative years of British Columbia history must, however, concern itself with the frontier, though an enlarged, more encompassing perspective is required than hitherto offered by historians of British Columbia.[3] Such an inquiry cannot be hagiographical in nature but must analyse the institutions and forces whereby British Columbia changed from Indian territory to fur trade realm, then to colony, and finally to province all within a brief span of forty years. During the years 1846 to 1871 an imperial tide lapped the shores of the Northwest Coast and in doing so changed the character of human occupation, and it brought with it at the flood new political, legal, and social institutions whose legacies are still apparent. This process forms a "frontier" and for the purposes of this paper "frontier" will be taken to mean the zone of influence of imperial administration emanating from London and from the colonial capitals of Victoria and New Westminster. Also for the purposes of this essay "frontier process" will be taken to meanthe methods by which Europeans extended their jurisdiction, occupied land, managed a resource base, developed an Indian policy, and established sites for the exploitation of the sea coast and the interior land mass. The first section of this essay examines environmental determinants, the second explores British and American influences, and the third provides a summary of the character of the British Columbia frontier and its legacies.

493

I

From the earliest European contact with the Northwest Coast, explorers understood that the nature of the environment would determine the type of human occupation in that locale. The European reconnaissance of British Columbia in the late eighteenth century revealed that the environment was generally devoid of level land suitable for agriculture. Rather they found a mountainous terrain bordering the Pacific, a land whose scale was impressive, whose physical landscape was varied. Rugged off-shore islands, inshore channels and inlets, coastal mountains and low-lands, river deltas, interior plateaus and narrow river valleys testified to the lack of level land at low elevation. Yet the sea and land provided resources for exploitation — sea otter and beaver, salmon, timber, and spars — and from the very beginning of European contact with this portion of the Northwest Coast the exporting of primary resources formed the central feature of white–Indian trade relations. Moreover, the potential resource wealth of the region brought international rivalry among Russia, Spain, Britain, and the United States, and by 1846 the present boundaries of British Columbia had been largely determined in this first rush for spoils.[4]

The British Columbia frontier properly dates from 1846 for it was in that year that British sovereignty over the region was determined by Anglo-American treaty, presumptuously without any compliance on the part of the Indians who now found that they had new political institutions with which to deal. That treaty had, the British government hoped, secured a great fur-trading preserve north of the boundary for the Hudson's Bay Company. The Oregon Boundary Dispute had underscored the conflict between fur trade and settlement on the Pacific slope: its resolution had left the Americans with lands more suitable for agricultural settlement, and it gave the British the rich fur preserve of the north.[5] Moreover, the dispute resulted in the retreat of the Hudson's Bay Company and its agricultural subsidiary, the Puget's Sound Agricultural Company, north from its Oregon holdings; and in the process the Company developed new sites of occupation and its agricultural subsidiary farmed some of the best lands available in Vancouver Island, then virtually the sole lands known to be suitable for settlement. Other lands might be available, but in some areas such as Cowichan the Indians were known to be hostile[6] and in others the availability of scarce land suitable for tillage was not discovered until the Vancouver Island Exploration Expedition of 1864. Perhaps in the end it was the mountainous, non-agrarian character of the British Columbia frontier that saved the area from American squatter settlement. Now the Hudson's Bay Company's dominance of the Pacific slope had to be confined within new political boundaries.[7]

Within this area the Hudson's Bay Company had already established a commercial network of posts, trails, and shipping routes. In 1843 Fort Victoria had been built as the focal point of Company seaborne commerce, and subsequently Forts Rupert and Nanaimo had been established to mine and market steamer coal. Forts Hope and Yale had been built to provide new transportation links north of the forty-ninth parallel.[8] Fort Langley acquired new importance on the lower Fraser while Port Simpson at the entrance to Portland Inlet became the focal point for northern trade extending to the Queen Charlotte Islands, Alaska, and the continental interior.

The patterns of resource exploitation, of corporate dominance, and of cluster settlement in and around forts had begun to appear long before miners searched tributaries of the Fraser River in 1858 for gold. The gold seekers, too, had to face environmental realities; the weather and climate were different than in some areas of California they had mined previously. Though on the lower reaches of the Fraser miners could use the "rocker" or "cradle;" on the upper Fraser they were obliged to tunnel into the pay-channel lying below the creekbed. In the dry diggings they engaged in sluicing, using quicksilver brought from California. But again, the environment determined that gold extraction would necessitate expensive hydraulic equipment and substantial financial outlay. These features influenced the early demise of the individual miners' rush of 1858–59 and the rise of companies such as the Van Winkle Company that prospered into the 1870s.[9] And not least among the geographical influences was the isolation of the area from California, the eastern seaboard of North America, Europe, and Asia — an isolation that determined costs of transportation, slowness of communication, modes of travel, and, for the early settlers, political and social perspectives. Not least, it influenced the character of official response, whether from the imperial or colonial capitals, when a threat to sovereignty within or on the border of British territory seemed real or when "troubles" with Indians in British or adjacent territories threatened the peaceful repose of the settler communities.

Environmental determinants also meant that governments had to put a premium on encouraging means of transportation. Coastal and river navigation had to be made safer by surveys and markers. River channels had to be widened and cleared of debris. New wagon roads beyond the headwaters of sternwheeler navigation had to be built and these required large government outlays that in some cases had to be recovered by a tolls system. And new way stations and administrative systems for a growing colonial bureaucracy had to be built to serve a governmental network that now, in the early 1860s, encompassed the Cariboo within its zone of influence.

By this time also the "heartland" of the region was the Georgia Strait area with its administrative and political leadership extending over a network of rivers and roads into the cordillera.[10] The Cariboo rush of the 1860s and the growth of lumbering on Vancouver Island extended commercial links inland and on the seaboard, and until the Canadian Pacific Railway reached Pacific tidewater and the Panama Canal shortened links with the Atlantic, Victoria remained the focus of the region. Vancouver City, important in the diversification of economic activities, was a latter-day corruption on this frontier. A functional unity based around the Fraser — Britain's Columbia, if you will — already existed by 1871.

II

Tempting as it might be to argue that the character of the British Columbia frontier was shaped by environmental realities, such a conclusion would exclude any study of the type of persons who came to British Columbia in its formative years and the form of government and authority emerging as a result of their migration. No sooner had the British government acquired sovereignty to Vancouver Island and continental territory north of the 49th parallel than it set about to establish means of countering the frontier tendencies of Americans.[11] Vancouver Island was established as a colony proper in 1849 to counter the threat of American squatter settlement, and the Hudson's Bay Company was assigned the task of developing a colony under strict regulations. Such a policy intended, at once, to encourage British immigration and to safeguard the interests of the Indians. The Colonial Office exhibited naivety on both counts, but it is important to note here that from the very beginning of settlement, the patterns of land occupation were government-directed.[12] Land by pre-emption was not available at first. Indian land title was alienated only in a few cases. The result was a different type of society than that emerging in adjacent American history.[13]

The second phase of government desires to protect British territory from American interest occurred only a few years later, in 1850 and 1851, when Victoria's political jurisdiction was extended to the Queen Charlotte Islands. London elevated the territory into a colonial territory administered by the Governor of Vancouver Island as a separate Lieutenant-Governorship, and the reason for this was that London intended to protect sovereignty there from "marauders without title."[14] In an age of American filibustering, Britain could take no chances. Gunboats were sent and signs erected in the islands, but the gold of the islands that had attracted five or six American ships out of San Francisco proved insufficient for economical exploitation and the environment proved unattractive to settlers. Nonetheless, an additional territory had been added to the formal British Empire's jurisdiction.

Two similar extensions of the imperial frontier subsequently occurred: first in New Caledonia with the establishment of the Colony of British Columbia in 1858, the second in the Stikine Territory in 1862 when a reorganization of British Columbia's boundaries allowed for the extension of imperial jurisdiction north to 60° North latitude (except to the Alaskan panhandle) and west to include the Queen Charlotte Islands.[15] The union of the colonies of Vancouver Island and British Columbia in 1866 was a natural successor to the administrative growth and consolidation that had gone on since 1849. In short, the means of formal control had been extended within a territory already British in sovereignty, and in every case the government's actions were motivated by a desire to pre-empt American squatter settlement and to protect the interests of the Crown.

Yet at the very same time, what Professor John S. Galbraith has rightly called "the imperial factor" — the Hudson's Bay Company — was fighting a rearguard action change.[16] The Company gave little encouragement to settlement on Vancouver Island. It sought to monopolize gold extraction from the Queen Charlotte Islands. It endeavoured to control means of transportation to the Fraser gold districts. It acted in a similar way during the Stikine rush of 1862. In each case it sought to exploit the resources of British Columbia in its own way as best it could, and it did so in an age when metropolitan and colonial critics of monopoly and of chartered companies — in others words, advocates of free trade — were making themselves heard in London. Indeed, from the very beginning of colonization on Vancouver Island, critics of the restrictive nature of Company control (particularly in land alienation and transportation control) objected to the domineering manner of the Company.[17] The Colonial Office's desire to end the Company's control on Vancouver Island was well advanced by the mid-1850s, and in 1856 the first legislative assembly met in Victoria — the first representative political institution in the Colony. In the following year a British parliamentary inquiry pointed to the end of Company monopoly in New Caledonia, and the Colonial Office was seeking ways of phasing out Company control on the mainland at the very time news reached London of the great rush to the Fraser in 1858. The result this time was a Crown Colony: a formal jurisdiction in which the colonial governor was answerable to London within rather confined limits. Now the governor was solely an imperial representative, and in a series of political moves initiated by London the Hudson's Bay Company's imperium came to an end. In its place London's authority held sway, more paternalistic than the Company regime and more anxious as time progressed to make the colonies on the Pacific seaboard not only united but self-sufficient and members of a British North American confederation.

497

By creating British Columbia as a colony proper, the imperial government could increase British executive control because, as the preamble to the 1851 act stated, "it is desirable to make some temporary provision for the Civil Government of such territories, until permanent settlements shall be thereupon established, and the number of Colonists increased . . . ."[18] Self-government was deliberately withheld because the Secretary of State for the Colonies, Sir Edward Bulwer Lytton, thought "the grand principle of free institutions" should not be risked "among settlers so wild, so miscellaneous, perhaps so transitory, and in a form of society so crude."[19] The Undersecretary of State for the Colonies, Herman Merivale, believed that only by providing security for settlers and affording the appropriate political climate could a responsible government free from the factiousness of American politics be fostered.[20] Moreover, central authority would provide trusteeship over the Indians, and prevent "cruelties and horrors that had been perpetrated in the early days of our colonies" and in the western United States.[21] In these respects, the British government devised a form of government that they thought suitable for the circumstances: it was arbitrary government, they admitted, but one in which there could be a relaxation of executive powers with the changing circumstances.[22]

This metropolitan form of control allowed the governor, James Douglas, and the first chief justice, Matthew Begbie, to establish a uniform judicial system throughout the colony. Californians, who formed the large majority of migrants into this frontier, by and large came to respect British law on this far western frontier. The reason for this, Begbie argued, was that the populace had willingly submitted to the powers of the executive — powers which, no matter how contrary to their wishes, were clearly and directly expressed.[23] At the same time Douglas devised a licence scheme (based on a system used in New South Wales in 1851 and the Colony of Victoria, Australia, in 1854) for miners that enabled the government to raise revenue for administration and public works, to keep a record of the number of adventurers entering the gold region, and to provide salaries for law enforcement officers and gold commissioners. Douglas attempted to establish a boat licence whereby the public were to observe the Company's exclusive rights of trade with the Indians, its rights of sole navigation to the mining region and elsewhere within its territories, and its requirement that all non-Company trading vessels possess licences issued by the Company. The Colonial Office declared this proclamation invalid because the Company's monopoly extended only to British trade with the Indians and instructed Douglas that it be removed. However, in the four-month interval that it was in force it alienated miners who rightly saw the governor acting for the private interests of the Company rather than the public interests of the Crown.[24] Another measure of the colonial government to regulate the activities of miners within their jurisdiction, the establishing of mining boards, provided the miners with regulation over the matters they were most concerned with — the size of claims and sluices and the rules for working and holding them. These boards provided a vent for miners' complaints and thus aided the British in their local administration.

In Indian relations as well, the executive exercised the initiative. Its principal aim was to prevent whites and Indians from taking the law into their own hands. Interracial conflict did occur during this critical phase of British Columbia's government, but a show of force was made by the governor, who took pains to explain to persons of both races that British law allowed for the protection of all men regardless of race. He appointed prominent members of Indian tribes as magistrates to keep order among the Indians and appointed justices of the peace at various

498

places on the Fraser River to whom whites and Indians alike could apply for redress of grievance. The governor's diplomacy among Indian peoples was important but the forbearance of the Indians themselves[25] allowed for the peaceful resolution of difference so uncharacteristic of race relations in adjacent American territory.

Certainly Californians who entered British territory objected to the domineering influence of the Company and Crown in British Columbia, but they came to respect the strong role of the executive. They found the boat licence "outrageous." They objected to the tolls of roads. They disliked mining licences. But they came to respect in British Columbia, as in New South Wales, Western Australia, and Victoria, the type of frontier government emanating from an empire that had once ruled their own country. They found the colonial government well managed, void of the graft and corruption of California politics, and contributory to the common good of the populace and the growth of the economy.[26]

There were, however, exceptions to the willingness of Californians to submit to British regulations. Case studies show that some Americans with not a little bravado attempted to violate British regulations in the Fraser River. Others attempted to continue the feuding of California mining camps in British territory. Still others of a criminal nature continued their careers north of the border. Many of them were opposed to British regulations *per se*; they were spirited gold seekers willing to "twist the Lion's tail" if they got the chance.[27] They were individuals bent on fortune, and they did not form agroup which might combine to subvert British authority as officials in Victoria and London feared. The United States Consular resident in Victoria, John Nugent, did attempt to marshal American complaints against the colonial government and courts with a view to fostering an annexation movement. But Douglas, in his own defence, prepared a lengthy memorandum for the British government in which he documented how American citizens in British Columbia were treated in a comparable manner to British citizens in California. Subsequently in Washington, D.C., General Lewis Cass, the United States Secretary of State, acknowledged that the regulations prevailing in British Columbia respecting the rights of foreign miners were in fact more liberal than those in force in California. As for Nugent, he was branded as a subversive by British colonial officials who believed that he intended to provoke a filibuster under the guise of protecting Americans from misrule. No such action occurred, Nugent returned to San Francisco, and the only organized American political protest against British rule in the region — a protest by and large the work of one man and without the support of the press — came to an end.[28]

The Nugent case and those of various Americans opposing British law and order tended to underscore the fears of British officials that Americans would indeed subvert the government unless checked by a strong executive authority. It has tended to glorify Douglas and Begbie as guardians of constitutional rights at the expense of ignoring how both had their critics within the ranks of British and Canadian colonists who did not believe that their rights as Englishmen were being protected by an arbitrary government. The birth of the *British Colonist*, a Victoria newspaper, came precisely from this political quarter, and for many years political factions took as their main point of contention the role of the executive in colonial government. The 1858 rush, therefore, had brought important American influences into British territory: influences that authorities feared, and influences which they used to establish strong, centralized administrations to prevent Americans from undermining legal authority.

The British Columbia frontier, then, was a British imperial frontier — a counterfrontier, so to speak, projected from London and Victoria in response to influences and pressures from neighbouring frontiers, particularly from Oregon in the case of Vancouver Island and California in the case of British Columbia. The frontier process occurred in a zone already occupied and exploited by the Hudson's Bay Company, and for a time (particularly on Vancouver Island and for a brief moment in British Columbia) a type of double-image executive authority existed whereby the interest of Company and Crown were often inseparable and often confused. The imperial government, however, forced the clarification of responsibilities between the two. Indeed, the 1858 rush afforded the Colonial Office the opportunity of pressing for full imperial jurisdiction in New Caledonia.[29]

This imperial extension of control allowed for the opening up of the colonies by new transportation routes and by settlement of lands hitherto controlled by the Company. These measures were undertaken by government in response to fears that large numbers of Americans and other foreign land or gold seekers might squat on British territory, establish a popular government and drumhead court, invoke their own crude legal remedies for existing lawlessness, and treat Indians in a violent and inhuman way. These inter-related forces — squatter settlement, the filibuster, and lawlessness — became in their own ways material determinants on the British Columbia frontier. They forced colonial and imperial governments to establish regulations, introduce judicial systems, and provide military aid in support of the civil power in order that similar developments could be avoided in British territory.[30] It was precisely the American frontiersman's propensity to manage his own political affairs (in Frederick Jackson Turner's words, "to preserve order, even in the absence of legal authority"[31]) which most disturbed governors of Vancouver Island and British Columbia and a succession of British Colonial Secretaries and Undersecretaries during the course of the timespan considered by this essay. Officials wanted a self-sufficient territory free from American lawlessness, and they responded in a fairly regular and predictable way in the founding of the Colony of Vancouver Island, in the extension of jurisdiction to the Queen Charlotte Islands, in the constituting of the gold colony of British Columbia, and in the extension of boundaries in the Stikine. Government's concerns for securing the boundaries of British Columbia adjacent to the Alaska Panhandle and the Yukon as well as in the San Juan archipelago were merely extensions of government's attempts to secure the outer fringes of the imperial frontier.

In this way the British Columbia frontier was markedly similar to that of the rest of Canada. It was structured, to employ the words of the Canadian economic historians Easterbook and Aitken, in "the interests of a unity threatened by United States' penetration." The American frontier, by contrast, with its security against outside intervention, constituted an expansive, emerging force which greatly accelerated the rate of economic advance."[32] The structured unity of the British Columbia frontier was provided by London, erected on foundations supplied by the Hudson's Bay Company, and made secure by the material means which the British government was able to provide in the form of ships of the Royal Navy and men of the Royal Marines and Royal Engineers. London provided the finance, the manpower, and, not least, the psychological support rendered by the world's pre-eminent nation and empire that made the British Columbia frontier an imperial frontier.

501

But such metropolitan dominance on this western North American frontier also meant that arbitrary government enjoyed a lingering death; responsible government did not appear until British Columbia joined the Canadian confederation in 1871. Myths of suspected American takeovers continued for some time.[33] The founding fathers of the new colonies, Douglas and Begbie, were lionized at the expense of others such as Richard Blanshard and Amor de Cosmos who fought for more democratic causes. Above all, metropolitan influence tended to reinforce colonial perspectives whereby things British were, as a colonist wrote enthusiastically, "burnished and made the most of!!!"[34] In these ways the metropolitan origins of the British Columbia frontier did much to define the uniqueness of that province in relation to adjacent American states, and, for that matter, to other provinces in Canada or to certain Commonwealth countries. The unique environment of the Pacific slope meant obviously that the founding of a new society in the area now known as British Columbia would be influenced by geographical features, particularly in land occupation, resource extraction, and spatial functions of hinterland and metropolis; but the British role in the extension of political jurisdiction and sovereignty, a role undertaken to counter American influences, also shaped the character of the political society emerging in this most distant west.

NOTES

[1] For reviews on the literature on Canadian frontiers, see J.M.S. Careless, "Frontierism, Metropolitanism and Canadian History," *Canadian Historical Review* 35, 1 (March 1954): 1–21, and Michael Cross, *The Frontier Thesis and the Canadas: The Debate on the Impact of the Canadian Environment* (Toronto, 1970), 1–7, 186–88.

[2] The typology provided by the frontier thesis of Frederick Jackson Turner as given in his "Significance of the Frontier in American History" (1893) and his *Significance of Sections in American History* (New York, 1932) has long been discredited by American historians. Nonetheless, American frontier experiences still invite comparative studies with adjacent Canadian territories and other former British Empire countries. See the guidelines offered by Paul Sharp, "Three Frontiers: Some Comparative Studies of Canadian, American, and Australian Settlement," *Pacific Historical Review*, 24 (November 1955): 369–77. The best interpretive work on comparative frontiers is Robin W. Winks, *The Myth of the American Frontier: Its Relevance to America, Canada and Australia* (Leicester: The Sir George Watson Lectures, 1971). These suggestive inquiries invite further empirical research.

[3] See, for instance, the narrow constitutional approach provided by W.N. Sage in "The Gold Colony of British Columbia," *Canadian Historical Review* 11 (1921): 340–59.

[4] R.W. Van Alstyne, "International Rivalries in the Pacific Northwest," *Oregon Historical Quarterly*, 46 (1945): 185–218.

[5] The outcome of the dispute also gave both nations access to ports in the lower straits area separating Vancouver Island and the mainland and freedom of navigation there. Norman Graebner, *Empire on the Pacific* (New York, 1955).

[6] Eden Colville to Sir John Pelly, 15 October 1849, in E.E. Rich, ed., *London Correspondence Inward from Eden Colville, 1849–1852* (London: Hudson's Bay Record Society, 1956), 19: 5.

[7] Not that the Company could not trade in American territory, but the United States government undertook to indemnify the Company for loss of their property in Oregon, and American politicians were anxious that the removal of the Company be effected as soon as possible. John S. Galbraith, *The Hudson's Bay Company as an Imperial Factor, 1821–1868* (Berkeley and Los Angeles, 1957), ch. 13.

[8] The new routes through the Similkameen Country were developed, in part to provide security for Company brigades so that they would not have to travel through the Cayuse Territory where an Indian War was in progress in the late 1840s. Gloria Griffin Cline, *Peter Skene Ogden and the Hudson's Bay Company* (Norman, Oklahoma, 1974)

[9] H.A. Innis and A.R.M. Lower, eds., *Select Documents in Canadian Economic History, 1783–1885* (Toronto, 1933), 771–77, 780–90, and W.J. Trimble, *The Mining Advance into the Inland Empire* (Madison, Wisconsin, 1914).

[10] J. Lewis Robinson and Walter G. Hardwick, *British Columbia: One Hundred Years of Geographical Change* (Vancouver, 1973), 12.

[11] W.P. Morrell, *Colonial Policy in the Age of Peel and Russell* (Oxford, 1930), 444–46.

[12] Land alienation was partially based on the theories of Edward Gibson Wakefield, whereby land was fixed at the "sufficient price" of £1 per acre. Land prices later were reduced in efforts to encourage colonization.

[13] The bailiff system attempted to introduce established society and deferential relationships into the Vancouver Island colony. Partially successful (though in a very small way), it tended to encourage the idea of a landed gentry in the Victoria area.

[14] James Doublas to Earl Grey, 29 January 1852, C.O. 305/3, Public Record Office, London; Lord Malmesbury to Admiralty, 23 June 1852, Admiralty Correspondence, vol. 1, Provincial Archives of British Columbia, Victoria.

[15] W.E. Ireland, "Evolution of the Boundaries of British Columbia," *British Columbia Historical Quarterly* 3 (October 1939): 263–82.

[16] Galbraith, *Hudson's Bay Company, passim*.

[17] Governor Douglas' identification with the Company was so strong that independent colonists tried to short-circuit imperial communications by sending delegations and petitions to London. During the Parliamentary Inquiry into the Company's affairs in 1857 the same critics were able to make their complaints known to the government.

[18] Great Britain, Statutes at Large, 21 and 22 *Vic.*, c. 99.

[19] Great Britain, *Hansard's Parliamentary Debates*, 3rd ser., 151 (1858), 1102.

[20] These views are set forth in E. Bulwer Lytton to Colonel Moody, 29 October 1858, C.O. 60/3. See also Merivale's article in *The Edinburgh Review* 107 (April 1858): 295–321.

[21] Hansard, 3rd ser., 151 (1858), 2102.

[22] Hansard, 3rd ser., 1769.

[23] M.B. Begbie, "Journey into the Interior of British Columbia," *Journal of the Royal Geographical Society* 3 (1861): 248.

[24] F.W. Howay in F.W. Howay, W.N. Sage, and H.F. Angus, *British Columbia and the United States* (Toronto and New Haven, 1942), 147.

[25] Indians have argued that the peace on the frontier was owing to their forbearance and willingness to allow whites "to use that country on equal terms with ourselves." One tribe, the Couteau, "saved the country from war when the Indians were about to combine and drive out the Whites." Evidence of Chief John Tedlenitsa of the Couteau tribe, in deputation to Sir Wilfred Laurier, 27 April 1916, in Borden Papers, MG 26 H 1(a), vol. 38, pp. 16394–5, Public Archives of Canada.

[26] W.E. Ireland, ed., "Gold Rush Days in Victoria, 1858–1859," *British Columbia Historical Quarterly* 12 (July 1948): 241. Also, Rodman W. Paul, " 'Old Californians' in British Gold Fields," *Huntington Library Quarterly* 17 (1954).

[27] Barry M. Gough, "Keeping British Columbia British: The Law-and-Order Question on a Gold Mining Frontier," *Huntington Library Quarterly* 38 (1975): 269–80.

[28] R.L. Reid, "John Nugent: The Impertinent Envoy," *British Columbia Historical Quarterly* 8 (1944): 53–76.

[29] John S. Galbraith, "Bulwer-Lytton's Ultimatum," *The Beaver*, Outfit 268 (Spring 1958), 20–24.

[30] On the question of military support for the civil power, see Barry M. Gough, " 'Turbulent Frontiers' and British Expansion: Governor James Douglas, The Royal Navy and the British Columbia Gold Rushes," *Pacific Historical Review* 41 (1972): 15–32.

[31] Turner's statement is quoted in H.C. Allen, *Bush and Backwoods: A Comparison of the Frontier in Australian and the United States* (East Lansing, Mich., 1959), 101.

[32] W.T. Easterbrook and H.G.J. Aitken, *Canadian Economic History* (Toronto, 1958), 356.

[33] W.N. Sage, "The Annexationist Movement in British Columbia," *Proceedings and Transactions of the Royal Society of Canada*, ser. 3, vol. 21 (1927), sec. 2, 97–110.

[34] Quoted in M.A. Ormsby, *British Columbia: A History* (Toronto, 1958), 107.

503

Topic Fifteen

Why Was Confederation Accepted?

Union of British North America had been considered as far back as 1790, but never achieved. A renewed interest arose in the 1850s when increased tension between British North America and the United States, and the emerging political deadlock in the Canadas, made the option of a larger colonial union attractive.

In the mid-1860s the right conditions prevailed for the politicians of the Canadas, New Brunswick, and Nova Scotia to bring about Confederation. The details of union were worked out at two important conferences in 1864. At the Charlottetown conference, the delegates agreed in principle on a number of the important features of the eventual federation, including the regional representation of the upper house (Senate) and "representation by population" in the lower house (House of Commons). They also arrived at the nature of the division of powers between provincial and federal governments. A second conference at Quebec in October 1864, only one month later, finalized these understandings in the Seventy-Two Resolutions. Between 1864 and 1867, the politicians worked to convince their respective colonial assemblies to adopt Confederation.

In Canada West, support for the proposals was widespread. Confederation was seen as a solution to the perennial problem of political deadlock. Moreover, an economic union would work to the advantage of Canada West, as the largest and most commercially advanced of the provinces. Union would also provide increased protection of the inland province at a time of acute American military threat. Canada West would also benefit from the eventual expansion of the new nation across the continent, particularly into the Northwest.

Elsewhere, however, the Confederation idea met with great opposition. In Canada East, as Jacques Monet explains in "True Blue, True Grit" (prepared with the assistance of Paul Litt), the anti-Confederate Rouge Party under Antoine-Aimé Dorion strongly opposed Confederation. In New Brunswick sentiments were decidedly mixed. Del Muise outlines Nova Scotia's response in "Railroaded into Union," and Rosemarie Langhout reviews the situation in New Brunswick in "About Face." The two islands, Newfoundland and Prince Edward Island — which looked eastward, not westward — rejected it. James Hiller outlines Newfoundland's position in "Confederation Defeated: The Newfoundland Election of 1869." Nova Scotia, too, opposed the scheme, and only Tupper kept the issue alive.

In light of such opposition to Confederation, several questions come to mind: why was there such urgency to establish a British North American federation? To what extent did the haste to form the union contribute to regional divisions and misunderstandings?

Many excellent books exist on the subject of British North American federation. A good starting point is Donald Creighton's *The Road to Confederation* (Toronto: Macmillan, 1964). W L. Morton's *The Critical Years, 1857–1873* (Toronto: McClelland and Stewart, 1968) is also extremely useful. A lively account of the confederation movement in the Canadas and the Atlantic region is P.B. Waite's *The Life and Times of Confederation, 1864–1867* (Toronto: University of Toronto Press, 1962). P.B. Waite has edited the original debates in the United Canadas in *The Confederation Debates in the Province of Canada, 1865* (Toronto: University of Toronto Press, 1967). *Confederation*, edited by Ramsay Cook (Toronto: University of Toronto Press, 1967), contains important articles on the subject, including the essay on New Brunswick by Alfred G. Bailey, "The Basis and Persistence of Opposition to Confederation in New Brunswick," and George F.G. Stanley's "Act or Pact: Another Look at Confederation." A full account of the Maritime colonies' position toward federation appears in William Menzie Whitelaw's *The Maritimes and Canada before Confederation* (Toronto: Oxford University Press, 1966; first published in 1934). J.M.S. Careless' *Brown of the Globe*, vol. 2 (Toronto: Macmillan, 1963) and Donald Creighton's *John A. Macdonald*, vol. 1, *The Young Politician* (Toronto: Macmillan, 1952) review the ideas and the important role of these leading figures in the Confederation movement. A recent article on the background to Confederation is Ged Martin's "Launching Canadian Confederation: Means to Ends, 1836–1864," *The Historical Journal*, 27, 3 (1984): 575–602.

True Blue, True Grit*

JACQUES MONET

The English-speaking Tory merchants of Montreal were out to restore their lost ascendancy, and the young, republican, radicals known as *les rouges* wanted a separate French Canadian state. With these widely divergent aims, the two groups became unlikely allies in a campaign to annex Canada to the United States in 1849.

*From *Horizon Canada* 46 (1986): 1081–87. Reprinted by permission.

Both groups were spurred by the loosening of ties with Britain, signalled by Britain's adoption of free-trade policies and the granting of responsible government to the united Canadas in the second half of the 1840s. Far from viewing these moves as positive steps in the development of Canada's economic and political independence, the Tory merchants, fearing that their political and economic prosperity was at an end, felt that their years of loyalty to the mother country had been repaid with a slap in the face. The French Canadian radicals also believed that Britain was rejecting its colonies and were heartened by the thought that British authorities might in fact look with favour on a complete break.

These odd allies put pen to paper in October 1849 and signed the Annexation Manifesto. It aroused immediate and overwhelming opposition. Loyalty to Britain was still strong; suspicion of the republican rabble to the south was rampant; and the recent achievement of self-government brought a fresh new identification with the Canadas themselves. The *rouges* held fast to their republicanism despite its unpopularity; but the Tories, who had acted more out of pique than conviction and who were denounced asself-seeking hypocrites, were soon chastened and apologetic. By the early 1850s, they had deserted the annexation cause.

506

A Radical Touch

The *rouges* of Canada East were not the only radical reformers to emerge in the 1840s. In Canada West, the Clear Grits had gained a large following by advocating similar republican principles, including demands for secret ballots, more elected rather than appointed officials, and an expanded franchise. The appearance of the *rouges* and Clear Grits signalled the re-emergence of radical reformers for the first time since the suppression of the rebellions of 1837–38.

In the intervening decade the Reform alliance had fought its battle for responsible government against the Tories. Now it found itself challenged in both sections of the province by reformers who were more democratic and less committed to bicultural cooperation than the La-Fontaine–Baldwin coalition had been.

Splits began to develop in that alliance too. Under Louis-Hippolyte LaFontaine and Robert Baldwin, French and English Reformers had been united in pursuit of their common goal of responsible government. But once in power, and with that goal achieved, conflicts began to emerge in their respective political agendas.

The most serious of these conflicts was exacerbated by George Brown, the editor of the influential Toronto *Globe*, whose Presbyterianism emphasized the separation of church and state. This brought him into direct conflict with LaFontaine's old followers, known as the *bleus* in opposition to the anti-clerical *rouges*. The *bleus* were bent on protecting a French Canadian society in which the Catholic Church was involved in education, health care, and social welfare. It was bad enough that this went on in Canada East, but Brown feared that the Reform alliance was allowing the Catholic Church to extend its influence in Canada West as well.

Some Reformers sympathized with Brown but there was no place for his anti-French stance in the Reform alliance. He found himself sharing the opposition benches with the Clear Grits and the *rouges*, even though he did not share the enthusiasm of both these groups for a Canadian republic.

A New Breed

Defeated in the assembly in 1854, the Reform alliance began casting about for reinforcement and found it among the Tories, who were no longer the rigid elitists of the bad old days but mostly moderate conservatives happy to work within the system. 507

The new breed of conservative was best represented by Kingston lawyer John A. Macdonald. Genial, persuasive, and a master of compromise, he had been working behind the scenes for years to secure the cooperation of Reformers with his conservative colleagues. Like most of the moderate Reformers, he was "progressive" in his belief that the fate of the Canadas hungon economic development. Macdonald also believed that that development would be impossible without cooperation between French and English Canadians.

In the *bleus* Macdonald found a French Canadian leader of like mind. George-Etienne Cartier, also a lawyer, was convinced that French Canada could best ensure its survival by continued political cooperation in a bicultural party. Pugnacious but practical, Cartier was anxious that French Canadians participate in the economic development of the country so that they would not be left behind by a progressive society. With their complementary goals, Macdonald and Cartier formed a new partnership that would prove even more successful than that of LaFontaine and Baldwin. The Reformers and moderate conservatives of Canada West joined with the *bleus* of Canada East, forming a Conservative party that, from 1854, would dominate the Canadian political scene for the next 40 years.

On taking office in 1854, the Conservatives carried out long-overdue reforms. In Canada West, they settled the decades-long controversy over the Clergy Reserves, redirecting the revenues from these reserved lands, originally meant to support the Church of England, to municipal administrations. In Canada East, they did away with the old seigniorial system of land tenure, settling on a formula that compensated *seigneurs* with cash payments and title to designated lands, and that allowed farmers to buy their land outright or rent it from the *seigneurs* who now became no more than landlords in the modern sense.

In both these cases, however, the Conservatives simply completed the reform agenda of previous decades. This was no new departure dictated by radical reformers. The real concern of the Conservative government was economic growth. In the 1850s, this came through Reciprocity and railways.

Canada and the United States signed the Reciprocity Treaty in 1854. It provided for free trade in natural products, thus compensating Canadian businessmen for the loss of their preferential position in British markets since Britain's adoption of free trade in 1846. But even before the Reciprocity Treaty, Canada was experiencing an economic boom, due largely to the railway building craze.

508

Sir George-Etienne Cartier

Cartier was LaFontaine's successor as leader of the *bleus* in Lower Canada. Unlike most of his predecessors, he came from a business family, and in his politics and his nationalism he mixed a very practical concern for the commercial development of the Canadas. He was an energetic man with a mercurial temperament. As a young man he became a hero of the *patriotes* for his courage in the battle of St. Denis during the rebellion of 1837. In the aftermath of the uprisings he became a follower of Lafontaine, sharing his strategy for attaining responsible government. His star rose as that of his leader fell, and by the mid-1850s, through determination, charm, and sheer ability, he had risen to become the acknowledged leader of the *bleus*.

As the leader of the largest block of votes in the assembly, he was, in effect, the leader of the government from 1857 on, although it was not until 1858 that he was actually made prime minister. Macdonald, his partner and leader of the Conservatives of Upper Canada, had neither his support nor his influence in the assembly. It was, in fact, mostly because of Cartier's influence that the political negotiations leading up to Confederation were successful.

There was another way, no less crucial, that Cartier made Confederation possible: He was one of the first Canadian politicians to recognize the potential of railways. His support for the Grand Trunk and other railway projects helped create the physical links between the colonies that became Canada.

This was the "Railway Age" in Canada. Promoters, businessmen, and governments invested in the construction of railways that promised prosperity for every town and region along their routes. The symbol of progress, it came to dominate politics. "My politics are railroads," said Sir Alan McNab, and so it was for most members of the Conservative government.

Running Out of Esteem

Cartier himself was the lawyer for the Grand Trunk, the biggest railway scheme of all, designed to link all the important regions of the Canadas along one railway line. Here politics and railways were most thoroughly

509

Sir John A. Macdonald

Macdonald is best known as the first prime minister of Canada, but his political career began in the late 1840s, and by the 1850s he was playing a leading role in political events. He was a new breed of conservative, opposed to the oligarchic control of the old Tories. The Family Compact had been a loyalist, Anglican elite, centred in Toronto, but Macdonald was a Kingston lawyer, a Presbyterian with liberal instincts.

Broad-minded and far-sighted, Macdonald possessed a rare talent for managing men and for transmuting determined opposition into workable compromise. He was instrumental in bringing about the alliance of moderate Reformers and conservatives in 1854. In cooperation with the *bleu* leader Cartier, he created the Conservative party.

Macdonald, however, was no angel. He enjoyed scrapping with opposition forces in the House. His taste for strong drink is legendary, and it was debatable what took more of his strength: his political battles in Parliament, or his bouts with the bottle.

Recognizing the impossibility of forever continuing the Union with its chronic sectionalism, Macdonald joined with Cartier in 1858 in embracing Alexander Galt's plan for Confederation. When Galt joined the cabinet, he did so on two conditions: first, that the Confederation plan be pursued, and second, that tariff barriers for the protection of domestic industry be adopted. In subsequent decades Macdonald, the consummate politician, was to adopt both these planks as his own, and earn himself unparalleled fame in the annals of Canadian history.

intertwined. The government supported the Grand Trunk with legislation and loans throughout the decade.

The enthusiasm for railways was well founded, but like manygood things, inflated hopes and speculation carried it too far, too fast. Construction problems and dubious financing plagued many schemes, including the Grand Trunk. The governments involved found themselves embarrassed and forced to extend further loans. By the end of the decade, the railway-led economic boom had gone bust. It was a setback, rather than a total collapse, for railways had boosted the Canadas to new heights of prosperity.

Cartier's fellow middle-class *bleus* jumped as eagerly as their allies in Canada West on the economic bandwagon of the Railway Age. But their support was always conditional on the maintenance of French Canadian rights. And this meant a separate school system for Catholics in Canada West that offered the same educational opportunities available to Protestants in Canada East.

510

The issue of separate schools was to provide a rallying point for the forces of opposition in Canada West. When *bleus* votes from Canada East carried a new separate-school bill in 1855 against a majority of opposing votes from Canada West, George Brown was quick to raise the cry of "French domination!" The Clear Grits agreed; and in mutual outrage, the two groups forgot their differences and began to unite as an opposition force.

Brown cemented the support of the Grits with his famous demand for "Rep by Pop." The Act of Union of 1840, with its clear aim of assimilating the French-speaking population of Canada East, had given both of the Canadas an equal number of seats in the legislature even though the population of CanadaEast far surpassed that of Canada West. Now the census of 1852 showed that for the first time, the population of Canada West had grown to outstrip that of Canada East. The original injustice of the Act of Union now worked against the English-speaking majority instead of to its advantage. "French domination!" cried Brown. He demanded that each section of the province be represented in proportion to its population. The assembly defeated his proposal, but it proved a popular issue which further eroded support for Macdonald's Conservatives in Canada West.

Opponents Link Up

In 1857, Brown's followers and the Clear Grits met at the Upper Canada Reform convention. Having forsaken their radical republicanism, the Grits joined Brown in a common platform that opposed Catholic separate schools and demanded "Rep by Pop." They also agreed that Canada should acquire control of the Northwest, the vast territory also known as Rupert's Land that had been ruled for almost two centuries by the Hudson's Bay Co.

Why the sudden interest in this territory? Canada West was filling up. The last large block of wilderness suitable for agricultural development had been sold. Farmers looked west, as did businessmen who saw territorial expansion as spelling an increase in trade. The Conservative government of Macdonald and Cartier showed interest and sent an emissary to Britain to present Canada's claim to the lands. But the Conservatives were not yet as eager as the Grits. They feared upsetting the territorial balance between the Canadas and disturbing the conditions on which the cooperation of French and English Canadians was based.

In the elections of 1857, the Conservatives were reduced to a minority in Canada West. In Canada East, however, the rouges were still a small minority, ever suspicious of the anti-French bias of Brown's Grits. So the Conservatives still held a slim majority in the assembly.

511

A Time of Instability

In its weakened state, the government fell in the summer of 1858 on a motion of non-confidence attacking its acceptance of Queen Victoria's choice of Ottawa as a permanent capital. The Macdonald-Cartier government resigned and was replaced by a ministry led by Brown and the *rouge* leader Antoine-Aimé Dorion. Their government survived only two days before Macdonald and Cartier once more took the helm.

The instability was crippling. The Conservatives had insufficient strength to pass any controversial legislation, and the opposition had even less support. Worse still, the standoff between the Grit majority in Canada West and the *bleu* majority in Canada East was polarizing Canada along racial lines. Was the guiding principle of French–English cooperation, so painfully learned, to become the first victim of the new political deadlock?

As the curtain fell on the 1850s, no solution had beenfound. But already some Canadians were drawing on the experience of the Union period to find ways to break the political deadlock while preserving bicultural accommodation.

In 1858, Alexander Galt, a businessman who held an independent seat in the assembly, proposed a radical idea: the union of all the colonies of British North America. This scheme, which he called "Confederation," involved nothing less than the creation of a new nation that would stretch from the Atlantic colonies to British Columbia on the Pacific Ocean, including all the empty western lands. It seemed an impossibly ambitious plan. Yet it also offered solutions to most of the problems that beset the Canadas.

The key lay in the federal constitution which would loosen the deadlock between French and English Canadians in the Canadas. In such a federation, provincial legislatures would preside over regional concerns, and a national government would provide economic unity and the trappings of nationhood.

Though the Union period ended in acrimonious deadlock, in death it preserved the basis for a reborn Canada: French–English cooperation and federalism. Macdonald and Cartier, the two leaders who personified and protected these ideals, were to carry them still further on a broader stage, in a new nation with a bilingual and bicultural character that would be admired throughout the world.

(The author thanks Paul Litt for his help in the preparation of this article.)

Railroaded into Union*

DEL MUISE

Only a modest public display greeted the dawn of the new union in Halifax on the first Dominion Day. Other communities in Nova Scotia were less reserved. The youth of Yarmouth, for instance, burned pro-Confederation politicians in effigy, along with a dead rat! For many Nova Scotians, the British North America Act was a bitter pill to swallow, rammed down their throats by the Conservative Dr. Charles Tupper and his followers. The bad taste and ill feelings would not go away.

In the first elections to the Dominion Parliament in September 1867, the dissatisfaction showed itself in the fact that 18 of the 19 members returned for Nova Scotia were pledged to push for the immediate release of the province from the "bondage" of Confederation. A provincial election the same day returned 36 of 38 members pledged the same way and led to the formation of a separatist provincial government.

Yet the early stages of the drive to Confederation had not been nearly so tumultuous in the "Bluenose" province. Political leaders of all stripes had flirted with the idea of colonial union long before the Charlottetown Conference of 1864. As a matter of fact, it was largely at the instigation of the Nova Scotia government that that conference, officially called to discuss Maritime Union, was convened in the first place. The idea of Maritime Union had a certain emotional pull in Nova Scotia, harking back as it did to the days before 1784 and 1769 when New Brunswick and Prince Edward Island respectively had formed part of the one colony of Nova Scotia.

*From *Horizon Canada* 56 (1986): 1321–27. Reprinted by permission.

A Question of Railways

Whenever colonial leaders spoke of colonial union before 1864, however, the subject was always treated as a kind of offshoot of railway negotiations, something to be worked out once satisfactory communications had been established to warrant a broader uniting of political objectives. Most colonial governments had been driven deep into debt by their expenditures on railway construction in the 1850s. The advocates of Confederation came to believe that the fragmented lines in the various colonies would remain money-losing bits and pieces so long as they were not linked in a larger system.

At Charlottetown, Nova Scotia's representatives became convinced that the only way of achieving Halifax's metropolitan ambitions was some form of political union, the first task of which would be construction of effective railway links to the other colonies. For them, the prospect of making Halifax the eastern terminus of a line stretching deep into the heartland of the continent was central to fulfilment of the union.

Railway ambition was only the most obvious plank in the platform of the pro-Confederation forces. Union promised continued development of the province's coal reserves and their integration in a new "national" economy, linking the resources and markets of the St. Lawrence and beyond to the Atlantic community.

Aggressive young politicians like Charles Tupper and Adams G. Archibald, the newly crowned leaders of the Conservative and Reform par-

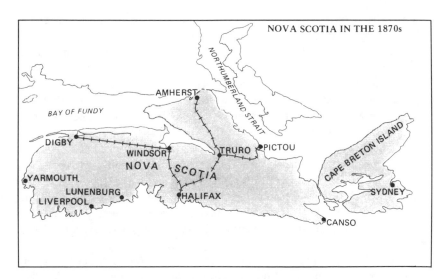

Dept. of Cartography, CEGEP de Limoilou, Que.

Railway age. The construction and operation of railways was the most significant political issue of the pre-Confederation decade in Nova Scotia.

ties respectively, were united in their support for union as a replacement for the 1854 Reciprocity Treaty with the United States, which was soon to expire. For them, the prospect of greater access to central Canadian markets and further development of Nova Scotia's industrial capacity were the prime objectives. At the same time, there was a decided nationalist streak in their pronouncements regarding the vast potential of the new "nation" they were creating.

It was not long after the Quebec Conference had come up with a detailed proposal for union in October 1864 that strong opposition surfaced in Nova Scotia. The "Quebec Scheme," as it came to be derisively termed, became the topic of a major debate in Halifax and throughout the colony, as many argued that there was much to lose and little to gain from such a scheme.

514   Opposition Hardens

Union and railways went hand in hand. But the reaction of various communities depended on how close the proposed railway would run to their town, or how much benefit they could draw from it. So there could be little reason to support the objectives of union in areas far removed from the narrow corridor to be served by the proposed lines. Where dependence on traditional export industries like fishing, lumbering, and shipping was most pronounced, the promises of Confederation seemed remote indeed.

Opposition hardened in January 1865 at a series of public meetings where representatives of all commercial classes, from country storekeepers to Halifax merchant princes, joined to oppose the measure. Commercial objections, including the prospect of higher taxes to support railway development, were reinforced by provincial or local patriotism. The loss of stature that Confederation would entail for a province that had been in the vanguard of the struggle for responsible government quickly became a central issue.

Joseph Howe, the hero of that earlier struggle, took a leading part in the opposition, publishing a series of 12 public letters, provocatively entitled "The Botheration Letters," in the Halifax *Morning Chronicle* starting Jan. 11, 1865. Howe's position as Her Majesty's Fisheries Commissioner required him to abstain from political controversy, so he published the letters anonymously, but his authorship was a secret to no one.

Howe's opposition to union has been the subject of much debate. Then, as later, many understood him to have previously favoured the idea. His adversaries charged that his opposition was purely partisan and spiteful, the work of a man frustrated by the fact that he had no direct role in what would undoubtedly be the most important act of statecraft in his lifetime.

That was of little immediate consequence, however, for by the early spring of 1865, the issue died down temporarily when Samuel Leonard Tilley's pro-union government in New Brunswick was forced to resign after losing a controversial election to an anti-Confederate coalition. Nova Scotia's Confederates could do little but wait on developments in the neighbouring province which stood between it and the Canadas.

Another Crack at It

The situation in New Brunswick was reversed within a year, thanks to pressure from the imperial government combined with financial backing from the Canadians for Tilley's forces and some opportune aggression by American-based Fenians on the Maine border. Tilley was swept back into office and in Nova Scotia, the way was clear for Tupper and his supporters to take another stab at Confederation.

515

At the tail end of the 1866 sitting of the Nova Scotia legislature, Tupper won guarded support for a new delegation to participate in a new conference under the auspices of the Colonial Office in London. Caught off guard by the swiftness of Tupper's initiative, anti-Confederates formed the "Anti-Confederation League," deciding on a campaign of peaceful petition and lobbying to counter the Conservative government's move.

Pros and Antis sailed for London in the summer of 1866. Tupper's official delegation was shadowed around the British capital as Howe and others lobbied intensively against the passage of any act of union to which the people of Nova Scotia had not given their consent. Recently freed from his duties as an imperial public servant, Howe led the opposition mission, repeating the economic arguments and patriotic sentiments against union outlined in his "Botheration Letters."

But eloquent speeches, massive petitions to the British Parliament, and active pamphleteering failed to sway British legislators. Firmly convinced that Confederation was in the interests of the Empire as well as of all parts of British North America, they were determined to see it through.

Back home following passage of the British North America Act in the spring of 1867, the Antis set out to give a forceful demonstration of Nova Scotia's opposition to the union, hoping thereby to bring the British legislators around to their point of view. Nova Scotia's first elections under the new regime were scheduled for Sept. 18. The Anti-Confederation League quickly transformed itself into the Nova Scotia Party and set to work.

The results, following a blistering summerlong campaign, offered a dramatic refutation of claims that Nova Scotians were behind Confederation. The only unionist survivor at the federal level was Tupper himself, who won his Cumberland County seat by a slim 98-vote majority. Nova Scotia's position in Confederation appeared in jeopardy.

The Fight Goes On

Determined to press their case in Ottawa at the first opportunity, the Antis were confident that their overwhelming strength would guarantee them a reasonable hearing and speedy release from the union. When MPs took their seats, the Nova Scotia members presented a motion to that effect. But after a polite hearing, the powerful Conservative majority decisively rejected their proposal.

516 In Nova Scotia, the provincial government of William Annand, owner and editor of the strongly anti-Confederation *Morning Chronicle*, was unwilling to let the issue die so easily. Massive public petitions were drawn up, and resolutions addressed to the imperial government were passed through the legislature.

Later in the autumn, a delegation of provincial government representatives and MPs from the Nova Scotia Party was sent to London under Howe's leadership. They were given a polite hearing but told they would have to work within Confederation. Any complaints regarding the actual workings of the union would have to be taken up with Ottawa. Some Antis saw this as a tremendous slap in the face, a denial of responsible government, an odious overriding of the clear wishes of free British subjects expressed through their elected representatives.

But a cautious streak in the movement's leaders kept them from taking any drastic step to carry their point. A tiny minority favouring annexation with the United States turned Howe and his federal associates away from continued agitation and opened the door for compromise. The only real option for those like Howe who remained loyal to the Crown was some sort of agreement with the hated government in Ottawa.

Aware of the necessity to let the Anti movement run its course, Prime Minister Sir John A. Macdonald was also determined to get out of the embarrassing position of having a key partner in the union so obviously disaffected. When the Nova Scotia delegates returned from London in June 1868, they were met in Halifax by a mission from Ottawa offering "Better Terms."

Six months of negotiations culminated in a rearrangement of the financial terms for the province within Confederation, allowing the provincial government sufficient funds to maintain levels of service in line with pre-Confederation realities. At the same time, a political accord drew Howe and a companion, Antigonish MP Hugh MacDonald, into the federal cabinet.

By the spring of 1869, the opposition to Confederation in Nova Scotia had been declawed. Whatever discontent lingered in the provincial government was left to fade as the province was drawn more and more into the political affairs of the new country.

Colouring the Future

Two major themes characterized the opposition to Confederation in Nova Scotia — the fear, particularly strong among a self-confident commercial elite, of a loss of control over the economic destinies of the province, and a feeling of having been railroaded into union. There was a cry at the time that Confederation had been negotiated for Nova Scotia by "Four Lawyers and a Doctor" who hardly represented the interests of the most advanced commercial community in British North America. It was doubted that Canadians could ever understand the special needs of a society and an economy largely shaped by the sea.

517

To allay some of those fears, Sir John A. Macdonald's government set out to protect and encourage the fishery and defend it against American competitors. Resolution of the issue of American access to territorial waters by the Treaty of Washington in 1871 helped to overcome the anxieties of fishermen and merchants.

But considerable rancour was still felt over the way union had been imposed on the province. The notion stuck that Tupper had pulled a dirty trick by failing to submit the issue to the people in an election before it had all been sewn up in London. The exclusion of the Anti government from the "Better Terms" negotiations was another sore spot left to fester at the heart of federal–provincial relations in the early years of the new Dominion.

In the end, the anti-Confederates were unprepared to carry the fight beyond the limits of strictly legal protests, and even the provincial government soon gave up trying to convince an uninterested imperial government of its mistake. By 1869–70, Nova Scotia anger at the Conservative government in Ottawa had taken a more productive turn as the discontented sought a loose alliance with Ontario Reformers who were becoming the real opposition to Macdonald's Tory government.

The set of alliances and attitudes forged in the heat of the Confederation struggle remained central to the outlook of the province's traditional parties for generations. They would colour Nova Scotia views of national issues for years.

About Face*

ROSEMARIE LANGHOUT

Following the Quebec Conference of October 1864, held to discuss the federation of British North America, delegates returned to their home colonies with a series of resolutions outlining the details of the Confederation scheme. Before they could be approved in Britain, the resolutions needed the agreement of each colony's legislature. The issue was not a foregone conclusion — many powerful groups opposed Confederation — and it was almostthree years before the Dominion of Canada emerged as a united country.

Geographically sandwiched between Nova Scotia and the colony of Canada, New Brunswick was pivotal to the success or failure of the scheme. No political union of British North America was feasible without its consent. Yet New Brunswick's response to the question of Confederation was mixed.

This is hardly surprising given that New Brunswick was a society divided by ethnic, religious, and linguistic differences, differences which not infrequently led to blows. About a third of the population was Roman Catholic, and a quarter was Baptist. Anglicans, Presbyterians, and Methodists also formed significant congregations and almost a quarter of all New Brunswickers were Acadians. The colony's economic activities also tended to divide the population. For the most part they were confined exclusively to one or another of the colony's watershed regions — the Saint John river valley in the south and west, or the Miramichi in the north and east. Even political and economic power was to some extent separate. The city of Saint John, which contained nearly a fifth of the population, was to its chagrin, not the colony's seat of government. For all these reasons, the response to the Confederation plan could hardly be expected to reflect a simple reality.

Many people welcomed the plan when it was announced by government leader Samuel Leonard Tilley in November, but there was a very strong "anti" faction; so strong, in fact, that Tilley did not immediately submit the issue to the assembly for fear it would be defeated. Instead he launched a propaganda campaign designed to win popular support for Confederation in the election to be held the following year. The strategy failed, however, and in the election of early 1865 Tilley's group went down to defeat and Albert J. Smith took over as leader of an anti-Confederation government.

It is testament to the volatility of New Brunswick political opinion at the time that just over a year later, opposition to Confederation had

*From *Horizon Canada* 53 (1986): 1249–55. Reprinted by permission.

crumbled. British colonial authorities strongly endorsed the idea of union and when this was formally announced it removed a fear among the anti-confederates that union with Canada meant breaking the imperial tie.

Another factor contributing to the voters' abrupt change of heart was a renewed suspicion of American aggression. The civil war in the U.S. was drawing to a close, and British North Americans feared in its wake an American attempt to seize the northern colonies. The military value of political union became one of the plan's major selling points as Fenian demonstrations across the border brought home the possibility of invasion.

As public opinion shifted, so did the position of the Smith government, but not fast enough. In April 1866, under pressure from Lieutenant Governor Arthur Hamilton Gordon, Smith resigned and a pro-Confederation government was appointed. The intervention of the lieutenant governor was controversial and his recall was widely demanded, but in the June election, Confederation won a strong endorsement: In an assembly of 41 members, only eight "antis" were elected. The House quickly passed resolutions in favour of union and Tilley set off for London at the head of the New Brunswick delegation to work out the final details with representatives of the other colonies.

519

The Railway Era

The immediate issues may have been reciprocity, the British connection, and military security, but two decades of economic change had already done much to pave the way for New Brunswick's acceptance of Confederation. The years between 1850 and 1880 have often been described as the "Golden Age" of the Maritimes. The building of wooden sailing ships, and their operation by Maritimers in a world-wide carrying trade, provided the basis for prosperity during these years. By far the largest fleet in the region was registered at Saint John.

In the 1850s, however, the government of New Brunswick opted to build, own, and operate railways. The European and North American Railway (E&NA), built across southern New Brunswick from Saint John to Shediac on the Northumberland Strait, was a precursor of a new technological age. The technology of coal, iron, and steam implied the formation of a new set of economic structures which had a significant impact on political developments in the 1860s.

Railway building was expected to complement and expand the colony's trade. It also accelerated the growth of a small industrial sector in Saint John. By 1865, much of the city's industry was composed of metal foundries and railway car shops. Between 1861 and 1865, manufactured goods nearly doubled as a proportion of total New Brunswick exports.

Traders and manufacturers tended to expect different things from government. In general terms, traders preferred low taxes and minimal government interference with free enterprise: They were happy with the colonial system. Manufacturers, on the other hand, encouraged governments to protect local industries by imposing taxes on imported goods. In general, they supported Confederation. Yet traders, especially those involved with the timber export trade, remained economically powerful and the Confederation question was another ingredient in the ongoing debate about the economic future of the colony.

The constituency to which both pro- and anti-confederates devoted the bulk of their attention was the "respectable working classes" — mechanics and crafts people. By 1861 this group contained over a third of the colony's enumerated working people, which made it the largest group of voters in New Brunswick. It was also growing rapidly. The number of mechanics and crafts people in New Brunswick had increased by 30 percent between 1851 and 1861. The group included most of those whose work was of an industrial or semi-industrial character; an election platform highlighting industrial over commercial growth could be expected to appeal to them.

520

A New Economy

A good cross section of Saint John's master trades people and manufacturers signed an address favouring Confederation, published in a local newspaper before the 1865 election. They argued that the money which Confederation-linked railway construction would attract would "enable our rising manufacturers to take a firm stand, and instead of the periodical stagnation of trade caused by the fluctuations of our only articles of export — Lumber and Ships — we shall have manufactures that will be a continual source of prosperity, not affected by the changes in the European Market, and giving our working people employment all the year round." Here was a clear statement opting for an alternative to the traditional Maritime economic system based on wood, wind, and sail. The old system had been evolving ever since Britain had withdrawn trade preferences from New Brunswick timber in the late 1840s. Denied a protected market for their most important export product, some New Brunswickers had turned to the idea of industrial growth and diversification within a protected domestic market.

Candidates for election in 1865 dealt directly with the economic implications of Confederation in terms of jobs and the costs of living. Anti-confederates claimed that, far from offering a larger market, Confederation would swamp New Brunswick's productive capacity with cheap Canadian labour, and reduce the value of New Brunswick's trade by raising customs duties. Confederates were quick to rebut these claims.

They argued that even if taxes under Confederation were higher, the burden would be placed not on the poor but on the wealthy — those to whom "it would not be very inconvenient." This was an unlikely argument to impress the colony's great merchant traders!

In more general terms, those in favour of union suggested that it would "give greater scope to the energies of employers and a larger market for their wares . . . [and would] afford to the industrious working man a greater probability of steady employment than he can now hope for." One confederate candidate, who was a self-proclaimed working man, argued that union would give "the working men of the province . . . labour and a market, the result of which to them would be increased wealth," and would "develop the resources of the country and divert hither capital."

The importance attached to attracting outside investment was linked to the prevalent belief that railways were the key to economic growth. New Brunswick did not have enough money to build railways. Even government railway-building initiatives had ceased in the colony in the early 1860s for lack of funds. Yet railways were demanded by the public as a means of opening up wilderness land to exploitation and settlement. The rhetoric of railway promotion was echoed by pro-confederates. Union, they argued, "will open up and colonize immense tracts of fertile lands . . . lying unreclaimed and desolate. It will multiply the sources of industry and intensify the demand for labour. It will tend to keep our young men at home and allure those of other lands to our shores."

The *Saint John Globe* had been off the mark in its 1864 prediction that "the country will soon recognize but two parties, a Railway and Anti-Railway party," for in 1865, both pro- and anti-confederates wanted railways. "Antis" favoured limiting railway works to a Western Extension of the E&NA from Saint John to the American border, on the grounds that this was the least costly of the schemes then bandied about, and that it would be of immediate and lasting value to New Brunswick in terms of commercial opportunities. Their opponents claimed that a confederated Canada would be able to afford both the Western Extension and an intercolonial railway (ICR), because it would not be subject to the doubts of English capitalists as to the safety of investing in "isolated and disunited" British North America. An intercolonial railway running from a terminus in Halifax, through Nova Scotia and New Brunswick to Quebec and Montreal, would bind together the new nation and provide a channel for communication and trade between the provinces. For New Brunswick this would mean access to a larger market, and the potential for economic growth.

Anti-confederates protested that the promised ICR would be of little immediate use to New Brunswick, because Canadian labourers would reap the benefits of the building of the line. Moreover, they argued that the line would inevitably follow the route favoured by the British, which hugged the north shore of New Brunswick, far from possible U.S. intervention. This played on the fears of southern New Brunswickers, that if the railway travelled the north-shore route, intercolonial trade would follow, bypassing Saint John. Halifax might then emerge the victor in its traditional metropolitan rivalry with Saint John. In any case, the "anti" argument ran, the cost of paying interest on loans needed to finance railway schemes would stifle development.

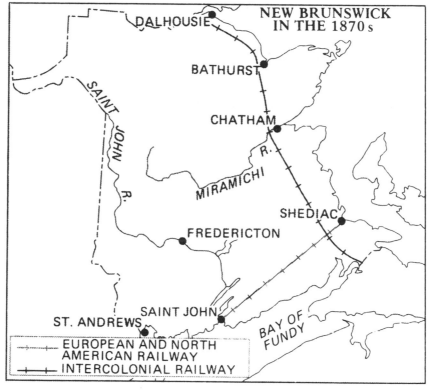

Dept. of Cartography, CEGEP de Limoilou, Que.

A Change of Mind

As one contemporary observer noted: "The rejection in New Brunswick of [Confederation] in 1865, and its almost unanimous adoption *unaltered* in 1866 is a queer commentary on the value of the popular vote on such a subject." But the voting public was perhaps not as quixotic as this journalist believed. Circumstances had changed between the two elections. For one thing, the Fenian threat and pressure from Britain had made more explicit New Brunswick's evolving relationships with the mother country and the threatening republic to the south.

Furthermore, a year of continuous debate served to clarify the issues involved. Initial suspicion of "upper Canadian" motives gave way to a belief that jobs and prosperity depended on railway construction and an enlarged, protected market for New Brunswick goods. Voters decided that Confederation would bring both these benefits, and accordingly gave the Quebec plan their support.

New Brunswick was in.

Confederation Defeated: The Newfoundland Election of 1869*

JAMES HILLER

523

It is entirely possible that Newfoundland would not have been represented at the Quebec conference had not Hugh Hoyles,[1] the colony's premier, approached Charles Tupper in the summer of 1864, when visiting his wife's family in Halifax.[2] Tupper blandly told Hoyles that Newfoundland had not been invited to Charlottetown because of "the belief that was generally entertained, that Newfoundland had no wish to become a party" to the proposed union, but it is more likely that the possibility had not crossed his mind, nor that of any other future father of confederation.[3] On the other hand, Newfoundland had shown no interest in mainland moves towards Maritime or federal union. The 1864 legislative debates contain no reference to the matter, and the newspaper editors were silent. So far as one can tell, Hoyles acted entirely on his own initiative. He was invited to Charlottetown, prudently declined on the grounds that he had to return home to bid farewell to his old political ally Governor Bannerman, and submitted Macdonald's subsequent invitation to Quebec to his government.[4]

Hoyles' exclusively Protestant Conservative party, which had the support of the most important merchants, had come into office in 1861 when Bannerman had unceremoniously dismissed the mainly Catholic Liberals led by John Kent.[5] This action precipitated a severe crisis, characterized by rioting in parts of ConceptionBay and St John's, and active political intervention by both Anglican and Roman Catholic bishops.[6] Once settled in power, however, the Conservatives put religious cries aside. Showing themselves to be, on the whole, cautious, moderate, and honest, their leaders maintained from the outset that effective and progressive government would depend upon the reconciliation of Protestant and Catholic, Conservative and Liberal, after the bitter fights of the

*From *Newfoundland in the Nineteenth and Twentieth Centuries: Essays in Interpretation*, ed. James Hiller and Peter Neary. Copyright 1980 by University of Toronto Press. Reprinted by permission of University of Toronto Press.

1850s. Hoyles can hardly have expected the Liberals to coalesce with the premier who had ousted them from office, but he kept cabinet posts symbolically open for them, and adopted fair and moderately nationalistic policies to which little exception could be taken.[7] His government's reaction to attending the Quebec conference was entirely in character. Union was a national question, and should not be treated as a party matter; thus the delegation should be bi-partisan and denominationally balanced. There had been no local debate on confederation in any forum, thus the delegates could make no binding commitment.[8] It was all very cautious, moderate, and reasonable. Frederick Carter,[9] the respected speaker, would represent Conservatives and Protestants; Ambrose Shea,[10] one of the leading and most energetic members of the opposition, Liberals and Catholics.

524   There is no need to summarize yet again the proceedings of the Quebec conference. Suffice it to say that the Newfoundland delegates became caught up in the spirit of the occasion, made enthusiastically confederate speeches at Quebec, Toronto, and Montreal, and arrived back in St John's on 14 November.[11] The resolutions which they had signed were printed in the local press on 1 December and debate on the issue that was to dominate local politics for the next five years began.[12]

It soon became clear that two important groups were opposed to federation. These were the major merchants of St John's and Conception Bay, who effectively dominated the local economy, and the Roman Catholic population. There were, of course, members of both groups who supported confederation from the start, but the overwhelming majority of each expressed either outright hostility or deep reservations. Foreshadowed in newspaper debate and correspondence, the character of the opposition became clearly defined when the legislature opened in January 1865. No vote on the Quebec resolutions was asked for or taken, but in debating a clause in the throne speech calling for a "calm examination" of the question and in subsequent discussion the assembly showed itself almost evenly divided.[13] Eight of the thirteen Liberals and five of the seventeen Conservatives spoke against confederation, all of the latter being merchants.[14] The sixteen members favouring union in principle, if not on the Quebec terms, included most of the lawyers and smaller businessmen, and five Liberals — John Kent, Ambrose Shea, his two co-members from Placentia–St Mary's district, and his brother Edward. The majority of speakers in the largely mercantile Legislative Council declared themselves undecided or opposed.[15]

In these circumstances it was clearly impossible for the government to push for a definite decision, as it had originally intended.[16] In the opinion of both Hoyles and Governor Anthony Musgrave,[17] it was better to have no decision than an adverse one, and given events in the Maritimes, speed no longer seemed essential. In any case, the government was under pressure from outside the legislature to avoid precipitate action. On 10 February the Commercial Society drafted a clearly anti-confederate petition asking for more information and an election on the issue.[18] The next day an impressive array of Water Street aristocrats addressed a well-attended public meeting, where a similar petition was unanimously approved.[19] Hoyles conceded the point on 14 February, when he moved a resolution in the assembly establishing that confederation would be decided by the electorate.[20]

The next election was due in the fall of 1865, and the leading confederates probably hoped that its results would provide the necessary *imprimatur*. When the session closed, Hoyles retired from politics to the bench, and was succeeded as premier by Carter, who had no difficulty in persuading Kent and the Shea brothers to join his government. This move had the effect of emasculating the Liberals and strengthening the confederate wing of the Conservatives, besides creating a strong, pansectarian administration, which could hope to split the Catholic vote. Carter and his new allies of course justified the amalgamation in loftier terms, arguing in essence that "Sectarianism had been tried and found wanting,"[21] and that the critical state of the colony demanded a strong government of all the talents.[22] The sincerity of these protestations need not be doubted; however, the anti-confederate press was right to howl indisbelief when the *Newfoundlander* claimed: "Into the consideration of the arrangements for the coalition Government the idea of Confederation has never entered."[23] Confederation was not a major issue in the 1865 election, though, because the new government had no wish to make it one. The situation in the Maritimes remained uncertain, the Conservatives divided, the merchants and Catholics hostile. A visitor to St John's found confederation "a very sore subject . . . the feeling against it being much more unanimous than in either New Brunswick, Nova Scotia or Cape Breton."[24] Time was needed, the confederates thought, to allow reason to work on the minds of the electorate; then, as Edward Shea put it, "the conversion will be easy and complete."[25] But even he must have had private doubts about his own district of Ferryland, where he had thought it prudent to retire from the contest after being burned in effigy.[26] In the absence of any significant opponents, Ambrose Shea delivered the three Placentia seats, but in St John's East John Kent found it necessary to assure his constituents that "no matter what my private convictions may be, I must renounce the advocacy of a measure at variance with the opinions of those on whom I rely for Parliamentary support."[27] Of the thirteen members elected for predominantly Catholic districts in 1865, only four were confederates; had confederation been a central issue, none would have succeeded.[28]

Though 93 per cent of the Catholic population was native born, it was still very Irish in character and orientation.[29] The priests and schoolteachers were for the most part Irish born and trained, and it is hardly surprising that they looked at the world through the prism of past and

525

contemporary Irish prejudices. Newfoundland Catholics of Irish descent, with few exceptions, accepted the view that the troubles of the homeland derived exclusively from the Act of Union. Confederation was viewed as a proposal to re-enact in a colonial context that infamous piece of legislation. "The Confederation or Union . . . of a small country with a large one is pretty much in the nature of a conquest," wrote Thomas Talbot, an Irish-born schoolmaster and journalist, "the relation between them must always be that of slave and master." The Irish Union demonstrated the point — it had resulted in "the almost total destruction of the Irish people as a Nation."[30] "In proportion as Ireland was made to suffer, Newfoundland would have to suffer also," echoed the ancient Peter Brennan.[31] "[H]ow has Ireland been under her Union with England?" asked John Kavanagh.

> Had she gained any benefits by that? How has it fared with that lovely land of the sun, which might be said, for its fertility, to be flowing with milk and honey — that land whose sons are brave, and its daughters virtuous, who sent forth saints and heroes to instruct man and combat tyrants. . . . Was Ireland benefitted by the union? On the contrary, she lost everything . . . she sank far below the level of a petty province, and is now steeped in misery and want. . . . With this fact before our eyes, let us, in the name of everything that is good, retain that great boon [responsible government] which the mother country bestowed on us. . . . [32]

This line of argument, casting Canada in the role of England, had an immense emotional force which Catholic confederates could not weaken. Ambrose Shea desperately stressed his O'Connellite credentials, and denied that any parallel could be drawn with Ireland since Newfoundland would join the union on just, negotiated terms.[33] But it was to no avail. To the Catholic mind, union spelled ruin, and its advocates were traitors.

On the whole, the Catholic community in Newfoundland was satisfied with the status quo and was loath to take any action that might destroy it. They had their own, state-funded schools — to the chagrin of the High Church Anglicans who wanted the same — and, in theory, a fair share of government patronage. Through the Liberal party they had fought for and won responsible government, widely perceived as local Home Rule. Change might well be for the worse. There was fear, for instance, that the denominational school system would be destroyed. Even Bishop John Mullock[34] of St John's, who ought to have known better, thought that "the education of our people [might] be taken out of the hands of the local clergy and transferred to a Board in a remote Province notorious for its anti-Catholic spirit. . . ."[35] In a chauvinistic outburst, Robert Parsons, editor of the *Patriot*, claimed that the Newfoundland school system, "probably the best in the world," would be "broken up, and we should be compelled to adopt the Canadian system."[36] Canada — meaning, in local parlance, Canada West — was seen as a hotbed of militant Orangeism, whose spread would accompany confederation to the detriment of the Catholic population. Hitherto, said Talbot, Newfoundland had been mercifully free of both Orangemen and Fenians, but "Let the Canadians come down here, and let us go up there, and very soon we should have both Fenian and Orange lodges established here."[37] Better continued independence than the importation of new religious feuds.

Linked with such arguments were patriotic effusions celebrating the glories of Newfoundland and denigrating Canada. A typical example can again be culled from the prolific Talbot:

> there is not a country in the world so happily circumstanced as is Newfoundland, and so open to the influences of civilization. She is situated between Europe on the one side, and the United States on the other . . . she is in constant communication, through the medium of her commerce, with . . . these two great and civilized Continents of the world; she lies on the pathway of both, with the full radiance of all their civilization flashing upon her; and . . . she is asked to surrender herself to Canada, a country placed outside the current of civilization, shut out by natural barriers from the Commerce of the world, and influenced in her civilization only by her association with the polar bear.[38]

527

Such inflated rhetoric was the common coin of all anti-confederates, but it was especially relevant to the Catholics in that it reinforced their belief that in Newfoundland they had built a society which should not be despised, in a country which, though underdeveloped, had great economic potential.

In the face of such deeply felt anti-confederate feeling, the "easy and complete" conversion of which Edward Shea spoke could only have been effected had the Catholic church chosen to make common cause with the Catholic confederates. In both Nova Scotia and New Brunswick (from 1866) bishops urged Irish Catholics to vote for confederation, and the *Newfoundlander* (edited by Edward Shea) gave prominence to their efforts. But the Newfoundland bishops, Mullock of St John's and John Dalton[39] of Harbour Grace, did not follow the trend. As Irishmen long settled in Newfoundland they shared the prejudices of their flocks, and such evidence as exists indicates that both were opposed to confederation.[40] Neither bishop made any directpublic statement on the issues, probably because they had no wish to revive sectarian animosity which, by the later 1860s, had died down significantly. Their withdrawal from active politics after the rowdy crisis of 1861 — for which Mullock had to bear at least some of the blame — made possible the denominational accommodation promoted by Hoyles and completed by Carter. Yet Mullock was a mercurial, outspoken man who, had he believed in it, would have fought for confederation. He did not need to fight against it; it was sufficient to leave the largely anti-confederate priesthood alone, and deny his support to Kent and the Sheas, politicians with whom he had always had uneasy relations. The position of the small band of middle-class Catholic confederates was therefore extremely weak, and their hope of gaining support slim. Lacking episcopal approval they were fair game for virulent anti-confederate attacks which exposed their lack of influence. The elderly Kent, nearing the end of a tortuous political career with prestige tarnished by the events of 1860–61, was no longer the populist of the 1830s and commanded little loyalty. The Sheas, though respected for their talents, were not trusted, and Ambrose in particular was thought to be more concerned with his own and his relations' ambitions than with the good of party or colony:

> I'm a cute old codger, fond of tin,
> And Ambo is my name;
> Tho' very few can take me in,
> At length I've lost my game.
> Sure, you'd think 'twould be a splendid hit,
> And worthy Castlereagh,
> To sway the country every bit,
> And then get dubbed Lord Shea.[41]

If the key to winning the Catholic districts was the support of the priesthood, the key to the predominantly Protestant constituencies was the support of the merchants who supplied the fisheries and otherwise provided employment. The Protestant clergy did not possess the same degree of influence as their Catholic counterparts, and were in any case less inclined to become openly embroiled in politics.[42] The influence of the merchant, on the other hand, was considerable. Running the fisheries on a credit system, he could exert pressure on his dealers at outfitting time in the spring, and again at settling-up time in the fall. Outfits and supplies could be refused or curtailed, debts suddenly called in. Their attitude was obviously crucial.

The initial reaction of the trade was almost unanimously hostile, and was neatly summarized in the report of the St John's Chamber of Commerce for 1865:

> So far as this Chamber is aware the project of a Confederation . . .
> was devised as a means of relieving Canada from the political difficulties which have for some time past embarrassed the action of the Legislature, and also of affording more available resources for repelling any act of agression upon that Province on the part of the adjoining republic and of providing access to the Atlantic Seabord at all seasons . . . for its products through territory under its own government . . . the latter two [objects] . . . would apparently

confer proportionate advantages on the Provinces of New Brunswick and Nova Scotia, but it is difficult to see what interest this Colony can have in any one of these objects to justify the sacrifice of its independent legislative position and the assumption of a share of the enormous expenditure that must be incurred for the support of the General Government; for the erection of efficient defensive works . . . for the maintenance of a Military and Naval force . . . and . . . for the construction of many public works of advantage to the Provinces only.

These expenditures . . . would necessitate the imposition of a very high tariff . . . which would press with peculiar and unequal severity on this Colony. . . .

It is moreover to be apprehended that the operation of such a tariff would divert much of our commerce from its accustomed and most convenient and advantageous channels, by compelling our Importers to have recourse not to the cheapest markets . . . but to the Confederated Provinces. . . .

It [confederation] can open no new or more extensive market for the products of our fisheries, nor does it hold out the prospect of developing new resources within the Colony or of extending those we now possess.[43]

529

In short, the purposes for which the union had been conceived were irrelevant to Newfoundland, and there was no point in paying higher taxes and dislocating trade to benefit the mainland — sentiments enthusiastically applauded by the Catholic anti-confederates.[44]

Isolated on the periphery of the continent, Newfoundlanders felt no threat to their security, which they assumed would be forever safeguarded by the British government. "[A]s long as Great Britain maintains her supremacy on the Sea, and has any possessions to protect in North America," wrote Newman and Company "we need not fear molestation, at any rate Canada could not help us."[45] Though St John's was rattled by the occasional scare, Fenianism was not regarded as a danger, and there was no mistrust of the United States. Many Newfoundlanders had relatives living there, even at this comparatively early date, and for economic reasons most merchants wanted as close and untroubled a relationship with the USA as possible. One of the threats of union was involvement in Canadian quarrels which would damage the chance of continued reciprocity, quite apart from costing Newfoundland dearly in terms of money and men.[46]

Newfoundland merchants had relatively little to do with the mainland provinces, which took only about 5 per cent of the colony's exports and provided about 16 per cent of its imports. The markets for Newfoundland produce were in southern Europe, the West Indies, and Brazil; imports came mainly from the United States and Britain, which together provided

70 per cent of the colony's needs.[47] To businessmen operating in this Atlantic economy it appeared essential that trade remain as free as possible, unhampered by tariffs that were high or protective. Engaged in a somewhat precarious business, they must be free to buy and sell where they would, keeping costs as low as possible. Confederation made no economic sense because the other provinces did not represent a promising market for imports or exports. Further, there was the threat of a tariff that would be high — to finance schemes dreamt up by the notoriously spendthrift Canadians for their own benefit — and also protective. Newfoundland merchants' costs would rise as a result, and they would lose the freedom to import from traditional markets. What Canada could not supply would be expensive, because subject to a protective duty. Had the Canadian tariff of 1864 been applied to the Newfoundland imports of the same year, taxes would have risen by nearly 44 per cent.[48] Even if remodelled to meet the needs of the Atlantic region, merchants did not see how taxes could fail to rise significantly, given the commitments of the future federal government. Confederation looked like a poor speculation.

530

Confederate counter-arguments seemed weak, because they could point to no immediate or tangible benefit. Though confederates were prepared to argue interminably about tariff levels and comparative costs, their most usual reply was to point to the appalling state of the colony and enquire what solution the merchants could offer if they rejected confederation, which at least offered a chance for material and cultural improvement. Many came close to saying that Newfoundland was in such straits that any change would be for the better.[49]

Newfoundland's economic condition, which contrasted so painfully with the relative prosperity of the Maritimes, was caused by a series of poor seal and cod fisheries beginning in the late 1850s, and complications in the Spanish and Brazilian fish markets. The catch of seals declined between 1856 and 1864, with 1862 and 1864 being particularly disastrous years, and did not approach the level of the early 1850s until 1870. Similarly, the catch of cod declined between 1857 and 1868, and though the worst failures were in the inshore fishery, the industry as a whole fared badly in the mid 1860s.[50] Over the same period the population increased by about 19.5 per cent (approximately 24,000), and since no other sector of the economy expanded, the per capita fish export fell steeply while expenditures on poor relief climbed.[51] Between 1861 and 1865, relief payments absorbed, on average, 23 per cent of current revenue before slightly improved conditions and firmer administration by Carter stopped the spiral.[52] In response to poor fisheries and difficult markets, most merchants cut back on their credit business. "[I]t is not our duty," wrote Newman and Company, "to maintain Paupers."[53] It was the duty of the government, and the merchants found it safer and more profitable to let the government look after the problem of fishermen who could not earn enough to buy a winter's diet. As a result, winter supply on credit became exceptional, and summer credit more difficult to obtain.[54] Poverty was endemic. Anglican missionary reports from all over the island comment monotonously on fishery failures, potato blight, short supplies, high food prices, and sickness. "At no time during my residence of more than twenty years . . . ," wrote the Reverend Bertram Jones from Harbour Grace in 1864, "has the condition of the whole people been more deplorable than it is this winter."[55]

There was fairly general agreement that the ultimate cure lay in economic diversification. The Conservative governments of the 1860s, as a result, attempted to stimulate mining and agriculture — by instituting a geological survey (1864), and by a scheme of bounty payments for the clearing and cultivation of waste lands (1866) which, it was hoped, would induce people to move to the heads of the bays and combine fishing with agriculture and lumbering.[56] Such initiatives had no immediate results. The area of cultivated land actually declined between the census years of 1857 and 1869, apparent confirmation of the contention that the agricultural traditions of the first generation immigrants largely died with them, their children being content with subsistence farming in a land where soils are poor and acidic, the market was small, and the fisheries left little time for tending fields and flocks.[57] The Geological Survey certainly stimulated interest in the island's mineral potential, but only one mine opened — at Tilt Cove in Notre Dame Bay — and that exploited an ore body discovered in the late 1850s. The more radical Liberals pressed for greater government initiative, urging the Conservatives to subsidize industry, provide tariff protection, and begin large-scale public works.[58] In essence free traders, the latter were not prepared to do more. In their view it was up to private capital to take the initiative.[59] The fact was, though, that local capital was loath to diversify out of the fisheries. Charles Fox Bennett,[60] the eventual anti-confederate leader, was the only merchant in this period who invested significantly in new ventures, possessing besides a share of the Tilt Cove copper mine, a foundry, a brewery, and a distillery. Why, it was asked, had not others done the same?

One possible answer was that the merchants, as importers, were naturally averse to the development of import substitutes; another was that in the absence of a protective tariff or an extensive drawback system, it was cheaper to import boats and nets, for instance, than to invest in their local manufacture; a third, widely accepted at the time, was that since many local houses were branches of English and Scottish firms, profits were drained out of the country leaving Newfoundland capital poor.[61] There was an element of truth in each of these points. As a group, the merchants were cautious and conservative; they were more concerned with the stability of their firms, and the creation of some personal wealth out of a hazardous trade, than with the long-term development of the

531

economy of a colony in which few of them would lay their bones. But critics took no account of the fact that merchants had large amounts of capital tied up in the fishery — in premises, inventory, and debts — and had little surplus cash for speculation in enterprises which, in a period of depression, were sure to lose money and in which they had no expertise. If government was not to intervene, and if the merchants were not prepared to diversify, how was stagnation to end?

One answer was confederation, and its supporters urged insistently that union would remove the colony's curse, the great impediment to economic diversification, its isolation from the rest of the world. Better communications, better government would create the climate in which businessmen would begin to invest in the colony. This rather dubious argument did not convince the merchants: if Newfoundland was worth investing in, men would have done so already — and why expect Canadian investment, when most Canadians hardly knew where Newfoundland was, and were borrowing abroad for their own purposes? In their view confederation would create an additional impediment to diversification by raising costs. They could not, however, show how diversification might be achieved, arguing only that taxation and government expenditure should be reduced, and that better times would bring about the desired change.[62] While agreeing on most points, the merchants' Liberal allies could not accept the passive role envisaged for government, a disagreement which spotlighted a fundamental divergence between the two wings of the nascent anti-confederate party, as well as a basic point of agreement among Conservatives, whether or not they favoured confederation.

The Liberal anti-confederates were among those who had fought most fiercely for the grant of responsible government in the 1850s, and they believed in it as a potential agency for promoting reform and progress. They were prepared to admit that there was a case for retrenchment and purification, but not that the system should be abandoned, or infused with principles that would reduce a government's sphere of action. The Conservatives, though, were prepared to admit that responsible government had been a failure. "Moving within the restricted circle of local politics," said Carter, "no matter what comparative amount of political skill a local government could possess, they must be powerless, as any have been powerless to confer any signal and enduring benefit upon the country." The constitution was cumbersome and expensive, unsuited to so small a colony.[63] Many merchants agreed with him, even if unprepared to accept confederation as the cure. Charles Bennett, who had served on the Executive Council in pre-responsible government days, was especially extreme in his condemnation of responsible government and advocated a return to crown colony status. "The sooner we get rid of the House of Assembly, and make Newfoundland a Crown Colony, the better," he wrote, "for there are but few persons among us who can afford to pay the taxes."[64] Thus the anti-confederate party emerged as a strange coalition of left and right, those espousing the maintenance of responsible government on principle, and those who hated responsible government but had to argue for its maintenance from a belief that confederation-would bring catastrophe.[65] The alliance between Liberal Catholic politicians and the Protestant Tories of Water Street did not go unremarked — Daniel Prowse thought it a "wonderful and affecting sight" to see these old enemies form "a solemn league and covenant" — and confederates derived enjoyment from watching Bennett, who had bitterly opposed the introduction of responsible government, pose as the champion and defender of Newfoundland's rights and liberties.[66]

Though united in opposition to confederation in 1864 and 1865, the mercantile community was clearly split on the issue by 1869 when the promised appeal to the electorate finally took place. The fundamental cause appears to lie with the muddled mercantile response to the economic future of the colony. The attitude of Bennett and his friends was basically Micawberish — economize, and something would turn up. But as economic depression continued wearily year after year, it was a point of view increasingly difficult to maintain. The confederate position, which offered a reduction in the cost of local government and the chance of economic recovery, became increasingly attractive as a result. Stephen Rendell, manager of the large St John's firm of Job Brothers, was originally anti-confederate; in 1869, he told the assembly:

533

> . . . many who were at first opposed . . . are now at all events quiet, and think it best to "accept the situation," make the best terms we can, and get instead of our present expensive local government, something cheaper, less cumbersome. . . . This he believed was the general idea that was entertained by those connected with the commerce of the country. . . . In our present condition we were now perfectly helpless and could do nothing of ourselves.[67]

Economic depression bred confederates out of pessimism and a sense of helplessness.

There were of course other factors. Fears of excessive taxation and trade dislocation were probably lessened by the character of the federal tariff, although there is no direct evidence on this point. A feeling of inevitability appears to have been growing, especially after Nova Scotia's acquiescence in the union, and it was strengthened by an awareness that the imperial government was determined that the colonies should accept the full implications of internal responsibility. "[W]e must look upon Confederation as a foregone conclusion . . . ," lamented J.S. Clift of St John's. "Were we to hesitate . . . a pressure would be brought to bear on us that would leave no other alternative."[68] A final and telling factor in the local context was the character of the anti-confederate coalition. Though Charles Bennett, the emerging leader, was a respected figure in the community, he had always been something of an outsider, and his followers were, for the most part, politically and culturally alien to the mercantile elite. In the last analysis, what troubled many of the Protestant gentry of the colony was the prospect of working with their old religious and political enemies. Sooner Carter and his confederates, who were at least respectable and moderate, than Bennett and his following of dangerously volatile Irishmen — "leagued with the disaffected rabble," as one critic said.[69]

In the early months of 1869, then, the prospects for confederation looked favourable. Draft terms of union passedthrough the legislature without difficulty, and the acquiescence of the merchants seemed final when, on 6 March, Robert Prowse failed to find a seconder for an anti-confederate motion at a meeting of the Commercial Society.[70] The Catholics still appeared obdurate, but in the absence of powerful opposition it seemed likely that Shea could at least win the Placentia seats, thus ensuring that confederation would not be carried by Protestants alone. It is not surprising, therefore, that Carter was urged to call a spring election to coincide with the issuing of fishery supplies. He refused on the grounds that it would be unfair.[71] This remarkably high-minded decision, deriving in part from overconfidence, and in part from a genuine conviction that there was no room for trickery or deceit when the future of a country was at stake, was fatal to confederate chances. During the summer of 1869 the situation was changed by two factors. First, the economy showed signs of improvement. A reasonable seal fishery was followed by a much improved catch of cod — the best since 1858 — accompanied by fair average prices. The upturn was not so dramatic that poverty was banished from the land, but it was sufficient to dispel much of the pessimism that had pervaded the colony during the sixties, and to allow many fishermen to eliminate or reduce their debts so that, as Governor Stephen Hill complained, they could feel "more or less free and in consequence . . . [able to] adopt opinions in opposition to the Merchants."[72] Secondly, Carter's delay in calling the election allowed Bennett and his allies to begin a vigorous and strident campaign, which profited from improved economic conditions, mobilised all anti-confederate elements — Catholic, Liberal, and mercantile — and placed the confederates very much on the defensive. When Hill arrived to replace the blithely optimistic Musgrave in early August, he found that the Protestant vote was no longer securely confederate, and that members of the government "entertain[ed] grave doubts as to the result of the Elections proving favourable. . . . "[73] Indeed, Carter and Shea must already have realized that the election was lost.

Of the thirty seats in the assembly, thirteen represented the predominantly Roman Catholic districts of the southeast.[74] Reason had so obviously failed to work on the minds of these voters that only four confederate candidates could be found. In St John's East, a Methodist clockmaker was soundly trounced, obtaining votes only in the few Protestant outharbours.[75] In Placentia–St Mary's, Ambrose Shea led a slate against Charles Bennett. At Paradise he was advised not to land; at Oderin he was sent on his way with flags at half-mast and three groans; at Placentia he was met by priest and people bearing pots of pitch and bags of feathers, and the moaning of cow horns. His defeat was overwhelming.[76]

Given the division of mercantile opinion, results in the Protestant districts were less predictable. There was, however, one foregone conclusion in the two-seat district of Twillingate-Fogo. The sitting members, William Whiteway — the future premier — and Thomas Knight,[77] faced the combined anti-confederate opposition of the area's two dominant employers. These were the fishery supply house of Muir and Duder, whichduring the 1860s had come to dominate the Notre Dame Bay business, and the mining company at Tilt Cove.[78] The anti-confederate candidates represented the two interests: Charles Duder the fishery business, Smith McKay, Bennett's partner, the mine. It is not to be wondered at that Whiteway appeared on the hustings trying "to be merry but it wouldn't do, his face seemed care worn," while Knight stayed up the bay canning salmon.[79] They collected only a quarter of the vote.

535

In other east coast districts the contests were more evenly balanced, even though the preponderance of mercantile influence was in favour of the confederates. Without exception, all the major Conception Bay merchants worked on Carter's behalf and as a result both Carbonear and Harbour Grace (three seats) were won by the confederates, though not without some hard campaigning. Their influence was also decisive in Bay de Verde, where John Bemister, a Carbonear merchant, beat his opponent with the active help of his relative, the Methodist clergyman, who no doubt had an interest in aiding the defeat of a former Methodist, recently turned Anglican.[80] The merchants were unable, however, to deliver the single-member district of Brigus–Port de Grave, where the election was unusually violent. Though the confederate candidate, R.J. Pinsent, had been born in the district of a prominent Conception Bay family he was hampered by the death in 1866 of the district's principal merchant, an event which had caused a political vacuum. When he appeared at Port de Grave in the company of John Munn, largest of the bay merchants, they "were . . . hooted and pelted with stones, sods and filth." Laterin his hazardous campaign Pinsent narrowly avoided ambush, and he was showered with stones and insults with some regularity. Had not troops been sent into the area, it is doubtful that he would have got the 101 votes that he did.[81]

The confederates' loss at Brigus, and the narrow majority at Harbour Grace, indicate that along with the Catholic minority in Conception Bay, many Protestant planters[82] and fishermen were passionately anti-confederate, and, given the economic climate of 1869, unafraid to show it. In Harbour Grace, the confederates fielded John Munn himself and W.S. Green, a prominent Bay Roberts merchant, against the relatively undistinguished opposition of J.L. Prendergast, a small Catholic merchant, and Captain Robert Dawe, a Bay Roberts sealing master. Their victory was narrow, and if the anti-confederate *Courier* can be believed, Munn found it necessary to spend £50 on "ardent spirits," close his business, and refuse to pay wages until the polls were declared.[83] It is evident that, had not the Conception Bay merchants used their influence to the fullest, anti-confederates would have swept the board.

In Trinity Bay (three seats) the confederate slate represented mercantile influence. Stephen Rendell, a sitting member, had once managed the Job Brothers' establishment at Hant's Harbour. The business there was, by 1869, run by Ellis Watson, another candidate, who was probably supplied by Jobs. The third candidate was Thomas Ridley of Harbour Grace, who operated branches at Catalina and Heart's Content.[84] Against this impressive trio the anti-confederates ran Stephen March, a locally born St John's merchant, and Robert Alsop, a failed businessman who was nevertheless able to exert considerable influence as chairman of the Board of Works, a position from which Carter did not remove him until just before the election.[85] They were backed by the principal firms of the town of Trinity, Grieve and Bremner and Brooking and Company. The election was hard fought, and very close, the confederates taking two seats, and the anti-confederates one.

Bonavista Bay (three seats) fell to the antis, although the confederates had probably counted on victory. The Protestant vote was almost equally divided. The principal firm in the bay, Brooking and Company, had branches at Bonavista and, more importantly, Greenspond. The local manager, J.L. Noonan, headed the anti-confederate slate, which also had the support of the St John's based firm of J. and W. Stewart. This influence was countered by Ridley's of Harbour Grace, which maintained a small operation at Greenspond and exerted a considerable amount of influence over the town of Bonavista and the southern shore of the bay from its branch at Catalina. The large local traders of Bonavista such as Michael Ryan and Jabez Saint — who dealt with the confederate St John's firm of Baine, Johnston, and Company[86] — were also active on the confederate side. Victory was given the anti-confederates by the Catholic voters living in and around King's Cove, whose natural antipathy to union was sharpened by the fact that one of the confederate candidates, Michael Carroll, had had to close his business there the previous autumn, causing some hardship. The sole confederate vote at King's Cove camefrom the Anglican minister who, alone among confederates in the village, was allowed to go to the polls.[87]

Of the three predominantly Protestant districts on the south coast, only one was contested. Burgeo–La Poile was handed to the confederates since the anti-confederate — T.R. Smith, Bennett's St John's manager

536

— failed to be properly nominated.[88] In Fortune Bay, the confederates did not oppose the election of the sitting member, Thomas Bennett, an English Harbour trader held in considerable local respect. The dominant firm in the area, Newman and Company of Harbour Breton, was probably anti-confederate (although Governor Hill claimed the opposite) and a confederate would also have had to contend with the hostility of the merchants on the French island of Saint-Pierre.[89]

The Newfoundland–Saint-Pierre trade has never been studied in any detail, but its volume was probably growing during the 1860s with the expansion of the bank fishery, which in turn created a demand for fresh bait. Bankers coming from France would habitually touch at Saint-Pierre to load fresh herring, supplied by Newfoundland fishermen, before making their first voyage. Newfoundlanders traded bait — as well as firewood and game — for supplies which were smuggled back to the island. The merchants of Saint-Pierre prospered as middlemen in this traffic, and Newfoundland fishermen profited from lower prices. Their mutual fear was that confederation would end this trade through the efficient enforcement of customs and fisheries laws. The available evidence indicates that the most politically active of the Saint Pierre merchants was J.P. Frecker, who did all he couldto ensure the defeat in Burin district of his brother-in-law Edward Evans, a Grand Bank merchant, and Frederick Carter, who had inherited this difficult seat from Hoyles.

The Burin election was the closest contest of all. Carter and Evans had to contend not only with Frecker, but also with the overt hostility of the Catholic priest, whose flock comprised 38 per cent of the population. Prominent antis campaigning on Bennett's behalf in the neighbouring district of Placentia–St Mary's made frequent incursions, and Carter was further handicapped by the necessity of his speaking on behalf of candidates elsewhere in the island. There is no evidence that the confederates received a significant amount of mercantile support, and there may well be truth in the *Courier*'s accusation that they had to encourage and exploit an adverse Protestant reaction to the strident campaigning of the local Catholics — a common enough tactic in a district where the electorate was fairly equally divided into Methodists, Anglicans, and Catholics.[90] In the event, the confederates won by five votes — proxies from Frenchman's Cove, whose authors were immediately visited by one of Frecker's agents and bidden to repair at once to Burin and change their minds. This they did, and the returning officer obligingly altered the poll book. Carter, however, persuaded him to change it back, fought off his opponents' charges that he had received pauper votes as well, and returned in triumph to St John's with the hapless returning officer in tow.[91]

The final election result gave the confederates nine seats,the antis twenty-one.[92] The analysis presented above has attempted to show that this was brought about by two basic factors: the implacable opposition

537

of the mass of Catholic voters to any scheme of union, and a division in mercantile ranks which made it impossible for Carter to carry all the Protestant seats. It does not, however, account for the close margins by which all victorious confederates won their seats. There was, obviously, a powerful groundswell of anti-confederate sentiment that was by no means confined to the Catholic districts. It has already been suggested that one cause of this was the improvement in the fisheries, which removed the apathy that was the confederates' best ally. Another was the fact that, on the Labrador coast in the summer of 1869, Newfoundland fishermen imbibed the anti-confederate opinions of Nova Scotians.[93] Licking their wounds after the election, confederates added two others: the abolition of able-bodied poor relief in 1868, and the highly emotional character of the anti-confederate campaign.

By proclamation in June 1868 the government confined relief to the sick, infirm, destitute widows, and orphans.[94] This measure was almost universally applauded by the colonial elite as a means of reducing expenditure and removing the pauperism that was thought to be demoralizing the populace. In the poverty-stricken outports it was predictably unpopular. At Fogo the magistrates offered a reward for the apprehension of those "who did wilfully and maliciously besmear the said Proclamation with *Cow dung* — thereby offering a gross and malicious insult to the Governor and Government of Newfoundland."[95] That Carter should risk such a move so near to a crucial election shows how he and his government were more concerned with satisfying the traditional moulders of opinion than with gratifying the electorate. It was, as he later admitted, a bad political mistake. "If anything could have kept the late government in power," said Carter in 1870, "that thing would be [*sic*] the continuance of pauper relief."[96] Likewise, Pinsent believed that "hundreds throughout the country would have voted for confederation if they could, as usual, have received the customary dole. . . ."[97] Governments associated with, and thought to have contributed to, hard times are usually unpopular; Carter's was no exception.

Confederates were agreed, however, that the character of the campaign was of greater significance. Carter complained bitterly of irresponsible rumour-mongering; people had been told "they would be sold into slavery. They had even been told that their young children would be rammed into guns, their young men taken away. Even the taking of the Census, it was said, was for the . . . information of the Canadian government."[98] Captain Edward White, a sealing skipper of Greenspond background who campaigned for the confederates in Bonavista Bay, said he had often been asked: "are our gardens to be sold; are our hoops, poles to be taxed; and some assured him they were told if they had a pig to be killed, they should send to Canada for a person to come and kill it, who would take half for his portion."[99] The antis worked on the ignorance, credulity, and conservatism of rural Newfoundland and without difficulty

538

created a deep fear of Canada and confederation against which "Influence . . . was ineffectual."[100] "[I]t was better to bide as us be," said McKay's seconder at Twillingate, "than to sill the country and have the 'Kennedy's' a comin down to make slaves of us."[101] Robert Kent, a prosperous St John's merchant, was laughed at by the labourers on his wharf who declared "they got enough of union at home."[102] The cries of excessive taxation, conscription, and selling the country "so bewildered the poor people that they did not know whether they were standing on their heads or their heels."[103] The confederates' position was difficult, for, as Nicholas Stabb remarked, it was far easier to inspire terror than remove it.[104] Rational argument was certainly attempted, and the electorate was provided with elaborate assurances that taxation would be reduced and the economy improved; but in the end, the confederates had to fight with the same weapons, confusing the issue even more. If the antis attacked them as a coterie of place-hunting lawyers, they in turn were branded as the reactionary dupes of a mining monopolist. If the antis bewailed the loss of the British connection, the confederates lambasted them as closet annexationists. The more the antis played on the prejudices of the Catholic voter, the more confederate candidates and newspapers played up the threat of a Catholic political ascendancy should Bennett win. The antis did not have a monopoly on exaggeration and slander. Nevertheless, it was they who set the tone of the campaign, turning it into a lusty brawl in which they held the superior weapon — fear of the unknown.

539

Confederation could only have been won had Carter beenwilling to abandon the pledge given by Hoyles in 1865 that the electorate would be consulted or, alternatively, had he been prepared to fight the election in the spring of 1869 and mount an overtly anti-Catholic campaign. There were fears that the mistrusted Ambrose Shea would persuade Carter to merely pass an address through the legislature, as provided for by the British North America Act, but the latter reaffirmed his policy on several occasions. For example, at a meeting in St John's in October 1867, he stated before a hostile audience that confederation would occur only "if the people wanted it . . . and that was *his* solemn promise and determination . . . (Loud cheers for Mr. Carter)."[105] He was not prepared to follow Tupper's example, believing, like his opponent Thomas Glen, that the "constitution was granted, not to the House of Assembly, but to the people of Newfoundland, and . . . the people were entitled to be consulted. . . . "[106] For the same reasons, he was not disposed to allow a spring election in 1869. The sectarian cries that were used by some confederate candidates in the election were the result of desperation rather than part of a planned strategy. An overtly sectarian campaign would have been abhorrent to Carter not only because a great question was to be decided, but also because it would have negated the basis of his coalition government, which enjoyed the support of many members of the Catholic bourgeoisie. He had denounced sectarian politics as sterile and, like many others, was haunted by memories of the violently sectarian battles of the 1850s and earlier, and their spectacular culmination in 1861. Given his principles, Carter had no alternative but to put the question in the fall of 1869.

Such justifications for Carter's actions should not obscure the fact that he lacked the dynamism imparted by personal ambition and thus tended to shy away from bold and decisive political action. He was temperamentally unable to turn the confederate campaign into a crusade, or to indulge in the sharp practice that might have brought success. From a Canadian perspective, which views confederation as an unquestionable good, Carter may seem to be a rather colourless failure; but it was his character which, from a Newfoundland point of view, made him an ideal premier for the later 1860s and gave him an important place in the country's history. Respected, trusted, honest, and broadminded, Carter was the only politician who could heal the divisions created by previous battles and pave the way for party politics based on issues other than religion. His great achievement was the establishment of the principle of denominational power sharing, a development which, though possessing harmful side effects, at least prevented Newfoundland from developing into a transatlantic Ulster.

Many confederates were bitter in defeat. Claiming that the election had been carried "by means the most fraudulent and flagitious," they argued that the result did not represent the "rational and dispassionate judgment of the community," and was therefore not a true verdict.[107] Governor Hill agreed with this assessment; supplying the Colonial Office with details of the uniquely rowdy election at Brigus, he suggested to Granville that Newfoundland be thrust into confederation by imperial order incouncil. The Colonial Office demurred.[108] Besides the legal impossibility was the traditional insistence that the consent of the colonies involved was essential. "I should deprecate anything like using violence," Blackwood had minuted in 1866, when Musgrave suggested the application of pressure. "This scheme of Union is the offspring of the Colonies. It is not initiated or forced on them by H.M. Govt."[109] Newfoundland was in any case thought to be less vital to the success of the scheme than any other colony, and officials were worried lest imperial bullying should lead to difficulties over the French Shore — the interminable question around which all Colonial Office thinking about Newfoundland revolved.[110] From the lack of any significant reaction in London to the results of the 1869 election it can be deduced that the officials felt sooner or later confederation would happen; in the meantime Newfoundland's political isolation posed no problem.

Ottawa reacted in a similar manner. Newfoundland had never been viewed as a vital component of the confederation, and Canadian politicians had taken no active interest in Carter's campaign. There had

540

been no delegations to the colony, no ministerial visits, no funds. Newfoundland was "of no importance to Canada," Macdonald told Lisgar, and the terms of union had been too generous. A reaction would soon occur.[111] An unidentified member of his cabinet told the French consul at Québec that "il ne fera une seule démarche pour ramener les récalcitrants; il se bornera à attendre. . . . 'Terre-Neuve est trop pauvre pour persister longtemps dans cette opposition,' ajoutait ce Ministre, 'et la faim nous la fera ramener'."[112]

Given what had occurred in Nova Scotia and New Brunswick, and the fact that Carter commanded the support of most of the colony's able politicians, the supposition that confederation had only been postponed was not unreasonable. It was based, however, on the expectation that the Newfoundland confederates would remain active supporters of union, and this was not to be the case. Within a few years they had decided to accept the obvious: that the electorate was overwhelmingly opposed to union, and was likely to remain so unless some compelling reason for changing its mind emerged. To remain wedded to confederation was to accept perpetual exclusion from office. Thus the Conservatives abandoned confederation, and having managed to convince the voters that the matter was indeed closed, regained control of the government in 1874. The basis from which all governments now had to work was the colony's continued independence. Newfoundland began to take independent, nationalistic attitudes towards such questions as the North Atlantic fisheries, reciprocity, and the French Shore, much to the annoyance of both Ottawa and London. The confederates of the

541

TABLE 1   Social Characteristics of Candidates for the 1869 Election

| | Total cands | Age[a] | | Occupation | | |
		Ave	Median	Mchnts & Busnsmen	Professions	Other
Confeds	20	49.4	47	13 (65%)	6 (25%)	1
Antis	27	54.5	55.5	15 (55.6%)	7 (25.9%)	5

| | Birthplace[b] | | | Residence | | Denomination[c] | | |
	British Isles	BNA	Nfld	St John's	Other	RC	CE	Dissent
Confeds	10	1	8 (42%)	10 (50%)	10	4 (20%)	9	7
Antis	8	4	13 (52%)	20 (74.1%)	7	9 (34.6%)	9	8

[a]Ages known for 17 confederates, 20 anti-confederates
[b]Birthplace known for 19 confederates, 25 anti-confederates
[c]Denomination known for all confederates, 26 anti-confederates

TABLE 2 1869 Election — Summary of Results

District	Population[a]	RC[a] / Prot.%	Turnout[b] %	Confederate candidates	Anti-confederate candidates
Twillingate/Fogo	13,067	15 / 85	70.3%	W.V. Whiteway (208), T. Knight (83)	C. Duder (1,025), S. McKay (1,063)
Bonavista Bay	11,560	20.9 / 79.1	77.1	J.H. Warren (539), J.T. Burton (537), M. Carroll (515)	J.L. Noonan (697), W.M. Barnes (650), F. Winton (657)
Trinity Bay	13,817	10 / 90	87.8	S. Rendell, T.H. Ridley, E.C. Watson	R. Alsop, S. March
Bay de Verde	7,057	24.5 / 75.5	70.9	J. Bemister	R. Reader
Carbonear	5,633	42 / 58	80.2	J. Rorke	F. Taylor
Harbour Grace	12,740	32.6 / 67.4	82.5	J. Munn, W.S. Green	J.L. Prendergast, R. Dawe
Brigus–Port de Grave	7,546	25.3 / 74.7	87.8	R.J. Pinset (101)	J.B. Wood (735)
St John's East	17,204	75.2 / 24.8	65.9	W.T. Parsons (412)	W.P. Walsh (1,327), J.A. Jordan (1,325), R.J. Parsons, Sr. (1,298)
St John's West	11,646	65.4 / 34.6	No contest	—	P. Brennan, T. Talbot, H. Renouf[c]
Harbour Main	6,542	76.2 / 23.8	No contest	—	J.I. Little, J. Kennedy

Ferryland	5,991	97.1	No contest	—	T. Glen
		24.8			T. Badcock
Placentia/St Mary's	8,794	84	71.1	A. Shea (100)	C.F. Bennett (882)
		16		P. Barron (90)	R.J. Parsons, Jr. (860)
				T. O'Reilly (103)	H. Renouf (872)
Burin	6,731	37.8	85.4	F.B.T. Carter	H.C. LeMessurier
		62.2			
Fortune Bay	5,233	24.7	No contest	E. Evans	J. Woods
		75.3			
Burgeo–La Poile	5,119	2.8	No contest	P. Emerson	T.R. Bennett
		97.2			
Total for colony including Labrador and French Shore	146,546			Total elected: 9	— Total elected: 21

aFigures from 1869 census
bFigures derived from 1870 Blue Book; percentage is of registered voters
cL. Tessier (anti) was elected in 1870 to fill the St John's West seat vacated by Renouf

1860s, then, became the nationalists of the late nineteenth century, but they never lost the continental orientation that had in part distinguished them from the antis. Thus when Carter and Whiteway looked for ways to develop the local economy, they took Macdonald as the exemplar and launched into a program of railway building designed to open up the "hidden resources" of the interior. There was no attempt to create an indigenous development strategy, with the result that a tiny political unit became burdened with a huge development debt, gradually sank into insolvency, and after a decent interval, confederation. In this sense the nineteenth-century confederates succeeded; in the short term they failed because most Newfoundlanders, rightly or wrongly, believed that the experiment of independence should at least be given a fair trial. "Let us try . . . ," urged Robert Parsons, "before we seek to absorb this country in the New Dominion to become the outharbor of another province."[113]

544 NOTES

[1] Hugh Hoyles, born St John's, 1815, lawyer; premier and attorney general, 1861-65, chief justice, 1865-80.

[2] A detailed narrative of events can be derived from the following: A.M. Fraser, "The Issue of Confederation, 1864-70," in R.A. MacKay, ed., *Newfoundland: Economic, Diplomatic and Strategic Studies* (Toronto, 1946); H.B. Mayo, "Newfoundland and Confederation in the Eighteen-Sixties," *CHR* 29 (1948): 125-42; P.B. Waite, *The Life and Times of Confederation*, 2nd ed. (Toronto, 1962); E.C. Moulton, "The Political History of Newfoundland, 1861-1860," unpublished M.A. thesis, Memorial University, 1960, ch. 5, 7; W.D. MacWhirter, "A Political History of Newfoundland, 1865-1874," unpublished M.A. thesis, Memorial University, 1963, ch. 1; F.J. Smith, "Newfoundland and Confederation, 1864-1870," unpublished M.A. thesis, University of Ottawa, 1970.

[3] Minute of council, 12 Sept. 1864, *JHA*, 1865, appendix 845.

[4] Minute of council, 13 Sept. 1864, *JHA*, 1865, appendix 846-47.

[5] John Kent, born Waterford, 1805; commission merchant; premier, 1858-61.

[6] E.C. Moulton, "Constitutional Crisis and Civil Strife in Newfoundland, February to November 1861," *CHR* 48 (1967): 251-72; John P. Greene, "The Influence of Religion in the Politics of Newfoundland, 1850-61," unpublished M.A. thesis, Memorial University, 1970, ch. 6; Gertrude Gunn, *The Political History of Newfoundland, 1832-1864* (Toronto, 1966), ch. 11.

[7] For an account of Hoyles' ministry, see Moulton, "Political History, 1861-1869."

[8] Minute of council, 13 Sept. 1864, *JHA*, 1865, appendix, 846-97.

[9] Frederick B.T. Carter, born St John's, 1819; lawyer; premier and attorney general, 1865-70, 1874-78; chief justice, 1880-1900.

[10] Ambrose Shea, born St John's, 1816; merchant; member of assembly, 1848-69, 1874-87; governor of the Bahamas, 1887.

[11] Their speeches at the Quebec conference on 10 Oct. 1864 can be found in "A.A. Macdonald's Notes on the Quebec Conference, 10-29 October 1864," printed in G.P. Browne, ed., *Documents on the Confederation of British North America* (Toronto, 1969), 129-30. The speech given by Carter to Quebec Board of Trade, printed in *Newfoundlander* (St John's), 3 Nov. 1864; at Toronto, printed in *Newfoundlander*, 24 Nov. 1864; by Shea at Montreal, printed in *Newfoundlander*, 17 Nov. 1864, which also reports their return.

[12] The resolutions appeared first in the *Newfoundlander*, owned by the Shea family and edited by Ambrose's brother Edward, also a Liberal politician. Born 1820, Edward was a member of the assembly, 1848-69, and member of the Legislative Council, 1873-1913.

[13] *JHA*, 1865, 2; for the assembly debate on this clause see *Newfoundlander*, 2-16, 21 Feb. 1865. For subsequent debates on confederation in 1865, see *Newfoundlander*, 9 March to 1 May 1865.

[14] Stephen Rendell of Job Brothers was absent from the house, but it is known that he was anti-confederate at this time. The standings were therefore 16 favourable to confederation, 14 opposed.

[15] For the Legislative Council debate on 13-14 Feb. 1865, see *Newfoundlander*, 16, 23, 27 Feb., 6, 9 March 1865.

[16] Hoyles in assembly debate, 14 Feb. 1865 (*Newfoundlander*, 16 Feb. 1865).

[17] Anthony Musgrave, born Antigua, 1828; governor of Newfoundland, 1864-69, and of British Columbia, 1869-71.

18 *Times and General Commercial Gazette* (St John's), 15 Feb. 1865. The petition was presented to the assembly, 23 Feb. 1865 (*Newfoundlander*, 6 March 1865), and to the Legislative Council, 13 Feb. 1865 (*Newfoundlander*, 16, 23 Feb. 1865).

19 For various accounts of the meeting, see *Day Book* (St John's), 13 Feb. 1865; *Times and General Commercial Gazette*, 15 Feb. 1865; *Courier* (St John's), 15 Feb. 1865; *Newfoundlander*, 13 Feb. 1865; *Telegraph* (St John's), 15 Feb. 1865. Presented to assembly, 20 Feb. 1865 (see *Newfoundlander*, 3 March 1865).

20 Hoyles in assembly debate, 14 Feb. 1865 (*Newfoundlander*, 16 March 1865).

21 Ambrose Shea in assembly debate, 8 Feb. 1866 (*Newfoundlander*, 19 Feb. 1866).

22 See Kent, Carter in assembly debate, 8 Feb. 1866 (*Newfoundlander*, 19, 22 Feb. 1866, and editorial, 23 Nov. 1865). See also CO 194/174. Musgrave to Cardwell, 19 April 1865.

23 *Newfoundlander*, 27 April 1865.

24 Extract from *Edinburgh Daily Review* printed in *Times and General Commercial Gazette*, 7 Oct 1865.

25 *Newfoundlander*, 21 Dec. 1865.

26 *Newfoundlander*, 6 Nov. 1865; Archives of the Roman Catholic Archdiocese of St John's, Edward Morris diary, 11 Oct. 1865. Morris, a member of the Legislative Council, was a cousin of John Kent.

27 John Kent, "To the Electors of the Eastern Division of the District of St John's," 29 Sept. 1865, printed in *Newfoundlander*, 6 Nov. 1865.

28 The predominantly Catholic districts were Placentia–St Mary's (3), Ferryland (2), St John's West (3), St John's East (3), and Harbour Main (2).

29 Figure derived from Newfoundland census of 1869.

30 Thomas Talbot, "A Few Brief Observations on Confederation, Its Nature and Effects," printed in *Chronicle* (St John's), 11–13 Sept. 1869.

31 Brennan in assembly debate, 1 March 1869 (*Newfoundlander*, 17 March 1869). A merchant and bone-setter, Brennan was 80 when elected for St John's West in 1866.

32 Kavanagh in assembly debate, 28 Feb. 1865 (*Newfoundlander*, 20 April 1865).

33 Shea in a speech at Harbour Grace in 1869, reported in *Chronicle*, 24 Sept. 1869, and *Courier*, 25 Sept. 1869; in assembly debates, 27 Jan., 21 Feb. 1865 (*Newfoundlander*, 6 Feb., 2 March 1865).

34 John Mullock, born Limerick, 1807; coadjutor bishop, 1848; bishop of St John's, 1850–69.

35 Lenten pastoral, 1867, in *Newfoundlander*, 6 March 1867.

36 Parsons in assembly debate, 26 Feb 1869 (*Newfoundlander*, 12 March 1865).

37 Talbot in assembly debate, 7 March 1866 (*Newfoundlander*, 5 April 1866). Compare speeches by Kearney, 16 Feb. 1866, and Brennan, 1 March 1869, reported in *Newfoundlander*, 8 March 1866, and 17 March 1869, respectively.

38 Talbot, "A Few Brief Observations," *Chronicle*, 23 Sept. 1869.

39 John Dalton, born Tipperary, 1821; arrived Newfoundland, 1839; bishop of Harbour Grace, 1856–69.

40 In 1866 Dalton signed an anti-confederate petition (see Arthur Fox, "The Merchants' 1866 Petition against Confederation," in J.R. Smallwood, ed., *The Book of Newfoundland*, vol. 5 (St John's, 1975), 190–93. In 1868 Mullock spoke strongly against confederation in private conversation (Edward Morris diary, 13 May 1868).

41 "Ambo's Lament," *Chronicle*, 1 Oct. 1869.

42 Scattered evidence from the press and letters from Anglican ministers to the Society for the Propagation of the Gospel (PANL, Society papers, Series E, microfilm) suggests that the Protestant clergy was generally in favour of confederation. Edward Feild, the Anglican bishop, was cautious, however: "[L]et us not build much . . . upon the proposed Confederation," he told his flock in the spring of 1869; "or the new laws and legislators under and bywhich we shall be governed. We may hope for some change for the better in our social, as well as political state. But he must have a greater faith in Dominion politics and politicians than I have, who expects to obtain much relief from that quarter" (The "Poor Pastoral" in H.W. Tucker, *Memoir of the Life and Episcopate of Bishop Feild, D.D.* (London, 1877), appendix A, 301.

43 CO 194/174, enclosure in Musgrave to Cardwell, 19 Aug. 1865.

44 For example, Parsons in assembly debate, 28 Feb. 1865 (*Newfoundlander*, 2 April 1865); Glen in assembly debate, 12 Feb. 1866 (*Newfoundlander*, 20 Feb. 1866).

45 PANL, Newman Hunt papers, Letterbook, 1858–65 (microfilm), Newman, Hunt and Co. (London) to J. and W. Stewart (St John's), 13 March 1865.

46 For the attitude towards Fenianism see, for example, Edward Morris diary, 23–31 March 1866; *Newfoundlander*, 12, 19 Jan. 1865; *Patriot* (St John's), 20 Oct. 1866. The attitude towards the USA can be seen in letters from C.F. Bennett to *Times* and *General Commercial Gazette*, 21 Nov., 5 Dec. 1868; Talbot, "A Few Brief Observations," *Chronicle*, 17 Sept. 1869.

47 The percentages represent averages for the period 1857–63.

48 Calculated from a table printed in *JHA*, 1865, appendix, 302–309. The average annual revenue per capita for the period 1860–64 was $4.18. Application of the Canadian tariff to the 1864 Newfoundland imports resulted in a per capita increase of $1.82.

49 For example, letter of Ambrose Shea to his constituents, 7 Feb. 1867, *Newfoundlander*, 12 Feb. 1867.

50 Sir W. MacGregor, *Report of the Foreign Trade and Commerce of Newfoundland*, 1905 (Cmmd. 2480), tables 6, 8. See also above.

545

51 Shannon Ryan, "The Newfoundland Cod Fishery in the Nineteenth Century," unpublished M.A. thesis, Memorial University, 1971, table 14, 41.

52 Figure derived from *PANL* Blue Books, 1861-70.

53 *PANL*, Newman Hunt papers, Letterbook, 1866-72, Newman, Hunt and Co. (London) to Newman and Co. (Newfoundland), 24 April 1869.

54 Glen in assembly debate, 3 Feb. 1864 (*Newfoundlander*, 18 Feb. 1864); *Day Book*, 19 May 1865, "Tyro" to *Courier*, 21 Dec. 1867.

55 Society for the Propagation of the Gospel papers, E series, microfilm, Jones to Hawkins, 31 Dec. 1864.

56 The Act to Reduce Pauperism by Encouraging Agriculture was passed in 1866. The Conservatives also provided small bounties to encourage ship-building and bank fishing.

57 Carter in assembly debate, 21 Feb. 1866 (*Newfoundlander*, 15 March 1866); Prowse in assembly debate, 1 March 1866 (*Newfoundlander*, 26 March 1866).

58 For example, Talbot in assembly debate, 8 Feb. 1866 (*Newfoundlander*, 19 Feb. 1866); Renouf in assembly debate, 11 Feb. 1868 (*Newfoundlander*, 14 Feb. 1868); Parsons in assembly debate, 27 Feb. 1868 (*Newfoundlander*, 28 Feb. 1868).

59 Carter in assembly debate, 21 Feb. 1866 (*Newfoundlander*, 15 March 1866); Prowse in assembly debate, 11 Feb. 1868 (*Newfoundlander*, 14 Feb. 1868); Kent in assembly debate, 6 March 1868 (*Newfoundlander*, 11 March 1868).

60 Charles Fox Bennett, born Dorset, 1793; merchant; premier, 1870-74.

61 "Bayman" to *Courier*, 30 Dec. 1865, expressed the first suggestion. For the second see M. Kearney to *Chronicle*, 10 Nov. 1866, and in assembly debate, 12 Feb. 1866 (*Newfoundlander*, 1 March 1866); see also "Vindex" to *Courier*, 31 Jan. 1866; *Chronicle*, 26 Feb. 1868. For examples of the third point of view, see Hogsett in assembly debate, 1 April 1867 (*Newfoundlander*, 3 April 1867); "Comus" to *Courier*, 25 Nov. 1868.

62 See C.F. Bennett's letters to *Times and General Commercial Gazette*, 2 Nov., 4, 12 Dec. 1868.

63 Carter in assembly debate, 23 Feb. 1869 (*Newfoundlander*, 3 March 1869).

64 Bennett to *Times and General Commercial Gazette*, 11 Feb. 1867. For a comparison see Bennett to *Chronicle*, 7 Dec. 1868.

65 "Senex" to *Chronicle*, 25 Feb. 1867; "Hampden" to *Chronicle*, 11 Oct. 1868; editorials, 13 Feb., 20 March 1867. Bennett's reactionary attitudes goaded Thomas Glen, a leading Liberal, to reply; for their bitter exchange, see *Chronicle*, November 1868 to January 1869.

66 Prowse in assembly, 6 Feb. 1865 (*Newfoundlander*, 20 Feb. 1965).

67 Rendell in assembly debate, 4 Feb. 1869 (*Newfoundlander*, 10 Feb. 1809).

68 Clift in Legislative Council debate. 12 March 1869 (*Times and General Commercial Gazette*, 24 March 1869).

69 "Comus" to *Courier*, 25 Nov. 1868.

70 For the draft terms, see *JHA*, 1869, 33-36. For the final terms, see Canada, *Sessional Papers*, 1869, vol. 5, no. 51. For the report of the Commercial Society meeting see *Newfoundlander*, 10 March 1869.

71 Prescott Emerson, "Carter: A Father of Confederation," reprinted in J.R. Smallwood, ed., *Book of Newfoundland*, vol. 6 (St John's, 1975), 58.

72 CO 194/178, Hill to Granville, 22 Oct. 1869. Hill (1809-91) was governor of Newfoundland from 1869 to 1876.

73 CO 194/178, Hill to Granville, 8 Aug. 1869.

74 See note 28 above. For a social analysis of the candidates, see Table 1.

75 *Patriot*, 16 Nov. 1869.

76 *Courier*, 16 Oct. 1869, and J.E. Collins, *Life and Times of the Right Honourable Sir John A. Macdonald* (Toronto, 1883), 311-12. The anti-confederate majority was about 770 votes.

77 For Whiteway's career see above, 38 n2O. Thomas Knight ran a small business in Green Bay and had represented the district since 1855.

78 Ryan, "Newfoundland Cod Fishery," 89-91. Muir and Duder absorbed the business formerly carried on by the Slades and W. Cox and Co.

79 "A Looker on at Twillingate" to *Telegraph*, 22 Dec. 1869.

80 *Courier*, 27 Nov. 1869.

81 For Pinsent's version of events, see CO 194/178, enclosures in Hill to Granville, 22 Nov. 1869.

82 See Table 2.

83 *Courier*, 27 Nov. 1809. The voting figures are not known forany of the Conception Bay districts except Brigus. For Munn, see *Dictionary of Canadian Biography* (hereafter *DCB*), 10: 538.

84 For Thomas Ridley, see *DCB* 10: 617-18.

85 For Robert Alsop, see *DCB* 10: 8-9. The voting figures for Trinity Bay are not known.

86 "In Re Jabez Saint. 1883," in E.P. Morris, ed., *Decisions of the Supreme Court of Newfoundland, 1874-84* (St John's, 1898), 477.

87 J.T. Lawton and P.K. Devine, *Old King's Cove* (St John's, 1944), 10-11, 17-18, 61-62. The Bonavista Bay results can be found in *Telegraph*, 1 Dec. 1869.

88 *Courier*, 22 Feb. 1870.

[89] CO 194/178, Hill to Granville, December 1869. The last reference to confederation in the firm's correspondence is in February 1869, and was not favourable (see Newman, Hunt papers. Newfoundland letterbook, 1866–72, 150, Newman, Hunt and Co. (London) to J. and W. Stewart (St John's), 22 Feb. 1869.

[90] *Courier*, 21 Jan., 8, 16 March 1870.

[91] "Vindex" to *Telegraph*, 16 March 1870; *Express*, 26 Feb. 1870; *Chronicle*, 21 Nov. 1869.

[92] H. Renouf was elected for both St John's West and Placentia. In 1879, Lewis Tessier (anti) was elected for the St John's vacancy. See Table 2.

[93] *Newfoundlander*, 15 Oct. 1869; *Courier*, 16 Oct. 1969.

[94] *Newfoundlander*, 19 June 1868.

[95] Public notice, July 1868 (copy in *PANL*, CS 2/80).

[96] Carter in assembly debate, 18 Feb. 1870 (*Chronicle*, 5 March 1870).

[97] Pinsent in Legislative Council debate, 3 Feb. 1870 (*Newfoundlander*, 11 Feb. 1870).

[98] Carter in assembly debate, 18 Feb. 1870 (*Chronicle*, 5 March 1870).

[99] White in Legislative Council debate, 9 Feb. 1870 (*Newfoundlander*, 18 Feb. 1870).

[100] Pinsent in Legislative Council debate, 3 Feb. 1870.

[101] "A Looker on at Twillingate" to the *Telegraph*, 22 Dec. 1869.

[102] Kent in Legislative Council debate, 9 Feb. 1870 (*Newfoundlander*, 18 Feb. 1870).

[103] "Retriever," Bonavista, to *Telegraph*, 6 April 1870.

[104] Stabb in Legislative Council debate, 11 Feb. 1870 (*Newfoundlander*, 15 Feb. 1870).

[105] *Chronicle*, 11 Oct. 1867.

[106] Glen in assembly debate, 27 Jan. 1865 (*Newfoundlander*, 2 Feb. 1865).

[107] *Newfoundlander*, 10 Dec. 1869; Pinsent in Legislative Council debate, 3 Feb. 1870.

[108] CO 194/178, Hill to Granville, 20 Nov. 1869; Granville to Hill, 24 Dec. 1869.

[109] CO 194/175, Minute by Blackwood, 28 July 1866.

[110] See, for example, CO 194/175, minute by Rogers, 31 July 1866. In 1868 Elliott wrote that he thought the existence of the French Shore problem made it undesirable for Newfoundland to confederate — "much embarrassment might arise if we had to deal upon those questions with so powerful a Community as Canada" (CO 194/177, minute, 3 June 1868).

[111] Macdonald to Lisgar, 8 Dec. 1869, in J. Pope, *Memoirs of the Rt. Hon. Sir John A. Macdonald* (Toronto 1930), 505–506.

[112] Public Archives of Canada, Ministère des Affaires étrangères, correspondence consulaire politique, Québec et Montréal, microfilm, vol. 44, 369, F. Gautier to secretary of state, 29 Nov. 1869.

[113] Parsons in assembly debate, 27 Feb. 1868 (*Newfoundlander*, 28 Feb. 1868).

Contributors

T.W. Acheson is a member of the History Department at the University of New Brunswick.

John F. Bosher teaches history at York University, Toronto.

George W. Brown (1894–1963) taught history at the University of Toronto.

James E. Candow is an historian with Parks, Environment Canada, Atlantic Region, in Halifax.

J.M.S. Careless is Professor Emeritus at the University of Toronto, where he taught Canadian history.

Ann Gorman Condon teaches Canadian Loyalist History at the University of New Brunswick, Saint John.

Gerald M. Craig (1916–1988) taught Canadian history at the University of Toronto.

W.J. Eccles is Professor Emeritus at the University of Toronto, where he taught Canadian history.

John C. Ewers is Ethnologist Emeritus, Smithsonian Institution, Washington, D.C.

Robin Fisher teaches Canadian history at Simon Fraser University, Burnaby, B.C.

Barry M. Gough teaches Canadian history at Wilfrid Laurier University, Waterloo.

Naomi Griffiths teaches Canadian history at Carleton University, Ottawa.

James Hiller teaches history at Memorial University, Newfoundland.

José Igartua teaches history at l'Université du Québec, Montréal.

Michael Katz is a member of the Department of History at the University of Pennsylvania, Philadelphia.

Rosemarie Langhout teaches history at the University of New Brunswick.

John Leslie is Chief, Treaties and Historical Research Centre, Department of Indian and Northern Affairs, Ottawa.

Paul Litt is a Ph.D. candidate in Canadian history at the University of Toronto.

Keith Matthews taught history at Memorial University, Newfoundland.

John McCallum is Chairman of Economics at McGill University.

Jacques Monet is President of Regius College, Toronto School of Theology, University of Toronto.

Del Muise teaches Canadian history at Carleton University, Ottawa.

Jan Noel teaches women's studies at Trent University, Peterborough.

Fernand Ouellet teaches Canadian history at York University, Toronto.

George A. Rawlyk teaches Canadian history at Queen's University, Kingston.

Arthur J. Ray teaches Canadian history at the University of British Columbia.

Ian Ross Robertson teaches history at Scarborough College, University of Toronto.

Jacques Rousseau (1905–1970) botanist, ethnobiologist, and ethnohistorian, taught at Université Laval, Quebec.

Elinor Kyte Senior (1926–1989) taught history at St. Francis Xavier University, Antigonish, Nova Scotia.

W.G. Shelton taught European history at the University of Victoria.

D.N. Sprague teaches Canadian history at the University of Manitoba.

C.P. Stacey (1906–1989) was Professor Emeritus at the University of Toronto, where he taught Canadian history.

549

S. Dale Standen teaches Canadian history at Trent University, Peterborough.

Gerald Tulchinsky teaches history at Queen's University, Kingston.

Sylvia Van Kirk teaches Canadian history at the University of Toronto.

Jean-Pierre Wallot is the National Archivist, National Archives of Canada, Ottawa.

To the Student:

We are interested in your reaction to *Readings in Canadian History: Pre-Confederation, 3rd ed.*, by Douglas Francis and Donald Smith. Through feedback from you, we can improve this book in future editions.

1. What was your reason for using this book?

   _____ university course   _____ continuing education course
   _____ college course   _____ personal interest

2. Approximately how much of the book did you use?

   ____ ¼   ____ ½   ____ ¾   ____ all

3. Which article did you like best? _____

   Least?_____ Why? _____

4. Have you any suggestions for improvement?

Fold here

To the Instructor:

We are interested in your reaction to *Readings in Canadian History: Pre-Confederation, 3rd ed.*, by Douglas Francis and Donald Smith. Through feedback from you, we can improve this book in future editions. Please help us by completing this questionnaire:

1. Type of school: Comm. coll. _____ University _____

2. Type of course: One ____ Two ____ semester; Other: _____

3. Size of class: _____

4. Total *annual* enrolment for *all* sections of this course: _____

5. Which articles did you like best/assign most often?

   _____

6. Which articles did you like least/assign least often? Why?

   _____

7. Any suggestions for readings/topics for future editions?

   _____

8. What are the strongest features of the book?

   _____

9. How could this book be improved?

   _____

Fold here